Communicating at Work

Strategies for Success in Business and the Professions

Thirteenth Edition

Ronald B. Adler
Santa Barbara City College, Emeritus

Michelle M. Maresh-Fuehrer
Texas A&M University–Corpus Christi

Jeanne Elmhorst
Central New Mexico Community College

Kristen Lucas
University of Louisville

COMMUNICATING AT WORK: STRATEGIES FOR SUCCESS IN BUSINESS AND THE PROFESSIONS, THIRTEENTH EDITION

Published by McGraw Hill LLC, 1325 Avenue of the Americas, New York, NY 10121. Copyright ©2023 by McGraw Hill LLC. All rights reserved. Printed in the United States of America. Previous editions ©2019, 2013, and 2010. No part of this publication may be reproduced or distributed in any form or by any means, or stored in a database or retrieval system, without the prior written consent of McGraw Hill LLC, including, but not limited to, in any network or other electronic storage or transmission, or broadcast for distance learning.

Some ancillaries, including electronic and print components, may not be available to customers outside the United States.

This book is printed on acid-free paper.

1 2 3 4 5 6 7 8 9 LWI 27 26 25 24 23 22

ISBN 978-1-264-30508-7 (bound edition)
MHID 1-264-30508-7 (bound edition)
ISBN 978-1-265-05342-0 (loose-leaf edition)
MHID 1-265-05342-1 (loose-leaf edition)

Executive Portfolio Manager: *Sarah Remington*
Product Development Manager: *Dawn Groundwater*
Product Developer: *Karen Moore*
Executive Marketing Manager: *Kate Stewart*
Content Project Managers: *Maria McGreal, Katie Reuter*
Buyer: *Laura Fuller*
Content Licensing Specialists: *Sarah Flynn*
Cover Image: *TierneyMJ/Shutterstock*
Compositor: *MPS Limited*

All credits appearing on page or at the end of the book are considered to be an extension of the copyright page.

Library of Congress Cataloging-in-Publication Data

Names: Adler, Ronald B. (Ronald Brian), 1946- author. | Elmhorst, Jeanne Marquardt, author. | Maresh-Fuehrer Michelle Marie, author | Lucas, Kristen, author
Title: Communicating at work : strategies for success in business and the professions / Ronald B. Adler, Michelle M. Maresh-Fuehrer, Jeanne Elmhorst, Kristen Lucas.
Description: 13e. | New York, N.Y. : McGraw Hill LLC, [2023] | Includes bibliographical references and index.
Identifiers: LCCN 2021011548 (print) | LCCN 2021011549 (ebook) | ISBN 9781264305087 (hardcover) | ISBN 9781265053420 (spiral bound) | ISBN 9781265055738 (epub)
Subjects: LCSH: Business communication–Study and teaching.
Classification: LCC HF5718 .A33 2023 (print) | LCC HF5718 (ebook) | DDC 658.4/5–dc23
LC record available at https://lccn.loc.gov/2021011548
LC ebook record available at https://lccn.loc.gov/2021011549

The Internet addresses listed in the text were accurate at the time of publication. The inclusion of a website does not indicate an endorsement by the authors or McGraw Hill LLC, and McGraw Hill LLC does not guarantee the accuracy of the information presented at these sites.

mheducation.com/highered

Ronald B. Adler is professor emeritus at Santa Barbara City College. Throughout his career, he has specialized in the study of organizational and interpersonal communication. He is the author of *Confidence in Communication: A Guide to Assertive and Social Skills* and coauthor of *Understanding Human Communication, Interplay: The Process of Interpersonal Communication,* as well as the widely used text *Looking Out/Looking In.* Professor Adler is a consultant for a number of corporate, professional, and government clients and leads workshops in such areas as conflict resolution, presentational speaking, team building, and interviewing.

Michelle M. Maresh-Fuehrer is professor of public relations at Texas A&M University–Corpus Christi, where she specializes in the areas of crisis communication, public relations, and social media. She is the author of *Creating Organizational Crisis Plans* and coauthor of *Public Relations Principles: Strategies for Professional Success.* Her work has also appeared in *Persuasion in Your Life, The Handbook of Crisis Communication, Computers in Human Behavior, Communication Teacher, Communication Education,* and the *American Communication Journal.* Professor Maresh-Fuehrer also works as a consultant for a variety of business and nonprofit organizations.

Jeanne Elmhorst is an instructor in communication formerly of Central New Mexico Community College in Albuquerque, New Mexico. Her courses reflect the variety in the communication discipline: business and professional, public speaking, listening, intercultural, and interpersonal. Ms. Elmhorst lived and taught in Asia for three years, and she continues to find opportunities to travel, study, and volunteer in other countries. She enjoys designing and presenting communication training for business and not-for-profit clients.

Kristen Lucas is associate dean for faculty affairs and associate professor of management & entrepreneurship at University of Louisville. She teaches courses, conducts research, and facilitates management training sessions on organizational communication, workplace dignity, and careers. Her research has appeared in *Journal of Business Ethics, Management Communication Quarterly,* and *Journal of Applied Communication Research.*

In a time of great upheaval for traditional workspaces around the globe, *Communicating at Work: Strategies for Success in Business and the Professions* reminds students that practical communication skills and competencies endure and remain essential to finding success in the business world. The thirteenth edition of this well-respected title provides current research and real-world best practices to help students make ethical choices, develop cultural intelligence, navigate virtual environments, and enhance their business speaking and writing skills. With Connect for Business Communication, students will have access to a suite of assessments and presentation tools to help them become successful and confident communicators in the workplace.

McGraw Hill Connect® offers full-semester access to comprehensive, reliable content and assessments for the Business Communication course. Connect's deep integration with most learning management systems (LMS), including Blackboard and Desire2Learn (D2L), offers single sign-on and deep gradebook synchronization. Data from Assignment Results reports synchronize directly with many LMS, allowing scores to flow automatically from Connect into school-specific gradebooks, if required.

• Instructor's Guide to Connect for *Business Communication*

Mc Graw Hill connect®

When you assign Connect, you can be confident—and have data to demonstrate—that your students, however diverse, are acquiring the skills, principles, and critical processes that are necessary for effective communication. This process allows you to focus on your highest course expectations.

Tailored to You

Connect offers on-demand, single sign-on access to students—wherever they are and whenever they have time. With a single, one-time registration, students receive access to McGraw Hill's trusted content.

Easy to Use

Connect seamlessly supports all major learning management systems with content, assignments, performance data, and SmartBook, the leading adaptive learning system. With these tools you can quickly make assignments, produce reports, focus discussions, intervene on problem topics, and help at-risk students—as you need to and when you need to.

A Personalized and Adaptive Learning Experience

Mc Graw Hill SMARTBOOK® SmartBook is the first and only adaptive reading and study experience designed to change the way students read and master key course concepts. As a student engages with SmartBook, the program creates a personalized learning path by highlighting the most impactful concepts the student needs to learn at that moment in time.

SmartBook is optimized for mobile and tablet and is accessible for with different abilities. For instructors, SmartBook tracks student progress and provides insights and reports that can help guide teaching strategies.

eBook

Alongside SmartBook, the Connect eBook offers simple and easy access to reading materials on smartphones and tablets. Students can study on the go even when they do not have an Internet connection, highlight important sections, take notes, search for materials quickly, and read in class. Offline reading is available by downloading the eBook app on smartphones and tablets. Any notes and highlights created by students will subsequently be synced between devices when they reconnect. Unlike with SmartBook, there is no pre-highlighting, practice of key concepts, or reports on usage and performance available with the eBook.

• *About Communicating at Work, Thirteenth Edition*

Focus on Practical Applications

A new feature, **A Professional Perspective**, helps students connect theoretical concepts with practical application. Twelve former business communication students share their perspectives on the value and relevance of course material in their professional lives, from experiences with conducting online networking to leading intercultural teams to conducting virtual meetings. Students will walk away with a variety of practical tips from professionals in fields as diverse as marketing, meteorology, sales, and government.

Part Four, Making Effective Presentations, has been reorganized to help students focus on the specific aspects of public speaking they will encounter in workplace situations. The unit begins with Chapter 9 which introduces the most common types of professional presentations as well as the types of audiences students will most likely encounter when speaking in the workplace. Subsequent chapters continue to develop relevant and business-oriented advice on how to develop, organize, support, and deliver presentations.

Appendix V continues to focus on the types of crises businesses today often face—including the COVID-19 pandemic—and how communication plays a role in recovering from such events. Special emphasis is placed on crisis prevention, including strategies for responding to specific types of conflicts, and on templates for developing crisis response messages.

Available in Connect, **Writing Assignments** offer faculty the ability to assign a full range of writing assignments to students with just-in-time feedback. You may set up manually scored assignments in a way that students can

- automatically receive grammar and high-level feedback to improve their writing before they submit a project to you;
- run originality checks and receive feedback on "exact matches" and "possibly altered text" that includes guidance about how to properly paraphrase, quote, and cite sources to improve the academic integrity of their writing before they submit their work to you.

The new writing assignments will also have features that allow instructors to assign milestone drafts (optional), easily re-use your text and audio comments, build/score with your rubric, and view your own originality report of student's final submission.

Strong Emphasis on Ethical Communication and Cultural Diversity

This edition features updated coverage of cultural diversity, with a new emphasis on developing cultural intelligence and respecting gender identity in the workplace. New topics include microaggressions, personal pronouns in a professional environment, inclusive language, current legal protections concerning diversity, personal dress choice and dress codes, and masculine and feminine language use. Students will also consider new ethical content related to supporting material for business presentations and persuasion in business contexts. Culture at Work and Ethical Challenge boxes appear throughout, engaging students in thinking critically about topics of diversity and ethics in the workplace.

Updated and Expanded Coverage of Evolving Communication Technologies

Integrated throughout the program, *Communicating at Work* offers instruction on using the latest mobile technologies to effectively conduct and participate in meetings and updated coverage of social media tools and the accepted etiquette for their use. In the wake of the COVID-19 pandemic, students will also consider the shift to remote work, virtual workplace relationships and teams, virtual dress codes, virtual meeting fatigue, and text messaging/group texting etiquette. This edition also includes enhanced and updated coverage of Internet job searches and applications, virtual networking and interviewing, as well as online résumés and interviews.

Boxed Features

The thirteenth edition of *Communicating at Work* includes a variety of boxed features to support students' learning and enhance their business communication skills.

- **Culture at Work** boxes highlight the ways in which culture applies to every aspect of business and professional communication. Topics covered include the danger of uniformity in teams and the use of inclusive language in workplace presentations.
- **Case Study** boxes present cases from the world of business and the professions and offer compelling examples of how the principles in the book operate in everyday life.
- **Career Tip** boxes give practical advice on how to be more successful in work-related situations. Topics include building positive workplace relationships, coping with unfair treatment, shifting to remote work, and combating virtual meeting fatigue.
- **Technology Tip** boxes demonstrate how students can use a variety of communication tools to achieve their goals. Topics include how to "un-Google" oneself, apps for teamwork, and online internship searches.
- **Self-Assessment** boxes help students see how well they are applying communication concepts and identify their own strengths and weaknesses as communicators.
- **Ethical Challenge** boxes invite students to consider ways of incorporating ethical considerations into day-to-day work contexts.
- **A Professional Perspective** boxes—a new feature for this edition—highlight the experiences of former business communication students who regularly use and apply the concepts and ideas they learned in the classroom in their professional lives.

• Video Capture Powered by GoReact

With just a smartphone, tablet, or webcam, students and instructors can capture video of presentations with ease. Video Capture powered by GoReact, fully integrated in McGraw Hill's Connect platform, does not require any extra equipment or complicated training.

Create your own custom Video Capture assignment, including in-class and online speeches and presentations, self-review, and peer review.

With our customizable rubrics, time-coded comments, and visual markers, students will see feedback at exactly the right moment, and in context, to help improve their speaking and presentation skills and confidence.

- The Video Capture tool allows instructors to easily and efficiently set up speech assignments for their course that can easily be shared and repurposed, as needed.

- Customizable rubrics and settings can be saved and shared, saving time and streamlining the speech assignment process.

- Allows both students and instructors to view videos during the assessment process. Feedback can be left within a customized rubric or as time-stamped comments within the video-playback itself.

• Instructor Reports

Instructor Reports allow instructors to quickly monitor learner activity, making it easy to identify which learners are struggling and to provide immediate help to ensure those learners stay enrolled in the course and improve their performance. The Instructor Reports also highlight the concepts and learning objectives that the class as a whole is having difficulty grasping. This essential information lets you know exactly which areas to target for review during your limited class time.

Some key reports include:

Progress Overview report—View learner progress for all modules, including how long learners have spent working in the module, which modules they have used outside of any that were assigned, and individual learner progress.

Missed Questions report—Identify specific assessments, organized by chapter, that are problematic for learners.

Most Challenging Learning Objectives report—Identify the specific topic areas that are challenging for your learners; these reports are organized by chapter and include specific page references. Use this information to tailor your lecture time and assignments to cover areas that require additional remediation and practice.

Metacognitive Skills report—View statistics showing how knowledgeable your learners are about their own comprehension and learning.

• Classroom Preparation Tools

Whether they are used before, during, or after class, a suite of products is available to help instructors plan their lessons and to keep students building upon the foundations of the course.

- **PowerPoint Slides** The PowerPoint presentations for *Communicating at Work* provide chapter highlights that help instructors create focused yet individualized lesson plans.

- **Test Bank and Test Builder** The *Communicating at Work* Test Bank is a collection of more than 1,000 examination questions based on the most important mass-communication concepts explored in the text. New to this edition and available within Connect, Test Builder is a cloud-based tool that enables instructors to format tests that can be printed or administered within a Learning Management

System. Test Builder offers a modern, streamlined interface for easy content configuration that matches course needs, without requiring a download. Test Builder enables instructors to:

- Access all test bank content from a particular title
- Easily pinpoint the most relevant content through robust filtering options
- Manipulate the order of questions or scramble questions and/or answers
- Pin questions to a specific location within a test
- Determine your preferred treatment of algorithmic questions
- Choose the layout and spacing
- Add instructions and configure default settings

- **PowerPoint Presentations** The PowerPoint presentations, lecture-ready and WCAG-compliant, highlight the key points of the chapter and include supporting visuals. All of the slides can be modified to meet individual needs.

- **Instructor's Manual** This comprehensive guide to teaching from *Communicating at Work* contains lecture suggestions and resources for each chapter.

• Support to Ensure Success

- **Support at Every Step**—McGraw Hill's Support at Every Step site offers a wealth of training and course creation guidance for instructors and learners alike. Instructor support is presented in easy-to-navigate and easy-to-complete sections. It includes the popular Connect how-to videos, step-by-step guides, and other materials that explain how to use both the Connect platform and its course-specific tools and features. Visit us at https://www.mheducation.com/highered/support.html

- **Implementation Consultant**—These specialists are dedicated to working online with instructors—one-on-one—to demonstrate how the Connect platform works and to help incorporate Connect into a customer's specific course design and syllabus. Contact your local McGraw Hill representative to learn more.

- **Digital Faculty Consultants**—Digital Faculty Consultants are experienced instructors who use Connect in their classrooms. These instructors are available to offer suggestions, advice, and training about how best to use Connect in your class. To request a Digital Faculty Consultant to speak with, please e-mail your McGraw Hill learning technology consultant.

Contact Our Customer Support Team

McGraw Hill is dedicated to supporting instructors and students. To contact our customer support team, please call us at 800-331-5094 or visit us online at http://mpss.mhhe.com/contact.php

---

• Changes to the Thirteenth Edition: Highlights

Chapter 1

- Coverage of formal communication networks has been updated with new content on Voice of Employee in regards to upward communication.
- An expanded discussion of personal networking equips students with tips they can begin using immediately.
- Sixteen new references highlight the most current research.
- Two revised Career Tip boxes help students get recognized by managers and practice the all-important "elevator speech."
- A revised Technology Tip reminds students of the importance of disconnecting from devices from time to time to enhance productivity.
- Meteorologist Albert Ramon shares tips on professional networking in the new "A Professional Perspective" feature.

Chapter 2

- A new section on legal protections appears in the discussion of "Diversity and Ethical Issues."
- Chapter 2 now offers guidance on cultural intelligence and microaggressions.
- New Career Tips boxes help students consider shifts to remote work (particularly in light of the COVID-19 pandemic), develop cultural intelligence, and cope with unfair treatment in the workplace.
- The chapter is thoroughly updated with 26 new references to ensure students are thinking through current, timely issues.
- Global media personality Melissa Mushaka shares the importance of finding a good fit in terms of workplace culture in "A Professional Perspective."

Chapter 3

- Updates to this chapter reflect the adaptations of listening in today's remote and virtual business environments.
- Barriers to listening when working remotely and being attuned to one's nonverbal cues when attending virtual meetings are now discussed to enhance students' understanding.
- Software developer Ahmad Mather shares why listening well is particularly important when communicating in highly technical fields in "A Professional Perspective."

Chapter 4

- The section on Masculine and Feminine Language Use has been thoroughly updated to reflect current understandings of sex, gender, and language.
- A new Career Tips box discusses dress codes and remote work while the new Ethical Challenge box tackles a related topic—dress codes and religious belief.
- Director of program management Lilly Vu describes the value of sense of humor as a tool for building workplace rapport in "A Professional Perspective."

Chapter 5

- Timely updates in light of the COVID-19 pandemic include new content on challenges for workplace relationships related to remote work as well as work–life balance issues related to working from home.
- A new Career Tip box invites discussion on how to build positive workplace relationships given their importance to success and satisfaction on the job.
- In "A Professional Perspective," digital marketer Josephine Christiani discusses the value of using interpersonal skills to build relationships and reduce high turnover within a corporate job in a high-context culture.

Chapter 6

- Updated content on the importance of cleaning up online identities when preparing for an interview (given the frequency with which organizations engage in cyber-vetting candidates) offers students immediate, actionable tasks.
- A new Technology Tip on un-Googling oneself provides tips to address common online identity red flags.
- The section on The Employment Interview now offers a discussion of the tricky topic of when (and how) to use humor when interviewing for a professional position.
- A new Career Tip provides advice for negotiating salary and benefits when accepting employment.
- In "A Professional Perspective," management consulting specialist KeAnna Whisenhunt argues that a thoughtful self-analysis of previous employment situations is essential for all types of interviews on the job.

Chapter 7

- A new Culture at Work box discusses a culturally insensitive video ad from designer Tori Burch and how diverse perspectives on teams can prevent such offensive and embarrassing events from occurring.
- The section on Virtual Teams has been updated in light of the coronavirus pandemic that forced many teams to make the move to virtual with little to no preparation.
- In "A Professional Perspective," Chelsea Childress (special assistant to the Secretary at the U.S. Department of Veteran's Affairs) discusses the role of asking hard questions, building networks, and taking risks to achieve success in the workplace.

Chapter 8

- This chapter offers the latest research with 22 new references on contemporary topics.
- The section on Virtual Meetings has been revised to reflect the reality of workplace life during the time of COVID-19 restrictions and what it might mean for the future of workplace meetings.
- A new Career Tip box on combatting virtual meeting fatigue explores why this phenomenon happens and how to prevent it or at least lessen its effects.
- In "A Professional Perspective," digital sales manager Nicole Plascencia discusses the challenges (and benefits) of prioritizing virtual meetings with teammates and clients, despite all parties' growing fatigue and frustration with on-screen interaction.

Chapter 9

- This chapter has been revised to offer readers a thorough overview of the types of business presentations that they will most frequently encounter on the job, and includes a new section on podcasting as a type of workplace presentation.

- An entirely new section on Common Audiences for Business Presentations prepares students to think about internal and external audiences, setting the stage for a later discussion of audience analysis.

- In "A Professional Perspective," communication consultant Jeffrey Riddle talks about the importance of knowing your audience and tailoring workplace presentations to their various needs.

Chapter 10

- New content on considering your own level of confidence when analyzing yourself as a speaker aims to help students think through their own communication apprehension when beginning to prepare a presentation.

- A new section on Analyzing Your Group offers tips specific to preparing for a group presentation, including learning the dangers of social loafing.

- A Culture at Work box gives tips on using inclusive language in presentations.

- New content encourages speakers to know their way around a digital platform when speaking virtually as well as they would know their way around the physical location of an in-person speech.

- In "A Professional Perspective," marketing and public relations professional Kristen Bily discusses the two questions that should guide most business presentations: "Why am I presenting?" and "To whom am I speaking?"

Chapter 11

- New content (as well as a new Case Study) on ethical quoting and paraphrasing helps students avoid this common pitfall when preparing content for an effective business presentation.

- Updated content on using visual aids in virtual presentations is covered throughout, including tips on optimizing and compressing photos, using virtual meeting platforms, screen sharing, and engaging with virtual whiteboards.

- A new section on interactive polls as a visual aid encourages students to find ways to make some business presentations more interactive.

- A comprehensive new section on using support ethically includes content on oral and textual citations for visual aids and inclusive language and physical depictions when sharing aids.

- In "A Professional Perspective," digital content, marketing strategy, and analytics specialist Stephanie Russell describes how to build trust with an audience using inclusive, clear language, and straightforward visual aids.

Chapter 12

- This thoroughly revised chapter offers updated and new content on building confidence to address communication apprehension related to business presentations. New sections encourage students to "Focus on the Positive" and "Draw from Negative Experiences" to manage nervousness, while recognizing that audience members cannot generally detect speaker anxiety.

- The section "Rehearse Your Presentation" now includes suggestions specific to rehearsing for virtual presentations.
- A new section, "Assess Your Delivery with Technology" offers specific steps to help students observe their own rehearsals using technology in order to discover opportunities to improve both visually and vocally.
- The chapter features two new Technology Tip boxes. The first explains how students might use a virtual teleprompter when giving a manuscript speech; the second explains security measures to help prevent the unfortunately common experience of videoconference hacking.
- In "A Professional Perspective," account specialist Curtis Falkner describes how he gained confidence in his delivery style after the COVID-19 pandemic forced him to move from in-person client presentations to the virtual realm.

Appendix I
Social media and video conference interviews are now discussed in this appendix.

Appendix II
This appendix has been updated to cover a variety of topics relevant to today's students as they transition to professional writing, including how to address someone if you don't know their preferred pronoun, how to treat slang in writing, when to use reply-all in an e-mail, how to use text messaging (and group texts) in professional contexts, and when to use exclamation marks in business communication. In addition, the discussion of resumes and cover letters is enhanced with advice on avoiding clichés and scanning signatures.

Appendix III
The content on problem-solving communication has been updated to address remote work. In addition, the discussion of "storming" now includes differences in this process between high and low context cultures.

Appendix IV
The sample presentations in this appendix are now organized by general speech purpose (to inform/instruct, to persuade, and to celebrate), corresponding to Chapter 9. The samples are updated with bracketed narrations of guidelines being used in the examples to boost clarity and aid in students' comprehension.

Appendix V
This appendix has been updated with information on the importance of having a crisis plan, including a discussion of the liability issues organizations face for not having a COVID-19 crisis plan.

acknowledgments

We are grateful for the suggestions from colleagues whose thoughts helped guide us in preparing this new edition:

Brandon Wood	College of DuPage
Carl Stoffers	Kean University
Heidi Bolduc	University of Central Florida
Kathy Castle	University of Nebraska-Lincoln
Karley Goen	Tarleton State University
Karen Otto	Florida State College at Jacksonville, North Campus
Minnie Roh	Saint Peter's University
Mandolen Mull	Rockford University
Patrick Daly	Faulkner University, Montgomery Campus
Ryan DePesa	Wentworth Institute of Technology
Renee Rallo	Florida Gulf Coast University
Stellina Chapman	The University of Arkansas
Tim Detwiler	Calvin University

We would like to express our gratitude to members of the McGraw Hill team whose ideas, feedback, and encouragement helped shape this edition of *Communicating at Work*:

- Sarah Remington and Dawn Groundwater: It is a pleasure working with both of you! Thank you for your guidance in the development of our revision plan.
- Karen Moore: We can't thank you enough for going above and beyond for this project! Your keen eye for detail and thoughtful insights made every chapter stronger.

A special thanks also to our production team, Surbhi Sharma and Maria McGreal, as well as Yashoda Rawat, the talented copyeditor whom we were fortunate to have contribute to this edition.

Finally, we thank our colleagues, students, families, and friends for their support. We would like to express a special note of gratitude to Warren "Josh" Maxwell for their contributions to the research-gathering process.

brief contents

contents

Verbal and Nonverbal Messages 88

Interpersonal Skills and Success 124

Principles of Interviewing 162

part three

Working in Groups
Strategic Case:
Museum of Springfield 210

7 Leading and Working in Teams 212

8 Effective Meetings 242

Matej Kastelic/
Shutterstock

12 Delivering the Presentation 380

Communicating at Work

Strategies for Success in
Business and the Professions

PART ONE

Sundown Bakery

laflor/Getty Images

When Carol Teinchek and Bruce Marshall first started Sundown Bakery, the business was fairly simple: Carol ran the shop up front, while Bruce ran the bakery and ordered supplies. When the business began to grow, Carol hired two part-time clerks to help out in the shop. Marina had moved to the country two years earlier from El Salvador, and Kim was a newly arrived Korean working his way through college. Bruce hired Maurice, a French Canadian, as an assistant.

The ovens were soon running 24 hours a day, supervised by Maurice, who was now master baker, and two assistants on each of three shifts. Marina and Kim supervised the shop because Carol was usually too busy managing general sales distribution to spend much time with customers. Bruce still spent 3 or 4 hours a day in the bakery whenever he could get out of his office, but he devoted most of that time to coordinating production and solving problems with Maurice.

Over the next year, Sundown expanded from its original location, adding two new shops as well as two kiosks in local malls. Carol and Bruce hired an operations manager, Hans Mikelson, formerly a regional manager of a national chain of coffee shops. Hans had plenty of new ideas about how to operate an expanding business: He launched a website, added an extensive range of drinks and meal items to the menu, and instituted two dress codes—one for all counter help and another for kitchen employees. He also put together an employee manual to streamline the process of orienting new employees. Hans announced all of these changes by memos, which store managers distributed to the employees.

Sundown's expanding size led to a change in the company. The "family feeling" that had been so strong when Sundown was a small operation became less noticeable. The new employees barely knew Bruce and Carol; as a result, there was less give-and-take of ideas between the owners and workers.

Hans's memos on the dress code and the employee manual created a crisis. Old-time employees were furious about receiving orders from "the bureaucrats," as management came to be called. Bruce and Carol recognized the problem and wanted to keep the lines of communication open, but they weren't sure how to do so. "I'm just a baker," Bruce confessed in exasperation. "I don't know how to run a big company."

Another set of challenges grew out of the changing character of the employees. In the original location alone, Sundown now employed workers from seven different countries. Nadheer, who was born in Yemen, confessed to Bruce that he felt uncomfortable being managed by Carol. "It's nothing personal," he said, "but where I come from, a man doesn't usually take orders from a woman." The Sundown employee profile was diverse in other ways as well: Two of the assistant bakers were gay; one of the sales clerks uses a wheelchair.

Carol, Bruce, and Hans know that good products alone aren't enough to guarantee Sundown Bakery's continuing success. They need to improve the quality of communication among the growing team who make and sell their products.

Basics of Business and Professional Communication

As you read the chapters in this unit, consider the following questions:

chapter 1

1. Apply the Communication Model (see Figure 1.1) to analyze Hans's communication with employees regarding the employee manual and uniforms. Consider the impact of the sender, message, decoding, feedback, context, and probable sources of noise. Which elements seem to contribute most to the apparent lack of shared understanding?
2. Identify the changes that have occurred in the communication channels between employees and management as Sundown Bakery has grown. Suggest alternative communication strategies that might have reduced employee resentment. Explain why these channels could help improve management's communication about workplace changes. How might an organization's culture affect its choice of communication channels?
3. Identify the instrumental, relational, and identity messages that employees seem to have received from management as Sundown's business grew. Which functions of downward communication do you notice? Can you find examples of upward and horizontal communication in this case study? How could Sundown improve its upward communication flow?
4. How have Sundown's formal and informal communication networks changed as the company expanded? In which ways have both the formal and informal networks contributed to Sundown's growing pains? In which ways can these networks be used to improve the relationships between management and employees?

chapter 2

1. How do the changes in the demographic makeup of Sundown Bakery reflect transformation of the larger workforce as described in Communication in a Diverse Society section?
2. Reflect on the six parts of the Customs and Behavior section. Cite a specific instance or predict the impact of three of these customs and behaviors in this workplace.
3. Consider the following hidden dimensions of culture as you describe the impact of culture on communication within the company: high- and low-context styles, individualism and collectivism, power distance, uncertainty avoidance, masculinity/femininity, and long-term orientation.
4. Using the guidelines in the Communicating across Diversity section, which specific advice would you give to Sundown's management team about how to communicate most effectively in the face of the company's growth?

Chapter One
Communicating at Work

chapter outline

chapter objectives

After reading this chapter you should be able to:

1. Explain the role of communication in career success, providing examples to support your claims.

2. Apply the key principles of communication, knowledge of the basic elements of the communication model, and considerations of effective communication channel use to a specific situation, showing how each one affects the outcome of the interaction.

3. Describe how formal and informal communication networks operate in a given situation in your career field; then create a strategic plan of personal networking to accomplish your goals within an organization.

4. Apply the concepts of ethical communication discussed here to one or more ethically challenging situations.

• Communication and Career Success

The next time you look for job postings online, talk to recruiters at a job fair or check out internship opportunities at your college's career services office, look a little closer. No matter which type of position you are seeking—from an entry-level job to a highly technical professional position—chances are you will see "excellent communication skills" listed as a job requirement.

Regardless of which occupations they pursue, people spend a staggering amount of time communicating on the job. At many companies, employees spend around 80% of the workweek on the phone, in meetings, and communicating by e-mail.[1] However, it is not just the amount of time spent communicating that is important. When it comes to communication, quality matters in almost every career.[2] Scientists must convey important findings—such as the transmission rate of viruses—to general audiences. Engineers spend most of their professional lives speaking and listening, mostly in one-to-one and small group settings.[3] Accountants may crunch numbers, but they also need to communicate

effectively to serve their clients. That is why certified public accountants (CPAs) and the firms that hire them constantly cite effective communication as essential for career success.[4]

Effective communication is an essential tool for achieving a healthy workplace culture and business success.[5] As a matter of fact, a global study found that companies with high communication effectiveness are three and a half times more likely to outperform their competitors.[6] On-the-job communication skills can also mean the difference between life and death. The Los Angeles Police Department cited "bad communication" as one of the most common reasons for errors in shooting by its officers.[7] Communication skills are also essential for doctors, nurses, and other medical professionals.[8] A survey by a major hospital accreditation group identified "communication failures" among the root causes of medical errors—including errors related to death, serious physical injury, and psychological trauma.[9] Research published in the *Journal of the American Medical Association* and elsewhere suggests there is a significant difference between the communication skills of physicians who have no malpractice claims against them and doctors with previous claims.[10]

CAREER **tip**

Communication skills are also essential for personal career success. Employees in technical careers who have effective communication skills earn more money than their counterparts who are weak communicators.[11] Table 1-1 summarizes the results of one survey in which employers list the skills and qualities for their ideal candidate. Included in the top ten skills are problem-solving skills, the ability to work in a team, written and verbal communication, and leadership.[12] Although this survey is distributed annually, communication skills are always near the top of the list. Executive coach and pharmaceutical recruiter Jim Richman made this point most emphatically: "If I give any advice, it is that you can never do enough training around your overall communication skills."[13]

Many people fail to realize the full extent of the role of communication in career success. One survey revealed that nearly 80% of students believe that they are competent in oral and written communication; however, only 42% of employers agreed that the students were proficient in these areas.[14] In other words, many students underestimate the importance of good communication while overstating their own abilities. This is not a recipe for success.

Because communication skills are an essential ingredient in professional and organizational accomplishment, this book is dedicated to helping you hone your talents in this important area.

Table 1-1	Top Qualities/Skills Employers Seek on a Candidate's Résumé
	1. Problem-solving skills
	2. Ability to work in a team
	3. Strong work ethic
	4. Analytical/quantitative skills
	5. Communication skills (written)
	6. Leadership
	7. Communication skills (verbal)
	8. Initiative
	9. Detail-oriented
	10. Technical skills

Source: *Job Outlook 2020,* National Association of Colleges and Employers.

• The Nature of Communication

Communication looks simple and almost effortless, especially when it goes smoothly. But every communicative exchange is affected by principles that are not always apparent. Understanding this process better can help you make strategic choices that help achieve both personal and organizational goals.

Communication Principles

A more sophisticated understanding of how communication operates begins with some fundamental principles.

Communication Is Unavoidable   A fundamental axiom of communication is "One cannot not communicate."[15] As you will learn in Chapter 4, facial expression, posture, gesture, clothing, and a host of other behaviors offer cues about our attitudes. The notion that we are always communicating means we send messages even by our absence. Failing to show up at an event or leaving the room suggests meaning to others. Because communication is unavoidable, it is essential to consider the unintentional messages you send.

Communication Is Strategic   Almost all communication is aimed at achieving goals. On the job, the most obvious type is **instrumental communication**, or messages aimed at accomplishing the task at hand. Your manager is communicating instrumentally when she says, "I need that report by noon," and you are pursuing instrumental goals when you ask, "How long does the report need to be?" People are not always direct in their communication about instrumental goals. Saying, "Wow—look at the time!" could be an implicit message designed to accomplish the task of ending a conversation. Furthermore, in a negotiation, your "final offer" may actually be a bargaining ploy to get a better deal.

Jose Luis Pelaez Inc/Blend Images LLC

The second set of goals involves **relational communication**, or messages that shape and reflect the way people regard one another. As we will explore in Chapter 5, building positive relationships is not just about being sociable. A positive climate in the workplace also helps us accomplish instrumental goals. Conversely, a negative relationship can make it difficult, or even impossible, to accomplish the task at hand.

Virtually all messages contain both instrumental and relational dimensions. When a customer service representative asks, "How can I help you?" the instrumental nature of this question is obvious. But the *way* the question is asked shapes the tenor of the relationship between the representative and the customer—rushed or deliberate, sincere or phony, friendly or unfriendly.[16]

A third, less obvious reason we communicate involves **identity management**, which is the practice of presenting yourself in ways that produce a preferred image and distinctive sense of self. To understand this concept, list 10 words or phrases that describe the way you would like others to see you on the job. Your list probably includes terms such as *competent*, *trustworthy*, and *efficient*. (Be sure to complete your own list before reading on.) Taken together, the attributes on this list (and many others) make up the professional identity you want to create. Next, think about the ways you communicate, both verbally and nonverbally, to get others to accept your identity. If being calm under pressure is part of your preferred identity, what do you say or do to project that quality? If you want others to see you as knowledgeable, how do you communicate to create that impression?

As these examples show, communication is often *strategic*; in other words, we intentionally craft messages for the purpose of achieving instrumental, relational, and identity goals. However, we do not always realize that we are being strategic in our communication. Think about the last time you met a new person. You probably did not have the following thoughts running through your mind: "Must look confident and friendly! Firm handshake! Direct eye contact! Remember to smile!" While many of these behaviors are performed subconsciously, crafting a thoughtful strategy to achieve your goals can boost the odds you will succeed.

The authors of this book suggest a variety of communication strategies you can use to achieve your goals and the objectives of the organizations with which you are involved. Many of these strategies focus on specific work-related contexts, such as interviews, meetings, and presentations. Others will be useful in almost every professional context where you want to enhance your professional identity, manage relationships, and get the job done most effectively.

At first, the notion of strategic communication might seem unethical. In reality, communicating purposefully is not necessarily dishonest. For example, organizational spokespersons must be strategic in how they phrase their messages when communicating with the public during a crisis event. If family members are grieving over the loss of a loved one due to a workplace accident, a spokesperson may strategically choose to acknowledge that they are hurting, rather than saying, "I know how you feel." The guidelines in the Ethical Dimensions of Communication section show that it is possible to be strategic while still respecting others' rights and needs.

Communication Is Irreversible

At one time or another, everyone has wished they could take back words they regretted uttering. Unfortunately, this is not possible. Our words and deeds are recorded in others' memories, and we cannot erase them. As the old saying goes, people may forgive, but they do not forget. In fact, the more vigorously you try to erase an act, the more vividly it may stand out.

Communication Is a Process

It is not accurate to talk about an "act" of communication as if sending or receiving a message is an isolated event. Rather, every communication event needs to be examined as part of its communication context. As an example, suppose your boss responds to your request for a raise by saying, "I was going to ask you to take a *cut* in pay!" How would you react? The answer probably depends on several factors: Is your boss a joker or a serious person? How does the comment fit into the history of your relationship—have your boss's remarks been critical or supportive in the past? How does the message fit with the ones you have received from other people? What kind of mood are you in today? All these questions show that the meaning of a message depends in part on what has happened before the message. Each message is part of a process: It does not occur in isolation.

Communication Is Not a Panacea

Panacea comes from the Greek word *panakeia,* meaning "all-healing." Just as alchemists during the Renaissance believed there was an elixir that would give eternal life, some individuals today believe that communication is a cure-all for problems. Although communication can certainly smooth out the bumps and straighten the road to success, misunderstandings and ill feelings may still occur.[17] Even effective communication cannot solve all problems. In some situations, the parties may understand one another perfectly yet still disagree. These limitations are important to understand as you begin to study communication on the job. Boosting your communication skills may increase your effectiveness, but improvements in those skills will not be a remedy for every situation that you encounter.

Derogatory E-mails Lead to Firings

Three employees of the Iowa Civil Rights Commission learned the hard way that digital gossip can be costly. They were fired after supervisors found they had used the state's e-mail system to disparage and ridicule coworkers. The culprits referred to colleagues by offensive nicknames, such as Monster, Psycho, Stoned Intern, Roid Rage, Extreme Makeover, Where's My Car?, and Albino. A representative message read,

"Where's My Car and Psycho are talking about food—a match made in stoner/fatty heaven!"

The workers called their e-mails harmless office chatter. "It was just talk, water cooler chat," one protested. An administrative law judge disagreed, characterizing their messages as "misconduct" that disqualified them from receiving unemployment insurance benefits.

Source: Foley, R. J. (2011, August 22)., Email exchanges gets three Iowa civil rights investigators fired. *Cedar Rapids Gazette*.

Basics of the Communication Model

No matter what the setting is or how many people are involved, all communication consists of the same elements. Understanding those elements can help explain what happens when one person tries to express an idea to others. It can also offer clues about why some of these attempts succeed and others fail.

The communication process begins with a **sender**, the person who transmits a **message**.[18] Some messages are deliberate, whereas others (such as sighs and yawns) may be unintentional. The sender must choose specific words or nonverbal methods to send an intentional message. This activity is called **encoding**. The **channel** (sometimes called the *medium*) is the method used to deliver a message. You will read much more about channels in the next section.

Even when a message reaches its intended receiver intact, there is no guarantee it will be understood as the sender intended it to be.[19] The **receiver** must still attach meaning to the words or behavior. Receivers actively interpret and respond to the messages they have received, both unintentionally and intentionally. The process of a receiver attaching meaning to a message—such as when a teacher interprets a student's yawn as signifying that the student is bored by the lecture—is called **decoding**.

Misunderstandings often arise because messages can be decoded, or interpreted, in more than one way. Consider a situation in which a customer responds to a slip-up by saying, "Don't worry about it." Perhaps the literal statement is accurate: "There's absolutely no need to worry." Or perhaps the customer means, "It isn't perfect, but I can tolerate the mistake." The customer could also be annoyed yet not want to say bluntly, "I'm really unhappy." In the coming chapters, you will learn a variety of strategies for reaching a shared understanding during these situations.

The receiver's observable response to a sender's message is called **feedback**. Some feedback is nonverbal—smiles, sighs, frowns, and so on. Sometimes it is verbal, as when you react to a colleague's ideas with questions or comments. Feedback can also be written, as when you respond by writing an e-mail to your coworker. In many cases, the lack of a message is a type of feedback. Failure to answer a letter or to return a phone call, for example, can suggest how a receiver feels about the sender.

Even though we have described sending and receiving as discrete roles, communication is actually a two-way process. Especially when communication is instantaneous—in face-to-face settings, phone conversations, and web conferencing—people are simultaneously senders and receivers. Imagine pitching an idea (sending a message) to your manager (receiver). While listening to your idea, your manager frowns (sending feedback), and you immediately attempt to adjust your communication (receiver). Both of you are sending and receiving messages at the same time. Because sending and receiving are simultaneous and connected, these two roles are combined into the "communicator" positions represented on both sides of the model pictured in Figure 1.1.

Once you understand that receiving and sending are simultaneous and connected, you start to recognize that successful communication is not something active senders do to passive receivers. Rather, it is a collaborative process in which the participants create a shared understanding through the exchange of messages. In other words, communication is not something we do *to* others, but rather a process we do *with* them. An effective way to build shared meaning is to practice other-orientation—that is, to try to understand the other person's viewpoint, whether or not we agree with it. Feedback helps us in this process of building shared meaning.

One of the greatest barriers to effective communication is **noise**—factors that interfere with the exchange of messages. The most obvious type of noise is *environmental,* or based on the communicators' surroundings. The babble of voices in the next room, the annoying ring of someone's mobile notifications during a meeting, and a smelly cigar are all examples of environmental noise. The second type of noise is *physiological*—physical issues such as hearing disorders, illnesses, disabilities, and other factors that make it difficult to send or receive messages. To appreciate the impact of physiological noise, recall how tough it is to process messages when you are recovering from a late-night study session or have a headache. The third type of noise is *psychological*—forces within the sender or the receiver that interfere with understanding, such as egotism, defensiveness, assumptions, stereotypes, biases, prejudices, hostility, preoccupation, and fear. If you were thinking strategically about communicating with someone at work, what steps could you take to reduce the amount of noise in your environment before delivering your message?

Communication Channels

As a business communicator, the channel you choose to deliver your message can have a big influence on your effectiveness. Should you express your ideas in a phone call? Put them into a text message or e-mail? Send them in hard copy? Or should you express yourself in person? Deciding which communication channel to use is not a trivial matter; communication researchers have extensively studied which factors lead to good channel

FIGURE 1.1
Communication
Model

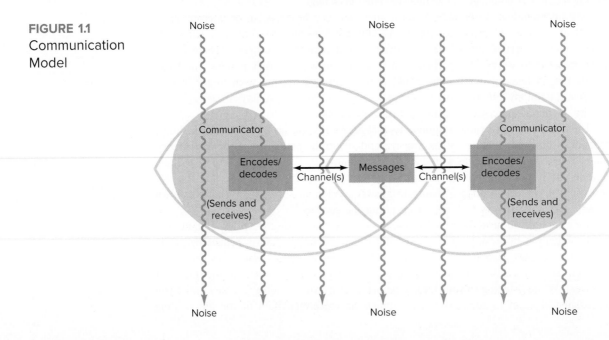

choice.[20] To select the best channel, you should consider several aspects related to the communication.

Consider Channel Characteristics New technologies have given business people a wider range of choices for communication than ever before. It was not that long ago when the choices were in-person communication, telephone call, fax, pager message, or written memo. Today, other options include e-mail messages, voice mail, live streaming, web conferencing, social media, mobile phone calls, texting, and more. One way to start evaluating these choices is to consider how each channel's different characteristics match up with your communication goals.

- *Richness.* Richness refers to the amount of information that can be transmitted using a given channel. Three aspects determine the richness of a channel: (1) whether it can handle many types of cues at once, (2) whether it allows for quick feedback from both senders and receivers, and (3) whether it allows for a personal focus.[21] Ideally, when announcing an important decision that may affect employees (e.g., the acquisition of another company), you would select a rich channel to convey this information. Face-to-face communication would likely be preferred in such a situation because it allows for the communication and decoding of verbal and nonverbal cues, simultaneous feedback, and a personal focus. In contrast, lean channels carry much less information. While a lean e-mail channel is a good choice for exchanging information efficiently, it is not as effective when factors such as tone and emotion are important. Even the inclusion of emojis such as "smiley faces" may not prevent e-mail misunderstandings.[22]

- *Speed.* The speed of the channel refers to how quickly the exchange of messages occurs. High-speed or instantaneous channels support **synchronous communication**; they include face-to-face conversations, video chat, and telephone conversations. A key benefit of synchronous channels is that no time lag separates the transmission and reception of messages, so immediate feedback is possible. That is, you can respond to questions as soon as they arise and rephrase or elaborate as necessary. If you need a price quote *now*, or if you need to discuss a complex idea that will need elaboration, a high-speed channel is probably the best choice. Nevertheless, high-speed, synchronous communication is not always desirable. Another option is **asynchronous communication**, which occurs through channels such as e-mail, interoffice memos, and voice mail. In these "low-speed" channels, there is a lag between the transmission and reception of messages. These channels can be effective for less urgent requests. In addition, if you want to avoid a knee-jerk reaction and encourage careful thought, you might be better off choosing an asynchronous method to deliver your message.

- *Control.* Control refers to the degree to which you can manage the communication process. Of course, because communication is a two-way process, you can never have complete control over it. Even so, different channels offer different types of control. In written channels (such as e-mail and social media posts), you can exert more control over how you encode a message because you will be able to write, proofread, and edit it as many times as you need until you get it exactly the way you want. If you have something highly sensitive to say, this might be a good channel to choose. But there are also some trade-offs to this kind of channel. Even though you might spend hours drafting a memo, letter, or report, the recipient may scan it superficially or not read it at all. In contrast, in a face-to-face channel, you have much more control over the receiver's attention. You can reduce noise, interpret nonverbal signals of understanding, or even explicitly ask the sender to pay more attention to your message.

Consider the Desired Tone of Your Message

In general, channels that utilize oral communication—face-to-face, telephone, video conference—are best for communicating messages that have a personal dimension. One corporate manager, whose company spends more than $4 million annually on employee travel, makes the case for face-to-face contact: "Nothing takes the place of a handshake, going to lunch, seeing their eyes."[23] These types of channels are also best for ideas that have a strong need for visual support, in the form of a demonstration, photos or slides, and so on. Spoken communication is also especially useful when immediate feedback is needed, such as in question-and-answer sessions or as a quick reply to your ideas.

Written communication works well when you want your message to have a relatively formal tone. Writing is almost always the best medium when you must choose your words carefully. Writing is also better than speaking when you want to convey complicated ideas that are likely to require much study and thought on the part of the receiver. Likewise, it is smart to put your message in writing when you want it to be the final word, with no feedback or discussion. Finally, writing is the best option for *any* message if you want a record of that communication. In business and the professions, sending confirming letters and e-mails is a common practice, as is keeping meeting minutes. These steps guarantee that what is said will be a matter of record, with the documentation being useful in case of later misunderstandings or disputes and in case anyone wants to review the history of an issue. Handwritten notes of thanks or sympathy also express thoughtfulness and add a personal touch that is lost in many electronic messages.

Consider the Organization's Culture

Besides message-related considerations, the culture of the organization in which you work may favor some communication channels over others.[24] Along with an organization's overall preference for certain channels, it is important to consider the preferences of particular departments or even individuals. For example, the computer support staff members in some organizations respond to e-mails, while in other companies a phone call to the help desk is the best way to get a quick response. If you know a coworker or your boss responds only to face-to-face reminders, your best bet is to use that approach. In fact, one study indicated that employees who followed corporate norms for e-mail and instant messaging received higher performance evaluations.[25]

Consider Using Multiple Channels

In some cases, it is wise to send a message using more than one channel. For example, you could:

- Distribute a written text or outline that parallels your presentation.
- Follow a letter, fax, or e-mail message with a phone call, or call first and then write.
- Send a report or proposal, and then make appointments with your readers to discuss it.

This redundancy capitalizes on the diverse strengths of the various channels and boosts the odds of getting your desired message across. One study revealed that following up a face-to-face exchange with an e-mail that included supplemental information was more persuasive than the single-channel approach. The dual-channel approach also enhanced the sender's credibility.[26]

Sometimes channel selection involves trade-offs. For example, face-to-face communication is rich and fast, and it allows you to have much control over the receiver's attention. It also has the potential to create personal bonds that are more difficult to forge through other types of communication. Unfortunately, personal contacts can be difficult to schedule, even when people work in the same building. A cross-town trip for a half-hour meeting

The Virtues of Going Offline

Today's array of communication technologies makes it possible to be connected to others on a nearly around-the-clock basis. Along with their benefits, however, the technologies that keep workers connected have a downside. When your boss, colleagues, and customers can reach you at any time, you can become too distracted to tackle the necessary parts of your job.

Communication researchers have discovered that remote workers have developed two strategies for reducing contact and thereby increasing their efficiency.[27] The first simply involves disconnecting from

time to time—logging off the computer, forwarding the phone call to voice mail, or simply ignoring incoming messages. The researchers labeled the second strategy *dissimulation.* With this approach, teleworkers discourage contact by disguising their activities—for example, changing their instant message status to "in a meeting" or posting a fake "out of the office" message online.

It's important to note that these strategies are typically used not to avoid work but rather to get more done. Too much connectivity is similar to many aspects of life: More is not always better.

---

can consume most of the morning or afternoon. Sometimes it is impossible to access contacts face-to-face when a colleague works in a different state or country, or during a situation like the COVID-19 crisis.

Ultimately, the question is not which communication channel to use, but when to use each one most effectively.[28] Knowing how to choose the optimal channel can have a strong impact on your career. In one survey, managers who were identified as "media sensitive"—those who carefully matched the channel to the message—were almost twice as likely to receive top ratings in their performance reviews when compared with less-media-sensitive peers.[29] Table 1-2 presents some guidelines that will help you decide how to deliver your message most effectively.

• Communicating in and beyond Organizations

For most of us, work is collaborative. Whether the people we work with are in adjacent cubicles or on the other side of the world, we are members of **communication networks**—patterns of contact created by the flow of messages among communicators through time and space.[30] Two kinds of networks exist: formal and informal.

Formal Communication Networks

Formal communication networks are systems designed by management that dictate who should communicate with whom to get a job done. In small organizations, these "chain of command" networks are so simple they may hardly be noticeable. In larger organizations, they become more intricate. The most common way of describing formal communication networks is with **organizational charts** like the one in Figure 1.2. Organizational charts provide clear guidelines indicating who is responsible for a given task and which employees are responsible for others' performance. They also depict optimal flows of communication, including downward, upward, and horizontal communication.

Downward Communication   **Downward communication**, sometimes referred to as top-down communication, occurs whenever leaders or managers send messages to their

Table 1-2	Considerations in Choosing a Communication Channel

	Richness	Speed	Control over Message	Control over Attention	Tone	Level of Detail
Face-to-Face	High	Synchronous	Low	High	Personal	Moderate
Telephone Calls, Teleconferencing, and Videoconferencing	Moderate	Synchronous	Low	Moderate	Personal	Moderate
Voice Mail	Moderate	Asynchronous	Moderate	Low	Moderate	Low
E-mail	Low	Asynchronous	High	Low	Impersonal-Moderate	High
Instant Messaging	Low	Asynchronous but potentially quick	Moderate	Moderate	Moderate	Low
Text Messaging	Low	Asynchronous but potentially quick	High	Low	Impersonal-Moderate	Low
Hard Copy (e.g., handwritten or typed message)	Low	Asynchronous	High	Low	Depends on writer's style	High

FIGURE 1.2
A Formal
Communication
Network

Organizational Chart

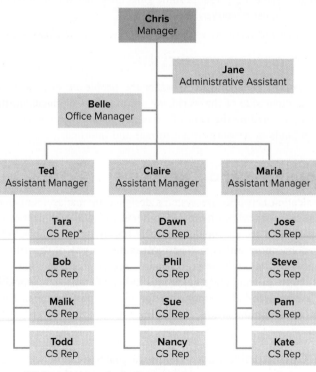

*CS Rep = Customer Service Representative

lower-level employees. Downward communication is usually one-directional; in other words; the higher-level communicator does not invite a response from the lower-level recipient.[31]

Examples of downward communication include explaining an organization's mission or vision, assigning directives or giving job instructions, and providing feedback. Business communication experts John Anderson and Dale Level have identified five benefits of effective downward communication:

- Better coordination
- Improved individual performance
- Improved morale
- Improved consumer relations
- Improved industrial relations[32]

Most managers would agree—at least in principle—that downward communication is important. It is hard to argue with the need for giving instructions, describing procedures, explaining rationales, and so on. Like their bosses, employees recognize the importance of downward communication. A study at General Electric (GE) revealed that "clear communication between boss and worker" was the most important factor in job satisfaction for most people. GE was so impressed with the findings of this study that it launched a program to encourage managers to communicate more, and more directly, with their employees, including holding informal meetings to encourage interaction.[33]

The desire for feedback is probably so strong among most employees because supervisors rarely provide enough of it. As two leading researchers put it: "The frequent complaint . . . by the individual is that he [sic] does not know where he stands with his superiors."[34] Many companies do take a more enlightened approach to feedback. Ed Carlson, former president of United Airlines, is generally credited with turning the company from a loser into a winner during his tenure. Part of his success was due to his emphasis on keeping United's employees—all of them—aware of how the company was doing. "Nothing is worse for morale than a lack of information down in the ranks," he said. "I call it NETMA—Nobody Ever Tells Me Anything—and I have tried hard to minimize that problem."[35] True to his word, Carlson passed along to the field staff information on United's operations that was previously considered too important to circulate.

Upward Communication

Messages flowing from the lower levels of hierarchy to upper levels are labeled **upward communication**. One form of upward communication is **Voice of Employee (VoE)**, or employees expressing ideas, grievances, and suggestions.[36] A variety of tools exist for providing such feedback, including annual employee surveys, posts on job sites like Glassdoor, and online employee sentiment tools. One study found that employees who hold central positions in the formal network are more likely to speak up with ideas and suggestions; however, their perceptions of peer support may influence their willingness to do so.[37]

Businesses that truly are open to upward communication can profit from the opinions of employees.[38] Mark Whitten, U.S. director of operations for Martinrea International, credited one-on-one meetings with each of his employees—a total of 550 meetings—for a host of positive changes in organizational culture. Among the benefits were increased employee satisfaction, $200 million in new business, and a supplier award from customers.[39] Bestselling author John Izzo emphasized the importance of listening to employees in an interview with Business News Daily, saying "the bottom line is that people want to

Getting Recognized by Your Bosses

According to career advisors Caroline Zaayer Kaufman and Tyler Omoth, no matter how great you are at your job, it's hard to advance if your boss isn't noticing you. Both offer tips for how you can showcase your talent, create interest in your work, and display your potential:

- **Be early to work.** Showing up just 10 minutes early can increase your chances of being noticed.

- **Speak up during meetings.** Employees who offer ideas and suggestions to problems are more likely to be noticed for their contribution.

- **Share your achievements.** Your boss may not realize the positive contributions you are making to the company; use your boss's preferred method of communication to share relevant updates.

- **Be involved.** Volunteer to participate on committees, service projects, or other events. Create opportunities to meet and build relationships with people at many levels of your organization.

- **Recognize your co-workers' success.** Take the time to praise others for their work to foster positive relationships and build a reputation as a supportive colleague.

Source: Kaufman, C. Z. (n.d.). 10 ways to get your work noticed by senior staff. *Monster*. Retrieved from https://www.monster.com/career-advice/article/employee-recognition-1117; Omoth, T. (n.d). 6 ways to impress your boss. *TopResume*. Retrieved from https://www.topresume.com/career-advice/6-ways-to-get-your-boss-to-notice-you

be heard and feel valued."[40] As the Career Tip suggests, getting recognized by your supervisor can pave the way to career advancement.

Upward communication can convey what employees are doing, which unsolved dilemmas they are facing, how problem areas might be improved, and how employees feel about one another and the workplace.[41] These messages can benefit both lower-level employees (subordinates) and upper-level management (superiors)—which explains why the most satisfied employees feel free to express dissent to their bosses.[42] Bennis emphasizes the critical role that upward communication plays in the success of an organization:

> The longer I study effective leaders, the more I am convinced of the underappreciated importance of effective followers. What makes a good follower? The single most important characteristic may well be a willingness to tell the truth. In a world of growing complexity, leaders are increasingly dependent on their subordinates for good information, whether the leaders want to [be] or not. Followers who tell the truth, and leaders who listen, are an unbeatable combination.[43]

Despite its importance, upward communication is not always easy. Almost every organization *claims* to seek upward messages, but many supervisors are not as open to employee opinions as they purport themselves to be. Being frank with superiors can be both important and risky, especially when the news is not what the boss wants to hear.[44] One executive gives an example:

> In my first C.E.O. job, a young woman who worked for me walked in one day and said, "Do you know that the gossip in the office is that the way for a woman to get ahead is to wear frilly spring dresses?" And I just looked at her and asked, "Where did this come from?" She said, "Well, you said, 'pretty dress' to four women who happened to be dressed that way. And so now it's considered policy."[45]

Some organizations have developed systems to promote upward communication in the face of potential challenges. British Airways launched an online suggestion box for its employees. One idea was to make the planes lighter by descaling the toilet pipes. As unusual as it might sound, the implementation of this idea cut the cost of fuel by over $900,000 a year.[46]

Most of the responsibility for improving upward communication rests with managers. One study showed the likelihood of reporting bad news was highest when employees trusted supervisors and when there was a history in the organization of leaders resolving problems.[47] They can begin the process by announcing their willingness to hear from subordinates. A number of vehicles can be used to facilitate upward messages—an open-door policy, grievance procedures, periodic interviews, group meetings, and the suggestion box, to name a few. Nevertheless, formal channels are not the only way to promote upward messages. In fact, informal contacts are often the most effective approach. Chats during breaks, in the elevator, or at social gatherings can sometimes tell more than planned sessions. Even so, no method will be effective unless a manager is sincerely interested in hearing from employees and genuinely values their ideas. Just talking about the desirability of upward communication is not enough; employees have to see evidence of a willingness to hear upward messages—both good and bad—before they will really open up.

Horizontal Communication   A third type of organizational interaction is **horizontal communication** (sometimes called *lateral communication*). This type of communication occurs between people, divisions, or departments that would be considered on an equal level in the organizational hierarchy. Communications occurring among office workers in the same department, coworkers on a construction project, and teachers at a middle school are all examples of horizontal communication.

Horizontal communication serves five purposes[48]:

- *Task coordination:* "Let's get together this afternoon and set up a production schedule."
- *Problem-solving:* "It takes three days for my department to get reports from yours. How can we speed things up?"
- *Sharing information:* "I just found out a big convention is coming to town next week, so we ought to get ready for lots of business."
- *Conflict resolution:* "I've heard you were complaining about my work to the boss. If you're not happy, I wish you would tell me first."
- *Building rapport:* "I appreciate the way you got that rush job done on time. I'd like to say thanks by buying you lunch."

Top-performing organizations encourage people from different areas to get together and share ideas. At Hewlett-Packard, worldwide personnel manager Barbara Waugh and her colleagues spent five years improving horizontal communication. "My role is to create mirrors that show the whole what the parts are doing—through coffee talks and small meetings, through building a network, through bringing people together who have similar or complementary ideas."[49]

Despite the importance of horizontal communication, several forces may discourage communication among peers.[50] *Rivalry* is one such factor. People who feel threatened by one another are not likely to be cooperative. This sense of threat can stem from competition for a promotion, a raise, or another scarce resource. Another challenge is the *specialization* required for people with different technical specialties to understand one another. A communication professor and a geographic information science professor may find it difficult to collaborate because of their individual specialties, despite being peers in the hierarchy of a university setting. *Information overload* may also discourage employees from reaching out to others in different areas. A simple *lack of motivation* is another problem. Finally, *physical barriers,* such as having offices scattered throughout different buildings, can interfere with horizontal connections.

Sydney Shaffer/Photodisc/Getty Images RF

Informal Communication Networks

So far, we have focused on networks within organizations that are created by management. Alongside the formal networks, every organization also has **informal communication networks**—patterns of interaction based on friendships, shared personal or career interests, and proximity. One business writer described the value of informal networks:

A firm's organizational chart will tell you about authority. It doesn't always show how things get done or created. You know the rules, but you don't know the ropes. For that, you need a map to the network, the corresponding informal structure that is usually invisible.[51]

Informal relationships within organizations operate in ways that have little to do with the formal relationships laid out in organizational charts.[52] Figure 1.3 shows how the actual flow of information in one firm is quite different from its formal structure. Moreover, beyond any sort of organizational connection, people are connected with one another through informal personal networks—with friends, neighbors, family members, and all sorts of other relationships.

Some informal networks arise because of personal interests. Two colleagues who are avid basketball fans or share a fascination with rare books are more likely to swap information about work than coworkers who have no such bonds. Personal friendships create connections that can lead to increased communication. Finally, physical proximity increases the chances of interaction. Shared office space or frequent meetings around the copying machine make it more likely that people will exchange information.

Informal networks are often a source of important job-related information, organizational resources, career advice, and social connections that help workers successfully navigate their careers. When someone is excluded from that network—even unintentionally—they are placed at a major disadvantage. For example, research has shown that isolation from informal communication networks has a real impact on career success.[53] The difference is even more pronounced for minority women, who face "concrete walls" that isolate them from informal relationships with superiors and peers.[54] It is important to identify the informal networks in your organization and try to get as involved as possible—especially if you are a minority.

Not all informal messages are idle rumors. Informal communication can serve several useful functions:

- *Confirming formal messages:* "The boss is really serious this time about cutting down on overnight travel. I heard him yelling about it when I walked past his office."

FIGURE 1.3
An Informal Communication Network

Source: Adapted from Orbe, M. P., & Bruess, C. J. (2007), *Contemporary issues in interpersonal communication.* New York: Oxford University Press.

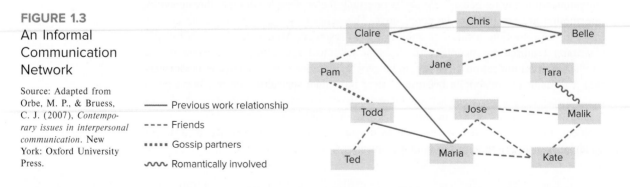

——— Previous work relationship

- - - - Friends

••••• Gossip partners

∿∿∿ Romantically involved

- *Expanding on formal messages:* "The invitation to the office party says 'casual dress,' but don't make it too informal."

- *Expediting official messages:* You might learn about openings within an organization from people in your network long before the vacancies are published.

- *Contradicting official messages:* You might learn from a friend in accounting that the deadline for purchases on this year's budget is not as firm as it sounded in the comptroller's recent memo.

- *Circumventing formal channels:* Your tennis partner who works in duplicating might sneak in an occasional rush job for you instead of putting it at the end of the line.

Many companies elevate informal communication to an official policy by encouraging open, unstructured contacts between people from various parts of the organization. Some observers consider informal contacts to be the primary means of communication within an organization. In one survey, 57% of the respondents said that communicating with informal contacts is "the only way to find out what's really happening" in their organizations.[55] A decade of research shows engineers and scientists are five times more likely to turn to a person for information than to impersonal sources such as databases or files.[56]

Writing in *Harvard Business Review,* David Krackhardt and Jeffrey Hanson capture the difference between formal and informal networks: "If the formal organization is the skeleton of a company, the informal [organization] is the central nervous system."[57] Like the human nervous system, informal networks are faster and often more dependable than formal channels.[58] They also provide a shortcut for (and sometimes a way around) the slower and more cumbersome formal channels, making innovation easier.[59] This fact helps explain why organizational decision-makers tend to base their decisions on verbal information from trusted associates.[60] Smart communicators do not just rely on informal contacts with peers for information, but rather take advantage of sources throughout the organization. One study revealed that general managers spent a great deal of time with people who were not direct subordinates, superiors, or peers—people with whom, according to the official chain of command, they had no need to deal. Although many of these people—administrative assistants, lower-level subordinates, and supervisors with little power—seemed relatively unimportant to outsiders, successful managers all seemed to cultivate such contacts.[61]

Enlightened organizations do everything possible to encourage constructive, informal interactions. Upon purchasing an old bank building to use as an office, England marketing agency Team Eleven hired an office design agency to design a floor plan that inspires creative ideas. Dubbed "The Bank of Brilliant Ideas," Team Eleven's office space uses centrally-located soft furniture, as well as a "freak show" themed meeting room to encourage workers to mingle and swap ideas.[62]

Informal networks do not just operate within organizations. Friends, neighbors, and community members increase their effectiveness by sharing information with one another. In some cities, chambers of commerce host networking events to encourage ties among community businesses. Even without these organized contacts, most people are surprised to realize just how many people they know who can offer useful information.

Personal Networking

While all of us have personal contacts, **networking**, as the term is typically used, has a strategic dimension that goes beyond being sociable. It is the process of deliberately meeting people and maintaining contacts to give and receive career information, advice, and leads.

CAREER **tip**

Your Elevator Speech

Often the chance to present yourself and your ideas last less than a minute. You meet a prospective customer at a party. You run into your boss on the street. You are introduced to a potential employer in a hallway. Whether networking opportunities like these turn out well may depend on your foresight and preparation.

When the opportunity arises, you can make a good impression by delivering what is called an "elevator speech" or "elevator pitch." (This type of communication gets its name because it should be brief enough to deliver in the length of an elevator ride.) Elevator speeches can accomplish a variety of goals. Besides serving as introductions, they can be a tool for seeking help, establishing a relationship, gaining visibility, marketing yourself or your organization, getting feedback, expanding your personal network, and doing an end-run around someone who is blocking your progress. A written version of your elevator pitch may also be included in your professional online profiles, such as LinkedIn.

Your speech should contain four parts and take 20 to 30 seconds to deliver.

1. State your name and your current job title or position.
   "Hi. I'm Mayra Alaniz. It's nice to meet you! I'm a senior, graduating in December."

2. Give a brief summary of your background, high-lighting strengths or experiences.
   "I'm completing my computer science major this semester with a 3.8 GPA, and I recently developed additional skills by attending a coding boot camp in Austin, Texas."

3. Depending on your audience, make your "pitch" by sharing what you can do for others *or* asking for their help.
   "If you or someone you know needs help with coding or web development, I can help," *or* "If you know of any openings in computer science, I'd like to hear about them."

4. Include a call to action, by sharing how the person can get in touch with you or how you plan to contact this person.
   "Here's my card with my e-mail address and a link to my career portfolio. I'd like to hear from you."

While modesty is a virtue, the best elevator pitch is one that is delivered with confidence. Chapter 4 contains tips for using verbal and nonverbal communication to demonstrate self-assurance. Improve your skill at presenting yourself briefly and effectively by planning and delivering an elevator speech to your classmates.

Source: Indeed Career Guide. (2020, July 7). How to give an elevator pitch (with examples). Retrieved from https://www.indeed.com/career-advice/interviewing/how-to-give-an-elevator-pitch-examples

For many, the concept of networking is intangible. In fact, one of the authors of your textbook commonly receives questions about how students can build a network while they are still in college. The answer is not as daunting as one might think. Think about networking as building an impression and name recognition, rather than finding ways to share your resume. Volunteering with on- and off-campus organizations, interning at an organization, helping your peers with a homework problem, attending career fairs, and actively engaging during class discussions are all ways to build an impression that may benefit you in the future. Attending face-to-face mixer events, being actively engaged on business sites like LinkedIn, and joining professional associations or service organizations like Rotary International are ways to expand your professional network while engaging in meaningful activities that benefit the community.

People with highly developed personal networks tend to be more successful in their careers.[63] Over their lifetimes, they earn more raises, are promoted more often, and are generally more satisfied with their jobs. With better networks, people have greater access to career sponsorship, resources, and information. Membership of just one network, however, probably will not accomplish these goals. Instead, the key is to have a wide and diverse network that incorporates all kinds of people. As you explore and expand your network, keep the following tips in mind.[64]

Using LinkedIn Effectively

The social networking site LinkedIn (http://www.linkedin.com) has been called "Facebook for professionals." More than 467 million members around the world use this service to advance their careers. Your profile is often your first impression with employers and recruiters. When used appropriately, LinkedIn can help you manage your professional identity, expand your network of contacts, and enhance career opportunities. The following guidelines can help you use LinkedIn effectively.

Improve Your Profile

- Upload a professional photo to your profile to increase your chances of being found and receiving messages. If you don't have a professional headshot, dress nicely and ask a friend to take your photo in a well-lit location.

- Write a concise summary that showcases your personality and tells a story of your experience, interests, and goals.

- Include your education to establish credibility and help you connect with alumni and friends.

- Input your work experience, past jobs, and internships. Include your job title, company name, and time period. If you are in transition or unemployed, use a title that describes what you wish to pursue.

- Maintain a list of at least five relevant skills in order of your strengths.

- Add your location.

Manage Your Professional Identity

- Start connecting with past and current colleagues, fellow students, and your professors. Use the search function to locate and connect with professionals who are working in jobs similar to those you hope to seek.

- Use LinkedIn for professional messages only. Do not link your page to your Facebook or Twitter identity if you use those tools to share nonprofessional information.

- Use LinkedIn's multimedia capabilities to showcase your work (and yourself).

- Request recommendations from professors, colleagues, supervisors, and clients who can comment on your work, attitude, skills, achievements, professionalism, and integrity.

- Proofread everything you post.

- Use status updates to share industry-relevant content to show that you are in-the-know.

Learn from Others

- Join, contribute to and use groups. Begin by searching for groups in your career field. Focus on trends, glean advice, and garner news and tips particular to your field. Connect with national and international groups as well as local groups to explore employment, training, and networking opportunities virtually and in person. When you understand the culture of different groups, contribute your knowledge, links to pertinent articles, upcoming events, or book reviews.

- Use the Answers Forum to discover which types of questions others are asking and to learn from the answers. Browse by topic and subtopic (e.g., résumé writing, start-ups and small business, nonprofit, work–life balance, mentoring, finance) or by language.

Source: Fisher, C. (2016, August 3). 5 steps to improve your LinkedIn profile in minutes. Retrieved from https://blog.linkedin.com; LinkedIn (n.d.) About LinkedIn. Retrieved from https://press.linkedin.com/about-linkedin; Serdula, D. (n.d.). LinkedIn makeover: Professional secrets to a powerful LinkedIn profile. Retrieved from http://www.linkedin-makeover.com/blog; Stokes, C. (2019, June). Developing a first-rate LinkedIn profile. *Strategies & Tactics*. Retrieved from https://apps.prsa.org/StrategiesTactics/Issues/view/2/6

View Everyone as a Networking Prospect   Consider the members of all the networks to which you already belong: family members, friends, neighbors, social acquaintances, fellow workers, members of your religious community, professionals (e.g., doctors, dentists, accountants, attorneys), and school contacts (e.g., faculty, fellow students, counselors). Beyond the people you already know, almost everyone you meet has the potential to be a source of useful information. The passenger seated next to you on a plane might be acquainted with people who can help you. The neighbor who chats

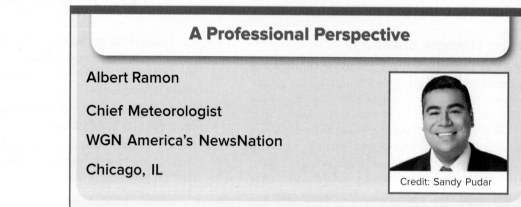

A Professional Perspective

Albert Ramon

Chief Meteorologist

WGN America's NewsNation

Chicago, IL

Credit: Sandy Pudar

We have all heard the saying, "it's all about who you know" when it comes to searching for an internship or first job. There is definitely truth to this, but how does someone with zero work experience connect with hiring managers and network with professionals at companies they want to one day work for? The age of social media has changed the meaning of "who you know." Some of my past hires have reached out to me via LinkedIn, Twitter, and Facebook.

I encourage interns with my organization to come up with a list of companies they would want to work for, then research the supervisor for the department they are most interested in. (This information can often be found on the company's website and/or on LinkedIn.) The company does not have to have a current opening, nor does the prospective employee need to be ready to be hired. A professional message expressing an interest in the career field and the company can make a positive impression for the future. Interested individuals may also explain what they are doing right now to obtain their professional goals or even ask for feedback on their resumes or advice on the job search process. Some managers may not reply, but I guarantee some will respond enthusiastically because they remember what it was like to search for that first job post-degree. Sometimes reaching out even yields a mentor/mentee relationship from which both parties benefit over many years.

Lastly, I always share one key piece of advice with interns and job hunters: When you do get that internship or first job, work hard. People notice and appreciate a solid work ethic, an enthusiasm to learn, and a passion for the craft.

with you at a block party might have the knowledge or skill to help you solve a problem. Within an organization, the best informants are often people you might overlook. Administrative assistants are exposed to most of the information addressed to their managers, and they usually serve as **gatekeepers** who can give or deny access to them. Custodial and maintenance people travel around the building and, in their rounds, see and hear many interesting things.

Be Sensitive to Personal and Cultural Factors   While everyone you meet is a potential networking prospect, it is important to think of each person as an individual. Some may welcome the chance to share information, whereas others may object to more than occasional contacts. It is also important to recognize that culture plays a role in networking practices.

Treat Your Contacts with Gratitude and Respect

Do not make the mistake of equating networking with being dishonest or exploitive. As long as you express a genuine desire for information openly, there is nothing to be ashamed of. Furthermore, seeking information does not mean you have to stop enjoying others' company for social reasons. When others do give you information, be sure to express your appreciation. At the very least, a sincere "thank you" is in order. Even better, let your networking contacts know exactly *how* the information they gave you was helpful.

Build Genuine Relationships

After meeting someone, jot down a few notes about the interaction in your phone contacts or on the back of their business card. Consider listing when and where you met them along with any details that might be worth mentioning in a future interaction, such as where they went to school or if they were recently married. Send an e-mail to them within 1-2 days to reinforce the connection. Tell them how great it was to meet them, remind them of where you met, thank them for their time and let them know you would like to remain connected. Continue your relationship by sending an "I hope you're well" e-mail around the holidays.

Help Others

Do not just be an information-seeker. Whenever possible, make an effort to put people who will benefit from a contact in touch with one another: "You're looking for a new bookkeeper? I know someone who might be right for you!" Volunteering for opportunities to serve on committees, or plan events or socials are also great ways to be a resource for others. The idea is to help people without seeking anything in return. Besides being the right thing to do, helping others will earn you a reputation for generosity that can serve you well.[65]

Get Referrals to Secondary Sources

The benefits of personal networks do not stop with your personal acquaintances. Each person you know has his or her own connections, some of whom could be useful to you. Researchers have demonstrated the "small world" phenomenon: A study on the "six degrees of separation" hypothesis involving more than 45,000 messages and more than 150 countries has demonstrated that the average number of links separating any two people in the world is indeed a half-dozen.[66] You can apply this principle to your own information by only seeking people removed from your personal network by one degree: If you ask 10 people for referrals and each of them knows 10 others who might be able to help, you have the potential to obtain support from 100 information-givers.

Secondary sources are so valuable that some online networking group sites exist to help users find the contacts they need. Having a network of people who can refer you to others can be especially helpful in today's workforce, where people often stay in their jobs for only a year or two.

If you are trying to connect to someone you have never met, let them know what you have in common and why you are reaching out. If you are requesting secondary connections on LinkedIn, for example, make an impression by liking or commenting on their posts, sending kudos messages recognizing their accomplishments, and actively posting content on your own page that shows your interests and expertise.

Seek a Mentor

A mentor is a person who acts as a guide, trainer, coach, and counselor; who teaches you the informal rules of an organization or a field; and who imparts the types of wisdom that come from firsthand experience. Many organizations have formal programs that match new employees with experienced ones. Other mentor-protégé relationships develop informally and unofficially. Sixty-four percent of recent graduates of U.S. colleges and universities say that a professor was their college mentor.[67] However you find one, a mentor can be invaluable. This is especially true for women, minorities, and people trying to break into nontraditional fields where "good old boy" networks can be hard to penetrate.[68]

A successful mentoring relationship is not a one-time affair. Instead, it passes through several stages.[69] In the initial phase, the parties get to know each other and gain confidence in their mutual commitment to the relationship. After the initial stage, a period of cultivation occurs in which the mentor guides the protégé through a series of conversations and tasks with the goal of building knowledge, confidence, and skill. By the third phase of the relationship, the protégé can function mostly on their own, with occasional guidance from the mentor. Finally, the fourth stage involves either separation or a redefinition of the relationship as peers. Not all mentoring relationships are quite so involved or long-lasting as this description suggests. Nevertheless, whether they are relatively brief or ongoing, they can provide great value and satisfaction for both mentor and protégé.

Whatever the relationship, some rules guide mentoring relationships.[70] Look for someone with a position in a field that interests you. Do not be bashful about aiming high: You may be surprised by successful people's willingness to give back by helping aspiring newcomers. Approach your mentor professionally, showing that you are serious about growing in your career. See The Career Research Interview section for guidelines on how to handle this process.

Once you have found a mentor, show respect for their time by keeping most of your contact to regularly scheduled times. Be sure to follow up on your mentor's suggestions about reading, checking websites, and attending activities.

Realize that a mentoring relationship should be primarily professional. If you have serious personal problems, turn to a counselor. A mentor may be able to help you with some personal problems as they affect your professional life, but a mentor should not become an emotional crutch. Also, remember that any personal insights that mentors and protégés share should be kept confidential. Finally, do not expect a mentor to grant you special favors, intervene on your behalf with your boss, or boost your chances for promotion. The advice you receive should be reward enough.

Network throughout Your Career   Networking is not just for job-seekers. Indeed, it can be just as important once you start climbing the career ladder. In an era when changing jobs and even changing careers is common, expanding your options is always a smart move.

• Ethical Dimensions of Communication

Some cynics have noted that the trouble with business ethics is that the phrase is an oxymoron. Despite this attitude, there is a growing recognition that behaving ethically is an essential part of being an effective, promotable employee. Scandalous business practices have led to the downfall of major corporations like Enron and WorldCom and have cost others millions of dollars. As a result of these ethical lapses, sensitivity to the need to communicate in a principled way has grown, and several hundred corporations and organizations now include an ethics officer in their organizational chart who reports

Guanxi: Networking Chinese-Style

Any savvy business person in China knows the value of *guanxi* (pronounced "gwan-shee")—the web of social relationships that help get a job done through the granting of favors. It takes *guanxi* to get a good job, find a good apartment, overcome bureaucratic hurdles, and line up suppliers and distributors. In other words, it is required to accomplish almost any transaction. As one observer put it, "In the West, relationships grow out of deals. In China, deals grow out of relationships."[71]

It may be tempting to think of *guanxi* as the Chinese equivalent of Western networking, but the concept has far more cultural and practical significance. The unwritten code of *guanxi* is rooted in the Chinese national character, reflecting the Confucian emphasis on loyalty, obligation, order, and social harmony.

Guanxi operates on three levels.[72] The strongest bond is with immediate family. In relationships linked by blood and marriage, higher-status members are obligated to perform favors for their lower-status relatives. In return, lower-status family members are obliged to demonstrate fierce loyalty. To a lesser extent, *guanxi* connects extended family members, friends, neighbors, classmates, and people with other strong commonalities. Unlike the closest form of *guanxi,* obligations in these relationships are usually reciprocal; receiving help creates an obligation to return the favor. The least powerful level of *guanxi* is between people who know one another but have no strong relational history. At this level, *guanxi* is similar to networking connections in the West. These relationships lack the history, trust, and power of stronger bonds.

Developing *guanxi* can be challenging for foreigners who want to do business in China, but it is not impossible. One strategy is to rely on intermediaries to make initial connections. This practice is widespread among native Chinese, so a foreigner will not stand out for using it. Once introduced, be prepared to socialize. Even more so than in the West, important business is often conducted outside of the workplace. When socializing, look for the chance to emphasize commonalties—business experiences, education, and mutual acquaintances are a few examples. After enough trust has developed to seek favors, be indirect. As you will read in the next chapter, Asian cultures consider oblique, "high-context" communication as a sign of sensitivity and skill. Finally, remember that *guanxi* is reciprocal. Accepting help from others obliges you to assist them in the future.

---

directly to the chairperson.[73] Employees share this concern for ethics. One survey revealed that 75% of Millennials would take a pay cut to work for an organization with a better reputation for corporate social responsibility (CSR) and ethics.[74]

Behaving ethically is not always easy. On a personal level, you are likely to face conflicts between what you believe is right and what is practical. For instance, you might have to deal with a customer or colleague whose business or approval you want, but who is behaving badly—perhaps making sexist or racist remarks. After a trip together, coworkers may turn in inflated expenses and expect you to do the same. Your team might be under pressure to finish a project when you recognize shortcuts are creating potential safety issues. Besides personal challenges, sooner or later you are likely to experience situations like these where others in your organization behave in ethically questionable ways. Do you speak up when a colleague makes promises to clients that you know the company cannot keep? Should you challenge your boss when he or she treats other employees unfairly or illegally?

It has been said that ethics centers on a sense of responsibility for someone other than yourself.[75] A blanket obligation to communicate ethically can be too vague to be helpful in specific situations. Many industries have developed codes of ethics to serve as a guide for employees in day-to-day decision-making. However, in the absence of such a code, five philosophical principles offer guidelines that can help you decide how to behave in a principled manner.[76]

There is no single right approach to ethics; these competing ethical perspectives often lead to conflicting actions. For example, what one group perceives as "virtuous" might not

ETHICAL **challenge**

Ethical Communication Choices

Descriptions for seven guidelines for judging ethical communication are provided in the text:

- Utilitarian approach
- Rights approach
- Fairness or justice approach
- Common-good approach
- Virtue approach
- Professional ethic
- Publicity test

Outline the range of ways you could handle each of the following situations. Use two or more of the ethical guidelines to compare courses of action, and then decide on a course of action you believe to be both principled and realistic. Justify your decision.

1. A coworker tells you he is about to buy an expensive car that will strain his budget to the maximum. You recently learned he is slated to be laid off at the end of the month but were told to keep this information in strictest confidence. What do you do?

2. Your friend is applying for a job and has given you as a reference. A questionnaire sent by the employer asks if there is any reason you cannot recommend the applicant. You know that your friend is struggling with an alcohol problem, which led to dismissal from a previous job. Do you mention this problem on the reference form? If so, how?

3. Your manager calls you into her office and praises you for doing excellent work on a recent project. She suggests that this level of performance is likely to earn you a promotion and a raise. In truth, a colleague made a far greater contribution to the project. How do you respond to your manager's praise?

4. As part of your job, you learn that some damaged equipment can be repaired for $15,000. Your supervisor tells you to claim the damage is much greater so the insurance company will pay closer to $100,000. What do you do?

5. While you are entertaining a customer, he makes a blatantly offensive joke. How do you respond?

Source: Adapted from Richardson, J. E. (Ed.) (2003). *Business ethics 03/04* (15th ed.). Guilford, CT: McGraw Hill/Dushkin; Soeken, D. (2008). On witnessing a fraud. In J. E. Richardson (Ed.), *Business ethics 07/08* (19th ed.). Dubuque, IA: McGraw Hill/Dushkin.

bring good to the greatest number; likewise, what one group considers moral might be considered immoral by another group. When faced with a decision about how to communicate ethically, it is helpful to ponder the situation from several viewpoints before proceeding.

1. *Utilitarian approach (Jeremy Bentham and John Stuart Mill):* Does this action provide the greatest good for the greatest number?

2. *Rights approach (Immanuel Kant):* Does this action respect the moral rights (truth, privacy, noninjury, promises) of everyone?

3. *Fairness or justice approach (Aristotle, John Rawls):* Is this action fair and free of discrimination or favoritism?

4. *Common-good approach (Plato, Aristotle, Cicero, John Rawls):* Does the action further the common or community good?

5. *Virtue approach:* Does this action promote the development of moral virtue (character) in me and my community?

Two additional guidelines can help you evaluate whether you are behaving ethically:

1. *Professional ethic:* How would an impartial jury of your professional peers judge this action?

2. *Publicity test:* Would you be comfortable having the public learn about your behavior in the broadcast or print media?[77]

review points

- Communication is important for career success.
- Communication is unavoidable, strategic, and irreversible. It is a process that involves instrumental and relational communication and identity management. It is not a panacea that will solve all problems.
- The communication model demonstrates how senders and receivers encode and decode messages in the process of developing a shared meaning. To improve communication, consider the characteristics of various channels, the desired tone of the message, the organization's culture, and the use of multiple channels.
- Noise can interfere with exchange of a message. This type of distraction can be environmental, physiological, or psychological in nature and can be present in the sender, receiver, message,

or channel. Good communicators reduce noise as much as possible.
- Formal communication networks (organizational charts) represent management's view of organizational relationships: upward, downward, and horizontal/lateral.
- Informal networks, based on proximity, shared interests, or friendships, serve to confirm, expand, expedite, contradict, or circumvent formal communication.
- Effective communicators cultivate and use personal networking for career success.
- Professional success necessitates an understanding of and ability to apply various ethical frameworks (utilitarian, rights, fairness/ justice, common good, virtue, professional ethic, publicity test) to consistently make principled decisions around ethical challenges.

key terms

asynchronous communication   11
channel   9
communication networks   13
decoding   9
downward communication   13
encoding   9
feedback   9
formal communication networks   13
gatekeeper   22
horizontal (lateral) communication   17
identity management   7
informal communication networks   18

instrumental communication   7
message   9
networking   19
noise   10
organizational charts   13
receiver   9
relational communication   7
sender   9
synchronous communication   11
upward communication   15
voice of employee (VoE)   15

activities

1. Invitation to Insight

Keep a log of your work-related (or school-related) communication over a three-day period. Include who you have communicated with (superior, subordinate, peer, external) and your level of satisfaction

with the communication. Based on your findings, analyze the following:

a. How much time you spend communicating.
b. With whom you communicate. (Identify each example as downward, upward, or horizontal flow of communication.)

c. Which channels of communication you tend to use most frequently.

d. Your level of satisfaction.

e. Areas where improving your communication skills would be desirable.

2. Invitation to Insight

Think about a situation you have experienced in which communication went wrong. Diagnose the problem by finding the parts of the communication process that contributed to the trouble. Suggest a remedy for each problem you identify.

a. Sender: Did the wrong person send the message?

b. Encoding: Did the sender use words or nonverbal cues that were confusing, inappropriate, or irrelevant?

c. Message: Was the message too short or too long? Were there too many messages? Was the timing wrong?

d. Channel: Was the most appropriate channel chosen?

e. Receiver: Was there no receiver at all? Was the message poorly formulated for the person(s) at whom it was aimed? Was it received by the wrong person?

f. Decoding: Did the receiver read in meanings that were not intended?

g. Feedback: How did the feedback affect the sender? Did the feedback help or hinder shared understanding?

h. Noise: In which ways did environmental, physiological, or psychological noise distort the message? Provide specific examples.

3. Invitation to Insight

Learn about upward communication in the workplace by asking several employees which types of information they share with their supervisors. Which types of information do they avoid sharing with their supervisors? How does the organization encourage or discourage accurate upward communication?

4. Skill Builder

Develop your skill at cultivating informal communication networks by following these instructions:

a. Choose one of the following information goals, or identify a school-related or work-related goal of your own.

1. Decide which instructors and/or courses in an academic department of your institution are worth seeking out and which you might want to avoid.

2. Identify the qualities that would help you get the job of your dreams.

3. Locate an organization where you could gain job experience as a volunteer or intern.

b. Identify the people who can help you acquire the information you are seeking. Locate people from a variety of positions within the organization so you will gain a complete perspective. For each person, decide which channel you could use to begin to develop your network.

5. Skill Builder

With your group members, formulate a hypothetical context for each of the following messages. Then use the information from the section on Communication Channels to decide which channel would be best for each message. Use the criteria from Table 1-2 to explain your choice.

a. Informing your supervisor about difficulties with a coworker.

b. Asking for a few days of leave from work to attend a friend's wedding.

c. Training a new employee to operate a complicated computer program.

d. Notifying the manager of a local business that you have not received the refund you were promised.

e. Reminding your busy boss about a long-overdue reimbursement for out-of-pocket expenses.

f. Apologizing to a customer for a mistake your company made.

g. Getting your boss's reaction to the idea of giving you more responsibility.

6. Invitation to Insight

Ask a few of your acquaintances to describe an ethical dilemma they have encountered in the workplace or in their personal lives. How did they handle the situation? Which factors influenced them?

With a group of classmates, determine which ethical perspectives your informants seemed to rely on as they decided how to act. Apply various ethical perspectives to the same situations. Would you have followed the same course of action your informants did? Why or why not?

![McGraw Hill logo] **LearnSmart**™

For further review, go to the LearnSmart study module for this chapter.

references

1. Cross, R., Rebele, R., & Grant, A. (2016, January-February). Collaborative overload. *Harvard Business Review*, 74-79. Retrieved from https://hbr.org/2016/01/collaborative-overload

2. Morreale, S. P., & Pearson, J. C. (2008). Why communication education is important: The centrality of the discipline in the 21st century. *Communication Education, 57,* 224-240.

3. Darling, A. L., & Dannels, D. P. (2003). Practicing engineers talk about the importance of talk: A report on the role of oral communication in the workplace. *Communication Education, 52,* 1-16.

4. Gray, E. F. (2010). Specific oral communication skills desired in new accountancy graduates. *Business Communication Quarterly, 73,* 40-67.

5. Kashyap, V. (2019, May 20). Effective communication in the workplace: How and why? *HR Technologist.* Retrieved from https://www.hrtechnologist.com/articles/employee-engagement/effective-communication-in-the-workplace-how-and-why/

6. Towers Watson Communication (2013, December 5). *2013-2014 change and communication ROI study.* Retrieved from https://pdpsolutions.com/research/test-to-add-to-research

7. Harper's index. (1994, December). *Harper's Magazine,* 13.

8. Mauksch, L. B., Dugdale, D. C., Dodson, S., & Epstein, R. (2008). Relationship, communication, and efficiency in the medical encounter. *Archives of Internal Medicine, 168,* 1387-1395; Holmes, F. (2007). If you listen, the patient will tell you the diagnosis. *International Journal of Listening, 21,* 156-161.

9. Joint Commission. (2019, February 5). *Most commonly reviewed sentinel event types.* Retrieved from https://www.jointcommission.org/resources/patient-safety-topics/sentinel-event/sentinel-event-data—event-type-by-year/

10. Levinson, W., Roter, D., & Mullooly, J. P. (1997). Physician-patient communication: The relationship with malpractice claims among primary care physicians and surgeons. *Journal of American Medical Association, 277,* 553-559. See also Rodriguez, H. P., Rodday, A. C., Marshall, R. E., Nelson, K. L., Rogers, W. H., & Safran, D. G. (2008). Relation of patients' experiences with individual physicians to malpractice risk. *International Journal for Quality in Health Care, 20,* 5-12.

11. Calandra, B. (2002, September 16). Toward a silver-tongued scientist. *The Scientist, 16,* 42.

12. National Association of Colleges and Employers (2020). *Job outlook 2020.* Retrieved from https://www.naceweb.org/about-us/press/2020/the-top-attributes-employers-want-to-see-on-resumes/.

13. Calandra, B. (2002, September 16). Toward a silver-tongued scientist. *The Scientist, 16,* 42.

14. National Association of Colleges and Employers (2018). *Job outlook 2018.* Retrieved from https://www.naceweb.org/job-market/trends-and-predictions/job-outlook-2018-college-hiring-to-increase-by-4-percent/

15. Watzlawick, P., Beavin, J. H., & Jackson, D. D. (1967). *Pragmatics of human communication.* New York: Norton.

16. Watzlawick, P., Beavin, J. H., & Jackson, D. D. (1967). *Pragmatics of human communication.* New York: Norton.

17. Byron, K. (2008). Carrying too heavy a load? The communication and miscommunication of emotion by email. *Academy of Management Review, 33,* 309-327.

18. Shannon, C. E., & Weaver, W. (1949). *The mathematical theory of communication.* Urbana, IL: University of Illinois Press; Adler, R. B., Rosenfeld, L. B., & Proctor, R. F. (2012). *Interplay: The process of interpersonal communication.* New York: Oxford University Press.

19. Powers, W. G., & Witt, P. L. (2008). Expanding the theoretical framework of communication fidelity. *Communication Quarterly, 56,* 247-267.

20. Flaherty, L. M., Pearce, K. J., & Rubin, R. B. (1998). Internet and face-to-face communication: Not functional alternatives. *Communication Quarterly, 46,* 250-268; Sheer, V. C., & Chen, L. (2004). Improving media richness theory: A study of interaction goals, message valence, and task complexity in manager-subordinate communication. *Management Communication Quarterly, 18,* 76-93; and Turner, J. W., & Reinsch, N. L. (2007). The business communicator as presence allocator: Multicommunicating, equivocality, and status at work. *Journal of Business Communication, 44,* 36-58.

21. Daft, R. L. (2008). *The leadership experience* (4th ed.). Mason, OH: Thomson South-Western.

22. Byron, K. (2008). Carrying too heavy a load? The communication and miscommunication of emotion by email. *Academy of Management Review, 33,* 309-327.

23. Bryant, A. (2000, October 23). Fare rage. *Newsweek*, 46.

24. Baxter, L. A. (1993). Talking things through and putting it in writing: Two codes of communication in an academic institution. *Journal of Applied Communication Research, 21,* 313–323.

25. Turner, J. W., Grube, J., Tinsley, C., Lee, C., & O'Pell, C. (2006). Exploring the dominant media: How does media use reflect organizational norms and affect performance? *Journal of Business Communication, 43,* 220–250.

26. Stephens, K. K., Sørnes, J. O., Rice, R. E., Browning, L. D., & Sætre, A. S. (2008). Discrete, sequential, and follow-up use of information and communication technology by experienced ICT users. *Management Communication Quarterly, 22,* 197–231.

27. Leonardi, P. M., Treem, J. W., & Jackson, M. H. (2010). The connectivity paradox: Using technology to both decrease and increase perceptions of distance in distributed work arrangements. *Journal of Applied Communication Research, 38,* 85–105.

28. Renischn, L., & Turner, J. W. (2006, July). Ari, r u there? Reorienting business communication for a technological era. *Journal of Business and Technical Communication, 20,* 339–356.

29. Lengel, R. J., & Daft, R. L. (1998). The selection of communication media as an executive skill. *Academy of Management Executive, 2,* 225–232.

30. Monge, P. R., & Contractor, N. S. (2003). *Theories of communication networks.* New York: Oxford University Press.

31. Boundless (2016, May 26). Downward Communication. *Boundless Management.* Retrieved from https://www .boundless.com/management/textbooks/boundless -management-textbook/communication-11 /management-and-communication-83/ downward-communication-397-847/

32. Anderson, J. & Level, D. (1980). The impact of certain types of downward communication on job performance. *Journal of Business Communication, 17*(4), 51–59.

33. Managers' shoptalk. (1985, February). *Working Woman,* p. 22.

34. Katz, D., & Kahn, R. (1978). *The social psychology of organization,* 2nd ed. New York: Wiley.

35. Peters, T. J., & Waterman, R. H., Jr. (1982). *In search of excellence: Lessons from America's best-run companies.* New York: Harper & Row.

36. Bhat, A. (n.d.). *Voice of employee: Definition, survey questions, and importance.* Retrieved from https://www.questionpro.com/blog/voice-of-employee/

37. Venkataramani, V., Zhou, L., Wang, M., Liao, H., & Shi, J. (2016). Social networks and employee voice: The influence of team members' and team leaders' social network positions on employee voice. *Organizational Behavior and Human Decision Processes, 132,* 37–48. https://doi.org/10.1016/j.obhdp.2015.12.001

38. See, for example, Kassing, J. W. (2000). Investigating the relationship between superior-subordinate relationship quality and employee dissent. *Communication Research Reports, 17,* 58–70.

39. Whitten, M. (2019, July 25). The importance of listening to employees. *Industry Week.* Retrieved from https://www.industryweek.com/leadership/article /22027966/the-importance-of-listening-to-employees

40. Business News Daily Editor (2020, February 28). If you listen up, your employees will step up. *Business News Daily.* Retrieved from https://www .businessnewsdaily.com/1934-leadership-listening -employee-input-initiative.html

41. Katz, D., & Kahn, R. (1978). *The social psychology of organizations* (2nd ed.). New York: Wiley.

42. Kassing, J. W. (2000). Investigating the relationship between superior-subordinate relationship quality and employee dissent. *Communication Research Reports, 17,* 58–70.

43. Bennis, W. G. (1993). *An invented life: Reflections on leadership and change.* Reading, MA: Addison-Wesley.

44. Dansereau, F., & Markham, S. E. (1987). Superior-subordinate communication: Multiple levels of analysis. In F. M. Jablin, L. L. Putnam, K. H. Roberts, & L. W. Porter (Eds.), *Handbook of organizational communication.* Newbury Park, CA: Sage.

45. Bryant, A. (2011, June 27). A sitting duck can't catch a moving turkey. *New York Times.*

46. Ellis, M. (2012, February 23). Flush with cash: British Airways saves £600,000 on fuel by descaling its toilet pipes. *Mirror.* Retrieved from https://www .mirror.co.uk/news/uk-news/ flush-with-cash-british-airways-saves-740383

47. Keil, M., Tiwana, M., Sainsbury, R., & Sneha, S. (2010). Toward a theory of whistleblowing intentions: A benefit-to-cost differential perspective. *Decision Sciences, 41,* 787–812.

48. Goldhaber, G. (1993). *Organizational communication* (6th ed.). Dubuque, IA: William C. Brown.

49. Mieszkowski, K. (1998, December). Change-Barbara Waugh. *Fast Company, 20,* 146–154.

50. Goldhaber, G. (1993). *Organizational communication* (6th ed.). Dubuque, IA: William C. Brown.

51. Ferguson, T. W. (1997, May 19). Who's mentoring whom? *Forbes,* 252.

52. Doloff, P. G. (1999, February). Beyond the org chart. *Across the Board, 36,* 43–47.

53. Gregory, M. (2009). Inside the locker room: Male homosociability in the advertising industry. *Gender, Work & Organization, 16,* 323–347.

54. Bell, E. L. J. E., & Nkomo, S. M. (2001). *Our separate ways: Black and white women and the struggle for professional identity*. Boston, MA: Harvard Business School Press; Baker, M., & French, E. (2018). Female underrepresentation in project-based organizations exposes organizational isomorphism. *Equality, Diversity and Inclusion, 37*(8), 799–812. Retrieved from https://doi.org/10.1108/EDI-03-2017-0061

55. Did you hear it through the grapevine? (1994, October). *Training & Development*, p. 20; Motlhamme, K. F. (2018). *Black female managers perceptions' of integration into informal social networks at work*. Retrieved from https://hdl.handle.net/10539/27216

56. Cross, R., & Parker, A. (2004). *The hidden power of social networks: Understanding how work really gets done in organizations*. Boston, MA: Harvard Business School Press.

57. Krackhardt, D., & Hanson, J. R. (1993, July). Informal networks: The company behind the chart. *Harvard Business Review, 71*, 104–111.

58. Kanter, R. M. (1989, November/December). The new managerial work. *Harvard Business Review, 67*, 85–92.

59. Bush, J. B., Jr., & Frohman, A. L. (1991). Communication in a 'network' organization. *Organizational Dynamics, 20*, 23–36.

60. Eisenberg, E. M., & Goodall, H. E., Jr. (1993). *Organizational communication: Balancing creativity and constraint*. New York: St. Martin's.

61. Murray, T. J. (1987, August). How to stay lean and mean. *Business Month*, pp. 29–32.

62. Interaction (n.d.). *Team Eleven*. Retrieved from https://www.interaction.uk.com/case-studies/team-eleven/

63. Seibert, S. E., Kraimer, M. L., & Liden, R. C. (2001). A social capital theory of career success. *Academy of Management Journal, 44*, 219–237.

64. R. E. Kelley interviewed by Webber, A. M. (2000). Are you a star at work? In *Fast Company career guide*. New York: Fast Company Media Group.

65. Feely, T. H. (2000). Testing a communication network model of employee turnover based on centrality. *Journal of Applied Communication Research, 28*, 262–277; Network inside your organization. (2000). In *Fast Company career guide* (p. 13). New York: Fast Company Media Group.

66. Dodds, P. S., Muhamad, R., & Watts, D. J. (2003). An experimental study of search in global social networks. *Science, 301*, 827–829.

67. Marken, S., & Auter, Z. (2018, October 30). Recent college grads say professors most frequent mentors. *Gallup*. Retrieved from https://news.gallup.com/poll/244019/recent-college-grads-say-professors-frequent-mentors.aspx

68. Lyness, K. S., & Thompson, D. E. (2000). Climbing the corporate ladder: Do female and male executives follow the same route? *Journal of Applied Psychology, 85*, 86–101; Gregory, M. (2009). Inside the locker room: Male homosociability in the advertising industry. *Gender, Work & Organization, 16*, 323–347.

69. Kram, K. E. (1983). Phases of the mentoring relationship. *Academy of Management Journal, 12*, 608–625.

70. Gardenswartz, L., & Rowe, A. (1997, January). Starting a mentoring program? *Managing Diversity, 6*, 1–2; Advancing Women. (2006). *Mentoring process*. Retrieved from http://www.advancingwomen.com/wk_mentprocess.html

71. Vanhonacker, W. R. (2004, September). Guanxi networks in China. *China Business Review, 31*, 48–53.

72. Zhang, Y., & Zhang, Z. (2006). Guanxi and organizational dynamics in China: A link between individual and organizational levels. *Journal of Business Ethics, 67*, 375–392.

73. Driscoll, D. M., et al. (1997, June). Who says ethics are nice? *Across the Board, 34*, 47–50.

74. Cone Communications (2016, November 2). *2016 Cone Communications millennial employee engagement study*. Retrieved from https://static1.squarespace.com/static/56b4a7472b8dde3df5b7013f/t/5819e8b303596e3016ca0d9c/1478092981243/2016+Cone+Communications+Millennial+Employee+Engagement+Study_Press+Release+and+Fact+Sheet.pdf

75. Roberts, C. R. (2005, May 16). He argues for ethics. *Tacoma News Tribune*. Retrieved from http://elibrary.bigchalk.com

76. Velasquez, M., Ande, C., Shanks, S. J. T., & Meyer, M. J. (2012). Thinking ethically: A framework for moral decision making. In J. E. Richardson (Ed.), *Business ethics 11/12*. New York: McGraw Hill.

77. O'Connor, P. J., & Godar, S. H. (1999). How not to make ethical decisions: Guidelines from management textbooks. *Teaching Business Ethics, 3*, 69–86; Tinsley, D. B. (2005). Ethics can be gauged by three rules. In J. E. Richardson (Ed.), *Business ethics 05/06*. Dubuque, IA: McGraw Hill/Dushkin.

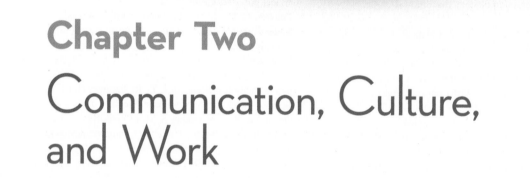

Chapter Two

Communication, Culture, and Work

chapter outline

chapter objectives

After reading this chapter you should be able to:

1. Define culture and co-culture.

2. Identify ways in which race or ethnicity, class, generation, region, disability, gender, and military experience can influence business communication.

3. Describe two key intercultural differences in formality, social customs, dress, time, tolerance for conflict, and gender roles.

4. Explain how the hidden dimensions of culture (e.g., context, individualism/collectivism, power distance, uncertainty avoidance, masculinity/femininity, long-term and short-term orientations) affect communication in a culturally diverse workforce.

5. Identify basic legal protections for employees and job applicants that make discrimination unlawful.

6. Describe additional factors of ethical communication.

7. Apply the guidelines in the section on Communicating across Diversity to describe six specific ways you and others can communicate more effectively in your workplace.

8. Describe the cultural challenges in a specific organization or career and identify specific approaches to communicate effectively within this culture.

Workplace diversity refers to the variety of differences that constitute the identities of people in an organization. As you will learn in this chapter, diversity encompasses many characteristics—race, ethnic affiliation, social class, generation, nationality, physical ability, gender, military experience, sexual orientation, and more.

Technological innovations, such as computer software and mobile apps, coupled with an increase in international trade and immigration mean that the likelihood of working with people from different parts of the world is greater today than at any other time in history. According to the Office of the Governor of Texas, more than 1,145 foreign companies and their subsidiaries operate in Houston alone.[1] In 2019, more than 28 million U.S. workers—17.4% of the country's total labor force—were born outside the United States.[2]

Workplace diversity concerns, however, are not limited to persons working in international business. Even the owners of a mom-and-pop pharmacy or local boutique in Kearney, Nebraska, will find themselves communicating with individuals from a variety of

FIGURE 2.1 U.S. Labor Force by Generation, 1994–2017

Note: Millennials became the largest generation in the labor force in 2016.

Source: Pew Research Center, https://www.pewresearch.org/fact-tank/2018/04/11/millennials-largest-generation-us-labor-force/

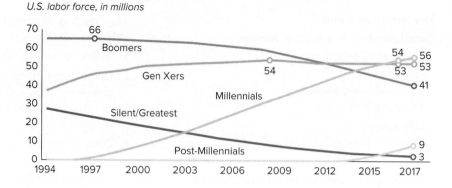

backgrounds on a regular basis. As Figure 2.1 shows, in 2016, Millennials became the largest generational component of the U.S. labor force.[3] As of 2017, 56 million Millennials were working or looking for work, and this number is expected to grow, partly due to immigration.[4]

Given these statistics, it is no surprise that intercultural competence has been identified as one of the top skills for the workforce in 2020.[5] For companies and individuals who can take advantage of the trend toward increasing cultural diversity, the opportunities are great. The quality of life services company, Sodexo, for example, has a policy of ensuring men and women have equal access to growth opportunities in the company. Its goal is to have women make up at least 40% of its senior leadership by 2025. In fact, Sodexo launched its Gender Balance Study in 2018 and found that gender-balanced management teams scored higher on operating margins, employee and client retention, safety, and employee engagement.[6]

Elena Rodriguez, global head of diversity and inclusion at Novartis, says, "Our business needs diverse people working in an inclusive environment in order to spark more innovation, improve our productivity and be sustainable."[7] According to Ajay Banga, president and CEO of MasterCard, "Diversity is what drives better insights, better decisions, and better products...It's what defines a great leadership culture..."[8] Whether you are working abroad, for or with foreign nationals at home, or with native-born people from different backgrounds, understanding cultural differences is an essential part of being an effective communicator.

• The Nature of Culture

When most people use the word *culture*, they think of people from different national backgrounds. National cultures certainly do exist, and they play an important role in shaping the way people communicate. In addition, differences related to factors such as race/ethnicity, socioeconomic class, gender, and age play a role in communication. Taking all these factors into account, we can define **culture** as a learned set of shared interpretations about beliefs, values, and norms that affect the behaviors of a relatively large group of people.[9]

It is important to realize that culture is learned, not innate. A Korean-born infant adopted soon after birth by non-Korean parents and raised in the United States will think and act differently from their cousins who grew up in Seoul. An African American may view the world differently depending on the region in which she was raised or where she chooses to live. For example, if she moves to France for a job opportunity, she will find that African heritage has a different significance from that in the United States.

Organizations are cultures, too. Every organization has its own way of doing business. Anyone who has worked for more than one restaurant or retail store, attended more than one college or university, belonged to more than one team, or volunteered for multiple worthy causes knows that even when the same job is being performed, the way it is done can be radically different. Theorists use the term **organizational culture** to describe these unique traits. An organization's culture is a relatively stable, shared set of rules that describe how to behave and a set of values that indicate what is important. In everyday language, culture is the insiders' view of "the way things are around here."

Organizational culture can affect you in many ways, large and small. Among other things, your organization's culture can determine where and how long you will work. For many professions or industries, designated work hours may not be the norm. A "workday" may consist of standard 9 a.m. to 5 p.m. work hours or it may be conducted 24/7, such as in the case of firefighters, first responders, or physicians. Organizational culture can shape the emotional environment, including the degree of cooperation or competition, and notions of how much and which kinds of fun are appropriate. Culture will surely influence the way you and others dress and the physical environment in which you will spend your time. Organizational culture will govern the amount and types of interactions you have (both on and off the job) with other employees, both coworkers and management.[10]

Your fit with an organization's culture can make all the difference between a satisfying experience and a disappointing job. A Workplace by Facebook study of more than 4,000 frontline workers and managers across the United States and United Kingdom found only 45% of workers share their ideas with managers; alternatively, 90% of managers feel that their frontline workers are empowered to share ideas with them.[11] This disconnect is part of the culture of these organizations and plays a role in whether employees will stay with the company. In this study, 21% of frontline workers claimed they'd consider quitting their jobs if they felt their voices were not heard.[12]

You can get a sense of a company's culture by talking with people who work there. Besides asking about culture in a formal job interview, off-the-record conversations with potential colleagues can provide valuable insights about the way the company operates. For example, ask how employees spend their time. A surprising amount of effort might go into activities only remotely related to getting the job done: dealing with paperwork, playing office politics, struggling with balky equipment, or attending one unproductive meeting after another. Even if you do not learn much about the organization as a whole, you will get a good picture of the kind of people with whom you will be working.

You can also get clues about an organization's culture by observing how it operates. Communication practices are a good place to begin. How are you treated when you visit a company or deal with its employees? Do e-mails and other written correspondence suggest a welcoming culture?[13] An organization's physical presence also says something about its culture. Are workers' areas personalized or standardized? Is the workplace clean or dirty? Does the organization seem prosperous, or is it operating on a shoestring? You are likely to spend more waking hours on the job than anywhere else. For this reason, thinking about the "personality" of an organization where you work can be just as important as the kind of person whom you desire as a life partner.

Organizational culture is constantly changing. The simple addition of a new employee in the workplace can change the vibe of the entire department, for example. Research from global staffing firm Accountemps reveals how office etiquette has evolved since 2009. Nearly all senior managers (91%) surveyed said workplaces are significantly less formal than they had been, and one in three employers said visible tattoos, casual attire, non-traditional hair colors and piercings, and the use of emojis in e-mails are now acceptable.[14] While this may be the case at some companies, it is

A Professional Perspective

Melissa Mushaka

Global Media Personality

Mushaka Productions

Brooklyn, NY

Credit: Melissa Mushaka

As a college student, I harbored two dreams: To work in television production and to live in New York City. Both dreams ultimately became reality, although the first job that brought me from Texas to New York was in publishing. In my position as a permissions assistant (one who gives legal permission for others to reuse content for non-promotional projects), I encountered an office culture that was intellectually stimulating, but also very professional and serious. It was not a culture that encouraged laughing or joking around with colleagues. Nonetheless, it was a great foot in the door to build my dream career in New York City.

I landed a job at VH1 working behind the scenes on a television show. The culture at VH1 was quite different—upbeat, energetic, and boisterous. Luckily, my personality naturally gravitated toward the laid-back nature of the crew and the laughter on set, despite the long hours. During my time there, I learned that MTV + VH1's organizational culture actually encourages a fun and collegial environment because of the long workday. When you are with the same people for 12 to 18 hours per day, it's best to enjoy each other's company!

Following a series of successful gigs in production, I was hired at NBC Universal. One of my duties in my new role was to hire our department interns. An internship at NBC headquarters is highly desirable, so we received hundreds of applications from highly qualified candidates. One thing that always made individual candidates stand out was a willingness to understand organizational culture and interviewing etiquette. For example, I was more likely to follow up with candidates who respected a level of corporate formality (and didn't treat me like a peer) and who knew to send a thank you note. (You would be surprised by how many failed to do this simple thing!) A candidate should be a good fit for the corporate culture and be persistent and polite. That screening begins during the interview process.

Shifting to Remote Work

Businesses around the world experienced a forced shift in organizational culture when the COVID-19 crisis hit in 2020. When faced with the choice of risking health by continuing business as usual, shutting down the business, or transitioning to remote work, many companies opted to go remote. As a result, employees had to adjust to changing workspaces (garages, dining tables, and bedrooms), new technology, and balancing the responsibilities of work and family, often simultaneously.

If you must work remotely, consider the following tips:

1. *Embrace the change.* Start by thinking about the benefits of your new situation. Do you no longer have a commute? Will you have more time to eat lunch? A positive mindset will go a long way in helping you adapt, even in non-ideal work situations.

2. *Develop a routine.* Giving your workday structure is helpful when adjusting to a new situation. If you are working from home, for example, try to follow your usual work hours rather than working sporadically.

3. *Achieve focus.* Think about what you need to be able to be productive: An organized workspace? Noise-canceling headphones? Create an environment that will allow you to not feel constantly distracted.

4. *Communicate with others.* Familiarize yourself with the communication guidelines your team will follow. For example, will your team have weekly meetings to check in and socialize? Keeping in regular communication will ensure that expectations are met and will help minimize feelings of isolation and loneliness.

Source: GitLab (n.d.). Remote work starter guide for employees: How to adjust to work-from-home. Retrieved from https://about.gitlab.com/company/culture/all-remote/remote-work-starter-guide/; Gonzalez de Villaumbrosia, C. (2020, April 14). How to adapt to remote work. *Forbes.* Retrieved from https://www.forbes.com/sites/forbesbusinesscouncil/2020/04/14/how-to-adapt-to-remote-work/#6ed846d953a7

important to adapt the cultural norms of your place of employment. Harvard Business School professors John Kotter and James Heskett flatly state that people who conform to the norms of their organization's culture will be rewarded, while those who do not will be penalized.[15]

● Communication in a Diverse Society

In addition to its symbols, mission statement, and values, an organization's culture is also made up of communication among and between its members. Today's business environment is comprised of a cross-section of many different people and cultures. Society in general is made up of a variety of **co-cultures**—groups that have a clear identity within the majority culture. Race, ethnicity, social class, generation, regional affiliation, disability, gender, religion, and military experience are a few examples of co-cultural markers that can make a difference in how we view ourselves and our coworkers.

Understanding how culture shapes communication is necessary for developing **cultural intelligence** (also referred to as *cultural quotient* or *CQ*), or the ability to adapt to new cultural settings. Cultural intelligence can help you avoid mistaken conclusions about what a certain message means. It may also help you understand more about how *you* communicate.

Developing Cultural Intelligence

In his book, *The Cultural Intelligence Difference*, Dr. David Livermore highlights four areas of focus when developing our cultural intelligence (CQ):

1. *CQ Drive* refers to the motivation to learn about different cultures. To strengthen this area, get to know people in different social groups or communities and learn another language.

2. *CQ Knowledge* is comprised of knowing how culture shapes people's behaviors, values, and beliefs. To grow in this area, observe how people from different cultures verbally and nonverbally interact. Aim to learn about the history of a culture in addition to its rules or norms.

3. *CQ Strategy* consists of using culturally-sensitive communication. To improve in this area, question your assumptions about cultures and make note of your cultural observations and interactions.

4. *CQ Action* relates to how you behave and react to difficult situations. Monitor your nonverbal communication, show an interest in asking respectful questions about someone's culture, and apologize if you make a mistake.

Source: Livermore, D. (2011). *The cultural intelligence difference: Master the one skill you can't do without in today's global economy.* AMACOM.

Race and Ethnicity

It is an oversimplification to describe a single race- or ethnicity-based style of communication, just as it is dangerous to claim that all young people, all women, or all New Yorkers are alike. Each person's communication style is a combination of individual and cultural traits.

Although the terms race and ethnicity are often erroneously used interchangeably, there are important distinctions. Both race and ethnicity are social constructs used to categorize distinct populations.[16] In general, the term *race* is associated with biology and refers to distinct physical characteristics—such as skin color—shared by groups of people. The U.S. Census Bureau lists five distinct categories of race: white; Black or African American; American Indian or Alaska Native; Asian; and Native Hawaiian or Other Pacific Islander.[17] On the other hand, *ethnicity* is a term that describes a person's cultural identity. For example, a person may list Black or white as their race, while *ethnically* identifying as Hispanic or Latino/a. Keeping in mind the risks of over-generalizing, researchers have found some patterns of communication that are common for many members of various races and ethnicities.

The amount of talk and silence that is appropriate can differ from one co-culture to another.[18] For example, most Native American and many Asian American cultures value silence more than mainstream U.S. culture does. By contrast, African American and Euro-American cultures place a high value on verbal skills, and their members tend to speak more. It is easy to imagine how the silence of, say, a Japanese American or Native American employee could be viewed by an African American or Euro-American colleague as a sign of dislike.

Attitudes toward conflict also differ from one ethnic co-culture to another. Because Asian cultures place a high value on saving face, or preserving one's credibility or reputation, some Asian Americans prefer to avoid clear expressions of disagreement. Native Americans may seek to deal with conflict through silence rather than direct confrontation. By contrast, many (though certainly not all) individuals with a Greek, Israeli, Italian, French, or South American background may prefer a direct, open conflict style.[19]

Even when communicators from different backgrounds speak roughly the same amount, the degree of personal information they reveal can differ dramatically. For

Race Discrimination

More than 1,000 labels have been used by Americans to degrade ethnic or racial groups. Known as *ethnophaulisms*, derived from the Greek words *ethnos* ("people") and *phaulisma* ("disparage"), these ethnic slurs are used to express a derogatory attitude toward the targeted group(s).[20]

Although the use of ethnophaulisms violates federal anti-discrimination laws and has been shown to create a hostile work environment, the use of slurs and other forms of racial discrimination remains prevalent in organizations.[21] A 2020 report of significant race discrimination cases by the U.S. Equal Employment Opportunity Commission contains multiple examples of the use of ethnophaulisms in the private and federal sectors.[22]

Research shows that members of socially dominant groups are often the perpetrators of this type of workplace discrimination. Specifically, socially dominant group members

- Are less likely to be targets of racial slurs than socially subordinate groups.

- Are more likely to use racial slurs than socially subordinate groups.

- Are less likely to speak up against users of racial slurs than socially subordinate groups.

- Tend to use racial slurs around members of the same dominant social groups.[23]

Individuals who engage in this type of behavior in the workplace are likely to experience hefty financial and reputational repercussions when it is made public. For example, in 2018, Papa John's founder John Schnatter resigned as chairman of the board after a recording of him saying a racial slur during a role-playing exercise in a conference call with marketing consultants was leaked to the media. Although Schnatter maintains that he did not use the term maliciously, this incident had a notable impact on his professional life, with the media and public backlash resulting in an extensive loss of reputation and financial standing. Furthermore, the Papa John's company continued to face declining sales for several years after the crisis.[24]

example, Euro-Americans disclose more than African Americans or Puerto Ricans, who in turn reveal more than Mexican Americans.[25] (Of course, varying social and cultural contexts may create different disclosure patterns.)

Nonverbal standards also vary by co-culture. Most communicators unconsciously assume that their rules for behaviors, such as eye contact, are universal. Researchers, however, have found that eye behavior can vary significantly. One study revealed that widely opened eyes are often interpreted in mainstream U.S. culture as a sign of surprise or wonder and in Hispanic culture as a call for help, signifying, "I don't understand." To some African Americans, the same kind of gaze is often regarded as a measure of innocence.[26] Cultural differences in nonverbal behavior are discussed in more depth in Chapter 4.

Because Euro-Americans often associate eye contact with honesty and respect, it is easy to misjudge the motives of others for whom steady eye contact would be a sign of disrespect. In all too many cases, attempts by Puerto Ricans and Native Americans to show respect to persons in authority by not looking at them have been interpreted as dishonesty or disrespect by those accustomed to greater eye contact. Traditionally, Hopi and Navajo people generally avoid steady eye contact, as it is considered offensive, disrespectful, and rude. Blacks tend to make more eye contact when speaking but will not direct such a steady gaze at the speaker when they are listening. Whites tend to make more continuous eye contact while listening to someone.[27]

Social Class

Even in egalitarian societies like those found in the United States and Canada, social class can have a major impact on how people communicate on the job. Research demonstrates that parents tend to raise their children with the social class values of their own workplaces.[28] For example, children raised in working-class families typically learn to be obedient, follow rules, and defer to authority. By contrast, those raised in middle- and upper-class households are taught how to make convincing arguments, think critically, and solve problems creatively.

These lessons can have consequences later in life. College professors often find that working-class and first-generation college students who are raised not to challenge authority can have a difficult time speaking up, thinking critically, and arguing persuasively.[29] The effects of social class continue into business and professional life, where skills such as assertiveness and persuasiveness are career-enhancers. People who come from working-class families and attain middle- or upper-class careers face special challenges in this environment. New speech and language, clothing, and nonverbal patterns are often necessary to gain acceptance.[30] Many of these individuals must also cope with emotional ambivalence related to their career success.[31]

Generational Differences

More than just a function of getting older over time, the historical period in which people live can affect their values, expectations, and, as a result, their communication. Today's workforce is largely composed of members of four generations: Baby Boomers, Generation Xers, Millennials, and Generation Zers.[32]

Baby Boomers (born 1946–1964) are the generation that is currently undergoing the most flux in the workplace. While this generation typically has the most seniority in organizations, its members are beginning to retire at an increasing rate. However, the oldest among them are staying in the labor force at higher rates than previous generations.[33] Born following World War II, the members of this generation were raised to be independent and to believe they have the power to effect meaningful changes. They witnessed and participated in an era of social reform and upheaval that included the Civil Rights movement and the Vietnam War, leading many Boomers to question the claims of authority figures—an ironic position now that they have become the authorities. In the workplace, Baby Boomers receive gratification from winning and achieving. They appreciate challenges and enjoy pressure to perform.[34]

Generation Xers (born 1965–1980) hold many of the management positions in today's organizations. In the workplace, Gen Xers are adept with technology, skeptical, and independent, and they possess a strong desire for work–life balance. They also place a high priority on fun, informality, and creativity on the job. They respect performance over tenure and are loyal to people, not organizations. The Pew Research Center found that Gen Xers believe their technology use, work ethic, conservative/traditional values, intelligence, and respectfulness distinguish them from other generations.[35]

Millennials (born 1981–1996) have also been labeled Generation Y, Net Generation, and Digital Natives. As of 2015, Millennials had become the largest generation by number in the U.S. workforce.[36] Older Millennials fill many of the mid-career positions in today's organizations and are beginning to shift into management roles. As a group, Millennials are technologically adept, ambitious, confident, hopeful, determined, and entrepreneurial. In the United States, Millennials are the

Igor Emmerich/Image Source

most ethnically diverse generation in history. They have an international worldview; more than half have passports and one-fourth expect to work outside the United States.[37]

Generation Zers (born 1997–2010) have also been labeled Post-Millennials, iGeneration, Founders, and Plurals. There is much debate surrounding the birth years that define this generation. For this chapter, we have chosen to utilize the range identified by consulting firm Frank N. Magid Associates.[38] The oldest members of this generation currently occupy entry-level positions in the workforce, while many of the members of this generation are coming of age to vote and compose much of the current college student population. Generation Z is the first generation to have access to the internet from a young age. As a group, they are viewed as being comfortable with technology and social media, demonstrating independence, and having an entrepreneurial desire.[39]

The characteristics that each generational cohort exhibits can be used to better understand the needs and preferences of its members. Marketing professionals, for example, use this information to guide companies in tailoring their products and services to their desired target audiences. Using the VALS ("Values, Attitudes, and Lifestyles") inventory, adults can be placed into one of eight distinct mindset categories that correspond with the major events and experiences of their generations. Consider the following key characteristics that tend to be associated with Millennials (Strivers) and Baby Boomers (Thinkers)[40]:

Strivers	Thinkers
Use video and video games as a form of fantasy	Enjoy a historical perspective
Have revolving employment; high temporary employment	Are not influenced by what's hot
Rely heavily on public transportation	Use technology in functional ways
Wear their wealth	Buy proven products

Because each generation brings its own unique qualities into the workplace,[41] it stands to reason that challenges may arise when members work intergenerationally. While many conversations have ensued concerning characteristics that cause problems in the workplace—such as Baby Boomers being workaholics[42] or Millennials being in need of recognition—a more productive goal is to focus on the positive qualities that each generation brings to the workplace.[43] For example, in 2018 Starbucks Mexico opened in a Mexico City location that is run entirely by employees aged 55 and older. When the location first opened, the company staffed younger employees to train their Baby Boomer counterparts to be able to run the location.[44] Just one year later, Starbucks Mexico opened a second location staffed by workers ages 52 and older in the state of Jalisco. The company was quoted as saying it's important that older workers participate in "a socially inclusive environment that cares about them and thinks of them as symbols of experience."[45]

Communication researchers Karen K. Myers and Kamyab Sadaghiani explain the importance of identifying the generational strengths of employees:

> Millennials are likely to be acutely affected by globalization, communication and information technologies, economics, and socialization by very involved parents. They are likely to have different, often broader, perspectives about the world marketplace, supervisor–subordinate relationships, cultural diversity, performance of tasks, and ways that communication and information technologies can be used to enhance organizational performance and to maximize productivity. Many of these Millennial stances and behaviors can be viewed by organizations as opportunities rather than obstacles.[46]

Building Intergenerational Relationships

It is a fact of life that the ages of most organizations' members span at least three generations. Thus, being successful in the workplace requires being able to embrace generational differences and build relationships with others. Consultants Kate Berardo and Simma Lieberman offer the following tips for improving your communication with members of differing generations:

- **Be flexible.** Be willing to adjust the channels you use to communicate (e.g., face-to-face, e-mail, social media).
- **Avoid generational jargon.** Speak in plain terms and avoid slang that other generations may not recognize (e.g., "the cat's pajamas," "wicked," "my bad," "yolo").
- **Be attentive.** Look for verbal and nonverbal signs that you may be misunderstanding each other.
- **Practice active listening.** Listen for expressions that suggest that the other person has different values or outlooks than you. Use these moments to better understand the individual.
- **Show respect.** Most generations have felt they do not get the respect they deserve. Use these strategies to show coworkers that you respect them and their experiences.

Source: Adapted from Berardo, K., & Lieberman, S. (2013). Strategies for cross-generational relationship building, *The Culturosity Group*. Retrieved from http://www.culturosity.com

Regional Differences

Even in an age of great mobility, regional differences in communication styles persist. For example, your manner of speaking can have a strong effect on how you are perceived. Speakers of the standard dialect are rated higher than nonstandard speakers in a variety of ways: They are perceived as more competent and more self-confident, and the content of their messages is rated more favorably.[47] In one experiment, researchers asked human resources professionals to rate job applicants' intelligence, initiative, and personality after hearing a 45-second recording of their voices. The speakers with identifiable regional accents—a Southern or New Jersey accent, for example—were recommended for lower-level jobs, while those with less pronounced speech styles were tagged for higher-level jobs that involved more public contact.[48] The judgment attached to identifiable accents is a key reason why many call centers for U.S. companies are located in Midwestern states. Gallup, the national telephone research agency, uses call centers in Nebraska because of the neutral accents of many of the people who live there.

The effect of non-native accents is even more powerful. In one study, jurors in the United States found testimony less believable when delivered by witnesses speaking with German, Mexican, or Middle Eastern accents.[49] Not surprisingly, other research shows that speakers with non-native accents feel stigmatized by the bias against them, often leading to a lower sense of belonging and more communication problems.[50]

Beyond accent, regional differences in communication can be significant. In the United States, for example, the unwritten rules about smiling differ from one part of the country to another. One communication researcher found Midwesterners from Ohio, Indiana, and Illinois smiled more than New Englanders from Massachusetts, New Hampshire, and Maine. None of those people smiled as much as people from Southern and border states like Georgia, Kentucky, and Tennessee.[51] Given these differences, it is easy to imagine how a manufacturer from Memphis might regard a banker from Boston as unfriendly, and how the New Englander might view the Southerner as overly demonstrative.

Disabilities

The Americans with Disabilities Act (ADA) and the ADA Amendments Act (ADAAA) define a person with a disability as someone who has a physical or mental impairment that substantially limits one or more major life activities, someone who has a history or record of such an impairment, or someone who is perceived by others as having such an impairment. Disability is diverse and nondiscriminatory: It will touch all of us at some point in our lives, either directly or through someone we love. In fact, the Social Security Administration estimates slightly more than one in four of today's 20-year-olds will become disabled before reaching the age of 67.[52]

According to the U.S. Bureau of Labor Statistics, 19.3% of persons with a disability were employed in 2019.[53] Workers with a disability were more likely to work in production, transportation, and material moving occupations, and less likely to work in management and professional occupations than those without a disability.[54]

Although the ADA and other laws have made great strides in improving accessibility and protecting the rights of persons with disabilities in the workplace, progress is still needed to educate members of the workforce about how to communicate with and about people with disabilities.

Perhaps one of the most important things to remember when interacting with others is to emphasize the person first, not the disability. For example, group designations like "the disabled" or "the blind" do not reflect the individuality of people with disabilities. Likewise, referring to someone as "normal" implies that people with disabilities are not normal. Replace this language with affirmative phrases, such as "person with a disability" or "person who is blind."

The following is a list of general tips distributed by the Department of Homeland Security to promote effective interactions with persons with disabilities[55]:

- When talking to a person with a disability, *look at and speak directly to that person,* rather than the individual's companion.

- *Be considerate of people's service animals.* Some people who have disabilities may use a service animal. Do not pet or play with the animal, as this activity may unsettle the person and may interrupt the animal from performing its assistive duties.

- *Avoid assuming the preferences and needs of people with disabilities.* People with disabilities are individuals and, therefore, have individual preferences and needs. If you have the impression that a person needs help, ask the person if, and then how, you may be of assistance.

- *Communicate clearly and comprehensibly.* As with all communication, an effective message is one that is spoken or written clearly and comprehensibly. This point is extremely important for people with disabilities who may have difficulty obtaining or comprehending messages. Be sure to convey your message in an understandable form and in multiple ways if necessary.

- *If you do not need to know about the specific nature of someone's disability, do not ask about that person's disability.* Your focus should be on what the person is communicating to you.

- *In your conversation, relax.* Don't be embarrassed if you happen to use accepted common expressions such as "See you later" or "Got to be running along" that seem to relate to the person's disability. Don't be afraid to ask questions when you are unsure of how to assist the person.

Disclosing Disability Status during an Interview

Although a job candidate is not required to disclose a disability to a prospective employer, there are several stages in the employment process when people with disabilities may feel compelled to disclose this information.

If accommodations are needed to complete an online application or participate in an interview, an applicant may need to disclose his or her disability. In this instance, an employer is able to ask the applicant for reasonable documentation—such as a note from an appropriate professional—that provides information about the disability, limitations, and accommodation needs.

The Americans with Disabilities Act prohibits interviewers from asking job candidates about a disability or the nature or severity of the disability. For a job candidate, however, questions may arise—for example, gaps in work history—that are difficult to explain. It is a good idea for the applicant to consider the questions that may be asked and rehearse the answers. Applicants who choose to disclose their disability status at this point should focus on showing their ability to deal with a difficult situation in a positive manner.

Many experts suggest that it is also helpful to anticipate concerns that an employer may have and find ways to address such concerns during the interview with anecdotes that demonstrate success. For example, persons with visible disabilities who wish to disclose their disability status during the interview can proactively describe an accommodation in a way that communicates self-confidence and an ability to perform the job effectively: "In my previous work, I was responsible for maintaining our inventory. I created a labeling system with a good color contrast that I could see easily. It turns out that this was a benefit for others as well."[56]

Sex and Gender

Although the terms sex and gender are often used interchangeably, when studying communication it is important to distinguish these terms from one another. The term sex traditionally refers to the biological sex of a person (male, female, or intersex), whereas one's *gender* is socially and culturally constructed.[57] Gender encompasses communication styles typically associated with masculinity, femininity, and androgyny (a blend of feminine and masculine traits), as well as sexual orientation, and gender identity (e.g., cisgender, androgynous, bigender, trans, transgender, etc.).[58]

As you will read in Chapter 4, communication among genders tends to differ in some significant ways. Unfortunately, perceptions of such differences have led to instances of sex-based discrimination in the workplace. This type of discrimination involves unlawfully treating someone unfavorably because of their biological sex, gender identity, or sexual orientation.[59]

Although improvements have been made, women continue to face some sex-based issues in the workplace today—most notably the wage gap. According to the Census Bureau data from 2018, female full-time employees of all races earned, on average, 82 cents for every dollar earned by males of all races, with the wage gap being larger for most women of color.[60] Several other factors have been suggested to hinder women in advancing in their careers, including a lack of mentors and role models, exclusion from informal communication networks, stereotyping of roles and abilities, lack of experience, and family responsibilities.[61]

If you accept the "different cultures" argument, then the guidelines for intercultural communication offered in the section on Communicating across Diversity suggest useful tips for communicating with members of different sexes and genders. Rather than "ethnocentrically" finding fault with the way they communicate, a more productive approach might be to think that they are speaking a different language to some degree.

Promoting sex equality in the workplace can also be achieved by providing training to management, providing employees with on-site child care facilities for parents, promoting successful employees of a variety of cultures in the company, publicizing efforts to promote equality, compensating employees equally for performing the same work, and establishing policies that forbid sexual harassment.[62]

Progress toward transgender-inclusive workplaces is also being made across the nation. According to the Human Rights Campaign's (HRC) 2020 Corporate Equality Index, 576 major employers have developed gender transition guidelines for their workforce, up from 382 in 2017.[63] Anticipating employees' needs and having a plan in place to communicate acceptance and respect during such a transition is an important part of today's work environment. The following strategies may be helpful in creating a culture of inclusion and community for individuals who are transitioning[64]:

- Create guidelines that explain expectations of transitioning employees, supervisors, colleagues, and staff.
- Host diversity training and educational programs (in-person or online).
- Offer employees an option to self-identify using anonymous surveys or confidential human resources records.
- Have formally recognized employee networks for diverse populations of the workforce.
- Provide networks related to such issues with access to resources, such as meeting rooms.
- Develop inclusive and visible philanthropic efforts.

Creating an inclusive culture benefits both the employee and the company. As an example, Patagonia provides company-paid health care and sick time to all employees, paid maternity and paternity leave, and access to on-site child care, among other benefits. The company's former chief executive officer, Rose Marcario, lists numerous benefits the company experienced from these actions: the ability to recoup 50% of costs in tax benefits, increased employee retention, increased employee engagement, more women in management, greater employee loyalty, and a stronger workplace culture of trust.[65]

Military Veterans

Military veterans have served or are serving in the armed forces, and some have had exposure to military conflicts, such as war. Many employers recognize the strengths that veterans can bring to the workplace, including working well with a team, taking responsibility for job performance, demonstrating self-confidence, being organized and disciplined, possessing a strong work ethic, having the ability to complete assignments under stressful circumstances, being able to adapt to situations, and being able to quickly and creatively solve problems.[66] As a result, the unemployment rate for veterans fell to 3.1% in 2019.[67]

Despite the increase in their employment rate in recent years, veterans' well-being in the workplace is lower than that of other Americans.[68] Among the challenges that veterans may face are being expected to go home at the end of the workday, even if the "mission" is not complete; being immersed in a competitive, rather than collaborative, workplace; adjusting to a new position and social changes; and worrying about possible job loss.[69]

In one study, a group of veterans discussed the need to educate supervisors about the nature of post-traumatic stress, as well as the need for supervisors to make the workplace a safe environment and to ask for resources and accommodations for veterans experiencing post-traumatic stress.[70] Other measures suggested as helpful for recruiting and retaining veterans in the workplace include the following[71]:

- Support/development of networking groups
- Offering educational components focused on professional development, leadership, or veterans community initiatives
- Programs addressing veterans' transition, networking, and post-traumatic stress needs
- Mandatory employee training on military-related issues
- Veteran internship programs
- Educating groups, such as chambers of commerce and Rotary clubs, on veteran recruitment

• Cultural Differences in International Business

Browse the travel and business sections of any bookseller or library, and you are likely to find many volumes detailing the cultures and business practices around the world. Some cultural differences in customs and behavior are obvious. For example, your work life will be simpler once you understand that punctuality is important in Switzerland and Germany but less important in most parts of Africa. As Table 2-1 later in this section shows, other differences are more subtle.

We begin this section by looking at the more obvious differences in customs and behavior that distinguish cultures. Next, we explore some fundamental dimensions of diversity that are less obvious but just as important. The following categories are not an exhaustive list of differences between countries, but they suggest the importance of learning the rules of the cultures in which you will operate.

Customs and Behavior

Before cataloging differences in communication around the world, it is important to note that people from varied backgrounds also share many similarities. For example, computer engineers from Singapore, Lima, Tel Aviv, and Vancouver would find plenty of mutual interests and perspectives due to their shared occupational and socioeconomic backgrounds.

Even when we acknowledge cultural variation, the fact remains that not everyone in a culture behaves identically. Figure 2.2 shows both the overlap in communication practices and the range of behavior within each one. Furthermore, within every culture,

FIGURE 2.2
Differences and Similarities within and between Cultures

Source: Adapted from Bond, M. H. (1991). *Beyond the Chinese face.* New York: Oxford University Press; Trompenaars, F. (1994). *Riding the waves of culture.* New York: McGraw Hill/Irwin.

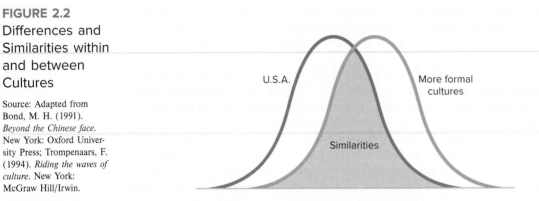

members display a wide range of communication styles. Ignoring similarities across cultures (*inter*cultural) and variations between members of the same cultural group (*intra*cultural) can lead to stereotyping people from different backgrounds.

Formality

Americans take pleasure in their informality and their quickness in getting on a first-name basis with others. With the exception of a few countries, including Thailand and Australia, business exchanges involving persons from other countries tend to be much more formal, especially at the beginning of a relationship.[72] In the United States and Canada, first names are seen as friendly and indicative of fondness and attachment. In contrast, in many other countries—Mexico, Germany, and Egypt, for example—titles are an important way of showing respect, and it is best to use them until you are invited to move to a first-name basis.[73]

Names and titles are not the only way to express degrees of formality. The way people do—or do not—converse with strangers varies from one culture to another. In North America, it is not uncommon to strike up a conversation with a stranger. This custom is not universal, however. The U.S. retail giant WalMart made the strategic decision not to hire greeters at its German stores for reasons expressed by a public relations expert from that country: "As a German, I find the idea of being greeted at the door uncomfortable. I would feel astonished if someone I didn't know started talking to me."[74]

Social Customs

Cultural differences begin as soon as communicators encounter one another. Greetings range from the bow (lower is more respectful) in Japan, to the *wai* (pressed palms with a head bow) in Thailand, to the handshake in Europe and South America.

In many countries, exchanging business cards is an important ritual. In Japan, especially, cards are given and received with care: The recipient should use two hands and study the card carefully, treating it with the same respect he or she would give its owner.[75] One U.S. businessman lost a deal in Japan because his inattention to the Japanese businesspersons' cards was taken as a measure of the lack of attention he would give to their business.[76]

In many cultures, gift-giving is a part of business protocol. Knowing the details of a specific culture can be important. For example, in India, where cows are sacred, gifts of leather are to be avoided. In China, avoid giving white flowers (associated with death) or gifts in sets of four because the sound of that number is the same as the word for death. Lavish gifts may put your host in an awkward position, so learn cultural specifics and choose carefully.

Another variable is the degree of overlap between doing business and socializing. While entertaining is part of business in almost all cultures, socializing after hours is a central part of building a working relationship in many parts of the world. In much of eastern Asia, drinking is regarded as a way of bonding that carries over into working relationships. One consultant alerts travelers to be prepared for a turn singing in the karaoke bars that are part of the scene in China, Japan, and other countries in the region.[77]

Styles of Dress

As travel and communication make the world feel like a smaller place, regional differences in clothing are becoming less pronounced. For men, the standard Western business suit is common in many urban settings. For both men and women abroad, conservative dress will take you much further than the latest fad or fashion. In Muslim countries, women can show respect with modest dress, including longer sleeves and lower hemlines than may be fashionable elsewhere. And women doing business in these countries might consider covering their hair, even if veiling is not part of their personal religion.

Chad Baker/Jason Reed/Ryan McVay/Photodisc/Getty Images RF

Even in an era of international business, local differences exist. For example, when United Parcel Service entered the German market, it belatedly discovered that the firm's signature brown uniforms evoked unpleasant memories of brown-shirted Nazi storm troopers. In Indonesia, the company had to modify its usual business suit dress rule and allow executives to wear more casual attire common in that hot and humid climate.[78]

Time   In international business, the first shock for travelers from the United States may be the way members of other cultures understand and use time. North Americans, like most northern Europeans, have what anthropologists term a **monochronic** view of time, seeing it as an almost tangible substance. American speech reflects this attitude when people talk about saving time, making time, having time, wasting time, using time, and taking time. In U.S. culture, time is money, so it is rationed carefully. People schedule appointments and rigidly adhere to them. Tasks are performed in a scheduled order, one at a time.

This monochronic orientation is not universal. Cultures with a **polychronic** orientation see time as more fluid. Meetings go on for as long as they take; they do not abruptly end because "it's time." Most Latin American cultures, as well as southern European and Middle Eastern cultures, have a polychronic orientation. In Mexico, for example, "you make friends first and do business later," according to R. C. Schrader, who once led California's trade office in Mexico City.[79]

Members of polychronic cultures are less concerned with punctuality than those raised with monochronic standards. It is not that being punctual is unimportant, but rather that other relational factors may take priority. This fact helps explain why the notion of being "on time" varies. Extremely monochronic cultures view even small delays as an offense. In polychronic cultures, varying degrees of lateness are acceptable—from roughly 15 minutes in southern Europe to part, or sometimes even all, of the day in the Middle East and Africa.[80]

Tolerance for Conflict

Tolerance for Conflict   In some cultures, each person is responsible for helping to maintain harmony of a group and of society. The maintenance and pursuit of harmony is expressed in the Japanese term *wa*. In Chinese, a similar term is *zhong he*.[81] In other places—the Middle East and southern Europe, for example—harmony takes a backseat to emotional expression. Figure 2.3 illustrates how the rules for expressing emotions vary around the world.

The cultural avoidance of conflict means that most Asian businesspeople will probably not say "no" directly to you, fearing you will lose face and suffer embarrassment. To help you maintain harmony and save face, they might spare you unpleasant news or information; the message will be softened so you do not suffer disgrace or shame, especially in front of others. You may be told they will consider the matter or that it would be very difficult. Mexican business culture also values harmony and discourages confrontation. This attitude creates problems when it clashes with more aggressive standards that U.S. businesspeople usually bring to transactions.

This sort of accommodation works both ways. People from cultures that seek harmony can learn to adapt to and accept conflict; communicators from more aggressive

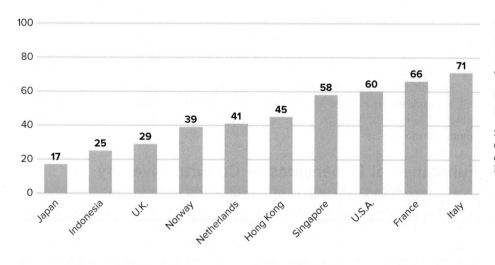

FIGURE 2.3

Percentage of Employees Who Would Openly Express Feeling Upset at Work

Source: Trompenaars, F. (1994). *Riding the waves of culture*. New York: McGraw Hill/Irwin.

societies like the United States can learn to appreciate the importance of harmony when communicating cross-culturally. Once communicators learn to appreciate the various sets of rules about how to express and handle disagreements, conducting business becomes much easier.

Gender Roles   Women from North America, Western Europe, and Australia/New Zealand who travel internationally are likely to be astonished and chagrined by the way they are regarded in some overseas cultures, where ideas of appropriate feminine behavior can be quite different from those in their home countries. In some countries, a woman who outranks a man may not be treated that way by hosts; the hosts may still speak to and prefer to negotiate with the male, assuming he is the woman's superior. In Asian countries and Muslim countries, women may find they are excluded from substantive

Table 2-1	Contrasting Chinese–Western Concerns and Communication Practices	
	Chinese	**Western**
Concerns	Saving face	Frankness, "honesty"
	Respect, politeness	Assertiveness
	Compromise, flexibility	Self-assurance
	General feeling, "spirit"	Specific terms
	Social status	Task at hand
	Patience	Time efficiency
Communication practices	Reserved	Extroverted
	Tentative	Firm
	Personal	Less personal
	No body contact	Hugging, backslapping acceptable
	No pointing	Index finger used to point

Source: Chen, M. (2001). *Inside Chinese business: A guide for managers worldwide*. Boston, MA: Harvard Business School Press.

conversations or overlooked in negotiations because of their designated gender roles. Sometimes, a woman can establish greater credibility by clarifying her title, role, and responsibilities in writing before making a personal visit, but even this step does not necessarily guarantee the desired effect.

The differences described here can present challenges when workers from different cultures work together. Table 2-1 illustrates some of these challenges by listing differences between Chinese and Western businesspeople in terms of both their concerns and their communication styles.

Fundamental Dimensions of Cultural Diversity

So far we have discussed obvious differences between cultures. As important as customs and norms are, they are just the tip of the cultural iceberg. Underlying what might appear to be idiosyncrasies in behavior are a number of fundamental values that shape the way members of a culture think, feel, and act. In this section, we look at some of these fundamental differences. Once you appreciate them, you will understand how and why people from different backgrounds behave as they do, and you will have ideas of how you can adapt to improve the quality of your communication with others.

High- and Low-Context Cultures   Anthropologist Edward Hall identified two distinct ways in which members of various cultures deliver messages.[82] A **low-context culture** uses language primarily to express thoughts, feelings, and ideas as clearly and logically as possible. To low-context communicators, the meaning of a statement lies in the words spoken. By contrast, a **high-context culture** relies heavily on subtle, often nonverbal cues to convey meaning, save face, and maintain social harmony. Communicators in these societies learn to discover meaning from the context in which a message is delivered: the speaker's nonverbal behaviors, the history of the relationship, and the general social rules that govern interactions between people. When delivering difficult or awkward messages, high-context speakers often convey meaning through context rather than plainly stated words to avoid upsetting their listeners. Consider a few differences between how a low-context Westerner and a high-context Chinese person might express the same idea[83]:

Western	Chinese
Do you understand? *(Responsibility placed on other.)*	Am I being clear? *(Speaker takes responsibility for understanding.)*
Is the project acceptable? *(Requires direct yes or no answer.)*	What do you think of the project? *(Gives respondent latitude to reply diplomatically.)*
We can't do that. *(Clear refusal could be perceived as harsh.)*	This may be a little difficult for us to do. *(Context makes it clear that the answer is still no.)*

Mainstream culture in the United States and Canada falls toward the low-context end of the scale. Long-time residents generally value "straight talk" and grow impatient with beating around the bush. By contrast, most Middle Eastern and Asian cultures fit the high-context pattern. In many Asian societies, for example, maintaining harmony is important, so communicators avoid speaking directly if that would threaten another person's dignity. One U.S. project manager describes how her insensitivity to high-context communication almost derailed an international team in developing a Japanese-language version of an Internet search service:

As an American project manager, I was expecting that if I was proposing something stupid, I would hear it from the people on the team. In reality, I had a plan with a fatal flaw, and the Japanese team members knew it, but it was not their style of communication to embarrass me by telling me.[84]

Even within a single country, co-cultures can have different notions about the value of direct speech. For example, the Puerto Rican language style resembles high-context Japanese or Korean more than low-context English. As a group, Puerto Ricans value social harmony and avoid confrontation, which leads them to speak in indirect ways to avoid offending their conversational partners.[85] The same holds true for Mexican Americans, as communication researcher Don Locke explains:

> Whereas members of the dominant culture of the United States are taught to value openness, frankness, and directness, the traditional Mexican-American approach requires the use of much diplomacy and tact when communicating with another individual. Concern and respect for the feelings of others dictate that a screen be provided behind which an individual may preserve dignity. . . . The manner of expression is likely to be elaborate and indirect, since the aim is to make the personal relationship at least appear harmonious, to show respect for the other's individuality. To the Mexican-American, direct argument or contradiction appears rude and disrespectful.[86]

A preference for high- or low-context communication is just one of many factors that distinguish one culture from another. One survey of 160,000 employees in 60 countries revealed several other ways in which the worldviews of one national culture can differ from those of another.[87] Table 2-2 lists those dimensions and the styles that are most common in some countries.

Daniel Adler

Individualism Members of **individualistic cultures** are inclined to put their own interests and those of their immediate family ahead of social concerns. Individualistic cultures offer their members a great deal of freedom in the belief that this freedom makes it possible for each person to achieve personal success. **Collectivist cultures**, in contrast, have tight social frameworks in which members of a group (such as an organization) feel primary loyalty toward one another and the group to which they belong. China, like most East Asian cultures, is highly collective.

In collectivist societies, members are expected to believe the welfare of the organization is as important as or even *more important* than their own.[88] Workers are less likely to strive to become organizational "stars," because that approach would dishonor other team members. "You seldom see an individual Japanese executive who stands above the rest until he is the most senior individual in the company," says international corporate recruiter Richard M. Ferry.[89] The power of collectivist beliefs was illustrated when PepsiCo rewarded one of its managers in China with a sizeable cash bonus, which he then divided equally among his subordinates.[90]

Power Distance The term **power distance** refers to attitudes toward differences in authority. Cultures with high power distance, such as Mexico and the Philippines, accept the fact that power is distributed unequally—that some members have greater resources and influence than others. In these cultures, differences in organizational status and rank are expected, routine, and clear-cut. Lower-level employees respect those in high positions.

Table 2-2	Cultural Values in Selected Countries

Long-Term Orientation	Short-Term Orientation
China	Pakistan
Hong Kong	Philippines
Taiwan	Norway
Japan	Canada
South Korea	East Africa*

Individualistic	Collectivistic
United States	Guatemala
Australia	Ecuador
United Kingdom	Panama
Canada	Venezuela
New Zealand	Pakistan
	Indonesia

Avoid Uncertainty	Tolerate Uncertainty
Greece	Singapore
Portugal	Jamaica
Uruguay	Denmark
Guatemala	Sweden
Belgium	Hong Kong
El Salvador	

High Power Distance	Low Power Distance
Malaysia	Austria
Philippines	Israel
Mexico	Denmark
Arab world**	New Zealand
China	Ireland

Masculine	Feminine
Japan	Sweden
Hungary	Norway
Austria	Netherlands
Italy	Denmark
Switzerland	Costa Rica

* Ethiopia, Kenya, Tanzania, Zambia.
** Egypt, Iraq, Kuwait, Lebanon, Libya, Saudi Arabia, United Arab Emirates.
Source: Adapted from Hofstede, G., Hofstede, G. J., & Minkov, M. (1997). *Cultures and organizations: Software of the mind* (3rd ed.). New York: McGraw Hill.

Other cultures, such as the United States, downplay differences in power. In these cultures, employees are more comfortable approaching—and even challenging—their superiors and may expect to gain greater power.

Colleagues with different approaches to power distance might find it difficult to work together. Imagine, for example, how a young business school graduate from a U.S. firm might grow frustrated after being transferred to the Guadalajara branch office, where the same relentless questioning that marked her as a free thinker in school is regarded as overly aggressive troublemaking.

Uncertainty Avoidance

Uncertainty Avoidance The world is an uncertain place. International politics, economic trends, and the forces of nature make it impossible to predict the future with accuracy. **Uncertainty avoidance** is a measure of a culture's tolerance for lack of predictability. Some cultures (e.g., Singapore and Hong Kong) are comfortable with uncertainty, allowing their members to take risks and being relatively tolerant of behavior that differs from the norm. Other cultures (e.g., Japan, Greece, and Portugal) are less comfortable with change. Their members value tradition and formal rules, and show less tolerance for different ideas.

Masculinity

Masculinity In the context of intercultural research, masculinity does not refer to biological traits. Instead, it addresses a culture's values, expressed in terms of stereotypical gender roles. For example, a culture that is made up of stereotypical male gender roles, such as a focus on material success, competition, power, and assertiveness, is termed **masculine**. A culture that embraces more stereotypically feminine characteristics, such as helping others and prioritizing relationships, is considered **feminine**.

More masculine cultures (e.g., Japan, Austria, and Switzerland) tend to focus on getting the job done. They are concerned with making the team more competent through training and the use of up-to-date methods. By contrast, more feminine cultures (Scandinavian countries, Chile, Portugal, Thailand, and much of Latin America) are more likely to be concerned about members' feelings and their smooth functioning as a team. They focus more on collective concerns, such as cooperative problem solving, maintaining a friendly atmosphere, and good physical working conditions. Relative to other countries, the United States falls slightly toward the masculine end of the spectrum, and Canada is almost exactly in the middle, balanced between task and social concerns.[91]

Future Orientation

Future Orientation Cultures with a **long-term orientation** defer gratification in pursuit of long-range goals, while those with a **short-term orientation** look for quick payoffs. The willingness to work hard today for a future payoff is especially common in East Asian cultures, while Western industrialized cultures are much more focused on short-term results.

As long as employees and employers share the same orientation toward payoffs, the chances for harmony are good. In contrast, when some people push for a quick fix while others urge patience, conflicts are likely to arise.

It is easy to see how a society's task or social orientation and its attitudes toward uncertainty, individuality, power distance, and short-term or long-term results can make a tremendous difference in how work situations evolve. Cultural values shape what people communicate about and how they interact. Of course, cultural differences do not account for every aspect of workplace functioning, but they do provide a set of assumptions that exert a subtle yet powerful effect on each person's workplace communication.

• Diversity and Ethical Issues

Some cultural differences may challenge your sense of what is normal or proper behavior without raising ethical questions. For example, you probably could readjust your sense of promptness or what to wear to a business meeting without facing any sort of moral dilemma. However, there may be moments when you might experience behavior that is hostile or derogatory. Some of these behaviors may be blatantly obvious and challenge your fundamental sense of right and wrong. For example, you might be offended by differing notions of gender equality. You should be shocked to learn that bribes or payoffs are considered a normal part of doing business. You could encounter favoritism toward friends and family members that offends your fair sense of play. You might see a profound disregard for the environment.

Other behaviors—like **microaggressions**—may be more difficult to decipher. For example, one of the authors of your textbook recalls feeling uncomfortable when a superior asked her why she wasn't "wearing her Latina business suit" when she arrived at the office. The superior was referring to the author's typical style of dress which consisted of high heels, dark jeans, and a blazer, but unwelcomingly attributed this style to the author's cultural identity. Although this comment was brief and may have been unintentional, such microaggressions communicate negative or stereotypical attitudes toward culturally marginalized groups and have no place in business.

It is important to know legal protections and business ethics to have the confidence to manage these challenges.

Legal Protections

In the United States, the Equal Employment Opportunity Commission (EEOC) offers protections for employees and job applicants that make discrimination unlawful. Despite these protections, the EEOC received over 72,000 allegations of workplace discrimination in 2019. The largest number of cases (over 39,000) were in reference to retaliation, followed by disability, race, sex, and age.[92] Knowing your basic legal rights will help you recognize workplace violations and seek help if your rights are violated.

- *Title VII of the Civil Rights Act of 1964*, as amended, protects employees and job applicants from discrimination on the basis of race, color, religion, sex, and national origin.[93] The *Pregnancy Discrimination Act of 1978* (PDA) amended Title VII to prohibit sex discrimination on the basis of pregnancy, childbirth, or related medical conditions.[94] In *Bostock v. Clayton County*, Georgia (2020), the U.S. Supreme Court ruled that sex discrimination on the basis of gender identity or sexual orientation is also protected by Title VII.[95] The Act also recognizes sexual harassment, as well as offensive remarks about a person's sex, as being unlawful.[96] These protections cover all companies and labor unions with more than 15 employees, employment agencies, state and local government, and apprenticeship programs.[97]

- *The Equal Pay Act of 1963* protects against sex-based wage discrimination between men and women in the same establishment who perform jobs requiring equal skill, effort, and responsibility under similar working conditions.[98]

- *The Age Discrimination in Employment Act of 1967* (ADEA), as amended, protects persons aged 40 or older from employment discrimination based on age. ADEA's protections apply to employees and job applicants and prevent age-based discrimination in hiring, firing, promotions, layoffs, compensation and benefits, job assignments, and more.[99]

- *Americans with Disabilities Act* (ADA), passed in 1990, prohibits discrimination against persons with disabilities in employment. The ADA requires employers to make reasonable accommodations to enable a qualified person with a disability to do their job.[100]

Responding to Ethical Challenges

There is a growing recognition that businesses that operate in a worldwide economy need a universal code of business ethics. Toward that end, the collaboration of business leaders in Japan, Europe, and the United States has resulted in the development of a code of ethics

Coping with Unfair Treatment

While all U.S.-based employers must follow federal laws regarding employment discrimination, it is understandable that victims of unfair treatment might feel apprehensive about reporting such behavior. Fear of retaliation or worsening workplace conditions, among other reasons, may cause employees to stay silent about such experiences.

Part of being empowered to address unfair treatment is knowing your rights and protections. Eric Kingsley, of Kingsley & Kingsley Lawyers, offers the following advice to persons who feel they may be victims of unfair treatment at work:

1. *Document the unfair treatment:* Keep a record of exchanges that illustrate unfair treatment. This may consist of e-mail messages, internal memos, office communications, voicemails, and written descriptions of anything you remember about instances of mistreatment.

2. *Report the unfair treatment:* To formalize your complaint, report the unfair treatment to your company's human resources (HR) department. If the treatment at work is criminal, such as sexual assault, immediately report it to law enforcement.

3. *Stay away from social media:* Avoid posting information about your experience on social media; this could aggravate the situation.

4. *Take care of yourself:* Self-care is important; talk to your family, spiritual advisor, friends, or a support group.

5. *Contact an experienced lawyer:* A lawyer can help you identify the proper approach for your situation and goals.

Source: Kingsley, E. (2020, January 2). How to deal with an unfair workplace. *Employee Rights Blog.* Retrieved from https://www.kingsleykingsley.com/how-to-deal-with-an-unfair-workplace

based on ideals from both East Asia and the West. This code, which is known as the Caux Round Table Principles for Business, includes many communication-related principles, such as treating all employees with honesty and dignity, listening to employee suggestions, avoiding discriminatory practices, dealing with all customers fairly, and avoiding industrial espionage and other dishonest means of acquiring commercial information.[101]

Despite this admirable effort to ensure good ethical practices on an international basis, you may encounter ethical challenges arising out of cultural differences. In such cases, you can respond in a variety of ways:

1. *Avoiding:* You might refuse to do business in cultures that operate according to ethical principles different from your own.

2. *Accommodating:* You could accept the different ethical system and conform to practices that are fundamentally different from your preferred practices.

3. *Forcing:* You could insist on doing business in a way you believe is ethically proper.

4. *Educating-Persuading:* You could try to convince the people with whom you want to do business that your set of ethical principles is more appropriate.

5. *Negotiating-Compromising:* You and the other party could each give up something to negotiate a settlement.

6. *Collaboration-Problem Solving:* You could work with the other party to confront the conflict directly and develop a mutually satisfying solution.[102]

All of these approaches have obvious drawbacks. It is easy to imagine a situation in which you may have to choose between compromising your principles to please your bosses and customers and staying true to yourself, which may put your career at risk.

Facing ethical dilemmas you never anticipated can be especially difficult. You can begin to prepare for this possibility by grounding yourself in ethical principles and learning about a new culture's ethical practices. When you do encounter new situations, ask yourself the following questions to help make the best possible decision:

ETHICAL **challenge**

- *How morally significant is this situation?* Not all ethical conflicts have the same moral significance. For example, while giving contracts to friends or family members may offend the sensibilities of a businessperson used to awarding jobs on the basis of merit, the practice may not be as morally offensive as exploiting child labor or damaging the environment.[103]

- *Is there home culture consensus regarding the issue?* If there is not widespread agreement in your home culture about the ethical principle, you justifiably may have more latitude about how to act. For example, corporations in the United States have a wide range of policies about supporting employees' families, so there might be less obligation for a company to provide family benefits in a host country.[104]

Communicating across Diversity

By now, it should be clear that communicating with others from different backgrounds is not always easy. Factors including culture, ethnicity, and gender may have made others' experiences quite different from yours.[105] Some of the responsibility for building bridges rests with management. As discussed in the Sex and Gender section, a growing number of businesses are now taking this job seriously and addressing it more formally. Even so, you do not need to join a corporate training program to benefit from cultural diversity.

Three ways to enhance your intercultural competency are to improve your knowledge, attitudes, and behaviors. These principles can be summarized in the three categories explored on the following pages. Adopting a more perceptive attitude can go a long way toward opening the door to more rewarding and productive communication.

Become Culturally Literate

Many cultural problems are caused not by malice, but rather by a lack of knowledge. Trainers in cultural sensitivity routinely cite examples of how mistaken assumptions can lead to trouble.[106] Lack of knowledge is most apparent in international settings. One engineer gives an embarrassing example:

> I was in a meeting with some Korean clients, and I had a red marker in my hand to make some corrections to a blueprint. . . . I used my red marker to write the name of one of the Korean guys that I was meeting with. The room got very silent, and everyone looked at me completely stunned.

Using Personal Pronouns

A pronoun is a word that refers to people who are being talked about. A personal pronoun is a pronoun that a person prefers to use to describe themselves. The following is a list of pronouns that persons may prefer:

- She, her, hers
- He, him, his
- They, them, theirs
- Ze or zie (pronounced "zee"; replaces she, he, they)
- Hir/hirs (pronounced "here"; replaces her/hers, him/his, or them/theirs)
- Some people prefer only their names be used ("Jessica's books are in Jessica's locker.")

Since you can't always tell what someone's pronoun is by their name or appearance, one of the most basic ways to show respect and avoid gender bias in the workplace is to adopt gender-inclusive language.

If you're not sure about a person's preferred pronouns, it's okay to ask ("What pronouns do you use?" or "I was wondering how you might like me to address you."). To make the situation more comfortable, you might even lead by sharing your own pronouns ("Hi, I'm Bobbie. My pronouns are she, her, hers."). Once someone has shared their pronouns with you, be sure to use them correctly. If you make a mistake or forget to use a person's pronoun, don't panic—simply apologize, correct it, and move on.

Source: Williams. (n.d.). Pronouns. Retrieved from https://lgbt.williams.edu/resources/trans-resources/pronouns/

One of the clients took pity on me and whispered that writing a living person's name in red is a bad idea. Apparently, in Korean culture, red is used to record a deceased person's name. Since my client was alive, I was wishing him dead.[107]

Lack of cultural knowledge can lead to similar problems closer to home. In one West Coast bank, officials were dismayed when Filipino female employees did not cooperate with the new "friendly teller" program. Management failed to realize that, in Filipino culture, overtly friendly women can be taken for prostitutes. A Taiwanese executive who was transferred to the Midwestern U.S. offices of a large company was viewed as aloof and autocratic by his peers, who did not understand that Asian culture encourages a more distant managerial style.

Misunderstandings like these are less likely to cause problems when workers understand one another's cultural backgrounds. As Paulette Williams, former senior manager at Weyerhauser's nurseries in Southern California, puts it, "If you don't learn how other people feel, you can hurt them unintentionally."[108]

Develop Constructive Attitudes

It is easy to think of cultural differences as an annoyance that makes it harder to take care of business. Dealing with others who have different attitudes or customs takes patience and time—both scarce commodities in a busy work schedule. With the right attitude, though, cultural diversity can stop being just a necessary cost of doing business and can become an opportunity.[109] In fact, one research study found that creating a culture of equality in the workplace can result in less fear of failure and more innovation.[110] Figure 2.4 shows the range of attitudes about cultural differences. It is easy to see which mindsets do and do not lead to productive relationships.

Another way to develop constructive attitudes is to avoid ethnocentrism. **Ethnocentrism** is the inclination to see all events from the perspective of your own culture and to evaluate your own culture as superior. It is evident when you judge someone to be less intelligent or less important because he or she does not keep up with your national teams, consider others to be less sophisticated because their dress does not match your culture's notion of fashion, or assume others have less business acumen because they communicate

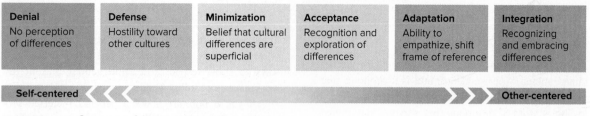

FIGURE 2.4 Stages of Intercultural Sensitivity

differently. Taking advantage of intercultural communication training and opportunities for multicultural interactions may help reduce your ethnocentrism.[111]

Adapt Your Behavior

Better knowledge of cultural differences and a constructive attitude can help you act in ways that achieve your goals and promote good working relationships.

Avoid Condescension   In his communication accommodation theory, Howard Giles outlines how people adjust their speech, vocal patterns, and gestures to accommodate to others and express liking. Although well-intentioned, sometimes these efforts to demonstrate an attitude of equality are perceived as being condescending. Individuals may try to accommodate another's physical disability by speaking more loudly to a person who has a hearing impairment, or they may mistakenly speak Spanish to a Mexican American person who speaks only English. One African American woman listed three statements that white women who want to treat black women with respect and friendship should never utter: (1) "I never even notice that you're black"; (2) "You're different from most black people"; and (3) "I understand what you're going through as a black woman, because I'm (Jewish, Italian, etc.)."[112]

Create Dialogue   Intercultural communication experts advise that an important first step toward intercultural competence is to enter into dialogue.[113] Dialogue occurs when two people acknowledge each other's common humanity and engage with each other authentically and spontaneously. Dialogue requires an attitude of mutual respect in which each person is listening to the other without having a preplanned agenda or relying on past prejudices and distortions.

When people from differing backgrounds do not listen to and talk with one another constructively, misperceptions can take root. In a study of American corporations, Charles Kelly found that Black persons perceived white persons as being reserved and ambitious and having an attitude of superiority. He found that white persons perceived Black persons as being easygoing and ambitious and feeling as if they are owed something.[114] Without understanding each other's concerns, attitudes like these are likely to persist.

Not all talk about diversity is constructive: The way people talk about differences can determine whether relationships improve or suffer. Journalist Ellis Cose describes two nonproductive styles:

> Discussions tend to be conducted at one of two levels—either in shouts or whispers. The shouters are generally so twisted by pain or ignorance that spectators tune them out. The whisperers are so afraid of the sting of truth that they avoid saying much of anything at all.[115]

Experts agree with Cose that ignoring differences can be just as dangerous as emphasizing them. The challenge, then, is to discuss differences openly without using inflammatory language. If you approach others with a constructive attitude, your odds of achieving a positive outcome increase.

MASTER the chapter

review points

- Society is increasingly diverse, making communicating with people from many cultures a business necessity.

- Co-cultures are groups with a clear identity within a major culture, based on characteristics such as race and ethnicity, social class, generation, region, disability, sex and gender, and military veteran status. Understanding co-cultures can improve workplace perceptions and behaviors.

- Employees need to be aware of the important international differences in formality, social customs, dress, time, tolerance for conflict, and gender roles. They must also recognize the existence of "hidden" cultural dimensions such as high- and low-context orientation,

individualism versus collectivism, power distance, uncertainty avoidance, masculinity versus femininity, and future orientation.

- Business success requires consideration of the complexity of multicultural ethical factors.

- Knowing your basic legal protections will help you recognize workplace violations and gain the confidence to seek help if you believe your rights have been violated.

- Astute business communicators strive to be culturally literate, develop constructive attitudes (such as seeing diversity as an opportunity and avoiding ethnocentrism), and adapt their behaviors for a diverse work environment by avoiding condescension and developing dialogue.

key terms

Baby Boomers 40
co-culture 37
collectivist culture 51
cultural intelligence 37
culture 34
ethnocentrism 57
feminine culture 53
Generation X 40
Generation Z 41
high-context culture 50
individualistic culture 51

long-term orientation 53
low-context culture 49
masculine culture 53
microaggressions 54
Millennials 40
monochronic time orientation 48
organizational culture 35
polychronic time orientation 48
power distance 51
short-term orientation 53
uncertainty avoidance 53

activities

1. Invitation to Insight

Through either personal interviews or research, identify several differences in communication practices between your own culture and another culture that interests you.

If you were interacting with a person from that culture, how would you bridge the differences?

2. Invitation to Insight

Choose one set of cultural values summarized in the Fundamental Dimensions of Cultural Diversity

section. and identify the characteristic that is not representative of your own culture. For example, if you are used to a low-context culture, you might focus on high-context communication. Now consider both the advantages and the disadvantages of working in an environment in which this unfamiliar norm is the dominant one. For instance, how might interactions be more effective or otherwise desirable if most people communicated in a high-context manner?

3. Skill Builder

Select one form of disability. Collaborate with several of your classmates to create a scenario illustrating effective communication with a person who is challenged by the disability. Share your scenarios with the class.

4. Skill Builder

Develop your ability to identify and communicate effectively within an organization's culture. Choose an organization in a field that interests you, or focus on an organization to which you already belong. By analyzing the organization's physical setting and literature, interviewing others, and making your own observations, construct a description of the organizational culture that addresses the dimensions listed in the chapter. On the basis of your findings, describe an optimal way to communicate in the following areas:

a. Introducing new ideas.
b. Interacting with superiors.
c. Dealing with conflict.
d. Managing time.
e. Socializing with fellow workers.
f. Using preferred methods of exchanging information (e.g., telephone, e-mail, face-to-face interaction).

5. Skill Builder

Choose three cultures around the world with which you might interact in the course of your career. To discover the keys to effective intercultural communication in your three chosen cultures, find some reputable sources on the Internet. For each of the three cultures describe:

a. The culture in general.
b. The business protocols for that culture.
c. The language(s).
d. Sources you could go to for additional training and/or e-mail contacts.

6. Skill Builder

Representatives from Japan, the United States, and European nations collaborated in an attempt to create an international code of business ethics. Read about the Caux Round Table by using a search engine to find articles on this process that began in 1994. Specifically, look for a document that discusses its seven principles and then complete the following exercises:

a. List the seven Caux Roundtable Principles for Business.
b. Describe how these seven principles relate to the ethical standards described in Chapter 1.
c. Write a short essay describing how your own personal sense of ethics corresponds to each of the seven principles.

7. Invitation to Insight

Choose one of the following options to better understand the importance of organizational culture. In each case, use the most relevant dimensions of communication described in the Communication in a Diverse Society section to structure your analysis and description.

a. Interview someone familiar with an organization or field that interests you, with the goal of learning about its culture. Identify the kinds of communication that shape this culture, and determine how the culture shapes the way communication operates in the organization or field.
b. Assume the administration of your college or university has asked you to brief newly hired faculty members on your school's academic culture from an undergraduate student's perspective. Describe how communication practices at your school both shape and reflect its culture. You can make your remarks clearer and more interesting by including one or more brief examples to illustrate how the culture operates.

8. Invitation to Insight

Find a video clip that demonstrates intercultural communication. With a group of classmates, analyze the video. Identify examples of assumptions and behaviors that either block or promote authentic relations. For those behaviors that block authentic relations, suggest ways to improve communication. Share your analysis with the class.

McGraw Hill LearnSmart

For further review, go to the LearnSmart study module for this chapter.

references

1. Office of the Governor Greg Abbott (2017). Foreign companies with operations in Texas. Retrieved from http://gov.texas.gov/fittexas/default.aspx

2. Bureau of Labor Statistics. (2020, May 15). Labor force characteristics of foreign-born workers summary. Retrieved from https://www.bls.gov/news .release/forbrn.nr0.htm/labor-force-characteristics -of-foreign-born-workers-summary

3. Fry, R. (2018, April 11). Millennials are largest generation in the U.S. labor force. Pew Research Center. Retrieved from https://www.pewresearch .org/fact-tank/2018/04/11/millennials-largest -generation-us-labor-force/

4. Fry, R. (2018, April 11). Millennials are largest generation in the U.S. labor force. Pew Research Center. Retrieved from https://www.pewresearch .org/fact-tank/2018/04/11/millennials-largest -generation-us-labor-force/

5. Davies, A., Fidler, D., & Gorbis, M. (2011). *Future work skills: 2020.* Palo Alto, CA: Institute for the Future. Retrieved from http://cdn.theatlantic.com /static/front/docs/sponsored/phoenix/future_work _skills_2020.pdf

6. Sodexo (2019, February 28). *Sodexo's gender balance study 2018: Expanded outcomes over 5 years.* Retrieved from https://www.sodexo.com/inspired-thinking /research-and-reports/gender-balance-study-2018.html

7. Novartis (2019, July 25). *Meet Elena Rodriguez, global head of diversity & inclusion at Novartis.* Retrieved from https://www.novartis.com/stories /people-and-culture/meet-elena-rodriguez-global-head -diversity-inclusion-novartis

8. Banga, A. (2014, May 22). *Lighting the way to a better, more equal world.* NYU Stern School of Business Commencement Address. Retrieved from https:// newsroom.mastercard.com/wp-content/uploads /2014/05/NYUStern-Commencement-Address-2014 -As-Prepared-for-Delivery.pdf

9. Lustig, M. W., & Koester, J. (2003). *Intercultural competence: Interpersonal communication across cultures* (4th ed.). Boston, MA: Allyn & Bacon.

10. Hansen, R. S. Uncovering a company's corporate culture is a critical task for job-seekers. Retrieved from http://www.quintcareers.com/employer_ corporate_culture.html

11. Carter, R. (2019, May 22). *Workplace by Facebook reveals employee/HQ disconnect.* UC Today. Retrieved from https://www.uctoday.com/collaboration/team -collaboration/workplace-by-facebook-reveals -employee-hq-disconnect/

12. Carter, R. (2019, May 22). *Workplace by Facebook reveals employee/HQ disconnect.* UC Today. Retrieved from https://www.uctoday.com/collaboration/team -collaboration/workplace-by-facebook-reveals -employee-hq-disconnect/

13. Waldvogel, J. (2007). Greetings and closings in workplace email. *Journal of Computer-Mediated Communication, 12,* 456–477.

14. Accountemps (2019, December 18). Office etiquette survey: Bad language, pets, political decor remain biggest offenses [Press Release]. Retrieved from https://www.prnewswire.com/news-releases/office -etiquette-survey-bad-language-pets-political-decor-re- main-biggest-offenses-300976607.html

15. Kotter, J., & Heskett, J. (1992). *Corporate culture and performance.* New York: Free Press.

16. Blakemore, E. (2019, February 22). Race and ethnicity: How are they different? *National Geographic.* Retrieved from https://www.nationalgeographic.com /culture/topics/reference/race-ethnicity/#:~:tex- t=%E2%80%9CRace%E2%80%9D%20is%20usually%20 associated%20with,and%20characterize%20seem- ingly%20distinct%20populations.

17. United States Census Bureau. (n.d.). About race. Retrieved from https://www.census.gov/topics/popula- tion/race/about.html

18. Orbe, M. P., & Harris, T. M. (2008). *Interracial communication: Theory into practice* (2nd ed.). Thousand Oaks, CA: Sage.

19. Hall, J. B. (2002). *Among cultures.* Fort Worth, TX: Harcourt College Publishers.

20. Allen, I. L. (1983). *The language of ethnic conflict: Social organization and lexical culture.* New York: Columbia University Press.

21. Rosette, A. S., Carton , A. M., Bowes-Sperry, L., & Hewlin, P. F. (2013). Why do racial slurs remain prevalent in the workplace? Integrating theory on intergroup behavior. *Articles in Advance,* 1–20.

22. U.S. Equal Employment Opportunity Commission. (2020). Significant EEOC race/color cases (covering private and federal sectors). Retrieved from https:// www.eeoc.gov/initiatives/e-race/significant-eeoc -racecolor-casescovering-private-and-federal-sectors

23. Rosette, A. S., Carton, A. M., Bowes-Sperry, L., & Hewlin, P. F. (2013). Why do racial slurs remain prevalent in the workplace? Integrating theory on intergroup behavior. *Articles in Advance,* 1–20.

24. Alcorn, C. (2019, November 5). *Papa John's is still haunted by its founder using the n-word.* CNN Business. Retrieved from https://www.cnn.com/ 2019/11/05/business/papa-johns-schnatter/index.html

25. Lustig, M. W., & Koester, J. (2003). *Intercultural competence: Interpersonal communication across cultures* (4th ed.). Boston, MA: Allyn & Bacon.

26. Condon, E. C. (1976). Cross-cultural interferences affecting teacher–pupil communication in American

schools. In F. L. Casmir (Ed.), *International and intercultural communication annual 3*. Falls Church, VA: Speech Communication Association.

27. Samovar, L. A., & Porter, R. (2004). *Communication between cultures* (5th ed.). Belmont, CA: Wadsworth.

28. Kohn, M. (1969). *Class and conformity: A study of values*. Homewood, IL: Dorsey Press; Lareau, A. (2011). *Unequal childhoods: Class, race, and family life* (2nd ed.). Berkeley, CA: University of California Press.

29. Kim, Y. K., & Sax, L. J. (2009). Student–faculty interaction in research universities: Differences by student gender, race, social class, and first-generation status. *Research in Higher Education, 50,* 437–459.

30. Kaufman, P. (2003). Learning to not labor: How working-class individuals construct middle-class identities. *Sociological Quarterly, 44,* 481–504.

31. Lubrano, A. (2004). *Limbo: Blue-collar roots, white-collar dreams*. Hoboken, NJ: John Wiley; Lucas, K. (2011). The working class promise: A communicative account of mobility-based ambivalences. *Communication Monographs, 78,* 347–369; Lucas, K. (2010). Moving up: The challenges of communicating a new social class identity. In D. O. Braithwaite & J. T. Wood (Eds.), *Casing interpersonal communication: Case studies in personal and social relationships*. Dubuque, IA: Kendall-Hunt.

32. Auby, K. (2008). *A Boomers guide to communicating with Gen X and Gen Y*. Retrieved from http://www.businessweek.com/magazine/content/08_34/b4097063805619.htm; Eisner, S. P. (2005). Managing Generation Y. *Advanced Management Journal, 70,* 13–17; Erickson, T. (2008, September 9). When Boomers work for Gen X and Gen Y. *Harvard Business Online*. Retrieved from http://www.business-week.com/managing/content/sep2008/ca2008099_258565.htm. See also Lyons, S., Duxbury, L., & Higgins, C. (2005). Are gender differences in basic human values a generational phenomenon? *Sex Roles: A Journal of Research, 53,* 763–779.

33. Fry, R. (2019, July 24). Baby Boomers are staying in the labor force at rates not seen in generations for people their age. *Pew Research Center*. Retrieved from https://www.pewresearch.org/fact-tank/2019/07/24/baby-boomers-us-labor-force/

34. Howe, N., & Strauss, W. (2007, July). The next 20 years: How customers and workforce attitudes will evolve. *Harvard Business Review, 85,* 41–52.

35. Taylor, P., & Keeter, S. (2010). *The Millennials: Confident. Connected. Open to change*. Washington, DC: Pew Research Center. Retrieved from http://pewsocialtrends.org/files/2010/10/millennials-confident-connected-open-to-change.pdf

36. Fry, R. (2015, May 11). Millennials surpass Gen Xers as the largest generation in U.S. labor force.

Pew Research Center. Retrieved from http://www.pewresearch.org/fact-tank/2015/05/11/millennials-surpass-gen-xers-as-the-largest-generation-in-u-s-labor-force/

37. Zogby, J. (2008). The way we'll be: *The transformation of the American dream*. New York: Random House; Zogby, J. (2008, October). The evolving American dream. *AARP Bulletin*, p. 37.

38. Magid Generational Strategies. (2014). The first generation of the twenty-first century. *Frank N. Magid Associates*. Retrieved from http://magid.com/sites/default/files/pdf/MagidPluralistGenerationWhitepaper.pdf

39. Dupont, S. (2015, May 1). Move over Millennials, here comes Generation Z: Understanding the 'New Realists' who are building the future. *Public Relations Society of America*. Retrieved from https://www.prsa.org/Intelligence/Tactics/Articles/view/11057/1110/Move_Over_Millennials_Here_Comes_Generation_Z_Unde#.WIE0uLYrLuS

40. Strategic Business Insights, "US Framework and VALS™ types" (2020) Retrieved from http://www.strategicbusinessinsights.com

41. Noble, S. M., & Schewe, C. D. (2003). Cohort segmentation: An exploration of its validity. *Journal of Business Research, 56,* 979–987.

42. McGuire, D., By, R. T., & Hutchings, K. (2007). Towards a model of human resource solutions for achieving intergenerational interaction in organizations. *Journal of European Industrial Training*, 31, 592–608.

43. McCann, R. M. & Giles, H. (2006). Communication with people of different ages in the workplace: Thai and American data. *Human Communication Research, 32,* 74–108.

44. Stump, S. (2018, September 6). Starbucks opens first store operated entirely by senior citizens. Today. Retrieved from https://www.today.com/food/starbucks-opens-first-store-mexico-operated-senior-citizens-t136950

45. Bolden-Barrett, V. (2019, January 23). Starbucks Mexico opens 2nd store run by older workers. *HR Dive*. Retrieved from https://www.hrdive.com/news/starbucks-mexico-opens-2nd-store-run-by-older-workers/546500/

46. Myers, K. K., & Sadaghiani, K. (June 2010). Millennials in the workplace: A communication perspective on Millennials' organizational relationships and performance. *Journal of Business Psychology, 25,* 225–238.

47. Bradac, J. J. (1990). Language attitudes and impression formation. In H. Giles & W. P. Robinson (Eds.), *The handbook of language and social psychology*. Chichester, UK: Wiley; Ng, S. H., & Bradac, J. (1993). *Power in language: Verbal communication and social influence*. Newbury Park, CA: Sage.

48. Bailey, R. W. (2003). Ideologies, attitudes, and perceptions. *American Speech, 88,* 115–142.

49. Frumkin, L. (2007). Influences of accent and ethnic background on perceptions of eyewitness testimony. *Psychology, Crime & Law, 13,* 317–331.

50. Gluszek, A., & Dovidio, J. F. (2010). Perceptions of bias, communication difficulties, and belonging in the United States. *Journal of Language & Social Psychology, 29,* 224–234.

51. Birdwhistell, R. L. (1970). *Kinesics and context.* Philadelphia, PA: University of Philadelphia Press.

52. Social Security Administration. (n.d.). Fact sheet. Retrieved from https://www.ssa.gov/news/press/fact-sheets/basicfact-alt.pdf

53. U.S. Bureau of Labor Statistics. (2020, February 26). Persons with a disability: Labor force characteristics summary [Press release]. Retrieved from https://www.bls.gov/news.release/disabl.nr0.htm

54. U.S. Bureau of Labor Statistics. (2020, February 26). Persons with a disability: Labor force characteristics summary [Press release]. Retrieved from https://www.bls.gov/news.release/disabl.nr0.htm

55. Department of Homeland Security. (2013, September 26). *A guide to interacting with people who have disabilities.* Retrieved from https://www.dhs.gov

56. Disclosing a disability. (2017). *CareerOneStop.* Retrieved from https://www.careeronestop.org

57. Ivy, D. K. (2016). *GenderSpeak: Communicating in a gendered world* (6th ed.). Dubuque, IA: Kendall Hunt Publishing.

58. Ivy, D. K. (2016). *GenderSpeak: Communicating in a gendered world* (6th ed.). Dubuque, IA: Kendall Hunt Publishing.

59. U.S. Equal Employment Opportunity Commission. (n.d.). Sex-based discrimination. Retrieved from https://www.eeoc.gov/laws/types/sex.cfm

60. U.S. Census Bureau (2018). PINC-05. Work experience-people 15 years old and over, by total money earnings, age, race, Hispanic origin, sex, and disability status. Retrieved from https://www.census.gov/data/tables/time-series/demo/income-poverty/cps-pinc/pinc-05.html

61. Catalyst. (2004). Women and men in U.S. corporate leadership. Retrieved from http://www.catalyst.org/system/files/Women%20and_Men_in_U.S._Corporate_Leadership_Same_Workplace_Different_Realities.pdf

62. White, C. (n.d.). How to promote gender equality in the workplace. *Houston Chonicle.* Retrieved from http://work.chron.com/promote-gender-equality-workplace-10258.html

63. Human Rights Campaign Foundation. (2020). Corporate equality index 2020. Retrieved from https://hrc-prod-requests.s3-us-west-2.amazonaws.com/files/assets/resources/CEI-2020.pdf

64. Human Rights Campaign Foundation. (2017). Corporate equality index 2017. Retrieved from http://hrc-assets.s3-website-us-east-1.amazonaws.com

65. Marcario, R. (2016, August 15). Patagonia's CEO explains how to make on-site child care pay for itself. *Fast Company.* Retrieved from https://www.fastcompany.com/3062792/second-shift/patagonias-ceo-explains-how-to-make-onsite-child-care-pay-for-itself

66. U.S. Department of Veterans Affairs. (2015). Veterans employment toolkit. Retrieved from https://www.va.gov/VETSINWORKPLACE/docs/em_good-employees.asp

67. Bureau of Labor Statistics. (2020, March 19). Employment situation of veterans summary [Press release]. Retrieved from https://www.bls.gov/news.release/vet.nr0.htm

68. Gallup, Inc. (2010, June 20). Active duty leads U.S. in wellbeing; Veterans lag. Retrieved from http://www.gallup.com/poll/141089/active-duty-military-leads-wellbeing-veterans-lag.aspx

69. U.S. Department of Veterans Affairs. (2015). Veterans employment toolkit. Retrieved from https://www.va.gov/vetsinworkplace/docs/em_challengesreadjust.asp

70. Competitive Edge Services, Inc., & Burton Blatt Institute at Syracuse University. (2013, April). Veterans in the workplace: Recruitment and retention. Retrieved from https://www.va.gov/VETSINWORKPLACE/docs/Veterans_in_Workplace_Final_Report.pdf

71. Competitive Edge Services, Inc., & Burton Blatt Institute at Syracuse University. (2013, April). Veterans in the workplace: Recruitment and retention. Retrieved from https://www.va.gov/VETSINWORKPLACE/docs/Veterans_in_Workplace_Final_Report.pdf

72. Zhu, Y. (2001). Comparing English and Chinese persuasive strategies in trade fair invitations: A sociocognitive approach. *Document Design, 2,* 2–17.

73. Boone, L. E., Kurtz, D. L., & Block, J. R. (1997). *Contemporary business communication* (2nd ed.). Englewood Cliffs, NJ: Prentice Hall.

74. Williams, C. J. (1999, August 15). Not all ways Wal-Mart as chain takes on Germany. *Los Angeles Times,* August 15, 1999, C1.

75. Glover, K. M. (1990, August 13). Do's and taboos. *Business America, 111,* p. 5.

76. Katayama, F. H. (1989, November 13). How to act once you get there. *Fortune's Pacific Rim Guide,* pp. 87–90.

77. Falkoff, R. (2006). The karaoke business meeting. Retrieved from http://workabroad.monster.com/articles/karaoke/

78. UPS: From local startup to global titan. (2007, June 27). *Business Week*. Retrieved from http://www.businessweek.com/smallbiz/content/jun2007/sb20070627_827624.htm

79. Padgett, T., & Lee, C. S. (1994, September 19). Go south, young yanquis. *Newsweek*, p. 48.

80. Trompenaars, F. (1994). *Riding the waves of culture*. Burr Ridge, IL: Irwin.

81. Chen, M. (2003). *Inside Chinese business: A guide for managers worldwide*. Boston, MA: Harvard Business School Press.

82. Hall, E. (1959). *Beyond culture*. New York, NY: Doubleday.

83. Chen, M. (2001). *Inside Chinese business: A guide for managers worldwide*. Boston, MA: Harvard Business School Press.

84. Melymuka, K. (1997, April 28). Tips for teams. *Computerworld, 31,* 72.

85. Morris, M. (1981). *Saying and meaning in Puerto Rico: Some problems in the ethnology of discourse*. Oxford, UK: Pergamon.

86. Locke, D. (1992). *Increasing multicultural understanding: A comprehensive model*. Newbury Park, CA: Sage.

87. Hofstede, G. (1997). *Cultures and organizations: Software of the mind*. New York, NY: McGraw Hill.

88. Nishishiba, M., & Ritchie, L. D. (2000). The concept of trustworthiness: A cross-cultural comparison between Japanese and U.S. business people. *Journal of Applied Communication Research, 28,* 347–367; Witteborn, S. (2006, June 16). Conceptualization and study of collective identities: Implications for research in culture and communication. Paper presented at the International Communication Association annual meeting, Dresden, Germany.

89. Taub, D. (1996, December 16). Global recruiting: Richard Ferry helped take Korn/Ferry International from two-man office to world's no. 1 executive search firm. *Los Angeles Business Journal,* 1.

90. Formula for success. (1992, December 8). *Financial World*, p. 40.

91. Hofstede, G. (1997). *Cultures and organizations: Software of the mind*. New York: McGraw Hill.

92. U.S. Equal Employment Opportunity Commission. (2020, January 24). EEOC releases fiscal year 2019 enforcement litigation data [Press release]. Retrieved from https://www.eeoc.gov/newsroom/eeoc-releases-fiscal-year-2019-enforcement-and-litigation-data

93. U.S. Equal Employment Opportunity Commission. (n.d.). Title VII of the Civil Rights Act of 1964. Retrieved from https://www.eeoc.gov/statutes/title-vii-civil-rights-act-1964

94. U.S. Equal Employment Opportunity Commission (n.d.). The Pregnancy Discrimination Act of 1978. Retrieved from https://www.eeoc.gov/statutes/pregnancy-discrimination-act-1978

95. *Bostock v. Clayton County*, No. 17-1618, 590 U.S. ___ (2020). Retrieved from https://supreme.justia.com/cases/federal/us/590/17-1618/

96. U.S. Equal Employment Opportunity Commission. (n.d.). Sexual harassment. Retrieved from https://www.eeoc.gov/sexual-harassment

97. U.S. Equal Employment Opportunity Commission. (n.d.). Title VII of the Civil Rights Act of 1964. Retrieved from https://www.eeoc.gov/statutes/title-vii-civil-rights-act-1964

98. U.S. Equal Employment Opportunity Commission. (n.d.). The Equal Pay Act of 1963. Retrieved from https://www.eeoc.gov/statutes/equal-pay-act-1963

99. United States Equal Opportunity Commission. (n.d.). The Age Discrimination in Employment Act of 1967. Retrieved from http://www.eeoc.gov/laws/statutes/adea.cfm

100. ADA National Network. (n.d.). An overview of the Americans with Disabilities Act. Retrieved from https://adata.org/factsheet/ADA-overview

101. Skelly, J. (1995, March/April). The Caux Round Table principles for business: The rise of international ethics. *Business Ethics,* 2–5.

102. Buller, P. F., Kohls, J. J., & Anderson, K. S. (1996, December 16). A model for addressing cross-cultural ethical conflicts. *Business & Society,* 36, 169–193.

103. Donaldson, T. (1996, September/October). Values in tension: Ethics away from home. *Harvard Business Review,* 74, 48–62.

104. Donaldson, T. (1996, September/October). Values in tension: Ethics away from home. *Harvard Business Review,* 74, 48–62.

105. Kiboski, J. F. (1999). Effective communication in the performance appraisal interview: Face-to-face communication for public managers in the culturally diverse workplace. *Public Personnel Management,* 28, 301–323.

106. Marby, M. (1990, May 14). Pin a label on a manager—and watch what happens. *Newsweek,* p. 43.

107. Raymond, J. (2010, December 13). The cobra was OK; the duck tongue not so much. *New York Times*, p. B6.

108. Copeland, L. (1988, June). Making the most of cultural differences in the workplace. *Personnel*, p. 53.

109. Millhous, L. M. (1999). The experience of culture in multi-cultural groups. Small *Group Research*, 30, 280–308.

110. Accenture. (n.d.). Getting to equal 2019: Creating a culture that drives innovation. Retrieved from https://www.accenture.com/us-en/about/inclusion-diversity/gender-equality-innovation-research

111. Dong, Q., Day, K. D., & Collaço, C. M. (2008). Overcoming ethnocentrism through developing intercultural communication sensitivity and multiculturalism. *Human Communication, 11,* 27–38.

112. Houston, M. (1994). When black women talk with white women: Why dialogues are difficult. In A. Gonzalez, M. Houston, & V. Chen (Eds.), *Our voices: Essays in culture, ethnicity, and communication.* Los Angeles, CA: Roxbury 133.

113. Martin, J. M., & Nakayama, T. K. (2004). *Intercultural communication in contexts.* Boston, MA: McGraw Hill.

114. Kelly, C. M. (1988). *The destructive achiever: Power and ethics in the American corporation.* Reading, MA: Addison-Wesley.

115. Cose, E. (1993). *The rage of a privileged class: Why are middle-class blacks so angry?* Why should America care? New York: HarperCollins.

PART TWO

GaudiLab/Shutterstock

STRATEGIC CASE

Omnicom Marketing

Mark's career at the marketing firm Omnicom is off to a good start. After spending a year as a rookie account representative, Mark was promoted to his first management position, supervising a team of reps. His group is mostly terrific: They work hard, get along well, and help one another. This is especially good news for Mark because his immediate compensation and his future at the firm depend on the team generating a significant number of billable hours.

Mark's only serious problem is with Kate. She was hired in an entry-level position with great expectations for her growth within the company. Now, after a few months on the job, Kate's performance has slipped dramatically. She missed two important deadlines, and some of the account reps are starting to complain about having to pick up the slack owing to her poor performance. She comes in late to the office, and she makes what are obviously social phone calls during work. Yesterday, Mark saw Kate checking Instagram several times. Mark knows that he can no longer ignore the situation. He has to confront Kate and get her to improve her performance, or else. Fortunately, Kate's upcoming performance review offers a good chance to discuss the problems.

Kate sees the situation very differently. After taking the job with great enthusiasm, she has come to believe that her contributions don't count for anything. "I suggest ideas," she says, "and they all get shot down." She feels overqualified for the job. "I'm ready to do serious work, but all they want me to do is take notes at meetings, make coffee, and run errands." Kate is also discouraged on the relational front. "I try to reach out to the rest of the team, but I just don't fit in. In fact, some of their jokes make me feel really uncomfortable. If I wanted, I could probably file a sexual harassment complaint." At this point, Kate has almost given up hope that things will get better. "If that's the way they want it, fine. I'll do my job, collect my pay, and look for a better place to work."

Personal Skills

As you read the chapters in this unit, consider the following questions:

chapter 3

1. Which barriers to listening might make it difficult for Mark and Kate to hear each other's perspectives when they meet to discuss this situation?
2. Consider the listening styles discussed in Chapter 3. Present evidence that indicates each person's style, and then describe how this knowledge might have created a different communication outcome for Kate and Mark.
3. Describe how Mark might have used the guidelines in Chapter 3 to deal more effectively with their disagreements.

chapter 4

1. Describe a series of messages, ranging from highly ambiguous to highly specific, that Mark and Kate could use to express their concerns to each other. Which approach(es) might have the best chance of success?
2. What specific advice would you give Kate and Mark if they wanted to improve their professional identities by using positive language and an optimal level of powerful language?
3. Give an example of how Mark and Kate might resort to each type of inflammatory language described in this chapter when they confront each other. For each statement, provide a noninflammatory alternative.
4. Which problematic nonverbal messages might Kate and her colleagues have been sending that contributed to the problem? Suggest alternative nonverbal messages that could help each party communicate more effectively.

chapter 5

1. How does the need to be treated with dignity affect Kate's perceptions and behaviors?
2. How might Kate use the guidelines about raising delicate issues to express her dissatisfaction to Mark?
3. Are there any ways Mark might have praised Kate that would have minimized her dissatisfaction and enhanced her performance?
4. How might Kate use the tips for responding to criticism to react when Mark raises the issue of her apparent lack of motivation?
5. Describe likely scenarios if Mark and Kate use each of the following approaches to deal with their conflict: win-lose, compromise, win-win.
6. How might Kate deal with her discomfort over her coworkers' jokes? How might Mark respond?

chapter 6

1. In hindsight, which questions might Kate have asked to explore the nature of her work environment and clarify her expectations during her employment interview?
2. How can Mark frame the opening of his performance review to protect Kate's dignity and set a tone that will help him get the information he needs?
3. If Kate does wind up seeking another job, how can she use the information in Chapter 6 to prepare for the interviews associated with her search?

Klaus Vedfelt/Getty Images

Chapter Three
Listening

chapter outline

chapter objectives

After reading this chapter you should be able to:

1. Describe how effective listening can contribute to your career success, and how false assumptions about listening could impede your career.

2. Identify three major barriers to listening effectively, and outline strategies for overcoming each barrier.

3. Analyze your listening style(s), and explain how you might use this knowledge to understand others better.

4. Apply the six guidelines for listening to understand and be able to create appropriate paraphrasing responses in given situations; apply the guidelines with regard to the evidence and appeals when listening to evaluate.

5. Evaluate various listening approaches you could use in a specific situation and describe the best approach to accomplish your goals and enhance your career relationships with others.

• Listening at Work

- "I told her we were meeting *this* Tuesday, not next Tuesday. Now we have to reschedule the meeting, and we may not make the deadline."

- "He said he was listening, but he didn't give me a minute to talk before he started interrupting. That's the last time I'll try to suggest a better way to do anything around here!"

- "Something went wrong down the line. I warned those people to watch the temperature carefully, but they don't listen. Now a whole batch is spoiled. What does it take to get them to understand?"

Situations like these are disturbingly common in business. They show how frequent listening failures are and how costly they can be. You may not be able to make others listen better, but you can certainly boost your own ability to listen carefully to the scores of important messages you are likely to hear every day.

As you will learn in this chapter, listening effectively is hard work. It involves far more than sitting passively and absorbing others' words. Listening occurs far more frequently than speaking, reading, or writing, and it is just as demanding and important as those aspects of communication.

The Importance of Listening

In his best-selling book, Stephen Covey identifies listening—understanding others' messages before making one's own understood—as one of the "seven habits of highly effective people."[1] Former Chrysler chairman Lee Iacocca endorsed this belief:

> You have to be able to listen well if you're going to motivate the people who work for you. Right there, that's the difference between a mediocre company and a great company. The most fulfilling thing for me as a manager is to watch someone the system has labeled as just average or mediocre really come into his own, all because someone has listened to his problems and helped him solve them.[2]

Research backs up these claims. In numerous studies, listening has proved to be the most important communication skill throughout one's career in terms of job and career success, productivity, upward mobility, and organizational effectiveness.[3]

Listening is valuable even before your career gets started. Job-hunters can respond best in employment interviews by engaging in active listening.[4] Once you have found a new job, listening can help you learn the ropes. Career consultant Andrea Sutcliffe puts it this way: "If you had to choose one interpersonal skill to work on in your first year on the job, pick listening. It will be the single most important tool you will have for getting along and getting ahead."[5]

Listening remains important throughout your career. Indeed, when 1,000 executives were asked to list the ideal manager's skills, listening ranked number one.[6,7] Mark Whitten, U.S. director of operations for Martinrea International, describes the benefits of listening to his employees using a series of 30-minute one-on-one meetings:

> After completing the one-on-ones, I had a clearer understanding of our employees' needs. Further, and equally important, I had a connection with every employee. I knew their names, and a little about them personally. They understood my expectations, and I understood theirs.[8]

Along with promoting individual success, effective listening is vital to organizations. As chairman and CEO of UPS, David Abney explains:

> One of the first things I did as a CEO of this company was to go on a worldwide listening tour, just letting our people and our customers tell me what they thought I should focus on . . . it's so important to listen. When you do that it's amazing what people will tell you if you will take time . . . we work together as a team, we enjoy success together, we learn from failures together . . . [9]

Assumptions about Listening

When it comes to communication, most people pay more attention to sending messages than to receiving them. This imbalance comes from several mistaken assumptions.

Faulty Assumption 1: Effective Communication Is the Sender's Responsibility   Both senders and receivers share responsibility for effective communication. Senders must communicate clearly and monitor the effectiveness of their communication by being attentive to receivers' feedback. Receivers should paraphrase and ask questions to ensure that they have understood the messages that senders communicate. As management expert Peter Drucker suggests, even the most thoughtful, well-expressed idea will be wasted if the intended receiver fails to listen. Both the speaker *and* the listener share the burden of responsibility in reaching an understanding.[10]

Faulty Assumption 2: Listening Is Passive   Some communicators mistakenly assume that listening is easy, requiring only the quiet absorption of a speaker's words. What these communicators are actually describing is *hearing*. As John A. Kline says, "Hearing is the reception of sound, listening is the attachment of meaning to the sound."[11] The latter activity is also referred to as **active listening**, or nonverbal and verbal attentiveness to a speaker. Active listeners maintain eye contact with speakers, nod their heads and smile, provide feedback, and reduce distractions such as mobile phones.

Good listeners are far from passive. Famous attorney Louis Nizer described how he would often emerge dripping with sweat from a day in court spent mostly listening. Sometimes listeners must also speak—to ask questions or paraphrase the sender's ideas, making sure they have understood those ideas. Therefore, active listening has been shown to be more effective for retaining information, and it also makes a speaker feel more comfortable.

Careless Listening Leads to Ridicule

On the first day of her social studies class, York University student Sarah Grunfeld was outraged when she heard Professor Cameron Johnston say, "All Jews should be sterilized." Grunfeld immediately reported her account of the lecture to a campus advocacy group, accused Johnston of being a bigot, and called for him to be fired. Within a few hours, the story went viral and Johnston came under immediate pressure and scrutiny.

The university's investigation found that Grunfeld missed an important point in Johnston's comment—one understood clearly by several hundred other students in the class. Johnston had explained that the belief that "all Jews should be sterilized" is an example of an unacceptable and dangerous opinion. When it became known that Professor Johnston (who is Jewish) did not make an anti-Semitic statement in class, Grunfeld came under attack. She was publicly ridiculed by bloggers and mainstream media for her poor listening skills, hair-trigger reaction, and unwillingness to accept even partial responsibility for the misunderstanding.

Source: Kennedy, B. (2011, September 14). Jewish prof. forced to defend himself against anti-semitism claims. *Toronto Star.*

Faulty Assumption 3: Talking Has More Advantages   At first glance, it seems that speakers control conversations while listeners are the followers. The people who do the talking are the ones who capture everyone's attention, so it is easy to understand how talking can be viewed as the pathway to success.

Talking instead of listening can lead professionals to miss important information. One analysis of physician–patient interviews revealed that the more doctors talked, the more they got off track and failed to address concerns raised by the patients.[12]

Despite the value of talking, savvy businesspeople understand that listening is equally important. Consider the advice of communication consultant Bill Acheson: "For every minute a salesperson spends listening, he or she will save four minutes overcoming objections."[13]

Communication expert Susan Peterson reinforces the value of superior listening skills:

> Too many times, whether it's with e-mail, voice mail, or Internet, we are concentrating on the art of telling, not listening. Yet good listening, in my opinion, is 80 to 90 percent of being a good manager and an effective leader. . . . Listening is one of the best ways to keep high touch in your organization. In your day-to-day meetings with customers, clients, or employees, if you listen—really listen with full eye contact and attention—you can own the keys to the communication kingdom.[14]

Faulty Assumption 4: Listening Is a Natural Ability   Listening might seem to be a natural ability—like breathing. "After all," you might say, "I've been listening since I was a child." Of course, we could all say the same thing about talking. Even though almost everyone listens, that does not mean most people do it well.

Evidence suggests that most people overestimate their ability to listen well. In one study, a group of managers rated their listening skills. Astonishingly, not one of them described himself or herself as a "poor" or "very poor" listener, while 94% rated themselves as "good" or "very good" listeners. The favorable self-ratings contrasted sharply with the perceptions of the managers' subordinates, many of whom said their bosses' listening skills were weak.[15]

Many companies are offering training to help their employees improve their listening skills. Xerox Corporation's program for improving listening has been used by more than 1.5 million employees in 71,000 companies, and Sperry Corporation invested more than

Working with a Poor Listener

We will all eventually have to work with someone who has poor listening skills. Whether they seem distracted or constantly interrupt you when you're speaking, it is no surprise that this behavior will have a negative impact on the work environment.

The following are tips for improving communication with ineffective listeners:

- **Consider differing learning styles.** Everyone has preferences for their learning methods. Some are visual learners, while others are auditory, kinesthetic, or reading-writing learners. It may seem like they're not listening, but perhaps they're having difficulty understanding. Offer to present the material in another format: "Would you prefer to see a graph depicting the changes in sales?"

- **Take time to analyze your communication style to better understand the other person's perspective.**

Perhaps you speak quickly or overwhelm your listener with statistics. Think about ways you can improve your communication to encourage better listening from others.

- **Emphasize the importance of your message before speaking.** "There is something really important I would like to talk to you about." Then, reinforce key points: "I want to repeat this because it's so important."

- **Demonstrate empathy by showing concern for someone who is not listening effectively.** For example, you might say, "You seem to have a lot on your plate that is requiring your attention. Is there anything I can do to help you?"

Source: Knight, R. (2017, September 5). How to work with a bad listener. *SHRM/Harvard Business Review.* Retrieved from https://www.shrm.org/resourcesandtools/hr-topics/employee-relations/pages/how-to-work-with-a-bad-listener.aspx

$4 million to advertise its message: "We know how important it is to listen." In addition, Sperry set up listening seminars for its 87,000 employees to ensure its advertising campaign was more than just a string of empty slogans.

Poor listening is often the source of conflict in organizations. According to one study, a typical U.S. employee spends 2.1 hours each week dealing with conflict; in many cases, this translates to sickness/absence, people leaving the organization, and project failure.[16]

• Barriers to Effective Listening

Despite the importance of understanding others, research suggests that misunderstandings are the rule, rather than the exception. Conversational partners typically achieve no more than 25% to 50% accuracy in interpreting each other's remarks.[17] Research shows that immediately after a 10-minute presentation, a normal listener can recall only 50% of the information presented. After 48 hours, the recall level drops to 25%.[18] As you read earlier in the book, three types of "noise" get in the way of receiving messages: environmental, physiological, and psychological.

Environmental Barriers

The sound of heavy machinery on a factory floor or the conversational buzz in a crowded room can make it difficult to hear and process messages. Nevertheless, not all environmental barriers involve sound. An overheated office or uncomfortable chairs can also make listening difficult. Ironically, some environmental distractions come from the tools we use to communicate. Incoming phone calls, text messages, notifications, and e-mails can all distract us from focusing on a conversational partner.

You cannot eliminate all environmental barriers, but you can often manage them. Suggest moving your conversation to a quieter location. Eliminate distractions and annoyances ("That perfume at the table next to us is getting to me. Can we move?"). Choose more reliable communication channels ("Let me call you back on a landline since my reception isn't great.").

Physiological Barriers

For some people, poor listening results from hearing deficiencies such as hearing loss. In some cases, these individuals can benefit from medical treatment and devices such as hearing aids. In other cases, hearing cannot be restored, although individuals in the d/Deaf community are certainly listening as they decode sign language, lip read, and so on. Other physiological issues that affect hearing, such as earaches, headaches, and even the common cold are temporary. Whether the problem is short-term or permanent, the effects can be problematic for communication.

Another physiological challenge comes from the difference between the relatively slow rate of most speech and the brain's ability to process messages more quickly. Listeners can process information at a rate of approximately 500 words per minute, while the rate of speech for most speakers is about 125 words per minute. This difference leaves us with a great deal of mental spare time. While it is possible to use this time to explore the speaker's ideas, it is all too easy to let your mind wander.

Psychological Barriers

Some of the most pervasive and daunting barriers to effective listening are psychological. These issues interfere with people's willingness to listen as well as their mental capacity for effective listening.

Preoccupation   Business and personal concerns can make it difficult to keep your mind on the subject at hand. Even when your current conversation is important, other unfinished business can divert your attention—the call to an angry customer, the questions your boss asked about your schedule delays, the new supplier you heard about and want to interview, or your child approaching you with homework questions during a virtual meeting. Figure 3.1 illustrates several ways in which preoccupation can cause listeners to stop focusing on a speaker's message.

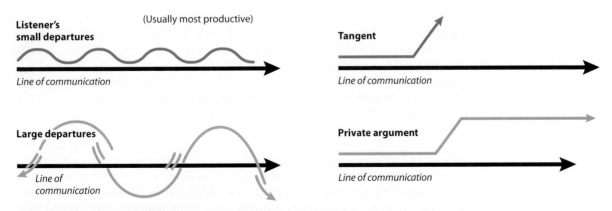

FIGURE 3.1 Thought Patterns

Source: Wolvin, A. D., & Coakley, G. (1993). *Perspectives on listening*. Norwood, NJ: Ablex.

CULTURE **at work**

Cultural Differences in Listening

Listening is often regarded as a fundamental aspect of business. Understanding how individuals from different national cultures perceive listening is especially important in today's globalized business world.

The distracted and attentive listening behaviors of managers and nonmanagers in India, Malaysia, and the United States were studied by one team of researchers. They found that differing national cultures, organizational position (manager versus nonmanager), and gender impact listening in the workplace. Their key findings include:

- Males are more prone to engage in distracted listening than are females.

- American females and males are less likely to be attentive.

- Managers are less likely to engage in distracted listening than nonmanagers.

- American managers are more distracted in their listening than nonmanagers.

- Indian and Malaysian managers are less distracted listeners than nonmanagers.

- Indian managers are more likely to be attentive.

- American and Malaysian managers are less prone to being attentive listeners than nonmanagers.

Source: Roebuck, D. B., Bell, R. L., & Ean, C. (2015). The effects of home country, gender, and position on listening behaviors. *Journal of Organizational Culture, Communications and Conflict, 19*(2), 93–120.

Message Overload In a world filled with smartwatches, tablets, laptops, and other personal digital devices, individuals face a challenge today that earlier generations never encountered: "multicommunicating."[19] It is difficult to listen carefully when people keep dropping in to give you quick messages; a coworker has just handed you cost estimates on a new product line; and your smartphone continuously beeps to let you know you have incoming calls, mail, text messages, and appointments. Working remotely poses a further challenge as personal and home-related distractions become more difficult to ignore. It is not uncommon to see a person turn off their video—presumably to step away from the computer or attend to another task—or surreptitiously check their phones while on a video call.

Coping with a deluge of information is like juggling—you can keep only a few things going at one time.[20] Many students pride themselves on their ability to multitask, but neurological evidence suggests that people really are not effective when they work on multiple tasks at the same time.[21] Human brains waste lag time each time we switch gears. As a consequence, we are much more effective and efficient when we complete one task at a time—and pay attention to one message at a time.

Egocentrism One common reason for listening poorly is the belief—usually mistaken—that your own ideas are more important or valuable than those of others. Besides preventing you from learning useful new information, such an egocentric attitude is likely to alienate the very people with whom you need to work. Self-centered listeners are rated lower on social attractiveness than communicators who are open to others' ideas.[22] As an old saying puts it, "Nobody ever listened themselves out of a job."

Ethnocentrism Cultural ignorance or prejudices can create psychological noise that interferes with understanding others. Consider accents: Some communicators mistakenly assume individuals with accented speech are less intelligent and less able to understand spoken words.[23] When operating a company in a foreign market, brands often suffer when staff at the company's headquarters refuse to listen to prospective customers and meet their cultural needs in the foreign market in which they wish to operate. Nissan experienced this form of ethnocentrism early in its international operations when it attempted to market the company's cars abroad using the same strategies it utilized in the domestic market (Japan). Tetyana Panchuk, director of a marketing company in London, explains, "[A]fter several years of its international trading, the company realized that [an] ethnocentric international marketing orientation is no longer relevant for some industries, including the automobile industry in which they were operating."[24]

Fear of Appearing Ignorant   Some businesspeople perceive asking for clarification as a sign of ignorance. Rather than seek clarification, they pretend to understand—often with unfortunate consequences. In truth, a sincere desire to seek clarification can pay dividends, as management guru Tom Peters recalls:

> My first boss . . . is one of the smartest people I know. He was smart enough and comfortable enough with himself to ask really elementary (some would say dumb) questions. The rest of us were scared stiff; we assumed that since we were being paid an exorbitant fee, we shouldn't ask dumb questions. But the result was we'd lose 90 percent of the strategic value of the interview because we were afraid to display our ignorance.
>
> Mostly, it's the "dumb," elementary questions, followed up by a dozen more elementary questions, that yield the pay dirt.[25]

• Listening Styles

Not everyone listens the same way. Research has identified that people have a general listening style, or a particular motivation for listening. Each style has its own advantages. Ideally, after you identify your preferred style, you should try to develop skill with the listening styles that do not come naturally to you, thereby expanding your listening capabilities. An effective listener is a flexible listener.

Relational Listening

People who are primarily focused on **relational listening** are most concerned with emotionally connecting with others. They listen to understand how others feel, are aware of their emotions, and are highly responsive to those individuals. Relational listeners are usually nonjudgmental about what others have to say. They are more interested in understanding and supporting people than in evaluating them.

A key strength of this listening style is that the people being "listened to" tend to be more satisfied with their relationships and life in general. Thus, when a relational listener attends to a subordinate or even a peer at work, there can be a positive benefit. Listening is not without drawbacks, however. It is easy to become overly involved with others' feelings, and even to internalize and adopt them. In an effort to be congenial and supportive, relational listeners may lose their ability to assess the quality of information others are giving. They also risk being perceived as overly expressive and even intrusive by speakers who don't want to connect on a personal level.

Analytical Listening

People who are most interested in **analytical listening** are concerned with attending to the full message before coming to judgment. They want to hear details and analyze an issue from a variety of perspectives. More than just enjoying complex information, these listeners have a tendency to engage in systematic thinking. Many companies have an ombuds staff to investigate and attempt to resolve complaints. Analytical listening is particularly

Graham Bell/Corbis

important to the ombuds personnel, as they must carefully consider all of the information they receive about the complaint before making a recommendation.

Analytical listeners can be especially helpful when the goal is to thoroughly assess the quality of ideas, and when there is value in looking at issues from a wide range of perspectives. On the downside, their thorough approach can be time-consuming. It may take them a long time to reach a conclusion, so when a deadline is approaching they may not respond as quickly as desired.

Task-Oriented Listening

People who are inclined to **task-oriented listening** are most interested in getting the job done. Because efficiency is their biggest concern, they expect speakers to get their point across quickly and to stay on topic. Not surprisingly, task-oriented listeners are often impatient.

In a fast-paced business environment, task-oriented listeners can help keep things functioning efficiently. Unfortunately, their impatience can sometimes strain relationships because task-oriented listeners are generally not good at responding empathetically and have a tendency toward verbal aggressiveness. Also, an excessive focus on time can hamper the kind of thoughtful deliberation that some jobs require.

Critical Listening

People engaged in **critical listening** have a strong desire to evaluate messages with the purpose of accepting or rejecting them. Critical listeners go beyond trying to understand the topic at hand by seeking to assess its quality. Not surprisingly, critical listeners tend to focus on the accuracy and consistency of a message.

Critical listening can be especially helpful when the goal is to investigate a problem, as in a forensic interview or a safety concern at an oil and gas refinery. More problematically, people who are critical listeners can frustrate others, who may think that they nitpick everything others say.

• Listening More Effectively

Social scientists have identified two levels of listening—mindless and mindful.[26] **Mindless listening** occurs when we react to others' messages automatically and routinely, without much mental investment. The term *mindless* sounds negative, but sometimes this sort of low-level processing can be useful because it frees us to focus our minds on messages that require more careful attention.[27] The challenge, of course, is to pay enough attention to decide which messages need more careful attention. By contrast, **mindful listening** involves giving careful and thoughtful attention and responses to the messages we receive.

You might imagine the value of mindful listening is so obvious that it hardly needs mentioning. In fact, business and professional communicators recognize that thoughtful listening is difficult and needs cultivating. At General Mills, for example, employees at all levels—including more than 80 vice presidents and directors—have voluntarily signed up for mindfulness programs ranging from a half-day to seven weeks in duration.[28] Participants of Google's most popular mindfulness course, "Search Inside Yourself," believe that the course has helped them become more effective listeners.[29]

Listening to Voice Mail

Hearing problems are not just an issue for communicators with physical impairments. The racket of background noise often makes it difficult to hear and understand messages—especially those played back on the tinny speakers in most telephones. Some products seek to decipher voice mail messages more clearly by transcribing the caller's spoken words into text that can be viewed on the display of a smartphone or computer. Besides saving you the time it takes to replay voice mail (perhaps more than once!), these services allow you to check for calls in a noisy environment, do so unobtrusively, and obtain a text record of what callers said. This technology, known as visual voicemail, became so popular that Apple included it as a key feature (rather than a third-party app) in September 2016.[30]

Of course, visual voicemail is not foolproof. It does not capture the vocal qualities that can affect the meaning of a message, and it often misses or bungles specific words. When in doubt about the accuracy of a transcription, it is smart to listen to the audio version of a message before jumping to conclusions.

One important step toward mindful listening is to be clear about your goal in a given situation. Are you listening to *understand* the other person, or are you listening critically to *evaluate* the message? Once you have answered this fundamental question, the following tips can help you listen more effectively.

Listening to Understand

Most of us would claim we always aim to understand what others are saying, but a little introspection will show we are often focused on other tasks: mentally (or overtly) arguing with the speaker, daydreaming, thinking about other tasks, and so on. Following the advice here can boost your accuracy in listening mindfully to the message.

Withhold Judgment In his study of highly effective people, Stephen Covey said it best: "Seek first to understand, then to be understood."[31] It is often difficult to try to understand another person's ideas before judging him or her, especially when you hold strong opinions on the matter under discussion. For example, you might ask for a customer's reaction to your company's product or service and then spend your mental energy judging the answer instead of trying to understand it. ("Doesn't this person have anything better to do than make petty complaints?" "Yeah, sure, he'd like us to deliver on a tighter schedule, but he'd scream his head off if we billed him for the overtime.") Or you might find yourself judging the ideas of a boss, coworker, or subordinate before he or she has finished explaining them. ("Uh-oh. I hope this doesn't mean I have to spend a week in the field, trying to get market information." "These college kids come in and want to take over right away.") Listen first. Make sure you understand. Then evaluate.

Talk and Interrupt Less Sometimes the best approach to listening is to stay out of the way and encourage the other person to talk. One marketing expert explained how, even in sales, silence can be more effective than talking:

> The 20/80 rule is a standard in small-business principles. Twenty percent of your customers account for 80 percent of your business. Here's a variation of the theme. . . . When meeting with prospective customers for the first time, listen 80 percent of the time and talk the other 20 percent. Your job is to listen attentively and determine what your prospects require. Before they are prepared to listen to your pitch, they want to tell you what they're looking for.[32]

If you are normally a talkative person, consider rationing your comments when trying to listen. Imagine you have only a finite number of words available so that you speak only when it is absolutely necessary. You may be surprised at how the quality of your conversations and your level of understanding improve.

Ask Questions   **Sincere questions** are genuine requests for information. They can be a terrific way to gather facts and details, clarify meanings, and encourage a speaker to elaborate. Former University of Kentucky basketball coach Rick Pitino learned the importance of asking questions after he lost a key recruit by trying to sell the virtues of his program instead of listening to what concerned his prospect. Later, when he courted another potential star (Tony Delk), he used a more effective approach:

> This time, instead of trumpeting Kentucky's virtues, he asked questions: what Delk wanted from a coach, what the family wanted for their son in college. For an hour, he just asked questions and nodded a lot, listening to their answers. . . .
> Not only did Pitino get Delk, but four years later, Delk helped lead Kentucky to its sixth national championship and Pitino's first. "That's one of my favorites," Pitino says. "That's one I like to tell business groups because it illustrates how important it is to listen to people."[33]

While sincere, focused questions can be a powerful tool, **counterfeit questions** are really disguised forms of advice or subtle traps: "Have you ever considered offering more money to get experienced people?" or "Why haven't you told me about this?" Counterfeit questions like these can pollute a communication climate just as quickly as any direct attack.[34]

Paraphrase   **Paraphrasing** involves restating a speaker's ideas in your own words to make sure you have understood them correctly and to show the other person that fact. Paraphrasing is often preceded by phrases such as "Let me make sure I understand what you're saying . . ." or "In other words, you're saying . . ." When you are paraphrasing, it is important *not* to become a parrot, mindlessly repeating the speaker's statements word for word. Understanding comes from translating the speaker's thoughts into your own language and then playing them back to ensure their accuracy. After paraphrasing, it is important that you invite the speaker to *verify* your paraphrase so you know whether you accurately understood him or her or to *clarify* your paraphrase and clear up what you have misunderstood.

The following conversations illustrate the difference between effective and ineffective paraphrasing:

Ineffective

Print Supervisor:	I'm having trouble getting the paper to run that job. That's why I'm behind schedule.
Plant Manager:	I see. You can't get the paper to run the job, so you're running behind schedule.
Print Supervisor:	Yeah. That's what I said.

After this exchange, the plant manager still does not have a clear idea of the problem—why the print supervisor cannot get the paper, or what he means when he says he cannot get it. Rather than paraphrasing the message by putting the print supervisor's statements into his or her own words, the plant manager simply repeats what was said. More effective paraphrasing could help get to the root of the problem:

Effective

Print Supervisor:	I'm having trouble getting the paper to run that job. That's why I'm running behind schedule.
Plant Manager:	In other words, your paper supplier hasn't shipped the paper you need for this job.
Print Supervisor:	No, they shipped it, but it's full of flaws.
Plant Manager:	So the whole shipment is bad?
Print Supervisor:	No, only about a third of it. But I've got to get the whole batch replaced, or the dye lots won't match—the paper won't be exactly the same color.
Plant Manager:	No problem—the colors can be a little off. But I need at least half of that order by Tuesday; the rest can wait a couple of weeks. Can you print on the good paper you have now, then do the rest when the new paper comes in?
Print Supervisor:	Sure.

At first glance, questioning and paraphrasing may seem identical, but a closer look reveals they are different tools. Questions seek new, additional information ("How far behind are we?" "When did it begin?"), whereas paraphrasing clarifies what a speaker has said. This is an important difference.

Three types of paraphrasing can be used. Although they all involve reflecting the speaker's message, each focuses on a different part of that statement.

Paraphrasing content The preceding example illustrates content paraphrasing, which plays back the receiver's understanding of the explicit message. It is easy to think you understand another person, only to find later that you were wrong. At its most basic level, paraphrasing is a kind of safety check that can highlight and clarify misunderstandings. People who practice paraphrasing are astonished to find out how many times a speaker will correct or add information to a message that had seemed perfectly clear.

Paraphrasing intent Besides helping you understand *what* others are saying, paraphrasing can help you learn *why* they have spoken up. Imagine that, at a staff meeting, the boss announces, "Next week, we'll start using this display board to show when we're out of the office and where we've gone." It's easy to imagine two quite different reasons for setting up this procedure: (1) to help keep customers and colleagues informed about where each person is and when he or she will return, or (2) to keep track of employees because the boss suspects some are slacking off on company time. Paraphrasing intent can help you understand what people mean when they make statements that can be interpreted in more than one way.

Michaeljung 123RF

Paraphrasing feeling   Often, the speaker's feelings are the most important part of a message.[35] Despite this fact, most people do not express—or even recognize—their emotions. Ask yourself which emotions might be contained in these statements:

1. "That's the third time he canceled an appointment on me—who does he think he is?"
2. "Whenever a deadline comes, I get excuses instead of results—this can't go on much longer."
3. "One minute she says we have to spend money to make money, and the next minute she talks about cutting costs—I can't figure out what she really wants."

In each of these examples, there are at least two or three possible emotions:

1. Statement 1: anger, hurt, and self-doubt.
2. Statement 2: anger, frustration, and worry.
3. Statement 3: anger and confusion.

Paraphrasing the apparent emotion can give the speaker a chance to agree with or contradict your interpretation: "Yeah, I guess it did hurt my feelings" or "I'm more worried than mad." In either case, this sort of response can help the other person clarify how he or she is feeling and deal with the emotions.

Attend to Nonverbal Cues   Focusing on a speaker's nonverbal cues may tell you more than their words. Watch for the "iceberg tips" that let you know if the speaker might say more, especially if encouraged to do so.[36] The next chapter explains in detail the wealth of nonverbal cues that are always available to you—gestures, postures, vocal tones, facial expression, and more.

Nonverbal cues can be especially useful in interpreting another person's feelings and attitudes. You can get a sense of how emotions are communicated nonverbally by imagining all the different messages that might be conveyed by the following statements. How many different ways can you imagine each could be expressed? Which different meaning might each set of nonverbal cues convey?

1. "No, nothing's the matter."
2. "We should get together one of these days."
3. "I would like to talk with you in my office."
4. "Nobody's ever had that idea before."

Besides attending to others' nonverbal cues, it is also useful to pay attention to your own. One of the authors of your textbook recently attended a Zoom meeting where one of the attendees was logged in from a phone or tablet, which they set down flat on a table. During the entire meeting, this individual ate dinner and watched TV while the other attendees were presented with an image of this person's chin and neck. What messages do you think this sent to the presenter and other meeting attendees? By contrast, what messages would this person be sending if the phone were positioned at face-level and the attendee looked up at the camera and maintained an interested expression?

As this example illustrates, you may *say* you're listening, but how you behave nonverbally will create a stronger impression.

Take Notes   When the conversation involves details or ideas you need to remember, notes can be essential. Note-taking can also signal to speakers that you care enough to

Use a Telephone Log

E-mail provides a virtually automatic record of your correspondence, but telephone conversations are ephemeral. Keeping a simple written log can help you maintain your records, prevent false claims, and re-establish contacts. For example, a log can remind you of the name of the agent to whom you spoke, the date and time of an appointment you have set up, or the model number of a product you are researching. Weeks later, it may be important to tell a client, coworker, or supervisor of all the attempts (successful and unsuccessful) you made to contact that person.

You can also rely on your notes to remind others about information and commitments they have made, such as a reservation, promised delivery date, or a price quote: "The job won't be ready until November 15? But last Friday, Rose in your office promised me that it would be done by the first of the month." A log can even remind people about what they *did not* say or do. For example, you might respond to a complaint that you have not kept a customer informed by explaining, "Actually, I've phoned three times before today: on April 4, 11, and 18. Each time your voice mail picked up, and I left a message telling you the job was ready."

For most purposes, a phone log does not have to be elaborate, but it should usually include the following information:

- Date and time the call was placed
- Subject of the call
- Phone number called
- Whether this call is a part of a series (i.e., a follow-up or response to an earlier call)
- Unsuccessful attempts to contact (busy signal, no answer, malfunctioning voice mail)
- Messages left on voice mail or with another person
- Name of the person with whom you spoke
- Key points you and the other person made

---

write down what they are saying. It can even cause speakers to consider their words more carefully. As an added bonus, if a question ever arises about the details of a conversation, you can say with confidence, "Let me check my notes."

Listening to Evaluate

Once you are sure you understand a message, you are ready to evaluate its quality. Most evaluations are based on two levels of analysis: evidence and emotion.

Analyze the Speaker's Evidence
As a critical listener, you need to ask yourself several questions about the evidence that a speaker gives to support his or her statements. What evidence does the order fulfillment manager give that the current computer system is causing problems or that a new one will be better? Does a sales representative back up the claim that a product will pay for itself in less than a year?

Once you have identified the evidence, you need to make sure it is valid. The success of the flexible-hours program instituted in the New York office does not mean the same program will work as well in the factory in West Virginia, where a certain number of people have to be operating the machinery at any given time. The two or three employees who are unhappy with the

"I'm not convinced that's the best strategy. Then again, I wasn't listening."

Used by permission of Marc Tyler Nobleman.

A Professional Perspective

Ahmad Mather

Software Developer

General Motors

Austin, TX

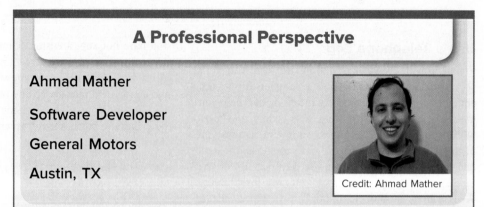

Credit: Ahmad Mather

In my highly technical role as a software developer, I have found listening to be an important tool to have in my arsenal. It sounds so simple, but it's an important skill that often gets overlooked.

For example, when I am in a meeting, I need to be able to decipher the interests of various business stakeholders and from that conversation extract actionable tasks. However, just listening to create a concrete list of tasks is not enough; it is also important to evaluate the scope of the assignment and determine risk factors or blockers that might come up while working on a project. I can save myself and my colleagues time and effort by anticipating issues and planning for them before something goes wrong.

While listening in a work environment, I appreciate it when my colleagues listen to my ideas without interrupting me and I always try to show them the same respect. This allows all of us to go further in depth and offer a more detailed explanation of what we are looking to accomplish with the conversation. I nod, make eye contact, or take notes to convey that I am listening and that I value the other person's ideas.

As a software developer, I am aware that my work involves very specific and technical language. In order to help colleagues and clients listen more easily, I have to be mindful of their background. Being too technical with someone like a business analyst or a marketing professional might not be a good idea, so I stick with the big picture and the main points.

new office furniture might be the exceptions rather than the majority, while the one or two satisfied customers you hear about could be the only happy ones. Carefully researched statistics that look at more than a few isolated cases are a much stronger form of proof than a few random examples.

The following questions can help you to examine the overall validity of supporting material:

- Is the evidence given true?
- Are enough cases cited?
- Are the cited cases representative of the whole being considered?
- Are there any exceptions to the points the speaker is making?
- Do these exceptions need to be considered?

Examine Emotional Appeals   Sometimes emotional reactions are a valid basis for action. The sympathy we feel for underprivileged children is a good reason for donating money to their welfare. The desire to cut down on your own fatigue may be a good reason to hire an assistant.

In other cases, emotional appeals can obscure important logical considerations that might otherwise dissuade you from accepting a proposal. We can see this by thinking about fund-raisers who seek money for underprivileged children. Your sympathy might not justify allowing a fund-raiser to wander around your building soliciting funds from employees: Your employees could resent being asked to give money to *your* favorite cause rather than one of theirs, especially if they have just been asked to donate to another cause. The particular agency asking for your donation might not be the best vehicle for helping underprivileged children: It may have excessive overhead so that much of your contribution never reaches any children, or other organizations might serve needier people.

In a business and professional environment, you will encounter a variety of messages daily. Effective listening will be crucial to making informed decisions when you receive persuasive messages that utilize emotional appeals and arguments that sound plausible. More information on persuasive appeals appears in Chapter 11.

MASTER **the chapter**

review points

- Listening is the most frequent communication activity at work. Listening effectively helps the organization and assists you in achieving your personal goals.

- A number of faulty assumptions about listening can impede effective understanding.

- Environmental, physiological, and psychological barriers (e.g., preoccupation, overload, egocentrism, ethnocentrism, and fear of appearing ignorant) can interfere with effective listening.

- Knowing and understanding the characteristics of your preferred listening style (relational, analytical, task-oriented, or critical) and others' listening styles will help you adapt to any given situation.

- Listening to understand requires withholding judgment, talking and interrupting less, seeking feedback by asking sincere (not counterfeit) questions, paraphrasing, attending to nonverbal cues, and taking notes.

- Evaluative listening involves analyzing both a speaker's evidence and emotional appeals.

key terms

active listening   70
analytical listening   75
counterfeit question   78
critical listening   76
mindful listening   76

mindless listening   76
paraphrasing   78
relational listening   75
sincere question   78
task-oriented listening   76

activities

1. Invitation to Insight

Recall three on-the-job incidents in which you had difficulty listening effectively. For each incident, describe which of the following factors interfered with your listening effectiveness:

a. Environmental barriers
b. Physiological barriers
c. Psychological factors

Develop a list of ways you could overcome the major barriers that prevent you from listening more effectively.

2. Invitation to Insight

Search online for two credible articles about multi-tasking. Then, write a short summary of what you learned about the impact of multitasking on listening. Next, identify all the tasks you try to attend to while you are engaging in an activity that requires listening (e.g., watching a movie, listening to a lecture, attending a team meeting). Think about the next listening activity in which you will participate and create a realistic schedule, setting aside separate times for the other activities you typically try to do during that listening activity. Try to stick to this schedule for the next week. Then, share your results with your classmates. What did you learn about multitasking? How did it affect your activity? Your relationships? Your other tasks? What did you learn about prioritizing? How might the things you learned about multitasking, prioritizing, and listening apply in the work environment?

3. Invitation to Insight

Survey several people with various careers to gather their opinions. Ask them to answer the following questions and to provide an example to support their answer.

a. Who do you think is more responsible for effective communication, the speaker or the listener?
b. Would you say listening is easier or harder than speaking?
c. Which do you think has more advantages—speaking or listening?

d. Do you think listening is a natural ability, or would it be a good idea to take classes in listening?
e. How does listening differ in face-to-face and virtual contexts?

In a small group, compare your respondents' answers with other classmates' results. With your group, create an explanation you could give to people who believe those faulty assumptions about listening, as identified in your text.

4. Invitation to Insight

For each of the following listening styles, describe a specific work situation in which this style would be effective and one situation in which the style would probably not be appropriate. Defend your answers.

a. Relational
b. Analytical
c. Task-oriented
d. Critical

5. Skill Builder

Explore the difference between sincere and counterfeit questions by answering the following questions:

a. How can you differentiate between sincere questions and counterfeit questions?
b. How do counterfeit questions affect the receiver? The interaction?
c. Give three examples of counterfeit questions. Supply a context that explains why the questions are counterfeit.
d. Convert the counterfeit questions to sincere questions.

6. Skill Builder

Practice your skill at questioning and paraphrasing in groups of four. Each group member should assume one of the following roles: speaker, listener 1, listener 2, or observer.

a. The **speaker** will talk about a problem they have recently experienced. If you can't think of a problem, talk about *one* of the following topics: how to perform a task with which you are already familiar, how to improve your chances of landing the job you want, or how to politely discuss a problematic behavior with a coworker.

b. The **listeners** should use vocalizations, sincere questions, and paraphrasing to *understand* the speaker's content, intent, and feeling.

c. After the conversation ends, the speaker should describe the degree to which he or she feels satisfied that the paraphrasing reflected his or her meaning accurately. This is the measure of success of the interaction.

d. The **observer** should point out specific examples of effective and ineffective techniques used by the listeners.

e. The listeners should answer the following questions:

1. Was paraphrasing difficult or awkward? Why?
2. How does this type of listening compare to your typical manner of responding?
3. What types of useful information did you gain from the conversations? Would you be likely to obtain the same quality of information by responding in your more usual manner?
4. How could you use paraphrasing and sincere questioning to help in your everyday work?

7. Skill Builder

Practice your evaluative listening skills by following these steps:

a. Listen to a short persuasive presentation. Identify what the speaker is asking the listeners to believe or do.

b. Evaluate the speaker's evidence by answering the following questions:

1. Does the speaker support the claim with evidence?
2. Does the speaker cite references for the evidence?
3. How accurate is the evidence? Explain.
4. Does the speaker represent opposing evidence fairly?

c. Identify at least two emotional appeals used by the speaker.

1. Do any of the emotional appeals obscure important logical considerations?
2. Do the emotional appeals stretch the truth? Why or why not?

d. Based on this analysis, do you believe the speaker's argument is trustworthy?

LearnSmart

For further review, go to the LearnSmart study module for this chapter.

references

1. Covey. S. (1989). *The seven habits of highly effective people*. New York: Simon & Schuster.
2. Iacocca, L., & Novak, W. (1984). *Iacocca: An autobiography*. New York: Bantam.
3. Flynn, J., Valikoski, T., & Grau, J. (2008). Listening in the business context: Reviewing the state of research. *International Journal of Listening, 22,* 141–151.
4. Sweet, D. H. (1993). Successful job hunters are all ears. *Managing your career*. New York: Dow Jones.
5. Sutcliffe, A. J. (1997). *First-job survival guide*. New York: Henry Holt.
6. Winsor, J. L., Curtis, D. B., & Stephens, R. D. (1997). National preferences in business and communication education: An update. *Journal of the Association for Communication Administration, 3,* 170–179.
7. Gabric, D., & McFadden, K. L. (2001). Student and employer perceptions of desirable entry-level operations management skills. *Mid-American Journal of Business, 16*(1), 51–59; Landrum, R. E., & Harrold, R. (2003). What employers want from psychology graduates. *Teaching of Psychology, 30,* 131–133.
8. Whitten, M. (2019, July 25). The importance of listening to employees. *IndustryWeek*. Retrieved from https://www.industryweek.com/leadership/article /22027966/the-importance-of-listening-to-employees
9. Pilon, A. (2017, June 9). UPS CEO explains why listening is so important to leaders. *Small Business Trends*. Retrieved from https://smallbiztrends.com /2017/06/why-leaders-should-listen.html
10. Franzen, J. (2003, October 6). The listener. *The New Yorker*, p. 85.

11. Kline, J. A. (1996, April). *Listening effectively*. Maxwell Air Force Base, AL: Air University Press. Retrieved from http://www.au.af.mil/au/awc/awcgate/kline-listen /kline-listen.pdf

12. McDaniel, S. H., Beckman, H. B., Morse, D. S., Silberman, J., Seaburn, D. B., & Epstein, R. M. (2007). Physician self-disclosure in primary care visits: Enough about you, what about me? *Archives of Internal Medicine, 167,* 1321–1326.

13. Cooper, E., (2001, July). Are you in the listening zone? Most times, it's not what you say that makes the sale—it's how you listen. *On Wall Street, 11*(7).

14. Peterson, S. (1995, January 1). Managing your communication.*Vital Speeches of the Day, 61,* 188–191.

15. Brownell, J. (1990). Perceptions of effective listeners: A management study. *Journal of Business Communication, 27,* 401–415.

16. CPP (2008). Workplace conflict and how businesses can harness it to thrive. *CPP Global Human Capital Report*. Retrieved from https://img.en25.com/Web /CPP/Conflict_report.pdf

17. Spitzberg, B. H. (1994). The dark side of incompetence. In W. R. Cupach & B. H. Spitzberg (Eds.), *The dark side of interpersonal communication*. Hillsdale, NJ: Erlbaum.

18. Nichols, R. G. (1957). *Are you listening?* New York: McGraw Hill.

19. Turner, J. W., & Reinsch, N. L. (2007). The business communicator as presence allocator: Multicommunicating, equivocality, and status at work. *Journal of Business Communication, 44,* 36–58.

20. Arsenault, A. (2007, May). *Too much information? Gatekeeping and information dissemination in a networked world*. Paper presented at the International Communication Association annual meeting, San Francisco, CA.

21. Hamilton, J. (2008, October 16). Bad at multitasking? Blame your brain. *National Public Radio*. Retrieved from http://www.npr.org/templates/story/story.php? storyId=95784052

22. Vangelisti, A., Knapp, M. L., & Daly, J. A. (1990). Conversational narcissism. *Communication Monographs, 57,* 251–274.

23. Thomlison, T. D. (1997). Intercultural listening. In D. Borisoff & M. Purdy (Eds.), *Listening in everyday life: A personal and professional approach*. Lanham, MD: University Press of America.

24. Panchuk, T. International marketing orientations. *Eleedan*. Retrieved from http://eleedan.com/articles /international-marketing-orientations/

25. Peters, T. (1987). *Thriving on chaos: Handbook for a management revolution*. New York: Knopf.

26. Langer, E. (1990). *Mindfulness*. Reading, MA: Addison-Wesley; Hajek, C., & Giles, H. (2003). New directions in intercultural communication competence: The process model. In J. O. Greene & B. R. Burleson (Eds.), *Handbook of communication and social interaction skills*. Mahwah, NJ: Lawrence Erlbaum.

27. Burgoon, J. K., Berger, C. R., & Waldron, V. R. (2000). Mindfulness and interpersonal communication. *Journal of Social Issues, 56,* 105–127.

28. Miller, A. (2008, September). The mindful society. *Shambhala Sun*, pp. 56–62, 106. Retrieved from http://www.shambhalasun.com/index.php?option= com_content&task=view&id=3253&Itemid=244

29. Schaufenbuel, K. (2015, December 28). Why Google, Target, and General Mills are investing in mindfulness. *Harvard Business Review*. Retrieved from https://hbr .org/2015/12/why-google-target-and-general-mills-are -investing-in-mindfulness

30. Apple. (2017). See a voicemail transcription on your iPhone. Retrieved from https://support.apple.com /en-us/HT207181

31. Covey, S. (1989). *The seven habits of highly effective people*. New York: Simon & Schuster.

32. Dollinger, T. (2004, March 29). Listen using the 20/80 rule. *Listening Leader*.

33. Delk, T. (1998, October). Rick Pitino. *Success, 45,* 68–71.

34. Borisoff, D., & Victor, D. A. (1989). *Conflict management: A communication skills approach*. Englewood Cliffs, NJ: Prentice-Hall.

35. Wyer, R. S., Jr., & Adaval, R. (2003). Message reception skills in social communication. In J. O. Greene & B. R. Burleson (Eds.), *Handbook of communication and social interaction skills*. Mahwah, NJ: Lawrence Erlbaum.

36. Marquardt, M. J. (2005). *Leading with questions: How leaders find the right solutions by knowing what to ask*. Hoboken, NJ: Jossey-Bass.

Chapter Four
Verbal and Nonverbal Messages

chapter outline

chapter objectives

After reading this chapter you should be able to:

1. Describe business situations in which ambiguous or specific language is preferable, giving an example of each type of statement.

2. Define, identify, and remedy examples of each type of inflammatory language described in this chapter.

3. Apply concepts of powerful and positive language to specific examples from your career field.

4. Compare and contrast characteristically feminine and masculine language use, and describe the potential benefits and problems arising from such differences.

5. Describe how you can apply the information on nonverbal behavior in this chapter to your own career.

6. Define and give examples of seven categories of nonverbal behavior, and summarize the importance of each in a specific organization or career field.

Although they are neighbors and see each other almost every day, Bob and Carolyn rarely speak to each other. Ever since their partnership broke up, the hard feelings have made even casual conversation painful.

"We both should have known better," Bob lamented. "It was such a simple misunderstanding. We went into the partnership agreeing that we would be 'equal partners,' but now I can see that we had different ideas about what being 'equals' meant. I saw each of us taking charge of the areas that we did best: I'm good at marketing and sales, and Carolyn knows product design and production backward and forward. So it made sense to me that, while we were each equally responsible for the business and deserving an equal share of the profits, we would each make the final decisions in the areas where we were experts."

"That's not what I meant by 'equal partners,'" stated Carolyn flatly. "Bob wasn't willing to take responsibility for the hard work of production. He kept saying, 'That's where you're the expert.' And he didn't have any faith in my ideas about sales and marketing. He wanted to make those decisions himself, whether or not I agreed. To me, being equal means you have just as much say as the other person in every part of the business."

In hindsight, both Bob and Carolyn realize there had been signs of trouble from the beginning of their partnership. "Even before we opened for business, I could tell that Carolyn was unhappy," sighs Bob. "I always saw the venture as a chance to make a fortune. But whenever I'd get excited and talk about how much money we could make, Carolyn would clam up and get this grim look on her face."

Carolyn also remembers early, unspoken signs of trouble. "I've always wanted to have a business that my kids could be proud of," she said. "But when I'd talk about that goal, Bob wouldn't have much to say. Even though he never said so, at times I got the feeling that he was laughing at my high ideals."

This story illustrates the importance of paying close attention to verbal and nonverbal messages. The ill-fated partnership between Bob and Carolyn could have been avoided if they had paid more attention to the unspoken but powerful nonverbal clues that warned of trouble in their relationship. Examining more carefully just what an "equal partnership" meant also could have helped them avoid the clash that finally led to their breakup.

This chapter looks at the two channels by which you communicate: your words and your nonverbal behavior. By applying its lessons, you will learn to recognize that significant problems can lurk in even the simplest statements, and you will discover some ways to avoid or overcome such problems. You will also become more aware of the wordless messages each of us constantly sends and receives.

• Verbal Messages

Misunderstandings are a fact of life; the process of encoding and decoding described earlier in this book is inherently imperfect. As Table 4-1 shows, a listener can understand the meaning of every word perfectly, yet still interpret a message completely differently from its intended meaning. In fact, most people vastly overestimate how well their explanations get through and how well they understand others.[1]

Clarity and Ambiguity

Because the most basic language problems involve misunderstandings, we begin our study of language by considering how to prevent this sort of miscommunication. We also look at times when a lack of clarity can actually be desirable.

Table 4-1	Even Simple Messages Can Be Misunderstood	
What the Manager Said	**What the Manager Meant**	**What the Subordinate Heard**
I'll look into hiring another person for your department as soon as I complete my budget review.	We'll start interviewing for that job in about three weeks.	I'm tied up with more important things. Let's forget about hiring for the indefinite future.
Your performance was below par last quarter. I really expected more out of you.	You're going to have to try harder, but I know you can do it.	If you screw up one more time, you're out.
I'd like that report as soon as you can get to it.	Drop that rush order you're working on, and fill out that report today.	I need that report within the next week or so.
I talked to the boss, but at the present time, due to budget problems, we'll be unable to fully match your competitive salary offer.	We can give you 95 percent of that offer.	If I were you, I'd take that competitive offer. We're certainly not going to pay that kind of salary to a person with your credentials.
We have a job opening in Los Angeles that we think would be just your cup of tea. We'd like you to go out there and look it over.	If you'd like the job, it's yours. If not, of course you can stay here in Denver. You be the judge.	You don't have to go to Los Angeles if you don't want to—but if you don't, you can kiss your career with this firm good-bye.
Your people seem to be having some problems getting their work out on time. I want you to look into this situation and straighten it out.	Talk to your people and find out what the problem is. Then get together with them and jointly solve it.	I don't care how many heads you bust, just get me that output. I've got enough problems around here without you screwing things up, too.

Source: Adapted from Altman, S., Valenzi, E., & Hodgetts, R. M. (1985). *Organizational behavior: Theory and practice.* Waltham, MA: Academic Press.

The Cost of Miscommunication

We often hear of communication errors disrupting productivity or even harming a person's professional reputation, but we do not always consider the more dire consequences of such errors.

In 2009, a 25-year-old Norwegian university student was severely injured in a bar fight in Copenhagen. The student tried to explain to the hospital staff that he was a hemophiliac. Hemophilia is a condition in which the body is unable to make blood clots, which are required to stop bleeding. The staff mistakenly thought the patient said he was homosexual, and sent him home without specialized treatment.

The communication error was caused by a language barrier. The Danish word for hemophilia is "haemofili," whereas the word for homosexual is "homofil." This miscommunication cost the young man his life: He was found dead from a brain hemorrhage less than 24 hours after being discharged from the hospital.

Source: Hauksson, K. M. (2009, May 21). Miscommunication costs Norwegian his life. *IceNews*.

Use Unequivocal Terms to Avoid Misunderstandings Most misunderstandings arise in casual conversation, where statements seem perfectly clear until you discover that others can interpret them differently.[2] This occurs with the use of **equivocal terms**, those with two different, but equally acceptable or common, meanings. Consider the examples in the following scenarios:

- A university president asks her executive assistant to book plane tickets and hotel reservations for an academic conference in Portland. Later, she finds that the tickets were booked for Oregon instead of the intended Maine destination.

- A client asks a contractor for a mid-project change: "Can you move that door from here to there?" The contractor replies, "No problem." Later, the client is astonished to find that they have been charged for the change order.

- You agree to visit a client at home at "dinner time" in a part of the country where "dinner" is midday and "supper" is in the evening. When you appear at 6:00 p.m., the client asks why you did not arrive at the promised time.

Sometimes equivocal problems arise because communicators from different fields use the same term in specialized ways. Former Hollywood agent Jerry Katzman describes just such a situation. In a meeting with representatives of a Silicon Valley software publisher, he used the phrase *in development* to mean that a project was in the rough-idea stage. The software people expected that phrase to mean the project had been funded and was being created. Katzman insinuated that the situation seemed to call for an interpreter, as though both parties could not understand each other's language.[3]

Equivocation sometimes arises from different cultural values. Compared with Americans, Mexicans are less inclined to express conflict and are more polychronic and relaxed about managing time. The Spanish word *ahorita* means "right now" or "immediately" in English. Despite its dictionary meaning, North Americans have found their Mexican counterparts use the term quite differently:

- When are those photocopies going to be ready? "*Ahorita,*" answers the secretary who knows the copy machine is broken.

- When will that delivery be made? "*Ahorita,*" answers the salesperson who has no truck.

- One U.S. financial officer sheepishly admits he finally prohibited his Mexican staff from giving him *ahorita* as an answer.[4]

case STUDY

Misunderstandings Lead to Airline Catastrophe

The worst accident in aviation history occurred on March 27, 1977—in large part due to a tragic misunderstanding. The lessons from that disaster are just as important today as they were more than four decades ago.

The airport on the Spanish island of Tenerife was shrouded in fog as two jumbo jets lumbered toward departure—one at each end of the single runway. As one plane headed into position, the second plane was pointed straight at it, hidden by the fog. The copilot of that plane radioed the control tower, saying, "We're now at take-off," to which the controller replied, "OK." The crew meant they were ready to begin take-off, while the controller assumed the plane was awaiting final clearance. He added, "Stand by for take-off; I will call you," but interference from another transmission blocked this critical part of the message.

Unaware the runway was occupied, the pilots of the doomed plane began their rush toward disaster. By the time the two aircraft were visible to each other, it was too late to avert impact. In the ensuing collision and fire, 583 lives were lost.

As a result of this catastrophe, aviation authorities now require the use of standard phrases to identify flight operations. The phrase *take-off* is used only when actual lift-off is due to take place. In all other cases, controllers and aircrews use the term *departure*. This simple change has helped prevent additional fatal misunderstandings like the one in Tenerife. Unfortunately, the clarification came too late for the almost 600 innocent travelers in the 1977 disaster.

Source: Subsecretaria de Aviacion Civil, Spain. (1978). Official report of the investigation translated into English. Retrieved from http://www.skybrary.aero/bookshelf/books/809.pdf; Tenerife Information Centre. (2009). The Tenerife Airport disaster. Retrieved from http://www.tenerife-information-centre.com/tenerife-airport-disaster.html

When possible, use unequivocal terms to ensure that your language is specific. When you agree to meet "Wednesday" with someone, mention the date to be sure you are both thinking of the same week. At least some equivocation problems can be avoided if you double-check your understanding of terms that might be interpreted in more than one way. When your supervisor says your ideas are "OK," ask follow-up questions to make sure the term means "well done" and not just "adequate." Also beware of the ubiquitous ASAP, which stands for "as soon as possible." What is considered "soon" by one person's standards is not always the same definition shared by others in the office.

Use Lower-Level Abstractions When Clarity Is Essential   Language varies in its level of abstraction, or vagueness. **Low-level abstractions** are concrete statements that provide specific details or descriptions. By contrast, **high-level abstractions** cover a broader range of possible objects or events without describing them in much detail. In business, it is important to communicate using low-level abstractions. High-level abstractions can create confusion and misunderstandings because they are often subject to a wide variety of interpretations. Consider the following examples:

High-Level Abstraction	Low-Level Abstraction
The job will take a little longer.	The job will take 48 hours to complete.
Please order some supplies.	Please order 5 easels and a case of paper.
We need some market research.	Please create a detailed survey that we can distribute to our customers to identify their preferences for learning about our events.
This team needs to take it to the next level.	This team needs to achieve a 3% increase in donations this month.

Poor Translations Create Marketing Blunders

When international firms fail to understand the culture of a new market that they are entering, the word-for-word translations of their product names can range from humorous to offensive. Here are a few examples:

1. Scandinavian vacuum manufacturer Electrolux didn't help its sales in the United States when it used the slogan, "Nothing Sucks Like an Electrolux."
2. Clairol introduced the curling iron "Mist Stick" into Germany, only to find out that "mist" is slang for manure in that country.
3. Pepsi lost market share in parts of Southeast Asia when it painted vending machines light blue—a color associated with death and mourning.
4. Gerber's baby food sales suffered in rural Africa when the company used the same packaging as in the United States with a smiling baby on the label. Later, the company discovered that in areas where many customers cannot read, product labels contain pictures of what's inside the package.
5. Colgate introduced a toothpaste in France called Cue, the name of a notorious porn magazine.
6. Ford's marketing of its Pinto cars flopped in Brazil, where that word is slang for "tiny male genitals."

Because both abstract language and specific language have their advantages, it is often best to use both. One way to achieve maximum clarity is to begin explaining your proposal, problem, request, or appreciation by making an abstract statement, which you then qualify with specifics:

- "I'm worried about the amount of time we seem to be spending on relatively unimportant matters [abstract]. In our last meeting, for instance, we talked for 20 minutes about when to schedule the company picnic and then had only 15 minutes to discuss our hiring needs [specific]."
- "I'd like to take on more responsibility [abstract]. Until now, the only decisions I've been involved in dealt with small matters [still abstract], such as daily schedules and customer refunds [more specific]. I'd like a chance to help decide issues such as buying and advertising [specific]."

Another type of ambiguous language that causes problems is the use of **relative words** such as *soon*, *often*, *large*, and *short* that have meaning only in relation to other (unspecified) terms. Telling your supervisor you will have the memo done *soon* or agreeing to do a *short* report can cause problems. If *soon* means "in a few weeks" to you, but "in a few days" to your boss, a conflict is brewing. Replacing relative words with numeric words can eliminate most of these problems. Use "in two days" rather than *soon* and "two paragraphs" rather than *short,* for example.

Use Slang with Caution   Casual, slang-laden speech may be fine off the job, but it can create the wrong impression with bosses, clients, and even colleagues. Some slang simply will not be understandable to others. For example, the British term "gobsmacked" is likely to draw a blank stare when used in conversation with someone outside the United Kingdom ("I was gobsmacked when they gave me that assignment"). Similarly, to compliment a colleague's presentation by calling it "sick" runs the risk of being interpreted as a deep insult. Other slang terms are also likely to cast you in an unprofessional light. You may call a friend "bro," but it is smart to use more professionally-oriented speech in business settings.

Use Jargon Judiciously   Every profession has its own specialized vocabulary, called **jargon**. For example, people who work in social media may talk about "SEO," "crowdsourcing," and "brandjacking," but these terms likely mean little to people outside of this profession. Nevertheless, using jargon has several benefits in the workplace.

First, jargon is often used to save time when communicating with colleagues. It is quicker to use a short term in place of a longer definition of a complex idea. For example, accountants use the term *liquidity* instead of saying "the degree to which an asset can be converted into cash." Acronyms are a special kind of jargon that saves time by giving people a shorthand way—an abbreviation—to refer to common things. For example, you may hear an organization's chief executive officer referred to as simply "the CEO."

Second, jargon can be used to evaluate people's expertise on a subject. If you have ever interviewed for a job, you may have noticed that some of the interview questions were peppered with jargon. One of the authors of this book recently learned that a former public relations student was asked an interview question about an organization's involvement in "CSR." This acronym refers to "corporate social responsibility," and it refers to the practice of engaging in efforts that illustrate the company's commitment to making an impact on environmental and social well-being. The interviewer was trying to determine whether the job candidate knew the insider language. If a candidate can "talk the talk," it is more likely that they possess the skills to do the job.

Finally, using a certain amount of jargon has value to outsiders. Speakers who sprinkle their comments with jargon will appear more credible to some listeners.[5] While incomprehensible language may impress listeners, it does not help them understand an idea. Thus, if your goal is to explain yourself (and not merely to build your image), the ideal mixture may be a combination of clear language sprinkled with a bit of professional jargon.

Despite these benefits, jargon may cause difficulty in the workplace. A customer shopping for a computer might be mystified by a sales associate's talk about bus speed, onboard circuitry, and data transfer rates. This could create noise for the listeners as they shift their focus to attempting to decipher the meaning or tune out altogether. However, when the same information is translated into language the buyer can understand—the length of time it takes to download a file, for example—a sale is more likely.

Use Ambiguous Language When It Is Strategically Desirable   In low-context cultures such as the United States and Canada, speaking directly is valued. "Don't beat around the bush" is a common phrase. Vague language can be seen as a sign of deliberate deception, as an old joke shows: A reporter warned a state senator, "Sir, your constituents were confused by today's speech." "Good," the senator replied. "It took me two days to write it that way."

Despite its bad reputation, ambiguous language does have its place. High-context cultures have made an art of *strategic ambiguity*,[6] or finding ways to express difficult messages indirectly. One U.S. author describes how indirectness works:

> Instead of criticizing a report, the manager asks for more information. . . . When they say "I'd like to reflect on your proposal a while," when the decision must be [made] soon, it means "You are dead wrong, and you'd better come up with a better idea very soon. But I don't tell you so, because you should know that yourself!"
>
> It seems to me that such indirectness in interpersonal communication is a virtue; it is just as efficient, and it is certainly more mature and polite than the affront, "You are dead wrong." We need not talk to one another as if we were children (or characters out of the pages of pulp fiction)—yes, children need clarity—but adults can deal with indirectness and multiple meanings.[7]

Even in normally low-context cultures such as the United States, Canada, Israel, and Germany, indirect speech may help communicators achieve three useful goals.[8] The first is *to promote harmony*. A group of workers who have been feuding over everything from next year's budget to funding the office coffee supply can at least reach consensus on an abstraction like "the need to reduce waste"—a step that represents a small but an important start toward greater cooperation.

A second function of ambiguous speech is *to soften the blow of difficult messages*. Business communicators face the constant challenge of delivering bad news: "This work isn't good enough." "We don't want to do business with you anymore." While these kinds of statements may be honest, they can also be brutal. Ambiguous language provides a way to deliver negative messages in a way that softens their blow and makes it possible to work smoothly with the recipients in the future. For example:

Brute Honesty	Strategic Ambiguity
This work isn't good enough.	I think the boss will want us to back up these predictions with some figures.
I don't want to work with you.	Right now, I don't see any projects on the horizon.

A final function of strategic ambiguity is to make a *point indirectly that cannot be expressed overtly*. In today's litigation-prone environment, business communicators often use strategic ambiguity to share critical messages without exposing themselves to lawsuits.[9] For example, consider this humorous letter of reference "endorsing" a former employee who was fired for being a slow, lazy, unmotivated worker with an inflated ego and who lacked qualifications, causing the company to lose money:

> I am pleased to say John Doe is a former colleague of mine. John left this job the same way he came, fired with enthusiasm. We are deeply indebted for the services he has given our firm over the years.
>
> John will do nothing that will lower your high regard for him. His job requires few skills which he lacks. I honestly don't think he could have done a better job for us if he had tried. I most enthusiastically recommend John Doe with no qualifications whatsoever. It will not take John long to get up to speed. No salary would be too much for him. You won't find many people like John.[10]

One problem with strategic ambiguity, of course, is that it can easily be misunderstood. This problem can be especially acute in medical settings when health care providers try to deliver bad news to patients in a way that softens its impact. For example:

> [A surgeon] took one look at a patient's badly infected foot and recognized that it would have to be amputated. "I don't think we're going to be able to deal with this with local treatments," he told the patient.
>
> When the surgeon left the examining room, the woman turned to the doctor and asked: "Does that mean I'm going to have to go to Los Angeles for treatment?"[11]

Even when misunderstandings are not a problem, strategic ambiguity works only when both the sender and receiver are willing to tolerate a deliberate lack of clarity. Without that understanding, the result can be confusion, and often feelings of being betrayed or manipulated.

Inflammatory Language

Language has the power to stir intense emotions. It can motivate, inspire, and amuse audiences. Unfortunately, it can also generate equally intense negative feelings:

antagonism, defensiveness, and prejudice. You can prevent these negative outcomes by following two guidelines.

Avoid Biased Language

Emotional problems arise when speakers intentionally or unintentionally use **biased language**—terms that seem to be objective but actually conceal an emotional bias. Consider, for example, the range of words you could use to refer to a 25-year-old man who disagrees with your proposal: *man*, *fellow*, *guy*, *young man*, or *dude*. Each of these terms paints a different picture in the listener's mind; none of them is neutral.

When faced with biased language, it is wise to recognize that the speaker is editorializing. Tactfully restate the term in language that does not contain an evaluation, paraphrase it with neutral language, or use terms that quantify the meaning.

Speaker's Biased Language	Listener's Restatement
It's a *gamble*.	So you don't think the idea is a reasonable risk. Is that it? (paraphrase)
He's *long-winded*.	Bill *has* been talking for a half-hour. (quantify)
She's so *wishy-washy*.	You think Susan isn't willing to make a decision? (rephrase in nonbiased language)

Self-Assessment   Recognizing Your Biases

Researchers coined the phrase "unconscious bias" to describe implicit bias that we are unaware of and that happens outside of our control. This bias has a considerable impact on the workplace, especially as it pertains to diversity. In one research study, science faculty from research-intensive universities were asked to rate the application materials submitted by two candidates—one male and one female—with the same qualifications for a laboratory manager position. Both male and female participants rated the male applicant as significantly more competent than the female applicant and were willing to offer more career mentoring and a higher starting salary to the male applicant. Although this example pertains to biological sex, unconscious bias can occur based on age, disability, nationality, religion, skin tone, sexuality, gender, and weight, among other factors.

The repercussions of unconscious bias are receiving quite a lot of attention in today's business environment. The Office of Diversity and Outreach at the University of California–San Francisco has started a campaign to address unconscious bias. Similarly, Google's roughly 60,000 employees around the world have been asked to complete 60- to 90-minute training sessions on unconscious bias.

One of the most popular tools available to assess unconscious bias is the Implicit Association Test (IAT). Scientists developed the IAT to detect biases by measuring their impact on behavior. The test takes the form of a simple sorting task, in which individuals are asked to sort images and words that appear on a computer screen into one of two categories. The idea is that when two concepts (fat, thin; good, bad) are highly correlated, people are able to pair those concepts more quickly than those that are not associated.

To assess your unconscious biases, visit the following site: https://implicit.harvard.edu/implicit/selectatest.html

Source: Moss-Racusin, C. A., Dovidio, J. F., Brescoll, V. L., Graham, M. J., & Handelsman, J. (2012). Science faculty's subtle gender biases favor male students. *PNAS*, *109* (41), 16474–16479; UCSF Office of Diversity and Outreach. (2016). Unconscious bias. Retrieved from https://diversity.ucsf.edu/resources/unconscious-bias; re:Work. (2016). Unbiasing. Retrieved from https://rework.withgoogle.com/subjects/unbiasing/; Project Implicit. (2011). Retrieved from https://implicit.harvard.edu/implicit/iatdetails.html

Strategic Swearing

Swearing serves a variety of communication functions.[12] It is a way to express emotions and to let others know how strongly you feel. It can be a compliment ("That was #$&@ing terrific!") or the worst of insults. Swearing can build solidarity and be a term of endearment, but it can offend and alienate, too.

Swearing on the job can have dire consequences. Such behavior may decrease morale among employees, influence how customers view the employees and brand, and create a hostile work environment. Moreover, some types of language can lead to complaints of sexual harassment, even when it is not directed at a particular employee.[13]

Communication researchers have investigated the effects of swearing in work settings.[14] Not surprisingly, they have found that the more formal the situation, the more negative the appraisal of swearing. The chosen swear word also makes a difference. "F-bombs" are judged to be more inappropriate than other, less-volatile terms. Perhaps most important, when listeners are caught by surprise by a speaker's swearing, they are likely to deem the person incompetent.

Despite these findings, Stanford University professor Robert Sutton notes that choosing *not* to swear can sometimes violate the norms of some organizations.[15] In addition, he maintains that swearing on rare occasions can be effective for its shock value. (The fact that Sutton authored a book called *The No Asshole Rule* suggests that he practices what he preaches.)

But even Sutton adds a cautionary note about swearing on the job: "If you are not sure, don't do it." This advice is especially important for workers who are new to the organization or whose position is not secure. The rules of communication competence always apply: Analyze and adapt to your audience; pay attention to both verbal and nonverbal feedback; and when in doubt, err on the side of restraint.

Beware of Trigger Words   Some terms have such strong emotional associations they act almost like a trigger, setting off an intense emotional reaction in certain listeners. These **trigger words** can refer to specific people (your boss, the president), groups or categories of individuals (union stewards, the human resources department, customers with complaints), issues (affirmative action, flexible scheduling), or other topics (imports, downsizing).

What is the best way to deal with trigger words? The first thing to realize is that, like everyone else, you almost certainly have your own trigger words. Therefore, you ought to begin by recognizing them, so when one comes up you will at least be aware of your sensitivity and avoid overreacting. If, for example, your parents are farmers and you are sensitive about people speaking condescendingly about farmers, you might catch yourself before you overreact when a coworker refers to someone on Casual Friday as "dressed like a farmer." It could be an innocent or uninformed remark.

Sometimes, however, you will discover too late that a term that seems innocuous to you is a trigger word for others. After the other person vents their strong feelings, you can acknowledge the misunderstanding, apologize, choose a more agreeable term, and proceed with the discussion.

Language and Identity Management

The way you speak can shape how others perceive you. Several speech habits can help you create a professional image.

Choose the Optimal Degree of Powerful Language   Some types of language make speakers sound less powerful, whereas other types create an air of power and confidence. Powerful language consists of clear language without unnecessary add-ons that make speakers sound as if they are doubting themselves or are not confident in their

own ideas. Notice the difference between the less powerful and more powerful speech examples in the following table.

Less Powerful Speech	More Powerful Speech
Tag questions "This report is good, *isn't it?*"	"This report is good."
Hesitations "We should, *um,* use the, *uh,* newer format."	"We should use the newer format."
Qualifiers *"I don't know if you'll like this idea, but* we could hire an outside consultant."	"We could hire an outside consultant."
Intensifiers "That was *such* a good job!"	"That was a good job!"
Questions "*Do you think* we should shorten the report?"	"We should shorten the report."

Speakers who use more powerful speech are rated as more competent, dynamic, and attractive than speakers who sound powerless.[16] One study revealed that even a single powerless speech mannerism can make a person appear less authoritative.[17] Thus, when your goal is to create an impression of power and conviction, it is best to use more powerful speech.

Conversely, sometimes powerful individuals might intentionally use less powerful language to avoid throwing their weight around. In some situations, less powerful forms of speech can even enhance a speaker's effectiveness.[18] For example, a boss might say to her assistant, "Would you mind making copies of these files before you go home?" Both the boss and the assistant know this is an order and not a request, but the questioning form is more considerate and leaves the assistant feeling better about the boss.[19] The importance of achieving both task and relational goals helps explain why a mixture of powerful and polite speech is usually most effective.[20]

Use Positive Language   One strategic way to enhance a professional identity is to use positive language. Imagine your boss comes to you at 4:45 p.m. and asks you to do a job as soon as possible. You could say, "I can't get to that tonight. It'll have to wait until tomorrow." Alternatively, you could reply, "I'll get to that first thing in the morning." It is easy to imagine which response would be viewed more favorably.

Unintentionally negative language habits can subtly damage a positive image. Negativity is often a reflex in simple exchanges: "*How are you?*" "Not bad." "*Can you handle this?*" "No problem." "*Thanks.*" "No big deal." Instead of using negative language, it is better to give quick, *positive* responses: "I'm fine." "Yes, I can." "You're welcome."

Limit Disfluencies   **Disfluencies** are utterances that add no meaning to a statement. Interjections such as "um," "you know," and "like" can make a smart idea sound less persuasive. When she was running for the U.S. Senate in 2008–2009, candidate Caroline Kennedy's disfluency habit may have helped sabotage her credibility. One critic reported counting more than 200 "you know's" in a single interview.[21] Another filler word often viewed negatively, especially by older generations, is "like." In fact, personal branding strategist Sylwia Dziedzic names "like" as one of the top filler words that can get in your way of getting hired.[22] No one expects colloquial speech to be flawless. In fact, perfect utterances would sound artificial and strange. Even so, practice can help keep the number of disfluencies under control.

Feminine and Masculine Language Use

As described in an earlier chapter 2, culture affects communication. Some social scientists have suggested that conversation between the sexes is a kind of cross-cultural communication in which members are not speaking different dialects but rather "**genderlects**."[23] They have argued that these stereotypically masculine or feminine approaches to speech profoundly affect the way we interact, but usually go unnoticed.

The words "masculine" and "feminine" are used to describe these language differences because they refer to traits characteristically linked to gender and not to biological sex. Thus, as you read about these linguistic differences, understand that masculine and feminine language may be used by persons of any sex or gender. Remember also that genderlect is not the only factor that influences conversational style. Cultural, geographical, and occupational influences play roles as well.

While these differences are important to consider, some researchers have argued that male and female communication styles are often indistinguishable.[24] In a series of studies involving the analysis of written transcripts of casual conversation, participants frequently incorrectly identified the sex of the speaker.[25] Ultimately, the differences outlined in this section reflect past communication patterns and, as gender roles in society evolve, speech styles may change in tandem.

Feminine Language Use   Feminine speech is characterized by what some researchers refer to as **rapport talk**—that is, talk used to create connections, establish goodwill, show support, and build community. For many, an important part of building rapport is using language as an *expressive tool*: to articulate emotions ("I'm worried about finishing those reports today"; "I'm glad everybody had a chance to speak") and clarify relationships ("We don't seem to be working well together").

Characteristically feminine speech often goes beyond just expressing emotions, by becoming *supportive*. Persons using this linguistic style are most likely to listen and respond to spoken and unspoken conversational clues about the other person's feelings. A characteristically feminine reply to a description of difficulties at work is "I know what that's like. Last year I had so much trouble with a client on the Bustos case . . ." This response lets the speaker know that they not alone, that they are understood.

Another characteristic of feminine conversational style is its *tentative* nature. This nature is reflected in questioning forms ("Could we go now?" "Would you type that for me?"), hedges and disclaimers ("I'm not sure about these figures . . ."; "This might not be a good time to bring this up, but . . ."), and tag questions ("The report is due today, isn't it?"). While these forms exhibit the less powerful characteristics described in the Choose the Optimal Degree of Powerful Language section earlier in this chapter, it may serve as more of a bid for solidarity than as a sign of weakness.[26] Another interpretation is that it builds rapport by avoiding dogmatism and supporting equality.

Conversational initiation and maintenance are also characteristic of feminine speech. Asking questions helps get a conversation going, find out what others are interested in, and show interest in a conversational partner: "Did you hear about . . . ?" "Are you going to . . . ?" "Did you know that . . . ?" In addition, "listening noises" ("uh, huh," "yeah," "mmhmm") may be used to show interest. If persons using a feminine language style do interrupt, that action is often intended to support or affirm the speaker, not to challenge or threaten them.

Masculine Language Use   Whereas a feminine style uses talk to build rapport, masculine style makes use of what linguists have labeled **report talk**—speech that focuses less on feelings and relationships and more on information, facts, knowledge, and competence. Persons using masculine language are more inclined to use speech to claim attention, assert a position, establish status, and show independence.

Characteristically masculine speech uses language *instrumentally* (as opposed to expressively) to get things done—that is, to report information, solve visible problems, achieve, accomplish, attain, execute, and perform. The results are often tangible and the reward is visible: "Fax these reports to accounting"; "I'll make reservations at Sara's"; "Finish that proposal by Monday." In addition, this type of language may be used to define status.

When dealing with personal problems, a characteristically masculine approach is to offer *advice* that will lead to a solution. Empathizing to show sympathy and establish solidarity just does not seem helpful or appropriate to those who use this style.

Masculine speech is more *assertive*, *certain*, *direct*, and *authoritative*. Statements of fact are preferred over opinion: "That deduction belongs on Schedule C" rather than "I think that's a Schedule C deduction." Declarative sentences and dropped pitch at the end of a sentence create a sense of sureness and authority. Persons are more likely to speak directly, giving clear and unambiguous commands rather than couching requests in the form of questions.

This speech style typically includes several characteristics of conversational *dominance* or *control*—namely, verbosity, topic control, and interruptions. It appears that the purpose of these interruptions is often to gain control of the conversational topic or the conversation itself. Table 4-2 summarizes research findings on the characteristics of feminine and masculine speech styles.

Meeting Gender-Related Language Challenges   Problems can arise when stereotypically masculine and feminine language styles clash on the job—often without anyone knowing exactly why. For instance, an employee who says, "I'm having difficulty with the Garcia account," may want to hear their concerns acknowledged and know that others have experienced similar problems. Their goal may be to gain support, establish connection, or seek rapport, or perhaps they may just want to talk about the situation. A colleague, conditioned to use speech to solve problems, might respond with advice: "Here's one way you could handle it . . ." If the employee wanted support and connection, being given advice might produce an effect just the opposite of the rapport they were looking for: The employee might feel like their colleague was trying to "one-up" them, coming across as a superior. From the colleague's frame of reference, however, they *were* being helpful by offering useful information at the request of someone in need.

Another gender-related problem can arise when one person in the conversation pays attention to the content of a message while the other focuses on the relational dimension of the words. If a supervisor says, "I can't do anything about your hours; the boss says they're set and can't be changed," the subordinate may hear a relational message of "I don't care" or "I don't want to be bothered." The superior, used to

Table 4-2	Characteristics of Feminine and Masculine Speech Styles

Characteristically Feminine Speech	Characteristically Masculine Speech
Builds rapport	Reports facts
Is expressive	Is instrumental
Offers support	Offers advice
Sounds tentative	Sounds certain
Initiates and maintains conversation	Controls conversation

A Professional Perspective

Lilly Vu

Director of Program Management Office

DataOceans LLC

Atlanta, GA

Credit: Lilly Vu

Sense of humor is often an underrated personal attribute in a corporate environment. However, throughout my years of working with and managing teams, I have come to believe that a sense of humor is a powerful tool for building rapport with others in the workplace.

One of the most obvious reasons is that having a sense of humor reduces stress levels for team members, especially when dealing with conflict or receiving bad news. Humor will also put people at ease because it allows them to understand that while team members take the work seriously, they do not take interpersonal conflict or intense discussions *personally.* This helps to create an atmosphere in which all team members can feel safe sharing their opinions and ideas. And when team members feel safe and respected, their productivity increases. Likewise, employee engagement and loyalty will be boosted.

Naturally, utilizing a sense of humor must be appropriate for the workplace culture and situation. It should be just enough to make people feel safe and comfortable communicating with managers and peers, especially in a formal setting with a large group or audience, but not so much that the joviality degrades into unprofessional conduct that calls the integrity of the team into question or embarrasses, demeans, or offends group members.

dealing with communication at the task level, is not being unsympathetic; they are just responding to a request.

Both masculine and feminine language styles work well—as long as listeners use the same rules. Frustration can arise when people expect others to use the same style as they do.[27] The following suggestions can help communicators understand and adapt to one another's differing uses of language:

- *Be aware of different styles.* Once you are aware that persons have been taught to use language differently, there is less likelihood of being dismayed at a style that does not match yours. The cultural analogy is apt here: If you were traveling in another country, you would not be offended by the inhabitants' customs, even if they were different from yours. In the same way, accepting language differences can lead to smoother relationships.

- *Switch styles when appropriate.* Being bilingual is an obvious advantage in a multicultural world. In the same way, using a communication style that differs from your usual style can be useful. If you routinely focus on the content of others' remarks, consider paying more attention to the unstated relational messages behind their words. If you generally focus on the unexpressed-feelings part of a message, consider being more task-oriented. If your first instinct is to be supportive, consider the value of offering advice; and, if advice is your reflexive way of responding, think about whether offering support and understanding might sometimes be more helpful.

- *Combine styles.* Effective communication may not be an either–or matter of choosing one style. In many situations, you may get the best results by combining typically masculine and feminine approaches. Research confirms what common sense suggests: A "mixed-gender strategy" that balances the traditionally masculine, task-oriented approach with the characteristically feminine, relationship-oriented approach is rated most highly.[28] Choosing the right approach for the other communicator and the situation can create satisfaction far greater than that achieved with an approach that relies on a single stereotypical style.

• Nonverbal Communication

Words are not the only way we communicate. You can appreciate this fact by imagining the following scenarios:

- Your boss has told the staff they welcome any suggestions about how to improve the organization. You take them at their word and schedule an appointment to discuss some ideas you have had. As you begin to outline your proposed changes, your boss focuses their gaze directly on you, folds their arms across their chest, clenches their jaw muscles, and begins to frown. At the end of your remarks, your boss rises abruptly from their chair, says, "Thank you for your ideas" in a monotone voice, and gives you a curt handshake.

- Despite the expense, you have decided to have a highly regarded certified public accountant (CPA) handle your tax matters. While waiting for the accountant to appear, you scan the impressive display of diplomas from prestigious universities and professional associations on the walls of the CPA's office. The accountant enters, and as the conversation proceeds, they yawn repeatedly.

Most people would find these situations odd and disturbing. This reaction would have nothing to do with the verbal behavior of the people involved. In each case, nonverbal behavior sends messages above and beyond the words being spoken: The boss does not really seem to want to hear your suggestions, and you wonder whether the accountant is capable or caring with regard to your taxes.

In the following pages, we examine the role of nonverbal communication in the working world. For our purposes, **nonverbal communication** involves messages expressed without words.

Characteristics of Nonverbal Communication

Nonverbal communication resembles verbal communication in some ways—but it is also quite different from verbal communication in other regards.

Nonverbal Behavior Always Has Communicative Value   You may not always *intend* to send nonverbal messages, but everything about your appearance, your every movement, your facial expressions, and the nuances of your voice have the potential to convey meaning.[29] You can demonstrate this fact by imagining your boss has "called you on the carpet," claiming you have not been working hard enough. How could you not send a nonverbal message? Nodding gravely would be a response; so would blushing, either avoiding or making direct eye contact, or shaking your head affirmatively or negatively. While you can shut off your linguistic channels of communication by refusing to speak or write, it is impossible to avoid behaving nonverbally.

One writer learned this fact from movie producer Sam Goldwyn while presenting his proposal for a new film. "Mr. Goldwyn," the writer implored, "I'm telling you a sensational story. I'm only asking for your opinion, and you fall asleep." Goldwyn's reply: "Isn't sleeping an opinion?"

Nonverbal communication operates even in mediated communication. Some nonverbal elements are obvious: The use of emojis, an abundance of exclamation points, and the impression of shouting when a message is typed in ALL CAPITAL LETTERS are clear examples. But even *not* responding to an e-mail or text message can suggest a put-down.[30]

Nonverbal Communication Is Powerful
Despite folk sayings like "you can't judge a book from its cover," we form impressions of others mostly from nonverbal observations about physical appearance and behavior. Once we form these impressions, they influence our subsequent impressions and judgments. Canadian communication consultant Lee McCoy gives an example:

> If I meet Susan and initially perceive her to be professional, attractive, and intelligent, I'm also likely to begin to attribute other positive characteristics to her. I might see her as organized, successful, and warm. This is not to suggest that I'll ignore negative characteristics, but it will take me longer to become aware of something negative if my initial perceptions of her are very positive. If, on the other hand, Susan presents herself to me as sloppily dressed, with bitten fingernails and a lack of eye contact, I may begin to attribute equally negative characteristics to her—insecurity, lack of knowledge, coldness.[31]

Even after first impressions have been made, the impact of nonverbal behavior is powerful. In fact, when nonverbal behavior seems to contradict a verbal message, the spoken words carry less weight than the nonverbal cues.[32]

Nonverbal Behavior Is Ambiguous
While nonverbal communication can create powerful impressions, the messages it conveys are ambiguous.[33] Does a customer's yawn signal boredom or fatigue? Are your coworkers laughing with or at you? Does your boss's frown reflect disapproval or preoccupation? Most nonverbal behaviors have a multitude of possible meanings, and it is a serious mistake to assume you can correctly determine which is true in any given case.

Nonverbal Communication Primarily Expresses Attitudes
While it is relatively easy to infer general interest, liking, disagreement, amusement, and so on from another person's actions, messages about ideas or concepts do not lend themselves to nonverbal channels. How, for instance, would you express the following messages nonverbally?

- Current sales are running 16% above last year's sales.
- Management decided to cancel the sales meeting after all.
- Let's meet at 2:00 p.m. to plan the agenda for tomorrow's meeting.

Obviously, such thoughts are best expressed in speech and writing. Nevertheless, nonverbal behavior can imply how the speaker *feels*: whether the speaker is pleased that sales are up or is worried that they are not as high as expected; whether the staff is relieved or frustrated about the canceled meeting, and so on.

Nonverbal Communication Affects Career Success   Not surprisingly, the ability to manage your nonverbal behavior plays a strong role in communicative success. For example, salespeople who are better at reading potential clients' nonverbal cues make more sales and earn higher incomes than their less astute colleagues.[34] Likewise, successful entrepreneurs owe a great deal of their success to their well-honed social skills, including the ability to manage their own nonverbal behavior and read that of others.[35] Similarly, managers who are good at reading and responding to nonverbal cues receive higher performance ratings from both their bosses and their subordinates.[36]

Much Nonverbal Behavior Is Culture Bound   Certain types of nonverbal behavior seem to be universal. For example, members of most literate cultures strongly agree about which facial expressions represent happiness, fear, surprise, sadness, anger, and disgust or contempt.[37] In contrast, many nonverbal expressions do vary from culture to culture.

In this age of international communication in business, it is especially important to understand cultural differences in the meanings assigned to nonverbal behaviors. Consider the different rules about how much distance is appropriate between speakers. One study revealed that the "proper" space between two speakers varies considerably from one culture to another: To a Japanese person, a comfortable space is 40 inches; for a U.S. resident, 35 inches; and to a Venezuelan, 32 inches.[38] It is easy to see how these differences could lead to challenges for a U.S. native doing business overseas.

Types of Nonverbal Communication

We have already mentioned several types of nonverbal messages. We now discuss each in more detail.

Voice   Your own experience shows the voice communicates in ways that have nothing to do with the words a speaker utters. You may recall, for instance, overhearing two people arguing in an adjoining apartment; even though you could not make out their words, their emotions and the fact they were arguing were apparent from the sounds of their voices. Similarly, you have probably overheard people talking in a language you did not understand, yet the speakers' feelings—excitement, delight, exhaustion, boredom, grief—were conveyed by their voices.

The term **paralanguage** describes a wide range of vocal characteristics, each of which helps express an attitude: pitch (high-low), resonance (resonant-thin), range (spread-narrow), tempo (rapid-slow), articulation (precise-imprecise), disfluencies (e.g., *um, er*), rhythm (smooth-jerky), pauses (frequency and duration), and volume (loud-soft).

Not surprisingly, voice contributes dramatically to business and professional communicators' success or failure. For example, surgeons with harsh, impatient voices are more likely to be sued by patients for malpractice compared to those with more friendly speech mannerisms.[39] One distinctive vocal trait is "uptalk"—the tendency to end sentences on a rising pitch. This vocal pattern makes assertions sound like questions: "Mr. Chen? It's Eliza Palmer? From Accounts Receivable?" In a July 2015 episode of National Public Radio's *Fresh Air*, journalist Jessica Grose discussed her experience being criticized for uptalk. She recalled an older man whom she was interviewing for an article in

Businessweek telling her that she sounded like his granddaughter. Grose said, "That was the first moment I felt [my voice] was hurting my career beyond just irritating a couple of listeners."[40]

Vocal fry—or a set of low, creaky vibrations—is another type of vocal trait that is often perceived negatively in the workplace. This particular vocal style has been popularized by musical artists like Britney Spears and Katy Perry, who use it to add style and variation to their singing. Some researchers note that vocal fry has become a common vocal trait in U.S. women, being used by as many as two-thirds of surveyed female college students aged 18–25 years.[41] Despite not equating vocal fry with confidence, college students tend to have a favorable impression of this trait and associate it with education/knowledge, intimacy, genuineness, and nonaggression.[42] When it comes to hiring decisions, however, research suggests employers have a more harmful perception of vocal fry. Specifically, females who use vocal fry are deemed less trustworthy, competent, and educated. As a result, listeners may be less willing to hire them than candidates who do not use vocal fry.[43]

While uptalk and vocal fry are used by both sexes, these traits appear to be more common among women. It is easy to imagine how these traits can contribute to perceptions of female unassertiveness. "If women always sound like they're asking for approval or agreement, they seem less sure of themselves," says communication consultant Mary-Ellen Drummond.[44]

Appearance   Personal appearance plays a tremendous role in determining how a communicator's messages will be received in business and elsewhere.[45] As a rule, people who *look* attractive are considered to be likable and persuasive, and they generally have more successful careers.[46] For example, research suggests that beginning salaries increase approximately $2,000 for every 1-point increase on a 5-point attractiveness scale and that more attractive men (but not more attractive women) are given higher starting salaries than their less handsome counterparts.

A number of factors contribute to how attractive a person seems. For instance, potential employers, customers, and coworkers are usually impressed by people who are trim, muscular, and in good shape. One study, in fact, shows that people who are overweight have more trouble getting job offers.[47] Some aspects of physical appearance cannot be changed easily. However, one significant factor in appearance—clothing—is one over which you may have the most control.

The kind of clothing one wears can influence how people react. Former Boeing Aircraft CEO Philip Condit is keenly aware of this fact. Having discovered that discussions were hard to get going when he appeared in a business suit and tie, Condit routinely dresses down when making trips to the shop floor to talk with the workers who build Boeing aircraft.[48]

Attitudes about which clothing is acceptable keep changing. By the mid-1990s, even conservative IBM abandoned its decades-long policy of requiring employees to wear a dark business suit. A spokesperson for IBM explained, "You try to dress like your customers do."[49]

The percentage of U.S. companies that allow employees to dress casually on a daily basis quickly grew from 32% in 2014 to 50% in 2019.[50] Additionally, close to two-thirds of companies allow casual dress at

Jupiterimages/Stockbyte/Getty Images

ETHICAL **challenge**

Dress Codes and Religious Beliefs

In September 2020, the Equal Employment Opportunity Commission (EEOC) filed a wrongful termination complaint on behalf of two employees who were fired from a Kroger supermarket in Conway, Arkansas. The ex-employees stated that they were required to wear a new apron with a new logo featuring a rainbow heart on the top left portion of the bib.

According to the lawsuit, they believed the logo was an "endorsement of the LGBTQ community," which violated their religious beliefs. The rainbow flag is a symbol associated with LGBTQIA+ pride, but it is unknown whether the symbol was intended to represent pride in this case.

Although the employees requested religious accommodations, such as being allowed to wear their name tags over the logo or wear different aprons, the employer allegedly denied their requests. According to the EEOC, both employees were fired for violating the store's dress code.

The lawsuit alleges Kroger violated Title VII of the Civil Rights Act of 1964 and Title I of the Civil Rights Act of 1991 by refusing to accommodate the employees' religious beliefs and terminating their employment "in retaliation for requesting a religious accommodation."

Did the employer act ethically in this case? How might companies address dress code policies in an effort to accommodate religious beliefs, social justice movements, and gender-neutrality?

Source: Smith, A. (2020, September 29). Dress-code policies reconsidered in the pandemic. *SHRM.* Retrieved from https://www.shrm.org /resourcesandtools/legal-and-compliance/employment-law/pages/coronavirus-dress-code-policies.aspx; Venkatraman, S. (2020, September 17). Kroger sued for allegedly firing workers who refused to wear rainbow symbol. *NBC News.* Retrieved from https://www.nbcnews.com/feature /nbc-out/kroger-sued-allegedly-firing-workers-who-refused-wear-rainbow -symbol-n1240252

least once per week.[51] Virgin Atlantic no longer requires female flight attendants to wear skirts and makeup, citing "an increased level of comfort" and "more choice" to express individuality.[52]

Although more companies are adopting a less formal dress code, whether to dress up or dress down depends on several factors, including the industry or field of work. California's outdoor gear and clothing manufacturer Patagonia may have one of the most liberal dress codes: Even shoes are not required.[53] By comparison, high-tech, utilities, and natural resources firms tend to allow the most informal attire while financial services and public administration businesses have some of the most conservative dress standards.[54] Although Goldman Sachs has updated its dress code policy to allow for flexible attire, professionalism is still of primary importance. An internal memo announcing the policy changes explains:

> Goldman Sachs has a broad and diverse client base around the world, and we want all of our clients to feel comfortable with and confident in our team, so please dress in a manner that is consistent with your clients' expectations . . . casual dress is not appropriate every day and for every interaction . . . All of us know what is and is not appropriate for the workplace.[55]

Knowing that an office has a business casual dress code is not enough to determine what is appropriate, however, as "casual" is itself an ambiguous term. As business etiquette expert Dana Casperson notes, business casual "means one thing on the West Coast, another thing on the East Coast, and no one knows in the middle."[56] An organization's culture also makes a difference in determining which attire is considered appropriate. Thus, two companies in the same field might have quite different appearance codes.

When choosing your wardrobe, consider the following tips:

- *Look around.* The best guide to an appropriate wardrobe is right in front of you: the key people in the industry and in the company where you work. Wearing a

Dress Codes and Remote Work

For many U.S. employees, the 2020 COVID-19 pandemic prompted a transition to remote work and, in many cases, a departure from typical dress code requirements. Although it may be enticing to spend the day wearing gym clothes or pajamas, at least one survey of 1,000 remote workers found that workers wearing business-professional or business-casual attire felt more productive throughout the day.[57]

While it may not be necessary to dress up for a day filled with fielding phone calls or e-mail messages, it is important to maintain a professional appearance when participating in videoconferencing. Wearing business casual attire and neutral colors helps speakers appear authentic and trustworthy.[58] It may also limit the risk of sexual harassment and other uncomfortable situations. As one attorney noted, "nobody wants a repeat of the infamous videoconference-in-no-pants moment."[59]

conservative, dark business suit in a freewheeling start-up company where everyone else comes to work in jeans would look just as odd as wearing workout clothes in a Wall Street stock brokerage. You may also ask the human resources staff about company dress codes.

- *Dress for the job you want.* If you are seeking advancement, consider dressing in a way that makes it easy for the people with the power to promote you to visualize you in a position of more responsibility.

- *Err on the side of dressing conservatively.* Standards of dress are always in flux. If you are unsure of which attire is appropriate in a given situation, choose the more conservative option. It is easier to loosen or remove a tie for a more casual look than it is to dress up a golf shirt.

- *Do not show too much skin.* What might be the norm on a college campus or when out with your friends may not be acceptable at your job. If you work with people from older generations, or in a particularly conservative environment such as the banking or energy industry, it will be crucial for your career success to dress modestly. For example, you should avoid wearing shorts, open-toed shoes, plunging necklines, short skirts, and shirts that show the midriff.[60]

- *Do not confuse "casual" with "sloppy."* A T-shirt and grubby denim jeans send a different message than pressed khakis and a button-down shirt or sweater. Looking good in casual dress can be at least as challenging (and expensive) as pulling off a more formal look. In any event, it is never acceptable to have dirty, stained, or wrinkled clothing.

Even though this double standard may be unfair, it is more important for women to dress professionally and conservatively than it is for men—especially if they have high career ambitions. In multiple studies on the effects of clothing choices, participants have been asked to evaluate the perceived competence of women who were wearing either professional clothes or "sexy" clothes. When the woman was in a low-status position (an administrative assistant), her choice of clothes had no effect on her perceived competence. In contrast, when she was in a high-status position (an executive), the sexily dressed woman was rated as significantly less competent.[61]

The Face and Eyes

On an obvious level, a person's face communicates emotions clearly: A subordinate's confused expression indicates the need to continue with an explanation; a customer's smile and nodding signal the time to close a sale; and a colleague's

Blend Images/Superstock

frown indicates that your request for help has come at a bad time. Facial expressions, like other nonverbal signals, may be ambiguous (a coworker's frown could come from a headache rather than the timing of your request). Nonetheless, researchers have found that viewers can often accurately judge facial expressions.[62]

The eyes themselves communicate a great deal. A skilled nonverbal communicator, for example, can control an interaction by knowing when and where to look to produce the desired results. Since visual contact is an invitation to speak, a speaker who does not want to be interrupted can avoid looking directly at people until it is time to field questions or get reactions.

Eye contact can be a good indicator of how involved a person is in a situation, although research partially contradicts the advice to always look people straight in the eye. In most two-person conversations, people seem to look at their partners somewhere between 50% and 60% of the time, often alternating short gazes with glances away. A person who makes little or no eye contact, however, may seem to have little involvement in the situation.

The rules for eye contact and facial expressions vary from one culture to another. In some cultures—Diné (Navajo), for example—lack of eye contact may indicate respect for elders, not a lack of interest. In Japan, smiling is less common than in North America, which can confuse visitors who mistakenly perceive formality for unfriendliness. Clerks greet customers with a simple "Irasshaimase"—"Welcome"—but typically do not accompany the greeting with a smile.[63] Some foreign companies, including McDonald's Corporation, have created "smile schools" to teach employees how to greet customers in a manner that seems friendlier.

Even among communicators who follow the rules of Euro-American culture, eye contact can be deceptive: Some people really *can* lie while looking you right in the eye. Even barely perceptible changes in eye contact can send messages that may or may not be accurate. The following story illustrates how eye contact can be misleading—and how misinterpretation of this cue can have serious repercussions:

> Discussing his corporation's financial future in front of television cameras, the chief executive officer of a *Fortune* 500 company lowered his eyes just as he began to mention projected earnings. His downcast eyes gave the impression—on television—that the executive wasn't on the level. Wall Street observers discounted the CEO's optimistic forecast, and the company's stock price dropped four points over the next few trading days. It took two years to build it up again—even though the projection had proved to be accurate.[64]

Posture and Movement

A person's body communicates messages in several ways. The first is through posture. The way you sit at your desk when you are working can reflect your attitude toward your job or how hard you are working to anyone who cares to look. A less obvious set of bodily clues comes from the small gestures and mannerisms that every communicator exhibits at one time or another. While most people pay reasonably close attention to their facial expressions, they are less aware of hand, leg, and foot motions. Thus, fidgeting hands might signal nervousness; a tapping foot, impatience; and clenched fists, restrained anger. Table 4-3 describes the way others may potentially interpret some of your gestures.

A study on privacy in the workplace by GF Business Equipment Company describes ways in which such gestures can be used to discourage visits from coworkers. In addition

Table 4-3	Common Gestures and Their Possible Perceived Meanings	
Gesture	**In Moderate Form**	**When Exaggerated**
Forward lean	Friendly feelings	Hostile feelings
Direct eye contact	Friendly feelings	Hostile feelings
Unique dress and hairstyle	Creativity	Rebelliousness
Upright posture	Expertise; self-confidence	Uptightness; hostility
Variability in voice pitch, rate, and loudness	Lively mind	Nervousness; anxiety; insecurity
Smiling	Friendliness; relaxed and secure composure	Masking hostility; submissiveness
Averting gaze	Shyness; modesty	Guilt; unreliability
Knitted brow	Involvement	Hostility
Nodding and reaching out the hands while talking	Self-confidence	Uncertainty

Source: Adapted from University of Northern Iowa College of Business Administration. (n.d.). Body language. Retrieved from http://business.uni.edu/buscomm/nonverbal/body%20Language.html

to avoiding eye contact with your visitor, the company suggests you shuffle papers or make notes to indicate a desire to return to work; keep pen or pencil poised, which communicates an aversion to engaging in conversation; and, if interrupted when dialing a call, do not hang up the phone.[65]

Good communicators are sensitive to these small cues and tailor their behavior accordingly. They will notice a forward-leaning position as an indication that their remarks are being well received and will capitalize upon the point that led to this reaction. When a remark results in a pulling back, a smart communicator will identify the source of the rejection and try to remedy it. Awareness of such subtle messages can make the difference between success and failure in a variety of business settings, including interviews, presentations, group meetings, and one-on-one interactions.

Body relaxation or tension is a strong indicator of who has the power in one-on-one relationships. As a rule, the more relaxed person in a given situation has the greater status.[66] This differential is most obvious in job interviews and high-stakes situations in which subordinates meet with their superiors—requesting a raise or describing a problem, for example. The person in control can afford to relax, while the supplicant must be watchful and on guard. While excessive tension does little good for either the sender or the receiver, total relaxation can be inappropriate for a subordinate. A job candidate who matched the interviewer's casual sprawl would probably create a poor impression. In superior–subordinate interactions, the best posture for the one-down person is probably one that is slightly more formal than the powerholder's stance.

Height also affects perceptions of power: Tallness usually equates with dominance. Standing up tall can help you appear more authoritative, whereas a slumped posture and slouched shoulders create an appearance of submissiveness or passiveness. Placing your body at the same level as your conversational partner is a way of nonverbally lowering your status, whether you are speaking with a colleague in a wheelchair or with someone who is shorter than you. To literally have to look up to someone may make the shorter person feel like a subordinate. Sitting down with someone could signal your desire for collegiality rather than an emphasis on status, while standing over or behind someone signals your greater power or status. Because women and people from some races or ethnicities may not be as tall as the average white male in the United States, and because people in wheelchairs interact at a shorter height, your relative height is a factor worth considering in professional interactions. If you are taller than others or are standing when others are sitting, they may see you as an authority figure or higher-status individual, even if you do not wish to appear as one.[67]

Personal Space and Distance

The distance we put between ourselves and others also reflects feelings and attitudes and, in turn, affects communication. Anthropologist Edward Hall identified four distance zones that middle-class Americans use: intimate (ranging from physical contact to about 18 inches), casual–personal (18 inches to 4 feet), social–consultative (4 to 12 feet), and public (12 feet and beyond).[68]

In some cases, these distance zones do not apply at all—or at least the distances are not flexible enough to reflect the parties' attitudes. Dentists and barbers, for instance, work within intimate distance—and actual physical contact—yet the relationship between dentist and patient or barber and client may be rather impersonal.

In other cases, the distance that people put between themselves and others is much more significant. For example, distance can reflect the attitude of the person who does the positioning. Research shows that a person who expects an unpleasant message or views the speaker as unfriendly takes a more distant position than does someone who expects good news or views the speaker as friendly.[69] An observant communicator, therefore, might use the distance others choose with respect to him or her as a clue about their feelings. ("I get the feeling you're worried about something, Harry. Is there anything wrong?")

Besides reflecting attitudes, distance creates feelings. In one study, subjects rated people who communicated at a greater distance as less friendly and understanding than those who positioned themselves closer.[70] Thus, an effective communicator will usually choose to operate at a casual–personal distance when establishing a friendly atmosphere is the goal. Closeness has its limits, of course. Intimate distance is rarely appropriate for business dealings.

Interpersonal distance is another nonverbal indicator of power. One unspoken cultural rule is that the person with higher status generally controls the degree of approach. As one psychologist puts it, "It is easy enough to picture an older person in this culture encouraging a younger business partner by patting him or her on the back; but it is very difficult to visualize this situation reversed; that is, with the younger person patting the older and more senior partner."[71] This principle of distance explains why subordinates rarely question the boss's right to drop into their work area without invitation but are reluctant to approach their superior's office even when told the door is open.

When a subordinate does wind up in a superior's office, both tension and distance show who is in charge. The less powerful person usually stands until invited to take a seat and, when given the choice, will be reluctant to sit close to the boss. Wise managers often try to minimize the inhibiting factor of this status gap by including a table or comfortable easy chairs in their offices so they can meet with subordinates on a more equal level.

Some managers try to promote informal communication by visiting employees in the employees' own offices. David Ogilvy, head of one of the largest advertising agencies in the country, says, "Do not summon people to your office—it frightens them. Instead, go to see them in *their* offices."[72]

Physical Environment   So far we have discussed how personal behavior sends nonverbal messages. The physical environment in which we operate also shapes how we communicate.

Consider the way space is allocated in a brick and mortar organization. Power locations become apparent when we look at the amount and location of existing space given to various employees and groups. In many organizations, for instance, an employee's status may be measured by whether their office is next to the boss's office or is in a dark alcove. An office with a window or an office on the corner often indicates higher status than an inside office with no window; moreover, any kind of office usually signals a higher status than a cubicle.

Another way in which environments shape communication is through proximity. The distance that separates people is perhaps the most important factor in shaping who talks with whom. Other things being equal, officemates will talk with one another more than with the people next door, and workers in the same area deal with one another more than with similarly employed people in another area. One researcher studied workers in research facilities, medical laboratories, and business schools. He found that the frequency with which a person spoke to colleagues was a direct function of the distance between their desks.[73] This sort of information can be useful on the job. You may be able to relocate your work to an area that will give you the interaction you want. If you are interested in making your bosses more aware of your work, it is important to be visible to them. Conversely, if you would just as soon be left alone, the old axiom, "Out of sight, out of mind" applies.

Furniture arrangement also influences the way people communicate. For example, in one study of a medical office, only 10% of the patients were "at ease" when conversing with a doctor seated behind a desk, but that proportion increased to 55% when the desk was removed.[74] Even when the location of furniture is fixed, choices about seating can influence interaction. Dominant, high-status persons often select the position at a table where they can see and be seen. This location allows them to engage in more interactions and to exert more influence over the interactions at the table. Not surprisingly, the person seated at the head of a table is more often perceived as a leader. Persons who want to diminish their potential for interaction and leadership often seat themselves in less visible spots along the sides of a table.[75]

Working remotely is becoming the norm in the business world. Unlike a traditional business environment that does not afford employees much sway over their assigned office location or furniture, working remotely allows for complete control of the workspace. In this work environment, organizational members interact from a variety of different locations, making the physical space surrounding each person more apparent.

When it comes to creating a professional remote workspace, it is important to designate an area that is free from clutter and distraction. While a funny Zoom photo background showing you sitting among stacks of toilet paper may be humorous among friends, it is likely not an appropriate choice when meeting with prospective clients. Additionally, meeting about a significant matter while sitting in your local coffee shop may not afford the privacy necessary for such a conversation.

When meeting remotely, a tidy and well-lit background that is free of clutter and noise is ideal. This does not mean that you have to spend a lot of money buying new furniture or renovating your home. Creating this environment can be as simple as moving your chair to the opposite side of your desk so the background is a wall instead of your bed, or repositioning your chair and computer to avoid the glare caused by a window. Clamp mounted selfie ring lights may be used to address issues with insufficient lighting, while noise-canceling headphones may filter out ambient sounds.

CAREER **tip**

Cubicle Etiquette

As the comic character Dilbert has shown, the world of daily life in a cubicle has its challenges. These tips can help you manage the communication dynamics of cubicle life.

Privacy

Treat others' cubicles as if they were private offices. Do not enter without verbal invitation or eye-contact permission—act as if the cubicle has a door. Never read other occupants' computer screens or borrow items from their desks just because you have access to them. Let others know when you are not available by hanging a "Do Not Disturb" sign or by avoiding eye contact. Resist the urge to shout out an answer to another cube-dweller's question just because you overheard it. Avoid popping up over the top of cubicles to talk to others; instead, walk over to the other person's cubicle or send an e-mail or instant message.

Remember, others can hear whatever you say in your own cubicle, so conduct meetings and personal conversations elsewhere. Keep conversations with your banker, family, doctor, and romantic partner out of the cubicle. Be polite enough to not listen to others' conversations, and certainly do not repeat anything overheard. Do not use speaker phone in a cubicle; it is rude to the person on the other end as well as to your colleagues.

Noise

Do not add to the noise of a cubicle farm. Keep your voice low. Set your phone ringer on low or vibrate, and turn it off when you are away from your desk. Do not let your mobile phone ring continuously when you are on another call. Use headphones when playing music.

Odors

Your favorite aroma, whether it is perfume or a scented candle, may be someone else's allergen, so think about its effect on others. When possible, eat in lunch areas and not at your desk, as your colleagues may not appreciate the odor of your food.

Children

In most organizations, children (especially if they are too young for school) are best kept away from work except on special occasions. No matter how well behaved, children may not be welcome or allowed by company policy into a shared cubicle.

Illness

Your determination to work when sick may be commendable, but you are not doing anyone any favors if you infect everyone else in the office. If you would not want someone in your state of health coming to work, try to stay away yourself.

Note: For more information, see Lockard, M. (2011, June 16). Cubicle etiquette: Sights, sounds and smells. *Forbes.* Retrieved from http://www.forbes.com/sites/work-in-progress/2011/06/16/cubicle-etiquette-sights-sounds-and-smells/; Smith, G. M. (2000). Cubicle etiquette. *Intercom, 47,* 10–11.

Time The way we use time sends a number of silent messages.[76] Many business advisors recommend that you be particularly scrupulous about your use of time during the first few months you are on the job:

> If . . . in that first ninety days, you're late or absent frequently, or seen as a clock watcher, you may earn yourself . . . negative scrutiny for a long time thereafter by your superiors. Rather than excusing any "infractions" of the rules, they'll be looking for slip-ups and a reason potentially to discharge you.[77]

As we discussed in the Customs and Behavior section in Chapter 2, there are differences in how members of various cultures value time. In monochronic cultures, speaking within the allotted time generally shows good planning and concern for the audience. Speaking longer inconveniences the listeners and communicates lack of regard for their schedules. In contrast, in some polychronic cultures, speaking only for the allotted time signals a lack of excitement or actual indifference toward the audience or the issue. Getting down to business quickly may be seen as a rude and insulting move on the part of a

potential business associate. In addition, in many polychronic cultures, the relationship is an important part of the business at hand. If the personal relationship is not established by taking time for dialogue and discussion, the business relationship will be at risk.

Improving Nonverbal Effectiveness

Now that you understand the elements of nonverbal communication, you can use the following guidelines to help achieve your professional goals.

Monitor Your Nonverbal Behavior   If you have ever asked yourself, "How am I doing?" you know something about **self-monitoring**—the process of paying close attention to your behavior and using these observations to shape the way you behave. Self-monitoring can be as simple as paying attention to the nonverbal feedback being communicated by the receiver(s) of your message and adjusting your communication accordingly. For example, if you notice a coworker glancing at her watch while you are running an idea past her at the end of the workday, you might conclude the conversation by telling your colleague, "I don't want to keep you—let's chat more about this tomorrow."

High self-monitors are good at knowing when to adapt their nonverbal behavior to suit the situation.[78] By contrast, low self-monitors do not recognize the negative impact of some of their behaviors. One study found that low self-monitors are blissfully ignorant of their shortcomings and more likely to overestimate their skill than are better communicators.[79] For example, experimental participants who scored in the lowest quartile on joke-telling skills were more likely than their funnier counterparts to grossly overestimate their sense of humor.

Self-monitoring is especially useful to ensure that you become integrated into the fabric of an organization. The results of one research study concluded that ostracized employees who rate high on self-monitoring are able to effectively use impression management tactics to increase their social acceptance over time.[80] While too much self-monitoring can make you overly self-conscious, keeping an eye on how you may look and sound to others is likely to enhance your image as a professional.

Demonstrate Interest in Others   The term **immediacy** describes verbal and nonverbal behaviors that indicate closeness and liking. Among these nonverbal cues are closer proximity (within social conventions, of course), more direct eye gaze, more forward lean, more relaxed posture, positive facial expression, and warmer vocal qualities.[81]

There is a strong link between high immediacy and career success.[82] For example, supervisors perceived as having high immediacy are regarded by their subordinates as more competent, credible, and attractive than less immediate bosses, and their subordinates are more cooperative. By contrast, low immediacy cues can be a put-off. Recall from your own experience how you reacted when you encountered someone with an unfriendly expression, a flat or hostile voice, and lack of animation.

Immediacy cues are especially important in the beginning stages of a relationship. First impressions have powerful implications, particularly when strangers do not have much other information available to form opinions of you. Even after you know someone well, immediacy may sometimes be especially important.[83]

With practice and self-monitoring, you can manage your nonverbal immediacy most effectively. You can begin by evaluating your current level of immediacy using the Self-Assessment inventory.

Observe Conventions   As described earlier in this book, some nonverbal conventions are cultural. For example, in northern Europe, you can expect to greet associates with a handshake; in contrast, in Mediterranean countries and Latin America, a hug and

Self-Assessment   Your Nonverbal Immediacy

Indicate in the space at the left of each item the degree to which you believe the statement applies to you, using the following five-point scale:

1 = Never

2 = Rarely

3 = Occasionally

4 = Often

5 = Very often

_____   1. I use my hands and arms to gesture while talking to people.

_____   2. I touch others on the shoulder or arm while talking to them.

_____   3. I use a monotone or dull voice while talking to people.

_____   4. I look over or away from others while talking to them.

_____   5. I move away from others when they touch me while we are talking.

_____   6. I have a relaxed body position when I talk to people.

_____   7. I frown while talking to people.

_____   8. I avoid eye contact while talking to people.

_____   9. I have a tense body position while talking to people.

_____   10. I sit close or stand close to people while talking with them.

_____   11. My voice is monotonous or dull when I talk to people.

_____   12. I use a variety of vocal expressions when I talk to people.

_____   13. I gesture when I talk to people.

_____   14. I am animated when I talk to people.

_____   15. I have a bland facial expression when I talk to people.

_____   16. I move closer to people when I talk to them.

_____   17. I look directly at people while talking to them.

_____   18. I am stiff when I talk to people.

_____   19. I have a lot of vocal variety when I talk to people.

_____   20. I avoid gesturing while I am talking to people.

even a ritual kiss or two might be more appropriate. Likewise, a non-Muslim Western woman traveling in an Islamic country probably would dress more conservatively and be more likely to wear a head covering than she would at home.

Some nonverbal conventions are just as strong within certain fields or organizations. The style of dress that personal trainers or website designers wear would look out of place at a meeting of investment bankers, and the way you would dress or act at a company

_____ 21. I lean toward people when I talk to them.

_____ 22. I maintain eye contact with people when I talk to them.

_____ 23. I try not to sit or stand close to people when I talk with them.

_____ 24. I lean away from people when I talk to them.

_____ 25. I smile when I talk to people.

_____ 26. I avoid touching people when I talk to them.

Scoring Procedure:

1. Start with a score of 78. Add to that the scores from the following items: 1, 2, 6, 10, 12, 13, 14, 16, 17, 19, 21, 22, and 25.

2. Add only the scores from the following items: 3, 4, 5, 7, 8, 9, 11, 15, 18, 20, 23, 24, and 26.

3. Subtract your total score in step 2 from your total score in step 1. This is your final score.

Scoring Norms:

Females	Mean = 96.7	S.D. = 16.1	High = > 112	Low = > 81
Males	Mean = 91.6	S.D. = 15.0	High = > 106	Low = > 77
Combined	Mean = 94.2	S.D. = 15.6	High = > 109	Low = > 79

When using this instrument, it is important to recognize that the difference in these self-reports between females and males is statistically significant and socially significant (that is, substantial variance in the scores on this instrument can be attributed to biological sex). Whether these differences are "real" (that is, females may actually be more nonverbally immediate than males) or a function of social desirability (that is, females think they should be more immediate than males think they should be) or of actual behavior has not yet been determined.

Source: Adapted from Richmond, V. P., McCroskey, J. C., & Johnson, A. D. (2003). Development of the nonverbal immediacy scale (NIS): Measures of self- and other-reported nonverbal immediacy. _Communication Quarterly_, 51, 505–517; McCroskey, J. C. (n.d.). Nonverbal Immediacy Scale: Observer report. Retrieved from http://www.jamescmccroskey.com/measures

picnic or weekend retreat would probably differ from the clothes you would wear or the way you would act back in the office on Monday morning.

In some cases, violating others' expectations can be effective, as long as your unexpected behavior is judged positively.[84] Dressing better and being more enthusiastic can generate positive reactions—as long as you do not overdo it to the extent that your violation is regarded as negative or phony.

review points

- Verbal messages are clearest when they use unequivocal and concrete language, with limited slang, jargon, and disfluencies. Strategically ambiguous messages are occasionally useful to promote harmony, soften difficult messages, and make a point indirectly.

- Avoiding inflammatory language (biased terms and trigger words that convey speaker attitudes and generate strong listener emotions) will help you be a better communicator, as will monitoring your own responses to others' inflammatory words.

- Use language to manage your professional identity by choosing the optimal degree of powerful language, using positive language, and limiting disfluencies.

- Masculine and feminine languages differ in some significant ways. Feminine language emphasizes rapport and relationships, while masculine speech focuses on reporting,

accomplishing tasks, and controlling situations. Overcome gender challenges by being aware of style differences and switching or combining communication styles to suit the situation.

- Nonverbal behavior is a part of every communication exchange. It is powerful, yet ambiguous; expresses attitudes more than ideas; and needs to be interpreted with caution because it affects career success and is culture-bound.

- Nonverbal messages can be expressed through the voice, appearance, face and eyes, posture and movement, personal space and distance, physical environment, and use of time.

- Achieve your workplace goals by monitoring your nonverbal behavior. Demonstrate interest in others through immediacy, and by observing and adapting to nonverbal cultural and organizational conventions.

key terms

biased language   96
disfluency   98
equivocal terms   91
genderlects   99
high-level abstractions   92
immediacy   113
jargon   94
low-level abstractions   92

nonverbal communication   102
paralanguage   104
rapport talk   99
relative words   93
report talk   99
self-monitoring   113
trigger words   97

activities

1. Skill Builder

Practice your skill at using unequivocal language by describing how each of the following sentences is likely to be misunderstood (or not understood at all). Then improve the clarity of each message by introducing your message with a high-level abstraction and qualifying it with low-level abstractions. To invent meaningful low-level abstractions, you will have to imagine a specific scenario.

a. You did a heck of a job on that proposal.
b. There are just a few small problems to clear up.
c. I just need a little more time to finish the job.
d. Your job performance hasn't been good this year.

2. Skill Builder

Practice clarifying your understanding of another person's ambiguous messages. For each of the following sentences, construct three polite, sincere questions you could ask the speaker to help clarify the meaning.

a. I need this report right away.
b. This presentation has to be perfect.
c. Whenever I leave to go to a meeting, nothing gets done in this office.
d. I'm on my own around here!

3. Invitation to Insight

Identify jargon in your own line of work, or interview a worker in a field that interests you and identify the jargon that they use. Then answer the following questions:

a. How does each term make communication more efficient?
b. What sorts of confusion might arise from the use of each term with certain listeners?
c. In cases where confusion or misunderstandings might arise, suggest alternative words or phrases that could convey the meaning more clearly.

4. Skill Builder

Develop strategically ambiguous ways to rephrase each of the following statements:

a. You have done a sloppy job here.
b. I cannot understand what you are trying to say in this letter.
c. Nobody likes your idea.
d. Would you hurry up and get to the point?

On the basis of your responses here, decide how honest strategically ambiguous statements are. If they are not completely honest, can they be considered ethical?

5. Invitation to Insight

Become more aware of your own emotional triggers by following these instructions:

a. In each category shown, identify two words that trigger positive reactions for you and two other words to which you react negatively:

   1. The label for a category of people (e.g., "fanatic")
   2. A rule, policy, or issue (e.g., "legalizing marijuana")

b. How do you react, both internally and observably, when you hear these terms? Consider the source of your reactions (the way you were raised? past experiences?). How might your reactions affect your communication?

c. Use the same categories to identify words that trigger positive and negative reactions in a coworker. What are the consequences of using these emotion-laden words with that person? Suggest neutral words you could use to replace the trigger words.

6. Invitation to Insight

Explore the characteristics of nonverbal communication as communicative, yet ambiguous.

a. Observe the nonverbal behaviors of a coworker. What interpretations do you attach to your observations? Describe an alternative interpretation for each nonverbal behavior you noticed. Speculate on which of your interpretations might be more accurate. Verify your perceptions by asking your coworker what the behavior means.
b. Ask a coworker to observe you during a meeting. After the meeting, have your coworker describe some of your nonverbal behaviors and speculate what meanings you intended. Did your coworker's perceptions match your intentions?

7. Skill Builder

Demonstrate the impact of nonverbal communication by describing effective and ineffective examples of behaviors in each of the following categories:

a. Voice
b. Dress
c. Face and eyes
d. Posture and movement
e. Personal space and use of distance

8. Skill Builder

Choose two countries that are likely to be a part of a specific career field or an organization you may work for. Find two or more gestures that have different meanings in those countries. Categorize the gestures into those that appear similar to a gesture in your culture but have a different meaning, those that appear unlike any gesture that would be recognized in your culture, and those that are very different from the gestures with the same meaning in your culture.

9. Skill Builder

For each of the following statements, indicate whether it is a less powerful or more powerful form of speech. If it is less powerful, indicate the type of speech it is. Then rewrite the statement, using the opposite type of speech.

a. Thank you so much.
b. You'd rather work late tonight, wouldn't you?
c. I'm not sure if this group will be OK with a new type of presentation, but I want to demonstrate it.
d. I think we need to update the color scheme in our ads.
e. I'm, uh, thinking that . . . well—we should hear the reports before we decide.

10. Invitation to Insight

Explore your present level of nonverbal effectiveness and consider how you might improve it.

a. Using the form that follows, identify an important business or professional context from your life (e.g., in meetings, with customers, on the phone). If you are not currently working, choose a context from school (e.g., in-class discussions, meeting with professors).
b. Using the information in this chapter, describe in the form given in this exercise both the aspects of your nonverbal behavior that are effective and those you could improve.
c. Interview someone who has seen you operate in the context you are analyzing (e.g., a colleague, supervisor, professor, fellow student). Using the Types of Nonverbal Communication section in this chapter, identify your behaviors. Consider the interviewee's opinion of your nonverbal communication in this context, and describe how you could communicate more effectively.
d. Based on the information you have compiled, develop an action plan that describes how you can improve your nonverbal effectiveness in the context you are analyzing.

WORKPLACE CONTEXT

	Effective Behaviors	Ineffective Behaviors	Suggestions for Improvement
Self-appraisal			
Self-appraisal			
Self-appraisal			
Self-appraisal			
Other's appraisal			
Other's appraisal			
Other's appraisal			
Other's appraisal			

Context _____

	Effective	Could Do Better (Describe How)
Self-appraisal		
Other's appraisal		
Action plan	1.	
	2.	
	etc.	

Mc Graw Hill LearnSmart™

For further review, go to the LearnSmart study module for this chapter.

references

1. Keysar, B., & Henly, A. S. (2003). Speakers' overestimation of their effectiveness. *Psychological Science, 13,* 207–212; Wyer, R. S., & Adaval, R. (2003). Message reception skills in social communication. In J. O. Greene & B. R. Burleson (Eds.), *Handbook of communication and social interaction skills.* Mahwah, NJ: Lawrence Erlbaum.

2. Bello, R. (2000). Determinants of equivocation. *Communication Research, 27,* 161–194.

3. Meyer, M., & Fleming, C. (1994, August 15). Silicon screenings: The marriage of Hollywood and Silicon Valley gets off to a rocky start. *Newsweek,* p. 63.

4. Miller, M. (1992, August 15). A clash of corporate cultures. *Los Angeles Times,* pp. A1, A8.

5. Armstrong, J. S. (1980). Unintelligible management research and academic prestige. *Interfaces, 10,* 80–86.

6. Eisenberg, E. M. (1984). Ambiguity as strategy in organizational communication. *Communication Monographs, 51,* 227–242.

7. Weiss, T. (1995). Translation in a borderless world. *Technical Communication Quarterly, 4,* 407–425.

8. Bavelas, J. B., Black, A., Chovil, N., & Mullett, J. (1990). *Equivocal communication.* Newbury Park, CA: Sage; Eisenberg, E. M., Goodall, H. L., Jr., & Tretheway, A. (2007). *Organizational communication: Balancing creativity and constraint* (6th ed.). New York: Bedford/St. Martin's.

9. Schneider, A. (2000, June 30). Why you can't trust letters of recommendation. *The Chronicle of Higher Education, 46,* pp. A14–A16. Retrieved from http://chronicle.com/article/Why-You-Can-t-Trust-Letters/2132; Conrad, C., & Poole, M. S. (2005). *Strategic organizational communication in a global economy* (6th ed.). Belmont, CA: Thomson Wadsworth.

10. Litigation-proof letters of recommendation. (n.d.). Retrieved from http://www.wildcowpublishing.com/other/letter.html

11. Rubin, R. (2003, May 1). Doctor-patient language gap isn't healthy. *USA Today,* p. 9D.

12. Jay, T., & Janschewitz, K. (2008). The pragmatics of swearing. *Journal of Politeness Research: Language, Behavior, Culture, 4,* 267–288.

13. *Reeves v. C. H. Robinson Worldwide, Inc.* (11th, 2010). Retrieved from http://www.ca11.uscourts.gov/opinions/ops/200710270op2.pdf

14. Johnson, D. I., & Lewis, N. (2010). Perceptions of swearing in the work setting: An expectancy violations theory perspective. *Communication Reports, 23,* 106–118.

15. Sutton, R. I. (2010, June 18). Is it sometimes useful to cuss when you are at work? The strategic use of swear words. *Psychology Today.* Retrieved from http://www.psychologytoday.com/blog/work-matters/201006/is-it-sometimes-useful-cuss-when-you-are-work

16. Bradac, J. J., Wiemann, J. M., & Schaefer, K. (1994). The language of control in interpersonal communication. In J. A. Daly & J. M. Wiemann (Eds.), *Strategic interpersonal communication.* Hillsdale, NJ: Erlbaum; Ng, S. H., & Bradac, J. J. (1993). *Power in language: Verbal communication and social influence.* Newbury Park, CA: Sage.

17. Hosman, L. A. (1989). The evaluative consequences of hedges, hesitations, and intensifiers: Powerful and powerless speech styles. *Human Communication Research, 15,* 383–406.

18. Tannen, D. (1995). *Talking from 9 to 5: Women and men in the workplace.* New York: Morrow.

19. Bradac, J. J. (1983). The language of lovers, flovers, and friends: Communicating in social and personal relationships. *Journal of Language and Social Psychology, 2,* 141–162.

20. Geddes, D. (1992). Sex roles in management: The impact of varying power of speech style on union members' perception of satisfaction and effectiveness. *Journal of Psychology, 126,* 589–607.

21. Hitchens, C. (2010, January 13). The other L-word. *Vanity Fair.* Retrieved from http://www.vanityfair.com/culture/features/2010/01/hitchens-like-201001

22. Dziedzic, S. (2011). 6 filler words that, like, won't get you hired, you know? *Brand-Yourself.com.* Retrieved from http://blog.brand-yourself.com/personal-brand/6-filler-words-that-wont-get-you-hired/

23. Tannen, D. (1990). *You just don't understand: Women and men in conversation.* New York: Morrow; Canary, D., & Emmers-Sommer, T. (1997). *Sex and gender differences in personal relationships.* New York: Guilford; Tannen, D. (1994). *Talking from 9 to 5: How women's and men's conversational styles affect who gets heard, who gets credit, and what get done at work.* New York: Morrow; Wood, J. T. (2011). *Gendered lives: Communication, gender, and culture* (9th ed.). Boston, MA: Cengage.

24. Brownlaw, S. Rosamond, J. A., & Parker, J. A. (2003). Gender-linked linguistic behavior in television interviews. *Sex Roles, 49,* 121–132.

25. Mulac, A. (1998). The gender-linked language effect: Do language differences really make a difference? In D. J. Canary & K. Dindia (Eds.), *Sex differences and similarities in communication* (pp. 127–155). Mahwah, NJ: Erlbaum; Mulac, A., Bradac, J. J., & Gibbons, P. (2001). Empirical support for the gender-as-culture hypothesis: An intercultural analysis of

male/ female language differences. *Human Communication Research, 27,* 121–152; Mulac, A., Bradac, J. J., & Palomares, N. (2003, May). *A general process model of the gender-linked language effect: Antecedents for and consequences of language used by men and women.* Paper presented at the meeting of the International Communication Association, San Diego, CA.; Mulac, A., Wiemann, J. M., Widenmann, S. J., & Gibson, T. W. (1988). Male/ female language differences and effects in same-sex and mixed sex dyads: The gender-linked language effect. *Communication Monographs, 55,* 315–335.

26. Tannen, D. (1994). *Talking from 9 to 5: How women's and men's conversational styles affect who gets heard, who gets credit, and what gets done at work.* New York: Morrow.

27. Mullany, L. (2007). *Gendered discourse in the professional workplace.* Houndmills, UK: Palgrave Macmillan.

28. Geddes, D. (1992). Sex roles in management: The impact of varying power of speech style on union members' perception of satisfaction and effectiveness. *Journal of Psychology, 126,* 589–607.

29. Clevenger, T., Jr. (1991). Can one not communicate? A conflict of models. *Communication Studies, 42,* 340–353.

30. Kalman, Y. M., Ravid, G., Raban, D. R., & Rafaeli, S. (2006). Pauses and response latencies: A chronemic analysis of asynchronous CMC. *Journal of Computer-Mediated Communication, 12,* 1–23.

31. McCoy, L. (1996, September/October). First impressions. *Canadian Banker,* p. 32–36.

32. Stiff, J. B., Hale, J. L., Garlick, R., & Rogan, R. G. (1990). Effect of cue incongruence and social normative influences on individual judgments of honesty and deceit. *Southern Speech Communication Journal, 55,* 206–229.

33. Friedman, H. S. (2001). Paradoxes of nonverbal detection, expression, and responding: Points to ponder. In J. A. Hall & F. J. Bernieri (Eds.), *Interpersonal sensitivity: Theory and measurement.* Mahwah, NJ: Erlbaum.

34. Byron, K., Terranova, S., & Nowicki, S. (2007). Nonverbal emotion recognition and salespersons: Linking ability to perceived and actual success. *Journal of Applied Social Psychology, 37,* 2600–2619.

35. Baron, R. A., & Markman, G. D. (2003). Beyond social capital: The role of entrepreneurs' social competence in their financial success. *Journal of Business Venturing, 18,* 41–60.

36. Byron, K. (2007). Male and female managers' ability to read emotions: Relationships with supervisor's performance ratings and subordinates' satisfaction ratings. *Journal of Occupational and Organizational Psychology, 80,* 713–733.

37. Ekman, P. (1973). Cross-cultural studies of facial expression. In P. Ekman (Ed.), *Darwin and facial expression.* New York: Academic Press.

38. Sussman, N., & Rosenfeld, H. (1982). Influence of culture, language and sex on conversational distance. *Journal of Personality and Social Psychology, 42,* 67–74.

39. Ambady, N., LaPlante, D., Nguyen, T., Rosenthal, R., Chaumeton, N., & Levinson, W. (2002). Surgeons' tone of voice: A clue to malpractice history. *Surgery, 132,* 5–9.

40. NPR. (2015, July 23). From upspeak to vocal fry: Are we "policing" young women's voices? *Fresh Air,* NPR. Retrieved from http://www.npr.org/2015/07/23 /425608745/from-upspeak-to-vocal-fry-are-we -policing-young-womens-voices

41. Wolk, L., Abdelli-Beruh, N. B., & Slavin, D. (2012). Habitual use of vocal fry in young adult female speakers. *Journal of Voice, 26*(3), 111–116.

42. Yuasa, I. P. (2010) Creaky voice: A new feminine voice quality for young urban-oriented upwardly mobile American women? *American Speech, 85*(3), 315–337.

43. Anderson, R. C., Klofstad, C. A., Mayew, W. J., & Venkatachalam, M. (2014). Vocal fry may undermine the success of young women in the labor market. *PLoS ONE 9*(5): e97506.

44. Word up. (2001, September 21). *The Guardian.*

45. Burgoon, J. K., Birk, T., & Pfau, M. (1990). Nonverbal behaviors, persuasion, and credibility. *Human Communication Research, 17,* 140–169.

46. Rothwell, J. D. (1998). *In mixed company* (3rd ed.). Ft. Worth, TX: Harcourt Brace Jovanovich.

47. Roan, S. (1990, December 18). Overweight and under pressure. *Los Angeles Times,* pp. E1, E4.

48. Philip Condit, CEO, Boeing/McDonnell Douglas: A true listening leader. (1997, November 24). *Listening Leader.* Retrieved from http://www.listencoach.com /SiteFrameSet.html

49. Matthews, J. (1994, January 31). In offices across America, attire is changing. *Washington Post,* p. 26.

50. Overmyer, S. (2019, August 20). How a casual dress code can help attract top talent. *Indeed.* Retrieved from https://www.indeed.com/lead/casual-dress-in -workplace

51. Overmyer, S. (2019, August 20). How a casual dress code can help attract top talent. *Indeed.* Retrieved from https://www.indeed.com/lead/casual-dress-in -workplace

52. Bhojwani, J. (2019, March 9). Not just fridays: More companies embrace casual dress codes. *NPR.* Retrieved from https://www.npr.org/2019/03/09 /701070560/not-just-fridays-more-companies-embrace -casual-dress-codes

53. Laabs, J. H. (2000). Mixing business with passion. *Workforce, 79*(3), 80–85.

54. Amiel, I. (1999). A nationwide survey on business casual conducted by a team of AICI professionals. *Association of Image Consultants International.* Retrieved from http://www.aici.org/dec99p5.html

55. Bhojwani, J. (2019, March 9). Not just fridays: More companies embrace casual dress codes. *NPR.* Retrieved from https://www.npr.org/2019/03/09/701070560/not-just-fridays-more-companies-embrace-casual-dress-codes

56. Marchetti, M. (2003, May 1). Barbarians at the buffet. *Successful Meetings.*

57. Smith, A. (2020, September 29). Dress-code policies reconsidered in the pandemic. *SHRM.* Retrieved from https://www.shrm.org/resourcesandtools/legal-and-compliance/employment-law/pages/coronavirus-dress-code-policies.aspx

58. Zandan, N. & Lnych, H. (2020, June 18). Dress for the (remote) job you want. *Harvard Business Review.* Retrieved from https://hbr.org/2020/06/dress-for-the-remote-job-you-want

59. Smith, A. (2020, September 29). Dress-code policies reconsidered in the pandemic. *SHRM.* Retrieved from https://www.shrm.org/resourcesandtools/legal-and-compliance/employment-law/pages/coronavirus-dress-code-policies.aspx

60. Lorenz, K. (2007, August 24). Too much skin: 10 taboos for office attire. *CareerBuilder.com.* Retrieved from http://www.careerbuilder.com/Article/CB-666-The-Workplace-Too-Much-Skin-10-Taboos-for-Office-Attire/?pf=true

61. Glick, P., Larsen, S., Johnson, C., & Branstiter, H. (2005). Evaluations of sexy women in low- and high-status jobs. *Psychology of Women Quarterly, 29,* 389–395; Wookey, M. L., Graves, N. A., & Butler, J. C. (2009). Effects of a sexy appearance on perceived competence of women. *Journal of Social Psychology, 149,* 116–118.

62. Wells, W., & Siegel, B. (1961). Stereotyped somatotypes. *Psychological Reports, 8,* 1175–1178.

63. Reitman, V. (1999, February 22). Learning to grin—and bear it. *Los Angeles Times*, p. A1.

64. Hunter, B. (1982, March 8). Are you ready to face *60 Minutes? Industry Week*, p. 74.

65. Memos. (1982, January 11). *Industry Week*, p. 11.

66. Mehrabian, A. (1980). *Silent messages: Implicit communication of emotions and attitudes* (2nd ed.). Belmont, CA: Wadsworth.

67. Borisoff, D., & Merrill, L. (1992). *The power to communicate: Gender differences as barriers* (2nd ed.). Prospect Heights, IL: Waveland Press.

68. Hall, E. (1969). *The hidden dimension.* New York: Doubleday.

69. Knapp, M. L., & Hall, J. A. (1992). *Nonverbal behavior in human interaction* (3rd ed.). Ft. Worth, TX: Harcourt Brace Jovanovich.

70. Knapp, M. L., & Hall, J. A. (1992). *Nonverbal behavior in human interaction* (3rd ed.). Ft. Worth, TX: Harcourt Brace Jovanovich.

71. Mehrabian, A. (1980). *Silent messages: Implicit communication of emotions and attitudes* (2nd ed.). Belmont, CA: Wadsworth.

72. Ogilvy, D. (1968). *Principles of management.* New York: Ogilvy & Mather.

73. Allen, T. (1969, November). Meeting the technical information needs of research and development projects. M.I.T. Industrial Liaison Program Report No. 13-314, Cambridge, MA.

74. Manning, P. (1965). *Office design: A study of environment.* Liverpool, UK: Pilkington Research Unit.

75. Andersen, P. A., & Bowman, L. L. (1999). Positions of power: Nonverbal influence in organizational communication. In L. K. Guerrero, J. A. DeVito, & M. L. Hecht (Eds.), *The nonverbal communication reader: Classic and contemporary readings* (2nd ed.). Prospect Heights, IL: Waveland Press.

76. McGrath, J. E., & Kelly, J. R. (1989). *Time and human interaction.* New York: Guilford; Ballard, D. I., & Seibold, D. R. (2000). Time orientation and temporal variation across work groups: Implications for group and organizational communication. *Western Journal of Communication, 64,* 218–242.

77. Are you really ready to change jobs? (1986, September 28). *Fall Job Market, Washington Post* [advertising supplement], p. 22.

78. Hamachek, D. E. (1987). *Encounters with the self* (2nd ed.). Ft. Worth, TX: Holt, Rinehart and Winston; Daly, J. A., Vangelisti, A. L., & Daughton, S. M. (1987). The nature and correlates of conversational sensitivity. *Human Communication Research, 14,* 167–202.

79. Dunning, D. A., & Kruger, J. (1999). Unskilled and unaware of it: How difficulties in recognizing one's own incompetence lead to inflated self-assessments. *Journal of Personality and Social Psychology, 77,* 1121–1134.

80. Wu, C. H., Kwan, H. K., Liu, J., & Lee, C. (2015). Regain acceptance from being ostracized: Effects of impression management and self-monitoring. *Academy of Management Proceedings, 2015*(1), 10962.

81. Mehrabian, A. (1972). *Nonverbal communication.* Chicago, IL: Aldine/Atherton.

82. Research summarized by Richmond, V. P., & McCroskey, J. C. (2004). *Nonverbal behavior in interpersonal relations* (5th ed.). Boston, MA: Allyn & Bacon.

83. Friedman, H. S., Riggio, R. E., & Casella, D. F. (1988). Nonverbal skill, personal charisma, and initial attraction. *Personality & Social Psychology Bulletin, 14,* 203–211.

84. Griffin, E. (2012). *A first look at communication theory* (8th ed.). New York: McGraw Hill.

Chapter Five
Interpersonal Skills and Success

chapter objectives

After studying this chapter you should be able to:

1. List important guidelines for giving effective praise, raising difficult issues, and offering and responding to criticism in a nondefensive manner.

2. Explain communication behaviors that exacerbate and alleviate workplace incivility and bullying.

3. Predict the outcomes of various verbal and nonverbal behaviors with regard to sexual harassment, and explain communication options for targets of harassment.

4. Identify coworker behaviors that may signal the use of peer-influence exit tactics, and explain how the recognition of such behaviors may be used to improve work performance.

5. Identify and give examples of key issues that underlie workplace conflicts.

6. Identify five approaches to conflicts, explain the advantages and disadvantages of each in specific situations, and predict likely consequences of each style in those situations.

7. Demonstrate how to plan for and conduct a work-related negotiation.

• Interpersonal Skills and Success

What does it take to succeed in your career? Talent, solid ideas, a good education, technical expertise, skills, hard work, motivation, initiative—all of these factors are important. In addition, because all jobs require you to get things done with other people—coworkers, customers, managers, people in other companies—your career success depends on your ability to build positive relationships, affirm others' dignity, and contribute to a positive organizational climate.

Building Positive Relationships

The importance of communication skills in a career cannot be overstated. In one survey, millennial employees were asked what they look for in a full-time job. The key findings of this survey overwhelmingly demonstrate the importance of **interpersonal communication** in today's workforce[1]:

- Millennials want to know why their organization or boss is having them do something.

- They expect their opinions to be heard and valued at work.

- They want to have primarily professional, friendly, and open communication with their supervisors.

- They want to feel comfortable asking their supervisors questions and talking to them about projects.

- They expect timely feedback from their supervisors that is communicated nicely and with suggestions for how to improve.

- They desire a combination of professional and personal communication with coworkers that is mostly professional.

These survey results emphasize the importance of effective communication with supervisors; however, the ability to work well with others is an important skill for *all* employees. Researchers have coined the terms **emotional intelligence (EQ)** or **social intelligence** to describe the ability and skills of interacting well with others.[2] One's intelligence quotient (IQ), actually takes a backseat to social intelligence in determining outstanding job performance.[3] Around the world and across the job spectrum, from copier repair technicians to scientists, IQ accounts for no more than 25% of entrepreneurial failure and success. The more difficult the job and the higher it is in an organization's hierarchy, the more important social intelligence becomes.

The majority of communication in the workplace occurs between peer coworkers,[4] and the quality of these relationships often has more influence on job satisfaction than the quality of supervisor–subordinate communication.[5] Research has shown that supportive peer coworker relationships can improve feelings of belonging[6] and commitment to the organization[7] and may help employees understand their job roles[8] and deal with stressful experiences.[9] Additionally, at least one team of researchers concluded that employees perform better on group tasks when they collaborate with persons they consider to be friends.[10]

On the other hand, work stressors related to organizational culture and poor interpersonal relations pose significant threats to the mental and physical health of workers.[11] Negative social interactions at work may cause stress and job dissatisfaction,[12] as well as medically diagnosed depression.[13]

Working from home or a remote location creates additional challenges for building positive relationships with colleagues. Remote employees may have fewer daily interactions than those in the office, which could lead to feelings of isolation from co-workers, bosses, and the workplace community. For example, one researcher found that both on-site and remote employees benefit from supervisors' engagement; however, the limitations posed by physical distance lead to remote workers feeling that they have fewer developmental opportunities available to them and fewer chances to present their ideas and opinions.[14] Tips for building effective workplace relationships can be found in the Career Tip callout box in this chapter.

Caiaimage/Paul Bradbury/OJO+/Getty Images RF

Affirming Dignity

A major ingredient of social intelligence involves showing respect to others. If you ask people to describe a bad communication experience at work, chances are they will tell you stories about being ignored, offended, belittled, and disrespected. Likewise, when you ask about positive experiences, you probably will hear

Building Positive Workplace Relationships

Building strong relationships is important for work satisfaction and productivity. Use the following guidelines to improve your relationships with coworkers, managers, customers, and other work partners:

- *Communicate often.* This can be as simple as stopping by a co-worker's office to say hello each afternoon or greeting a customer that you see regularly. In a remote work environment, this might include setting up a virtual gathering using a program like Zoom, Slack, or Microsoft Teams.

- *Adapt to each other's needs.* Ask about the person's preferred method of communication and share

your preferences. As discussed in Chapter 2, **generational differences** may impact the way one communicates in the workplace. Perhaps a Baby Boomer prefers e-mail or face-to-face communication, while a GenXer prefers text messaging. Adapting to these preferences may result in more frequent and satisfying communication for both parties.

- *Build rapport.* Utilize a few moments of rapport talk, as discussed in the **Feminine and Masculine Language** Use section of Chapter 4, at the beginning of phone or e-mail conversations to help you get to know someone and create a sense of caring. A simple question asking about their day or referring to a previous conversation can go a long way in developing a relationship.

---

about people feeling appreciated and respected—even in difficult situations.[15] The term **workplace dignity** refers to a person's ability to gain a sense of self-respect and self-esteem from their job and to be treated respectfully by others.[16]

In addition to enhancing self-esteem and self-respect, dignity creates conditions in the workplace that improve the bottom line, including increased job satisfaction, self-confidence, and work efforts.[17] By contrast, the effects of reduced dignity can be disastrous for both employees and organizations. For example, one study found that LGBTQ employees engage in strategic behaviors to avoid the potential for dignity threats. These behaviors include seeking safe work environments and attempting to pass as heterosexual or remaining closeted at work.[18] As one might infer from this example, employees facing dignity threats suffer both emotionally (increased stress, anxiety, depression) and physically (headaches, ulcers, increased blood pressure) in such circumstances.[19] Along with the individual damage, disregard for dignity costs organizations through decreased productivity, higher turnover and absenteeism, employee resistance and sabotage, and even increased risks of lawsuits.[20]

Workplace dignity arises from three kinds of communication: respectful interaction, recognition of competence and contribution, and messages that communicate equality and being valued as a unique individual within an organization.[21] This chapter focuses on communication skills and strategies that can be used to handle difficult messages while respecting and enhancing each person's dignity.

Enhancing Organizational Climate

The quality of communication in an organization affects the way people feel about their work and about one another. The term **organizational climate** describes the underlying nature of relationships in work groups. The weather metaphor is apt: Workplace climates can range from comfortable and pleasant to cold and stormy. Each organization has its own overall climate, which can be either healthy or polluted. Within that larger environment, small workgroups can then have their own microclimates. For example, your interactions with one team might be described as chilly, while you might enjoy a warm relationship with another group.

The climate of an organization results less from the specific tasks that members perform, and more from the feelings that they have about those tasks and one another. In fact, a positive climate can exist under the worst working conditions: in a cramped and understaffed office, during the graveyard shift in a factory, or even in a road gang cleaning up trash by the highway. Conversely, the most comfortable, prestigious settings can be polluted by a hostile climate.

An organization is a system and, as such, each of its members is interdependent. Because we rely upon each other to complete tasks, changes in our attitudes can impact the attitudes of others and the overall organizational climate. One factor that may impact our attitudes about the workplace is our perceptions of **work–life balance**, or the extent that an organization supports the harmony between its employees' work and personal lives. A lack of perceived work–life balance can lead to feelings of burnout, as well as mental and physical ailments.[22] In a survey of over 7,900 American surgeons, only 36% felt their work schedules left enough time for personal and family life. Of those surveyed, 40% met the criteria for being burned out, and a majority of those who felt burned out screened positive for symptoms of depression.[23]

Work-life balance lines may be especially blurred while working remotely or from home, as technology keeps us connected to our jobs 24/7, and family members may be physically present in (or even sharing) our workspaces. While a perfect balance between work and family roles may not be achieved or even ideal at times, employees' mental health is important. One research study of workers in China and Finland found that exhausted employees failed to achieve work–life balance, which then leads to burnout and a lack of engagement with their organizations.[24]

Conversely, when you feel good about your tasks, your coworkers, and the role of work in your life you help create a positive organizational climate. As suggested by the aforementioned research studies, organizational climates have a powerful effect on performance. They have been linked to productivity, job satisfaction, and employees' willingness to express dissent.[25] Climates are important in almost every kind of business and professional setting. For example, positive climates enhance job-related learning in sales organizations,[26] the ability of advertising agencies to win awards,[27] patients' trust in their doctors,[28] and entrepreneurs' passion for inventing.[29]

The remainder of this chapter introduces communication skills and practices that can help create and enhance positive organizational climates as well as help you achieve your personal goals on the job.

• Sharing Feedback

Some types of feedback are a pleasure, whereas other messages are necessary but tough to deliver. Whether feedback is pleasant or difficult, the guidelines provided in this section can help you communicate in ways that get the job done respectfully.

Giving Praise

There is truth to the old saying, "You can catch more flies with honey than with vinegar." Sincere praise, delivered skillfully, can work wonders. The following tips can help you make sure the praise you dole out gets the desired results.

Praise Promptly   The more quickly you can provide positive feedback, the more meaningful it will be. It does not take much time to praise positive behavior, and the results will most likely be well worth the investment.

The Zappos "Holacracy"

Zappos, an online-based shoe and clothing shop, is well known for its unique organizational climate. Former CEO Tony Hsieh (pronounced "Shay") operated his company as a *holacracy*. This style of governance is based on individual autonomy, such that everyone has an equal say and employees are evaluated and rewarded by their peers. The following list highlights a few of the unique characteristics that make Zappos a "fun and weird" place to work:

- The company operates based on 10 core values, most notably "deliver WOW through service" and "create fun and a little weirdness." Every employee learns these values and is expected to act on them.

- A "cultural fit interview" is conducted with prospective employees and is given 50% of the weight in hiring decisions.

- Everyone who is hired (including company lawyers) goes through the same four-week training as the call center representatives. During the training experience, new employees take calls from customers for two weeks.

- At the end of the training, Zappos employees are offered pay for the time they spent training, as well as extra pay if they wish to leave the company. The purpose is to eliminate employees who do not buy into the culture.

- Employees receive pay raises based on their performance on skills tests and other measurable actions.

- "Cultural assessments" are provided in lieu of performance evaluations. Employees are given feedback on their fit within the company culture as well as suggestions for improvement.

- Zappos sponsors several family events each year, as well as additional company events throughout the year.

Source: Heathfield, S. M. (2016, June 28). 20 ways Zappos reinforces its company culture. *The Balance*.

Make Praise Specific Almost any sincere praise will be appreciated, but describing exactly *what* you appreciate makes it easier for the other person to continue that behavior. Notice how the following specific compliments add clarity:

Broad	Specific
Good job on handling that complaint.	You really kept cool, calm, and collected when the customer complained.
I appreciate the support you have given me lately.	Thanks for being so flexible with my schedule while I was sick.
You have really been on top of your work lately.	You have finished every job this month within two days.

Of course, being specific does not mean you have to avoid making broad comments. Rather, along with giving general praise, consider the value of adding enough particulars to help the other person understand exactly what you appreciate.

Praise Progress, Not Just Perfection You might wonder whether some people do much of anything that deserves sincere praise. If you look for outstanding performance, the answer may be no. Even so, you can still deliver genuine compliments by looking for progress. Consider a few examples:

- "This draft of the report is a lot clearer. Adding a detailed budget really helps explain where the money will go. I think the same level of detail would help make the schedule clearer."
- "I know we still see things differently, but I'm glad we were able to work so well together on the Baretti job."

Praise Intermittently   Too much praise can sound insincere, and social scientists have discovered it is not as effective as occasional compliments. Praise others from time to time, when your remarks will have the best effect, but do not go overboard.

Relay Praise   If you already believe that complimenting someone sincerely can improve the communication climate in your relationship, wait until you see the benefits of singing that individual's praises to others who deserve to know. When you relay praise in this way, you win the gratitude of the person you are complimenting, but you also show your own sense of security and team spirit, and you share information that your audience will probably find valuable. Praising others takes little time, and it benefits everyone.

Similarly, you can become a "praise messenger" by letting people know you have heard others saying complimentary things about them. They will be more likely to continue the behavior, and they will feel better both about the person who praised them and about you for delivering the good news.

Praise Sincerely   Insincere praise is worse than no praise at all. It casts doubt on the validity of all your other compliments. It also suggests that you cannot think of anything the other person has done that deserves genuine acknowledgment. Finally, it insinuates that the recipient is naive enough to believe in your phony compliments.

As you consider when and how to give praise, it is important to be aware of the cultural rules that may influence both the person receiving compliments and the larger audience who hears those compliments. In some collectivist cultures, it can be embarrassing to be singled out for praise, especially in front of others. In such cases, giving private reinforcement is probably wiser than lavishing compliments publicly.

Go Social with Recognition   Many organizations view social media as a place to raise public awareness of their brands, but social media also represent an effective platform for praising employees and their accomplishments. Retweeting photos, news stories, or videos highlighting employees' successes are simple ways to show appreciation.

Raising Difficult Issues

It is not pleasant, but sometimes you must communicate about problematic behavior. For example, a colleague may not be doing their share of the job. Your manager may not have followed through on their promise to change working conditions. A supplier might be late on a promised delivery. The list of problematic behaviors can seem endless! Communicating about these kinds of issues can be difficult because your message may be perceived as an attack on the person whose behavior is causing a problem—and perceived attacks often trigger defensive responses.

Even the most experienced managers dread having conversations in which difficult issues are raised. One study of nurse managers revealed that they had feelings of "uneasiness, anger, frustration, churning in the stomach, feeling drained and stressed, lost sleep, and reduced self-confidence" when anticipating an upcoming conversation.[30]

Differing Cultural Expectations for Praise

Performance feedback norms differ across cultures. In Germany, for example, it is unusual to offer praise to employees. Employees are expected to do their jobs effectively and are praised only when they do something extraordinary. As one can imagine, this particular style of management may be demotivating or uninspiring for members of other cultures who expect positive reinforcement for a job well done.

The following tips may be used to adapt to performance feedback expectations when working in a multicultural environment:

- Learn the cultural norms for your geographic location.
- Ask your team what their desired preferences are for receiving feedback.
- Proactively discuss the feedback norms for your culture with your team.
- Adjust your feedback style in a way that is comfortable for you and accommodates the team.

Source: Molinsky, A. (2013, February 15). Giving feedback across cultures. *Harvard Business Review*.

More than 60 years ago, psychologist Jack Gibb identified six kinds of messages likely to evoke defensiveness, and six alternative approaches that boost the odds of achieving a more positive response (Table 5-1)—even when its subject means the message has the potential to be perceived as an attack.[31] As you read about these constructive approaches, imagine how you could use them when you need to raise a difficult issue on the job.

Use Descriptive "I" Language   Many communicators phrase their messages in a way that can be perceived as a direct attack on the other person. Statements worded in this way are often called **"you" language** because they point a verbal finger of accusation at the receiver:

1. "*Your* report is too sloppy. *You'll* have to clean it up."
2. "*You're* always late."
3. "That was a dumb promise *you* made. We can never have the job done by the end of the month."

Rather than focusing on the other person, you should instead use **descriptive statements** (often termed **"I" language**). "I" language is phrased in a way that focuses on the

Table 5-1	Defense-Reducing and Defense-Arousing Messages
Defense-Reducing	**Defense-Arousing**
Descriptive (Use "I" language)	Evaluative
Problem-oriented	Controlling
Honest	Manipulative
Concerned	Indifferent
Equal	Superior
Open-minded, provisional	Dogmatic, certain

speaker, instead of judging the other person. Notice how each of the evaluative statements given earlier can be rephrased using descriptive "I" language:

- *"I'll* get in big trouble if we turn in a report with this many errors. We'll get a better reaction if it's reworked."

- *"I've* made a lot of excuses when people call asking for you when you are running late. That's why *I* need you to start showing up on time."

- *"I'm* worried about the promise you made. *I* don't see how we can get the job done by the end of the month."

These kinds of statements show that it is possible to be nonjudgmental and still say what you want without landing any verbal punches. In fact, descriptive statements are actually *more* complete than typical everyday complaints because they express both the speaker's feelings and the reason for bringing up the matter—information that most evaluative remarks do not convey.

Focus on Solving Problems, Not Controlling Others

Even if you are in charge, others can become defensive if you force them to accept an idea they do not agree with or understand. If you are up against a tight deadline, it is easy to say, "Just do it my way." Because wielding power in this way shows a lack of regard for the other person's needs, interests, or opinions, it can cause problems in the relationship, even if it gets you what you want now.

In contrast, **problem-oriented messages** aim at solving both persons' needs. The goal is not to solve a problem either my way ("You need to purchase more advertising to increase our sales") or your way, but rather to develop a solution that meets everyone's needs ("I would like to work with you to find a solution for the recent drop in sales"). You will learn more about how to achieve problem-oriented solutions when we discuss win–win negotiating strategies in the section on Negotiation Strategies and Outcomes.

Be Honest: Do Not Manipulate

Once people discover they have been manipulated, a defensive reaction is almost guaranteed. As Roger Fisher and Scott Brown explain, "If one statement of mine in a hundred is false, you may choose not to rely on me at all. Unless you can develop a theory of when I am honest and when I am not, your discovery of a small dishonesty will cast doubt over everything I say and do."[32]

By contrast, simple honesty is less likely to generate defensiveness, even when the news shared is not welcome. Even though others may sometimes dislike what you have to say, your reputation for candor can earn you the respect of subordinates, coworkers, and management.

Show Concern for Others

Indifference—lack of acknowledgment or concern for others—is likely to trigger a defensive reaction. By contrast, a genuine message indicating interest can do wonders. The customer support agent who takes the time to find the right person to answer your questions can leave you feeling grateful and worthwhile, encouraging you to do business with that company again. The manager who seems genuinely concerned with your opinion—even if they do not agree with you—is easier to work with than one who brushes your concerns aside.

Demonstrate an Attitude of Equality

Neither talent nor job title justifies arrogance. Al Neuharth, founder of *USA Today*, earned a reputation as a tough, abrasive boss. Comments like the following one suggest why: "When I criticize a female or when I criticize a grossly overweight person or anybody else, it's because, damn it, I think they ought to do better, just as I do."[33]

Is Total Honesty Always the Best Policy?

In principle, few people would dispute the ethical principle that honesty is the best policy. At the same time, it is hard to imagine a world in which everyone told the whole truth all the time.

Explore how you can reconcile the need to be honest with other goals by listing all the opportunities you had to tell the truth during a typical day. Identify each occasion when you chose the following options:

1. Told even a partial lie (e.g., said, "Nothing's wrong," when you were bothered)
2. Hedged the truth by equivocating (e.g., said, "That's an interesting idea," instead of "I don't think that idea will work")
3. Kept quiet instead of volunteering the truth

Based on your self-analysis, construct a principled yet pragmatic code of ethics related to honesty.

The essence of a positive attitude is *respect*. Communication expert Kerry Patterson explains that respect is essential, just like the air we breathe: "If you take it away, it's all people can think about. At that point, the conversation is all about defending dignity."[34] Respect is often conveyed—or not conveyed—by how we construct messages. As an example, consider the difference between saying, "Could you get me the files?" and demanding, "Get me the files." As this example illustrates, *how* we speak and act can be more important than which words we use.

When expressing yourself, pay close attention not only to the words that you say, but also to your nonverbal behavior, including your vocal tone and facial expression. One group of researchers found that a sender's facial expression, when giving feedback to someone and looking directly at that person, affects the receiver's self-esteem.[35] For example, self-esteem will be reduced among employees who are greeted with an angry expression as opposed to a neutral or happy expression.

Keep an Open Mind   When raising difficult issues, it pays to approach the situation with an open mind. Be willing to hear what the other person has to say before reaching a conclusion. Hearing someone out may teach you something useful. Besides providing useful information, listening with an open mind can show respect and promote positive relationships.

Offering and Responding to Criticism

Criticism is a fact of life, especially in the workplace. Sometimes you have to deliver a complaint; at other times you are on the receiving end of others' gripes. Either way, criticism can start a cycle of defensiveness that pollutes the communication climate between people or working groups. Despite their risks, critical messages do not have to create problems. With enough skill, you can learn to both deliver and respond to them in ways that can maintain—or even improve—working relationships.

JUPITERIMAGES/Comstock Images/Alamy Stock Photo

Offering Constructive Feedback   Despite its fault-finding nature, criticism does not have to trigger a defensive reaction. The way you present criticism can make the difference between your comments being accepted and considered or being disputed and rejected.[36] You can maximize the chance of a good outcome by strategically choosing the best sender of the message, carefully framing your message, and paying attention to your delivery.

Who delivers the criticism can make a big difference in how the feedback is received. Follow these guidelines when you choose the sender:

- *Choose the most credible critic.* Sometimes the recipient will be more receptive to one person than to another. If a choice is available, make sure the message comes from whoever can deliver it most effectively.

- *Make sure the criticism is appropriate to the critic's role.* Even accurate criticism is likely to be rejected if you have no business delivering it. For example, most comments about someone's personal life are out of place unless they affect a working relationship. Job-related comments should be appropriate for your relationship to the other person.

Once you have chosen the appropriate sender, you can decide *how to frame* the message. This involves several considerations:

- *Limit the criticism to one topic.* You may have several complaints, but it is smart to focus on only one at a time. The respondent may be able to handle a single problem, but they could grow understandably defensive if you pile on one gripe after another.

- *Make sure the criticism is accurate.* Be absolutely sure you get the facts straight before voicing them to the recipient. If even a small detail is out of line, the other person may argue about that minor point, sidetracking the discussion from the real problem at hand.

- *Define the problem clearly.* List the facts in enough detail that the recipient knows exactly what you are talking about. Be prepared to give some examples to back up your point, but do not overwhelm the other person with an avalanche of examples.

- *Show how your criticism can benefit the recipient.* Whenever possible, describe the payoffs for responding to your remarks. At the very least, addressing your feedback will be a valuable learning opportunity.

- *Remember to acknowledge the positives.* Let the other person know that your specific criticism does not diminish your respect or appreciation for the person in other areas. Sincerely acknowledging the positives can make the negatives easier to accept. Taking an even-handed approach will also go a long way toward maintaining a positive relationship and preserving that person's dignity.

Finally, how you *deliver* criticism can make a big difference in the way it is received. The most effective feedback is delivered respectfully.[37] These guidelines can help you select your approach:

- *Deliver feedback privately.* Criticizing someone in front of others is likely to trigger embarrassment and resentment.

- *Allow enough time.* Waiting until the problem turns into a full-blown crisis can be a recipe for disaster. It is far better to discuss the problem in depth when there is plenty of time to remedy it before things boil over.

- *Avoid sounding and looking judgmental.* Avoid using emotive language: Don't call someone names or use inflammatory labels, and don't attribute motives to the other person. Instead, try to use the kind of descriptive "I" language described earlier in this chapter instead of defense-arousing "you" statements. Avoid condescending nonverbal behaviors such as shaking your finger, raising your voice, or rolling your eyes.

- *Listen to the other person.* If you genuinely want to improve a performance problem, listening can be as important as talking. Ask what the recipient of the criticism views as the problem. You will make the other person feel appreciated, and you may be able to generate some creative ideas for improving performance.

- *Remain calm and professional.* Even when your criticism is delivered in a face-saving manner, the other person might respond in highly emotional ways—anything from cursing to crying. Even if such a reaction leaves you feeling angry or defensive, it is important to remain calm. If necessary, you may need to request that the conversation continue at a later time.

Responding to Criticism

When people are faced with criticism, the two most common responses are "fight" and "flight." Fighters react by counterattacking and blaming others: "I'm not the only one who's at fault here." Your own experience probably shows that fighting with your critics seldom persuades them to back down.

Most businesspeople are too mature to run away from a critic, but there are other ways of evading negative remarks. Sometimes you *can* physically avoid your critics—steering clear of their offices or not returning their phone calls, for example. Even when you cannot escape unpleasant remarks, you can mentally disengage by refusing to listen thoughtfully to the criticism. While keeping quiet can seem to work in the short run, it is seldom a satisfying way to deal with an ongoing relationship in which you are constantly under attack.

Since neither fighting nor fleeing is likely to satisfy your critics or help you understand legitimate criticism, you need alternative techniques that allow you to listen nondefensively without losing face. Fortunately, three such alternatives exist.

Seek More Information

Asking your critic to explain the problem gives you a constructive option that avoids either fighting or fleeing. By asking your critic for more information, you show that you take the criticism seriously, but you do not necessarily take the blame for the problem. There are several ways to seek more information:

- *Ask for examples or clarification.* "You've said I'm not presenting a good attitude to customers. Can you describe exactly what I'm doing?"

- *Guess about details of the criticism.* Even if the critic is not willing or able to offer specifics, you can guess: "Was it the way I spoke to Mr. Tyson when the bank sent back his check for insufficient funds?"

- *Paraphrase the critic.* "When you say I have a bad attitude toward customers, it sounds as if you think I'm not giving them the service they deserve."

- *Ask what the critic wants.* "How do you think I should behave differently around customers?"

It can be hard to listen sincerely when you are being criticized. Even so, it is easier to keep your cool if you realize that trying to understand the objections does not mean you have to agree with them—at least not at this point. You may find that making notes about your critic's comments can give you something to do besides defend yourself in the heat of the moment. In addition, this approach will show your critic that you take his or her comments seriously.

Agree with the Criticism   An obvious but often overlooked way of responding is to agree with the criticism. Although this approach might seem like a form of self-punishment, it can be extremely effective. There are three ways to agree with a critic:

- *Agree with the facts.* Sometimes you are confronted with facts that cannot be disputed. In these cases, your best approach is probably to fess up to the truth: "You're right. I *have* been late three times this week." Notice that agreeing with the facts does not mean you are accepting responsibility for every imaginable fault. In the case of being late to work, you might go on to point out that your recent lateness is a fluke in an otherwise spotless work record. Arguing with indisputable information is not likely to satisfy your critic, however, and it will probably make you look bad.

- *Agree with the critic's right to their own perception.* Sometimes you cannot honestly agree with the criticism. For example, a customer might unjustly accuse you of not caring about good service. After asking for more information to find out the basis of the criticism (a shipment did not arrive on time, for example), you can acknowledge how the other person might view you as being at fault: "I can understand why it might seem that I don't care about your needs. After all, you did tell me you absolutely had to have that shipment by last Friday, and I told you it would be there. I'd be mad, too, if I were you." Notice that agreeing with the perception does not require you to *accept* your critic's evaluation as accurate, although you might find that it really does have some merit. Instead, with this response, you acknowledge the other person's right to view the issue in a way that may differ from yours; you agree that you can see how this perception makes sense to the critic, whether or not you see it the same way.

- *Emphasize areas of common ground.* As much as possible, point out areas where you and the other person share the same point of view. For example:

Critic: The customers will never go for this idea.

Response: We *do* have to keep the customers satisfied. What if we test market the idea? If they hate it, of course I'll drop the suggestion.

Even when the criticism is extreme, you can probably find something in the other person's position to agree with:

Hysterical Critic: You're going to ruin the whole job!

Response: I know how important it is to you. (Then let the critic talk about the job's importance, reinforcing your agreement.)

Work for a Cooperative Solution   Once your critic believes you have understood their position and acknowledged at least some parts of it, they will be as ready as possible to hear your point of view. A few strategies can maximize the chances for a constructive solution[38]:

- *Ask for the chance to state your point of view.* If you push ahead and state your position before the critic is ready to listen, your words probably will not get through. It is far more productive to give your critic a thorough hearing, agree with whatever points you can, and then ask, "May I tell you my perspective?" Doing so does not guarantee you will get a respectful hearing, but it gives you the best chance of attaining this outcome.

- *Focus on finding a solution, not on finding fault.* Your own experience likely has taught you that playing the blame game rarely works. A far more productive approach is to focus on finding a solution that will work for both you and the critic by asking, "What would make this situation better?" or "How can we handle this situation in a way both of us can accept?"

A Professional Perspective

Josephine Christianti

Experienced Digital Marketer & Communications

E-Commerce in Indonesia and Southeast Asia

Jakarta, ID

Credit: Josephine Christianti

In 2018, I was offered the role as a Head of Seller Communication within my organization. In this role, I led a team of five people, most of whom were Millennials and Gen-Z. One of my responsibilities was to retain my team members. That might sound straightforward, but it can be challenging in a startup environment where employee turnover rates are high. To succeed in this role, I learned that interpersonal skill is crucial, especially in building positive relationships with peers and subordinates. I put a lot of effort into treating my team members with respect and valuing their opinions. With these efforts, I was able to build positive relationships and I lowered the turnover rate.

In a leadership role, I learned that my success was deeply intertwined with the success of my team. To ensure that my team members succeeded, I frequently gave feedback on their performance. However, giving *constructive* feedback can be challenging in countries like Indonesia that have a high-context culture. In such cultures, we do not explicitly give criticism, so I had to proceed cautiously.

One communication skill that helped me was descriptive "I" language. Utilizing "I" language enabled me to deliver feedback more effectively because it allowed the other person to share their opinion or perspective as well. I might say, "This is how I feel, but what is your perspective?" When feedback is effectively delivered, it motivates peers and subordinates instead of lowering their self-esteem or confidence.

• Dealing with Difficult People and Situations

So far in this chapter, we have described ways of creating respectful communication climates. Unfortunately, sometimes other people behave badly despite your best efforts. Everyone can tell stories about coworkers, bosses, and customers whose communication style made life unpleasant. Table 5-2 details some types of communication that surveys have found are especially irritable. You can probably recognize at least some of these behaviors in people with whom you have worked, and possibly even in yourself.

Now we will discuss different types of difficult behavior that you are likely to experience in a professional environment and offer strategies for dealing with these situations.

Table 5-2	Communication Traits of Unpleasant Coworkers

Busybody	**Unprofessional Behavior**
● Butts into conversations	● Gossips and bad-mouths others to a third party
● Butts into others' business	● Criticizes others
● Expresses opinions on matters that do not concern him/her	● Yells or screams
Controlling/Bossy	**Unprofessional Focus of Attention**
● Gives orders without having the proper authority	● Talks about personal problems at work
● Is condescending/talks down to others	● Brings personal problems to work
● Wants his/her own way	● Talks about non–work-related issues
Self-promoting	**Defensive and Judgmental**
● Competitive, wants to be number one	● Sees others as a threat to his/her job
● Tries to promote himself/herself	● Attacks others' behavior and judgments
● Is self-centered	● Critical rather than constructive
● Tries to make himself/herself look good	
	Distracting
	● Distracts others from work
	● Behaves in irritating ways

Source: Fritz, J. M. H. (2003). How do I dislike thee? Let me count the ways: Constructing impressions of troublesome others at work. *Management Communication Quarterly, 15*, 410–438.

Incivility

Incivility is the exchange of seemingly inconsequential, inconsiderate words and deeds that violate the conventional standards of workplace conduct.[39] The severity of incivility can range from insensitive (checking messages during a meeting) to blatantly rude (name-calling). As economic pressures mount and working conditions become more difficult, uncivil communication is on the rise.[40]

Sometimes incivility carries a tinge of aggression—for example, casually mocking or belittling others, spreading rumors, talking down, or excluding someone from a meeting. Incivility does not even have to be intentional to have an impact.[41] Small discourtesies like interrupting, not expressing thanks, showing up late, and failing to return phone calls can take a toll, especially over time.

Like most types of messages, what counts as uncivil communication depends more on the receiver's reaction than on the sender's intentions. Swearing can offend certain employees, even though it is an accepted part of the culture in some organizations. Humor is another example of how perceptions are more important than intentions. One employee described her boss's attempt at wit, which she perceived negatively:

> When I was out on disability due to a severely broken ankle, my supervisor wrote an obnoxious letter about my injury. He was trying to be funny, but it was very disrespectful. I guess some people got some laughs from it, but I didn't.[42]

As this example illustrates, in many cases the offenders and the targets have different amounts of power. Approximately 60% of the time, the offender has a higher job status than the target.[43] For example, bosses are more likely to interrupt their subordinates rather

The Costs of Incivility

On September 8, 2016, a truck driver complained that a human resources employee at the company in which he was employed made a racist comment about Mexicans. Shortly after he logged his complaint, he was reassigned from a long-distance route to a city route.

Imagine yourself as the truck driver's employer: *How might you handle this difficult issue?*

Ultimately, the truck driver filed a civil action lawsuit claiming that the route change was due to retaliation. The judge eventually dismissed the lawsuit because the employer was able to cite poor performance (being consistently late with his deliveries) as the reason for the driver's reassignment.

Source: *Marlow v. McClatchey*, No. 15-2147, SD TX, 2016.

than the reverse. Supervisors can use humor as a putdown without the same consequences that lower-level employees would face if the tables were turned. Moreover, if you are in charge, you can lose your temper in ways that might permanently sabotage the career of a subordinate. By comparison, uncivil communication between equals or from subordinates to superiors is likely to be subtle—withholding information, spreading rumors, or anonymously posting criticism online.

The culture of connectedness that has resulted from technical innovations has caused managers and employees to feel pressured to be constantly available via social media, e-mail, and text messaging. As a result, **multicommunicating (MC)**—managing multiple conversations at the same time—has quickly emerged as an uncivil behavior in the workplace.[44] It is not uncommon to see employees checking their phones during a physical or virtual meeting or speaking on the phone while responding to customers' inquiries on social media.

Across the various professions, there is a continuum of acceptable multicommunicating behavior. Most organizations fall somewhere in the middle of this continuum, with acceptance being largely dependent on the situation at hand.[45] Some organizations may encourage or even require multicommunicating. After all, this behavior can increase efficiency and productivity.[46] In other organizations, it may be considered unprofessional or rude to multicommunicate.[47] With this behavior comes an increased risk of misunderstanding or sending a message to someone other than the intended receiver, and an inability to keep the pace of one or more of the conversations.[48]

Cyber incivility—that is, rude or discourteous behaviors occurring through communication technologies such as e-mail, text messages, and social media—is also on the rise. These technologies lack nonverbal cues and participants can choose to be anonymous, which can lead to both intended and unintended messages being perceived as harmful by recipients.[49]

Cyber incivility can be quite damaging to employees, especially if their supervisors put them down or communicate in a condescending manner online. Research has found that employees who experience high levels of cyber incivility from their supervisors are more likely to miss work, experience burnout, and think about quitting their jobs more often.[50]

Workplace Bullying

Whereas incivility can be relatively mild and unintentional, **workplace bullying** is more intense, malicious, ongoing, and damaging.[51] Because of the intensity of this abuse, bullied employees are likely to leave the organization in an effort to avoid the constant aggression and humiliation.[52]

Bullying can come in several forms[53]:

- Aggression: Controlling through fear and intimidation, using aggressive language, making threats, and sometimes even throwing objects.

TECHNOLOGY **tip**

- Criticism: Nitpicking that destroys the target's confidence and competence by making unreasonable demands for work, such as setting impossible deadlines and expectations of perfection.

- Deviousness: Exhibiting passive–aggressive, dishonest, and indirect behavior; sabotaging victims behind their backs.

- Gatekeeping: Controlling the resources needed to succeed, including money, staffing, and time.

A study commissioned by the Workplace Bullying Institute found that 27% of adults surveyed had current or past direct experience with abusive conduct at work.[54] Although bullying occurs among peer coworkers, it more often takes place in supervisor–subordinate relationships. Bullies—especially those in positions of authority—tend to be effective at making their targets look bad to others. In turn, the target's appeals to management for help are often met with skepticism. (Is the complainer a troublemaker?) If higher-ups do not take the complaint seriously, the target is left isolated and silenced. In such cases, the bullying becomes an ongoing cycle, typically ending only after the target quits or is fired. This outcome rarely satisfies the bully, who typically moves on to a new victim.[55]

The digital age has also led to a form of workplace bullying known as cyberbullying. Cyberbullying is similar to traditional workplace bullying, but occurs via electronic devices and online communications such as text messaging, instant messaging, e-mail, social media, websites, and blogs. The prevalence of cyberbullying in the workplace is troublesome. In one study, 20% of respondents reported that they had been cyberbullied at least once per week.[56]

Cyberbullying behavior includes, but is not limited to, the following types of abuse:

- Malicious or threatening messages or posts
- Jokes about ethnicity, religion, sexual orientation, or other uncomfortable topics
- Public shaming
- Sharing embarrassing, offensive, or altered images or videos of an individual
- Spreading lies, rumors, and gossip

Cyberstalking, a more extreme form of cyberbullying, also occurs in the work environment. This form of stalking largely occurs when a prospective employee is not hired, or when an employee has been fired, has been laid off, or has an issue with management or coworkers.[57]

Strategies for Dealing with Incivility and Bullying   It is natural to feel helpless and victimized in a workplace characterized by incivility or bullying. But you do

Workplace Cyberbullying

In *Maldonado-Cátala v. Municipality of Naranjito* (D. P.R. 2015), an emergency medical technician who was employed by a municipality claimed that she was the victim of a hostile work environment after receiving threatening messages on Facebook from an office director.

One message sent at 9:46 p.m. called the employee several derogatory names and said, "I will see you fall you dirty lesbian and every one of you one by one [for] what you did to that man, the one from emergency management. . . . Remember that you have children. . . . By the way, the boy is gay and the girl is a lesbo."

The victim filed a police report, and the police traced the message to a computer in the municipality's emergency management office that only the director and the secretary could access. In court, the victim alleged that she was subjected to a gender-based hostile work environment. The court denied the municipality's request to resolve the lawsuit outside of a trial, ruling that the use of the derogatory names raised Title VII hostile work environment concerns.

How does the anonymity of social media platforms create complications for workplace cyberbullying cases?

Source: *Maldonado-Catala v. Municipality of Naranjito et al.,* No. 3:2013cv01561 · Document 126 (D.P.R. 2015).

---

have choices. Based on more than a decade of research, management professors Christine Pearson and Christine Porath provide several options.[58]

SpeedKingz/Shutterstock

- *Negotiate with the offender.* Even if you use the best communication practices, this can be a risky approach—especially if the other person has the power to affect the course of your career. Before you decide to take this step, it can be smart to conduct a risk-benefit analysis. Are you prepared to accept the worst outcome if things go badly? Do you have career options if the worst-case scenario comes to pass? If not, it may be wise to consider one or more of the other options outlined in this section. If you decide to approach the offender, consider whether you want to do so one-on-one, or whether a mediator might be able to help manage the meeting. Choose a neutral meeting place—perhaps a semi-public spot like a restaurant where bystanders' presence might moderate the other person's behavior. Review the strategies in this chapter, as well as the listening skills described in Chapter 3. Imagine how you could apply these approaches and, ideally, rehearse the meeting with a trusted partner who can play the role of the person you will be approaching.

- *Appeal to a third party.* If your risk-benefit analysis argues against speaking directly to the offender, a third party may be able to manage the situation in your best interests. This individual might be a coworker who can command the offender's attention and respect, or perhaps your boss. If your boss is the offender, your situation might be bad enough for you to take the unconventional step of going up the chain of command. Again, this approach has its risks. Your boss almost certainly will not appreciate the move, and it is possible the authority to whom you appeal might support the offender. For these reasons, be cautious when considering this high-risk approach.

- *Back off.* You may decide that retreating from the offender is the best approach. Some strategic options include communicating via phone or e-mail whenever possible rather than in person, working at different times and places (perhaps including from home if the job permits), or working with the offender's assistants or associates. It may even be necessary to back off from your workplace physically and emotionally until you can find a better situation. Avoid company social events, take the sick days and vacation time you have earned, and do not participate in committees that put you in uncomfortable settings. This is not a recommendation to do less than your best work, but rather a strategy for protecting yourself.

- *Reframe your thinking.* When you are the target of demeaning communication, it is easy to start believing you somehow deserve the abuse. In the world of business and the professions, though, there is no justification for bullying or consistently acting uncivil. Once you recognize this fact, it is clear that anyone who acts rudely or abusively is at fault for behaving badly.

    Despite this fact, you may feel like less of a victim if you recognize the ways you have contributed to the painful communication pattern. Perhaps you let uncivil behavior slide in an effort to get along. Or perhaps you accepted a job working with or for a bully when your gut feeling or other people warned you against doing so.

Sexual Harassment

Sexual harassment on the job has always existed, but in recent decades it has been identified as a problem significant enough to warrant legal prohibitions and penalties. The Civil Rights Act of 1964 and subsequent legislation and court decisions have identified two types of sexual harassment:

- **Quid pro quo**. (a Latin term meaning "this for that"). Examples of this form of harassment include directly or indirectly threatening not to promote someone who will not date you or implying employment depends on granting sexual favors.

- **Hostile work environment**. This category includes any verbal or nonverbal behavior that has the intention or effect of interfering with someone's work or creating an intimidating, offensive, or hostile environment. Unwelcome remarks ("babe," "hunk"), humor, stares ("elevator eyes"), hand or body signs, and invasions of physical space all can create a hostile work environment.

Of the two types of harassment, there is less confusion about blatant quid pro quo propositions, and most people agree on what constitutes blatant harassment.[59] By comparison, there is less agreement on which kinds of behavior create a hostile working environment. One person's harmless joke can be deeply offensive to someone else, and what seems like a sincere compliment to the person who offers it can sound like a come-on to the receiver.

Sexual harassment is not necessarily restricted to a single individual behaving inappropriately. It can be caused by an organizational culture that, intentionally or not, allows and even encourages perpetrators while dismissing the concerns of targets.[60]

Sexual harassment can occur in a variety of circumstances. It may arise among persons of the same or different gender identities. The harasser can be the target's supervisor, an agent of the employer, a supervisor in another area, or a coworker. Even behavior by nonemployees (e.g., customers or people from other organizations) can be grounds for a harassment claim. The target does not have to be the person harassed, but rather could be anyone affected by the offensive conduct. (Situations like this are termed *third-party harassment.*) Unlawful sexual harassment may occur without economic injury to or discharge of the target.[61]

Avoiding Sexual Harassment Problems   Beyond the normal precautions and courtesy, it is smart to be especially sensitive in situations in which others might take offense at your words or behaviors. Look at the situation from the other person's point of view. Could your language be considered offensive? Could your actions lead to discomfort? Read your company's sexual harassment policies carefully, know the Equal

Employment Opportunity Commission (EEOC) guidelines, and be familiar with any training and other information that human resources professionals at your organization provide. If you wonder whether a behavior might be construed as harassment, not engaging in it is probably the safest course of action.

If you have a position of power within your organization—for example, if you are a supervisor or work in human resources—you can play an even bigger role in avoiding sexual harassment problems. Strategies you can employ include implementing and monitoring policies that will not tolerate sexual harassment, providing training to all managers and workers, enlisting employees who are supportive of stopping harassment, and carefully examining day-to-day interactions to ensure that the organizational climate remains positive.[62]

Responding to Sexual Harassment   Most organizations have written policies prohibiting sexual harassment and reporting procedures that people can use when they believe they are being harassed. Options for reporting abuse may include hotlines and human resources representatives. If you believe you have been the target of harassment, make sure you understand the policies and resources available to you.

In addition to being protected by company policy, targets of sexual harassment are entitled to legal protection from such abuse. The EEOC, state and local agencies, and the court system all enforce civil rights regulations relating to harassment.

Despite the government's determination to protect employees, fighting sexual harassment through legal channels requires stamina on the target's part. The process can be time-consuming, and targets sometimes experience retaliation, psychological distress, and lowered job satisfaction.[63] For these reasons, taking care of harassment at the lowest, most informal level possible may solve the problem in a way that does not punish the target. Listed here are several options for managing harassment, in escalating order. They are not meant as a step-by-step guide for how to respond, but they can help you decide which options may best suit a given situation.

1. *Consider dismissing the incident.* This approach is appropriate only if the remark or behavior does not interfere with your ability to perform your job or does not cause high stress or anxiety. Pretending to dismiss incidents you believe are important can lead to repetition of the offensive behavior, self-blame, and diminished self-esteem.

2. *Keep a record of the incident for possible future action.* A record of what happened can be important if you later decide to pursue a grievance. Include the date and location where the incident occurred and create a detailed log of the problematic behavior and your reaction. Include the names of any observers. You can save this record in an e-mail to yourself or a trusted colleague.

3. *Write a personal letter to the harasser.* A written statement may help the harasser to understand which behavior you find offensive. Just as important, it can show you take the problem seriously. Put the letter in a sealed envelope (keep a copy for yourself). Use information from your log to detail specifics about what happened, which behavior you want stopped, and how you felt. You may want to include a copy of your organization's sexual harassment policy. Keep a record of when you delivered the letter. If you want to be certain that the delivery of the letter will be acknowledged, take a friend along when you present it or send it via certified mail.

4. *Ask a trusted third party to intervene.* Perhaps a mutual acquaintance can persuade the harasser to stop. The person you choose should be someone who understands your discomfort and supports your opinion. Be sure this intermediary is also someone who the harasser respects and trusts.

5. *Use company channels.* Report the situation to your supervisor, the human resources office, or a committee that has been set up to consider harassment complaints.

6. *File a legal complaint.* You may file a complaint with the federal EEOC or your state agency. You have the right to retain an attorney to explain and pursue your legal options. (See http://www.eeoc.gov for detailed explanations of this procedure.)

Problematic Communication

Most employees have at least a basic understanding of how to recognize when incivility, bullying, or sexual harassment is occurring in their work environment. In contrast, they may not be equally as adept at recognizing the influence that their coworkers have on their motivation to work for an organization.

A fascinating line of research has found that some employees intentionally communicate messages and behaviors for the purpose of influencing their peers to leave the organization.[64] These **peer-influence exit tactics** include the following steps:

- Criticizing the coworker's performance and competencies
- Advising the coworker to find an occupation more congruent with their personality or skill set
- Berating the company, other employees, or the job
- Speaking favorably of other careers and occupations, emphasizing the advantages of working elsewhere
- Politely advising coworkers to think about their situation in the workplace
- Providing messages about job openings
- Warning the coworker of the possible negative consequences of staying at the organization, such as layoffs
- Talking to the coworker about their personal views on life and how these views do not match the coworker's work experience or goals
- Persuading the coworker to leave immediately without thinking about the future
- Encouraging the coworker to leave by highlighting the advantages of doing so voluntarily, such as avoiding being fired
- Commending the coworker's positive qualities and telling them that these skills can be of great use in another organization
- Giving an ultimatum to change the coworker's behavior or risk being fired, or choose between resigning and being fired[65]

Research has shown that employees encourage their peers to leave the organization when they believe the coworker is difficult to work with or is a detriment to the workplace, when they wish to improve their own standing in the organization, and when they want to improve the work situation of the coworker.[66] Understanding these strategies and the motives for their use may help you recognize when you are a target of peer-influence exit tactics. In this situation, you may wish to evaluate your performance and relationship with colleagues by consulting veteran members of the organization about areas for improvement, or recognizing when these messages are being delivered for positive reasons, such as a genuine desire to see you excel in your career.

• Managing Conflict

Like it or not, conflict is part of every job. In one study, human resources managers reported spending as much as 60% of their time dealing with employee disputes, and more than half of workers said they lost time at work worrying about past confrontations or fretting about future conflicts.[67]

To most people, the fewer conflicts, the better. Since conflict is unavoidable, however, an inability or refusal to face problems can lead to job-hopping or feelings of intense stress. As we briefly explored earlier in this chapter, **job burnout**—a syndrome of physical, emotional, or mental exhaustion that is often caused by prolonged exposure to stressful situations[68]—can be a result of workplace conflict. Individuals who experience burnout may feel physically and mentally exhausted, perceive themselves as lacking personal accomplishments, and harbor negative attitudes toward their coworkers and supervisors.[69]

John Lund/Nevada Wier/Blend Images/Getty Images

The good news is that, with the right approach, conflict can produce good results and reduce burnout.[70] Management consultant and former Harvard Medical School psychologist Steven Berglos argues flatly that constructive conflict is an essential ingredient in organizational success:

> If you're not looking for ways to promote healthful conflict between people of different backgrounds who cannot possibly see the world the same way, don't be surprised if anarchy ensues or if the best and the brightest abandon you.[71]

Conflict is both a threat and an opportunity; what matters most is how the conflict is managed. A poorly handled organizational conflict can certainly be dangerous: Relationships may suffer, and productivity may decline. Conversely, a skillfully handled conflict can result in several benefits.[72] The incident can function as a safety valve, letting people vent frustrations that are blocking their effective functioning, and it can lead to a resolution for troublesome problems.

Causes of Conflict

There are at least five types of conflicts you may experience in a professional environment.[73]

The Topic at Hand   The most obvious source of conflict is the subject at hand. Topic-related disagreements are a fact of life in the workplace. They involve issues such as pay and other compensation, resources, scheduling and job assignments, level of autonomy, the quality of products and services, and budgeting.

The Process   Some disputes are about *how* to do something rather than *what* to do. For example:

- A project team might agree that the work at hand needs to be divided, but they could disagree on how to decide who does what.
- Members of a nonprofit group might decide to hold a fundraiser, but disagree on how to choose the type of event.

Relational Issues   Substantive content issues are just one source of conflict; *relational* disputes that center on how parties want to be treated by one another may also arise. Relational issues can involve affinity, control, and respect.

- Are we a big family, or are we a group of professionals who keep our personal lives separate from work? (affinity)
- Should the company allow employees to book their own hotels and flights on business trips as long as costs are within the organization's cost guidelines? (respect, control)

- Does management really welcome ideas from rank-and-file employees, or is the suggestion box just a prop? (respect, control)

Ego/Identity Issues

Researchers use the term *face* to describe the identity that each of us strives to present. In a work context, most people try to present a face of competence, honesty, commitment, reasonableness, fairness, and professionalism. Relationships thrive when others acknowledge our presenting face, whereas conflicts intensify when others communicate in ways that challenge our identities–a practice referred to as a *face-threat*.[74] When someone's face is threatened, it can add a whole new dimension to the dispute.

Privacy Issues

Concerns about privacy have always occurred in organizations. On an interpersonal level, employees have always been concerned about the consequences of sharing private information with coworkers. According to communication privacy management theory, once private information is shared with another party, the partner gains ownership of the information and may share it with whomever the partner wishes, even if the partner has been asked to keep it a secret. **Boundary turbulence** may be created in such a scenario either intentionally or unintentionally (as in the case of another coworker overhearing and sharing the private information).

Alternatively, boundary turbulence may occur due to a lack of preexisting rules for a situation. In a world filled with social media and other public platforms, perceptions of privacy invasion may readily become sources of conflict.[75] As organizations adapt to these technologies, issues such as access to text messages that are sent on employees' private phones while logged into the company's Wi-Fi network are emerging and causing concern among employees. These privacy concerns may cause employees to perceive the organization's monitoring policies as being unfair and to feel less committed to their organizations.[76]

The next section presents five types of conflict. Although these types are listed separately here, most disputes actually involve a combination of issues. When you deal with a conflict, it is important to explore all of the dimensions on which it operates.

Approaches to Conflict

When faced with a conflict, you have several choices about how to respond. Each of these approaches is likely to lead to different results.[77] While some researchers have touted controlling emotions and engaging in problem-solving as ways to manage conflict "professionally,"[78] new research suggests that this may hinder employees' ability to empathize and cope with the situation.[79] Organizational members draw on individual and organizational values and norms when managing conflict (especially in the case of coping with offensive behavior) and, thus, may cope differently or have different expectations for appropriate conflict management styles.[80] Regardless of the conflict management strategy you choose to enact, researchers suggest encouraging members of an organization to dialogue about possible coping responses and their individual approaches and expectations.[81]

Avoiding

One way to deal with conflict is to avoid it whenever possible and withdraw when confronted. In some cases, avoidance is physical such as refusing to take phone calls, staying barricaded in the office, and so on. In other cases, however, avoidance can be psychological such as denying that a problem exists or is serious, repressing emotional reactions, and so on. In the workplace, a communicator who avoids conflicts might accept constant schedule delays or poor-quality work from a supplier to avoid a confrontation or might pretend not to see a coworker's dishonest behavior. As these examples suggest, avoidance may have the short-term benefit of preventing a confrontation, but it usually carries long-term costs, especially in ongoing relationships. "I think it's better to face whatever the conflict is head on and deal with the situation as it comes up and not side-step it or go to someone else about the problem," advises Jean Stefani, a senior operations analyst at Comcast Communication.[82]

Despite its drawbacks, avoidance may sometimes be a wise choice. Table 5-3 lists some circumstances in which keeping quiet may be the most appropriate course of action.

Table 5-3	Factors Governing Choice of a Conflict Style

Consider Avoiding:

1. When an issue is genuinely trivial or when more important issues are pressing.
2. When you have no chance of winning.
3. When the potential for disruption outweighs the benefits of resolution.
4. To let others cool down and regain perspective.
5. When the long-term costs of winning may outweigh the short-term gains.
6. When others can resolve the conflict more effectively.

Consider Accommodating:

1. When you find you are wrong.
2. When the issue is important to the other party and not important to you.
3. To build social credits for later issues.
4. To minimize your losses when you are outmatched and losing.
5. When harmony and stability are more important than the subject at hand.
6. To allow others to learn by making their own mistakes.

Consider Competing:

1. When quick, decisive action is vital (e.g., in emergencies).
2. On important issues where unpopular actions need implementing (e.g., cost-cutting, enforcing unpopular rules).
3. When others will take advantage of your noncompetitive behavior.

Consider Collaborating:

1. To find solutions when both parties' concerns are too important to compromise.
2. When a long-term relationship between the parties is important.
3. To gain the commitment of all parties by building consensus.
4. When the other party is willing to take a collaborative approach.

Consider Compromising:

1. When goals are important but not worth the effort or not worth the potential disruption associated with more assertive modes of conflict resolution.
2. When opponents with equal power are committed to mutually exclusive goals.
3. To achieve temporary settlements of complex issues.
4. To arrive at expedient solutions under time pressure.
5. As a backup, when collaboration is unsuccessful.

Source: Thomas, K. W. (1987). Toward multi-dimensional values in teaching: The example of conflict behavior. *Academy of Management Review, 2*, 484–490.

For example, when standing up for your rights would be hopeless, silence might be the best policy. You might simply tolerate a superior's unreasonable demands while you look for a new job, or you might steer clear of an angry coworker who is out to get you. In many cases, however, avoidance has unacceptable costs: You lose self-respect, you become frustrated, and the problem may just get worse.

Accommodating

Whereas avoiders shy away from conflicts, accommodators give ground as a way of maintaining harmony. Accommodating can be an effective strategy in some circumstances (Table 5-3). If you realize that you are wrong, then giving up your original position can be a sign of strength, not weakness. If harmony is more important than the issue at hand—especially if the issue is minor—then accommodating is probably justified. For example, if you do not have a strong opinion about whether the new stationery is printed on cream or gray paper and fighting for one color might be a big concern for others, then giving in is probably smart. Finally, you might choose the accommodation strategy if satisfying the other person is important enough to your welfare. You might, for example, put up with an overly demanding customer to make an important sale.

Accommodating is not always an effective strategy. In some circumstances, it can be equivalent to appeasement, sacrificing your principles, and putting harmony above dealing with important issues. When safety or legality is the issue, accommodating can be downright dangerous.

Competing

A competitive approach to conflict is based on the assumption that the only way for one party to reach its goals is to beat the other party. This zero-sum approach is common in many negotiations, as you will see in the Negotiation Strategies and Outcomes section later in this chapter.

Sometimes competition may be necessary. When an adversary is out to win at your expense and refuses to cooperate, you probably need to protect your own interests. Likewise, when the principle at stake is too important to compromise on, you may need to fight for your position.

In other cases, a competitive attitude is unnecessary. It is often possible for both sides in a conflict to achieve their goals. For instance, an employer might find the cost of providing on-site exercise equipment is more than offset by reduced absenteeism and greater appeal when recruiting new employees. Furthermore, a competitive orientation may sometimes generate ill will that is both costly and unpleasant. Continuing the physical fitness example, those workers whose needs are ignored are likely to resent their employer and act in ways that ultimately wind up costing the company a great deal.

Despite its drawbacks, competition is not always a bad approach. In some cases, an issue is not important enough to spend time working it out. In other instances, there is not enough time to collaborate on solutions. Finally, if others are determined to gain an advantage at your expense, you might compete out of self-defense.

Collaborating

Collaborative communicators are committed to working together to resolve conflicts. Collaboration is based on the assumption that it is possible to meet both one's own needs and the needs of the other person.

Whereas avoiding and accommodating are based on the assumption that conflict should be avoided, and competing is based on the belief that conflict is a

PeopleImages/DigitalVision/Getty Images RF

struggle, collaboration assumes that conflict is a natural part of life and that working with the other person will produce the best possible solution. The benefits of collaboration are clear: Not only can the issue at hand be resolved, but the relationship between the parties can also be improved.

Despite its advantages, collaborative conflict resolution is not a panacea. It takes time to work with others, and a mutually satisfactory outcome is not always possible. Furthermore, collaboration requires the cooperation of everyone involved. If the other party is not disposed to work with you, then you may be setting yourself up for exploitation by communicating openly and offering to work cooperatively.

Compromising   In a **compromise** to reach an agreement, each party sacrifices something they are seeking. On the one hand, this approach is cooperative, recognizing that both parties must agree to resolve a conflict. On the other hand, compromise is self-centered because the parties act in their own self-interest to get the best possible deal.

Compromise is a middle-range approach. It is more assertive than avoiding and accommodating, yet less aggressive than competing. It is cooperative, yet less so than collaboration. While it does not give any party in a dispute everything they seek, compromise provides an outcome that, by definition, everyone involved can live with. As Table 5-3 shows, compromise may not be the perfect approach, but under many circumstances it produces the best possible outcome.

Handling Conflicts Constructively

When you avoid a conflict or accommodate another party's demands, few communication skills are necessary. In contrast, if you decide to address an issue directly—either to collaborate, compete, or seek a compromise—you will need to negotiate.

Negotiation occurs when two or more parties—either individuals or groups—discuss specific proposals and seek a mutually acceptable agreement. Although we do not always use the term, we negotiate every day. As one consultant explains, "Negotiations are seldom formal, sit-around-the-table affairs. In fact, almost any form of business problem or disagreement—from scheduling work shifts to 'Who's going to pay this $500 expense?'—is resolved by some form of negotiation."[83]

There is nothing magical about negotiation. When poorly handled, it can leave a problem still unsolved and perhaps even worse than before. ("I tried to work things out, but he just tried to railroad me. I'm going to file a lawsuit this time.") When negotiation is handled skillfully, though, it can improve the position of one or even both parties. The remainder of this chapter focuses on communication strategies that can produce the best possible outcomes in your negotiations.

Negotiation Strategies and Outcomes   A common negotiating strategy is the competitive **win-lose approach**. It is based on the assumption that only one side can reach its goals, such that any victory by that party will be matched by the other party's loss. As Table 5-3 shows, you probably will need to take a competitive win-lose approach to protect your interests if others insist on gaining at your expense or when resources are truly scarce. For example, your company and a rival might compete for the same customers, and you might compete with another candidate for the same once-in-a-lifetime job.

No one seeks out **lose-lose** outcomes, but they can arise when two competitors try to gain an advantage at the other's expense. Like armies that take mortal losses while trying to defeat their enemies, disputants who go for a competitive victory often find they have hurt themselves as much as their opponents. For example, if you push for an unrealistically low price, you might antagonize the seller so much that you do not get the product you

Self-Assessment   Your Conflict Management Style

Instructions: Below are 15 statements that describe possible strategies for dealing with a conflict. Use the following scale to describe how you typically behave in conflicts.

1 = Always   2 = Usually   3 = Sometimes   4 = Not very often   5 = Rarely, if ever

____ a.   I argue the merits of my position forcefully.

____ b.   I try to work out compromises between my position and others.

____ c.   I try to meet others' expectations as much as possible.

____ d.   I try to explore differences with others to find mutually acceptable solutions.

____ e.   I am firm in resolve when it comes to defending my side of the issue.

____ f.   I prefer to avoid conflict, keeping disagreements to myself as much as possible.

____ g.   I defend my solutions to problems.

____ h.   I'm willing to compromise to reach solutions.

____ i.   I like to exchange important information with others so our problems can be solved together.

____ j.   I avoid discussing my differences with others.

____ k.   I try to accommodate the wishes of my peers and colleagues.

____ l.   I prefer to bring everyone's concerns into the open to resolve disputes in the best possible way.

____ m.   I advocate middle positions in an effort to break deadlocks.

____ n.   I accept others' recommendations about how to resolve conflicts.

____ o.   I avoid hard feelings by keeping my feelings and ideas to myself.

Scoring

The 15 statements you just read are organized into five categories below. Each category contains the letters of three statements. Record the number you placed next to each statement. Calculate the total for each category.

Style				Total
Competing	a. ____	e. ____	g. ____	____
Collaborating	d. ____	i. ____	l. ____	____
Avoiding	f. ____	j. ____	o. ____	____
Accommodating	c. ____	k. ____	n. ____	____
Compromising	b. ____	h. ____	m. ____	____

Results

My dominant style is _____
(your **LOWEST** score),
and my backup style is _____ (your second-lowest score).

Source: Adapted from Falikowski, A. (2007). *Mastering human relations* (4th ed.). Don Mills, ON: Pearson Education; Hamilton, K. (n.d.). What's your conflict style? Retrieved from http://webhome.idirect.com/?kehamilt/ipsyconstyle.html

are seeking and the seller does not make the sale. On the job, feuding parties may ruin their own careers by gaining reputations as difficult employees or poor team players.

Sometimes it seems better to *compromise* than to fight battles competitively and risk a lose-lose outcome. In some cases, compromise is truly the best attainable outcome—usually when disputed resources are limited or scarce. If two managers each need a full-time assistant but budget restrictions make hiring two new workers impossible, they may have to compromise by sharing one employee's services. While compromises may be necessary, they are less than ideal because both parties lose at least some of what they were seeking. Buyers, for instance, may pay more than they can afford, while sellers may receive less than they need.

When negotiators collaborate, they can often—though not always—achieve a **win-win** outcome in which everyone involved is satisfied. Win-win solutions are easiest when each party's needs are compatible, as in the following example:

> Even though they were paid overtime, teachers at a preschool resented working weekends to keep school equipment clean and organized. A brainstorming session between the teachers and director produced a solution that satisfied everyone's needs: Substitutes covered for the teachers during some school hours while the teachers sorted and cleaned equipment. This approach had several benefits: Teachers' weekends were free, and they got a weekly change-of-pace from child care. Furthermore, the director welcomed the chance to observe the substitutes who were seeking full-time teaching jobs. She was also happy because the substitutes' pay was lower than the teachers' overtime.

This example illustrates that parties working together can often find no-lose solutions to their problems. Not surprisingly, research shows that a win-win approach is preferred to other problem-solving styles.[84] In one study, researchers compared the problem-solving styles used in six organizations. They found the two highest-performing organizations used a win-win approach to a greater degree than did the less effective companies, while the lowest-performing organizations used that style less than the others.[85]

Win-win outcomes are ideal, but are not always realistic. Table 5-4 offers guidelines about when the chances are best for using this approach, as well as the alternative.

Preparing to Negotiate   Successful negotiations begin before you say a word to the other person. You can take several steps to think out your position and approach your negotiating partners in a way that boosts the odds of getting your message across and getting a constructive response.

Table 5-4	When to Use Competitive and Win–Win Negotiating Styles
Consider a Competitive Approach:	**Consider a Win–Win Approach:**
When your interests and the other party's clearly conflict	When you and the other party have common interests
When the other party insists on taking a win–lose approach	When the other party is willing to consider a win–win approach
When you do not need a long-term harmonious relationship	When a continuing, harmonious relationship is important
When you are powerful enough to prevail	When you are weaker or power is approximately equal
When short-term goals are more important	When long-term goals are more important

Clarify your interests and needs   Communicators can doom negotiations by prematurely focusing on means instead of ends. *Ends* are the goals you want, whereas *means* are ways of achieving those goals. In their best-selling book *Getting to Yes*, Roger Fisher and William Ury show that win–win results come from focusing on ends instead of means.[86] To illustrate the difference, we can adapt a story that these authors tell.

Imagine a dispute between two office workers. John wants to open a window, and Mary wants it closed. (This issue may seem trivial, but long-standing feuds have developed over smaller issues.) At this point, the issue seems irreconcilable. But suppose that a colleague asks each worker what he wants. John replies, "To get some fresh air." Mary replies, "To avoid a draft." "I have an idea," the mediating colleague suggests. "What if we open a window in the next room? That would give John the fresh air he needs and prevent the draft Mary wants to avoid."

This simple example illustrates the difference between means and ends:

Issue	Ends	Means
John	Fresh air	Open window
		or
		Open window in adjoining room
Mary	No draft	Keep window closed
		or
		Open window in adjoining room

If Mary and John stayed focused on the first means that occurred to them, the issue would never be resolved to their satisfaction. Once they identified the end that each was seeking, however, the pathway to a mutually acceptable means became perfectly clear. It is far better to identify the real end you are seeking and leave a discussion of means for later.

Consider the best time to raise the issue   Timing can have an impact on the quality of your interactions—whether it is the time of day or the time of year. Raising a difficult issue when the other person is tired, grumpy, or distracted by other business is likely to decrease your odds of getting the results you want. Asking, "Is this a good time?" or "Would another time be better for you?" can help you boost your chances of negotiating successfully.

Consider cultural differences   As you plan your approach, consider the cultural sensibilities of your negotiating partners. As described in an earlier chapter, the approach that seems comfortable to you may not align with the cultural background of your partner. For example, the following Culture at Work box illustrates some of the differences that could distinguish the approaches of Western and Chinese negotiators.

Prepare your statement   Think about how you can best express yourself, following the advice in the Offering Constructive Feedback section earlier in this chapter. Practicing your message can help you make your point quickly and clearly, and it will prevent you from blurting out an angry statement that you may regret later. When planning your remarks, be sure to think about how you can use "I" language instead of delivering defense-arousing "you" messages.

Rehearsing your statement does not mean you should memorize your remarks word for word; this approach would sound canned and insincere. Instead, you should think about your general ideas and perhaps a few key phrases you will use to make your ideas clear.

Chinese and Western Negotiating Styles

Along with apparently conflicting goals, Chinese and Western negotiators can struggle with different cultural approaches to bargaining. Recognizing these differences can be an important first step toward reaching successful outcomes.

Chinese	*Western*
Less direct communication (high context)	More direct communication (low context)
Incremental gains	Winner takes all
Finesse	Overt power
Avoidance of confrontation	Head-to-head disagreement expressed
Niche and local context focused	Broad-based and overall market dominance
Risk-averse	Prone to take bigger risks
Privacy valued	Transparent flow of information valued

Source: Adapted from Chen, M. J. (2001). *Inside Chinese business: A guide for managers worldwide.* Boston, MA: Harvard Business School Press.

Conducting the Negotiation   The win–win approach is most successful when it follows the steps described next.

Identify the ends both parties are seeking   Identify the outcomes that each party wants. As you read earlier, seemingly irreconcilable conflicts can be resolved if negotiators focus on their needs and not on their positions. Consider the example of a parent who has found that the traditional work schedule is not compatible with their child care responsibilities. Here are the ends that the employee and the boss identified:

Employee: Make sure the children are cared for after school.

Boss: Make sure the employee's productivity does not drop.

Both: Keep the employee on the job. Keep a positive relationship.

Brainstorm a list of possible solutions   Once both parties have identified the ends they are seeking, the next step is to develop a list of solutions that might satisfy each party's needs. Recall the problem-oriented approach introduced earlier in this chapter: Instead of working against each other (*How can I defeat you?*), the parties work together against the problem (*How can we beat the problem?*).

Consider again the case of the employee trying to have their child cared for after school. In this case, a number of potential win–win solutions are worth exploring:

- The employee could do some work at home during nonbusiness hours.
- The company could offer flexible work hours so employees can get their jobs done when children are at school or being cared for by others.
- The employee could share their full-time position with another worker, giving the boss the coverage they need while also allowing the employee to take the time that they need. If the employee needs additional income, they could take part-time work that could be performed at home at their convenience.
- The boss could subsidize after-school child care on the assumption that productivity would rise and absenteeism would decline when employees' children are being cared for.

While not all of these options are likely to be workable, the key to successful brainstorming is to avoid judging any possible solutions for the time being. Nothing deflates creativity and increases defensiveness as much as saying, "That won't work." You can judge the quality of each idea later; for now, the key is to focus on quantity—on finding a lot of potential solutions. Perhaps one person's unworkable idea will spark a productive suggestion.

Evaluate the alternative solutions   After brainstorming as many ideas as possible, decide which ones are most promising. During this stage, it is still critical to work toward a solution that meets all parties' important needs. Cooperation will come only if everyone feels satisfied with the solution.

Implement and follow up on the solution   Once the best plan is chosen, make sure everyone understands it; then give it a try. Even the most appealing plans may need revision when put into action. After a reasonable amount of time, plan to meet with the other parties to discuss how the solution is working out. If necessary, identify the needs that are still unmet, and then repeat the problem-solving procedure.

MASTER the chapter

review points

- Interpersonal skills are essential for a successful career. They help create positive relationships, improve organizational climates, and affirm others' dignity.

- A key ingredient of social intelligence is the ability to treat others with respect, even when you disagree.

- Effective praise creates and maintains positive communication climates. Praise is most effective when it recognizes progress, and when it is specific, prompt, and sincere.

- When raising difficult matters, the odds of success are increased by using descriptive "I" language rather than accusatory "you" language, focusing on solving problems rather than imposing solutions, being honest, showing concern for others, and demonstrating an attitude of equality and open-mindedness.

- Criticism is most likely to be successful when delivered by the most credible sender and framed to benefit the recipient. It should be delivered respectfully, privately, and without judgment.

- Criticism can be handled nondefensively by seeking more information and finding ways to agree with the critic without compromising one's principles.

- Whether it is unintentional or deliberate, sexual harassment is always illegal. The target of harassment can employ a variety of escalating response options, depending on the circumstances.

- Recognizing problematic communication, such as peer-influence exit tactics, may help the target understand a coworker's motives and improve their own personal work situation.

- On-the-job conflicts can be handled most constructively by exploring the root causes, choosing the best conflict-resolution approach (avoiding, accommodating, competing, collaborating, or compromising), and negotiating a mutually acceptable agreement.

- When possible, preferred and expected conflict management styles should be discussed among coworkers before a problem exists to improve the potential for empathy. Successful conflict management may lead to reductions in negative outcomes, such as job burnout.

- Successful negotiations require clarifying interests and needs (ends and means), careful timing and preparation, and managing issues respectfully. Parties in a negotiation can employ several strategies, with the ideal option being a win–win approach in which the best solution that satisfies all parties is implemented.

key terms

activities

1. Invitation to Insight

Recall two or three instances in which you have enacted defensive communicative behaviors (see Table 5-1).

   a. Identify which types of behaviors you enacted. Which circumstances led you to engage in these behaviors?
   b. What were the results of these behaviors for you and the other people involved?
   c. Describe specifically how you could have behaved less defensively.

2. Skill Builder

Convert each of the following defense-arousing messages into a defense-reducing statement. In each statement, use descriptive "I" language and unequivocal terms as we discussed in Chapter 4. Create details for the situation as necessary.

   a. "I sure wish I had someone to help me with this project."
   b. "Look—stop asking questions and just get it done."
   c. "You may think you know how to handle the situation, but you really don't have enough experience. I'm the boss, and I know when an assignment is over your head."
   d. "What a lame idea. A formal reception with paper plates! I can't believe you'd even suggest that."
   e. "If you want to keep your job, you better round up 10 new accounts by Monday."

3. Invitation to Insight

Familiarize yourself with effective praise by completing the following exercise:

   a. Recall three situations in which someone praised you. Using the guidelines outlined in the section on Giving Praise, evaluate the praise you received. Was it specific? Sincere? How did the praise impact you?
   b. Think of three coworkers or acquaintances whom you could praise sincerely. How could you deliver the praise effectively? For each person, write a short statement or paragraph expressing your praise.

4. Skill Builder

Practice your ability to manage criticism constructively by discussing the following scenarios with a partner. Take turns describing how you would respond to the criticism and critiquing each other's responses.

   a. A coworker accuses you of trying to ingratiate yourself with (kiss up to) the boss.
   b. A hard-to-please client snaps at you about not returning phone calls in a timely manner.
   c. You forgot to proofread the budget committee's minutes before you distributed them; you accidentally mistyped several of the budget figures and the boss is upset.
   d. You walk through a coworker's work area on the way to the water cooler. They bark, "Can't you give me some space to do my job?"

e. At a meeting, you present a proposal that angers two of your coworkers. They attack you verbally, claiming you don't have your facts right.

f. Your supervisor criticizes you for taking too long to finish a job.

Discuss the impact each approach is likely to have on (1) the relational climate and (2) future interactions between these employees. Explain your answer by using the communication model in Chapter 1.

5. Invitation to Insight

Recall two conflicts you've been involved in recently.

a. For each incident, identify the primary source of conflict as described in the Causes of Conflict section of this chapter. Do you think the other party(ies) would agree about the primary source of the conflict? Why or why not?

b. Identify any secondary sources for each conflict.

c. How did each dimension affect the way the participants approached the conflict?

6. Skill Builder

Describe an avoiding, accommodating, competing, collaborating, and compromising response to each of the following situations. Then decide which approach you would recommend. Because the meaning of a message varies with the context, you will need to decide on the specifics of the situation to make an informed choice. Explain your choice, using the information in the Approaches to Conflict section of this chapter.

a. At 4:30 p.m., just before an assistant is scheduled to leave work for the day, the boss asks the assistant to work late to retype a 25-page report that is due the next morning. The assistant has purchased nonrefundable tickets to attend a concert that evening.

b. The coworker with whom you share a small cubicle habitually leaves papers, files, and books strewn all over the floor and desk. The litter bothers you. In addition, you are concerned it gives your clients a bad impression.

c. The assistant manager of a bookstore is confronted by a customer who demands a refund for a book they claim was a gift. The book has several crumpled pages and a torn cover.

d. You are the facilitator of a student group that is writing a research report worth half of your

grade for the term. One group member misses two meetings without contacting you. When they return, they disclose that they had a family emergency and asks what they can do to make up the work.

7. Skill Builder

Sharpen your skills in knowing when and how to raise difficult issues by following these steps:

a. Develop a defensiveness-reducing message for each of the following situations in your professional life:

1. Making a difficult request.
2. Describing a problem involving the recipient of your message.
3. Offering a suggestion.

b. Practice each message with a partner until you are confident that it is organized and you are delivering it as effectively as possible. Recording your rehearsal can provide valuable feedback.

c. Discuss with your partner the potential benefits and drawbacks of delivering each assertive message.

8. Skill Builder

In the following conflicts, identify the type(s) of conflict (topic, process, relational, ego/identity) and the ends each party desires. For each situation, identify solutions (means to the end) that can satisfy the needs of everyone involved.

a. A landlord and a tenant disagree about who should pay for an obviously necessary paint job for the office space.

b. Two coworkers contributed equally to the development of a proposal for an important client. Both want to be the person who delivers the final proposal.

c. A sales manager and sales representatives disagree over the quota necessary to earn bonuses.

d. In a company with limited resources to spend on a new project, the marketing manager wants more money to be spent on advertising, while the product development manager wants a larger budget for researching new product lines.

9. Skill Builder

With a partner, select one of the following situations. Plan how you would prepare for and conduct the negotiation, working through each step in the Handling Conflicts Constructively section. Provide details as necessary to explain the situation.

a. You want to ask for a raise.
b. You and your coworkers would like your boss to hire an additional worker so you can accomplish all the necessary work in a timely fashion, without burnout.
c. You want to rent office space for your small business at a rate that is 5% to 10% less than the advertised price.

d. You need an extra week to complete a long, complex assignment.

10. Invitation to Insight

With your group, refer to the Ethical Challenge titled "Is Total Honesty Always the Best Policy?" Describe two equivocal statements you (or someone you know) once used purposefully to disguise the blunt truth. Select one statement you believe was ethical and one you believe was not ethical. Explain your reasoning. You may wish to refer to the section "Ethical Dimensions of Communication" presented in Chapter 1.

LearnSmart™

For further review, go to the LearnSmart study module for this chapter.

references

1. Hall, A. (2016). Exploring the workplace communication preferences of millennials. *Journal of Organizational Culture, Communications and Conflict, 20*, 35–44.
2. Goleman, D. (1995). *Emotional intelligence: Why it can matter more than I.Q.* New York: Bantam; Weisinger, H. (1997). *Emotional intelligence at work: The untapped edge for success.* San Francisco, CA: Jossey-Bass; Goleman, D. (2006). *Social intelligence: The new science of human relationships.* New York: Random House.
3. Goleman, D. (2000). *Working with emotional intelligence.* New York: Bantam; Suliman, A. M., & Al-Shaikh, F. N. (2007). Emotional intelligence at work: Links to conflict and innovation. *Employee Relations, 29*, 208–220.
4. Sias, P. M., Krone, K. J., & Jablin, F. M. (2002). An ecological systems perspective on workplace relationships. In M. L. Knapp & J. A. Daly (Eds.), *Handbook of interpersonal communication* (3rd ed.). Thousand Oaks, CA: Sage.
5. Chiaburu, D. S., & Harrison, D. A. (2008). Do peers make the place? Conceptual synthesis and meta-analysis of coworker effects on perceptions, attitudes, OCBs, and performance. *Journal of Applied Psychology, 93*, 1082-1103. Retrieved from https://doi.org/10.1037/0021-9010.93.5.1082
6. Kramer, M. W., Meisenbach, R. J., & Hansen, G. J. (2013). Communication, uncertainty, and volunteer membership. *Journal of Applied Communication Research, 41*, 18–39.

7. Hart, Z. P., Miller, V. D., & Johnson, J. R. (2003). Socialization, resocialization, and communication relationships in the context of an organizational change. *Communication Studies, 54*, 483–495.
8. Chiaburu, D. S., & Harrison, D. A. (2008). Do peers make the place? Conceptual synthesis and meta-analysis of coworker effects on perceptions, attitudes, OCBs, and performance. *Journal of Applied Psychology, 93*(5), 1082-1103. Retrieved from https://doi.org/10.1037/0021-9010.93.5.1082
9. Tracy, S. J., Myers, K. K., & Scott, C. W. (2006). Cracking jokes and crafting selves: Sensemaking and identity management among human service workers. *Communication Monographs, 73*, 283–308.
10. Chung, S., Lount, Jr., R. B., Park, H. M., & Park, E. S. (2017). Friends with performance benefits: A meta-analysis on the relationship between friendship and group performance. *Personality and Social Psychology Bulletin.* Retrieved from https://doi.org/10.1177/0146167217733069
11. Stoewen, D. L. (2016). Wellness at work: Building healthy workplaces. *The Canadian Veterinary Journal, 57*(11), 1188–1190.
12. Rosales, R. M. (2016). Energizing social interactions at work: An exploration of relationships that generate employee and organizational thriving. *Open Journal of Social Sciences, 4*(9), 29–33. doi: 10.4236/jss.2016.49004.
13. Oksanen, T., Kouvonen, A., Vehtera, J., Virtanen, M., & Kivimäki, M. (2010). Prospective study of workplace social capital and depression: Are vertical and horizontal components equally important?

Journal of Epidemiology and Community Health, 64(8), 684–689.

14. Tavenner, Jr., F. B. (2019). *Supervisors' dyadic relationship with remote workers compared with traditional colocated workers: A case study* (Doctoral dissertation, ProQuest Dissertations Publishing). (UMI No. 10978973).

15. Lucas, K. (2011, May). *Communicating workplace dignity: An exploratory study.* Paper presented at the International Communication Association annual conference, Boston, MA.

16. Hodson, R. (2001). *Dignity at work.* Cambridge, UK: Cambridge University Press.

17. Hodson, R., & Roscigno, V. J. (2004). Organizational success and worker dignity: Complementary or contradictory? *American Journal of Sociology, 110,* 672–708.

18. Baker, S. J., & Lucas, K. (2017). Is it safe to bring myself to work? Understanding LGBTQ experiences of workplace dignity. *Canadian Journal of Administrative Sciences, 34,* 133–148.

19. Lucas, K. (2012, May). *Toward a conceptual understanding of communicating workplace dignity.* Paper presented at International Communication Association annual conference, Phoenix, AZ.

20. Sutton, R. I. (2007). *The no asshole rule: Building a civilized workplace and surviving one that isn't.* New York: Warner Business Books; Wood, M. S., & Karau, S. J. (2009). Preserving employee dignity during the termination interview: An empirical examination. *Journal of Business Ethics, 86,* 519–534; Hodson, R. (2001). *Dignity at work.* Cambridge, UK: Cambridge University Press.

21. Lucas, K. (2015). Workplace dignity: Communicating inherent, earned, and remediated dignity. *Journal of Management Studies, 52,* 621–646.

22. Raja, S., & Stein, S. L. (2014). Work-life balance: History, costs, and budgeting for balance. *Clinics in Colon and Rectal Surgery, 27*(2), 71–74.

23. Shanafelt, T. D., Balch, C. M., Bechamps, G. J., Russell, T., Dyrbye, L., Satele, D., et al. (2009). Burnout and career satisfaction among American surgeons. *Annals of Surgery, 250*(3), 463–471.

24. Zeng, C., & Chen, H. (2020). An exploration of the relationships between organizational dissent, employee burnout, and work-family balance: A cross-cultural comparison between China and Finland. *Communication Studies, 71*(4), 633–648.

25. Kassing, J. W. (2008). Consider this: A comparison of factors contributing to employees' expressions of dissent. *Communication Quarterly, 56,* 342–355.

26. Bell, S. J., Mengüç, B., & Widing, R. E., II (2010). Salesperson learning, organizational learning, and retail store performance. *Journal of the Academy of Marketing Science, 38,* 187–201; Evans, K. R.,

Landry, T. D., Po-Chien, L., & Shaoming, Z. (2007). How sales controls affect job-related outcomes: The role of organizational sales-related psychological climate perceptions. *Journal of the Academy of Marketing Science, 35,* 445–459.

27. Verbeke, W., Franses, P., le Blanc, A., & van Ruiten, N. (2008). Finding the keys to creativity in ad agencies. *Journal of Advertising, 37,* 121–130.

28. Kowalski, C., Nitzsche, A., Scheibler, F., Steffen, P., Albert, U., & Pfaff, H. (2009). Breast cancer patients' trust in physicians: The impact of patients' perception of physicians' communication behaviors and hospital organizational climate. *Patient Education & Counseling, 77,* 344–348.

29. Kang, J. H., Matusik, J. G., Kim, T., & Phillips, J. M. (2016). Interactive effects of multiple organizational climates on employee innovative behavior in entrepreneurial firms: A cross-level investigation. *Journal of Business Venturing, 31*(6), 628–642.

30. Bradley, G. L., & Campbell, A. C. (2016). Managing difficult workplace conversations: Goals, strategies, and outcomes. *International Journal of Business Communication 53*(4), 443–464.

31. Gibb, J. R. (1961). Defensive communication. *Journal of Communication, 11,* 141–148.

32. Fisher, R., & Brown, S. (1988). *Getting together: Building relationships as we negotiate.* Boston, MA: Houghton Mifflin.

33. "Nineteen eighty-nine turkeys of the year." (1989, November 23). *San Jose Mercury News*, p. 1D.

34. Patterson, K. (2005, July 20). Mutual respect: The continuance condition of safety [e-newsletter]. *VitalSmart.*

35. Lamer, S. A., Reeves, S. L., & Weisbuch, M. (2015). The nonverbal environment of self-esteem: Interactive effects of facial-expression and eye-gaze on perceivers' self-evaluations. *Journal of Experimental Social Psychology, 56,* 130–138.

36. Carson, C., & Cupach, W. R. (2000). Facing corrections in the workplace: The influence of perceived face threat on the consequences of managerial reproaches. *Journal of Applied Communication Research, 28,* 215–234.

37. Wittenberg, P. M. (1995). Discipline with dignity: A positive approach for managers. *Federal Probation,59*(3), 40–42.

38. Anderson, K. (2000). Handling criticism with honesty and grace. *Public Management, 82,* 30–34.

39. Andersson, L. M., & Pearson, C. M. (1999). Tit for tat? The spiraling effect of incivility in the workplace. *Academy of Management Review, 24,* 452–471.

40. Jayson, S. (2011, August 7). Incivility a growing problem at work, psychologists say. *USA Today.* Retrieved from http://usatoday30.usatoday.com/news/

health/wellness/story/2011/08/Incivility-a-growing -problem-at-work-psychologists-say/49854130/1

41. Sypher, B. D. (2004). Reclaiming civil discourse in the workplace. *Southern Communication Journal, 69,* 257–269.

42. Pearson, C. M., & Porath, C. L. (2009). *The cost of bad behavior: How incivility is damaging your business and what to do about it.* New York: Portfolio.

43. Pearson, C. M., Andersson, L., & Porath, C. L. (2000). Assessing and attacking workplace incivility. *Organizational Dynamics, 29,* 123–137.

44. Cameron, A-F, & Webster, J. (2011). Relational outcomes of multicommunicating: Integrating incivility and social exchange perspectives. *Organization Science, 22*(3), 754–771.

45. Reinsch, N. L., Jr., Turner, J. W., & Tinsley, C. H. (2008). Multicommunicating: A practice whose time has come? *Academy of Management Review, 33*(2), 391–403.

46. Reinsch, N. L., Jr., Turner, J. W., & Tinsley, C. H. (2008). Multicommunicating: A practice whose time has come? *Academy of Management Review, 33*(2), 391–403.

47. Reinsch, N. L., Jr., Turner, J. W., & Tinsley, C. H. (2008). Multicommunicating: A practice whose time has come? *Academy of Management Review, 33*(2), 391–403.

48. Cameron, A-F, & Webster, J. (2011). Relational outcomes of multicommunicating: Integrating incivility and social exchange perspectives. *Organization Science, 22*(3), 754–771.

49. Giumetti, G. W., McKibben, E. S., Hatfield, A. L., Schroeder, A. N., & Kowalski, R. M. (2012). Cyber incivility @ work: The new age of interpersonal deviance. *Cyberpsychology, Behavior, and Social Networking, 15*(3), 148–154.

50. Giumetti, G. W., McKibben, E. S., Hatfield, A. L., Schroeder, A. N., & Kowalski, R. M. (2012). Cyber incivility @ work: The new age of interpersonal deviance. *Cyberpsychology, Behavior, and Social Networking, 15*(3), 148–154.

51. Lutgen-Sandvik, P. (2003). The communicative cycle of employee emotional abuse: Generation and regeneration of workplace mistreatment. *Management Communication Quarterly, 16,* 471–501.

52. Lutgen-Sandvik, P. (2003). The communicative cycle of employee emotional abuse: Generation and regeneration of workplace mistreatment. *Management Communication Quarterly, 16,* 471–501.

53. Namie, G., & Namie, R. (2009). *The bully at work: What you can do to stop the hurt and reclaim your dignity on the job.* Naperville, IL: Sourcebooks.

54. Namie, G. (2014). 2014 WBI U.S. workplace bullying survey. Workplace Bullying Institute. Retrieved from http://www.workplacebullying.org/wbiresearch/ wbi-2014-us-survey/

55. Lutgen-Sandvik, P. (2003). The communicative cycle of employee emotional abuse: Generation and

regeneration of workplace mistreatment. *Management Communication Quarterly, 16,* 471–501.

56. Economic and Social Research Council (ESRC). (2012). Cyberbullying in the workplace "worse than conventional bullying." *ScienceDaily.* Retrieved from http://www.sciencedaily.com/releases/2012/11 /121102084650.htm

57. Hall, R., & Lewis, S. (2014). Managing workplace bullying and social media policy: Implications for employee engagement. *Academy of Business Research Journal, 1,* 128–138.

58. Pearson, C. M., & Porath, C. L., (2009). *The cost of bad behavior: How incivility is damaging your business and what to do about it.* New York: Portfolio.

59. Jansma, L. (2000). Sexual harassment research: Integration, reformulation, and implications for mitigation efforts. In M. E. Roloff (Ed.), *Communication yearbook 23.* Thousand Oaks, CA: Sage.

60. Dougherty, D. S. (2009). Sexual harassment as destructive organizational process. In B. D. Sypher & P. Lutgen-Sandvik (Eds.), *Destructive organizational communication: Processes, consequences, and constructive ways of organizing.* New York: Routledge.

61. The U.S. Equal Employment Opportunity Commission. (2002, June 27). Facts about sexual harassment. Retrieved from https://www.eeoc.gov/facts/fs-sex.html

62. Dougherty, D. S. (2009). Sexual harassment as destructive organizational process. In B. D. Sypher & P. Lutgen-Sandvik (Eds.), *Destructive organizational communication: Processes, consequences, and constructive ways of organizing.* New York: Routledge.

63. Bergman, M. E., Langhout, R. D., Palmieri, P. A., Cortina, L. M., & Fitzgerald, L. F. (2002). The (un) reasonableness of reporting: Antecedents and consequences of reporting sexual harassment. *Journal of Applied Psychology, 87*(2), 230–242.

64. Sollitto, M., Weber, K., & Chory, R. M. (2013, June). *Communication organizational exit: The development and validation of the Peer-Influenced Exit Measure.* Paper presented at the annual meeting of the International Communication Association, London, UK.

65. Cox, S. A. (1999). Group communication and employee turnover: How coworkers encourage peers to voluntarily exit. *Southern Communication Journal, 64,* 181–192.

66. Sollitto, M. (2015). *Why and how organizational members encourage their peer coworkers to voluntarily exit the organization: An investigation of peer-influence exit tactics* [Doctoral dissertation]. Dissertation Abstracts International Section A, 76.

67. Zupek, R. (2007, December 31). Six tips to managing workplace conflict. *CNN.* Retrieved from http://www. cnn.com/2007/LIVING/worklife/12/31/cb.work.conflict/

68. Rahim, M. A. (2016). Reducing job burnout through effective conflict management strategy. *Current Topics in Management, 18,* 201-212.

69. Maslach, C., Jackson, S. E., & Leiter, M. P. (2001). Job burnout. *Annual Review of Psychology, 52,* 397-422.

70. Rahim, M. A. (2016). Reducing job burnout through effective conflict management strategy. *Current Topics in Management, 18,* 201-212.

71. Berglos, S. (1995, May). Harmony is death: Let conflict reign. *Inc.,* 56-58.

72. Coser, L. (1956). *The functions of social conflict.* New York: Free Press.

73. Wilmot, W. W., & Hocker, J. L. (2007). *Interpersonal conflict* (7th ed.). New York: McGraw Hill.

74. Folger, J. P., Poole, M. S., & Sturtman, R. K. (2004). *Working through conflict: Strategies for relationships, groups, and organizations* (5th ed.). Boston, MA: Allyn & Bacon.

75. Kanter, M., & Robbins, S. (2012). The impact of parents "friending" their young adult child on Facebook on perceptions of parental privacy invasions and parent-child relationship quality. *Journal of Communication, 62*(5), 900-917.

76. Chory, R. M., Vela, L. E., & Avtgis, T. A. (2016). Organizational surveillance of computer-mediated workplace communication: Employee privacy concerns and responses. *Employee Responsibilities and Rights Journal, 28,* 23-43.

77. Wilmot, W. W., & Hocker, J. L. (2007). *Interpersonal conflict* (7th ed.). New York: McGraw Hill.

78. Cheney, G., & Ashcraft, K. L. (2007). Considering "the professional" in communication studies: Implications for theory and research within and beyond the boundaries of organizational communication. *Communication Theory, 17,* 146-175; Fineman, S. (2006). Emotion and organizing. In S. R. Clegg, C. Hardy, T. B. Lawrence, & W. R. Nord (Eds.), *The Sage handbook of organization studies* (pp. 675-700). Thousand Oaks, CA: Sage; Lammers, J. C., & Garcia, M. A. (2009). Exploring the concept of "profession" for organizational communication research: Institutional Influences in a veterinary organization. *Management Communication Quarterly, 22,* 357-384.

79. Paul, G. P., & Putnam, L. L. (2016). Moral foundations of forgiving in the workplace. *Western Journal of Communication, 81*(1), 43-63.

80. Paul, G. P., & Putnam, L. L. (2016). Moral foundations of forgiving in the workplace. *Western Journal of Communication, 81*(1), 43-63.

81. Paul, G. P., & Putnam, L. L. (2016). Moral foundations of forgiving in the workplace. *Western Journal of Communication, 81*(1), 43-63.

82. Starkey, D. (1998, February 20). Finding common ground. *Sacramento Business Journal,* 12-13.

83. McCormack, M. H. (1984). *What they don't teach you at Harvard Business School.* New York: Bantam.

84. Pavitt, C., & Kemp, B. (1999). Contextual and relational factors in interpersonal negotiation strategy choice. *Communication Quarterly, 47,* 133-150; Friedman, S. D., Christensen, P., & DeGroot, J. (1998, November/December). Work and life: The end of the zero-sum game. *Harvard Business Review, 76,* 119-129.

85. Burke, R. J. (1970). Methods of resolving superior-subordinate conflict: The constructive use of subordinate differences and disagreements. *Organizational Behavior and Human Performance, 5,* 393-411.

86. Fisher, R., & Ury, W. (1981). *Getting to yes: Negotiating agreement without giving in.* Boston, MA: Houghton Mifflin.

Chapter Six
Principles of Interviewing

chapter outline

chapter objectives

After reading this chapter you should be able to:

1. Plan and conduct an information-gathering interview to assist you in a current work or school project.

2. Plan and conduct a career research interview that will help you clarify and/or achieve your goals.

3. Describe the features of various types of employment interviews, including video interviews, and explain ways to prepare for each type of interview.

4. Identify the purpose of a performance appraisal interview and the steps involved in preparing for this type of interview.

5. Distinguish between legal and illegal employment interview questions, and identify the advantages and disadvantages of each of four methods of responding to illegal questions.

6. Explain how to define interview goals, identify and analyze the other interview party, and choose the best interview structure.

7. Demonstrate knowledge of the uses and limitations of each type of interview question: primary, secondary, closed, open, factual, opinion, direct, indirect, hypothetical, and critical incident.

8. Describe the purpose of and appropriate conduct during each stage of an interview (opening, body, and conclusion).

9. Describe and observe the ethical obligations of interviewers and respondents.

W hen most of us hear the word *interview*, we naturally think of the screening process employers use to identify the best candidates for a job. However, there are several other types of interviews that occur in the business world. As illustrated later in this chapter in the Case Study titled "The Coffee Bar," each of the conversations Gina needs to have is an **interview**—a two-party interaction in which at least one party has a specific, serious purpose and that usually involves the asking and answering of questions.[1]

Interviews play a central role in the world of work. Organizations use *employment interviews* (sometimes called *selection interviews*) to identify the best candidates for a job. Supervisors use *performance appraisal interviews* to review employees' performance and help set targets for the future. When problems arise, they use *disciplinary interviews* to deal with misconduct or poor performance. Human resources personnel use *exit interviews* to help determine why a person is leaving an organization and to solicit feedback on possible problems in the organization.

Health care providers, attorneys, counselors, and salespeople regularly use *diagnostic interviews* to detect problems and gather information that helps them respond to their clients' needs. Police officers, journalists, and social workers use *investigative interviews* to help determine the causes of a problem. Businesspeople conduct *research interviews* to gather information as the basis for making future decisions. For example, advertising, marketing, and public relations professionals use *survey interviews* to gather information from a number of people with the intent of using that information to better understand the people they want to reach with their messages. Because interviews are important to many aspects of working life, some communication authorities claim interviews are the most common form of planned communication.[2]

Whatever their specific type, all interviews share some common characteristics. First, while there may be several interviewers (as sometimes occurs in employment situations) or multiple respondents (as in a "meet the press" journalistic format), there are always *at least two parties* involved: an interviewer and a respondent. Second, interviewing is always *purposeful.* Unlike in more casual conversations, at least one participant in the interview has a serious, predetermined goal. Third, there is a focus on asking and answering *questions.* Indeed, questions are the basic tools of an interview. They are developed and used to gather information and direct the flow of the exchange.

By now, you should begin to see that interviews differ from other types of communication exchanges in several ways. Most important, interviews are more *structured* than most conversations. As you will soon learn, every good interview has several distinct phases. Interviews also have an element of *control* not present in more casual interaction. The interviewer's job is to keep the conversation moving toward a predetermined goal. A final difference between interviewing and other conversations involves the *amount of speaking* by each party. While persons in most informal conversations speak equally, experts suggest that participation in most interviews ought to be distributed in roughly a 70-to-30 ratio, with the person being interviewed doing most (70%) of the talking.[3]

• Types of Interviews

Of all the interview types described in the opening section of this chapter, the ones most essential in almost every occupation involve information-gathering, career research, employment, and performance appraisal. The following pages outline the skills required for each of these important types of interviews.

The Information-Gathering Interview

Many businesspeople owe their success in great part to the lessons they learned in information-gathering interviews. Sam Walton, founder of the Walmart empire, used this approach early in his career by visiting businesses and asking to speak to executives who might have helpful information:

> I would just show up and . . . as often as not, they'd let me in, maybe out of curiosity, and I'd ask lots of questions about pricing and distribution, whatever. I learned a lot that way.[4]

Suppose you are interested in proposing a job-sharing plan—a system in which two people share the responsibilities and salary of one full-time job. You might first conduct interviews with persons experienced in this approach to gather information about some basic questions: How common is job-sharing? Has it been tried by any firms in your field? What have been the results of such arrangements?

Information-gathering interviews follow the general approach described next.

Define Interview Goals and Questions   As an interviewer, you should define your goal for the interview as clearly as possible. Your goal statement should be worded in a way that will tell you whether you have the answers you were seeking. The following are examples of clear goals for information-gathering interviews:

- Could the accident have been prevented?
- Will tax-free municipal bonds give me better liquidity, appreciation, safety, and tax sheltering than my present investments?
- Will a database management system improve our efficiency enough to justify the purchase?

Once you have identified your goal, you can develop questions that will help you achieve it. For example:

> *Goal:* To learn what steps I need to take to have a job-sharing arrangement approved by management.
>
> *Questions:*

- Who will be the key decision-maker on this issue?
- Whom should I approach first?
- Should I present my formal proposal, or should I start by mentioning the subject informally?
- What objections might management raise regarding the proposal?
- Is anyone else in the company (non-management personnel) likely to oppose or support the idea?
- What arguments (such as precedent, cost savings, or employee morale) will most impress management?
- Which influential people might support this idea?

Choose the Right Respondent   Who you interview is likely to shape the value of what you learn. It might be naive to talk with your boss about the job-sharing proposal before you have consulted other sources who could suggest how to best broach the subject. Perhaps conducting an information-gathering interview with a politically astute coworker, someone who has experience making proposals to management, or even the boss's administrative assistant—if you have a good working relationship—would be helpful.

After you have identified the purpose and the appropriate person to interview, follow the interviewing strategies discussed later in this chapter to plan and conduct the interview.

The Career Research Interview

The **career research interview** is a special type of informational interview in which you meet with someone who can provide information that will help you define and achieve your career goals. It is based on the principle that speaking with the right people can give you valuable ideas and contacts you simply cannot find from books, magazines, the Internet, or any other source.

The Value of Networking   The old phrase, "It isn't what you know, it's who you know" is certainly true when it comes to getting a job. More than 30 years of research confirms that the vast majority of people do not find jobs from advertisements, headhunters, or other formal means.[5] Despite the popularity of web-based services, such as Indeed.com, the majority of new hires get offers for employment through contacts in their personal

The Coffee Bar

Not bad for a 20-year-old, thinks Gina deSilva. I'm the youngest store manager in the history of The Coffee Bar. With this job, it will take me a little longer to get my degree, but I won't have to take out student loans and I'll leave school with some real management experience. That should make me much more employable after I graduate.

Gina knows this job won't be easy. As a starting point, she makes a mental to-do list and thinks about the people whom she needs to interview.

- *Clarify Marty's expectations of me.* Now that I'm the store manager, Marty (the regional manager) will be my boss. I don't know him well, and I need to understand what he wants me to do. What are his priorities? What problems does he see with the store? What does he think of me?

- *Hire an assistant manager to replace me.* Interview Rashid and Samantha, the top candidates. Rashid is more experienced and sociable, but can I count on him to put the store first when it conflicts with his band's plans? Samantha is serious, but her in-your-face style rubs some clerks the wrong way. Can she learn to be a little less aggressive? Also, I need to be sure whoever I hire is committed to staying with the job for at least one year.

- *Hire two new clerks.* We need to hire two new salesclerks soon. What skills and attitudes are we looking for? How can I handle the interviews to make sure we get the best people?

- *Solve the issue of employee turnover.* We had to replace 7 out of 10 baristas last year. I'm not sure why so many people have left. Training new staff takes a lot of time, and new people don't serve the customers well until they have figured out our routine. I need to talk with the three veteran clerks who are still here and the new ones. I could also track down people who left the store and find out why they quit.

- *Do market research with customers.* Sales have been low since Starbucks opened in the mall. I need to talk with our customers to find out how to keep them here. I also need to track down customers we've lost and find out how to get them back.

networks. The reverse is also true: Most employers find good employees through their personal networks.[6] In fact, the *hidden job market* is a term used to describe available jobs that are filled through networking rather than being advertised or posted online.[7] One corporate recruiter explained why networking is superior to web-based employment sites:

> In the rare instances where I actually post a position online, I get résumés from all over the world. Many of them bear no relationship to the job I am trying to fill. It's as though people just "point and shoot."
>
> The last professional position I posted—with extremely explicit qualifications laid out in the posting—received almost 1,000 responses, of whom only 25 or so even met the technical and educational qualifications for the position. My time is much better spent networking personally with people to find good candidates than reviewing and responding to these résumés.[8]

Finding a job is just one goal when you engage in a career research interview. These interviews can also have the following purposes:

- *To learn more* about the field and specific organizations that interest you.

- *To be remembered* by making contacts who will recall you at an appropriate time and either offer you a position, inform you of employment opportunities, or suggest you to a potential employer.

- *To gain referrals* to other people whom you might contact for help in your job search. These referrals can easily lead to meetings with more useful contacts, all of whom might mention you to their friends and associates.

Internet Job and Internship Searches

When job-seekers think of searching for employment online, sites such as Indeed.com or ZipRecruiter.com typically come to mind. However, the Internet is filled with an array of resources that offer valuable information that can prove even more helpful in locating a job or internship.

- **Company Websites:** If you have a goal to work for a specific company, go directly to their official website. Most company websites contain a career section dedicated to job and internship openings.

- **LinkedIn:** Employers can pay to list a job opportunity in the "Jobs" tab. They may also post a job in a specific Group that can be seen only by Group members. Each available position features a list of members in your personal network that are affiliated with the organization, making it easier for you to use networking to your advantage.

- **Twitter:** Company representatives will often tweet a job or internship vacancy. Additionally, services such as CareerArc allow job-seekers to create a free account and have notifications of new jobs within their skill sets and interests sent directly to their Twitter feed.

- **Professional Organization Job Boards:** Many professional associations post job listings for their members. Individuals interested in public relations jobs, for example, might visit the Public Relations Society of America's (PRSA) Jobcenter. Other associations with job boards include the National Communication Association (NCA), the American Institute of Architects (AIA), and the American Institute of CPAs (AICPA).

- **Specialty Job Boards:** Some industry-specific boards advertise job positions for candidates interested in a particular profession. Examples include Medzilla for biotechnology, pharmaceuticals, medicine, and health care, and Dice for information technology (IT) jobs.

- **College Alumni Groups:** Many colleges and universities offer job boards. One of the authors of this book graduated from Texas Tech University, which provides a job board called "Hire Red Raiders" for students and alumni, with viewing privileges for faculty/staff and parents.

Choosing Respondents   The key to finding the wealth of unadvertised positions is to cultivate a network of contacts who can let you know about job opportunities and pass along your name to potential employers. We offered tips on how to build and nurture a personal network in Chapter 1.

There is no doubt that the people in your immediate networks can be helpful. Perhaps surprisingly, you can benefit even more from distant connections who are connected to other, less familiar communication networks that often contain valuable information about new jobs.[9]

You might wonder why the important person you have targeted for a career research interview would be willing to meet with you. There are actually several reasons. First, if you have made contact through a referral, the respondent will probably see you as a courtesy to your mutual acquaintance. If you can gain a referral, you are most likely to get a friendly reception. Second, they might be willing to meet with you for ego gratification. It is flattering to have someone say, "I respect your accomplishments and ideas," and it is difficult for even a busy person to say no to a request that accompanies such a comment. A third reason is altruism. Most successful people realize they received help somewhere along the line, and many are willing to do for you what others did for them. Finally, you may get an interview because the person recognizes you as ambitious—someone who might have something to offer their organization.

Contacting Prospective Respondents

When you approach a prospective respondent—especially one whom you do not know well—it can be smart to make your first contact in writing through e-mail. A telephone call runs the risk of not getting through and, even if you do reach the respondent, your call may come at a bad time. Your first message, like the one in Figure 6.1, should introduce yourself, explain your reason for the interview (stressing that you are *not* seeking employment), state your availability for a meeting, and promise a follow-up telephone call. If you are requesting to interview a professional in another geographic location, be sure to specify your time zone and/or technology requests (e.g., phone, Zoom).

If your interview will occur more than a few days after the date the respondent agreed to your request for a meeting, you should compose a second e-mail no more than a week before the interview to confirm its date, place, and time. This sort of follow-up can save you the frustration of being stood up by a forgetful respondent. Just as important, it shows that you know how to handle business engagements professionally.

Giving your respondent an advance list of topic areas and questions you hope to cover will distinguish you as a serious person, worth their time and effort. Supplying this list will also give your respondent a chance to think about the areas you want to discuss and ideally come to your meeting well-prepared to help you. Figure 6.2 illustrates a confirming e-mail with a list of questions.

Following Up

After the meeting, take the time to compose an e-mail or handwritten card to express appreciation for the respondent's time and mention how

FIGURE 6.1
Request for Career Research Interview

From: Emily Park <eprk112@sunnet.net>
Sent: Thursday, May 19, 2022 12:51 PM
To: Vanessa J. Yoder <v.yoder@DGHattysatlaw.com>
Subject: Seeking your advice

Dear Ms. Yoder:

I am currently a junior at the University of New Mexico, majoring in political science and communication. After graduating from UNM, I plan to attend law school and focus my studies on immigration law.

From several news accounts and also from several of my professors, I've learned that you are an expert in immigration law and have a stellar reputation for representing women when the cases involve both domestic violence and immigration issues. I also heard of your work during my internship at the Women's Workforce Training Center.

I would appreciate the opportunity to meet with you to discuss how I might best prepare myself for an eventual career in immigration law. I would also like to know which law schools you would recommend and hear about the challenges and rewards of this type of practice.

Let me stress that I am not seeking employment at this time. Your advice would be invaluable as I prepare myself for a career in law. I will call your office next week hoping to schedule an appointment. I know you are a busy person and I would be grateful for 30–45 minutes of your time.

I look forward to benefiting from your insights and recommendations.

Sincerely,
Emily Park
9971 Washoe St., NE
Albuquerque, NM 87112
(505) 793-3510

FIGURE 6.2
Confirming
E-mail with List
of Questions

From: Emily Park <eprk112@sunnet.net>
Sent: Friday, June 10, 2022 8:26 AM
To: Vanessa J. Yoder <v.yoder@DGHattysatlaw.com>
Subject: Interview confirmation and questions

Dear Ms. Yoder:

Thank you again for agreeing to speak with me about how I can best prepare myself for a career in immigration law. I am looking forward to our meeting at your office this coming Thursday, June 15, at 2:00 p.m. I know how busy you must be, and I'm grateful for your giving me 45 minutes of your time.

In order to use our time together most efficiently, here is a list of some questions I hope we can discuss at our meeting:

TRENDS IN IMMIGRATION AND LAW
- What trends do you anticipate in immigration patterns?
- How do you view the field of immigration law changing to reflect these conditions?

EDUCATION
- What law schools do you recommend for someone interested in practicing immigration law?
- Do you recommend any courses I should take in my senior year at the university?

EXPERIENCE
- What types of work experience (paid or volunteer) could help prepare me for law school and eventual employment?
- Can you recommend ways I might pursue positions in these areas?

EMPLOYMENT
- What types of jobs are there for attorneys who specialize in immigration law?
- How easy/difficult do you anticipate it will be to secure employment in these sorts of jobs?
- What, if any, are the pros and cons I might expect as a woman practicing law in this area?

LIFESTYLE
- How would you describe the benefits and challenges of working in the field of immigration law?
- What are some ways a person interested in this career might maintain work-life balance?

OTHER CONTACTS
- Can you recommend other people who might be willing to talk with me about preparing for a career in immigration law?

helpful the information was. Besides demonstrating common courtesy, your message becomes a tangible reminder of you and provides a record of your name and contact information that will be useful if the respondent wants to contact you in the future. Of course, all correspondence should be composed using impeccable format, spelling, and grammar.

The Employment Interview

An **employment interview** explores how well a candidate might fit a job. The exploration of fit works both ways: Employers certainly measure job candidates during this conversation, and prospective employees can decide whether the job in question is right for them. In July 2019, 56.2% of persons in the United States between the ages of 16 and 24 years old were employed—so your probability of facing at least one employment interview in the near future is high.[10]

The short time spent in an employment interview can have major consequences. Consider the stakes: Most workers spend the greatest part of their adult lives on the job—roughly 2,000 hours per year or upward of 80,000 hours during a career. The financial difference between a well-paid position and an unrewarding one can also be staggering. Even without considering the effects of inflation, a gap of only $200 per month can amount to almost $100,000 over the course of a career. Finally, finding the right job has considerable emotional implications. A frustrating job not only makes for unhappiness at work, but this dissatisfaction also has a way of leaking into nonworking hours.

How important is an interview in getting the right job? The Bureau of National Affairs—a private research firm that serves both government and industry—conducted a survey to answer this question. It polled 196 personnel executives, seeking the factors that were deemed most important in hiring applicants. The results showed the employment interview is the single most important factor in landing a job.[11] In turn, communication skills are one of the most important factors in making a hiring decision during these critically decisive interviews.

Pre-Interview Steps

Scanning the Internet for openings and then filing an application is often not the most effective way to find a job. Many employers never advertise jobs and, even when a company does advertise, the odds do not favor a candidate who replies with an application and résumé. Employment expert Richard Bolles explains:

> I know too many stories about people who have been turned down by a particular
> company's personnel department, who then went back to square one, found out
> who, in that very same company, had the power to hire for the position they wanted,
> went to that woman or man, and got hired—ten floors up from the personnel depart-
> ment that had just rejected them.[12]

Since most job announcements attract many more applicants than an employer needs, the job of the human resources department becomes *elimination,* not selection. Given this process of elimination, any shortcoming becomes welcome grounds for rejecting the application and the applicant. Many consultants, therefore, suggest identifying and contacting the person who has the power to hire you *before* an opening exists. The process has several steps.

Clean up your online identity   In spite of your best efforts to craft an effective résumé and present yourself as a qualified job applicant, prospective employers have other ways of forming impressions of you, including all of the information available online.[13] Many employers engage in **cybervetting**, or using Internet information and social networks to screen applicants.[14] One CareerBuilder study found that 57% of employers who research job candidates on social media said they have rejected a candidate because of the content that they found. Some of the most common reasons for rejection included provocative photos and videos; information about drinking or using drugs; discriminatory comments; criminal behavior; and poor communication skills.[15]

Research shows that young people may use some social media sites for personal reasons and others (such as LinkedIn) for professional reputation management and are not comfortable having personal sites used for cybervetting.[16] Some job candidates perceive cybervetting to be unethical due to a loss of information privacy; these candidates respond in one of five ways: refusal, negative word of mouth, complaining to friends, complaining to the company, and complaining to third parties.[17] Although these responses have important implications for the reputations of the companies in question, cleaning up your "digital dirt" is well worth the effort.

To discover what others can easily see about you, begin by typing your name into a search engine such as Google or Bing. Sometimes, the only hits may be advice you gave about training your Jack Russell terrier or a review you wrote about a great restaurant. However, you may also find comments you made at meetings you attended, links to your social media profiles, information about you in newspaper articles, public hearings, or court actions. You may be able to get site owners to remove things you would rather not have on record. See the Technology Tip titled "How to 'un-Google' Yourself" for more tips on handling undesirable search results.

One set of researchers suggest viewing publicly available online information as an extension of your résumé. The results of their research indicate that those job candidates with Facebook profile photos perceived as attractive with positive personality traits obtained 38% more job interview invitations than their counterparts.[18]

It is a good idea to review your profile on social media sites such as Facebook, Twitter, and Instagram and on blogs or websites you have created. Think about how prospective employers might

bloomua/123RF

perceive your profiles, and consider untagging or removing posts, photos, and videos you no longer want to share with the world—or at least change your privacy settings. The photo of you from the Halloween party your sophomore year or the comments others wrote and tagged you in might not create the best impression. Furthermore, other people's content you have liked or shared may be inconsistent with the image on your page and may also appear on your profile. Be aware that, in today's highly networked world, it is possible that an employer could gain access to your profile from one of your mutual connections.

In addition, it is good practice to link a different e-mail address to your accounts than the one you include on your résumé and application. You might also opt to modify your name or the geographic location on your account to limit your appearance in search results.

TECHNOLOGY **tip**

How to "un-Google" Yourself

Prior to applying for a job, it is a good idea to look for your full name, nicknames, and aliases using a search engine like Google. If the search results surface undesirable content, there are a few steps you can take to attempt to remove the content:

- Contact the owner of the website or social media site to request that the information be removed.
- For content you can control, such as tweets, follow the link from the search result and delete the post.

- Use an app such as Timehop to conduct daily purges of outdated content that may no longer fit your image.
- Close old accounts that you no longer use.

It is important to remember that deleted information will remain in a search engine's cache for several weeks after it has been removed. It is recommended to proactively follow these steps as far in advance of a job search as possible.

Source: wikiHow Staff (2020, March 25). How to unGoogle yourself. Retrieved from https://www.wikihow.com/Ungoogle-Yourself

Conduct background research   A second step for the job-seeker is to explore the specific organization(s) that sound appealing to you. This step involves reading, researching, and talking to anyone who might have useful information.

When conducting background research on a company, avoid limiting your search to the company's mission statement, products and services, and location(s). Consider digging a bit deeper into the company's culture by searching for information on its ethical standards and community involvement. This information can help you make a decision about whether you can foresee a future for yourself with the company.

Besides helping you find organizations where you want to work, your knowledge of a company will distinguish you as a candidate worth considering for a job. A simple review of Starbucks' corporate website, for example, allows you to see the company's "Social Impact" efforts. For example, Starbucks has had an environmental mission statement since 1992 and encourages its employees to proactively identify the environmental impacts of their operations.[19] If you have a passion for the environment, you can easily see how Starbucks' emphasis on its environmental footprint might mesh with your personal values. Inserting this type of information into your interview will show that you have done your research and identified your ability to fit into the company's culture.

Desiree Crips of Salus Media in Carpinteria, California, aptly sums up most potential employers' view: "If someone walks in here and doesn't know anything about our company, that's a real negative. There's just no excuse for not being up to speed on any company you're applying to these days."[20] Doing your homework is just as important in the workforce as in school.

Contact potential employers   At some point, your research and networking will uncover one or more job leads. You might read a newspaper story about a local employer's need for people with interests or training like yours. Perhaps a career research interview subject will say, "I know someone over at Company X who is looking for a person like you." You might learn through a friendly contact that a desirable firm is about to expand its operations. In such a case, it is time to explore how you can help meet the company's needs.

Most career counselors recommend directing your request for an interview to a person who has the power to hire you rather than to the company's human resources department. We have already discussed why personnel departments are not the best avenue for getting hired: They are usually charged with screening large numbers of applicants, so they look for reasons to reject as many candidates as possible to arrive at a manageable number of finalists to interview.

The mechanical nature of this screening process is well illustrated by the growing reliance on computer screening techniques. Retailers such as Best Buy, Nordstrom, and Target have replaced paper applications with computer kiosks for initial applicant screening. Additionally, many companies now utilize **scannable résumés** that are read by document-scanning devices, not humans. The software searches for keywords and phrases that describe the qualifications and education required for the position. Applications that contain these words are passed on to a human, who then evaluates them further.

Appendix II offers tips for creating effective scannable résumés. Nevertheless, even the best document may not capture the unique traits you can offer an employer. For this reason, you will maximize your chances of being recognized as a stellar candidate by developing a relationship with people who know both your talents and the characteristics of the job. In most cases, the best way to approach the hiring manager is with written correspondence, usually a cover letter, a copy of your résumé, and a link to your career portfolio. Appendix II also has advice on constructing and formatting standard cover letters and résumés.

A Professional Perspective

KeAnna Wisenhunt

Executive Coordinator

Management Consulting

Dallas, TX

Credit: KeAnna Whisenhunt

One of my best tips for successful interviews is to be in an ever-present state of evaluating and reflecting on professional experiences. I've learned through my own experience that you never know when you might find yourself in an interview situation (given that not all interviews are formal employment interviews). Always be prepared.

For example, as a local news intern working in a city with a large Latino population, I needed to consider cultural factors relevant to my bilingual readers. Studying previous news articles provided me with a blueprint to understand the events and issues that mattered to my community, but I also conducted informational interviews. I talked with other reporters about the types of questions I should ask and how I could ensure that the voices of people in my community were heard in my articles. A senior colleague advised me to go into every interview with the intention of learning three things about the interviewee that I didn't know from my own research and allow their responses to shape the story. In addition, I do not have a background or formal training in photography, but my job required me to capture images to tell a compelling, yet authentic story. I studied photos taken by the newspaper's photojournalist and I asked him questions about lighting and proper angles. He was a busy professional, but took the time to meet with me because I approached him with clear goals and direct questions, thereby showing that I valued his time and expertise.

Evaluating my own experiences has also given me the confidence to know what I am looking for in a job or company. The job interview is a two-way street. They are interviewing me, but I am also interviewing them. Will this job allow me to use my talents and be productive? Will I experience work–life balance, inclusion, and professional development? Will I be excited to get out of bed in the morning to do this work, with these people, in this environment? By knowing what I value, I can effectively engage in discussions with potential employers in order to find a mutually beneficial match.

Prepare for possible interview formats The standard one-on-one, question-and-answer interview format is not the only one you may encounter. Employers today use a variety of interview formats. If you are prepared for all of them, you are not likely to be surprised.

In a **panel interview** (sometimes called a *team* or *group interview*), the candidate is questioned by several people. Panel interviews save the company time and provide the people with whom you may work an opportunity to compare their perceptions of you. When setting up an interview, it is appropriate to ask whether you will be facing a team of questioners. If you

TECHNOLOGY **tip**

Video Résumés

Video résumés (sometimes referred to as visumés or video profiles) are a way for candidates to creatively share additional information about their job qualifications, beyond what can be explained by a cover letter or standard résumé.

Before submitting this kind of profile, you should determine whether the prospective employer will accept your video résumé. While some may refuse—likely due to fears of claims of bias from applicants—employers in career fields that require presentation or multimedia skills (e.g., public relations, marketing, advertising, training, sales, journalism, film) may be more receptive to this approach.

The following tips will help you if you choose to submit a video résumé:

- Ensure that your video expands upon or adds to the content of your standard résumé and cover letter.

- Outline or create a script of your main points so you can speak extemporaneously to the camera.
- Make sure your nonverbal communication is polished (eye contact; no distracting gestures).
- Stay within a 60- to 90-second time limit.
- Test the lighting and sound before recording your video.
- Use equipment that will create a high-quality video.
- Be creative! Digital marketer Todd Cavanaugh submitted a video résumé that featured a short campaign about explaining Dropbox to grandparents; it concluded with him briefly explaining his qualifications on camera. This résumé has been viewed more than 30,000 times.[21]

Shannon Fagan/Image Source

are, do your best to learn and use the names of each person. Search the company website for photos of the interviewers; this will make it easier to match their names to their faces. When you answer questions, make sure you look at everyone in the group. Some employers use a **stress interview** to evaluate your behavior under pressure; researching this type of interview and being prepared for such ploys will help you remain calm and in control.

In an **audition interview,** you will be asked to demonstrate skills that the employer is seeking. You might be asked to create a project, solve a problem, or respond to a typical scenario in the job, such as dealing with a difficult client. For example, one of your authors' students recently completed an audition interview at a public relations firm: She was given details about a campaign and was asked to write a news release, develop social media content, and edit a short video.

The audition shows the potential employer how you are likely to do on the job. The prospect of an audition can be especially helpful if you will be competing against candidates with more experience or stronger credentials. For that reason, you might even volunteer for an audition if you are confident you can handle the job well.[22]

A **behavioral interview** is based on the assumption past experience is the best predictor of future performance. In this approach, interviewers explore specifics about the candidate's past accomplishments. John Madigan, president and CEO of Executive Talent Services explains the way behavioral interviews work: "We actually ask what you did in specific situations. Concrete examples will demonstrate a person's preferred way of dealing with those situations and give you a better idea of that person and how they're likely to act on the job."[23]

Here are some questions you might encounter in a behavioral interview:

- Provide a specific example of when you sold your supervisor or professor on an idea or concept. What was the result?
- Tell me about a time when you came up with an innovative solution to a challenge you or your company was facing. What was the challenge? What roles did others play?
- Describe a situation where you faced the need to manage multiple projects. How did you handle it?[24]

If you have a proven record of accomplishments that clearly mesh well with the job you are seeking, a behavioral interview should sound ideal. If you do not have work experience that is clearly relevant to the new position, however, you should find ways to demonstrate how things you have done in other contexts apply to the job you are seeking. The PAR (problem-action-result) method is useful for answering behavioral interview questions.

Problem: What was the problem or goal? What constraints or challenges did you face?

Action: What did you do to manage these challenges? What resources did you use?

Result: What were the results? What did you learn from the experience?

Using this method, you might be able to show how experience in retail sales taught you how to deal with the difficult customers you may encounter in a customer service job, or how being a volunteer for a nonprofit charity gave you an appreciation for working with limited resources—an attitude most employers will welcome.

Prepare for the possibility of a virtual interview As a result of the COVID-19 pandemic companies that historically relied on face-to-face employment interviews began conducting interviews virtually. A Gartner, Inc. poll of over 300 human resources managers found that 86% of organizations are incorporating virtual technology to interview candidates due to the pandemic.[25] While this may seem like a response to an unprecedented time, Lauren Smith, Gartner HR vice president, suggests that virtual interviews may become the new standard long after social distancing guidelines are lifted.[26] While the format and questions asked during an online interview are similar to those encountered in a face-to-face setting, online interviewing requires additional considerations.

In advance of your interview date:

- Verify the date, the time (be aware of time zone differences), the person(s) with whom you will be speaking, and any other pertinent details. For example, some interviewers may opt to conduct an interview over a Skype call, which does not require video.
- Verify that you have access to a working webcam and microphone, and that you have installed the latest software update for the app you will be using for the interview (e.g., Skype, Zoom, Microsoft Teams, WebEx).
- Select a professional and private location for the interview, such as a home office or tucked away corner of your living area. Avoid interviewing from your car or a noisy coffee shop.
- Ensure a neutral background that is free of distractions (noises and visuals) and clutter.
- Test the lighting in the room that you will be using for your interview at the same time of day that you will be interviewing. Position your computer so that your face will be lit with natural lighting and free of shadows.
- Position your webcam at eye level so you are looking directly into the camera instead of looking up or down.

Andrey_Popov/Shutterstock

On the day of your interview:

- Dress professionally, just as you would for a face-to-face interview. While the interviewers may only see what you are wearing on the upper half of your body, it is good practice to make sure all of your attire is professional. Not only will your confidence be boosted when you look and feel good, but there will also be fewer chances for embarrassing mishaps.

- Inform others in your home that you will be in an interview. If possible, you might lock or put a sign on the door as a reminder. However, life happens and this may not prevent all unexpected intrusions. If someone barges into the room while you are interviewing, politely acknowledge and apologize for the situation and move on with the interview.

- Silence any notifications or ringers from apps, phones, or computer programs before the interview begins.

- Ask if your interviewer can see and hear you clearly.

- Make eye contact and smile at your interviewer.

- Become comfortable with pauses. Connection delays can cause you to awkwardly interrupt the interviewer. Wait for the interviewer to stop speaking, pause for a second or two, and then begin speaking.

Think constructively   The way you think about an upcoming interview can affect how you feel and act during the session. A study by Everest College and Harris Interactive found that 92% of U.S. adults are anxious over job interviews. The most common fears include "seeming nervous" and "arriving late."[27] Feelings of anxiety can have negative effects on the outcome of the interview. A research team at Washington State University interviewed both highly anxious and more confident students and the differences between groups were startling.[28] Anxious students avoided thinking about an interview in advance, so they did little research or preparation. When they did think about an upcoming interview, they tended to dwell on negative self-talk: "I won't do well" or "I don't know why I'm doing this." Not surprisingly, thoughts like these created negative self-fulfilling prophecies that led to poor interview performances. Students who handled interviews better did not completely avoid anxiety, but they thought about the upcoming challenge in more productive ways. We can imagine them thinking, "The interviewer isn't trying to trick me or trip me up" and "I'll do a lot better if I prepare."

Dress appropriately and act professionally   Looking good when you meet a potential employer is vitally important. In one survey, recruiters ranked clothing as the leading factor in shaping their initial impressions of applicants (ahead of physical attractiveness and résumé). Furthermore, 79% of the recruiters stated that their initial impressions influenced the rest of the interview.[29] In fact, one survey found that 49% of employers can discern whether a candidate is a good fit for the job within the first five minutes of meeting them.[30] The best attire to wear will depend on the job you are seeking: The professional business suit appropriate for a banking job would almost certainly look out of place if you were interviewing for a job in the construction industry, and it might look overly formal at many software companies. When in doubt, it is always safest to dress on the conservative side. Of course, cleanliness and good personal hygiene are essential.

Be sure to arrive at the interview approximately 10 minutes early, but avoid arriving more than 15 minutes before your scheduled time. Arriving too early may inconvenience the interviewers who are preparing for your visit. If you are running late, immediately contact the individual with whom you set up the interview to apologize and inform them of the delay and estimated arrival time.

Arrive with extra copies of your résumé on quality paper, a tablet or notepad and pen, and a portfolio of your work. Be polite to everyone in the office. While you wait, choose reading material about the business or company, not about entertainment. When introduced, shake hands firmly, no more than three shakes, avoiding a limp or hand-crushing grip. Smile, make eye contact, and take your lead from the interviewer about how to proceed.

During the Interview   If your fate in the selection process were determined by a skilled, objective interviewer, the need for strategic communication might not be essential. Research shows, however, that the rating you receive from an interviewer can be influenced by factors as varied as the time of day, the sex of the interviewer and the respondent, whether the candidates before you did well or poorly, and the interviewer's mood.[31] Because an interview is not a scientific measure of your skills, it is especially important to do everything possible to make the best impression.

Your background research will pay dividends during the employment interview. One criterion that most interviewers use in rating applicants is "knowledge of the position," and a lack of information in this area can be damaging. Table 6-1 lists common mistakes that hiring managers say will instantly destroy a candidate's chances for obtaining their desired position.

Anticipate key questions   Most employment interviewers ask questions in five areas:

1. *Educational background.* Does the candidate possess adequate training for a successful career? Do the candidate's grades and other activities predict success in this organization?

2. *Work experience.* Did any previous jobs or internships prepare the candidate for this position? What does the candidate's employment history suggest about their work habits and ability to work well with others?

Table 6-1	Common Mistakes by Respondents

Lying
Answering mobile phone or texting during the interview
Appearing arrogant or entitled
Appearing to have a lack of accountability
Swearing
Dressing inappropriately
Talking negatively about current or previous employers
Knowing nothing about the job or company
Using unprofessional body language
Knowing nothing about the industry or competitors

Source: CareerBuilder (2018, February 22). The most unusual interview mistakes and biggest body language mishaps according to a CareerBuilder survey. Retrieved from http://press.careerbuilder.com/2018-02-22-The-Most-Unusual-Interview-Mistakes-and-Biggest-Body-Language-Mishaps-According-to-Annual-CareerBuilder-Survey

3. *Career goals.* Does the candidate have clear goals? Are they compatible with a career in this organization?

4. *Personal traits.* Do the candidate's actions and attitudes predict good work habits and good interpersonal skills?

5. *Knowledge of organization and job.* Does the candidate know the job and organization well enough to be certain they will feel happy in them?

While the specifics of each job are different, many questions are the same for any position. Table 6-2 lists the questions that interviewers most commonly ask.

In addition, knowledge of the company and the job position should suggest other specific questions to you. There is a good chance you will be asked at least some of the common questions identified in this section. The tips offer advice about how to approach them, while keeping the focus on what you can do for the organization.

Question	What to Emphasize
Why should we hire you?	Do not give a generic answer: Nearly everyone says they are hardworking and motivated. Briefly list your unique strengths and qualifications, showing **how they will help you perform the job in question**.
Why do you want to work here?	If you have researched the organization, this question gives you an opportunity to explain **how your experience and qualifications match the company's needs**.
Tell me about yourself.	Keep your answer focused on those parts of your life that relate to the job. Pick a couple of points that show how you possess skills or have experiences that **show what you can contribute to this organization**.

You cannot anticipate every question a prospective employer will ask. Nevertheless, if you go into the interview with a clear sense of yourself—both your strengths and your limitations—and the nature of the job you are seeking, you can probably handle almost any question. Consider a few examples of unusual questions and what the interviewers who asked them were seeking.

Question	What the Interviewer Was Seeking
What's the biggest career mistake you have made so far?	Have you learned from your errors? Which mistakes are you not likely to make if you work for us?
If I asked your previous coworkers what I should watch out for from you, what would they say?	How aware are you of your own strengths and weaknesses?
Who else are you interviewing with, and how close are you to accepting an offer?	How committed are you to our organization? How do others view your potential as an employee?[32]

Because most employers are untrained in interviewing, you cannot expect them to ask every important question.[33] If your interviewer does not touch on an important area, look for ways of volunteering information that they probably would want to have. For instance, you could show your knowledge of the industry and the company when you respond to a question about your past work experience: "As my résumé shows, I've been

Table 6-2   Commonly Asked Questions in Employment Interviews

Educational Background

- How has your education prepared you for a career?
- Why did you choose your college or university?
- Describe your greatest success (or biggest problem) in college.
- Which subjects in school did you like best? Why?
- Which subjects did you like least? Why?
- What was your most rewarding college experience?

Work Experience

- Tell me about your past jobs. What did you do in each?
- Which of your past jobs did you enjoy most? Why?
- Why did you leave your past jobs?
- Describe your greatest accomplishments in your past jobs.
- What were your biggest failures? What did you learn from them?
- How have your past jobs prepared you for this position?
- What were the good and bad features of your last job?
- This job requires initiative and hard work. How have you demonstrated these qualities?
- Have you supervised people in the past? In which capacities? How did you do?
- How do you think your present boss (subordinates, coworkers) would describe you?
- How do you feel about the way your present company (past companies) is (were) managed?

Career Goals

- Why are you interested in this position?
- Where do you see yourself in 5 years? In 10 years?
- What is your career goal?
- Why did you choose the career you are now pursuing?
- What are your financial goals?
- How would you describe the ideal job?
- How would you define success?
- Which things are most important to you in a career?

Self-Assessment

- In your own words, how would you describe yourself?
- How have you grown in the last years?
- What are your greatest strengths? Your greatest weaknesses?
- Which things give you the greatest satisfaction?
- How do you feel about your career up to this point?
- What is the biggest mistake you have made in your career?
- Do you prefer working alone or with others?
- How do you work under pressure?
- What are the most important features of your personality?
- Are you a leader? (A creative person? A problem solver?) Give examples.

Knowledge of the Job

- Why are you interested in this particular job? Our company?
- What can you contribute to this job? Our company?
- Why should we hire you? What qualifies you for this position?
- What do you think about (job-related topic)?
- Which part of this job do you think would be most difficult?

Other Topics

- Do you have any geographical preferences? Why?
- Would you be willing to travel? To relocate?
- Do you have any questions for me?

working in this field for five years, first at Marston-Keenan and then with Evergreen. In both jobs, we were constantly trying to keep up with the pace you set here. For example, the VT-17 was our biggest competitor at Evergreen. . . ."

Listen actively and give clear, detailed answers   Careful listening can assure you understand the questions the interviewer asks, so you do not go off on a tangent or give an answer unrelated to what is asked. An off-the-track answer suggests the respondent did not understand the question, is a poor listener, or might even be evading the question. Considering your answers to what the interviewer has previously said shows both listening and critical thinking skills.

Respond to the employer's needs and concerns   While you may need a job to repay a college loan or finance your new car, these concerns will not impress a potential employer. Companies hire employees to satisfy *their* needs, not yours. Although employers will rarely say so outright, the fundamental question that is *always* being asked in an employment interview is, *"Are you a person who can help this organization?"* In other words, *"What can you do for us?"* One career guidance book makes the point clearly:

> It is easy to get the impression during an interview that the subject of the interview, the star (so to speak) of the interview is, well, you. After all, you're the one in the hot seat. You're the one whose life is being dissected. Don't be too flattered. The real subject of the interview is the company. The company is what the interviewer ultimately thinks is important.[34]

Within the broad question of "What can you do for us?" potential employers have three concerns:

1. Are you qualified to do the job?
2. Are you motivated to do the job?
3. Will you fit with the organization's culture and get along with your colleagues?[35]

No matter how the question is worded, these are potential employers' key concerns. A smart candidate will answer in ways that address them. Background research will pay off here: If you have spent time learning about what the employer needs, you will be in a good position to show you are motivated and can satisfy the company's needs and concerns. Consider an example:

Interviewer:	What was your major in college?
Poor Answer:	I was a communication major.
Better Answer:	I was a communication major. I'm glad I studied that subject because the skills I learned in school could help me in this job in so many ways: dealing with customers from many cultures, working in the department teams, and creating presentations for the external contractors who are part of the job. . . .
Interviewer:	Tell me about your last job as a sales rep.
Poor Answer:	I handled outside sales. I called on about 35 customers. My job was to keep them supplied and show them new products.
Better Answer:	(elaborating on previous answer) As part of that job, I learned how important it is to provide outstanding customer service. I know the competitive edge comes from making sure the customers get what they want, when they need it. I know this company has a reputation for good service, so I'm really excited about working here.

Just because you respond to the employer's needs, that does not mean you should ignore your own goals. Even so, during an interview, you need to demonstrate how you can help the organization or you will not have a job offer to consider.

Because most employers have had poor experiences with some of the people they have hired, they are likely to be concerned about what might go wrong if they hire you. In Richard Bolles's words, employers worry you will not be able to do the job; you lack the skills; you will not work full days regularly; you will quit unexpectedly; it will take you a long time to master the job; you will not get along with others; you will do the minimum; you will need constant supervision; you will be dishonest, irresponsible, negative, a substance abuser, or incompetent; and you will discredit the organization or cost it a lot of money.[36]

You can ease these fears without ever addressing them directly by answering questions in a way that showcases your good work habits:

Interviewer:	What were the biggest challenges in your last job?
Answer:	The work always seemed to come in spurts. When it was busy, we had to work especially hard to stay caught up. I can remember some weeks when we never seemed to leave the office. It was hard, but we did whatever it took to get the job done.
Interviewer:	How did you get along with your last boss?
Answer:	My last manager had a very hands-off approach. That was a little scary at times, but it taught me I can solve problems without a lot of supervision. I was always glad to get guidance, but when it didn't come, I learned I can figure out things for myself.

Be honest   Whatever else an employer may be seeking, honesty is a mandatory job requirement. If an interviewer finds out you have misrepresented yourself by lying or exaggerating about even one answer, then everything else you say will be suspect.[37]

Being honest does not mean you have to confess to every self-doubt and shortcoming. As in almost every type of situation, both parties in an employment interview try to create desirable impressions. In fact, some ethicists have noted the ability to "sell" yourself honestly but persuasively is a desirable attribute since it shows you can represent an employer well after being hired.[38] During the interview, then, you should highlight your strengths and downplay your weaknesses, but always be honest.

Emphasize the positive   Although you should always be honest, it is also wise to phrase your answers in a way that casts you in the most positive light. Consider the difference between the positive and negative responses to this question:

Interviewer:	I notice you've held several jobs, but you haven't had any experience in the field you've applied for.
Negative Answer:	Uh, that's right. I decided I wanted to go into this field only last year. I wish I had known that earlier.
Positive Answer:	That's right. I've worked in a number of fields, and I've been successful in learning each one quickly. I'd like to think this kind of adaptability will help me learn this job and grow with it as technology changes the way the company does business.

Notice how the second answer converted a potential negative into a positive answer. If you anticipate questions that have the ability to harm you, you can compose honest answers that present you favorably.

Even if you are confronted with comments that cast you in a negative, you can reframe yourself more positively. In the following list, notice how each negative trait could be reframed as a positive attribute[39]:

Negative Trait	Positive Attribute
Overly detailed	Thorough, reliable
Cautious	Careful, accurate
Intense	Focused
Slow	Methodical, careful
Naive	Open, honest
Aggressive	Assertive

Do not misunderstand: Arguing with the interviewer or claiming you have no faults is not likely to win you a job offer. In contrast, reframing shortcomings as strengths can shift the employer's view of you.

Employer: If I were to ask your colleagues to describe your biggest weaknesses, what do you think they'd say?

Candidate: Well, some might say that I could work faster, especially when things get frantic. But I think they would agree I'm very careful about my work and I don't make careless errors.

Another important rule is to avoid criticizing others in an employment interview. Consider the difference between these answers:

Interviewer: From your transcript, I notice you graduated with a 2.3 grade-point average. Isn't that a little low?

Negative Answer: Sure, but it wasn't my fault. I had some terrible teachers during my first two years of college. We had to memorize a lot of useless information that didn't have anything to do with the real world. Besides, professors give you high grades if they like you. If you don't play their game, they grade you down.

Positive Answer: My low grade-point average came mostly from very bad freshman and sophomore years. I wasn't serious about school then, but you can see my later grades are much higher. I've grown a lot in the past few years, and I'd like to think I can use what I've learned in this job.

Most job candidates have been raised to regard modesty as a virtue, which makes it hard to toot their own horns. Excessive boasting certainly may put off an interviewer, but experts flatly state that showcasing your strengths is essential if you want to win out as a job candidate. Texas State University management professor Micki Kacmar found that job-seekers who talked about their good qualities were rated higher than those who focused on the interviewer.[40] Pre-interview rehearsals will help you find ways of saying positive things about yourself in a confident, nonboastful manner.

Back up your answers with evidence   As you read earlier, behavioral interviewers figure the best predictor of a potential employee's performance is what they have done in

Demonstrating Your Ethical Standards

Employers often use behavioral interviews to assess whether a candidate's individual ethics match the values of their company. Using what you have learned in this chapter about emphasizing the positive and backing your answers up with evidence, construct an answer to the following interview prompt:

Tell me about a time when you were challenged ethically.

---

the past. Even if you are not engaged in a behavioral interview, it is usually effective to back up any claims you make with evidence of your performance.

One good framework for answering questions is the "PAR" approach. This acronym denotes the three parts of a good answer: identifying the *problem,* describing the *action* you took, and stating the *results* your actions produced. You can see the value of this approach by comparing the two answers to this interviewer's question:

Interviewer:	Which strengths would you bring to this job?
Weak Answer:	I am a self-starter who can work without close supervision [unsupported claim].
Stronger Answer:	I am a self-starter who can work without close supervision [claim]. For example, in my last job, my immediate supervisor was away from the office off and on for three months because of some health issues [problem]. We were switching over to a new accounting system during that time, and I worked with the software company to make the change [action]. We made the changeover without losing a single day's work, and without any loss of data [results].

Keep your answers brief   It is easy to rattle on in an interview out of enthusiasm, a desire to show off your knowledge, or nervousness but, in most cases, highly detailed answers are not a good idea. The interviewer probably has a lot of ground to cover, and long-winded answers will not help. A general rule is to keep your responses to less than 2 minutes. An interviewer who wants additional information can always ask for it.

Be enthusiastic   If you are applying for jobs that genuinely excite you, the challenge is not to manufacture enthusiasm but rather to show it. This can be difficult when you are nervous during what feels like a make-or-break session. Just remember that the interviewer wants to know how you really feel about the job and the organization. Sharing your interest and excitement can give you a competitive edge. Career center director Gregory D. Hayes says, "If I talk to five deadbeat people and have one who is upbeat, that's the one I'm going to hire."[41]

Use humor when appropriate   Laughter is a powerful communication tool that, when used appropriately, can create a positive impression that helps you stand out from the crowd. One study of executives interviewing for leadership positions found that outstanding leaders were able to get the interviewer to laugh with them twice as often as the average executives.[42] However, humor is also risky. Not everyone shares the same idea of what is funny, which can be a recipe for disaster during an employment interview. One team of researchers found that self-denigrating humor, where the speaker is the target, is the safest and most successful form of humor whereas humor directed at others was riskier.[43]

As with all business communication, it is important to analyze your audience before using humor. Executive coach Natalia Autenrieth shares an example of successful use of humor that she used during an interview:

> As an auditor, I am no stranger to having to ask sensitive questions, dig into mistakes that could potentially damage someone's career, and poke around when people are just trying to do their jobs. To be effective at what I do, I had to come up with something that would lighten the mood and get me better results. I decided that I would bribe my clients–with chocolate and cookies![44]

Correct any misunderstandings   Being human, interviewers sometimes misinterpret comments. Interviewees, for their part, want to ensure the messages they send have been received accurately. Obviously, you cannot ask the interviewer, "Were you listening carefully?" but two strategies can help get your message across.

First, you can orally restate your message in either the body or the conclusion phase of the interview. For instance, in the body phase, while reporting on a list of exhibit preparations, the interviewee might mention the brochures will have to be hand-carried. The following exchange could then come later in the body phase or at the conclusion:

Interviewer: So if we hire you, everything will be at the exhibit booth when we get to the convention, and all we have to do is set up the exhibit?

Respondent: Not quite. The brochures won't be ready in time to ship to the convention, so you'll have to carry them with you on the plane.

Second, you can put your ideas in writing. It is sometimes wise to summarize important ideas in an e-mail after the interview so both the recipient and you will have a permanent record of your message.

Have your own questions answered   After you have answered the interviewer's questions, be prepared for them to ask you if you have any questions of your own. When you are asked this question, it is good practice to respond with a question. Realize that your questions make indirect statements about you, just as your answers to the interviewer's inquiries did. Be sure your questions are not all greedy ones that focus on salary, vacation time, benefits, and so on. Instead, this is a great time to highlight your fit for the role ("As part of my undergraduate coursework, I worked with a team to create a crisis communication plan for a client. If I were hired for this role, is there a possibility that my job responsibilities will include crisis response?") and to get a sense of the company culture ("What are the company's goals for the upcoming year?"). Table 6-3 lists some questions to consider asking when you are invited to do so.

Rehearsing an Interview
No athlete would expect to win without practicing, and no performer would face an audience without rehearsing. The same principle holds when you are facing an important employment interview. Effective practicing involves several steps:

1. Use your pre-interview research to identify the nature of the job you are seeking. What skills are required? What personal qualities are most desirable for this position? What kind of person will fit best with the organization's culture?

2. Draft a series of questions that explore the job description; use the lists in Table 6-2 as a guide to include each key area.

3. Think about how you can answer each question. Each answer should contain a *claim* ("I have experience making presentations using Apple Keynote") and

Table 6-3	Questions to Consider Asking the Interviewer during an Employment Interview

- Why is this position open?
- How often has this position been filled during the past five years?
- What have been the reasons for people leaving in the past?
- Why did the person who most recently held this position leave?
- What would you like the next person who holds this job to do differently?
- What are the most pressing issues and problems in this position?
- What kind of support does this position have (e.g., people, budget, equipment)?
- What are the criteria for success in this position?
- What might be the next career steps for a person who does well in this position?
- What do you see as the future of this position? This organization?
- What are the most important qualities you will look for in the person who will occupy this position?

evidence to back it up ("I used it to train customer service representatives in my last job"). In every case, make sure your answer shows how you can satisfy the employer's needs.

4. Role-play the interview several times with the help of a friend. Be sure you include the orientation and conclusion phases of the interview and practice the questions you plan to ask the interviewer. If possible, record and review your performance twice: once to evaluate the content of your answers, and again to check your appearance and the image you are projecting.

Many colleges have student job placement centers that offer a wealth of resources on interviewing. They may also provide a way to schedule and record a mock interview with a professional job counselor, who will then review your video with you and give you constructive advice.

Post-Interview Follow-up Without exception, every employment interview should be followed by a thank you note to the person who interviewed you within 24- to 48-hours. As Figure 6.3 shows, this note serves several purposes:

- It demonstrates common courtesy.
- It reminds the employer of you.
- It gives you a chance to remind the interviewer of important information about you that came up in the interview and to provide facts you may have omitted.
- It can tactfully remind the interviewer of promises made, such as a second interview or a response by a certain date.
- It can be used to correct any misunderstandings that may have occurred during the interview.[45]

Unlike most business correspondence, a thank you note can be handwritten. Whatever style you choose—whether a handwritten card, a formal letter, or an e-mail message—the note should be neat, well written, error-free, and carefully composed. Additionally, connect with the interview team on LinkedIn. This step will help you build your professional network and may open the door for future opportunities.[46]

Self-Assessment   Your IQ (Interview Quotient)

Assess how ready you are to handle employment interviews skillfully by answering the questions below, using the following scale:

5 = strongly agree; 4 = agree; 3 = maybe, not certain; 2 = disagree; 1 = definitely not

Pre-Interview Planning

1. I have conducted background research and understand the organization and the field.   5 4 3 2 1

2. I know the nature of the job (responsibilities, skills, how it fits in the company).   5 4 3 2 1

3. When possible and appropriate, I have asked members of my personal network to give the prospective employer favorable information about me.   5 4 3 2 1

4. I am prepared for any interview format.   5 4 3 2 1

5. I think constructively about the upcoming interview rather than dwell on negative thoughts.   5 4 3 2 1

6. I will dress and groom appropriately for this company and position.   5 4 3 2 1

7. I know how to arrive at the interview site.   5 4 3 2 1

During the Interview

8. I can handle the small talk that arises in the opening phase of the interview.   5 4 3 2 1

9. I nonverbally communicate my interest and enthusiasm for the job.   5 4 3 2 1

10. I am prepared to answer the kinds of questions likely to be asked (see Table 6-2) in a way that shows how I can meet the employer's needs.   5 4 3 2 1

11. I back up all my answers with examples that help clarify and prove what I'm saying.   5 4 3 2 1

12. I give concise answers to the interviewer's questions.   5 4 3 2 1

13. I present myself confidently and enthusiastically.   5 4 3 2 1

14. I am prepared to respond to illegal questions the interviewer might ask.   5 4 3 2 1

15. I know when and how to deal with salary questions.   5 4 3 2 1

16. I have prepared a list of references.   5 4 3 2 1

17. I am prepared to ask my own questions about the job and organization.   5 4 3 2 1

18. I practiced asking and answering questions until I am comfortable and articulate.   5 4 3 2 1

After the Interview

19. I know how to write an effective thank you letter.   5 4 3 2 1

20. I am prepared to follow up with the interviewer to determine my status, if necessary.   5 4 3 2 1

Scoring

Total the numbers you have circled. If your score is between 80 and 100, you appear to be well prepared for interviews. If your score is between 60 and 80, you are moderately prepared. If your score is less than 60, you would do well to make additional preparations before any employment interviews.

Source: Krannich, C., & Krannich, R. (2002). *Interview for success: A practical guide to increasing job interviews, offers, and salaries* (8th ed.). Manassas Park, VA: Impact Publications.

FIGURE 6.3
Sample of Thank
You Message

From: Susan Mineta [stm@comnet.net]
Sent: Friday, March 25, 2022 9:14 AM
To: Leslie Thoresen [lesthor@blogsite.com]
Subject: Thank you!
Attached: 📄 S Mineta articles.pdf

Dear Mr. Thoresen:

I left our meeting yesterday full of excitement. Your remarks about the value of my experience as a student journalist and blogger were very encouraging. I also appreciate your suggestion that I speak with Mr. Leo Benadides. Thank you for promising to tell him that I'll be calling within the next week.

Since you expressed interest in the series I wrote on how Asian women are breaking cultural stereotypes, I am attaching copies to this e-mail. I hope you find them interesting.

Your remarks about the dangers of being typecast exclusively as a writer on women's issues were very helpful. Just after we spoke I received an assignment to write a series on identity theft and the elderly. I'll be sure to let you know when these articles appear online.

Thank you again for taking time from your busy day. I will look forward to hearing from you when the job we discussed is officially created.

Sincerely,

Susan Mineta
8975 Santa Clarita Lane
Glendale, CA 90099
(818) 214-0987

If you do not get the job, consider contacting the person who interviewed you and asking which shortcomings kept you from being chosen. Even if the interviewer is not comfortable sharing this information with you (it might not have anything to do with your personal qualifications), your sincere desire to improve yourself can leave a positive impression that could help you in the future.

Interviewing and the Law   Many laws govern which questions are and are not legal in employment interviews, but the general principle that underlies them all is simple: Questions may not be asked for the purpose of discriminating on the basis of race, color, religion, sex, disabilities, national origin, or age. Employers may still ask about these areas, but the U.S. government's Equal Employment Opportunity Commission (EEOC) permits only questions that investigate a **bona fide occupational qualification (BFOQ)** for a particular job. This means any question asked should be job-related. The Supreme Court says "the touchstone is business necessity."[47] Table 6-4 lists questions that are generally not considered BFOQs, as well as those that are legitimate.

The Americans with Disabilities Act of 1990 (ADA) requires equal access to employment and provision of reasonable accommodations for persons with disabilities. It defines *disability* as a physical or mental impairment that substantially limits one or more major life activities. As with any other job-related issue, the key question pertains to what is considered reasonable. The law clearly states, however, that candidates with disabilities can be questioned only about their ability to perform essential functions" of a job, and that employers are obligated to provide accommodations for candidates and employees with disabilities. If a person indicates a need for reasonable accommodation during the application process, the company is required to provide it. For example, a person who is hearing impaired can request an interpreter at company expense for the interview.[48]

Table 6-4   Questions Interviewers Can and Cannot Legally Ask

Federal law restricts employer interviewer questions and other practices to areas clearly related to job requirements. The following are some questions and practices that are generally considered legitimate and others that are not.

Subject	Unacceptable	Acceptable
Name	"What is your maiden name?" "Have you ever changed your name?"	"What is your name?" "Is there another name I'd need to check on your work and education record?"
Residence	"Do you own or rent your home?"	"What is your address?"
Age	Age Birth date Dates of attendance or completion of elementary or high school Questions that tend to identify applicants who are older than age 40	Statement that hiring is subject to verification that the applicant meets the legal age requirements "If hired, can you show proof of age?" "Are you older than 18 years of age?" "If you are younger than age 18, can you, after employment, submit a work permit?"
Birthplace, citizenship	Birthplace of the applicant, applicant's parents, spouse, or other relatives "Are you a U.S. citizen?" *or* citizenship of the applicant, applicant's parents, spouse, or other relatives Requirement that the applicant produce naturalization, first papers, or alien card *prior to employment*	"Can you, after employment, submit verification of your legal right to work in the United States?" *or* a statement that such proof may be required after employment
National origin	Questions as to nationality, lineage, ancestry, national origin, descent, or parentage of the applicant, applicant's parents, or spouse "What is your mother tongue?" or the language commonly used by the applicant How the applicant acquired the ability to read, write, or speak a foreign language	Languages that the applicant reads, speaks, or writes, if use of a language other than English is relevant to the job for which the applicant is applying
Sex, marital status, family	Questions that indicate the applicant's sex Questions that indicate the applicant's marital status Number and/or ages of children or dependents Provisions for child care Questions regarding pregnancy, childbearing, or birth control Name or address of a relative, spouse, or children of an adult applicant "With whom do you reside?" or "Do you live with your parents?"	Name and address of a parent or guardian if the applicant is a minor; statement of company policy regarding work assignment of employees who are related
Race, color	Questions about the applicant's race or color Questions about the applicant's complexion or color of skin, eyes, or hair	

(continued)

Table 6-4	Questions Interviewers Can and Cannot Legally Ask *(Continued)*

Subject	Unacceptable	Acceptable
Religion	Questions regarding the applicant's religion Religious days observed *or* "Does your religion prevent you from working weekends or holidays?"	Statement by the employer of regular days, hours, or shifts to be worked
Arrest, criminal record	Arrest record *or* "Have you ever been arrested?"	"Have you ever been convicted of a felony?" Such a question must be accompanied by a statement that a conviction will not necessarily disqualify an applicant from employment
Military service	General questions regarding military service, such as dates and type of discharge Questions regarding service in a foreign military	Questions regarding relevant skills acquired during the applicant's U.S. military service
Organizations	"List all organizations, clubs, and societies to which you belong."	"Please list job-related organizations or professional associations to which you belong that you believe enhance your job performance."
References	Questions of the applicant's former employers or acquaintances that elicit information specifying the applicant's race, color, religious creed, national origin, ancestry, physical handicap, medical condition, marital status, age, or sex	"By whom were you referred for a position here?" Names of persons willing to provide professional and/or character references for applicant

Source: Doyle, A. (n.d.). Illegal interview questions. Retrieved from http://jobsearchtech.about.com/od/interview/l /aa022403_2.htm; Cobb, L. (2007). Illegal or inappropriate interview questions. Retrieved from http://www.gsworkplace .lbl.gov/DocumentArchive/BrownBagLunches/IllegalorInappropriateInterviewQuestions.pdf

Choosing the best response style to an illegal interview question depends on several factors.[49] First, it is important to consider the interviewer's probable intent. The question may indeed be aimed at collecting information that will allow the employer to discriminate, but it may just as well be a naive inquiry with no harm intended. Some interviewers are unsophisticated at their jobs. A study of 200 interviewers in *Fortune* 500 corporations revealed that more than 70% of them thought at least five of 12 unlawful questions were safe to ask.[50] In another survey, employers at 100 small businesses were presented with five illegal interview questions. All of the respondents said they either would ask or have asked at least one of them.[51] Results like these suggest an illegal question may be the result of ignorance rather than malice. The interviewer who discusses family, nationality, or religion may simply be trying to make conversation. Be careful not to introduce these topics yourself, as doing so may open the door to conversations and questions you would rather not deal with.

Second, when considering how to respond to an illegal question, think about your desire for the job at hand. You may be more willing to challenge the interviewer when a position is not critical to your future; however, if your career rides on succeeding in a particular interview, you may be willing to swallow your objections.

Third, consider your feeling of comfort with the interviewer. For example, a candidate with school-age children might welcome the chance to discuss child care issues with an interviewer who identifies as a single parent who faces the same challenges.

Fourth, think about your own personal style. If you are comfortable asserting yourself, you may be willing to address an illegal question head-on. If you are less comfortable speaking up, especially to authority figures, you may prefer to respond less directly.

There are several ways to answer an unlawful question[52]:

1. *Answer without objection.* Answer the question, even though you know it is probably unlawful: "I'm 47."

2. *Seek explanation.* Ask the interviewer firmly and respectfully to explain why this question is a BFOQ: "I'm having a hard time seeing how my age relates to my ability to do this job. Can you explain?"

3. *Redirection.* If the interviewer asks, "How old are you?" a candidate might shift the focus toward the position requirements: "What you've said so far suggests age isn't as important as willingness to travel. That isn't a problem for me." Redirection can also involve strategic ambiguity and humor. "I'm old enough to do this job well and young enough to have fresh ideas."

4. *Refusal.* Explain politely but firmly that you will not provide the information requested: "I'd rather not talk about my religion. That's a personal matter for me." If you are sure you are not interested in the job, you could even end the interview immediately: "I'm very uncomfortable with these questions about my personal life, and I don't see a good fit between me and this organization."

Being interviewed does not mean you are at the interviewer's mercy; laws do govern your rights as a candidate. If you choose to take a more assertive approach to illegal questioning you believe resulted in discrimination, you have the right to file a complaint with the EEOC and your state's Fair Employment Practices Commission within 180 days of the interview. In practice, the EEOC will hold off on beginning its investigation until the state commission has completed its inquiry. Federal and state agencies have a backlog of cases, however, so it may take years to complete an investigation. The commission may mediate the case, file a suit, or issue you a letter to sue.[53] Keep in mind that just because you can file a lawsuit, it does not mean this will always be the best course of action: A suit can take many months, or even years, to be settled, and a ruling in your favor may not result in a large settlement. Furthermore, knowledge that you have filed this kind of suit is not likely to make you an attractive candidate to other employers who hear of your action. Seeking professional counsel can help you make a decision that balances your personal values and practical considerations.

The Performance Appraisal Interview

Performance appraisal interviews are a special kind of interview in which superiors and subordinates meet at regularly scheduled intervals (usually annually) to discuss the quality of the subordinate's performance. These interviews have several functions:

- *Letting the employee know where they stand.* This kind of feedback includes praising good work, communicating areas that need improvement, and conveying to the employee their prospects for advancement.

- *Developing employee skills.* The review can be a chance for the employee to learn new skills. Among their other roles, managers and supervisors should be teachers. The performance appraisal interview can be a chance to show an employee how to do a better job.

- *Improving employment relationship.* Performance reviews should improve superior-subordinate relationships and give employees a sense of participation in the job.

Negotiating Salary and Benefits

Many job candidates assume the interviewing process is over once they've received a job offer. However, it is important not to let your excitement rush your judgment. When a job offer is presented to you, ask for the details in writing along with a reasonable amount of time (no more than 24 hours) to review the offer before responding with a final decision.

While considering the offer, you may decide that you would like to try to negotiate for a higher salary or more benefits. One of your authors found that her students often express feeling a lack of confidence in negotiating compensation during a job offer. When prompted to explain why they lacked confidence, most stated that they didn't know what salary would be considered appropriate nor did they truly understand what constituted benefits. To help you know your worth and feel more comfortable entering negotiations, consider the following tips:

- *Research rates of pay for your industry, city, and position level (entry, midcareer, manager).* Sites like Glassdoor.com and LinkedIn.com provide salary ranges and market averages that may be helpful for getting an idea of what is reasonable. Additionally, Job Search Intelligence offers a free salary calculator that may be used to guide your negotiation. It is also useful to communicate with your professional network and mentors to ask for advice regarding appropriate salary ranges.

- *Use a cost-of-living calculator* to get a sense of how your take-home pay (after taxes, insurance, retirement, etc.) will measure up. You may be able to use this information to negotiate for higher base pay.

- *It is also important to realize that salary is not the only form of compensation that can be negotiated.* Many employers offer benefits which can make up to 30% of your salary. Examples of benefits you might negotiate include insurance, retirement, hiring bonuses, vacation time, sick leave, relocation cost reimbursement, tuition assistance, family leave, company cars or phones, gym memberships, etc.

Be sure to prepare for the possible outcomes of this conversation. Consider how you will react if the hiring manager says that negotiation is not an option or if they are only willing to budge a little. Ultimately, it is up to you to make the choice that is best for you. Regardless of your choice, being kind and genuine will go a long way.

Ideally, employees will leave the interview feeling better about themselves and the organization.

- *Helping management learn the employee's point of view.* A performance appraisal should include upward as well as downward communication. It provides a chance for subordinates to explain their perspective to managers.

- *Counseling the employee.* An appraisal interview provides a chance for managers to learn about personal problems that may be affecting an employee's performance and to offer advice and support.

- *Setting goals for the future.* One result of every performance appraisal interview should be a clear idea of how both the superior and the subordinate will behave in the future.

Even though performance appraisal interviews serve valuable functions, they are not always a positive experience for employees or managers—especially when there are problems that must be addressed. As you learned earlier in this title, receiving criticism can be a challenge. The interviewing strategies outlined in this section can help make sure a performance review meets the needs of both management and employees. While following these guidelines will not guarantee a successful performance review, it can increase the chances that the meeting will be genuinely constructive and serve the interests of both the superior and the subordinate.

Provide an Overview   After an initial exchange of pleasantries—usually brief—the manager should provide a rationale for the interview, an outline of what information will be covered and how it will be used, and a preview of the interview's probable length. After the preliminaries, the body of an appraisal interview should go on to cover three areas: a review of the criteria established in past meetings, a discussion of the employee's performance, and establishing goals for the future.

Review Progress   The first step in the body of any appraisal interview should be to identify the criteria by which the employee is being evaluated. Ideally, these criteria will already be clear to both the manager and the employee, but it is wise to restate them. A manager might say:

> Will, as I'm sure you remember, we decided at our last meeting to focus on several targets. We agreed that if you could reach them, you'd be doing your present job very well and you'd be setting yourself up for an assistant sales manager's position. Here's the list of targets we developed last time [shows employee list]. So these are the areas we need to look at today.

Discuss Successes, Problems, and Needs   After the criteria have been defined, the discussion can focus on how well the employee has satisfied them. This part of the discussion will be easiest when the goals are measurable: Are sales up 15%? Have jobs been completed on time? If the employee has explanations for why targets were not reached, it is the manager's job to consider these fairly. When goals are subjective, the evaluation of their performance will be a matter of judgment. Even seemingly vague goals such as "being more patient with customers" can be at least partially clarified by turning them into low-level abstractions such as "letting customers talk without interrupting them."

When evaluating past performance, it is important to maintain a balance among the points under consideration. Without meaning to let it happen, a manager and an employee can become involved in discussing (or debating) a relatively unimportant point at length, throwing the overall look at the employee's performance out of perspective. A skillful interviewer will focus only on the most important criteria, usually dealing with no more than three areas that need work. Even the most demanding manager will realize upon reflection that changing old habits is difficult and it is unrealistic to expect dramatic improvement in too many areas within a short time frame.

Even when an appraisal is conducted with the best of intentions, its evaluative nature raises the odds of a defensive response. Feedback will be best received when it meets several criteria. Observing these guidelines can boost the chances of keeping the interview's tone constructive:

- *Feedback should be accurate.* Perhaps the worst mistake an evaluator can make is to get the facts wrong. Before you judge an employee, make sure you have an accurate picture of their performance and all the factors that affected it. A tell-and-listen approach can help the manager understand an employee's performance more fully.

- *Feedback should be relevant to the job.* For example, commenting on an employee's appearance in a job that involves contact with the public may be appropriate, but it is out of line to be critical about the way they handle personal matters after business hours.

- *Feedback should include a balance of praise and constructive criticism.* Both everyday experience and research have demonstrated the power of positive reinforcement. Nevertheless, mentioning only the positives means forgoing the possibility of identifying areas for growth and improvement.

- *Feedback should be delivered in a way that protects people's dignity.* Sooner or later, even the most outstanding employee will need to hear criticism about their work. Delivering negative information is one of the biggest challenges a manager or supervisor can face. The guidelines in the previous chapter offer tips on how to offer negative feedback in a supportive manner. Handling critical situations well is not just the boss's responsibility; the subordinate needs to behave responsibly, too. The guidelines for responding in a non-defensive way to criticism outlined in the previous chapter should be helpful when it is your turn to receive critical messages.

Set Goals   Once the employee and the manager have discussed past successes, problems, and needs, the task becomes defining goals for the future. These goals should meet several criteria:

- The goals should focus on the most important aspects of the job. The tried-and-true 80:20 rule applies here: Changing 20% of a worker's behavior will usually solve 80% of the problems.

- The goals should be described as specifically as possible so both the manager and employee will know which actions constitute the target.

- A time period should be stated for each target. People often work best when faced with a deadline, and setting dates lets both parties know when the results are due.

- The targets ought to provide some challenge to the worker, requiring effort yet being attainable. A manageable challenge will produce the greatest growth and leave workers and managers feeling pleased with the changes that occur.

Review and Respond to the Written Record   The appraisal process commonly has a written dimension in addition to the interview itself. Before the meeting, the manager often completes an evaluation form listing characteristics or behaviors that are important for the job. Ideally, the information on this form will be taken from the goals set at the previous interview. In some organizations, the subordinate also completes a self-rating form covering similar areas.

After the meeting, the performance review is typically summarized and documented with a written evaluation. In most cases, the manager completes a final report that summarizes the results of the session. The employee usually has the option of adding their own response to the manager's report. This document then becomes part of the employee's record and is used as a basis for future evaluations and as a source of information for decisions about promotions.

• Interviewing Strategies

Every good interview shares some common characteristics and communication strategies. This section introduces skills you can use in almost every interview you will conduct in your career.

Planning the Interview

A successful interview begins before the parties face each other. Interviewers must make important choices with the purpose of structuring the interview in a way that will elicit the desired information from the respondent.

Define the Goal   Although it may seem obvious, it is important to first identify a clear goal for the interview. You will keep this goal in mind as you prepare the list of topics and the structure of questions. As an interviewer, you should make your goal as clear as possible:

Vague: Learn about prospective web designers.

Better: Evaluate which web designer can do the best job for us.

Best: Determine which web designer can create and maintain an affordable website that attracts and retains customers.

Identify and Analyze the Other Party   You cannot always choose who you will interview, but when you do have options, choosing the right person can make your conversation more useful and successful. Mark McCormack, the owner of a sports promotion agency, once explained:

> One of the biggest problems we have had as a sales organization is figuring out who within another company will be making a decision on what. Very often in our business we don't know if it's the advertising department, the marketing department, or someone in PR, or corporate communications. It may very well turn out to be the chairman and CEO of a multibillion-dollar corporation if the subject is of personal interest to him.[54]

Finding the right interviewee is important in other fields besides sales. For example, if you want to know more about the safety procedures in a manufacturing area, the plant manager can tell you more about them than, say, the publicity staff—who probably get their information from the plant manager anyway.

Chris Ryan/Ojo Images/AGE Fotostock RF

Prepare a List of Topics   To help you get all the information you need to accomplish your goal, you should prepare a list of topics that support your goal. An office manager who is purchasing new tablet computers for the staff might consider the following goal and topics when interviewing sales representatives from different companies:

- *Goal:* To purchase tablet computers that will be affordable, reliable, and compatible with our current setup.
- *List of Topics:*
  - Wireless and networking capabilities
  - Compatibility with existing software and operating systems
  - Pricing and quantity discounts
  - Warranties and tech support

Choose the Best Interview Structure   Several types of interview structures may be used. As Table 6-5 illustrates, each calls for different levels of planning and produces different results.

A **structured interview** consists of a standardized list of questions that allow only a limited range of answers with no follow-up: "How many televisions do you own?" "Which of the following words best describes your evaluation of the company?" Structured

Table 6-5	Differences between Structured and Unstructured Interviews

Structured Interview	Unstructured Interview
Usually takes less time than an unstructured interview	Usually takes more time than a structured interview
Easier for interviewer to control	More difficult for interviewer to control
Provides quantifiable results	Results more difficult to quantify
Requires less interviewer skill	Requires high degree of interviewer skill
Low flexibility in exploring responses	High flexibility in exploring responses

interviews are preferable when the goal is to get standardized responses from a large number of people, as in market research and opinion polls. They are less appropriate in most other situations.

The **moderately structured interview** consists of a set of major questions that the interviewer would like to explore but leaves room for follow-up questions that may emerge from the interview discussion. Specifically, the interviewer prepares a list of topics, anticipates their probable order, and then designs major questions and possible follow-up probes. The planned questions ensure coverage of important areas while allowing for examination of important but unforeseen topics. Moderately structured interviews are well suited for most situations because they provide measures of both control and spontaneity.

As its name suggests, an **unstructured interview** stands in contrast to its structured and moderately structured counterparts. The interviewer has a goal and perhaps a few topical areas in mind but no list of questions. Unstructured interviews allow considerable flexibility about the amount of time they take and the nature of the questioning. They permit the conversation to flow in whatever direction seems most productive. Unstructured interviews are usually spur-of-the-moment events. For example, you might meet a useful contact at a party and use the opportunity to explore career options.

Consider Possible Questions As you might expect, the type and quality of questions asked are likely to be the biggest factor in determining the success or failure of an interview. As Table 6-6 shows, a question can fit into several categories. For instance, the prompt "Describe some experiences that demonstrate your leadership abilities" is primary, open, factual, and direct. A question could also be secondary, closed, and hypothetical: "You said you welcome challenges. If the chance arose, would you be interested in handling the next round of layoffs?" A good interviewer considers these question types as tools and chooses the right combination to get the information they want to discover.

Some questions look legitimate but have no place in most interviews. **Leading questions** suggest the answer the interviewer expects: "You're interested in helping us work on this year's United Way campaign, aren't you?" "You aren't really serious about asking for a raise now, are you?"

Arrange the Setting The physical setting in which an interview takes place can have a great deal of influence on the results. The first consideration is to arrange a setting free of distractions. Sometimes it is best to choose a spot away from each person's normal habitat. Not only does this lessen the chance of interruptions, but people often speak more freely and think more creatively when in a neutral space, away from familiar settings that trigger habitual ways of responding.

Table 6-6	Types of Interview Questions

Type	Use
Primary Introduces a new topic.	• *To open a new line of discussion:* "Tell me about your past experience . . ."
Secondary Gathers additional information on the topic under discussion.	• *When a previous answer is incomplete:* "What did she say then?" • *When a previous answer is vague:* "What do you mean you *think* the figures are right?" • *When a previous answer is irrelevant:* "I understand the job interests you. Can you tell me about your training in the field?" • *When a previous answer seems inaccurate:* "You said everyone supports the idea. What about Yuki?"
Closed Restricts the interviewee's response.	• *When specific information is needed:* "When do you think the order will be ready?" "How long have you worked here?" • *To maintain control over the conversation:* "I understand you're upset about the delay. When was the shipment supposed to arrive?" • *When time is short:* "If you had to name one feature you want, what would it be?" • *When a high degree of standardization between interviews is important:* "On a scale of 1 to 10, how would you rate the importance of each of these features . . .?"
Open Invites a broader, more detailed range of responses.	• *To relax the interviewee (if the question is easy to answer and non-threatening):* "How did you hear about our company?" • *To discover the interviewee's opinions, feelings, or values:* "What do you think about . . .?" • *To evaluate the interviewee's communication skills:* "How would you handle an extremely irate customer?" • *To explore the interviewee's possession of information:* "What do you know about the missing documents?"
Factual Seeks concrete information.	• *To seek objective information:* "Can we apply lease payments to the purchase price, if we decide to buy?"
Opinion Explores the respondent's viewpoint.	• *To seek the respondent's analysis:* "Do you think the investment is worth it?" • *To evaluate the respondent's judgment:* "Which vendor do you think gives the best service?" "Do you think Priti is being sincere?"
Direct Straightforward request for information.	• *When the respondent is willing and able to provide the information being sought:* "Do you have a list of the employee benefits that come with this position?"

(continued)

Table 6-6	Types of Interview Questions *(Continued)*

Type	Use
Indirect Elicits information without directly asking for it.	• *When the respondent is not in a position to answer a direct question (e.g., "Do you understand?"):* "Suppose you had to explain this policy to other people in the department. What would you say?" • *When the respondent is unwilling to answer a direct question (e.g., "Are you satisfied with my leadership?"):* How do you think most of your coworkers view my leadership?
Hypothetical Seeks an answer to a "what if?" question.	• *When the respondent lacks experience to answer a direct question:* "If you were manager of this department, which changes would you make?" • *To get input that will help the interviewer make a good decision:* "If you were me, what would you do under these circumstances?"
Critical Incident Asks about a specific account of a real—rather than hypothetical—situation.	• *To evaluate the respondent's experience:* "Think of a time when you felt you had to break an implicit company policy to achieve the larger company vision. Describe the situation and how you handled it."

A manager at a major publishing company often interviews subordinates over lunch at a restaurant where company employees frequently eat together. The manager explains:

> The advantage of meeting here is we're both relaxed. They can talk about their work without feeling as though they've been called on the carpet to defend themselves. They're also more inclined to ask for help with a problem than if we were in the office, and I can ask for improvements and make suggestions without making it seem like a formal reprimand.

The physical arrangement of the setting can also influence the interview. Generally, the person sitting behind a desk gains power and formality. Sitting together at a table or with no barrier promotes equality and informality. Distance, too, affects the relationship between interviewer and respondent. Other things being equal, two people seated 40 inches apart will have more immediacy in their conversation than those separated by a distance of 6 or 7 feet.

As with other variables, the degree of formality depends on your goal. A supervisor who wants to assert their authority during a disciplinary interview might increase distance and sit behind a desk. In contrast, a health care provider who wants to gain a patient's trust may avoid the barrier of a desk.

The right time is as important as the place for a successful interview. When you plan an interview, give careful thought to how much time you will need to accomplish your purpose, and let the other person know how much time you expect to take. Consider the time of day and people's schedules before and after the interview. For example, you might avoid scheduling an important interview right before lunch so neither person will be more anxious to eat than to accomplish the goal of the interview.

Successfully Navigating Job Fairs

Job fairs offer the chance to network with employers and to secure job interviews, sometimes on the spot. In this respect, job fairs serve as initial interviews.

Some job fairs are set on college and university campuses, where employers look for graduating students. Community fairs are open to the public at large. Some target a specific field such as health care or engineering, while others feature a diverse array of organizations and fields.

Before You Go:

- Ask yourself what will make you stand out from the hundred people a recruiter might see in a day.
- Gain a competitive edge by learning about the employers that interest you. Learn what positions they are hiring for and what qualifications are required. If possible, discover whether companies will be conducting job interviews at the fair or soon thereafter. You may be able to discover this sort of information from the career fair sponsor. Also, if you contact the target company, you may be able to find out whether the person at the table is doing the hiring or if a human resources representative screens for quality candidates to recommend.
- Rehearse your "elevator" speech so you can present yourself clearly and professionally. Bring copies of both your generic résumé and customized versions for positions you will be seeking. Dress conservatively and professionally.
- Carry a professional leather tote or briefcase (a shoulder strap leaves your hands free for handshakes and writing notes) with a portfolio that allows you to easily retrieve résumés and letters of recommendation. Pack tissues and breathe mints.

At the Fair:

- Arrive early. Spend a few minutes getting a feel for the way the fair operates. Is the atmosphere formal or informal?

- Don't ever ASK what an employer does. KNOW before you go.
- Manage your time efficiently: Approach your second-tier choices first to "warm up" so you are confident when approaching your first choices. Some employers pack up an hour or so before the designated closing time, so don't wait until the last minute.
- If you must stand in line, use that time to talk with other candidates: Find out what they've found about employers and positions.
- Approach the company's representative with confidence: "Hello. I'm Janya Greer. I'm a journalism and English major, and I'm interested in the writing positions." Remember, you are being evaluated from the moment you make contact.
- Always think about how your career objectives and qualifications meet the employer's needs. Ask specific questions that show you've done your homework.
- Ask for the business card of anyone with whom you speak.

After the Fair:

- For employers that look like a good match, follow up with a phone call or an e-mail to express thanks and confirm your interest.
- Remind the person where you met, what you talked about, and how your skills and qualifications match the company's needs. Add any information you neglected to mention at the job fair. Express your interest in learning more about the fit between you and the organization.

Source: University of New Mexico Career Center (n.d.). Retrieved from http://www.collegegrad.com and www.career.unm.edu

Conducting the Interview

After careful planning, the interview itself takes place. An interview consists of three stages: an opening (or introduction), a body, and a closing. In this section, we examine each of these stages in turn.

Opening   A good introduction can shape the entire interview. Research suggests people form lasting impressions of each other in the first few minutes of a conversation. Dave Deaver, a national management recruiter, describes the importance of first impressions in a job interview:

> "The first minute is all-important in an interview. Fifty percent of the decision is made within the first 30 to 60 seconds. About 25% of the evaluation is made during the first 15 minutes. It's very difficult to recover the last 25% if you've blown the first couple of minutes."[55]

Monkey Business Images/Shutterstock

These initial impressions shape how a listener regards everything that follows.

A good opening contains two parts: a greeting and an orientation. The opening is also a time for motivating the respondent to cooperate and giving a sense of what will follow.

Greeting and Building Rapport   The interviewer should begin with a greeting and a self-introduction, if necessary. In formal situations—when taking a legal deposition or conducting a structured survey, for example—it is appropriate to get right down to business. In most situations, however, building rapport is both appropriate and useful. If the interviewer and the respondent are comfortable with each other, the results are likely to be better for both. Small talk tends to set the emotional tone of the interview—formal or informal, nervous or relaxed, candid or guarded.

The most logical openers involve common ground, focusing on shared interests or experiences. "How are you coping with our record snowfall?" "Did you find your way around the airport construction?" Another type of common-ground opener involves job-related topics, though they are usually unrelated to the subject of the interview itself. For example, a manager interviewing employees to help design a new benefits package might start the conversation by asking, "How's the new parking plan working out?"

Orientation   In this stage of the opening, the interviewer gives the respondent a brief overview of what is to follow. This orientation helps put the respondent at ease by removing a natural apprehension of the unknown and helps establish and strengthen the interviewer's control. In the orientation, be sure to do the following:

Explain the reason for the interview.   A description of the interview's purpose can both put the respondent at ease and motivate them to respond. If your boss called you in for a "chat about how things are going," curiosity would probably be your mildest response. Are you headed for a promotion or being softened up for a layoff? Sharing the reason for an interview can relieve these concerns: "We're thinking about opening a branch office soon, and we're trying to plan our staffing. I'd like to find out how you feel about your working situation now and what you want so we can consider your needs when we make the changes."

Explain what information is needed and how it will be used.   A respondent who knows what the interviewer wants will have a greater likelihood of supplying it. In our example, the boss might be seeking two kinds of information to plan staffing at the new branch office. In one case, a statement of needed information might be, "I'm not interested in having you provide names of people you like or dislike. I want to know which parts of the business interest you and what you'd consider to be an ideal job." A quite different request for information might be, "I'd like to hear your feelings about the people you work with. Who would you like to work with in the future, and who do you have trouble with?"

A description of how the information will be used is also important. In our current example, the boss might explain, "I won't be able to tell you today exactly which changes we'll be making, but I promise you that this talk will be off the record. No one else will hear what you tell me."

Clarify any ground rules.   Make sure that you and the other party understand any operating procedures. For example, you might say, "I'd like to record our conversation instead of taking notes."

Mention the approximate length of the interview.   A respondent who knows how long the session will last will feel more comfortable and give better answers.

Motivation   Sometimes you need to give respondents a reason to feel that the interview is worthwhile for them. In some cases, you can simply point out the payoffs: "If we can figure out a better way to handle these orders, it will save us both time." If the interview will not directly benefit the other person, you might appeal to their ego or desire to help other people: "I'd like to try out a new promotional item, and you know more about them than anyone."

Body   Once pleasantries have been exchanged and an overview of the interview has been provided to the respondent, the main portion—or body—of the interview begins. Questions and answers are exchanged in the body of an interview. The interviewer performs several tasks during the question-and-answer phase of the discussion:

Control and focus the conversation.   If an interview is a conversation with a purpose, then it is the interviewer's job to make sure the discussion focuses on achieving the purpose. A response can be so interesting that it pulls the discussion off track: "I see you traveled in Europe after college. Did you make it to Barcelona?" Such discussion about backgrounds might be appropriate for the rapport-building part of the opening, but it can get out of control and use up time that would better be spent achieving the interview's purpose.

A second loss of control occurs when the interviewer spends too much time in one legitimate area of discussion, thereby slighting another. Difficult as it may be, an interviewer needs to allot rough blocks of time to each agenda item and then follow these guidelines.

Listen actively.   Some interviewers—especially novices—become so caught up in budgeting time and planning upcoming questions they fail in the most important task: listening carefully to the respondent. Multitasking can present problems. It can be hard to juggle the tasks of asking and answering questions, taking notes, keeping eye contact, and budgeting time. Skillful listening will ensure that you focus on the most important aspect of the interview—the message being sent by the respondent.

Use secondary questions to probe for important information.   Sometimes an answer may be incomplete. At other times, it may be evasive or vague. Because it is impossible to know in advance when probes will be needed, the interviewer should be ready to use them as the occasion dictates.

Antonio M. Rosario/Photodisc/Getty Images RF

An interviewer sometimes needs to *repeat* a question to get a satisfactory answer:

Interviewer:	You said you attended Arizona State for four years. I'm not clear about whether you earned a degree.
Respondent:	I completed the required courses in my major as well as several electives.
Interviewer:	I see. Did you earn a degree?

When a primary question does not deliver enough information, the interviewer needs to seek *elaboration*:

Interviewer:	When we made this appointment, you said Ricky has been insulting you. I'd like to hear about that.
Respondent:	He treats me like a child. I've been here almost as long as he has, and I know what I'm doing!
Interviewer:	Exactly what does he do? Can you give me a few examples?

Sometimes an answer will be complete but unclear. This requires a request for *clarification*:

Respondent:	The certificate pays 6.3% interest.
Interviewer:	Is that rate simple or compounded?

A *paraphrasing* probe restates the answer in different words. It invites the respondent to clarify and elaborate on a previous answer:

Interviewer:	You've been with us for a year and have been promoted once. How do you feel about the direction your career is taking?
Respondent:	I'm satisfied for now.
Interviewer:	So far, so good. Is that how you feel?
Respondent:	Not exactly. I was happy to get the promotion, of course. But I don't see many chances for advancement from here.

Often *silence* is the best probe. A pause of as long as 10 seconds (which feels like an eternity) lets the respondent know more information is expected. Depending on the interviewer's accompanying nonverbal messages, silence can indicate interest or dissatisfaction with the previous answer. *Prods* ("Uh-huh," "Hmmmm," "Go on," "Tell me more," and so on) accomplish the same purpose. For example:

Respondent:	I can't figure out where we can cut costs.
Interviewer:	Uh-huh.
Respondent:	We've already cut our travel and entertainment budget 5%.
Interviewer:	I see.
Respondent:	Some of our people probably still abuse it, but they'd be offended if we cut back more. They think of expense accounts as a fringe benefit.
Interviewer:	(silence)
Respondent:	Of course, if we could give them something in return for a cut, we might still be able to cut total costs. Maybe have the sales meeting at a resort—make it something of a vacation.

Closing   An interview should not end with the last answer to the last question. Instead, it should include a good closing that brings the conversation to a satisfactory conclusion.

Review and Clarify the Results of the Interview   Either party can take responsibility for this step, though in different ways. The person with the greater power (usually the interviewer) is most likely to do so in the most forthright manner. For example, in an interview exploring a grievance between employees, a manager might say, "It sounds like you're saying both of you could have handled it better." When the party with less power (usually the respondent) does the reviewing and clarifying, the summary often takes the form of a question. A sales representative might close by saying, "So the product sounds good to you, but before you make your final decision you'd like to talk to a few of our clients to see how it has worked out for them. Is that right?"

Establish Future Actions   When the relationship between interviewer and respondent is a continuing one, it is important to clarify how the matter under discussion will be handled. A sales representative might close by saying, "I'll e-mail a list of our customers to you tomorrow. Then why don't I give you a call next week to see what you're thinking?" A manager might clarify the future actions by saying, "I'd like you to try out the arrangement we discussed today. Then let's all get together in a few weeks to see how things are going. How does the first of next month sound?"

Conclude with Pleasantries   A sociable conclusion need not be phony. You can express appreciation, concern, or talk about what comes next:

1. "I appreciate the time you've given me today."
2. "Good luck with the project."
3. "We'll follow up on this at the staff meeting tomorrow."

• The Ethics of Interviewing

Basic ethical guidelines and responsibilities should guide the exchange of information that occurs between interviewer and respondent.[56] In addition to the moral reasons for following these guidelines, there is often a pragmatic basis for behaving ethically: Because the interview is likely to be part of an ongoing relationship, behaving responsibly and honorably will serve you well in future interactions. Conversely, the costs of developing a poor reputation are usually greater than the benefits of gaining a temporary advantage by behaving unethically or irresponsibly.

Obligations of the Interviewer

A conscientious business communicator will follow several guidelines when conducting an interview.

Make Only Promises You Are Willing and Able to Keep   Do not make offers or claims that may later prove impossible to honor. For example, it is dishonest and unfair for an employer to excite a job applicant about the chances of receiving an offer until they are sure an offer will be forthcoming. Likewise, a candidate should not indicate a willingness to start work immediately if they must first sell their home and move to the town where the new job is located.

Handling Difficult Questions

1. You know an employee has been leaving work early for the past several months. You hope they will volunteer this information without your having to confront them. During a performance appraisal, how can you raise the issue with this employee?

2. You are conducting a series of half-hour interviews with consumers, exploring their attitudes toward a variety of social issues, as part of a market research project for your employer. In the first few minutes of one session, the respondent makes several racist comments. How do you respond?

3. You are interviewing for a job you really want. The employer asks about your experience with a particular type of database software. You don't know much about this type of program, but you are confident you can teach yourself before the job begins. How do you reply to the interviewer?

Keep Confidences Interviewers and respondents should not reveal confidential information or disclose any private information gained during a session to people who have no legitimate reason to have it. Be certain to let the respondent know if you plan to record the session, and make it clear who else may be reviewing the recording.

Allow Free Responses An interview that coerces the respondent into giving unwilling answers is a charade of an honest conversation. For example, a supervisor conducting a performance appraisal who asks a subordinate, "Who do you think is responsible for the problems in your area?" should be willing to accept whatever answer is given and not automatically expect the employee to accept the blame. Trying to *persuade* a respondent is a normal part of doing business, but coercing one is unethical.

Treat Every Respondent with Respect With rare exceptions, the interviewer's job is to help the respondent do well. This means making sure the respondent feels comfortable and understands the nature of the session. It also means the interviewer must design clear questions so the respondent may answer them as well as possible.

Obligations of the Respondent

The respondent is also obliged to behave ethically and responsibly during a session. Several guidelines apply here.

Do Not Misrepresent the Facts or Your Position Whether the setting is an employment interview, a performance review session, or an information-gathering survey, it can be tempting to tell interviewers what they want to hear. The temptation is especially great if your welfare is at stake. But besides being unethical, misrepresenting the facts is likely to catch up with you sooner or later and harm you more than telling the truth in the first place.

Do Not Waste the Interviewer's Time If the choice exists, be sure you are qualified for the interview. For example, it would be a mistake to interview for a job you have little chance of landing or would not accept. Likewise, it would be unethical to volunteer for a customer survey if you are not a member of the population being studied. If preparation for the interview is necessary, do your homework. Once the interview has begun, stick to the subject to use the time most wisely.

review points

- Interviews are purposeful and structured, use questions as the main tool, and allow one party greater control and the other party more speaking time.

- Information-gathering interviews allow individuals to collect information about an occupation, industry, or other topics in which they are interested.

- A career research interview helps the interviewer research a career field, be remembered by the respondent, and gain referrals.

- Employment interviews are an important way to communicate your professional identity. Before an employment interview, clean up your online identity, conduct background research, and prepare for a variety of formats. During the interview, put your best foot forward by communicating professionally and dressing appropriately.

- Respondents need to prepare for key questions, engage in active listening and give clear and detailed answers, respond to the employer's needs, and support answers with evidence honestly, positively, briefly, and enthusiastically. Interviewees can demonstrate their professionalism by clearing misunderstandings, using appropriate humor, asking pertinent questions, and following up with a thank you note.

- Under the law, interviewers are not supposed to ask questions that are not related to the BFOQs of a job. Respondents should know which kinds of questions are legal or illegal and prepare for the possibility that they might be asked illegal questions.

- Once an offer has been made, job candidates should be prepared to discuss (and potentially negotiate) salary and benefits with their prospective employers.

- Performance appraisal interviews allow superiors and subordinates to meet at regularly scheduled intervals to discuss the quality of the subordinate's performance.

- Interviewers can plan for the interview effectively by defining their goals, identifying and analyzing the other party, listing topics, choosing the best structure and questions, and arranging the setting.

- Interviewers should strategically use primary and secondary questions, including closed, open, factual, opinion, direct, indirect, and hypothetical questions, while avoiding leading questions.

- Interviews consist of three parts: an opening that creates rapport, orientation, and motivation; a body that focuses on the conversation with active listening and clear answers; and a closing that reviews, clarifies, and concludes the encounter.

- Ethical interviewers treat respondents respectfully, keep confidences, honor promises, and avoid coercion. Ethical respondents are sincere and prepared, and present themselves honestly.

key terms

activities

1. Skill Builder

Imagine you are conducting a research interview with an employee of a company where you might like to work.

a. Develop a list of topics you will need to cover to get a complete picture of the organization.
b. Decide which structure (structured, moderately structured, unstructured) would be best for this interview. Defend your choice.
c. For each topic, write several appropriate questions.

2. Skill Builder

Become more familiar with types of questions through the following activity.

a. For each of the following situations, describe whether an open or closed question would be more appropriate. Explain your choices. If you think more than one question is necessary to discover the essential information, list each one.

1. You want to find out whether your boss will support your request to attend a convention in a distant city.
2. A manager wants to know whether a project will exceed its projected budget.
3. An insurance sales representative wants to determine whether a customer has adequate coverage.
4. An employer wants to find out why an applicant has held four jobs in five years.

b. For each of the following situations, write one factual question and one opinion question. Decide which of these questions is most appropriate for the situation. Then write two secondary questions as follows-ups for the primary question you have chosen:

1. You want to know whether you are justified in asking your boss for a raise, and you decide to question a coworker.
2. A supervisor wants to discover whether an employee's request for a one-month personal leave of absence to visit a sick parent is essential.
3. You are planning to buy a laptop or a desktop computer. You want to decide whether the laptop computer is worth the extra $250 it will cost.

c. For each of the following direct questions, create an indirect question that could elicit the same information:

1. "How hard a worker are you?" (selection)
2. "Do you agree with my evaluation?" (appraisal)
3. "Does the product have any drawbacks?" (diagnostic)
4. "Are you telling me the real reason you're leaving?" (exit)
5. "Do you really believe this idea has merit, or are you just going along with it?" (research)

3. Skill Builder

With a partner, role-play how you, as an interviewer, could follow the interview guidelines presented in this chapter as you conduct the opening stages of each of the following interviews:

a. You are a real estate broker meeting a potential home-buying client for the first time.
b. You are considering opening a new restaurant in town (you choose the kind), and you are interviewing the owner of a similar type of establishment in another city about how you can be successful.
c. You are thinking about taking a specific college course (you choose which one) that will help you in your career, and you are meeting with the professor to get a better idea of what is involved.
d. You are interviewing the manager of an assisted care facility to see if it would be a suitable place for your grandmother.

4. Invitation to Insight

Select a person in your chosen career field who plays a role in hiring new employees. Conduct an information-gathering interview to discover the following:

a. What methods are used to identify job candidates?
b. What format is used to interview applicants?
c. What formal and informal criteria are used to hire applicants?
d. What personal qualities of applicants make positive and negative impressions?

205

5. Skill Builder

For each of the following topics, identify at least two people you could interview to gather information. Write a specific objective for each interview:

a. Learning more about a potential employer. (Name a specific organization.)

b. Deciding whether to enroll in a specific class. (You choose which one.)

c. Deciding which type of personal computer or software application to purchase.

d. Exploring career opportunities in a city of your choice.

e. Determining the best savings or investment vehicle for you at this time.

f. Finding a service activity you would like to participate in.

6. Skill Builder

You can develop your skill and gain appreciation for the value of the informational interview by doing one of the following activities:

a. Conduct an informational interview with a professional in a career field that interests you. Possible goals are to learn more about the field, to learn how to advance in your current job, or to learn what it would take to switch fields. Follow these steps:

1. Identify a promising interviewee.
2. Write an e-mail requesting an interview.
3. Follow up your e-mail with a phone call to arrange a date for the interview.
4. Develop a list of questions that will achieve your stated purpose. Be sure that these questions follow the guidelines presented in this chapter.
5. Conduct the interview and report your results. Analyze how well you performed. Suggest how you could improve in conducting future interviews.
6. Write a thank you letter to your interviewee.

b. Identify a specific organization you would like to work for. Complete the following pre-interview steps:

1. Identify the person—by title and name, if possible—who has the power to hire you.
2. Using research and the results of informational interviews, analyze the requirements for the position you would like to hold.

3. Develop a list of questions that a potential boss might ask in a selection interview.
4. Prepare answers to those questions using the PAR method.

c. Role-play an actual interview, with a companion filling the role of your potential employer.

1. Record a video of the interview.
2. View the interview and analyze both your verbal and nonverbal performance.

7. Invitation to Insight

Brainstorm five to 10 specific actions you have taken (in classes, on the job, or in volunteer activities) that demonstrate your ability to perform well. Include specific evidence for each. Recall the positive results of your actions.

For added practice, team up with a classmate. Use the PAR approach to role-play asking and answering interview questions. As your classmate asks questions, use your brainstormed accomplishments to answer with actions and results. Then switch roles.

8. Skill Builder

In a group, practice your skill at answering behavioral interview questions using the PAR approach:

a. Describe a time when you needed to work as part of a team.

b. Describe a time when you used creativity and problem-solving skills to solve an important problem.

c. Explain how you handled a situation when you had to make an important ethical decision.

d. Describe a time when you didn't succeed at something you were trying to accomplish.

e. Describe a time when you took on a greater share of responsibility or decision making than was required by your job.

9. Skill Builder

With your group, consider each of the following questions. Decide whether they would be lawful or unlawful to ask in an interview. Explain your reasoning.

a. "Have you ever been arrested?"
b. "When and where were you born?"
c. "What are your greatest weaknesses?"
d. "Do you own your own car?"
e. "Are you married, divorced, or single?"

f. "Which personal qualities do you have that you think would be helpful in working with the teams within our organization?"

g. "You look Vietnamese. Are you?"

h. "Do you own, rent, or lease your home?"

i. "Do you have any disabilities?"

j. "Your address is in an interesting part of town; isn't that the Cuesta Verde area?"

k. "What is your maiden name?"

l. "What do you know about our company?"

m. "Can you show proof of your age if you are hired?"

In your group, prepare five more potential job interview questions. Challenge your classmates to determine whether they are lawful or unlawful.

McGraw Hill LearnSmart™

For further review, go to the LearnSmart study module for this chapter.

references

1. Stewart, C. J., & Cash, W. B., Jr. (2011). *Interviewing: Principles and practices* (13th ed.). Boston, MA: McGraw Hill.

2. Stewart, C. J., & Cash, W. B., Jr. (2011). *Interviewing: Principles and practices* (13th ed.). Boston, MA: McGraw Hill.

3. Stewart, C. J., & Cash, W. B., Jr. (2011). *Interviewing: Principles and practices* (13th ed.). Boston, MA: McGraw Hill.

4. Walton, S., & Huey, J., *Made in America*. New York: Bantam, 1993.

5. Granovetter, M. (1995). *Getting a job: A study of contacts and careers* (2nd ed.). Chicago, IL: University of Chicago Press.

6. Baker, W. (2000). *Achieving success through social capital*. San Francisco, CA: Jossey-Bass.

7. Doyle, A. (2020, January 30). What is the hidden job market? *The Balance Careers*. Retrieved from https://www.thebalancecareers.com/what-is-the-hidden-job-market-2062004

8. Tugend, A. (2008, December 19). Readers weigh in with tips on jobs and money. *New York Times*.

9. Rogers, E. M. (1983). *Diffusion of innovations* (3rd ed.). New York: Free Press.

10. U.S. Bureau of Labor Statistics (2020, August 18). Employment and unemployment among youth—summer 2020 [News release]. Retrieved from https://www.bls.gov/news.release/pdf/youth.pdf

11. Peterson, M. S. (1997). Personnel interviewers' perceptions of the importance and adequacy of applicants' communication skills. *Communication Education, 46,* 287–291.

12. Bolles, R. N. (1997). *What color is your parachute? A practical manual for job-hunters and career-changers.* Berkeley, CA: Ten Speed Press.

13. Berkelaar, B. (2008, May). *Cyber-vetting (potential) employees: An emerging area of study for organizational communication.* Paper presented at the International Communication Association annual meeting, Montreal, QC.

14. Berkelaar, B. L., & Harrison, M. A. (2017). Cybervetting. In C. R. Scott, & L. Lewis (Eds), *The international encyclopedia of organizational communication* (pp. 1-7). Hoboken, NJ: Wiley.

15. CareerBuilder. (2018, August 9). More than half of employers have found content on social media that caused them not to hire a candidate, according to recent CareerBuilder survey [Press release]. Retrieved from http://press.careerbuilder.com/2018-08-09-More-Than-Half-of-Employers-Have-Found-Content-on-Social-Media-That-Caused-Them-NOT-to-Hire-a-Candidate-According-to-Recent-CareerBuilder-Survey#:~:text=Employers%20who%20found%20content%20on,or%20using%20drugs%3A%2036%20percent

16. Jacobson, J., & Gruzd, A. (2020). Cybervetting job applicants on social media: The new normal? *Ethics and Information Technology, 22,* 175–195. Retrieved from https://link.springer.com/article/10.1007/s10676-020-09526-2

17. Drake, J., Hall, D., Brecton, B., & Posey, C. (2016). Job applicants' information privacy protection responses: Using social media for candidate screening. *AIS Transactions on Human–Computer Interaction, 8*(4), 159–183.

18. Baert, S. (2018). Facebook profile picture appearance affects recruiters' first hiring decisions. *New Media & Society, 20*(3), 1220–1239.

19. Starbucks. (n.d.). Business ethics and compliance. Retrieved from https://globalassets.starbucks.com/assets/eecd184d6d2141d58966319744393d1f.pdf

20. Murphy, S. (1999, December 19). The second interview. *Santa Barbara News Press*, p. E1.

21. Cavanaugh, T. [Todd Cavanaugh]. (2014, January 22). Explaining Dropbox to your grandparents [Video file]. Retrieved from https://www.youtube.com/watch?v=NIWOy5Sb59M

22. Ace your audition interview. (2001). Retrieved from http://www.wetfeet.com/asp/article.asp?aid562

23. Trotsky, J. (2001, January). Oh, will you behave? *Computerworld, 35*(2), 42–43.

24. Farmery, P. (2000). Recruiters offer a new view of the job interview. In *Job choices: Diversity edition.* Bethlehem, PA: National Association of Colleges and Employers.

25. Gartner. (2020, April 30). Gartner HR survey shows 86% of organizations are conducting virtual interviews to hire candidates during coronavirus pandemic [Press release]. Retrieved from https://www.gartner.com/en/newsroom/press-releases/2020-04-30-gartner-hr-survey-shows-86–of-organizations-are-cond

26. Gartner. (2020, April 30). Gartner HR survey shows 86% of organizations are conducting virtual interviews to hire candidates during coronavirus pandemic [Press release]. Retrieved from https://www.gartner.com/en/newsroom/press-releases/2020-04-30-gartner-hr-survey-shows-86–of-organizations-are-cond

27. Everest College. (2013, September 4). 92% of Americans have job interview nerves [Blog]. *Everest College: The Official Blog.* Retrieved from https://everestcollege.wordpress.com/2013/09/04/92-of-americans-have-job-interview-nerves/#:~:text=A%20recent%20survey%20done%20by,top%20fear%20of%20the%20process.

28. Ayres, J., Keereetaweep, T., Chen, P., & Edwards, P. A. (1998). Communication apprehension and employment interviews. *Communication Education, 47,* 1–17.

29. Goodall, D. B., & Goodall, H. L., Jr., (1982). The employment interview: A selective review of the literature with implications for communications research. *Communication Quarterly, 30,* 116–122.

30. CareerBuilder (2018, February 22). The most unusual interview mistakes and biggest body language mishaps, according to CareerBuilder survey [Press release]. Retrieved from http://press.careerbuilder.com/2018-02-22-The-Most-Unusual-Interview-Mistakes-and-Biggest-Body-Language-Mishaps-According-to-Annual-CareerBuilder-Survey

31. Eder, R. W., & Ferris, G. R. (Eds.). (1989). *The employment interview: Theory, research, and practice.* Newbury Park, CA: Sage.

32. Caggiano, C. (1998, October). "What were you in for?" and other great job-interview questions of our time. *Inc., 20*(14), 117.

33. Cooper, C. L. (1993, May/June). No more stupid questions. *Psychology Today, 26*(3), 14–15.

34. Martz, G. (1996). *How to survive without your parents' money.* New York: Villiard.

35. Brandt, G. (2011, April 27). Executive recruiters agree there are only three true job interview questions. *Forbes.*

36. Bolles, R. N. (2012). *What color is your parachute? A practical manual for job-hunters and career-changers.* Berkeley, CA: Ten Speed Press.

37. Ralston, S. M., & Kirkwood, W. (1999). The trouble with applicant impression management. *Journal of Business and Technical Communication, 13,* 190–207; Ralston, S. M. (2000). The "veil of ignorance": Exploring ethical issues in the employment interview. *Business Communication Quarterly, 63,* 50–52.

38. Rosenfeld, P. (1997). Impression management, fairness and the employment interview. *Journal of Business Ethics, 16,* 801–808.

39. Beatty, R. H. (2003). *The interview kit* (3rd ed.). Hoboken, NJ: John Wiley & Sons.

40. Silverstein, S., & Brooks, N. R. (1993, March 1). And be sure to mention your favorite subject: You. *Los Angeles Times,* p. D3.

41. Quoted in Kleiman, C. (2003, February 16). Passion play. *The Salt Lake Tribune and the Deseret News,* p. F1.

42. Sala, F. (2000). Relationship between executive's spontaneous use of humor and effective leadership. Unpublished doctoral dissertation, Boston University.

43. Van De Mieroop, D., & Schnurr, S. (2018, July). Candidates' humour and the construction of co-membership in job interviews. *Language & Communication, 61,* 35–45. Retrieved from https://doi.org/10.1016/j.langcom.2018.01.002

44. Autenrieth, N. (n.d.). How to appropriately use humor in an interview. *TopResume.* Retrieved from https://www.topresume.com/career-advice/how-to-appropriately-use-humor-in-an-interview

45. Chen, H. (2009). Can this interview be saved? Maybe with a proper thank you note and follow up. *Vault.* Retrieved from http://www.vault.com/nr/main_article_detail.jsp?article_id=8801822&cat_id=0&ht_type=10

46. Stokes, C. (2019, May). Interviewing 101 for the recent graduate. *Strategies & Tactics, 7.*

47. Medley, H. A. (1978). *Sweaty palms: The neglected art of being interviewed.* Belmont, CA: Wadsworth.

48. Dickson, M. B. (1993). *Supervising employees with disabilities: Beyond ADA compliance.* Menlo Park, CA: Crisp.

49. Springston, J. K., & Keyton, J. (1988). So tell me, are you married? When the interviewee knows you're asking an illegal question. In J. W. Robinson (Ed.),

Proceedings of the 1988 Annual National Conference of the Council of Employee Responsibilities and Rights. Virginia Beach, VA.

50. Woo, J. (1992, March 11). Job interviews pose risk to employers. *Wall Street Journal*, B1, B5.

51. McShulskis, E. (1997, June). Be aware of illegal interview questions. *HR Magazine, 42*(6), 22-23.

52. Sincoff, M. Z., & Goyer, R. S., *Interviewing.* New York: Macmillan, 1984.

53. Fry, R. (2002). *Your first interview* (4th ed.). Franklin Lakes, NJ: Career Press.

54. McCormack, M. H. (1984). *What they don't teach you at Harvard Business School.* New York: Bantam.

55. Shepherd, S. J. (1986, March). How to get that job in 60 minutes or less. *Working Woman, 10*, 118.

56. Wilson, G. L., & Goodall, H. L., Jr. (1991). *Interviewing in context.* New York: McGraw Hill.

PART THREE

Fuse/Corbis/Getty Images

STRATEGIC CASE

Museum of Springfield

Paul Georgakis, the new media coordinator at the Museum of Spring-field, is working on a career-defining assignment: developing the web-site for the museum's forthcoming new show, "Images of Springfield." Midwestern Industries is underwriting the exhibit, and museum curator Mary Weston has told Paul that the board of trustees is counting on the exhibit's success to open the door to more corporate support. "If that happens, we'll have a shot at becoming a top-quality regional museum," Mary tells Paul. "I don't have to tell you how important that is to the board of trustees." Mary might as well have said, "I don't have to tell you how important this is to your career."

Along with Paul, the project team for the website includes four other members. Elaine Cortez is the site's designer. Bringing San Francisco-based Elaine on board was a coup for Paul. Elaine has created sites for several world-class organizations, and took the museum job for a deeply discounted fee to give something back to the community. Dwayne Henderson, a history professor at the local branch of the state university, is the content expert for the exhibit and the accompa-nying website. Dwayne's specialty is the influence of business and government institutions on underprivileged groups in nineteenth-century U.S. society. Hieu Phan is the corporate liaison with Midwestern Industries. Hieu has made it clear that their company is glad to support the museum and expects to be recognized for doing so. "Doing good can help Midwestern Industries do well," Hieu told Paul. Mary Weston, Paul's boss, represents the museum's administration and board of trustees.

The website project got off to a good start. Lately, however, several problems have developed. On a practical level, it has proved almost impossible to get all members to attend the last few meetings. Because Elaine is based in San Francisco and Hieu's office is in Minneapolis, it has been difficult for both of them to squeeze in visits to Springfield.

Even more alarming has been a growing tension that has arisen as it has become clear that Dwayne's exhibit includes some disturbing images and stories. Hieu recently sent the team an e-mail saying, "Midwestern Industries isn't contributing several hundred thousand dollars to upset the community." Dwayne replied, "It isn't a historian's job to make people happy." Paul is growing worried that Dwayne or Hieu might pull out of the project, and either scenario would be a disaster.

Finally, it has become clear that Elaine views any suggestion for revising her design as an assault on her artistic talent. "I don't tell you how to run your museum or Midwestern Industries," Elaine says. "You're the experts in your own fields, and I am the expert in mine. I know what I'm doing, and you just have to trust me." Mary has made it clear she is counting on Paul to keep the team together and the project on track.

Working in Groups

As you read the chapters in this unit, consider how answers to the following questions might help Paul manage this difficult job.

chapter 7

1. Which type of power listed in Chapter 7 does each team member have? How can the members use their power to help the team achieve its goal?
2. Which approaches to leadership outlined in Chapter 7 can Paul use to keep the team functioning well?
3. What are each member's personal goals? How do these goals contribute to or interfere with the team's job?

chapter 8

1. How can the team use the systematic problem-solving method outlined in Chapter 8 to overcome the challenges it faces?
2. Which decision-making method(s) should the members use in deciding how to resolve their disagreements?
3. Are there ways the team can handle some of its tasks without meeting in person?
4. What might an agenda for the team's next meeting look like?
5. Which techniques outlined in Chapter 8 can Paul use when leading face-to-face meetings?

Chapter Seven
Leading and Working in Teams

chapter outline

chapter objectives

After reading this chapter you should be able to:

1. Identify the kinds of communication that distinguish a group from a team.

2. Explain the advantages and disadvantages of face-to-face and virtual teams, and describe ways to address the disadvantages.

3. Compare and contrast various approaches to leadership, leader–member relations, and power distribution, and explain their impact on teams.

4. Identify and apply guidelines for effective communication in teams with regard to roles, goals, norms, cohesion, conformity, and creativity.

P olitical economist Robert Reich describes the importance of teamwork in an increasingly technological age:

Rarely do even Big Ideas emerge any longer from the solitary labors of genius. Modern science and technology is too complicated for one brain. It requires groups of astronomers, physicists, and computer programmers to discover new dimensions of the universe, teams of microbiologists, oncologists, and chemists to unravel the mysteries of cancer. With ever more frequency, Nobel prizes are awarded to collections of people. Scientific papers are authored by small platoons of researchers.[1]

Working with others is a vital part of almost every job.[2] In many companies, employees spend 80% or more of their time collaborating.[3] A national survey of architects and landscape architects found that more than 75% of respondents reported "always" or "often" working in teams.[4] Indeed, the amount of research done by teams has increased in virtually every scientific field.[5] Even the surgical profession is increasingly becoming a team effort.[6]

Given the prevalence of teams, no matter how talented you are, being a solo player is not an option in the modern business world. Gary Kaplan, owner of a Pasadena, California, executive recruiting firm, offers one explanation of why team players are more highly valued today than rugged individualists: "The single-combat warrior, that bright, purposeful worker, tends to suck up a lot of oxygen in an organization. And now they're often seen as too innovative and too difficult."[7] As legendary baseball manager Casey Stengel once put it, "Gettin' good players is easy. Getting 'em to play together is the hard part."

Teams have several notable advantages over individuals working alone.[8] One of these advantages is greater productivity. Research shows that the old saying, "Two heads are better than one," can be true: Well-conceived and efficiently operating teams produce more solutions than individuals working alone, and those solutions are likely to be better than one developed by a solo practitioner. In addition to the greater productivity, the accuracy of an effective team's work is higher than the accuracy of isolated individuals' work. Consider the task of creating a new product. A team of people from sales, marketing, design, engineering, and manufacturing is likely to consider all the important angles, whereas one or two people without this breadth of perspective would probably miss some important ideas.

Teams not only produce better products, but also generate more commitment and enthusiasm from the

FS Stock/Shutterstock

members who created them. People are usually more committed to a decision if they have had a part in making it. Recognizing this principle, many companies create participatory management programs and quality circles that involve employees in important decisions. For example, William Deardon, former chief executive officer of Hershey Foods Corporation, established a corporate planning committee to make the major plans and decisions for the company. "I figured that if we worked it out together," he explained, "the members of the group would feel that it was their plan and our plan—not my plan—and they'd work harder to implement it."[9]

• The Nature of Teams

As Table 7-1 shows, teams play an important role in the world of business and the professions. Unfortunately, you or one of your classmates may have had a negative experience while working with others in the past. It is important that you do not let such an experience affect your perception of teamwork in general. As you will read in this chapter, there are some key differences between working in groups and working as a team. In the workplace, teamwork is often crucial for the success of an organization.

Characteristics of Workgroups

The word *group* is often used to refer to any assembly of people—the sightseers gathering for a walking tour of the downtown area, the rock band at a local nightspot, the group of neighbors assembled online for a virtual library program. However, when we talk about people interacting at work, we use this term differently. Nevertheless, not all collections of people—even people who come together in working settings—are groups.

For our purposes, a **workgroup** is a small, interdependent collection of people with a common identity who interact with one another over a period of time to reach

Table 7-1	Team vs. Individual Performance	

Team Superior to Individuals	Individuals Superior to Team
Task requires broad range of talents and knowledge	Task requires limited knowledge and information (which individuals possess)
Complicated task (requires division or coordination of labor)	Simple task (can be done by one person or individuals working separately)
Time available for deliberation	Little time available
Members are motivated to succeed	Members don't care about the job
High standards of performance	"Social loafing" is the norm

Source: Adapted from Rothwell, J. D. (2013). *In mixed company* (8th ed.). Boston, MA: Cengage; Hare, A. P. (2003). Roles, relationships, and groups in organizations: Some conclusions and recommendations. *Small Group Research, 34,* 123–154.

a goal. Based on this definition, we can single out several significant characteristics of workgroups that can help you develop ways to work more effectively with others on the job.

Size Most experts would say that a pair is not a group because the partners do not interact in the same way three or more people do. For instance, two people working together can resolve disputes only by persuading each other, giving in, or compromising. By comparison, in groups, members can form alliances and outvote or pressure the minority.

Although less agreement exists about when a collection of people becomes too large to be considered a group, almost every small group expert argues that a collection much larger than 20 people loses many of the properties that define groups—at least, effective ones.[10] Research on a number of companies has shown that 10-person groups and teams often produce better results more quickly and with higher profits than do groups consisting of several hundred people.[11] Most communication experts suggest the optimal size for groups focused on decision making is either 5 or 7 members.[12] The odd number of participants eliminates the risk of tie votes. Decision-making groups with fewer than 5 members lack the resources to come up with good ideas and to carry them out, while larger groups suffer from the problems of anonymity, domination, and lack of commitment. Research suggests that groups composed of 5 to 12 members can succeed, provided the type of task and the group composition are given primary consideration.[13]

Shared Purpose Guests at a reception or attendees at a convention might talk with one another, but unless they share a mutual goal, they will not collectively accomplish anything. One challenge facing anyone leading a newly created group is to give its members a clear sense of shared purpose.

Interaction over Time A collection of people studying in a library or working out at the gym are merely co-acting. Likewise, a roomful of trainees at a seminar is not considered a group unless and until the individuals start interacting. A group that interacts over a period of time develops particular characteristics. For example, it will tend to develop shared standards of appropriate behavior that its members are expected to meet. Typical expectations involve how promptly meetings begin, what contribution each member is expected to make to certain routine tasks, what kind of humor is appropriate, and so on.

Interdependence Group members do not just interact—they depend on one another. Consider the workers in a restaurant: If the kitchen crew fails to prepare orders promptly or correctly, the servers' tips will decline. If the employees who clear tables do not perform their jobs quickly and thoroughly, the servers will hear complaints from their customers. If the waiters fail to take orders accurately, the cooks will have to prepare some meals twice.

Identity Both members of a group and outsiders view groups as distinct entities. Some groups have a formal title, such as "benefits committee" or "accounting department." Others have an informal identity, such as "lunchtime power walkers" or "the ones who carpool together." In either case, the fact that the group is seen as distinct has important consequences. To a greater or lesser extent, members feel their own image is tied to the way the group is regarded. In addition, the group's identity means the addition or loss of a member feels significant to the people involved, whether the change in membership is cause for celebration or disappointment.

Learning Teamwork from Firefighters, Comedians, and Musicians

For one action-packed afternoon, a group of corporate workers traded in their office garb for gas masks, heavy boots, and turnout gear. Coached by New York City firefighters, they assembled in four-person teams to learn about teamwork from first responders.

Dousing fires and staging subway rescues might seem far removed from routine office life. Even so, the intense demands of performing in an emergency taught the participants a great deal about what it takes for a team to perform successfully.

"Firefighting is very complex and interdependent, and that has obvious applications to the business world," said one program planner. "Since our training puts people into crisis situations, hopefully they will be better prepared to handle any crisis that arises in the workplace."

Firefighting isn't the only nontraditional venue for developing teamwork. Chicago's Second City Communications offers comedy workshops for almost 400 corporate clients, who learn that the flexibility and creativity required in an improvisational comedy troupe can transfer to organizations facing business challenges. Music offers another setting in which to teach collaboration. The Minneapolis firm Jazz Impact has trained workers from *Fortune* 500 companies to interact more effectively. Employees take turns performing improvisational solos in a jazz song. This impromptu technique teaches employees how to integrate solo performances and accompanying players into a successful piece of work.

Whether the setting is a burning building, a nightclub, or an office, the same principles of teamwork apply: Assemble a group of talented and trained members. Be flexible. Forget about personal glory and do whatever it takes to get the job done.

Source: Kranz, G. (2011, May). Corporate leaders train in fire drills and funny skills. *Workforce Management*, 28–30, 32.

What Makes a Group a Team?

The term **team** appears everywhere in the business world. The positive connotations of a team—spirit, cooperation, and hard work—lead some managers to label every collection of workers as a team. You do not have to be an athlete to appreciate the value of teams, and you do not need to be a cynic to know calling a group of people a team does not make them one.[14] True teams have all the attributes of a group, but they have other distinct qualities that make them more satisfying to work in and more productive.[15]

Groups	Teams
Members are primarily concerned with their own challenges and goals.	Members focus primarily on team challenges and goals.
Members produce individual products.	Members produce collective products.
Work is shaped by the manager.	Work is shaped collectively by the team leader and members.

Several types of teams exist in business. Project teams work on a specific task, usually for a finite period of time. For example, a team of marketing experts might design a publicity program to accompany the rollout of a new software product. Service teams support customers or employees. For example, public utilities have service agents available around the clock to help customers. Management teams work collaboratively on a daily basis within organizations to help them perform their missions. At a university, for example, top officials meet regularly to coordinate their divisions: academic, student support, financial, recreational facilities, and so on. Action teams offer immediate responses and are activated in (typically) emergency situations. For example, community health workers form teams to deal with public health threats.[16]

Although teams are more productive and successful than groups, not all teams are equally effective. Researchers Carl Larson and Frank LaFasto spent nearly three years interviewing the members of more than 75 successful teams. The teams came from a wide range of enterprises, including a Mount Everest expedition, a cardiac surgery team, the presidential commission that studied the space shuttle Challenger accident, the team that developed the IBM personal computer, and two championship football teams. Although the teams pursued widely different goals, they all shared eight important characteristics that distinguished them from regular workgroups[17]:

- *Clear and inspiring shared goals.* Members of successful teams know why their teams exist, and they believe that purpose is important and worthwhile.

- *A results-driven structure.* Members focus on getting the job done in the most effective manner. They are organized and efficiently structured.

- *Competent team members.* Members have the skills necessary to accomplish their goals.

- *Unified commitment.* Members put the group's goals above their personal interests. While this commitment might seem like a sacrifice to others, the personal rewards are worth the effort.

- *Collaborative climate.* Another word for collaboration is *teamwork*; members trust and support one another.

- *Standards of excellence.* Doing outstanding work is an important norm. Each member is expected to do their personal best.

- *External support and recognition.* Successful teams need an appreciative audience that recognizes their effort and provides the resources necessary to get the job done. The audience may be a boss, or it may be the public whom the team is created to serve.

- *Principled leadership.* Winning teams usually have leaders who can create a vision of the team's purpose and challenge members to get the job done. Those leaders also have the ability to unleash the members' talent.

You may not be able to single-handedly transform your entire organization into a team-friendly environment, but it is still possible to influence the group of people with whom you work. Examine the eight characteristics of teams listed here and ask yourself whether you are communicating in a manner that makes that small, but important, leap possible.

Virtual Teams

Virtual teams interact and function without being in the same place at the same time.[18] As one observer put it, virtual team members are "working together apart."[19] Globally, virtual teams are becoming the norm. Prior to the coronavirus pandemic, approximately 30% of Dell's employees were working from home either a few days of the week or full-time.[20] There has been a surge in virtual workspaces due to COVID-19, with employees from a variety of fields working from home for extended periods of time—a trend that is likely to continue long after the pandemic. In fact, Dell plans to have over half of its workforce permanently working virtually once business returns to normal operations.[21]

TECHNOLOGY **tip**

Apps for Teamwork

A simple search for "to do" apps in your smartphone's or tablet's app store is likely to turn up thousands of results. Although it may seem daunting to scroll through the results, task management apps can be especially useful when you are working in a team.

To choose the best app for the job, consider the needs and preferences of the team. Will team members be working on interdependent tasks? Will a visual element (such as a checklist) help the team track its progress? Would an integrated chat or comment feature be helpful? Would it be useful if the app could sync to external calendars?

Once you have determined which features are most important, your options will narrow. For example, if team members answered "Yes" to all of the questions in the preceding paragraph, you would likely choose an app like Trello, which allows users to create a board (e.g., fundraising event) and organize lists of tasks (pre-event, event, post-event) that contain a set of to-do actions (post-event: send thank-you cards to donors; publish final amount of money raised; write a news release). This particular app would also give team members the option to assign individuals to tasks, color-code items, comment and receive notifications, and add labels, descriptions, photos, attachments, and subtasks.

Furthermore, as technology-savvy generations enter the workforce, new norms for communicating among teams are being established.[22] Technology permits virtual teams to transcend boundaries of location and time. Barry Caldwell, former supervisor of computer-aided industrial design (CAD) technologies at Ford Motor Company's Corporate Design division, concurs, explaining how Ford's virtual teams span the globe: "We can't change the fact that Europe is five or six hours ahead [of Michigan]," he says. "But virtual teams can be extremely effective if you can have people working in Italy or Germany—five hours ahead of you—and they can hand work off to Dearborn at the end of their day, and you can carry it further and then pass it back. Instead of an eight-hour day, you can get 14 hours."[23]

Virtual teams are not always—or even usually—on separate continents. Nevertheless, technology can keep members connected while they are telecommuting or on the road. Even when people work under the same roof, being digitally connected can make work more efficient. Some human resources experts claim that when people work more than 50 feet apart, their likelihood of collaborating more than once a week is less than 10 percent.[24] Given this fact, virtual meetings can even boost the efficiency of people who work under the same roof.

Travelerpix/Shutterstock

Another advantage of virtual teams is the leveling of status differences. On networked teams, rank is a much less prominent characteristic than it is in face-to-face groups.[25] When sent by e-mail, the ideas of a new or mid-level worker look identical to those of a senior manager. Back-and-forth dialogue is much less intimidating in a mediated format than it might be when you have to face the boss in person.

Despite the advantages of virtual teamwork, computer networking cannot replace all aspects of personal contacts. Furthermore, it is an oversimplification to suggest that teams are always either virtual or face-to-face. In truth, many teams are hybrid; that is, members meet from time to time and keep in touch electronically between sessions.

• Leadership and Influence in Teams

In group endeavors, successes or failures often are attributed to leadership. Coaches of losing sports teams risk being fired, while winning coaches are celebrated. CEOs of bankrupt companies are ousted by their boards of directors, while CEOs of profitable companies earn sizeable bonuses. When ethical lapses occur in an organization, a "lack of leadership" is often cited as the culprit. In this section, we look at the role of communication in effective—and ineffective—leadership.

Perspectives on Leadership

Throughout much of the history of organizations, leadership was considered to be a role held by an individual. More recently, researchers have come to recognize leadership is a process and different team members can take part in providing leadership to the team—with or without an official leadership role. This section summarizes several of the key approaches to understanding leadership.

Trait Approach   The **trait approach** is based on the belief that all leaders possess common traits that lead to their effectiveness. The earliest research sought to identify these traits, and by the mid-1930s scores of studies pursued this goal. The conclusions reached by the various researchers were contradictory, however, casting doubt on the validity of the trait approach. Certain traits did seem common in most leaders, including physical attractiveness, sociability, desire for leadership, originality, and intelligence.[26] Despite these similarities, the research also showed these traits were not predictive of leadership. In other words, a person possessing these characteristics would not necessarily become a leader. Another research approach, it became clear, was necessary.

Style Approach   Beginning in the 1940s, researchers began to consider the **style approach**. They asked whether the designated leader could choose a way of communicating that would increase effectiveness. This research identified three managerial styles. Some leaders are **authoritarian**, using the power at their disposal to control members. Others are more **democratic**, inviting members to help make decisions. A third leadership style is described as **laissez-faire**: The designated leader gives up the power of that position and transforms the group into a leaderless collection of equals.

Early research seemed to suggest that the democratic style produced the best results,[27] and contemporary studies suggest members of groups with democratic leadership are slightly more satisfied than those run by autocratic leaders.[28] For example, one pair of researchers found that subordinates perceived more solidarity and higher levels of job satisfaction with democratic supervisors than authoritarian leaders.[29]

Even so, it is an oversimplification to say that a democratic approach always works best. For instance, groups with autocratic leaders are more productive in stressful situations, while democratically led groups do better when the conditions are nonstressful.[30] Furthermore, subordinates with laissez-faire supervisors are less likely to experience job burnout than those with authoritarian leaders.[31]

One of the best-known stylistic approaches is the Leadership Grid developed by Robert Blake and Jane Mouton (Figure 7.1),[32] which shows that good leadership depends on skillful management of the task and the relationships among group members. The horizontal axis of the grid measures a manager's concern for task or production—getting the job done. The vertical axis measures the leader's concern for people and relationships. Blake and Mouton's grid counteracts the tendency in some naïve managers to assume that if they focus solely on the task, good results will follow. These theorists argue the most effective leader is one who adopts a 9,9 style, showing high concern for both product *and* people.

FIGURE 7.1 The
Leadership Grid

Source: From Robert R.
Blake and Anne Adams
McCanse [formerly the
Managerial Grid by Blake,
R. R., & Mouton, J. S.
(1991). *Leadership
dilemmas-grid solutions.*
Gulf Publishing Company.]

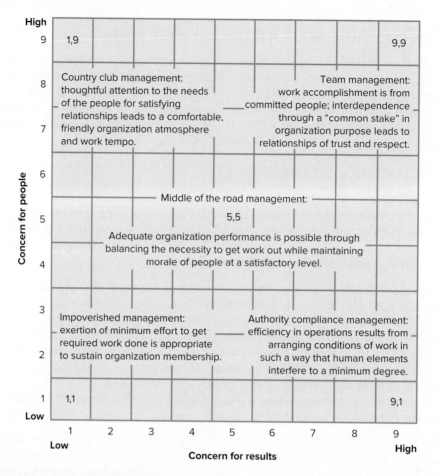

Contingency Approaches

Unlike the style approach, **contingency approaches** are based on the idea that the "best" leadership style is flexible—it changes from one situation to the next. For instance, a manager who successfully guides a project team to develop an advertising campaign might flop as a trainer or personnel officer.

Psychologist Fred Fiedler conducted extensive research in an attempt to discover when a task-oriented approach works best versus when a relationship-oriented style is most effective.[33] He found that the decision whether to emphasize task or relationship issues in a situation depends on three factors: (1) *leader–member relations*, including the manager's attractiveness and the followers' loyalty; (2) *task structure*, involving the degree of simplicity or complexity of the job; and (3) *the leader's power*, including job title and the ability to coerce and reward the followers.

Generally, Fiedler's research suggests a task-oriented approach works best when circumstances are extremely favorable (good leader–member relations, highly structured tasks) or extremely unfavorable (poor leader–member relations, unstructured task, weak leader power). In moderately favorable or unfavorable circumstances, a relationship-oriented approach works best. While these findings are useful, it is important not to overstate their implications. In most cases, good leadership requires a mixture of relationship and task concerns. The question is not which dimension to choose, but rather which one to emphasize.

Another contingency approach to leadership is the situational leadership model, developed by Paul Hersey and Kenneth Blanchard.[34] Originally termed life-cycle theory, the **situational leadership model** suggests that successful leaders adapt their leadership style to the ability of the individual or group they are attempting to lead. A worker with a low level of readiness to work independently needs a highly directive and task-related style of leadership. As the subordinate becomes able to perform the task without guidance, the manager gradually withdraws the task-related supervision. Finally, when the worker's ability to handle a task is superior, the boss can cut back the amount of socioemotional support, knowing the worker is functioning at the highest level and any reinforcements are now primarily internal.

Transformational Leadership Approach   Leadership expert, historian, and presidential biographer James MacGregor Burns introduced the concept of **transformational leadership** in his 1978 book *Leadership*.[35] In this approach, leaders' personality traits and ability to define a clear vision for the organization enable them to inspire subordinates to work toward common goals and empower those subordinates to exceed their normal levels of performance. Bernard M. Bass expanded upon this idea, suggesting that transformational leadership is measured in terms of the leaders' influence on their subordinates. Transformational leaders:

- Model integrity and fairness
- Set clear goals
- Have high expectations
- Encourage others
- Provide support and recognition
- Stir the emotions of people
- Get people to look beyond their self-interest
- Inspire people to reach for the improbable[36]

One approach to transformational leadership is known as **servant leadership**. If we visualize traditional leadership as a pyramid, where the leader sits at the top and makes requests of subordinates, then servant leadership would flip the pyramid upside down. The servant leader serves their subordinates by putting their needs first, based on the belief that empowered employees are able to do their jobs more effectively when the leader supports them. The servant leader approaches the job by asking a simple question: What can I do for you?

Research has shown that servant leadership improves the well-being of followers[37] and affects employees' performance through the development of an ethical work climate. Servant leaders are ethical role models and, as such, contribute to the creation of an organizational culture where doing the right thing is expected and encouraged.[38] As such, servant leadership creates a higher level of ethics that results in increased performance[39] and creativity, and less turnover.[40]

Leader–Member Exchange

So far we have been assuming leaders treat all group members equally. But your own experience probably shows that leaders have different relationships with each person on their team. Some of these relationships are characterized by positive communication and mutual satisfaction. Others can be more distant or even fraught with dissatisfaction on both sides. Recognizing this fact, **leader–member exchange (LMX)** theory views leadership as a collection of multiple relationships with organizational members, with each of those relationships being unique.

The basic premise of LMX is that leaders—no matter how good they are—have a limited amount of time and energy. As a result, they cannot give every member an equal amount of resources. Inevitably, some people get more, and some get less.[41] This "differential distribution" of resources is both the cause and the effect of some leader–member relationships being "high quality" (i.e., richer and more satisfying) and others being lower quality.

Servant Leadership in Action

In her book, *Dare to Serve: How to Drive Superior Results While Serving Others*, Cheryl Bachelder discusses how servant leadership has helped her revive the Popeyes Louisiana Kitchen brand.

When Bachelder became CEO of Popeyes in November 2007, she faced the challenge of solving several problems that had plagued the company for years, including a decline in guest visits, negative restaurant sales and profit trends, and a steep drop in the company's stock price.

Bachelder found that the relationship between the company and its franchise owners was strained. As a result, she and her team focused on serving the franchise owners well. They created a workplace where people were treated with respect and encouraged to collaborate as a team and perform at the highest level. The new leadership standard led to improved guest ratings, an increase in restaurant sales and profit, and a growth in market capitalization from less than $300 million to more than $1.4 billion. The franchisees began reinvesting in the brand by remodeling restaurants in record time and opening new locations around the world.

In an interview with *Business Insider*, Bachelder summarized her efforts: "This company hadn't been performing well in years. We asked ourselves who we would serve, and we decided on the franchise owners. We put every decision we made through the filter of how well it served the franchise owner. Then, over the course of the next several years we checked performance against the measures of what makes franchise owners successful. Together, we've created this high-performing company."

Source: Bachelder, C., (2015). *Dare to serve: How to drive superior results by serving others.* Berrett-Koehler Publishers; Goudreau, J. (2015, March 24). The CEO of Popeyes says becoming a 'servant leader' helped her turn around the struggling restaurant chain. *Business Insider*; Popeyes Louisiana Kitchen, Inc. (2017). *Cheryl A. Bachelder.* Retrieved from https://company.popeyes.com/company/leadership/cheryl-bachelder/

Communication in high-quality LMX relationships is typically positive and reinforcing, characterized by support statements, coaching, and joint decision-making. When disagreements arise, they are handled respectfully and constructively. This treatment marks certain members as "insiders." Communication in low-quality LMX relationships, by comparison, is dramatically different. There is often less interaction, and what does occur can include more face-threatening acts, competitive conflict, power games, and defensiveness.[42] Such patterns mark these group members as outsiders. Not surprisingly, there is a strong connection between the quality of a member's relationship with their leader and the member's overall satisfaction with that boss, coworkers, and the organization as a whole.[43]

As a leader, you should strive to engage employees by coaching and motivating them, and being consistent with your communication.[44] As a member, you can communicate in ways that lead to a high-quality "insider" relationship with your leader.[45] Research suggests that leaders are most impressed by "work-related currencies," such as taking initiative, exercising responsibility, and going beyond the official job description.[46] Basic as it may sound, doing a good job and exceeding the leader's expectations can be the best route to forging a high-quality relationship.

Becoming a Leader

Sometimes leaders are appointed by an individual with higher authority or by the team itself. For example, a football team may select a captain, or a board of directors may appoint a director as chair of a committee. In other cases, leaders emerge organically from a group. **Emergent leaders** evolve into this role over time as a result of the group's interaction.

Emergent leaders do not always have official titles. For example, a group of disgruntled employees might urge one person to approach the boss and ask for a change. A team of students assigned to develop a class project might agree that one person is best suited to take the lead in organizing and presenting their work. Sometimes emergent leaders are officially recognized, but at other times their role is never acknowledged overtly. In fact, the designated leader may be the titular head of a group, while an emergent leader really runs the show. Fans of late-night movies will recall how the young, inexperienced lieutenant learns to defer to the grizzled, wise sergeant. This pattern often repeats itself in everyday working situations when new managers or supervisors recognize the greater knowledge of old-timers who are their subordinates on the organizational chart. In such cases, the new manager is smart to defer to the unofficial, emergent leader—at least until they gain more experience and wisdom.

Communication researcher Ernest Bormann studied how emergent leaders gain influence, especially in newly formed groups.[47] According to Bormann, a group selects a leader by the *method of residues*—a process of elimination in which potential candidates are gradually rejected for one reason or another until only one remains. This process of elimination occurs in two phases. In the first round, members who are clearly unsuitable are rejected. The surest path to rejection is being quiet; less talkative members were never chosen as leaders in the groups Bormann studied. Failing to participate verbally in a group's work leaves the impression of indifference and lack of commitment. Another ticket to early rejection is dogmatism: Members who express their opinions in strong, unqualified terms are usually perceived as being too extreme and inflexible to take a leading role. A third cause of elimination as a potential leader is a lack of skill or intelligence: Competence is obviously a necessary condition for successful leadership, and members who lack this quality are rejected early.

In the method of residues, quietness, dogmatism, and incompetence are almost always grounds for disqualification. Beyond these factors, a communication style that members find irritating or disturbing is likely to knock a member out of consideration as a leader. A variety of behaviors may fall into this category, depending on the composition of the group. In one case, being too serious might be grounds for rejection, but in a different situation, a joker might earn disapproval. Using inappropriate language could also be a disqualifier. In a group with biased members, gender or ethnicity might be grounds for rejection.

After clearly unsuitable members have been eliminated, roughly half of the group's members may still be candidates for leadership. This second phase can be a tense time for the group, as the jockeying for a role of influence may pit the remaining candidates against one another. In some groups, the contenders for leader acquire what Bormann calls "lieutenants," who support the contenders' advancement. If only one candidate has a lieutenant, their chances of becoming the leader are strong. If two or more contenders have supporters, the process of leader emergence can drag out or even reach a stalemate.

In their book *Getting It Done: How to Lead When You're Not in Charge,* Roger Fisher and Alan Sharp describe "lateral leadership" as a way to avoid the extremes of doing nothing or taking charge and bossing others. They suggest a team member can lead others by doing three things: (1) *asking* thoughtful, sincere questions to get others to think creatively and contribute their ideas; (2) *offering* ideas to help the team while inviting others to challenge your thoughts; and (3) *doing* something constructive needed by the team and modeling the behavior needed.[48]

Power and Influence of Members

Many teams have a **designated leader**—the supervisor, chairperson, coach, or manager who has formal authority and responsibility to supervise the task at hand. Other groups, called **self-directed work teams**, are responsible for managing their own behavior to get a task done.[49] For example, in 2015, Lokai launched a limited-edition blue bracelet in partnership with charity: water. The company donated $3 to charity: water for every blue Lokai bracelet sold between March 1 and March 22 in commemoration of World Water Day. When the partnership was launched, however, Lokai's e-commerce site could not keep up with

Sleep Deprivation and Leadership

It is no secret that leaders have demanding schedules and often find themselves burning the midnight oil to complete tasks and meet deadlines. This practice can be detrimental to their ability to be successful leaders, however. Recent research shows that sleep deprivation can undermine leaders' influence on their followers. Sleep-deprived leaders tend to be perceived as less charismatic than those who have had a normal night's sleep and, therefore, have a more difficult time inspiring their subordinates.

Interestingly, researchers have also found that sleep-deprived subordinates attribute less charisma to their leaders, meaning that they are more difficult to inspire.

When possible, leaders should eliminate practices that may cause sleep deprivation for themselves and their employees, such as responding to text messages or e-mail after hours.

Source: Barnes, C. M., Guarana, C. L., Nauman, S., & Kong, D. J. (2016). Too tired to inspire or be inspired: Sleep deprivation and charismatic leadership. *Journal of Applied Psychology, 101*(8), 1191–1199.

---

the customer demand and crashed. Lokai CEO and founder Steven Izen told *Entrepreneur* that he allowed his employees to take over; within an hour, the site was back and running. According to Izen, "I need to be able to rely on my team and the people around me. . . . If I really put my trust in them, they will be able to execute."[50]

Whether or not a team has a designated leader, every member has the power to shape events. More than a half-century ago, John French and Bertram Raven identified seven forms of power that are usually possessed by one or more members of a group—not necessarily just the designated leader.[51] Depending on how they are used, these forms of power can make or break a team's success.

Position Power   **Position power** is the ability to influence that comes from the position one holds. We often do things for our managers precisely because they hold that title. While position power usually belongs to designated leaders, people in lesser positions sometimes have jobs that involve telling higher-ups what to do. For example, a media expert might have the position power to tell the CEO or board chairperson what will and will not work in a presentation to stockholders.

Coercive Power   The power to punish is known as **coercive power** because we often follow another's bidding when failure to do so would lead to unpleasant consequences. Designated leaders have coercive power: They can assign unpleasant tasks, deny pay raises, and even fire people. Other members have coercive power, too, though it is usually subtle. Committee members or officemates who act as blockers when things do not go their way are coercing others to take their views into account, implying, "If you don't follow at least some of my suggestions, I'll punish the team by continuing to object to your ideas and refusing to cooperate with you."

Reward Power   The flip side of coercive power is **reward power**—the ability to reward. Designated leaders control the most obvious rewards, such as pay raises, improved working conditions, and the ability to promote. Even so, other members can give their own rewards. These may take the form of social payoffs, such as increased goodwill, and task-related benefits, such as voluntary assistance on a job.

Expert Power   **Expert power** comes from the group's recognition of a member's expertise in a certain area. Sometimes one expert is better suited to make a decision than an entire team. Designated leaders, however, are not always the experts in a group. In a manufacturing firm, for example, a relatively low-ranking engineer could influence management to alter a project by using their knowledge to declare that a new product will not work. Problems can arise either when management does not recognize a knowledgeable member as an expert or when unqualified people are granted expert status.

Referent Power   The term **referent power** alludes to the influence members possess due to the way others in the group feel about them—that is, out of respect, attraction, or liking. It is here that the greatest difference between designated leaders and members with true influence becomes evident. An unpopular boss might have to resort to wielding their job title and the power to coerce and reward that comes with it to gain compliance, whereas a popular person, with or without a leadership title, can get others to cooperate without threatening or promising.[52] Mike Zugsmith, chairman and founder of NAI Capital, captures the importance of referent power, even for a boss: "When I started this company in 1979, I was 28. I was supervising salespeople who were 20 to 30 years my senior. It readily became apparent that simply because your name is on the door doesn't mean you'll get respect. You have to earn it."[53]

Information Power   **Information power** is the ability of some members to influence a group because of the information they possess. This information is different from the kind of knowledge that gives rise to expert power. Whereas an expert possesses some form of talent based on training or education, an information-rich group member has access to otherwise obscure knowledge that other members value. A new employee who was hired away from a competitor, for example, is likely to play a key role in decisions about how their new company will compete against the old one. Likewise, a member who is well connected to the organizational grapevine can exert a major influence on how the group operates: "Don't bring that up now. Galardi is going through a divorce, and is saying no to everything." "I just heard there's plenty of money in the travel and entertainment budget. Maybe this is the time to propose that reception for the out-of-town distributors we've been thinking about."

Connection Power   In the business world, a member's influence can often come from the connections they have with influential or important people inside or outside the organization—hence the term **connection power**. The classic example of connection power is the boss's child. While the official word from the top may be "Treat my kid just like any other employee," this is easier said than done. Of course, not all connection power is harmful. If one member of the organization sees a potential customer socially, they are in a good position to help the business. If another one knows a government official, that employee might be able to get off-the-record advice about how to handle a government regulation.

If we recognize the influence that comes with connection power, the old saying "It isn't what you know that counts, it's who you know" seems true. If we look at all the types of power described in this section, however, we can see that a more accurate statement is "What counts is whom you know [connection power], what you know [information and expert power], who respects you [referent power], and who you are [position power]." This range of power bases makes it clear that the ability to influence a group is truly shared among members, all of whom have the potential to affect how well a group works as a unit and which quality of product it turns out.

● Effective Communication in Teams

Whether you are in a team with a powerful leader or one with shared decision-making power, you can communicate in ways that help the team operate effectively and make the experience satisfying. For the team to function well, each member must take into account the issues and problems that may arise whenever people try to communicate.

The Danger of Uniformity

In an ideal situation, our teams and workgroups will be diverse. We will be able to bounce ideas around with others who have different life experiences and cultural backgrounds, and who come from varying geographic locations. Realistically, however, we are often faced with situations where our groups lack diversity and differing viewpoints. Without being able to draw on diverse perspectives, it becomes easy to make a mistake that can have major consequences.

In 2017, designer Tory Burch was criticized for a video ad titled, "Tory Story: An American Road Trip," which features model Poppy Delevigne and two other Caucasian models dancing to the hip hop song "Juju on that Beat."

Not only did the ad fail to include any Black models, but it also incorporates shots of a monkey-shaped handbag in the backseat of a car and on the yacht with the models.

Comments on the Internet expressed outrage, calling the ad *tone-deaf* and culturally insensitive. This ultimately led to an apology from Tory Burch, along with the removal of the video from its website and social media.

Many times, when brands experience criticism for being tone-deaf, it is because they did not have a diverse team who could identify the ways their messaging might be perceived by others. If you are faced with a workgroup or team that lacks diversity, it is important to seek out the opinions of others before launching a project. For example, many companies utilize focus groups to test ideas with diverse groups representative of the audience(s) they intend to reach with their message.

For more tips on how to prevent these types of situations, refer to the "Avoid Excessive Conformity" section later in this chapter.

Fill Functional Roles

One way every member can shape the way a team operates is by acting in whatever way is necessary to help get the job done. This approach has been labeled the "functional perspective" because it defines influence in terms of fulfilling essential functions, not formal titles. These essential contributions have earned the name **functional roles** because they involve functions that are necessary for the team to do its job. Table 7-2 lists these functional roles and notes some dysfunctional behaviors that reduce the effectiveness of a team. As the table shows, there are two types of functional roles. **Task roles** play an important part in accomplishing the job at hand. **Relational roles** help keep the interaction between members running smoothly.[54]

Table 7-2 is a valuable diagnostic tool. When a team is not operating effectively, you must determine which functions are lacking. In some cases, your diagnosis of a troubled team might show that all the necessary task functions are being filled but members' social needs are not being met. Perhaps members need to have their good ideas supported ("That's a terrific idea, Lucia!"). Maybe personal conflicts need to be acknowledged and resolved ("I know I sound defensive about this. I've worked on this idea for a month, and I hate to see it dismissed in 5 minutes."). When social needs like these go unfilled, even the best knowledge and talent often are not enough to guarantee a team's smooth functioning.

Sometimes a team will transform important functional roles into formal ones. For example, at financial services giant Charles Schwab, one person in every meeting serves as an observer-diagnoser.[55] This person does not take part in the discussion; instead, they create a list of what went right (e.g., "Good creativity," "Excellent use of time") and what went wrong (e.g., "Lots of digressions," "Personal criticism created defensiveness") in the meeting. This list is included in the minutes, which management reviews. It is easy to imagine how the observer's comments can help a team improve its effectiveness.

Table 7-2	Functional Roles of Team Members

Task Roles

1. *Information- or opinion-giver.* Offers facts or opinions relevant to the team's task.
2. *Information- or opinion-seeker.* Asks others for task-related information or opinions.
3. *Starter or energizer.* Initiates or encourages task-related behavior (e.g., "We'd better get going on this").
4. *Direction-giver.* Provides instructions regarding how to perform the task at hand.
5. *Summarizer.* Reviews what has been said, identifying common themes or progress.
6. *Diagnoser.* Offers observations about task-related behavior of team (e.g., "We seem to be spending all of our time discussing the problem without proposing any solutions").
7. *Gatekeeper.* Regulates participation of members.
8. *Reality-tester.* Checks feasibility of ideas against real-world contingencies.

Relational Roles

1. *Participation encourager.* Encourages reticent members to speak, letting them know their contributions will be valued.
2. *Harmonizer.* Resolves interpersonal conflicts between members.
3. *Tension-reliever.* Uses humor or other devices to release members' anxiety and frustration.
4. *Evaluator of emotional climate.* Offers observations about socio-emotional relationships between members (e.g., "I think we're all feeling a little defensive now" or "It sounds as if you think no one trusts you").
5. *Praise-giver.* Reinforces accomplishments and contributions of members.
6. *Empathic listener.* Listens without evaluation to personal concerns of members.

Dysfunctional Roles

1. *Blocker.* Prevents progress by constantly raising objections.
2. *Attacker.* Aggressively questions others' competence or motives.
3. *Recognition-seeker.* Repeatedly and unnecessarily calls attention to self by relating irrelevant experiences, boasting, and seeking sympathy.
4. *Joker.* Engages in joking behavior in excess of the tension-relieving needs, distracting members.
5. *Withdrawer.* Refuses to take a stand on social or task issues; covers up feelings; does not respond to others' comments.

Having too many people fill a particular functional role can be just as troublesome as having no one fill it. For example, you might discover that several people are acting as opinion-givers but no one is serving as an opinion-seeker. If two or more people compete for the role of direction-giver, the results can be confusing. Even social roles can be over-done. Too much tension-relieving or praise-giving, for example, can become annoying.

Once you have identified the missing roles, you can fill them. Supplying these missing roles often transforms a stalled, frustrated team into a productive one.[56] Other members probably will not recognize what you are doing, but they will realize you somehow know how to say the right thing at the right time.

Recognize Both Team and Personal Goals

Every team operates to achieve some specific goal—selling a product, providing a service, getting a job done, and so on. In addition to pursuing a team's goals, members usually have their own individual goals. Sometimes an individual's goal in a team is identical (or nearly identical) to the group's shared goal. For example, the owner of a retail store might join the community holiday fund-raising campaign out of a sincere desire to help the needy. In most cases, however, people also have more personal motives for joining a team. The retailer, for instance, might realize that working on the fundraising campaign will improve both their visibility and image in the community—and ultimately lead to more business. Notice the relationships between some common team and individual goals in the following list:

Team Goal	Individual Goal
Sales department wants to meet annual sales target.	Sales representative wants to earn a bonus.
Retailer wants to expand hours to attract new business.	Employees want to avoid working nights and weekends.
Company wants an employee to attend a seminar in Minneapolis.	Employee wants to visit family in Minneapolis.

Individual goals are not necessarily harmful to a team or an organization if they are compatible with the overall objectives. In fact, under these circumstances, they can actually help the team to achieve its goals. For instance, sales representatives who want to increase their commissions will try to sell more of the company's products. Similarly, an otherwise reluctant employee might volunteer to attend a January seminar in Minneapolis if they can see their family during the visit.

Only when an individual's goals conflict with the organization's or team's goals do problems occur. If Amir and Liam dislike each other, their arguments could keep the team from getting much accomplished in meetings. If Morgan is afraid of losing her job because of a mistake that has been made, she may concentrate on trying to avoid being blamed rather than on solving the problem.

The range of personal goals that can interfere with team effectiveness is surprisingly broad. One or more team members might be concerned with finishing the job quickly and getting away to take care of personal business. Others might be more concerned with being liked or appearing smart than with doing the job as quickly or effectively as possible. Someone else might want to impress the boss. All these goals, as well as dozens of others, can sidetrack or derail a team from doing its job.

As Table 7-3 shows, teams will be harmonious and most efficient when the members are also reaching their personal goals. You can boost your team's effectiveness by doing everything possible to help members satisfy those goals. If the people in your team are looking for fun and companionship, consider ways to tackle the job at hand that also give them what they want. Conversely, if they are in a hurry because of busy schedules, concentrate on keeping meetings to a minimum. If some members like recognition, offer compliments whenever you can sincerely do so. The extra effort you spend attending to members' individual needs will pay dividends in terms of the energy and loyalty the team gains from happy members.

In some cases, team members announce their individual goals. In other cases, though, stating a personal goal outright could be embarrassing or counterproductive. A committee member would not confess, "I volunteered to serve on this committee so I could find new people to date." An employee would never say openly, "I'm planning to learn everything I can here and then quit the firm and open my own business." Personal goals that are not made public are called **hidden agendas**.

Table 7-3	Team Process Variables Associated with Productivity

1. Members are clear about and agree with team goals.

2. Tasks are appropriate for team versus individual solutions.

3. Members are clear about and accept their formal roles.

4. Role assignments match members' abilities.

5. The level of the leader's direction matches the team's skill level.

6. All team members are encouraged to participate.

7. The team gets, gives, and uses feedback about its effectiveness and productivity.

8. The team spends time defining and discussing problems it must solve or decisions it must make. Members also spend time planning how they will solve problems and make decisions.

9. The team uses effective decision-making strategies that were outlined in advance.

10. The team evaluates its solutions and decisions.

11. Norms encourage high performance and quality, success, and innovation.

12. Subgroups are integrated into the team as a whole.

13. The team contains the smallest number of members necessary to accomplish its goals.

14. The team has enough time to develop cohesiveness and accomplish its goals.

15. The team has a cooperative orientation.

16. Disagreements occur frequently but are usually resolved quickly.

Source: Wheelan, S. A., Murphy, D., Tsumura, E., & Kline, S. F. (1998). Member perceptions of internal group dynamics and productivity. *Small Group Research, 29*, 371–393.

Hidden agendas are not necessarily harmful. A member's dating goals need not interfere with team functions. Similarly, many other personal motives are not threatening or even relevant to a team's business. Some hidden agendas may even be beneficial. For instance, an up-and-coming young worker's desire to communicate their competence to the boss by volunteering for difficult jobs might help the team. According to international team consultant Frank Heckman, the "bottom line is that we all have personal agendas and to some degree, some are hidden even to us."[57] Other hidden agendas, however, are harmful. As Heckman notes, "the problem will come in if the individual is duplicitous and undermines what the team is trying to achieve."[58] Two feuding members who use meetings to disparage each other can only harm the team, and the person collecting ideas to go into business alone will most likely hurt the organization when they take their ideas elsewhere.

There is no single best way to deal with harmful hidden agendas. Sometimes the best course is to bring the goal out into the open. For example, a manager might speak to feuding subordinates one at a time, letting them know they recognize the problem and working with them to solve it directly and constructively (probably using the conflict management skills described in Chapter 5). When you do decide to bring a hidden personal goal into the open, it is almost always better to confront the member privately.

A Professional Perspective

Chelsea N. Childress

Special Assistant to the Secretary

United States Department of Veterans Affairs

Washington, DC

Credit: Chelsea N. Childress

Career success comes in many forms; it is a very personal thing, and perceptions of success can vary as infinitely as people themselves. Definitions of success can even change across the lifespan as we learn, grow, and change our minds. Each of us should determine our own definition of success wherever we currently find ourselves and strive to meet our goals, reflect on our progress, and adjust as needed.

I find that I must be willing to take calculated risks to be successful because taking big risks can generate significant rewards. For example, throughout my career with the Department of Veterans Affairs (VA), I have worked at the Hospital Management Level. After five years, I decided to take a position that was located on the other side of the United States at the VA Headquarters. This position is known to have a high level of stress and a high turnover rate due to the nature of the position. In fact, within the first six months, I found myself as the most senior person in my position. Nonetheless, the risk has absolutely been worth the reward of gaining invaluable knowledge at the national level and the opportunity to network with individuals throughout the world.

I've also learned not to be afraid to ask questions as it allows me to be a successful lifelong learner. By asking hard questions or asking for help, I built a network of people that I can trust. And each of these authentic encounters is a possible networking opportunity, whether it occurs in person or virtually. In other words, our success is tied to our ability to communicate effectively with others—whether that is getting the answers we need or negotiating our next position.

The embarrassment of being unveiled publicly is usually so great the person becomes defensive and denies the hidden goal exists.

At other times, it is best to treat a hidden personal goal indirectly. For example, if a member's excessive talking in meetings seems to be a bid for recognition, the best approach might be to make a point of praising that individual's valid contributions more frequently. If two feuding subordinates continue to have trouble working together, the manager can assign them to different projects or transfer one or both of them to different teams.

Self-Assessment Evaluating Your Team's Communication Effectiveness

Use this inventory to identify how well your team is performing these important communication practices.

As a team, how well did you:	Not Well				Very Well
Define or clarify the task	1	2	3	4	5
Exchange and share information	1	2	3	4	5
Encourage expression of various points of view	1	2	3	4	5
Evaluate and analyze data	1	2	3	4	5
Use the best decision-making approach (e.g., consensus, majority rule)	1	2	3	4	5
Focus on tasks, not on individuals	1	2	3	4	5
Demonstrate respect for all	1	2	3	4	5
Encourage feedback	1	2	3	4	5
Encourage expression of opinion	1	2	3	4	5
Build on others' ideas	1	2	3	4	5
Ask for clarification of ideas	1	2	3	4	5
Demonstrate equality	1	2	3	4	5
Address disagreements or misunderstandings	1	2	3	4	5
Stay on task	1	2	3	4	5

Promote Desirable Norms

Norms are informal, often unstated rules about what behavior is appropriate.[59] Some norms govern the way tasks are handled, while others shape the social interaction of the team. A team's norms are often shaped by the culture of the organization to which it belongs. For example, 3M's success has been attributed to its "bias for yes": When in doubt, employees are encouraged to take a chance instead of avoiding action out of fear of failure.[60] Likewise, Motorola's turnaround has been attributed to its changing norms for conflict. The company's culture now makes it acceptable to disagree strongly (and loudly) in meetings instead of keeping quiet or being overly diplomatic.[61] As Table 7-4 shows, the norms in some teams are constructive, whereas other teams have equally powerful rules that damage their effectiveness.[62]

The challenge of establishing norms is especially great when members come from different cultural backgrounds.[63] For example, team members from a low-context culture (such as the United States or Canada) would be more likely to address conflicts directly, whereas those from high-context backgrounds (East Asia or the Middle East, for example) would be inclined to use indirect approaches. Likewise, members from a background where high power distance is the norm would be less likely to challenge a team's leader than those from a background where low power distance is the norm.

Once norms are established, members who violate them may create a conflict for the rest of the team, who may respond in a series of escalating steps.[64] Consider, for example,

Table 7-4	Typical Constructive (and Destructive) Norms for a Team

- Handle (Ignore) business for coworkers who are away from their desks.
- Be willing (Refuse) to admit your mistakes.
- Occasional time off from work for personal reasons is (is not) okay, as long as the absence won't harm the company.
- Do (Do not) be willing to work overtime without complaining when big, important deadlines approach.
- Say so (Keep quiet) if you disagree. Do not (Do) hint or go behind others' backs.
- Avoid (Hold) side conversations during meetings.
- Do not (Do) interrupt or ignore others' ideas.
- Arrive on time (Be late) for meetings.
- Celebrate (Do not celebrate) successes.
- Honor (Shirk) your commitments.

Source: Baum, J. A. C. (n.d.). Avoiding common team problems. *Rotman School of Management*. Retrieved from http://www.rotman.utoronto.ca/?baum/mgt2003/avoid.html

a worker who violates the norm of not following up on their obligations between team meetings. Their teammates might react with increasing pressure:

- *Delaying action.* Members talk among themselves but do not approach the violator, hoping they will change without pressure.
- *Hinting about the violation.* Members tease the violator about being a "flake" or about being lazy, hoping the message behind the humor will cause them to do their share of the work.
- *Discussing the problem openly.* Members confront the nonconformist, explaining their concerns about the behavior.
- *Ridiculing and deriding the violator.* Persuasion shifts to demands for a change in behavior; the team's pressure tactics may well trigger a defensive response in the nonconforming member.
- *Rejecting or isolating the deviant.* If all other measures fail, the team member who does not conform to team norms is asked to leave the group. If the person cannot be expelled, other members can excommunicate the violator by not inviting them to meetings and by disregarding any attempts at communicating they might make.

There are two ways in which an understanding of norms can help you to function more effectively in a team.

Create Desirable Norms Early

Norms are established early in a team. Once they exist, they are difficult to change. Thus, when you participate in a team that is just being established, you should do whatever you can to create norms you think will be desirable. For example, if you expect committee members to be punctual at meetings, it is important to begin each session at the appointed time. If you want others to be candid about their feelings, it is important to be frank yourself and encourage honesty in others at the outset.

The Unproductive Teammate

You are a member of what was once a dream team of productive workers. Until recently, everyone worked well together to meet the team's goals. When one member took time off to care for a child who was hospitalized a few months ago, everyone was happy to cover for them. Over the next months, however, the same member began missing more work because of other problems—a spouse needing care, a sports injury, a move to a new home. The rest of the team has begun to doubt their unproductive colleague will ever contribute a fair share to the team again, and they agree it is time to raise this issue.

Describe how the team can deal with this issue in a way that acknowledges both the unproductive member's legitimate problems and the team's need for all members to do their share.

Comply with Established Norms Whenever Possible   In an established team, you have the best chance of reaching your goals if you handle the task and social relationships in the team's customary manner. If your coworkers are in the habit of exchanging good-natured insults, you should not be offended when you are the target—and you will be accepted as one of them if you dish out a few quips yourself. In a team in which the norm is never to criticize another member's ideas directly, a blunt approach probably will not get you very far. When you are entering an established team, it is wise to learn the norms by personal observation and by asking knowledgeable members about them before plunging in.

The national or regional culture can also shape the way team members communicate with one another. Differences in managing conflict are a good example. The straight-talking, low-context style that is accepted in many parts of the English-speaking world is not the norm in other places.[65] Of course, it may not always be possible to follow established norms. If a team is in the habit of cracking offensive jokes, doing shabby work, or stealing company property, for example, you would probably be unwilling to go along just to be accepted. This sort of conflict between personal values and team norms can lead to a major dispute in values. If the potential for conflict is great enough and the issue is sufficiently important, you may decide to do whatever you can to join a different, more compatible team.

Promote an Optimal Level of Cohesiveness

Cohesiveness can be defined as the degree to which members feel part of a team and want to remain with that team. You can think of cohesiveness as a magnetic force that attracts members to one another, giving them a collective identity. As you might suspect, highly cohesive teams have happier members than less closely knit groups. Workers who belong to cohesive teams are likely to have higher rates of job satisfaction and lower rates of tension, absenteeism, and turnover than those who belong to less cohesive ones.[66] They also make better decisions.[67]

Not all cohesive teams are productive—at least not in terms of the organization's goals. In strikes and slowdowns, for example, highly cohesive workers can actually shut down operations. (Of course, the workers' cohesiveness in such cases may help them to accomplish other team goals, such as higher pay or safer working conditions.) In less dramatic cases, cohesiveness in observing anti-organizational norms ("Don't work too hard," "Go ahead and report our lunch as a business expense—we always do that," "If you need some art supplies for your kids, just take them from the supply closet") can leave team members feeling good about one another but raise ethical issues and harm the organization's interests. Finally, too much cohesiveness can lead to the kinds of "groupthink" described in the forthcoming section titled "Avoid Excessive Conformity."

Cohesiveness develops when certain conditions exist in a team. Once you understand these conditions, you can apply them to groups on or off the job. You can also use them to analyze why a team's cohesiveness is high or low and choose ways to reach and maintain a desirable level of cohesiveness. The remainder of this section presents seven factors that promote an optimal level of cohesiveness.[68]

Shared or Compatible Goals

Team members draw closer together when they have a similar aim or when their goals can be mutually satisfied. For instance, the members of a construction crew might have little cohesiveness when their pay is based on individual efforts, but if the entire crew receives a bonus for completing stages of the building ahead of schedule, the members are likely to work together better.

Progress Toward Goals

When a team makes progress toward its target, members are drawn together; when progress stops, cohesiveness decreases. Members of the construction crew just mentioned will feel good about one another when they reach their target dates or can reasonably expect to do so. However, if they consistently fall short of meeting those targets, they are likely to get discouraged and feel less attraction to the team. When talking to their families or friends, there will be less talk about "us" and more about "me."

Shared Norms or Values

Although successful teams tolerate or even thrive because of some differences in members' expressed attitudes and behaviors, wide variation in what members consider appropriate behavior reduces cohesiveness. For example, a person who insists on wearing conservative clothes in a business where everyone else dresses casually probably will not fit in with the rest of the group.

Minimal Feelings of Threat among Members

In a cohesive team, members usually feel secure about their status, dignity, and material and social well-being. When conflict arises over these issues, results can be destructive. For example, if all of the junior executives in a division are competing for the same senior position—especially if senior positions rarely open—the team's cohesiveness is likely to suffer, at least until the job is filled.

Ingram Publishing

Interdependence among Members

Teams become more cohesive when members need one another to satisfy team goals. When a job can be done by one person alone, the need for unity decreases. An office team in which each member performs a different aspect or stage of a process will be less cohesive than one in which members rely on one another.

Competition from Outside the Team

When members perceive an external threat to their existence or dignity, they draw closer together. Almost everyone knows of a family whose members seem to fight constantly among themselves until an outsider criticizes one of them. The internal bickering stops for the moment, and the team unites against the common enemy. A fractured team could draw together in a similar way when another group competes with it for such things as use of limited company resources or desirable space in a new office building. Many wise managers deliberately set up situations of competition between teams to get tasks accomplished more quickly or to generate more sales.

Shared Team Experiences   When members have shared an experience together, especially an unusual or trying one, they draw closer together. This phenomenon explains why soldiers who have gone through combat together often feel close for the rest of their lives. Teams that have accomplished difficult tasks are also likely to be more cohesive. Some organizations also provide social events such as annual retreats for their executives. These retreats might include ropes courses, workshops, sports events, and parties. Annual sales meetings, although not the most cost-efficient way to distribute sales information, are often partially intended to increase team cohesiveness.

Avoid Excessive Conformity

Bad group decisions can also come about through too much agreement among members. Irving Janis calls this phenomenon **groupthink**, an unwillingness, for the sake of harmony, to examine ideas critically.[69] Janis describes several characteristics of groups that succumb to groupthink:

- *Illusion that the group is invulnerable:* "We can afford to raise the price on our deluxe-model kitchen appliances because they're so much better than anything else on the market. Even if our competitors could develop comparable models, we'd still outdo them on style."

- *Tendency to rationalize or discount negative information:* "I know the market research says people will buy other brands if our prices go up any more, but you know how unreliable market research is about things like that."

- *Willingness to ignore ethical or moral consequences of the team's decision:* "The waste we're dumping in the river may kill a few fish, but this company provides jobs and a living for all the people who live in this town."

- *Stereotyped views of other teams:* "The only thing those people at the head office care about is the bottom line. They don't care about what we think or what we need."

- *Team pressure to conform:* "Come on, none of the rest of us is interested in direct-mail marketing. Why don't you forget that stuff?"

- *Self-censorship:* "Every time I push for an innovative ad campaign, everybody fights it. I might as well drop it."

- *Illusion of unanimity:* "Then we all agree: Cutting prices is the only way to stay competitive."

- *"Mindguards" against threatening information:* "They're talking about running the machines around the clock to meet the schedule. I'd better not bring up what the supervisor said about how their staff feels about working more overtime."

Diversity of voices can serve as an antidote to groupthink by broadening outlooks and enriching discussions. However, one study found multicultural teams might be inclined toward groupthink if their awareness of cultural differences creates a desire to avoid conflict.[70]

A second type of harmful conformity, sometimes casually referred to as "mob mentality," has been labeled **risky shift**, referring to the likelihood of a group taking positions that are more extreme than the members would choose on their own.[71] Although risky shifts may result in teams taking unjustified risks and suffering the costs, some evidence suggests that many individuals are more willing to take a significantly higher level of risk for themselves than when others' payoffs are at stake.[72]

Devil's Advocate and Other Anticonformity Tools

Since medieval times, the Catholic Church has appointed a "devil's advocate" to present all possible arguments—even seemingly slight ones—against promoting a candidate toward sainthood. The church recognizes the danger of one-sided enthusiasm and relies on the advocate to make sure decision-makers consider all sides of the issue. This approach can serve nonreligious groups just as well, especially when an undisputed consensus arises regarding an important decision. If your team does not have the foresight to appoint a devil's advocate, you can take on this role by challenging the majority's thinking.

Other approaches can serve as antidotes to groupthink. If the team has enough members, it can be helpful to set up two (or more) subgroups to consider approaches independently. Another approach is to request the opinions of respected outsiders who have not been influenced by the collective enthusiasm of members.

At the opposite end of the spectrum, some people in groups shift toward a safer, more conservative behavior, known as **cautious shift**. When group members are conservative, their collective decisions are likely to be more cautious than their individual positions.[73] Thus, risky shift results in avoiding necessary steps that the team needs to take to survive and prosper.

Paradoxically, cohesive teams are most prone to groupthink and shift. When team members like and respect one another, the tendency to agree is great. The best way to guard against this sort of collective blindness—especially in highly cohesive teams—is to seek the opinions of outsiders who may see things differently. In addition, influential leaders should avoid stating their opinions early in the discussion.[74]

MASTER **the chapter**

review points

- Small groups share characteristics of size, shared purpose, interdependence, regular interaction and communication, and identity.

- Effective teams have clear and inspiring shared goals with a unified commitment to achieving those goals, a results-driven structure and collaborative climate, competent team members and principled leadership, as well as standards of excellence, and external support and recognition.

- Virtual teams transcend time and space boundaries, but present both advantages and challenges.

- Researchers suggest that the best approach to group leadership is one whereby leaders are flexible and adapt based on the circumstances.

- Although leaders enjoy unique relationships with the members of their teams, effective leaders provide a shared vision and empower their subordinates by putting employees' needs first.

- Some groups have a designated or appointed leader. In groups with no designated leader, a predictable process occurs in which a single leader often emerges.

- Team members possess various types of power: position, coercive, reward, expert, referent, information, and connection.
- Members contribute to team effectiveness by enacting functional roles (both task and relational) while avoiding dysfunctional roles.

- Teams can be more successful when members fill functional roles, recognize both personal and team goals, promote desirable norms, promote an optimal level of cohesiveness, and avoid excessive conformity.

key terms

authoritarian leadership style   219
cautious shift   236
coercive power   224
cohesiveness   233
connection power   225
contingency approaches to leadership   220
democratic leadership style   219
designated leader   223
emergent leader   222
expert power   224
functional roles   226
groupthink   235
hidden agenda   228
information power   225
laissez-faire leadership style   219
leader–member exchange (LMX)   221

norms   231
position power   224
referent power   225
relational roles   226
reward power   224
risky shift   235
self-directed work teams   223
servant leadership   221
situational leadership model   220
style approach to leadership   219
task roles   226
team   216
trait approach to leadership   219
transformational leadership   221
virtual team   217
workgroup   214

activities

1. Invitation to Insight

Consider an effective team you have observed or participated in. Identify the characteristics that contributed to this team's productivity. Provide an example of how the team enacted each of these characteristics. Then use concepts from this chapter to suggest at least one way the team could have improved.

2. Invitation to Insight

Interview a professional who regularly participates in virtual meetings. Identify what the person likes most and least about virtual meetings. In this person's opinion, what contributes most to the success of virtual meetings?

3. Invitation to Insight

Analyze the types of power that exist in a workgroup you are familiar with. Which members use each type of power? Who exerts the most influence? Which kinds of power do you possess? Which types

of power contribute most and least to your group's effectiveness?

4. Skill Builder

Using Table 7-2, identify the role that each of these statements represents: task, relational, or dysfunctional.

a. "Troy, could you hold on and let Mateo speak first?"
b. "So far we have discussed six funding sources. . . ."
c. "Although you seem to disagree, both of you are concerned with. . . ."
d. "I think you're really on to something. That seems like the information we need."
e. "What else do you think we should consider?"
f. "Debby, that is a really stupid idea."
g. "This is an exciting idea we're considering. Before we commit, let's look at how much it's going to cost to see if we can really do it."

h. "If you ask me, this is just too much work. Let's quit and play a video game instead."
i. "Now that we've finished brainstorming ideas, our next step is to evaluate them."
j. "I spent all yesterday evening making this graph. Why doesn't anyone at least thank me for it?"
k. "I found three websites with research studies we can use in this project."

5. Invitation to Insight

Which of the functional roles in Table 7-2 do you generally fill in groups? Do you fill the same role in most groups at most times or do you switch roles as circumstances require? Do you tend to fill task roles or relational roles? How could you improve the functioning of one group to which you belong by changing your role-related behavior?

6. Invitation to Insight

Although it may be larger than most of the groups discussed in this chapter, your class is a good model of the principles described here. Answer the following questions about your class or about a group in which you participate:

a. What are the stated goals of the class or group? Does the group have any unstated, shared goals?
b. What are your individual goals? Which of these goals are compatible with the group's goals, and which are not compatible? Are any of your individual goals hidden agendas?
c. What are your instructor's or the group leader's individual goals? Were these goals stated? If not, how did you deduce them? How compatible are these goals with the official goals of the class or group?
d. How do the other members' individual goals affect the functioning of the group as a whole?

7. Skill Builder

Suggest several norms that would be desirable for each of the following groups. In your list, include norms that address tasks, relationships, and procedures. How could you promote development of these norms as the group's leader? As a member?

a. A student fundraising committee to develop scholarships for your major or department.
b. The employees at a new fast-food restaurant.
c. A group of new bank tellers.
d. A company softball team.

8. Skill Builder

Use the skills you learned in Chapter 6 to interview one member of a work-related group. Identify the following:

a. What is the level of the group's cohesiveness? Is this level desirable, too high, or too low?
b. Which of the factors in the section of Chapter 7 titled "Promote an Optimal Level of Cohesiveness" contribute to the level of cohesiveness in this group?
c. On the basis of your findings, develop a report outlining specific steps that might be taken to improve this group's cohesiveness.

9. Skill Builder

Recall a group in which you participated that demonstrated an excessive level of conformity. Identify negative outcomes that resulted from the excessive conformity. Which characteristics of groupthink did the group exhibit? What allowed these characteristics to exist? Develop at least three suggestions that might have helped the group prevent over-conformity.

Mc Graw Hill LearnSmart

For further review, go to the LearnSmart study module for this chapter.

references

1. Reich, R. (1987). *Tales of a new America*. New York: Time Books.
2. Devine, D. J., Clayton, L. D., Phillips, J. L., Dunford, B. B. & Melner, S. B. (1999). Teams in organizations: Prevalence, characteristics, and effectiveness. *Small Group Research, 30*, 678–711.
3. Cross, R., Rebele, R., & Grant, A. (2016). Collaborative overload. *Harvard Business Review*.

Retrieved from https://hbr.org/2016/01 /collaborative-overload

4. Redmond, M. V. (1986). A plan for the successful use of teams in design education. *Journal of Architectural Education, 17*(4), 27–49.

5. Jones, B. (2009). The burden of knowledge and the death of the Renaissance man: Is innovation getting harder? *Review of Economic Studies, 76,* 283–317.

6. Gawande, A. (2011, May 26). *Cowboys and pit crews.* Commencement address at Harvard Medical School. Retrieved from http://www.newyorker.com/online/ blogs/newsdesk/2011/05/atul-gawande-harvard-medical -school-commencement-address.html

7. Lazzareschi, C. (1994, September 12). Being part of the team at work. *Los Angeles Times,* p. 13.

8. Forsutj, D. R. (2010). *Group dynamics.* Boston, MA: Cengage.

9. Rachman, D. J., & Mescon, M. H. (1990). *Profile kit for business today* (4th ed.). New York: Random House.

10. Katzenbach, J. R., & Smith, D. K. (1993, March/ April). The discipline of teams. *Harvard Business Review, 86*(2), 111–120.

11. Peters, T. J., & Waterman, R. H., Jr. (1982). *In search of excellence: Lessons from America's best run companies.* New York: Harper & Row.

12. Bormann, E. (1990). *Small group communication: Theory and practice.* New York: Harper & Row.

13. Is your team too big? Too small? What's the right number? (2006, June 14). Retrieved from http:// knowledge.wharton.upenn.edu/article. cfm?articleid=1501

14. Gribas, J. (1999). Organizational sports metaphors: Reconsidering gender bias in the team concept. *Communication Research Reports, 16,* 55–64.

15. Brounstein, M. (n.d.). *Differences between work groups and teams.* Retrieved from http://www.dummies.com /how-to/content/differences-between-work-groups-and -teams.html; Michelman, P. (2004). *How will you make your team a team?* Cambridge, MA: Harvard Management Press.

16. Basic types of virtual teams. (2009). *Free Management Library.* Retrieved from http:// managementhelp.org/groups/virtual/defined.pdf

17. LaFasto, F., & Larson, C. (2000). *When teams work best: 6,000 team members and leaders tell what it takes to succeed.* Thousand Oaks, CA: Sage.

18. Hirokawa, R. Y., Cathcart, R. S., Samovar, L. A., & Henman, L. D. (Eds.). (2003). *Small group communication: Theory & practice.* Los Angeles, CA: Roxbury.

19. Fisher, K. (2000). *Leading self-directed work teams: A guide to developing new team leadership skills.* New York: McGraw Hill.

20. Egan, J. (2020, May 13). Massive Austin employer predicts permanent shift to work-from-home for most workers. *Culture Map Austin.* Retrieved from https://austin .culturemap.com/news/city-life/05-13-20-one-of-austins -biggest-employers-guarantees-work-from-home-surge/#:~: text=The%20Associated%20Press%20quoted%20 Jen,after%20the%20pandemic%20lets%20up.

21. Egan, J. (2020, May 13). Massive Austin employer predicts permanent shift to work-from-home for most workers. *Culture Map Austin.* Retrieved from https:// austin .culturemap.com/news/city-life/05-13-20-one-of- austins -biggest-employers-guarantees-work-from-home -surge/#:~ :text=The%20Associated%20Press%20 quoted%20 Jen,after%20the%20pandemic%20lets%20up.

22. Wright, L. (2018, April 19). New survey explores the changing landscape of teamwork. *Microsoft.* Retrieved from https://www.microsoft.com/en-us/microsoft-365 /blog/2018/04/19/new-survey-explores-the-changing -landscape-of-teamwork/

23. Melymuka, K. (1997, April 28). Tips for teams. *Computerworld, 31*(17), 70–72.

24. Wigglesworth, D. C. (1997, July). Bookshelf. *HR Magazine, 42*(7), 133–134.

25. Herndon, S. L. (1997). Theory and practice: Implications for the implementation of communication technology in organizations. *Journal of Business Communication, 34,* 121–129.

26. Rothwell, J. D. (2013). *In mixed company: Small group communication* (8th ed.). Boston, MA: Cengage.

27. Lewin, K., Lippitt, R., & White, R. K. (1939). Patterns of aggressive behavior in experimentally created social climates. *Journal of Social Psychology, 10,* 271–299.

28. Foels, R., Driskell, J. E., Mullen, B., & Salas, E. (2000). The effects of democratic leadership on group member satisfaction. *Small Group Research, 20,* 676–701.

29. Kelly, S., & MacDonald, P. (2019). A look at leadership styles and workplace solidarity communication. *International Journal of Business Communication, 56*(3), 432–448. doi: 10.1177/2329488416664176

30. Rosenbaum, L. L., & Rosenbaum, W. B. (1971). Morale and productivity consequences of group leadership style, stress, and type of task. *Journal of Applied Psychology, 55,* 343–358.

31. Kelly, S., & MacDonald, P. (2019). A look at leadership styles and workplace solidarity communication. *International Journal of Business Communication, 56*(3), 432–448. doi: 10.1177/2329488416664176

32. Blake, R. R., & Mouton, J. S. (1985). *The new managerial grid.* Houston, TX: Gulf.

33. Fiedler, F. E. (1967). *A theory of leadership effectiveness.* New York: McGraw Hill.

34. Hersey, P., & Blanchard, K. (1982). *Management of organizational behavior* (4th ed.). Englewood Cliffs, NJ: Prentice-Hall; Blanchard, K. (1988, September). Selecting a leadership style that works. *Today's Office, 23,* 14.

35. Burns, J. M. (1978). *Leadership.* New York: Harper & Row.

36. Hersey, P., & Blanchard, K. (1982). *Management of organizational behavior* (4th ed.). Englewood Cliffs, NJ: Prentice-Hall; Blanchard, K. (1988, September). Selecting a leadership style that works, *Today's Office, 23,* 14.

37. Parris, D. L., & Peachey, J. W. (2013). A systematic literature review of servant leadership theory in organizational contexts. *Journal of Business Ethics, 113*(3), 377–393.

38. Brown, M. E., Treviño, L. K., & Harrison, D. E. (2005). Ethical leadership: A social learning perspective for construct development and testing. *Organizational Behavior and Human Decision Processes, 97*(2), 117–134.

39. Jaramillo, F., Bande, B., & Varela, J. (2015). Servant leadership and ethics: A dyadic examination of supervisor behaviors and salesperson perceptions. *Journal of Personal Selling & Sales Management, 35*(2), 108–124.

40. Liden, R. C., Wayne, S. J., Liao, C., & Meuser, J. D. (2014). Servant leadership and serving culture: Influence on individual and unit performance. *Academy of Management Journal, 57*(5), 1424–1452.

41. Graen, G. B., & Scandura, T. A. (1987). Toward psychology of dyadic organizing. In B. M. Staw & L. L. Cummings (Eds.), *Research in organizational behavior* (Vol. 9). Greenwich, CT: JAI Press.

42. Becker, J. A. H., Halbesleben, J. R. B., & O'Hair, D. H. (2005). Defensive communication and burnout in the workplace: The mediating role of leader-member exchange. *Communication Research Reports, 22,* 143–150; Fairhurst, G. T. (1993). The leader-member exchange patterns of women leaders in industry: A discourse analysis. *Communication Monographs, 60,* 321–351; Lamude, K. C., Scudder, J., Simmons, D., & Torres, P. (2004). Organizational newcomers: Temporary and regular employees, same-sex and mixed-sex superior-subordinate dyads, supervisor influence techniques, subordinates communication satisfaction, and leader-member exchange. *Communication Research Reports, 21,* 60–67.

43. Mueller, B., & Lee, J.(2002). Leader-member exchange and organizational communication satisfaction in multiple contexts. *Journal of Business Communication, 39,* 220–244.

44. Shannon, C. W. (2018). *Effective management communication strategies* [Doctoral dissertation, Walden University]. ScholarWorks. Retrieved from https://scholarworks.waldenu.edu/cgi/viewcontent.cgi?article=7058&context=dissertations

45. Madlock, P. E., Martin, M. M., Bogdan, L., & Ervin, M. (2007). The impact of communication traits on leader-member exchange. *Human Communication, 10,* 451–464.

46. Abu Bakar, H., Dilbeck, K. E., & McCroskey, J. C. (2010). Mediating role of supervisory communication practices on relations between leader-member exchange and perceived employee commitment to workgroup. *Communication Monographs, 77,* 637–656; Graen, G. B., & Uhl-Bien, M. (1991). The transformation of professionals into self-managing and partially self-designing contributors: Towards a theory of leadership making. *Journal of Management Systems, 3,* 33–48.

47. Bormann, E. (1990). *Small group communication: Theory and practice.* New York: Harper & Row; Rothwell, J. D. (2013). *In mixed company: Small group communication* (8th ed.). Boston, MA: Cengage.

48. Fisher, R., & Sharp, A. (1998). *Getting it done: How to lead when you're not in charge.* New York: Harper Business.

49. Wellins, R. S., Byham, W. C., & Wilson, J. M. (1991). *Empowered teams: Creating self-directed work groups that improve quality, productivity, and participation.* San Francisco, CA: Jossey-Bass.

50. Reader, G. (2016, September 19). How this founder learned to trust his team. *Entrepreneur.* Retrieved from https://www.entrepreneur.com/video/280987

51. French, J. R. P., & Raven, B. (1959). The bases of social power. In D. Cartwright (Ed.), *Studies in social power.* Ann Arbor, MI: University of Michigan Institute for Social Research; Raven, B., & Kruglanski, W. (1975). Conflict and power. In P. G. Swingle (Ed.), *The structure of conflict.* New York: Academic Press; Hersey, P., & Blanchard, K. (1982). *Management of organizational behavior* (4th ed.). Englewood Cliffs, NJ: Prentice-Hall.

52. Pescosolido, A. T. (2001). Informal leaders and the development of group efficacy. *Small Group Research, 32,* 74–93.

53. Loh, S. T. (1993, March 1). You say the boss is how old? *Los Angeles Times,* p. 9–10.

54. Keyton, J. (1999). Relational communication in groups. In L. R. Frey (Ed.), *Handbook of group communication theory and research.* Thousand Oaks, CA: Sage.

55. Matson, E. (1996, April). The seven sins of deadly meetings. *Fast Times, 2,* 122–125.

56. Mayer, M. E. (1998). Behaviors leading to more effective decisions in small groups embedded in organizations. *Communication Reports, 11,* 123–132.

57. Heckman, F. (2001, May). A purpose and a place: Harmonizing elements to create an organization with rhythm. *News for a Change, 5*(5), 1–3.

58. Heckman, F. (2001, May). A purpose and a place: Harmonizing elements to create an organization with rhythm. *News for a Change, 5*(5), 1–3.

59. Anderson, C. M., Riddle, B. L., & Martin, M. M. (1999). Socialization processes in groups. In L. R. Frey (Ed.), *Handbook of group communication theory and research*. Thousand Oaks, CA: Sage.

60. Eisenberg, E. M., Goodall, H. L., & Trethwey, A. (2010). *Organizational communication: Balancing creativity and constraint* (6th ed.). New York: Bedford/ St. Martin's.

61. Browning, L. (1992, May). *Reasons for success at Motorola*. Paper presented at the International Communication Association annual meeting, Miami, FL.

62. Mulvey, P. W., Bowes-Sperry, L., & Klein, H. J. (1998). The effects of perceived loafing and defensive impression management on group effectiveness. *Small Group Research, 29,* 394–415.

63. Oetzel, J. G., Burtis, T. E., Chew Sanchez, M. I., & Perez, F. G. (2001). Investigating the role of communication in culturally diverse work groups: A review and synthesis. In W. B. Gudykunst (Ed.), *Communication yearbook 25*. New York: Routledge.

64. Wenberg, J. R., & Wilmot, W. (1973). *The personal communication process*. New York: Wiley; Daniels, T. D., & Spiker, B. K. (1997). *Perspectives on organizational communication* (4th ed.). Dubuque, IA: Wm. C. Brown.

65. Melymuka, K. (1997). Tips for teams. *Computerworld, 31*(17), 70–72.

66. Janis, I. L. (1972). *Victims of groupthink*. Boston, MA: Houghton Mifflin.

67. Gammage, K. L., Carron, A. V., & Estabrooks, P. A. (2001). Team cohesion and individual productivity. *Small Group Research, 32,* 3–18.

68. Bormann, E. G. (1975). *Discussion and group methods* (2nd ed.). New York: Harper & Row; Adler, P., & Adler, P. (1988). Intense loyalty in organizations: A case study of college athletics. *Administrative Science Quarterly, 33,* 401–418.

69. Janis, I. L. (1972). *Victims of groupthink*. Boston, MA: Houghton Mifflin; Ross, J. A. (2008). *Team camaraderie: Can you have too much?* Retrieved from http://blogs.hbr.org/hmu/2008/02/team-camaraderie-can-you-have-1.html

70. Goby, V. (2007). Business communication needs. *Journal of Business and Technical Communication, 21,* 425–437; Sharon, A. (2008, February 5). The death of groupthink. *Business Week*. Retrieved from http://www.businessweek.com/print/managing/content/feb2008/ca2008025_687188.htm

71. Myers, D. G., & Lamm, H. (1976). The group polarization phenomenon. *Psychological Bulletin, 83,* 602–627; BarNir, A. (1998). Can group- and issue-related factors predict choice shift? *Small Group Research, 29,* 308–338.

72. Reynolds, D. B., Joseph, J., & Sherwood, R. (2009). Risky shift versus cautious shift: Determining differences in risk taking between private and public management decision-making. *Journal of Business & Economics Research, 7,* 63–77.

73. Stoner, J. A. F. (1968). Risky and cautious shifts in group decisions: The influence of widely held values. *Journal of Experimental Social Psychology, 4,* 442–459.

74. Robbins, S. P. (1990). *Organizational behavior: Concepts, controversies, and applications* (4th ed.). Englewood Cliffs, NJ: Prentice-Hall.

Chapter Eight
Effective Meetings

chapter outline

chapter objectives

After reading this chapter you should be able to:

1. Describe various purposes and types of meetings.
2. Describe the various types and characteristics of virtual meetings.
3. Identify reasons to hold (or not hold) a meeting.
4. Construct a complete meeting agenda.
5. Identify methods to set the tone for a meeting.
6. Apply various methods for conducting business: parliamentary procedure, decision-making methods, enhancing creativity, encouraging participation, keeping discussions on track, and keeping a positive tone.
7. Effectively bring a meeting to a close and follow up appropriately.

Meetings are a fact of life on the job. The most recent studies state that over 11 million business meetings take place each day in the United States. However, given that this statistic is from 1998, the figure is likely to be significantly higher today. In fact, some online meeting software professionals estimate that this figure is closer to 36 and 55 million meetings per day.[1] A typical American employee will attend 62 meetings per month,[2] at an average length of 31 to 60 minutes per meeting.[3] Perhaps even more astonishing is the fact that CEOs spend 60% of their working hours in meetings. Another 25% of their time is devoted to phone calls, conference calls, and events.[4]

Just because meetings are commonplace does not mean they are always worth the time and effort.[5] In fact, hours spent in meetings are not always considered productive. In addition to the time lost during an inefficient meeting, employees often spend additional time after such a meeting having to cool off due to frustration—a concept referred to as *meeting recovery syndrome*.[6] Unproductive meetings also have financial repercussions. One study commissioned by Doodle found companies and business professionals around the world lost more than $541 billion of resources in 2019 because of fruitless meetings.[7]

Beyond wasting precious time and money, pervasively inefficient meetings contribute to an overall atmosphere of cynicism. "Meetings matter because that's where an organization's culture perpetuates itself," says William R. Daniels, senior consultant at American Consulting & Training.[8] Meetings—whether good or bad—are a sign of an organization's health. Efficient meetings can leave employees feeling energized and excited about their work, and are a crucial part of a productive business culture.[9]

This chapter introduces some methods for planning and participating in meetings that will produce efficient, satisfying results. We focus specifically on how teams operate in face-to-face and virtual meetings—that is, on those occasions when their members communicate simultaneously to deal with common concerns.

• Types of Meetings

People meet for many reasons. Whether they occur in person or online, in most business and professional settings, meetings can be classified into three categories: information-sharing meetings, problem-solving meetings, and ritual activities. Of course, some meetings may serve more than one purpose.

Information-Sharing Meetings

In many organizations, people meet regularly to exchange information. **Information-sharing meetings** are appropriate for brainstorming, sharing updates, and gaining additional knowledge or training. Information-sharing meetings typically adhere to the format of a regular office meeting, though they may be informal or formal. You will experience many information-sharing meetings in your professional life, but the most common types are described next.

Briefings
A briefing is a type of meeting where important messages—typically status updates and instructions—are shared with team members to provide a clear understanding of their roles. Police officers and nurses, for example, begin every shift with a meeting in which the people going off-duty brief their replacements on what has been happening recently. Members of a medical research team experimenting with a new drug may meet regularly to compare notes on their results. In many office teams, the Monday morning meeting is an important tool for informing members about new developments, emerging trends, and the coming week's tasks. For example, Perkin Elmer Corporation, a producer of scientific measuring instruments and precision optical equipment, schedules a weekly meeting of all corporate and top executives to keep them up to date on the activities of the company's more than 20 divisions, which are located around the world.

Staff Meetings
It is necessary for members of an organization to be informed of issues that affect their work. Staff meetings allow employees and supervisors to come together to discuss this type of information. Staff meetings are often held at regular intervals (a *standing meeting*)—such as biweekly or monthly—but may also be spontaneously scheduled (known as an *ad hoc meeting*) when important matters arise. A group of college football officials might be asked to gather for an impromptu meeting to discuss a new rule change. Employees at two different fast-food restaurants might be required to attend a series of meetings leading up to a merger uniting the two companies.

Board Meetings
A board of directors (or *board*) is a group of individuals elected to act as a governing body representing the interests of key stakeholders or shareholders of an organization. All public companies and some private and nonprofit organizations have a board, which meets regularly to discuss the company's activities. The board oversees the company's actions, offers advice, engages in decision-making, and is involved in problem-solving and crisis management. The Children's Advocacy Centers of Texas, for example, consist of 25 to 35 volunteers from throughout the state—former prosecutors, healthcare workers, crisis counselors, and communication professionals—who each bring expertise to the role.

Planning Meetings
An excellent way to gain shared information, brainstorm ideas, discuss progress ideas, and make group decisions is via planning meetings. This type of meeting is commonly held when launching a project or campaign, preparing for an event, or meeting with a client to gain insight into their needs and goals. A hockey team might approach a public relations agency with a need for building a campaign to bring more fans into the stands. A planning meeting with the client would allow the agency to gain perspective as to the causes the client attributes to the attendance issue, as well as the organization's budget constraints and allowances. Furthermore, a group of volunteers with the local Rotary club may meet to discuss the steps needed to host a major fundraising luncheon and to divvy up tasks among themselves.

Workshops
Information-sharing meetings may also take the form of workshops. These types of meetings are for smaller groups, where attendees improve their knowledge

and skills of a certain task. A group of elementary school employees may take a First Aid and CPR course offered by The American Red Cross to gain the necessary skills for handling an emergency. Alternately, an information technology (IT) engineer may take online courses to satisfy continuing education hours required to maintain a professional license.

Seminars   A seminar is a meeting—such as a convention—designed to facilitate discussion about a specific topic or area of common interest with small or large groups of attendees. It is likely that your professors attend yearly conventions to share their research with colleagues and learn more about what other researchers are contributing to the field.

Problem-Solving and Decision-Making Meetings

While almost every meeting consists of attendees sharing information, in **problem-solving meetings**, the focus is on analyzing a situation or issue and identifying potential solutions. Problem-solving is the most common reason why business meetings are held. In **decision-making meetings**, a team may decide to take some action or make changes to existing policies or procedures. Because problem-solving and decision-making meetings are the most challenging type of group activity, considerable attention is given to this topic in Appendix III.

Some level of problem solving or decision-making may occur during each of the information-sharing meetings we discussed in the previous section. Questions may emerge during these meetings that require sharing ideas: Which supplier should we contract? Should we delay production so we can work out a design flaw in our new keyboard? How can we best schedule vacations? However, there are at least three additional types of meetings where problem solving and decision-making is the main purpose of the gathering.

Committees   A formal team consisting of a small group of persons performing a function on behalf of the larger group is a committee. These individuals may be selected, elected, or volunteers. Organizational by-laws may list specific standing committees, but companies may choose to create ad hoc committees as the need arises. Ad hoc committees typically include a deadline for completing a specific charge. A group of County employees may be selected to make sure financial reports are accurate and oversee the County budget, thus comprising a formal finance committee; whereas, a homeowners association may establish an ad hoc committee to help redesign its community clubhouse.

Task Forces   Small workgroups consisting of experts in specific areas of knowledge are often brought together to form a task force to accomplish a specific objective. Once the task has been completed, the group will disband. A university might create a task force of faculty which has experience in teaching online to pilot new video conferencing software with the purpose of deciding whether to adopt the software on campus. Furthermore, a technology company may create a task force to address a recurring problem with customers complaining about defective parts. The task force will need to discuss how to resolve the existing customer complaints, as well as identify the cause of the problem and develop a solution.

Executive Sessions   In the United States, each state's Open Meetings Act (OMA) stipulates that a governmental body must open its meetings to the public unless there is an authorized reason for a closed session, known as an executive session.[10] This type of closed session allows a board or elected governing body the ability to meet privately to handle confidential or sensitive matters. For example, a school board may hold an executive session to deliberate about an alleged violation of ethics by a school superintendent.

Ritual Activities

While information-sharing, problem-solving, and decision-making meetings are quite task-oriented in nature, for **ritual activities**, the social function is far more important than any specific task. Despite the setting and seemingly un-businesslike activity, these meetings serve several important purposes.[11] First, they reaffirm the members' commitment to one another and to the company. Choosing to socialize instead of rushing home is a sign of belonging and caring. Second, the sessions provide a chance to swap useful ideas and stories that might not be appropriate in the office. Who is in trouble? What does the boss really want? Three forms of ritual activities are described next. Finally, teams who score in the top 20% in engagement experience a marked reduction in absenteeism and turnover. They are more likely to show up to work with passion and energy.[12]

Social Functions   Festivities held on- or off-site with the purpose of socializing or celebrating are types of rituals in professional life. Ceremonial events like retirement parties or awards galas, or informal holiday parties and coffee chats are commonplace for many organizations. In one firm, Friday afternoon "progress review sessions" are a regular fixture. This apparently serious title is really an insider's tongue-in-cheek joke: The meetings take place at a local bar and might look like little more than a party to an outsider. Virtual and remote employees at Great Place to Work participate in a "spooky place to work meme fest" to generate laughs and bond over shared experiences.[13] In a more elaborate example, Grundfos, a pump manufacturing company headquartered in Denmark, hosts "Grundfos Olympics"—a five-day Olympics-style sports event bringing together over 1,000 employees from 55 countries. The participants from abroad are invited to lodge at the homes of their Danish colleagues. A company news release cites the event as a way to give staff an opportunity to create friendships and closer ties with colleagues they've never met or have only met online.[14]

Team-Building Meetings   Team building is essential for every company's overall health. Team-building events are internal events that are used to foster collaboration, resolve conflict, and improve communication among colleagues. Team-building meetings are especially useful after major turning points in the organization, as in the case of a merger, yearly kick-off, or before a large project. Remote employees at Great Place to Work volunteered to digitally transcribe documents for the Smithsonian, whereas Salesforce employees hosted an online talent show for Latina SafeHouse.[15] A ropes course is another example of a team-building meeting where employees participate in a variety of challenging activities that require the cooperation of the entire group to build trust and confidence.

Enrichment Meetings   Other rituals for some organizations are enrichment-based meetings that allow employees to use part of their workday to discuss issues that bridge their work life and personal well-being. For example, companies such as Target, Nike, Google, and Apple offer their employees meditation and yoga classes with the hope of reducing stress-related maladies.[16]

As you read in Chapter 1, this sort of informal communication can be invaluable, and ritual activities provide a good setting for it. Finally, ritual meetings can be a kind of perk that confers status on the

Hero Images Inc./Alamy Stock Photo

attendees. "Progress review committee" members charge expenses to the company and leave work early to attend the sessions. Thus, being invited to join the "meetings" is a sign of having arrived in the company.

• Virtual Meetings

Not long ago the term *meeting* might have conjured an image of people seated around a table, transacting business. In reality, in less than a generation, there has been a monumental shift in organizational life. What began due to an exciting influx of technological capabilities was accelerated by the global COVID-19 pandemic. This shift has resulted in many employees attending more virtual meetings than face-to-face get-togethers.[17] Virtual meetings may be held in real-time, so that everyone attends at the time when the event is scheduled regardless of their respective time zones, or they may utilize asynchronous communication so participants are able to contribute to the meetings at different times.

As we discussed in the previous section, meetings serve one or more purposes. Just like with face-to-face meetings, there are several types of virtual meetings that can be used to achieve your goals. No matter which type of virtual meeting is used, there are several benefits to meeting online. First, virtual meetings are an inexpensive way to gather participants and build engagement and productivity among teams.[18] The conversation and documents/materials being presented during virtual meetings can often be recorded, which allows participants to replay portions of the meeting or catch up on a meeting that they have missed. Additionally, participants can be patched in instantaneously to answer questions or share information, which eliminates the need for individuals to sit through an entire meeting if they are needed only briefly. Employees certainly enjoy the ability to have productivity meetings from the comfort of their own homes.[19] According to 2020 Gallup Panel data, 59% of U.S. employees would prefer to continue working from home once COVID-19 restrictions have been lifted.[20]

Of course, these types of meetings are not without some disadvantages. Being able to attend virtual meetings from almost anywhere allows attendees to call or log in from noisy locations such as coffeehouses, airport lounges, and busy home environments, making individuals prone to distractions.[21] A concern with inequality also arises as work–life balance needs become challenged by this arrangement. Employees attending to family members while working from home, communicating synchronously at sporadic intervals throughout the day, or commuting to find an effective workspace or Wi-Fi connection may negatively impact employees' productivity and wellness.[22] Some employees may also feel derailed by the lack of social interaction with colleagues.[23] As we discussed in Chapter 5, supportive peer coworker relationships have significant and positive impacts on employees' well-being, so a lack of interaction poses concerns. Additionally, just as with face-to-face meetings, poor facilitation can make virtual meetings seem awkward and dull.[24] Another downside is a new phenomenon known as **virtual meeting fatigue**, or feelings of tiredness, worry, or burnout caused by overusing virtual communication platforms.[25] Virtual meeting fatigue became particularly problematic in 2020 and is the topic of the Career Tip feature in this section.

Conference Calls

Conference calls are essentially multiparty telephone calls. To begin a conference call, the party hosting the call (the "calling party") may call other participants to add them to the call; however, many software platforms allow participants to dial a phone number

A Professional Perspective

Nicole Plascencia

Digital Sales Manager

FOX Sports West | FOX Sports San Diego | Prime Ticket

San Diego, CA

Credit: Nicole Plascencia

The sudden onset of COVID-19 changed my professional landscape overnight. On a Wednesday evening, mid-game, the NBA announced it would shut down for at least one month. That Friday, my colleagues and I went to the office and were told to pack up our things and be prepared to work from home. The following week, California Gov. Gavin Newsom issued a statewide shelter-in-place order.

After the dust settled and my team members and I adjusted working from home, we had to begin to define our new normal. For example, how often we should meet as a team and how often we should be in front of our clients? As salespeople, we are encouraged to spend most of our time with clients and potential clients, making it challenging in ordinary times to schedule internal meetings. Now add the additional challenges of a global pandemic—Zoom fatigue, colleagues trying to school their children while working, lack of face time with clients—and it became even tougher to prioritize team meetings. Nonetheless, these meetings matter. They help us feel connected to each other and allow us to share relevant information and engage in problem-solving discussions.

Most of the meetings I host are information-sharing. It's my job to develop team trainings on digital advertising. In a remote work setting, it is particularly important to set the tone for a meeting so that participants are engaged and feel that the meeting is worthwhile. I like to encourage the team members to keep their cameras on so that we can see each other's smiling faces—the same as we would in a face-to-face environment. Having an agenda is also helpful so attendees feel at ease about the content. Now more than ever it is important to schedule meetings with a clear purpose and think outside of the box to make high-quality connections in a virtual setting.

and enter a personal identification number (PIN) that enables them to access a meeting. Videoconferencing services like Zoom, GoToMeeting, and UberConference also provide conference call capabilities by allowing participants to use the audio-only feature to dial in via phone or computer. Conference calls may be designed to allow callers to speak on the line during the meeting, or callers may only be allowed to listen in on the meeting.

Businesses use conference calls on a daily basis to meet with internal and external participants, as they are a useful way for parties to hash out details that would take much longer to settle via e-mail or a chain of two-person phone conversations. Common uses for conference calls include regular team meetings, training sessions, client meetings, project meetings, and sales presentations. For example, public corporations in the United States are required by the Securities and Exchange Commission (SEC) to provide quarterly earnings reports. Many of these corporations utilize conference calls to discuss the financial results with interested stakeholders.

Web Conferences

Web conferencing is an online event using one-way audio/video communication, allowing a presenter to share information with a geographically dispersed group of attendees. Web conferences take place over the Internet, with participants connecting to a meeting using a web browser and link to the event. The link may direct participants to a web browser, or it may require software application to be installed on a computer, tablet, or mobile phone. Although web conferencing typically takes place in real-time, most applications allow presentations to be recorded for later viewing or distribution. Common features of web conferencing include:

- Audience tracking
- Whiteboard with annotation
- Instant messaging and text chat
- Live polling and surveys
- Slideshow presentations
- Live or streaming video of the presenter(s)
- Desktop, mouse, and keyboard sharing
- Automated e-mail
- Automated reminders and follow-ups
- Promotion tools

One type of web conference commonly used in a business setting is a **webinar**, or web-based seminar. A webinar is a presentation, lecture, workshop, or seminar that is transmitted over the Internet with limited audience interaction. Webinars are great tools for professional development and training meetings. HootSuite, for example, hosts a variety of webinars approximately one hour in length on topics related to social media management. Webinars are discussed in more depth in Chapter 9.

Video Conferences

Video conferencing provides real-time, two-way audio/video interaction among users in various locations. This meeting format enables participants to utilize webcams, microphones, or other audio/video equipment connected to a network to communicate with each other. Common features of video conferencing include:

- Personal meeting room
- Waiting room
- Password-enabled and open meetings
- Live or streaming video of the presenter(s)

Combatting Virtual Meeting Fatigue

Professionals all over the world quickly adapted to working and socializing in a virtual space amid the COVID-19 pandemic. From attending classes and business meetings to happy hours and memorial services, videoconferencing became a daily norm. While staying connected has its advantages, overusing virtual platforms of communication may lead to virtual meeting fatigue (referred to by some researchers as "Zoom fatigue").

A few possible reasons for virtual meeting fatigue include:

- The positive benefits of eye contact between two people may be impeded by having to look in the camera.[26]
- Audio delays may be associated with negative perceptions and distrust between people.[27]

- Impaired nonverbal cues among participants prompt a more intense focus on verbal communication.[28]
- "Brady Bunch"-style gallery views require listeners to decode the communication of many people at once.[29]

The following strategies may be used to combat virtual meeting fatigue:

- Avoid multitasking to help you pay attention
- Take breaks between calls to rest your eyes and move your body
- Reduce stress and self-consciousness by hiding your own video
- Avoid overstimulation by using plain backgrounds or agreeing as a group to turn off their videos when not speaking
- When possible, use other forms of communication in place of video[30]

- Participant list
- Text chat and private chat
- Breakout rooms
- Screen sharing; Multi-screen sharing
- Closed captioning
- Recordings available in the Cloud for streaming or download
- Integrated calendar functions

During the COVID-19 pandemic, many companies adapted by shifting their face-to-face meetings to video conferences. While the name implies a requirement of the use of video, participants can join these meetings by means of teleconferencing or audio conferencing if they do not have microphones, speakers, or webcams on their personal computers, or are unable to access an Internet connection while on the road. However, in a professional setting, it is always best to consult with your employer or meeting leader to verify their expectations for video participation during meetings and virtual events.

Diego Cervo/Shutterstock

Collaborative Technologies

According to Chicago-based research firm, dscout, the average person taps, pinches, or swipes their smartphone over 2,600 times per day across 76 separate phone sessions–most of which occurs during work hours.[31] The mobile environment is rapidly becoming the primary place where social networking, video viewing, reading, and location-based searching occur.[32]

Collaboration in Cyberspace: Geography Makes a Difference

How important is communication when team members from across the country and around the world meet in cyberspace? To answer this question, corporate giants Verizon and Microsoft commissioned a study to determine how virtual teams in a variety of industries and countries collaborate.

The study revealed that the importance of collaboration on performance was consistent across various industries (e.g., health care, government, financial services, manufacturing) and around the world. As one participant of the study remarked, "Global companies that collaborate better, perform better. Those that collaborate less, do not perform as well. It's just that simple."

The researchers also discovered cultural differences in workers' communication preferences. For example, Americans were more likely to enjoy working alone. They expressed a preference for using e-mail rather than the telephone. They were more comfortable with audio, video, and web conferencing technologies than people of other regions of the world, and they were more likely to multitask when on conference calls.

By comparison, Europeans expressed a preference for communicating in real-time with colleagues. They felt more obligated to answer the phone, and they expected others to call them back rather than leave a voicemail. Professionals in the Asia Pacific region, more than anywhere else, expressed a desire to keep in touch throughout the workday. As a result, they found the phone an indispensable tool and preferred instant messaging to e-mail. Differences like these suggest that teams can be more productive if their members take cultural differences into account when planning to communicate.

Source: Frost & Sullivan (2006). Meetings around the world: The impact of collaboration on business performance. Retrieved from https://e-meetings.verizonbusiness.com/maw/pdf/MAW_white_paper.pdf

The mobile revolution has also infiltrated the workplace. Given that there is little difference in accuracy and speed between face-to-face and virtual groups[33], many organizations are encouraging virtual engagement by providing employees with tools to access and share information on the go. Examples of these tools include the following:

- **Wikis** are interactive websites that allow teams to add, remove, share, exchange, and edit content. The National Aeronautics and Space Administration (NASA) uses wikis to internally share and discover information.[34]

- **Project management tools** are apps that allow teams to develop a timeline and assign tasks to one another. One example, Trello, was discussed in the "Technology Tip: Apps for Teamwork" box in Chapter 7.

- **Team communication platforms** (TCPs), like Cisco Jabber and Slack, are instant messaging applications that provide a way for colleagues to stay connected, share files, and work across multiple devices without having to access their e-mail accounts.[35]

- **Internal social networks/enterprise social networks** (ISNs/ESNs) are online communities that are accessible only to members of the organization and incorporate the same tools as regular social media. Microsoft Yammer is one example of this type of tool. Only individuals with e-mail addresses from their organization's domain may join the social network.

Most ISNs mimic the look and functionality of popular mainstream social networking sites; however, within the ISN platform, one may also have the ability to utilize blogs and wikis, social tagging, and document sharing.[36] The adoption of such technologies has numerous implications for workplace communication. For example, they may influence interactions with new hires, knowledge sharing, and employees' abilities to form relationships.[37] Additionally, the use of ISNs may contribute to a sense of belonging for employees, as some of the discussions of organizational issues that take place on ISNs can develop into organizational stories that are then shared in informal conversations among coworkers.[38] Employees at Lenovo used their ISN, "Lenovo Social Champions," to share a CRN magazine article titled "10 Hottest Laptops of 2015," which featured their La Vie Z laptop sixth on the list. Lenovo encourages its employees to share internal content—such as photos and videos from company gatherings—and external content that is related to the brand.

TCPs tend to boast similar features: communication being located in one place; integration with other media services, such as project management tools and e-mail support systems; searchable content; file sharing; private groups; and accessibility.[39] Some of the documented benefits of TCPs include centralized, visible communication; strengthened knowledge sharing and social cohesion; increased self-initiative; and being able to monitor conversations about projects.[40]

● Planning a Meeting

Thinking strategically about how to plan for a successful meeting is an important step in reducing "time-wasting meetings" in the workplace. Effective meetings can boost your team's performance and productivity.

When to Hold a Meeting

Public-sector businesses and organizations governed by boards of directors do not have a choice when it comes to holding meetings. These types of organizations are legally mandated to conduct any business that affects the public in the open. As an example, as part of this mandate, the Corporation for Public Broadcasting must make board meetings, board committee meetings, and community advisory board meetings open to the public. The organization must also provide the public with reasonable notice (at least seven days in advance) of the meeting. For a session to be recognized as an official meeting, a *quorum* (a majority of the membership) must be present, and discussions pertaining to issues that influence the membership must occur. The public must be given the opportunity to share their input during these discussions.

For other businesses that do not operate in this manner, meetings are essential but are not always required. Given the cost and effort necessary to bring people together, the most fundamental question is whether to hold a meeting at all. When considering scheduling a meeting, stop for a moment and think about the meeting's purpose. There are many times when a meeting may not be the most effective method to address the purpose:

- The matter could be effectively handled over the phone.
- You could achieve the goal with a memo or e-mail.
- Key people are not available to attend.
- The subject would be considered trivial by many of the participants.
- There is not enough time to handle the business at hand.
- Members are not prepared.
- The meeting is simply routine and there is no compelling reason to meet.
- The job can be handled just as well by one or more people without the need to consult others.
- Your mind is made up, or you have already made the decision.

How to Handle "Time Waster" Meetings

What should you do when you are expected to attend a meeting that you know will be a waste of time? On some occasions, you cannot escape such meetings—for example, when you are formally obligated to attend, when your absence would damage your reputation, or when your boss insists you show up. Although you must attend these meetings, it might be helpful to ask the host to provide an agenda that includes start and end times. It might also be productive to make a friendly suggestion at the beginning of the meeting that team members put away their mobile phones to minimize multicommunicating.

If you believe that you can miss a meeting without incurring negative consequences, you might consider using one of the following strategies to make your absence acceptable:

- Set aside your most productive hours each day by adding them to a shared calendar. Avoid making exceptions.

- Try starting a grassroots movement to have one or more "no-meeting days" each week. Setting aside Friday as a no-meeting day, for example, may boost everyone's productivity.

- Provide written input. If your sole reason for showing up is to provide information, a memo or written report may be a good substitute for your physical presence.

- Suggest a productive alternative. There may be other ways for you—and maybe even other attendees—to achieve your objectives without meeting, such as through an exchange of e-mails, teleconferencing, or delegating the job to a smaller group. Suggesting these alternatives may earn you the gratitude of others who do not want to attend the meeting any more than you do.

- Tell the truth. In some cases, you may choose to diplomatically explain your reasons for not wanting to attend: "I'm not sure my attendance would serve any useful purpose."

Source: Lippincott, S. M. (1999). *Meetings: Do's, don'ts, and donuts* (2nd ed.). Pittsburgh, PA: Lighthouse Point Press; Mock, L. (2016, August 30). How to cut down on useless meetings. *Gliffy*. Retrieved from https://www.gliffy.com/blog/2016/08/30/how-to-cut-down-on-useless-meetings/

Employees are likely to resent an unnecessary intrusion into their schedules.[41] Keeping these points in mind, a planner should call a meeting (or appoint a committee) only when they can answer yes to the following questions.

Is the Job Beyond the Capacity of One Person? A job might be too much for one person to handle for two reasons. First, it might call for more information than any single person possesses. For example, the job of improving health conditions in a food-processing plant would probably require a health professional's medical background, employees' experience, and a manager who knows the resources.

Second, a job might take more time than one person has available. For instance, even if one employee were capable of writing and publishing an employee handbook, it is unlikely the person would be able to handle the task and have much time for other duties.

Are Individuals' Tasks Interdependent? Each member at a committee meeting should have a different role. If each member's share of the task can be completed without input from other members, it is better to have the members co-acting under a manager's supervision. Consider the job of preparing the employee handbook: If each person on the handbook team is responsible for a separate section, there is little need for them to meet frequently to discuss the task.

Sometimes people who do the same job can profit by sharing ideas with a group. Members of the handbook team, for example, might get new ideas about how the book could be improved by talking to one another. Similarly, sales representatives, industrial designers, physicians, and attorneys who work independently might profit by exchanging experiences and ideas. In fact, generating such synergy is part of the motivation for holding professional conventions.

Many companies schedule quarterly or annual meetings of people who perform similar job functions but work independently. While this may seem to contradict the requirement for interdependence of members' tasks, there is no real conflict. A group of people who do the same kind of work can often improve their individual performance through meetings by performing some of the complementary functional roles. For example, one colleague might serve as reality tester: "Writing individual notes to each potential customer in your territory sounds like a good idea, but do you really have time to do that?" Another might take the job of being information-giver: "You know, there's a printer just outside Boston who can do large jobs like that just as well as your regular printer, but cheaper. Call me, and I'll give you the name and address." Others serve as diagnosers: "Have you checked the feed mechanism? Sometimes a problem there can throw the whole machine out of whack." Some can just serve as empathic listeners: "Yeah, I know. It's tough to get people who can do that kind of work."

Is There More Than One Decision or Solution?

Questions that have only one right answer are not well suited to discuss in meetings. Whether the sales team made its quota last year and whether the budget will accommodate paying overtime to meet a schedule, for instance, are questions best answered by checking the figures, not by getting the regional sales managers or the department members to reach an agreement.

In contrast, tasks that do not have fixed outcomes are appropriate targets for committee discussion. Consider the job facing the employees of an advertising agency who are planning a campaign for a client. There is no obvious best way to sell products or ideas such as yearly physical examinations, office equipment, or clothing. Instead, developing such campaigns calls for the type of creativity a talented, well-chosen group can generate.

Are Misunderstandings or Reservations Likely?

It is easy to see how meetings can be useful when the goal is to generate ideas or solve problems. However, meetings are often necessary, when confusing or controversial information is being communicated. Suppose, for instance, that changing federal rules require employees to document their use of company cars in far more detail than was previously required. It is easy to imagine how this sort of change would be met with grumbling and resistance. In this situation, simply issuing a memo outlining the new rules might not gain the type of compliance that is necessary. Only after voicing their complaints and hearing why the new policy is being instituted will employees see a need to go along with the new procedure. "It is always better to have the hard conversations face-to-face," says entrepreneur and best-selling author, Andrew Griffiths, "so much gets lost in translation otherwise, and a small problem can grow in a big problem..."[42]

Setting an Agenda

An **agenda** is a list of topics to be covered in a meeting. A meeting without an agenda is like a ship at sea without a destination or compass: No one aboard knows where it is or where it is headed. Smart organizations appreciate the importance of establishing agendas. At computer chip giant Intel, for example, company policy requires planners

Dealing with Opposing Viewpoints

Your manager has asked you to provide suggestions from your department about the company's policy on flex time. Flex time allows employees to choose their workday start and end times. These suggestions will be taken seriously and have a strong chance of being adopted. You are in a position to call a meeting of key people in your department to discuss the issue.

Two of the most vocal members of the department have diametrically opposed positions on flex time. One of them (whose position on the issue is different from yours) will be out of the office for a week, and you could call the meeting while they are gone. What do you do?

to circulate an agenda before every meeting. You can start building an agenda by asking four questions:

1. What is our objective?
2. What do we need to do in the meeting to achieve our objective?
3. What conversations will be important to the people who attend?
4. What information will we need to begin?[43]

As Figure 8.1 illustrates, a complete agenda contains the following information: a list of the attendees (and whoever else needs to see the agenda); the meeting's start and end

<table>
<tr><td colspan="2">

MEETING AGENDA

Louisville Design Group
Marketing Advisory Task Force

</td></tr>
<tr><td>**Meeting time:**</td><td>November 27, 9:00–10:00 a.m.</td></tr>
<tr><td>**Location:**</td><td>Conference Room A</td></tr>
<tr><td>**Invitees:**</td><td>Frank Brady, Monica Flores, Ted Gross, Scott Hendrickson, Kevin Jessup, Pat Rivera, Carly Woods</td></tr>
</table>

Call to Order (5 minutes)
- Review and approval of minutes from November 13 meeting (Ted)

Reports (10 minutes)
- Client Appreciation Event (Monica)
- Budget (Ted)

Unfinished Business (20 minutes)
- Website Redesign (Frank)
  Frank will present two design options for the LDG website redesign.

New Business (20 minutes)
- Client Research Project (Carly)
  Please bring ideas for what your team needs to know about our clients and their design needs.

Adjournment

FIGURE 8.1

Format for a Comprehensive Agenda

time and location; necessary background information; and a brief explanation of each item. Consider the following tips when creating an agenda:

- For virtual meetings, include the time zone.

- Unless you announce the length of the meeting, expect some members to leave early.

- Failure to note the location or instructions for accessing the meeting may result in members entering late.

- If the agenda includes one or more problem-solving items, it is best to keep the group size small (fewer than seven members) so everyone can participate in the discussions.

- Background information can educate members on the meeting's significance or provide participants with a reminder of information they may have forgotten.

Agenda items can come from many sources, including the group leader, minutes from previous meetings, team members, or standing items (e.g., committee reports).[44] A good agenda goes beyond listing topics, however, by describing the goals for the discussion. For example, rather than listing a general topic such as "Discuss the website redesign," an action-based goal can be provided: "Choose the website design that best represents our company's image and has the greatest functionality."

For virtual meetings, avoid trying to squeeze too many items into a single meeting. Rick Maurer, author of *Beyond the Wall of Resistance* and *Why Don't You Want What I Want*, advises planners to keep the focus on one or two topics at approximately 30 minutes each. If you must cover more items, Maurer suggests giving people time to stretch, take a restroom break, or replenish their coffee in between segments.[45] Communications expert Nick Morgan suggests an even smaller time frame of 10 minutes dedicated to each topic, as evidence suggests that attention spans may be only 10 minutes long in the information age.[46]

The order of agenda items is also important. Some experts suggest the difficulty of items presented should form a bell-shaped curve (Figure 8.2). The meeting ought to begin with relatively simple business: minutes, announcements, and the easiest decisions. Once members have hit their stride and a good climate has developed, the team can move on to the most difficult items. The final third of the meeting should focus on easier items to allow a period of decompression and goodwill.

You might argue such a detailed agenda would take too much time to prepare. Once you see how providing the attendees with this sort of information produces better results, though, you will realize the advance work is well worth the effort.

FIGURE 8.2 A Bell-Shaped Agenda Structure

Source: Tropman, J. E. (1995). *Effective meetings: Improving group decision making* (2nd ed.). Thousand Oaks, CA: Sage.

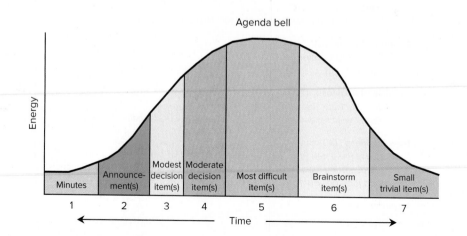

Pre-Meeting Work

Pre-meeting work helps ensure that the time spent in a meeting is focused and productive. Copies of the agenda should be distributed to attendees in advance. This will provide attendees with time to review the items that will be discussed, formulate ideas or questions, and prepare their thoughts. The meeting planner should set the tone by requesting that the agenda be read in advance.[47] This can easily be done by adding preparation instructions to the agenda. If certain members have specific jobs to do, the meeting organizer can jot down these tasks on their individual copies: "Sarah, be sure to bring last year's sales figures." Attendees of face-to-face meetings should be provided with an additional copy of the agenda once they arrive to the meeting to help keep them focused. Other documents that will be reviewed and discussed in the meeting, such as budget information, should be e-mailed to participants ahead of time for review.

Additionally, for virtual meetings, planners must also prepare to consider which technology will best help the team achieve its goals. Evidence suggests that video makes people feel more engaged because attendees can see one another's nonverbal reactions.[48] Audio is considered the next best option, as it allows attendees to hear what speakers are saying and interact with others.[49]

To ensure that the meeting proceeds smoothly, planners must ensure that their Internet connection is reliable and should know how to operate the various meeting-related software features:

- Toggling mute on and off
- Posting questions
- Retrieving responses or questions
- Transferring control between participants
- Screensharing
- Changing the window (such as toggling between the presentation and camera view)[50]

Once the technology has been determined, planners should send login information (call-in numbers, access codes, or URLs) to attendees at least one day in advance. Attendees should be asked to log in at least 15 minutes prior to the start of the meeting to test their connectivity.[51] Planners should also enlist someone to serve as a back-up host that can be ready to launch the meeting if the host has trouble with their connection.

• Conducting the Meeting

Effective openings get the meeting off to a good start. First, they give everyone a clear picture of what is to be accomplished. Second, they define how the team will try to reach its goal. Finally, they set the stage for good teamwork and, therefore, good results. The first few remarks by the person who called the meeting can prepare the team for a constructive session.

Setting the Tone

Creating a comfortable and professional environment will go a long way toward fostering good relationships and problem-solving discussions. Two great ways to set the tone include establishing etiquette and creating goodwill.

Blend Images/Alamy Stock Photo

Establish Etiquette In a virtual environment, establish some rules for etiquette and remind attendees of these guidelines. Participants may be asked to mute their microphones when they are not speaking to reduce background noise.[52] Participants may also be encouraged to say their names aloud before speaking if the meeting is audio-only.[53] Multitasking should be addressed as well. Some virtual meetings—particularly those without a video component—are ineffective because participants have their phones on mute and are using the time to work on unrelated tasks.

Additionally, virtual meetings present several unique challenges associated with the technology used. Because there is always the potential for technology to fail, technical support personnel should be on standby. The meeting planner should always have a backup plan ready for the meeting (such as moving to a conference call) and should make that plan known to the participants. Another challenge is the awkwardness that comes with the common 2- to 3-second video delay. To combat this issue, instruct participants to move at a slightly slower pace, make sure there are sufficient pauses after speaking, and call attention to themselves by providing a verbal or nonverbal signal (such as raising their hand, saying "question," or using the software's "raise hand" feature) and then waiting a few seconds before speaking.[54]

Create Goodwill Once etiquette has been established, begin the meeting with a personal–professional check-in to help create goodwill among attendees. In a virtual setting, conduct a roll call and introduce all participants. In any setting, attendees of small team meetings may be prompted to take one minute to share something that is going on in their personal or professional lives.[55] Remind them that they should provide only information that they are comfortable sharing. Go first to model the approach.

Upon conclusion of these informal pleasantries, identify the goals of the meeting. This will remind everyone of the purpose for meeting and help focus the discussion. For example:

> "We're faced with a serious problem. Inventory losses have almost doubled in the last year, from 5 percent to 9 percent. We need to decide what's causing these losses and come up with some ideas about how to reduce them."

Even though members should have reviewed the agenda, it can be helpful to spend a few moments previewing the agenda and goals. Background information may also be provided to explain the context of the meeting and ensure everyone has the same picture of the subject being discussed. This step prevents misunderstandings and helps members understand the nature of the information the group will consider. The format of the preview can range from referring to copies/files containing budget information or other key documents to delivering a short informational presentation to the team at the meeting.

Conducting Business

No meeting will be successful without committed, talented participants. But even the best attendees do not guarantee success. Someone—either the leader or a responsible member—has to be sure all important business is covered in a way that takes advantage of the talents of everyone present.

Parliamentary Procedure   One of the most common practices in business meetings is to follow **parliamentary procedure**, or a set of rules that govern the way groups conduct business and make decisions in meetings.[56] Often referred to as Robert's Rules of Order, this format can keep discussions clear and efficient while safeguarding the rights of everyone involved in deliberations. Parliamentary procedure is an appropriate way to operate a meeting when the team is faced with the following situations:

- The group's decisions are of interest to an external audience.
- A sense of urgency or being rushed may obscure critical thinking.
- Emotions are likely to be strong.

According to the rules of parliamentary procedure, a standard meeting agenda has the following parts:

1. *Reading of the minutes.* A good set of **meeting minutes**, or a written record of a meeting, is more than formality; it gives everyone involved a chance to make sure the record describes what really happened.

2. *Reports.* Teams often use committees to handle specific tasks that do not require the involvement of everyone in the group. Reports function as a place in which these committees, as well as individual members, share information with the rest of the group.

3. *Unfinished business.* If any matters from previous meetings have not yet been settled or if ongoing projects need attention, this "old business" is covered next.

4. *New business.* During this part of the meeting, members can bring up new issues for the group to discuss and decide on.

Whenever a decision needs to be made on an item raised during discussion, an attendee may introduce a **motion**, or a specific proposal for action. Good motions address a single issue briefly and clearly: "I move we redirect 10% of the Annual Fund contributions to the endowment." Once introduced, a motion must be seconded by someone other than its sponsor. At this point, the group may discuss the motion. This procedure ensures the group only discusses those motions that at least two members deem worthy. As discussion progresses, motions can be amended by members. Once discussion is complete, a motion is decided by a public vote.

Decision-Making Methods   Decision-making is an important component of an effective meeting. As business instructor Joel Baum put it, "How you decide is just as important as what you decide. The process you use has a direct impact on how members feel about the decision. It can influence commitment, excitement, and buy-in; or it can create feelings of resentment and exclusion."[57] There are a number of ways to make business decisions.

Consensus   When a collective decision is made and every member is willing to support the decision, the group has achieved **consensus**. The purest form of consensus is unanimous, unequivocal support, indicating every member's belief that the decision reached is the best possible. For instance, an entire employee search committee might agree that a particular candidate is perfect for a job. This state of unanimity is not always possible, however, and it is not necessary for consensus. Members may support a decision that is not their first choice, accepting the fact that it is the best option possible for the group at that time. In the case of the new employee, committee members might agree on a

How to Take Meeting Minutes

Minutes are a tangible record of a meeting and its associated actions, as well as a reference for members who were unable to attend. Effectively taking minutes requires capturing important details, such as the names of attendees, decisions that were made (e.g., motions, votes), and the identification of action items. Meeting minutes are typically reviewed by the group, and suggestions for amendments or corrections are raised at the next meeting.

The following tips will help you take minutes the next time you are tasked with this important role:

- Ask your supervisor (or committee chair) what their expectations are for minute-taking
- Obtain a copy of the meeting agenda and use it as an outline for taking notes
- Sequence your notes using the same order and numbering of items on the agenda
- Include the names of all meeting attendees ("Present")

- List the names of participants who were unable to attend ("Absent")
- List the date and time of the meeting
- Outline the discussion surrounding each agenda item
- Identify voting outcomes (including details regarding who made motions, seconded, approved, and so on)
- Include the next meeting date and time
- Store copies of handouts that were distributed at the meeting along with the minutes
- Ask your supervisor about the preferred procedure for distribution and storage of the minutes

While taking minutes, you may need to ask for clarification at times. This is perfectly acceptable! You may also want to ask participants for permission to record the meeting (e.g., on your phone or tablet) to help you capture any information you may have missed.

---

candidate who is some members' second choice because the people who will be working most closely with them are the candidate's most enthusiastic supporters.

Some cultures value consensus more highly than others. For example, British and Dutch businesspeople value the "group must be aboard" approach. By comparison, German, French, and Spanish communicators depend more on a strong leader's decision and view a desire for consensus as somewhat wishy-washy.[58]

Cultural norms aside, consensus has both advantages and drawbacks. While it has the broadest base of member support, reaching consensus takes time. It requires a spirit of cooperation among team members, a willingness to experience temporary disagreements, a commitment to listening carefully to other ideas, and a win–win attitude. Given these challenges, it is wise to limit consensus decisions to important issues when the need for agreement is high and when the team can dedicate the time and effort necessary to reach agreement.[59]

Majority Vote   Whereas consensus requires the agreement of the entire group, deciding by **majority vote** needs only the support of most of the members. Thus, majority voting decisions are much quicker and easier to reach. A 10-member staff choosing a decorating scheme for the new office might talk almost endlessly before reaching consensus; with a majority vote, however, the decision would require the agreement of only six members, which might be more readily achieved. The majority vote approach works well for relatively minor issues, but it is not usually the best approach for more important decisions because it can leave a substantial minority dissatisfied and resentful about being railroaded into accepting a plan they do not support.

Minority Decision   In a **minority decision**, a few members make a decision affecting the entire group. This is frequently the case in business situations. For instance, the executive committee of a corporation often acts on behalf of the board of directors, which in turn represents the shareholders. As long as the minority has the confidence of the larger group, this method works well for many decisions.

Expert Opinion   When a single person has the knowledge or skill needed to make an informed decision, the group may be best served by relying on that person's **expert opinion**. Some team members are experts because of specialized training—for example, a structural engineer who is working with a design team on a new building, or a senior airline mechanic who decides whether a flight can depart safely. Other people gain their expertise by experience—for example, the purchasing agent who knows how to get the best deals or a labor negotiator seasoned by years of contract deliberations.

Despite the obvious advantages of relying on expert opinion, following an expert's suggestions is not always as wise an approach as it might seem. It is not always easy to tell who the expert is. Length of experience is not necessarily a guarantee of wisdom or expertise.

Enhancing Creativity
One advantage of teams is the greater chance for creativity.[60] As more members bring their different perspectives to a task, the chances of coming up with a winning solution increase. As one executive put it, "innovation is a team sport."[61]

One way to boost the creativity of the group is through **brainstorming**—an approach that encourages free thinking and minimizes conformity. This term was coined by advertising executive Alex Osborn, who noticed groups were most creative when they let their imaginations run free.[62] Three cardinal rules must be followed to ensure the success of brainstorming:

1. All evaluation and criticism of ideas are forbidden during the early phases of the process.
2. Quantity—not quality—of ideas is the goal.
3. New combinations of ideas are sought.

One expert offers several other tips for healthy brainstorming:

- Do not let the boss speak first
- Encourage members to speak whenever they have an idea. Do not follow a set speaking order
- Include a variety of members in a session, not just experts[63]

Brainstorming can be even more effective in virtual groups than in face-to-face meetings.[64] More ideas are generated when brainstorming is anonymous than when members know who is contributing suggestions.

Encouraging Participation
Loosely structured, informal meetings may appear to give everyone an equal chance to speak out, but—because of personality, gender, culture, and style differences—every member may not have the same access.[65] Unbalanced participation can cause two sorts of problems. First, it discourages people who do not get a chance to talk. Second, it prevents the group from considering potentially useful ideas.

To improve participation at meetings, consider giving each person adequate time to speak to foster collaboration and avoid groupthink. Keith Ferrazzi, founder and CEO of the Los Angeles, California-based research and consulting firm Ferrazzi Greenlight, suggests having attendees write down an idea or question that they have or an issue they have been struggling with in advance of the meeting. During the meeting, time should be allotted to bring these issues to the table, one at a time, with a 5-minute discussion period. The group members should all go around and either ask a question or pass. Then, participants are given an opportunity to offer advice using the phrase "I might suggest" or pass.[66]

Especially in virtual meetings, it is easy to become fatigued by information overload and one-way communication. Nick Morgan, president of consulting company Public Words Inc., suggests that meeting leaders "take everyone's temperatures" at regular intervals during the meetings.[67] To do so, simply go down the list of participants and ask each person for input. Meetings should also be interactive. No more than three presentation slides or 10 minutes should pass without an interactive activity taking place.[68] Web tools, such as interactive polls, can be used to encourage participation among members.

Another method for ensuring that every member's ideas have an equal chance of being considered is the nominal group technique (NGT). Researchers have found that NGT generates a larger number of high-quality suggestions than brainstorming.[69] The name of the method suggests that, for much of this process, the participants are a group in name (nominal) only because they are working independently. The NGT method consists of five phases:

1. Each member anonymously writes down their ideas, which a discussion leader then collects. This method ensures good ideas from quiet members will have a chance for consideration.

2. All ideas are posted for every member to see. By keeping the authorship of ideas private at this point, perceptions of them are less likely to be based on personal factors such as authority or popularity.

3. Members discuss the ideas to better understand them, but criticism is prohibited. The goal here is to clarify the possibilities, not to evaluate them.

4. Each member privately rank-orders the ideas from most to least promising. Individual ranking again prevents domination by a few talkative or influential members.

5. The group critically and thoroughly discusses those items that received the greatest number of votes. At this point, a decision can be made using whichever decision-making method (e.g., consensus, majority rule) is most appropriate.

Using questions to draw out listeners is another way to encourage participation. Four types of questions can balance members' contributions.

Overhead Questions   Questions directed toward the group as a whole that anyone is free to answer are termed **overhead questions**: "Sales have flattened out in the western region. Can anybody suggest what's going on?" As long as overhead questions draw a response from all members, it is wise to continue using them. When a few people begin to dominate, however, it is time to switch to another type of question.

Direct Questions   When a question is aimed at a particular individual, who is addressed by name, it is considered a **direct question**: "Anahi, how's the new plan working in your department?" Direct questions are a useful way to draw out quiet members, but they must be used skillfully. Never start a discussion with a direct question, because doing so suggests that individuals should not speak unless they have been called on, which is hardly a desirable norm in most meetings. It is also important to phrase questions in such a way that they give respondents a way out of potentially embarrassing questions: "Tony, can you give us the figures for your department now, or will you need to check them and get back to us?"

Reverse Questions   When a member asks the leader a question and the leader refers the question back to the person who originally phrased it, the response qualifies as a **reverse question**: "That's a good question, Lauro. Do you think it's a practical idea?" Reverse questions work well when the leader senses a member really wants to make a statement but is unwilling to do so directly. It is important to use reverse questions with care: The member could be asking for information, in which case a direct answer is appropriate.

Relay Questions   A **relay question** is a response in which the leader refers a question that one member asks to the entire group: "Tamron has just raised a good question. Who can respond to it?" Relay questions are especially useful when the leader wants to avoid disclosing their opinion for fear of inhibiting or influencing the group. Relays should be phrased as overhead questions directed at the entire group.

Keeping Discussions on Track   Sometimes the problem is not too little discussion, but too much. Teams can often talk on and on without moving any closer to accomplishing their goal. When this happens, the leader or another team member needs to get the discussion back on track by using one of the following techniques.

- *Remind the group of time pressures.* Acknowledge the value of the comments being made, then remind everyone about the importance of moving quickly: "Radio ads sound good, but for now we'd better stick to the newspaper program. Mason wanted copy from us by noon, and we'll never make it if we don't get going."
- *Use* **relevancy challenges**. This technique involves tactfully asking a member to explain how an apparently off-track idea relates: "I'm confused, Sam. How will leasing new equipment instead of buying it help us to boost productivity?"
- *Promise to deal with good ideas later.* Sincerely suggest a way to deal with the idea at the appropriate time and mention exactly when you would like to follow up on the matter: "A graphics package seems important to you, Liu. Why don't you look into what's available and then we can schedule a meeting to decide whether the change would be worth the cost."

Keeping a Positive Tone   In meetings, getting along can be especially tough when others do not cooperate with your efforts to keep the meeting on track—or, even worse, when others attack your ideas. The following suggestions can help you handle these irritating situations in a way that both gets the job done and keeps potential enemies as allies.

Ask Questions and Paraphrase to Clarify Understanding   Criticizing an idea—even an apparently ignorant one—can result in a defensive reaction that will waste time and generate ill will. It is also important to remember that even a seemingly foolish remark can have some merit. Given these facts, it is often wise to ask for some clarification: "Why do you think we ought to let Troy go?"

You can also paraphrase to get more information about an apparently hostile or foolish remark: "It sounds as if you're saying Troy's doing a bad job." Paraphrasing accomplishes two things. First, it provides a way to double-check your understanding. If your replay of the speaker's ideas is not accurate, they can correct you. Second, even if your understanding is accurate, paraphrasing is an invitation for the other person to explain the idea in more detail.

Enhance the Value of Members' Comments   It is obvious that you should acknowledge the value of good ideas by praising or thanking the people who contribute them. Surprisingly, you can use the same method with apparently bad ideas. Most comments have at least some merit. Take advantage of their potential by using a three-part response[70]:

- Acknowledge the merits of the idea
- Explain any concerns you have
- Improve the usefulness of the idea by building on it or asking others for suggestions

Reframing Complaints in Meetings

Problem-solving meetings can generate complaints, defensiveness, and even outright hostility. Reframing members' complaints can nudge the discussion toward constructive solutions. Here are some reframing strategies:

Reframe complaints about the past as hopes for the future:

Statement: "Why do we always have to drive across town for these meetings?"

Reframe: "From now on, you'd like to find a way to keep everybody's travel time equal, right?"

Reframe negative statements as positive desires or visions:

Statement: "I've got work to do! All this long-range planning is a waste of time."

Reframe: "You want to be sure the time we spend planning makes a difference in the long run, right?"

Reframe personal attacks as issues:

Statement: "Jaclyn is always butting in when I have a customer, stealing my commissions."

Reframe: "So, we need to make sure we have clear lines about communicating with customers."

Reframe individual concerns as community or team interests:

Statement: "I've got kids at home and no child care! I can't keep working weekends on short notice."

Reframe: "All of us have lives outside of work. Let's talk about how we can handle rush jobs without creating personal emergencies or burning out."

Source: Littlejohn, S., & Domenici, K. (2007). *Communication, conflict, and the management of difference.* Long Grove, IL: Waveland Press.

"I'm glad you're so concerned about the parking problem, Saanvi [acknowledges merit of the comment]. But wouldn't requiring people to carpool generate a lot of resentment [balancing concern]? How could we encourage people to carpool voluntarily [builds on original idea]?"

Pay Attention to Cultural Factors As with every other type of communication, the rules for conducting productive, harmonious meetings vary from one culture to another. For example, in Japan, problem-solving meetings are usually preceded by a series of one-on-one sessions between participants to iron out issues, a process called *nemawashi*.[71] This practice arises from the Japanese cultural pattern that two people may speak candidly to each other, but when a third person enters the discussion, they become a group, requiring communicators to speak indirectly to maintain harmony. Automotive manufacturer Toyota utilizes nemawashi to seek employees' opinions and build consensus of opinion before making important decisions and changes.[72]

By contrast, in countries where emotional expressiveness is the norm, volatile exchanges in meetings are as much the rule as the exception. "I've just come back from a meeting in Milan," stated Canadian management consultant Dennis Stamp. "If people acted the same way in North American meetings you'd think they were coming to blows."[73]

Concluding the Meeting

When the scheduled closing time has arrived, when the group lacks resources to continue, or when all of the items on the agenda have been covered, it is time to conclude the meeting. The way a meeting ends can have a strong influence on how members feel about the group and how diligently they follow up on any decisions made or instructions given.[74] A good conclusion has three parts. In many discussions, the leader will be responsible for performing these steps. In leaderless groups or in groups with a weak leader, one or more members can take the initiative.

1. *Signal when time is almost up.* A warning allows the group to wrap up business and gives everyone a chance to have a final say.

2. *Summarize the meeting's accomplishments and future actions.* For the sake of understanding, review what information has been conveyed and what decisions have been made. Just as important is reminding members of their responsibilities.

3. *Thank the group.* Acknowledging the group's good work is more than just good manners. This sort of reinforcement shows you appreciate the group's efforts and encourages good performance in the future. Besides acknowledging the group as a whole, be sure to give credit to any members who deserve special mention.

Following Up the Meeting

It is a mistake to assume that even a satisfying meeting is a success until you follow up to make sure the desired results have really been obtained. A thorough follow-up involves four steps and will help the team maintain momentum between meetings.

Prepare and Distribute Meeting Minutes   It may be tempting to think a meeting is over when the group members leave the room or log off of the virtual meeting space. In fact, after the meeting ends, there is still important work to be done. One of the most important follow-up steps to a meeting is to prepare and distribute the meeting minutes. For virtual meetings, the minutes may be sent to group members along with a link to a recording of the meeting.

A good set of minutes should be thorough enough that someone who was not at the meeting should be able to know exactly what happened; at the same time, they should be short and to the point. Irrelevant and play-by-play information should be omitted. See Figure 8.3 for sample meeting minutes.

Build an Agenda for the Next Meeting   Most groups meet frequently, and they rarely conclude their business in a single sitting. A smart leader plans the next meeting by noting which items need to be carried over from the preceding one. What unfinished business must be addressed? What progress reports must be shared? What new information should members hear?

Furthermore, progress on action items and team goals should be tracked and shared. Celebrate the achievements of members between meetings, and include a place to recognize these achievements on the agenda for the following meeting.

Follow Up on Members   You can be sure the promised outcomes of a meeting actually occur if you check up on other members. If the meeting provided instructions—such as how to use the new accounting software—see whether the people who attended are actually following the steps outlined. If tasks were assigned, determine whether they are being performed. You do not have to be demanding or snoopy to do this sort of checking. A friendly phone call or personal remark can do the trick: "Is the new phone system working for you?" "Did you manage to get hold of Williams yet?" In the case of virtual teams, a good rule of thumb is to strive for one-on-one communication at least once per month.[75]

MEETING MINUTES

Louisville Design Group
Marketing Advisory Task Force

Meeting date: November 27

Attendees: Frank Brady, Monica Flores, Ted Gross, Kevin Jessup, Pat Rivera, Carly Woods

Absent: Scott Hendrickson

1. Ted called the meeting to order. The meeting minutes from the November 13 meeting were approved.

2. Monica reported on the Client Appreciation Event that was held on November 15. We had a great turnout, with 28 clients and their guests attending the invitation-only event. Clients were treated to hors d'oeuvres and cocktails, given a tour of the offices, and had their caricatures sketched by LDG's best cartoonist, Dave Ketchum. Monica received more than a dozen emails after the event thanking her for a terrific time. Based on the success, Monica suggested that we make this an annual event.

3. Ted provided an update on the budget. The committee was allotted $25,000 for marketing expenses during the year, and the total expenditures year-to-date come to $22,500. This leaves a balance of $2,500 that must be used by the end of the year, as the funds will not carry forward to next year.

   Action Item: Everyone must submit all outstanding marketing expense reports to Ted immediately. (Due 11/30)

4. Frank presented the committee with two designs for the LDG website redesign. Design A was a "clean" style with monochromatic colors, sleek fonts, and geometric graphics. Design B was a "splashy" style with a brightly colored palette, bolder fonts, and photos. Both designs incorporated the website navigation hierarchy agreed to by the committee. Ted thanked Frank for his hard work on the project.

   After the initial presentation, the committee debated the pros and cons of each design. They thought that the clean feel of Design A presented a more professional image. But they thought that the colorful palette of Design B showed LDG's fun side. There was no clear favorite.

   Action Item: Frank will create a mock-up of a third design option that will merge the sleek look of Design A with the color palette of Design B for consideration at the next committee meeting. (Due: 12/11)

5. Carly solicited input on the upcoming Client Research Project. The last research project conducted by LDG was five years ago. But with the advent of new social media technologies and the opening of two new firms in town, it is important that LDG get the most up-to-date info available. Carly asked for input into what topics to cover and how to administer the survey.

   The committee brainstormed several areas and agreed to ask about clients' primary design needs, familiarity with social media platforms (Twitter, Facebook), annual budgets for advertising and web design, and relative importance of cost/turnaround time/artistic quality/copywriting quality/firm reputation in selecting a firm for a job.

   There was some discussion on how to administer the surveys. The committee unanimously agreed to use an online survey system. However, Kevin said that it would be valuable information to have clients identified on the surveys, while Monica argued that we might get better quality information if the surveys were anonymous. The majority vote was for anonymous data collection.

   Action Item: Pat and Carly will use committee input to generate a preliminary survey, which will be reviewed and critiqued at the next committee meeting. (Due: 12/11)

FIGURE 8.3 Format for Meeting Minutes

Take Care of Your Own Action Items   Being a good team member means taking care of your action items. As you participate in the meeting, you should keep track of the tasks you have been assigned or have agreed or volunteered to complete. When you receive the meeting minutes, double-check that you have not missed any tasks. By taking care of your assigned tasks prior to the deadlines, you will solidify your reputation as a valuable team member.

review points

- Meetings are common, often time-consuming, and costly.

- Meetings serve one or more of the following purposes: sharing information, solving problems/making decisions, and engaging in ritual activities.

- Virtual meetings present both advantages and challenges for leaders and participants.

- Virtual meetings may take several forms: conference calls, web conferences, videoconferences, or use of collaborative technology.

- Meetings should be held only when the job at hand requires more than one person to handle, requires a division of labor, and has more than one right answer. If misunderstanding or resistance to a decision is likely, it is also wise to hold a meeting to overcome those hazards.

- Well in advance of each meeting, an agenda should be shared that announces the time, length, and location of the session; those who will attend; background information; goals; and advance work that the meeting participants need to do.

- Planners of virtual meetings must select technology based on its ability to meet goals, familiarize themselves with the features of the chosen technology, and distribute login information to attendees at least one day in advance.

- At the start of a meeting, the leader must set the tone for a professional environment by establishing etiquette and creating goodwill.

- Leaders may choose to follow parliamentary procedure, which requires reading the minutes, sharing reports, discussing unfinished business, and raising new business. If a decision needs to be made, attendees may raise and second a motion, discuss the motion, and then vote publicly.

- Choosing the best decision-making method (consensus, majority vote, minority decision, expert opinion) ensures the group uses time effectively and generates an outcome members support.

- Brainstorming may be used to enhance creativity among meeting participants.

- Member participation can be encouraged by giving each person time to speak, asking questions to draw out listeners, or applying the nominal group technique (NGT). In virtual meetings, additional steps include asking each person for input and hosting short interactive sessions.

- The leader and members can keep the discussion on track during the meeting by referring to time pressures, summarizing and redirecting remarks of members who have digressed, using relevancy challenges, and arranging to deal with tangential issues after the meeting.

- The tone of meetings will stay positive if members make an attempt to understand one another by asking questions and paraphrasing, enhancing the value of one another's comments, and being culturally aware.

- A meeting should close at its scheduled time, when the group lacks resources to continue, or when the agenda has been completed—whichever comes first. The leader should give notice that time is almost up, summarize accomplishments and future actions, and thank group members for their contributions.

- Leaders' duties after a meeting include preparing meeting minutes, building the agenda for the next session, following up with other members, and honoring their own commitments.

key terms

activities

1. Invitation to Insight

You can gain an appreciation of the importance of meetings by interviewing one or more people in a career field that is of interest to you.

Ask questions such as the following:

a. How frequent are meetings in your work?
b. How long do these meetings typically take?
c. What kinds of topics are covered in your meetings?
d. Which formats are used (parliamentary procedure, following an agenda, open-ended discussions with no clear agenda, virtual versus face-to-face)?
e. How effective are meetings? What factors contribute to their effectiveness or ineffectiveness?

Compare your findings with your classmates' findings.

a. Which types of meetings occur most frequently (e.g., informational, problem solving, ritual)?
b. Which types of formats occur most frequently?
c. Are the advantages mentioned by interviewees similar to those identified in the text?
d. Based on concepts from the text, suggest remedies for the challenges identified by the interviewees.

2. Skill Builder

Use the information in this chapter to decide which of the following tasks would best be handled by a problem-solving group and which should be handled by one or more individuals working separately.

Be prepared to explain your reasons for each choice.

a. Developing procedures for interviewing prospective employees
b. Tabulating responses to a customer survey
c. Investigating several brands of office machines for possible purchase
d. Choosing the most desirable employee health insurance program
e. Organizing the company picnic
f. Researching the existence and cost of training programs for improving communication among staff members

3. Invitation to Insight

Ask someone you know to provide you with a copy of an agenda from a workplace meeting, or provide one of your own from a meeting you have attended. With a group of classmates, analyze the agenda.

a. Which elements of an effective agenda are present? Which are absent?
b. To what degree does the agenda illustrate result-oriented, specific, and realistic goals?
c. Suggest improvements for future agendas. If result-oriented goals are missing, write some examples.

4. Skill Builder

You are chairing a meeting in which one member whom everyone dislikes is aggressively promoting an idea. Time is short, and everyone in the group is ready to make a decision that will go against the disliked member's position. You realize the unpopular idea does have real merit, but lending your support and urging further discussion will put the group further behind and leave the other members annoyed with you.

Suggest three different ways you could handle this situation. For each option, write out the specific comments you would make. Using concepts and vocabulary from this chapter, discuss advantages and disadvantages of each scenario.

5. Skill Builder

Use the skills introduced in the "Conducting Business" section to describe how you would respond to the following comments in a meeting. Identify which skill you are using:

a. "There's no way people will work on Sundays without being paid double-overtime."
b. "No consultant is going to tell me how to be a better manager!"
c. "I don't think this brainstorming is worth the time. Most of the ideas we come up with are crazy."
d. "Talking about interest rates reminds me of a time in the 1980s when this story about President Carter was going around. . . ."
e. "Sorry, but I don't have any ideas about how to cut costs."

6. Skill Builder

With a group of your classmates, simulate a group decision-making process using the nominal group technique. Use one of the following scenarios or create one of your own:

a. Choosing a topic from this class about which you could deliver a group oral presentation
b. Deciding where you and your classmates might go for a field trip
c. Selecting the next novel your book club will read and discuss

After you complete the role play, discuss advantages and disadvantages of the nominal group technique as a decision-making procedure.

7. Skill Builder

With three to six of your classmates, decide which method of decision-making would be most effective for your group in each of the following situations:

a. Choosing the safest course of action if you were lost in a dangerous area near your city or town
b. Deciding whether and how to approach your instructor to propose a change in the grading system of your course
c. Designing the most effective campaign for your school to recruit minority students
d. Duplicating for distribution to your instructor and classmates the solutions to this exercise that your group developed
e. Hiring an instructor for your department
f. Choosing the name for a new brand of breakfast cereal
g. Selecting a new computer system
h. Deciding which of three employees gets the desirable vacant office
i. Planning the weekend work schedule for the upcoming month
j. Deciding whether the employees should affiliate with a labor union

LearnSmart™

For further review, go to the LearnSmart study module for this chapter.

references

1. NFO Worldwide. (1998). *Meetings in America: A study of trends, costs, and attitudes toward business travel and teleconferencing, and their impact on productivity.* Greenwich, CT: Infocom; Keith, E. (2015, December 4). 55 million: A fresh look at the number, effectiveness, and cost of meetings in the U.S. *Lucid.* Retrieved from https://blog.lucidmeetings.com/blog/fresh-look-number-effectiveness-cost-meetings-in-us

2. Atlassian. (n.d.). You waste a lot of time at work. Retrieved from https://www.atlassian.com/time-wasting-at-work-infographic

3. Attentiv. (n.d.). America meets a lot: An analysis of meeting length, frequency and cost. Retrieved from http://attentiv.com/america-meets-a-lot/

4. Bandiera, O., Guiso, L., Prat, A., & Sadun, R. (2012). What do CEOs do? *Centre for Economic*

Performance. Retrieved from http://cep.lse.ac.uk /pubs/download/dp1145.pdf

5. Rogelberg, S. G., Leach, D. J., Warr, P. B., & Burnfield, J. L. (2006). "Not another meeting!" Are meeting time demands related to employee well-being? *Journal of Applied Psychology, 91,* 83–96.

6. Doyle, M., & Straus, D. (1982). *How to make meetings work.* New York: Jove Books.

7. Doodle. (2019). The state of meetings report 2019. Retrieved from https://meeting-report.com/ financial-impact-of-meetings/0

8. Matson, E. (1996, April). The seven sins of deadly meetings. *Fast Company, 2,* 122–125.

9. Hartman, N. (2014, February 5). Seven steps to running the most effective meeting possible. *Forbes.* Retrieved from http://www.forbes.com/sites/forbes leadershipforum/2014/02/05/seven-steps-to-running -the-most-effective-meeting-possible/#53a5d2941054

10. Texas Municipal League. (2019, September). Texas open meetings act laws made easy. Retrieved from https://www.tml.org/DocumentCenter/View/1332 /The-Texas-Open-Meetings-Act-Made-Easy-2019–Final

11. Williams, F. (1983). *Executive communication power: Basic skills for management success.* Englewood Cliffs, NJ: Prentice-Hall.

12. Harter, J., & Mann, A. (2017, April 12). The right culture: Not just about employee satisfaction. *Gallup Workplace.* Retrieved from https://www.gallup.com /workplace/236366/right-culture-not-employee-satisfaction.aspx

13. Hastwell, C. (2020, November 11). 7 things you can do today to give your remote teams social support. *Great Place to Work.* Retrieved from https://www .greatplacetowork.com/resources/blog/x-ideas-to -keep-your-remote-team-socially-connected

14. Grundfos. (2015, November 5). Bigger and better than ever: Grundfos Olympics is back. Retrieved from https://www.grundfos.com/about-us/news-and -media/news/bigger-and-better-than-ever-grundfos -olympics-is-back

15. Hastwell, C. (2020, November 11). 7 things you can do today to give your remote teams social support. *Great Place to Work.* Retrieved from https:// www.greatplacetowork.com/resources/blog/x-ideas -to-keep-your-remote-team-socially-connected

16. English, B. (2015, August 7). Mindful movement makes its way into the office. *Boston Globe.* Retrieved from https://www.bostonglobe.com/metro/2015/08/06 /mindfulness-takes-hold-corporate-setting/3Kxojy6XFt 6oW4h9nLq7kN/story.html

17. Morgan, N. (2012, October 2). 5 fatal flaws with virtual meetings. *Forbes.* Retrieved from http://www .forbes.com/sites/nickmorgan/2012/10/02/5-fatal-flaws -with-virtual-meetings/#79503c4866b6

18. Ferrazi, K. (2015, March 27). How to run a great virtual meeting. *Harvard Business Review.* Retrieved from https://hbr.org/2015/03/how-to-run-a-great -virtual-meeting

19. Puranam, P., & Minervini, M. (2020, April 2). What newly remote teams need, right now. *INSEAD Blog.* Retrieved from https://knowledge.insead.edu/blog /insead-blog/what-newly-remote-teams-need-right-now -13706#:˜:text=On%20average%2C%2040%20percent% 20of,note%20a%20decline%20in%20productivity.

20. Brenan, M. (2020, April 3). U.S. workers discovering affinity for remote work. *Gallup.* Retrieved from https:// news.gallup.com/poll/306695/workers-discovering -affinity-remote-work.aspx

21. Thomas, F. (n.d.). Five tips for conducting a virtual meeting. *Inc.* Retrieved from http://www.inc.com/guides /2010/12/5-tips-for-conducting-a-virtual-meeting.html

22. Puranam, P., & Minervini, M. (2020, April 2). What newly remote teams need, right now. *INSEAD Blog.* Retrieved from https://knowledge.insead.edu/blog /insead-blog/what-newly-remote-teams-need-right-now -13706#:˜:text=On%20average%2C%2040%20percent% 20of,note%20a%20decline%20in%20productivity.

23. Puranam, P., & Minervini, M. (2020, April 2). What newly remote teams need, right now. *INSEAD Blog.* Retrieved from https://knowledge.insead.edu/blog /insead-blog/what-newly-remote-teams-need-right-now -13706#:˜:text=On%20average%2C%2040%20percent% 20of,note%20a%20decline%20in%20productivity.

24. Ferrazzi, K. (2015, May 3). Five ways to run better virtual meetings. *Harvard Business Review.* Retrieved from https://hbr.org/2012/05/the-right-way-to-run-a -virtual&cm_sp=Article-_-Links-_-End%20of%20Page% 20Recirculation

25. Lee, J. (2020, November 17). A neuropsychological exploration of Zoom fatigue. *Psychiatric Times.* Retrieved from https://www.psychiatrictimes.com /view/psychological-exploration-zoom-fatigue

26. Lee, J. (2020, November 17). A neuropsychological exploration of Zoom fatigue. *Psychiatric Times.* Retrieved from https://www.psychiatrictimes.com /view/psychological-exploration-zoom-fatigue

27. Roberts, F., & Francis, A. L. (2013). Identifying a temporal threshold of tolerance for silent gaps after requests. *Journal of the Acoustical Society of America, 133*(6), EL471-EL477. https://doi.org/10.1121/1.4802900

28. Sklar, J. (2020, April 24). 'Zoom fatigue' is taxing the brain. Here's why that happens. *National Geographic.* Retrieved from https://www.national geographic.com/science/article/coronavirus-zoom -fatigue-is-taxing-the-brain-here-is-why-that-happens

29. Sklar, J. (2020, April 24). 'Zoom fatigue' is taxing the brain. Here's why that happens. *National Geographic.* Retrieved from https://www.national geographic.com/science/article/coronavirus-zoom -fatigue-is-taxing-the-brain-here-is-why-that-happens

30. Fosslien, L., & Duffy, M. W. (2020, April 29). How to combat Zoom fatigue. *Harvard Business Review.*

Retrieved from https://hbr.org/2020/04/how-to -combat-zoom-fatigue

31. Winnick, M. (2016, June 16). Mobile touches: A study on how humans use technology. *dscout*. Retrieved from https://blog.dscout.com/mobile-touches

32. Danova, T. (2014, January 23). The mobile revolution is the biggest tech shift in years, and companies are in a race to keep up. *Business Insider*. Retrieved from http://www.businessinsider.com/mobile-media-consumption-grows-2-2014-1

33. Dobosh, M. A., Poole, M. S., & Malik, R. (2019). Small group use of communication technologies: A comparison of modality on group outcomes. *Communication Research Reports, 36*(4), 298–308. https://doi.org/10.1080/08824096.2019.1660869

34. APPEL News Staff. (2012, February 27). Uses of wikis across NASA. *APPEL News*. Retrieved from https://appel.nasa.gov/2012/02/27/5-2_wikis _across_nasa-html/#:˜:text=Collaborative%2C%20 accessible%2C%20and%20efficient%2C,NASA%20 a%20powerful%20knowledge%20solution.&text =Rober%20has%20championed%20use%20of, regular%20email%20updates%2C%20and%20videos.

35. MacDonald, C. (2015, June 26). Team communication apps: Top 5 for business messaging. *Handshake*.

36. Leonardi, P. M., Huysman, M., & Steinfield, C. (2013). Enterprise social media: Definition, history, and prospects for the study of social technologies in organizations. *Journal of Computer-Mediated Communication, 19,* 1–19.

37. Leonardi, P. M., Huysman, M., & Steinfield, C. (2013). Enterprise social media: Definition, history, and prospects for the study of social technologies in organizations. *Journal of Computer-Mediated Communication, 19,* 1–19.

38. Madsen, V. T. (2016). Constructing organizational identity on internal social media: A case study of coworker communication in Jyske Bank. *International Journal of Business Communication, 53*(2), 200–223.

39. Warner, A. W. (n.d.). 7 reasons why Slack team communication strengthens our business. Retrieved from http://fooplugins.com/slack-team-communication-tool/

40. Anders, A. (2016). Team communication platforms and emergent social collaboration practices. *International Journal of Business Communication, 53*(2), 224–261.

41. Katelin (2013, January 10). Business and professional meetings. *Writing Commons*. Retrieved from http://writingcommons.org/open-text/genres/profes-sional-business-and-technical-writing/business-writing -in-action/business-and-professional-meetings

42. Griffiths, A. (n.d.). 10 reasons face to face meetings are more important than we think. *Inc*. Retrieved from https://www.inc.com/andrew-griffiths/10-reasons-face-to -face-meetings-are-more-important-than-we-think.html

43. 3M Meeting Network. (2003). *Building great agen-das*. Retrieved from https://www.nonprofnetwork.org

/Resources/Documents/Resources/Governance /building%20great%20agends.pdf

44. 3M Meeting Network. (2003). *Building great agen-das*. Retrieved from https://www.nonprofnetwork.org /Resources/Documents/Resources/Governance /building%20great%20agends.pdf

45. Thomas, F. (n.d.). 5 tips for conducting a virtual meeting. *Inc*. Retrieved from http://www.inc.com /guides/2010/12/5-tips-for-conducting-a-virtual -meeting.html

46. Morgan, N. (2011, March 1). How to conduct a virtual meeting. *Harvard Business Review*. Retrieved from https://hbr.org/2011/03/how-to-conduct-a-virtual -meeti&cm_sp=Article-_-Links-_-End%20of%20 Page%20Recirculation

47. Ferrazzi, K. (2015, March 27). How to run a great virtual meeting. *Harvard Business Review*. Retrieved from https://hbr.org/2015/03/how -to-run-a-great-virtual-meeting

48. Ferrazzi, K. (2015, March 27). How to run a great virtual meeting. *Harvard Business Review*. Retrieved from https://hbr.org/2015/03/how -to-run-a-great-virtual-meeting

49. McCauley, K. L. (n.d.). How to have virtual meetings. *Lovetoknow*. Retrieved from http://business .lovetoknow.com/business-communications/how-have -virtual-meetings#o6mWq0zYLl4ZJtYT.97

50. Schindler, E. (2008, February 15). Running an effective teleconference meeting. *CIO*. Retrieved from https://www.cio.com/article/2437139/running-an -effective-teleconference-or-virtual-meeting.html

51. Thomas, F. (n.d.). 5 tips for conducting a virtual meeting. *Inc*. Retrieved from http://www.inc.com /guides/2010/12/5-tips-for-conducting-a-virtual -meeting.html

52. Walton, A. (n.d.). The best practices for facilitation of virtual meetings. Retrieved from http://small business.chron.com/practices-facilitation-virtual -meetings-71353.html

53. Walton, A. (n.d.). The best practices for facilitation of virtual meetings. Retrieved from http://small business.chron.com/practices-facilitation-virtual -meetings-71353.html

54. Thomas, F. (n.d.). 5 tips for conducting a virtual meeting. *Inc*. Retrieved from http://www.inc.com /guides/2010/12/5-tips-for-conducting-a-virtual -meeting.html

55. Ferrazzi, K. (2015, March 27). How to run a great virtual meeting. *Harvard Business Review*. Retrieved from https://hbr.org/2015/03/how-to-run-a-great -virtual-meeting

56. Introduction to Robert's Rules of Order. Retrieved from http://www.robertsrules.org/rulesinttro.htm

57. Baum, J. A. C. (2003). Running an effective team meeting. Retrieved from http://www.rotman.utoronto. ca/˜baum/mgt2003/meetings.html

58. Day, B. (1990, October 6). The art of conducting international business. *Advertising Age, 61*(42), 46.

59. Crucial Skills. (2008, May 14). Crucial tip: Using consult decisions. *Crucial Skills Newsletter, 6*(20), 1.

60. Catmull, E. (2008, September). How Pixar fosters collective creativity. *Harvard Business Review, 86*(9), 64–78.

61. Rae-Dupree, J. (2008, December 7). For innovators, there is brainpower in numbers. *New York Times,* p. BU 3.

62. Osborn, A. (1959). *Applied imagination.* New York: Scribner's; Hurt, F. (1994, November). Better brainstorming. *Training & Development, 48*(11), 57–59.

63. Thompson, K. (2008). Six ways to kill a brainstorm. Retrieved from http://www.masternewmedia.org/news/2008/04/23/how_not_to_brainstorm_your.html.

64. DeRosa, D. M., Smith, C. L., & Hantula, D. A. (2007). The medium matters: Mining the long-promised merit of group interaction in creative idea generation tasks in a meta-analysis of the electronic group brainstorming literature. *Computers in Human Behavior, 23,* 1549–1581.

65. Tannen, D. (1994). *Talking from 9 to 5: How women's and men's conversational styles affect who gets heard, who gets credit, and what gets done at work.* New York: Morrow; Bonito, J. A., & Hollingshead, A. B. (1997). Participation in small groups. In B. R. Burleson (Ed.), *Communication yearbook 20.* Newbury Park, CA: Sage.

66. Ferrazzi, K. (2015, March 27). How to run a great virtual meeting. *Harvard Business Review.* Retrieved from https://hbr.org/2015/03/how-to-run-a-great-virtual-meeting

67. Ferrazzi, K. (2015, March 27). How to run a great virtual meeting. *Harvard Business Review.* Retrieved from https://hbr.org/2015/03/how-to-run-a-great-virtual-meeting

68. Young, J. (n.d.). Six critical success factors for running a successful virtual meeting. Retrieved from https://www.facilitate.com/support/facilitator-toolkit/docs/Six-Critical-Success-Factors-for-Successful-Virtual-Meetings.pdf

69. Rietzschel, E. F., Nijstad, B. A., & Stroebe, W. (2006). Productivity is not enough: A comparison of interactive and nominal groups in idea generation and selection. *Journal of Experimental Social Psychology, 42,* 244–251.

70. Xerox Learning Systems. (n.d.). *Leading meetings.* Great Neck, NY: Xerox Learning Systems.

71. Copus, M. (2013, May 31). Nemawashi: Toyota production system guide. *Toyota UK Magazine.* Retrieved from https://mag.toyota.co.uk/nemawashi-toyota-production-system/

72. Copus, M. (2013, May 31). Nemawashi: Toyota production system guide. *Toyota UK Magazine.* Retrieved from https://mag.toyota.co.uk/nemawashi-toyota-production-system/

73. Allard, C. (1992, August). Trust and teamwork: More than just buzzwords. *En Route Technology*, 41.

74. Blake, R. R., & Mouton, J. S. (1985). *The new managerial grid.* Houston, TX: Gulf.

75. Young, J. Six critical success factors for running a successful virtual meeting. Retrieved from https://www.facilitate.com/support/facilitator-toolkit/docs/Six-Critical-Success-Factors-for-Successful-Virtual-Meetings.pdf

PART FOUR

Flamingo Images/Shutterstock

STRATEGIC CASE

Fresh Air Sports

Fresh Air Sports Rentals began eight years ago in a southern California beachfront hut. At that hut, Brandon and Sara Belmont rented out fat-tired cruiser bikes to tourists. Business was good—so good, in fact, that within a year Fresh Air customers could also rent a variety of other outdoor gear, including surfboards, mountain bikes, and paddleboats.

Over the years, Fresh Air has grown into a network of 18 locations throughout the western United States and Canada. The company is now big enough that name recognition is feeding the business: Customers who have rented from Fresh Air in one location look for it in other vacation spots. Brandon and Sara are now just weeks away from expanding their business to resorts on the East Coast, in Mexico, and in Central America.

Next month, Fresh Air is having its first-ever associates' meeting in San Diego. Brandon and Sara need to develop several presentations for that event:

- A keynote speech, welcoming the employees and building enthusiasm for the company and the upcoming meeting. During this speech, Sara and Brandon will also introduce Fresh Air's new management team.

- An informative program on how to avoid sexual harassment claims. Fresh Air's new human relations director will deliver this talk, but Sara wants to play a major role in its development.

- A session introducing the company's new incentive plan, under which employees will receive bonuses for increasing sales. While the potential for greater compensation is good, base salaries will decline under this arrangement. Brandon knows it is important to sell the plan to employees if it is to have a chance of succeeding.

- A series of awards presentations at the closing dinner. At this session, employees will be honored for their exceptional service. Brandon and Sara want to include enough employee awards to boost morale, without creating so many awards that they appear meaningless.

- A public announcement of the business's expansion, allowing for a series of formal question-and-answer sessions with interested members of the media.

Making Effective Presentations

As you read the chapters in this unit, consider the following questions for each presentation:

1. What types of presentations will Brandon and Sara give? Will their audience members be internal, external, or a mixture?
2. What is the general goal for each presentation? Create a specific goal for each one.
3. Which factors outlined in Chapter 10 (audience, occasion, speaker) should Sara and Brandon consider for each presentation?
4. Construct an outline for at least one of the presentations, based on your analysis in question 2. Include material for the introduction, the main points, and the conclusion.
5. For each main point in the body of the presentation you developed in question 3, identify at least one type of supporting material you could use to make the point clearer, more interesting, or more persuasive.
6. Describe the style of delivery that would be most effective for each of the presentations to be delivered at the San Diego meeting. In addition to addressing the speaker's style, discuss ways in which the speaking environment could be arranged to help achieve the presentation's goal.

Fizkes/Shutterstock

Chapter Nine

Types of Business Presentations and Their Audiences

chapter outline

chapter objectives

After reading this chapter you should be able to:

1. Understand strategies for preparing and delivering the following types of informative presentations: briefings, status reports, final reports, webinars, media interviews, podcasts, and training sessions.

2. Understand the elements of and be able to construct persuasive feasibility reports, motivational speeches, goodwill speeches, proposals, and sales presentations.

3. Prepare and deliver remarks for various special occasions: civic and social presentations, welcoming remarks, introducing another speaker, honoring a person or institution, giving a toast, and presenting and accepting an award.

4. Understand the specific types of internal and external audiences you are likely to encounter when speaking in professional settings.

Whatever your field, regardless of your job, speaking to an audience is likely to be a fact of life. While the word *presentation* may conjure up intimidating images of formal speeches being delivered to large audiences, the reality is that you are more likely to encounter informal talks with a few people or even a single person on a regular basis.

If you drop into your boss's office and say, "Do you have a few minutes? I have some information that may help us cut down our travel expenses," you are arranging a presentation. You are also delivering presentations when you show the office staff how to use the new database, explain the structure of your department to a new employee, or explain to management why you need a larger budget.

Regardless of whether the presentation is formal or informal, the quality of your spoken remarks may be the measure of your success. During these interactions, you are exposed to a variety of audiences whose members may be inside and outside of your organization. Thus, your reputation as a professional depends on how you handle yourself in front of your audiences. Furthermore, as your career progresses, presentational

speaking skills become even more important.[1] One automobile executive explained:

> When I was just an engineer somewhere down the line working on a technical problem, everything affecting me was in my grasp. All I had to do was solve this particular problem, and I was doing my job. But now, as head of advanced engineering, I have to anticipate and predict product trends and then sell my programs for capitalizing on those trends.[2]

As you will learn in this chapter, being a successful speaker requires an understanding of the variety of presentations you will most often encounter on the job, as well as the types of audiences in which you are likely to engage.

• Common Business Presentations

Business professionals use presentations to meet the following **general goals**: to inform and instruct, persuade, and celebrate special occasions. You may be called upon to update your boss on the status of your project, relay information to your teammates that you learned from a customer survey, propose a new strategy to a client, recruit volunteers for an ad hoc committee, or welcome guests that are touring your facility.

In this section, we will start with the basic types and characteristics of informative presentations to help you organize your remarks. These principles are also the building blocks for persuasive and special occasion speaking, which are also topics covered here. Note that samples of many of the presentation types discussed are available in Appendix IV.

Presentations to Inform and Instruct

In business and industry, informative presentations are used to provide audiences with information that they need to understand an important issue or situation, perform their jobs, or make decisions. Even when you create a written report for your supervisor, you should prepare to be asked to summarize its contents in an oral presentation. The quality of your spoken remarks may be the measure of your success.

Briefings   As you learned in Chapter 8, **briefings** are often presented during information-sharing meetings. Briefings are typically directed at an already interested and knowledgeable audience to give them the information they need to do their jobs. Some briefings update listeners on what has happened in the past. For example, nurses attend pre-shift briefings to learn what has happened with their patients since their last shift. Other briefings focus on the future. The executive chef of a restaurant might brief waiters about the details of the day's menu specials; the representative handling an advertising account might brief the agency's team about a client's interests and quirks before an important meeting.

When presenting a briefing, keep the following characteristics in mind:

- *Length.* As the name suggests, most briefings are short—usually no more than 2 or 3 minutes on a given subject.
- *Organization.* Because of their brevity, speakers may organize information by topic or in chronological order.
- *Content.* Briefings may summarize a position ("As you know, we're committed to answering every phone call within 1 minute"), but they do not make complex arguments in its favor. Most briefing attendees already know why they are there, and the main focus should be getting them ready to complete the job at hand.
- *Presentation aids.* Some briefings may include simple visuals ("Here's what our new employee ID badges will look like"), but they rarely contain the kind of detail found in longer and more complex presentations.
- *Language and delivery.* Because of their informal nature, briefings are usually conversational. Delivery is more matter-of-fact than dramatic.

Reports   In a **report**, you give your audience an account of what you or your team has learned or done. Reports come in an almost endless variety. In this section, we discuss two of the most common types of informative reports: status and final reports. The third type of report—the feasibility report—is discussed later in this chapter.

Some reports are internal, meaning they are given to audiences within your organization. Others are external, delivered to outsiders such as clients, industry professionals, or the general public. Some reports are long and detailed, while others are brief. Some reports are presented formally and others informally. An organization's culture determines the manner in which you should present a report: brief or elaborate, with or without visual aids and question-and-answer sessions, and so on. Learn the conventions for your audience by watching accomplished colleagues and asking experienced (and successful) coworkers.

Status Reports   The most common type of informative presentation is the **status report**, sometimes called a *progress report*. In many meetings, you can expect to hear someone ask, "How's the project going?"

The person asking this question usually does not want a long-winded account of everything that has happened since your last report. You will gain your audience's appreciation and boost your credibility by presenting a brief, clear summary of the situation. The following format will serve you well in most situations. Cover each of the points briefly, and expect your listeners to pose additional questions when they want more information.

1. *Review the project's purpose.*

2. *State the current status of the project.* When relevant, include the people involved (giving credit for their contributions) and the actions you have taken.

3. *Identify any obstacles you have encountered and attempts you have made to overcome those obstacles.* If appropriate, ask for assistance.

4. *Describe your next milestone.* Explain what steps you will take and when they will happen.

5. *Forecast the future of the project.* Focus on your ability to finish the job as planned by the scheduled completion date.

Final Reports   As its name suggests, a **final report** is delivered upon completion of an undertaking. The length and formality of a final report will depend on the scope of that undertaking. If you are describing a weekend conference to your colleagues, it would most likely be short and informal. In contrast, a task force reporting to top management or the general public on a year-long project would most likely deliver a more detailed and formal report. You can adjust the following guidelines to fit your situation:

1. *Introduce the report.* State your name and your role unless everyone in the audience already knows you. Briefly describe the undertaking you are reporting on.

2. *Provide necessary background.* Tell your listeners what they need to know to understand why the project was undertaken, why you and others became involved, and any other factors that affected your approach.

3. *Describe what happened.* Explain what happened during the undertaking. Aim this discussion at the level of interest appropriate for your audience. For example, if others will be following in your footsteps, give details of challenges and explain how you dealt with them. If other persons were involved, mention them and offer your thanks for their assistance.

4. *Describe the results.* Report on the outcomes of the undertaking. Include a discussion of successes and failures. Describe any future events related to your topic.

5. *Tell listeners how to get more information.*

Webinars   As discussed in Chapter 8, *webinars*, or web-based seminars, are a type of virtual meeting commonly encountered in business settings. Webinar sessions are typically viewed in real-time, but may be recorded and e-mailed to participants and/or uploaded

online for on-demand viewing. Webinars may be used for the purpose of sharing information or providing instructions for how to do something. There are at least 10 uses for informative webinars[3]:

- *e-Learning/continuing education*: Covers a topic for educational purposes; may allow learners to earn credits to maintain their professional licenses or fulfill other field-based requirements.

- *Employee training*: Provides employees with information about specific topics that apply to their jobs.

- *Customer onboarding*: Helps new customers learn how to take full advantage of your products or services.

- *Product demonstration*: Teaches new customers how a service or product works.

- *Corporate communications*: Brings remote employees together to discuss information and/or solicit feedback.

- *Lead generation*: Shares free content with the purpose of collecting participants' information (e.g., names, e-mail addresses).

- *Customer retention*: Creates a dialogue with customers by keeping them informed and/or answering their questions.

- *Reputation management*: Familiarizes participants with a brand and establishes credibility by sponsoring content.

- *Providing association members with content*: Provides members with free content, while charging a fee to nonmembers to see the same content.

- *Panelist discussion*: Provides a round-table discussion of various topics of interest with a panel of industry experts.

The following tips will help you design and present a webinar that will keep your participants interested:

- *Length.* Webinars usually run 45 to 60 minutes in length.

- *Topic.* The topic of the webinar should clearly convey to participants what they will be doing or learning if they attend the webinar.

- *Organization.* Webinars should have a host who will welcome the audience, explain the format for the session, introduce the speaker, ensure that the speaker stays on topic, open the floor for questions, and conclude the session.

- *Presentation aids.* Because of their length, speakers must be able to engage the audience to keep them interested. This may be done with the use of multiple types of visual aids, as well as integrating interaction mechanisms, such as polls or links to additional information.

Vadym Pastukh/Shutterstock

Finally, some additional considerations must be made when organizing informative or persuasive presentations that will be delivered as webinars. The webinar session must be arranged in a format that maximizes clarity for presenters and participants. Table 9-1 provides a description of the five most common formats, along with the respective pros and cons of each.

Table 9-1	Organizational Formats for Webinars	
Description of Format	**Pros**	**Cons**
Presentation: The presenter gives a rehearsed speech using presentational software (e.g., Prezi).	Easy to create; scripted; allows the opportunity to provide viewers with the slides or other bonus content	Less engaging
Interview: An expert is interviewed by the host using a set of preselected questions.	Engaging; allows the speaker to prepare with a predetermined set of questions	Guest may go off-script
Q&A: An expert answers questions directly from the audience. Questions may be asked live or collected beforehand.	Highly engaging; offers the audience an opportunity to access an expert; requires interaction; gathers important information on topics the audience finds important	Unscripted; possibility that there will not be enough questions to fill the allotted time; potential for poor questions from the audience
Panel: Several speakers discuss a predetermined topic.	Highly engaging; offers various perspectives and experts	Potential for conflict between panelists
Product Demonstration: The presenter demonstrates how to use a product or showcases a service for new or prospective clients.	Provides an opportunity to engage with prospective clients; generates leads	Potential for failure

Source: Mazereeu, A. (2015, July 28). 5 memorable webinar formats to try. *LifeLearn*. Retrieved from http://www.lifelearn.com/2015/07/28/5-memorable-webinar-formats-to-try/

In addition to selecting an organizational format for the webinar session itself, individual presenters must assemble their talks using one of the organizational patterns discussed in Chapter 10.

Media Interviews

Media Interviews   Media coverage can significantly impact businesses. While positive coverage may help an organization gain credibility and new clients, negative attention can result in public skepticism and financial loss, and require strategic change.[4] Building a positive relationship with media personnel is an important part of business success. At some point in your career, you may be asked to serve as a spokesperson by communicating with the media on behalf of your organization.

Two types of presentations are common in this context: individual media interviews and press conferences. In both of these instances, an executive or leader from the organization typically serves as the primary speaker; however, other members of the organization may be prompted to speak based on their individual expertise about the situation at hand.

Media interviews may be impromptu or planned. A reporter might run up to you as you are leaving work to obtain a quote about a crisis that just broke. In other situations, you might be able to schedule a time to meet and provide your remarks about a new initiative or special occasion. In all scenarios, you must remember that the interviews will be recorded and that your words, if not chosen carefully, may sound differently than intended if used out of context.

A **press conference** (or **news conference**) is a specific type of media interview where a meeting is organized with the purpose of sharing important information about an organization and giving journalists an opportunity to ask questions. Press conferences have many purposes[5]:

- Political candidates can communicate their stance on important issues.
- Political activists can state their opinion on proposed legislation.
- Presidents can share important information and/or calm public fears.
- Officials (such as mayors, governors, police officers) may respond to emergencies or disasters.
- Organizations can issue an apology or official statement during a crisis.
- Companies can introduce a new product or service.
- Researchers can reveal a scientific breakthrough.
- Organizations can unveil a campaign or new branding.
- Nonprofits can announce a charity event with a featured celebrity or strategic partnership.
- Organizations can announce new leadership.
- Sports teams can announce the acquisition of a new player.
- Companies can release their financial information.

Several considerations should be taken into account when planning an effective press conference:

- *Length.* Most press conferences are 20 to 45 minutes in length, including a question-and-answer period.
- *Time.* The media are the audience for a press conference, which makes it important to research the deadlines of journalists whom you are inviting and schedule the event accordingly.
- *Location.* Press conferences can be held in a meeting room (at the organization's headquarters, for example) or on location, such as at the site of a new store's groundbreaking ceremony. Locations should be within a reasonable traveling distance, be free of noise distractions, and meet the technical requirements necessary for media setup.
- *Topic.* Press conferences should be reserved for major newsworthy announcements. A story is considered newsworthy if it is timely, affects many people, happens locally or to people with whom the audience relates, happens to a famous person or a notable organization, and has human interest.
- *Invitations.* Invitations, in the form of a news release or media advisory, should be sent to journalists who have an interest in your news or event announcement at least 24 hours in advance. A sample news release and media advisory can be found in Appendix II.
- *Organization.* Similar to a webinar, press conferences need a host to introduce speakers and facilitate the question-and-answer session. It is helpful to limit the event to two speakers to reduce the risk of communicating inconsistent information.
- *Language and delivery.* Hosts and speakers should be trained in working with the media. A few tips for them follow:
  - Anticipate and prepare answers for a variety of questions.
  - Rehearse in front of a camera, paying attention to nonverbal communication.

- Identify "talking points" or key messages that you wish to communicate.
- Keep statements brief.
- Consider using visual aids.
- Address questions with short, clear answers.

Podcasts   Another presentation tool that organizations may use to share information and connect with new and existing audiences is a **podcast**. Audiences can download or stream these digital audio files on their personal devices and listen at their leisure. Podcasts may contain interviews with guests, be conversational or educational in nature, or incorporate storytelling.

- *Length.* Most podcasts are between 15 and 60 minutes. According to Dan Misener, head of audience development at Pacific Content, the average length of all podcasts, regardless of popularity is about 37 minutes,[6] whereas the length of a top 100 podcast is approximately 53 minutes.[7]
- *Topic.* Rather than using the podcast to overtly promote your products or services, instead devote episodes to topics of interest related to your industry. For example, a crop insurance provider could discuss current changes in agricultural commodities trade policies that might affect the price of soybeans.
- *Organization.* Regardless of length, podcasts should be well-organized. Clear segments make it easy for listeners to pause the presentation and come back to finish listening at another time.
- *Language and delivery.* Podcasts should be conversational. Audiences will tune in because they enjoy the personalities of the host(s) and feel connected to them.

Training   A **training presentation** teaches listeners how to *do* something: operate a piece of equipment or use software, relate effectively to the public, avoid or deal with sexual harassment—the range of training topics is almost endless. Training can be informal, such as an experienced employee demonstrating how to transfer a telephone call for a new hire. At the other end of the spectrum, some training is extensive and highly organized. Corporations including Disney, Anheuser-Busch, Dell Computer, Harley-Davidson, and General Electric have full-blown institutes dedicated to training their employees.[8]

Some training is done by experts. Large organizations have staffers who design and deliver instructional programs. In addition, independent firms and freelancers create and deliver training on a fee-for-service basis. Despite the existence of a training industry, the U.S. Bureau of Labor Statistics says that almost 75% of all work-related training is delivered informally on the job.[9] This fact suggests that, sooner or later, you will be responsible for designing and delivering training, no matter what your job may be. Most training experts agree about the importance of each of the following steps[10]:

- *Define the training goal.* Training always aims to change the way your audience acts, so begin by identifying who you want to teach and the specific results you want to bring about. For example: "Employers who are authorized to buy new and replacement equipment will know how to use the new online purchasing system to locate vendors, place orders, track shipments, and check their department's purchasing budget."
- *Develop a schedule and a list of resources.* Determine the amount of time you will need to plan and publicize the training; identify the staffing and physical resources you need and make sure they are available; line up the facility and make sure its furnishings and layout suit your design; create and/or purchase necessary training materials.

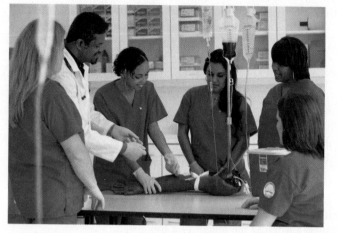

Ariel Skelley/Blend Images LLC

- *Involve the audience.* Listeners who are actively involved in a presentation will understand and remember the material far better than members of a passive audience.[11] For example, Lever Corporation trains its representatives to sell industrial cleaning equipment by teaching them to operate the machines themselves.[12] Audience members can be asked to read a manual or instructions, look at diagrams or displays, watch live demonstrations or videos, go on a site visit, complete worksheets, or simulate an experience.

- *Organization.* The most reliable format for training is a problem-solution approach: Listeners are more likely to pay attention to the information you provide when they view it as solving a problem they are currently experiencing.

Presentations to Persuade

Unlike purely informative presentations, which do not advocate a position, there are many times when we must use **persuasion** to motivate an audience to voluntarily change a particular belief, attitude, or behavior.[13] When you convince an interviewer you are the right person for the job, when you make a pitch to a prospective client for a new business project, and when you sway your team to adopt your great idea, you are delivering a persuasive presentation.

The following discussion covers the types of persuasive presentations you are most likely to deliver in the workplace, as well as strategies to create presentations that change minds and produce the results you are seeking in an ethical manner.

Motivational Speeches

A **motivational speech** attempts to generate enthusiasm for the topic being presented. When delivered effectively and at the proper time, such presentations can produce excellent results. For example, the organizers of a fundraising event can generate enthusiasm to recruit and energize volunteers. A team leader can inspire an otherwise skeptical workforce to work extra hard to cut costs. A manager can encourage an unmotivated employee to turn their performance around and become a top producer for the company.

Goodwill Speeches

As its name implies, a **goodwill speech** aims to create a favorable image of the speaker's cause in the minds of the audience. Representatives of organizations frequently speak to audiences to promote interest or support for their organizations. For example, a corporate recruiter who addresses graduating seniors and a bank economist who explains an economic forecast are making goodwill speeches.

These goodwill speeches might seem informative, but they also try to change the listeners' attitudes or behavior. The corporate recruiter is trying to encourage some students to apply for jobs with their company; the economist is trying to build the image of their institution as a leading business bank.

Feasibility Reports

A **feasibility report** evaluates one or more potential action steps and recommends how the organization should proceed. Would a bonus system increase

Using Training to Retain Employees

English Under the Arches (EUA) is a training program sponsored by McDonald's that has the purpose of educating employees for whom English is a second language. EUA is available to crew members and managers. McDonald's covers the tuition cost for the program, which provides English skills on restaurant-related topics such as shift basics, shift conversations, shift writing, and conducting performance reviews. The courses are a blend of face-to-face and virtual delivery.

McDonald's has experienced a 70% retention rate after three years for employees who complete EUA.

Source: "Archways to opportunity," *English Under the Arches* (n.d.) Retrieved from http://www.archwaystoopportunity.com/english_under_the_arches.html#; Patten, B. (n.d.). "10 companies with great training programs: An extensive rundown," *Innovation Enterprise*. Retrieved from https://channels.theinnovationenterprise.com/articles/7314-10-companies-with-great-training-programs-and-what-you-can-learn-from-them

profitability and retain employees? Is job-sharing a good idea? Would subsidizing the expenses incurred by employees who use public transportation solve the parking problem? Feasibility studies help answer questions like these.

Most feasibility reports should follow these steps:

1. *Introduction.* Briefly define the problem and explain its consequences. Explain why it is important to consider the alternatives you will be discussing. Consider explaining your recommendations if the audience will not object strongly. If listeners are likely to object to your conclusion, consider postponing it until later in your presentation.

2. *Criteria.* Introduce the standards you used to evaluate alternative courses of action. For example:

   - Will the course of action really achieve the desired goal?
   - Can we implement it?
   - Will implementation fit within our time constraints?
   - Can we afford it?

   It is hard for anyone to argue with criteria like those presented here, so getting listeners to accept them before they hear your recommendations can be an effective way to sell your conclusions.

3. *Methodology.* Describe the process you used to identify and evaluate the plan(s) under consideration. The amount of detail you supply will depend on the audience and the situation. For a relatively minor project, your explanation will probably be brief. For a major feasibility study—especially when it is controversial or when your credibility is in question—you will probably need to describe your approach in detail.

4. *Possible solutions.* Provide a detailed explanation of each solution you considered.

5. *Evaluation of the solutions.* Measure the suitability of each solution against the criteria you listed earlier. Offer whatever supporting material is necessary to show how you arrived at your conclusions.

6. *Recommendations.* Describe the solution that best fits the criteria provided earlier. If you have done a good job in evaluating the possible solutions using the

CAREER **tip**

How to Request a Raise

Asking for a raise is a kind of proposal, even though you typically will present your arguments informally to your boss. Here are tips that can increase your chances for success:

The Best Time to Seek a Raise:

- When you or your department has been recognized for doing a good job
- After you have volunteered to take on additional responsibilities (and have handled them successfully)
- If the organization cannot easily replace you or do without your services
- After you have contributed directly to the company's profitability and success (and you can demonstrate this connection)
- When the organization is in strong financial shape
- When your relationship with your boss is good

What to Ask For:

- Research the compensation range for jobs like yours in the industry. Check with professional associations in your field or web-based salary surveys. Demonstrate your request is reasonable by providing comparative figures.
- Consider asking for benefits other than cash. For many people, pay is not the only kind of compensation. For example, you might also seek more vacation time, a more flexible schedule, discounts on company products, or use of a company vehicle.

Do Not:

- Get emotional. Losing your temper is unlikely to be persuasive, and it can damage your long-term relationship with your boss.
- Confuse effort with contribution. Working hard is admirable, but effort alone probably will not be enough to earn you a raise. Show your boss that the *results* you produce justify better compensation.
- Rely on longevity ("I've been here for 8 years") or personal need ("My rent just went up 20%"). It is better to demonstrate that you *deserve* a raise.

criteria already introduced, the recommendation should be relatively brief and straightforward.

7. *Conclusion.* Briefly summarize your findings, showing how they can help solve the problem at hand.

Proposals In a **proposal** you advocate that your audience takes a specific action. Some proposals are aimed at external audiences, whereas others are focused on internal audiences. You might, for example, try to persuade management to support a ride-sharing program or reimburse employees for education costs, or you might try to convince your boss to give you more staffing support or a raise in pay. (See the Career Tip for advice on requesting a raise.)

Whatever the topic and the audience, the following two-step approach is the most straightforward for a proposal presentation:

1. *Introduce the problem.* Demonstrate the nature of the problem in terms that the audience will understand; show undesirable consequences of the problem; highlight ethical dimensions of the situation if the current situation is morally wrong; and provide causal analysis of the situation. (How did this problem develop?)

2. *Provide a solution (with supporting evidence).* Describe the positive consequences of your proposal; show how your proposal will avoid bad consequences; highlight the

ethical reasons for your approach and show why it is the right thing to do; then address the feasibility of your proposal. Show it can be done, in terms of cost, time, motivation, and other factors. Include an operation timeline to strengthen the proposal.

Sales Presentations   In a **sales presentation**, one party presents remarks aimed at persuading another party to purchase a product or service. Unlike the communication in retail settings, sales presentations are planned in advance. Sales presentations range from platform speeches in front of large audiences to less formal sit-down talks with small groups of decision-makers.

Whatever their size, sales presentations will adhere to the following guidelines:

- *Establish client relationships before your presentation.* Getting to know the people whom you hope to persuade will give you valuable information on what they want and suggest how you can satisfy their needs. Just as important, preexisting relationships will make your listeners more comfortable with you.

- *Put your clients' needs first.* Focus on the buyer's problems and concerns rather than on your products, company, services, or needs. What is not working well for the client right now? What do they want to happen? Once you know what is missing, you can find out how your product or service can fill that gap.

- *Listen to your clients.* Unlike most other presentations, sales-oriented talks call for greater audience involvement. One study of salespeople found that the difference between top and average performers was the willingness to listen. The prospective buyers of top performers spoke between 30% and 70% of the time.[14] Rather than viewing questions and comments as interruptions, welcome them as a chance for you to learn what the client wants.

- *Emphasize benefits, not features.* Features are qualities of a product or service that make it desirable and distinguish it from the competition. Salespeople understandably get excited about features, and they are often tempted to promote them to prospective customers. But features will not ultimately impress customers—the benefits that flow from those features will. For example, one feature of a customer service product might be that it is 100% web-based. The benefit would be that the customer does not have to host the product on their own server or maintain it. To be successful, you must "sell the benefit, not the feature."[15]

- *Use an effective closing strategy.* An effective close summarizes the primary benefits and the ways in which the benefits meet or exceed the client's needs. It then calls for any action that moves the sale along: agreement to a test or trial run, agreement to another meeting, agreement to attend a demonstration or arrange for your presentation to higher-level decision-makers. When developing your close, think long-term. As consultant Hans Stennek states, "I've never been a believer in closing because my objective is not to close the sale but to open a relationship."[16]

Presentations for Special Occasions

In business settings, many special speaking occasions and events arise, some of which you may be asked to participate in or be given a chance to volunteer for. You may be asked to introduce a speaker at a staff meeting or annual banquet, present an award to an employee, or accept an award you have won. Perhaps you will present a tribute to a member of a civic organization to which you belong or bid farewell to a supervisor who was promoted out of your department.

ETHICAL challenge

Keep in mind that every context is unique; you will want to adjust to the physical, social, chronological, and cultural context of each occasion. The following guidelines will help you feel confident and achieve your goals when delivering special-occasion remarks.

Welcoming a Guest or Group   When you deliver **welcoming remarks**, your words often set the tone for the whole event. Warmth and sincerity in words and behavior are important. Whether you are welcoming a special guest for a 2-hour banquet or a group of new employees, try to follow these guidelines:

- Say who you are (if the audience does not know) or on whose behalf you are speaking.

- Identify the person or people you are welcoming (unless you are welcoming the entire audience).

- Thank the guest or the group for coming (if either had a choice).

- Explain why the occasion is especially important or significant.

As you deliver your remarks, be sure to speak to the person or the group whom you are welcoming. If appropriate, turn to the audience and invite your listeners to participate in the welcome by clearly stating or showing them how you want them to behave.

Introducing Another Speaker   When handled well, your **speech of introduction**, which presents another speaker to your audience, will help make that person's remarks a success. This section offers some guidelines that will help you deliver an effective introduction. You may choose to switch the order of the information here, but you will almost always need to include it in some way unless the audience is already aware of the information.

- *Briefly preview the topic about which the person will speak.* If the speaker's topic is familiar, you may need to mention it only briefly. If the audience is unfamiliar with the topic, you may need to include more background information about the topic and explain why it is significant for the group.

- *Give the audience reasons to listen to the person you are introducing.* Share interesting and relevant parts of the speaker's background. Whenever possible, show how their remarks will have value for the audience.

- *Enhance the credibility of the person you are introducing.* Share information that will showcase their qualifications. Select the most interesting biographical information for your audience to describe the forthcoming speaker. It is best to give some general information and a few specifics rather than rattling off long lists: "John has done training with many groups, including the Air Force, IBM, and Baxter

Healthcare." Avoid being vague ("John has done a lot of training for big groups"), but do not burden the audience with too much time-consuming detail either ("John has done training for . . ." followed by a list of 20 companies).

A good introduction requires that you learn about the person you are introducing in advance. If you can, meet virtually or in person or interview the speaker over the phone. If possible, obtain a résumé or biographical information in writing ahead of time. The more you know, the better you can make your introduction.

Make sure all the information in your introduction is accurate. Check and practice the pronunciation of unfamiliar names, cities, and companies. Also, be sensitive to culture and gender differences. For example, members of many cultures prefer to be identified by formal titles (such as "director") that are not commonly used in the United States or Canada. Likewise, the humor that may be appreciated in the United States could easily offend listeners—or the individuals being introduced—if they are from cultures with more formal communication styles. Ask the person for their pronouns and how they would like to be referred to (pronoun or job title and last name, first and last name, or first name only). Strive for consistency if you are introducing more than one person.

The following tips will help ensure your introduction of another speaker is a success[17]:

- Plan your remarks carefully in advance. Do not take an impromptu approach.

- Your introduction should *appear* spontaneous and natural, even though it is planned. Practice your delivery so you will not have to rely on notes.

- When making your introduction, look at the audience, not at the person being introduced.

- Keep the introduction short. You are not the main attraction. In most cases, a 1- or 2-minute introduction will be enough. If the audience already knows the person you are introducing, this presentation can be even shorter.

Honoring a Person or an Institution   When you are asked to give a **speech of tribute**, you will be honoring a person or group's achievements or characteristics. When delivering such remarks, you can follow the person's life or career chronologically and pay tribute to achievements and characteristics along the way, or you might choose some themes or traits from the person's life and organize your remarks around those topics. If you do choose to pay tribute along theme lines (bravery and commitment, for example), anecdotes and examples can illustrate your points. For example, rapper and producer, T.I., presented a tribute to Nipsey Hussle at the 2019 BET Awards. During this tribute speech, T.I. discussed Hussle's community and social activist work in addition to his musical achievements.

Many of the guidelines for tributes parallel those for introductions: Ensure accuracy of names and details, and be sensitive to culture, gender, and personal desires. Check your information with the person to whom tribute is being paid if possible or practical; if not, check with an extremely authoritative source.

Giving a Toast   Sooner or later you are likely to be asked to deliver a special type of tribute—a **toast**. Besides honoring the person to whom it refers, a well-crafted toast can boost your visibility and reputation in any organization. Remember, toasts usually express appreciation, recognize accomplishments, and offer hopes and wishes for the future. Here are some hints to help you choose the right words.

- *Choose the time wisely.* If it is up to you to choose the moment, make sure everyone is present. At a dinner, choose the moment when the group has just been seated or wait until just before dessert. At a stand-around cocktail party or outdoor barbecue, wait until most people have drinks.

- *Be prepared.* Think ahead about the occasion, the attendees, and the person or people whom you are toasting. Delivering an impromptu toast can be risky. Use some inside information or little-known facts that compliment the person.

- *Look spontaneous.* Even though you have planned your remarks in advance, try to avoid reading notes or sounding as if you have memorized your speech.

- *Be brief.* A 30- to 60-second toast is the norm; 2 minutes is the maximum. If in doubt, say less, not more. End by raising your glass and gently clinking the glass of a person near you and saying, "Cheers," "Salud," or a similar expression.

- *Be visible and audible.* Make sure your presence commands the attention of your audience. For formal affairs, you may be asked to be on stage. If it is an unorganized mill-around affair, look for an elevated spot—a hillside, a stair step (not a chair), the back porch. Be certain you have everyone's attention before speaking, and begin loudly enough to be effective.

- *Be inclusive.* Alternate your gaze between the audience and the person or people whom you are honoring.

- *Be appropriate.* If you are debating whether a remark or story would be humorous or offensive, leave it out. If you think something is funny but are unsure if the honoree and guests will appreciate the humor, leave it unsaid.

Presenting an Award   Sometimes persons may know they are recipients of awards, but at other times the announcement may come as a surprise. Depending on the situation, you will choose whether to let the audience (and winner) know who is receiving the award at the beginning of the speech or save that information until the end. For an effective **award presentation**, follow these tips:

- If everyone knows who is receiving the award, mention the person's name early in your remarks. If the audience does not know who is receiving the award, you might want to build suspense by withholding their name until the end.

- State the name and nature of the award.

- State the criteria for selection.

- Relate the way (or ways) in which the recipient meets the criteria, using specific examples.

- Be sure the person receiving the award—not you, the presenter—is the center of attention and focus.

Hill Street Studios/Blend Images/Alamy Stock Photo

Accepting an Award   When you accept an award, a few brief remarks are usually all that are necessary. Recalling the long-winded speeches at the annual Academy Awards ceremony will help you appreciate the sentiment behind Marlene Dietrich's advice to Mikhail Baryshnikov when she sent him to accept her award from the Council of Fashion Designers: "Take the thing, look at it, thank them, and go."[18] This

The Show Must Go On

As with any speech, mistakes or unanticipated issues can happen during a special occasion presentation. At the 2017 Academy Awards, Warren Beatty mistakenly announced *La La Land* as the winner for Best Picture. As the producers of *La La Land* presented their acceptance speeches, they were told that *Moonlight* was the actual winner. Photos later confirmed that Beatty was handed the envelope containing the winner for Best Actress in a Leading Role.[20] Although the nominees, presenters, host, and Academy showed grace in their response to the mistake, there is no denying that the situation was uncomfortable for everyone involved.

Following is a list of issues you may encounter during a special-occasion presentation and suggestions for handling them[21]:

Announcing the winner of an award who is not present to accept the award. Consider asking the audience if anyone is present from the recipient's family or organization to accept the award on the winner's behalf. If you are aware of the winner's absence in advance, make arrangements to call upon this individual to accept the award.

Presenting an award with an error (such as a spelling mistake) printed on it. If you do not notice the error far enough in advance to correct the mistake, present the award. After the event, pull the recipient aside to apologize for the error and let them know that a corrected award will be provided as soon as possible.

Managing photo-ops that take too much time. As the master of ceremonies, you may restrict the amount of time allowed for each photo opportunity. You may also announce that award recipients will be available for photos at the conclusion of the ceremony. If you choose this route, be sure to make yourself available for the photos.

Signaling that time is up when a recipient's acceptance speech runs long. There are subtle, nonverbal ways to intervene when a speaker is out of time. Standing right beside the speaker may be enough to encourage them to wrap up. Otherwise, you will need to politely interject and then lead the applause: "What a treat to hear . . . but unfortunately, we will need to move on to the next . . . to stay on schedule. . . . Let's all give one more hand to . . ."

---

approach is probably too extreme, but brevity is certainly an important element of most acceptances. So, too, is gratitude. The following plan can help you organize your presentation in an effective way[19]:

- Express your sincere gratitude (and surprise, if appropriate).
- Acknowledge and show appreciation to contributors.
- Describe how the award will make a difference.
- Say thank you again.

• Common Audiences for Business Presentations

Effective presentations are tailored to the audiences to which they are directed. As business professionals, we often need to engage a variety of audiences to achieve our goals. Each of these audiences has a set of expectations for what they hope to learn from your presentation. In fact, you can most likely recall a time when you left a presentation feeling like your time could have been better spent elsewhere. In order to meet the needs of our audiences, we must consider the types of audiences we may encounter. As renowned astrophysicist and science communicator Neil de Grasse Tyson explains, effective communication with internal and external audiences is crucial:

> I'm not giving the same exchange with each host: If the host is playful I can be serious, or maybe take them one notch into the playful zone. If it's a conservative host, then I frame it in conservative context. If there's a liberal host, I can frame it that way. If the audience is old, I know they may [have] lived [through] the second World War or the Cold War or the Space Race. The core information is not altered. The science is intact. But if I'm going to be an effective communicator, I'm going to shape the content in a way that can best be received by the receptors of that audience.[22]

Internal Audiences

An **internal audience** consists of individuals or groups that are members of or are closely associated with an organization. Because of their affiliation, internal audiences tend to share common points of reference and have at least basic knowledge or understanding of the topic at hand. Consider a member of an oyster restoration team presenting a status report on the construction of a new oyster reef in Texas' Galveston Bay. They will not need to spend time providing background information explaining the need for such a project to internal audiences. These audiences will already be familiar with the existing threats to marine habitats.

Consider the following internal audiences and their interests:

- *Supervisors and Executives:* Members of these audiences expect an efficient presentation of facts, supporting details, and results. They need information illustrating the resources, costs, and potential benefits associated with your proposals or tasks.

- *Colleagues:* As coworkers, your colleagues must be aware of information that impacts the business or how they perform their jobs. They will likely privilege a more simplified approach rather than the detail-specific focus needed by supervisors and executives.

- *Board of Directors:* As we discussed in Chapter 8, the board of directors oversees the company's actions. Presentations to these members should be brief, with a focus on sharing information that is needed to engage in problem-solving and decision-making. Background information, current actions as well as proposed solutions should be prioritized.

- *Shareholders:* A shareholder legally owns shares in the financial capital of public or private corporations; as such, these individuals are considered members of the corporation and must be made privy to information that could impact their investments. As a result, these audiences will expect direct communication that explains the current financial situation, as well as any visual aids—such as quarterly earnings graphs—that will help them understand the information.

External Audiences

Presentations are not just delivered to internal audiences: Many people also give work-related addresses to listeners outside their organizations. **External audiences** typically have a vested interest in your organization. These audiences consist of individuals or groups

A Professional Perspective

Jeffrey Riddle

Military, Corporate & Non-Profit Communication Consultant

San Antonio, TX

Credit: Jeffrey Riddle

As a struggling college student, I once had a job that involved presenting a lesson on critical thinking to young kids. How do you get children to pay attention and engage with a speaker on such an abstract topic? Easy—you dress up like Peter Pan when presenting! It worked and it was one of my earliest lessons in customizing all aspects of a presentation to the audience— whether a group of high-energy elementary school students or a team of high-powered executives.

In my professional, post-college life, I continue to have many opportunities to practice adapting presentations to a variety of audiences. For example, in one position, I was asked to develop a briefing for leaders to use to save millions of dollars in funding for a federal program. Small task, right? I researched other federal committee communications and found that briefings are usually under 5-minute presentations that provide essential information to help knowledgeable audience members get their jobs done. Clearly, the presentation must be simple and to the point—because 5 minutes can seemingly pass in an instant. To keep everyone focused, I prepared a key presentation aid: a one-page fact sheet with statistics and a progress report of the program. I found out later that the late Senator John McCain ended up requesting the fact sheet and used it to help save the 21 million dollars in federal funding for the program. In other words, it was a successful briefing!

Regardless of where you find yourself in your public speaking career, always know your audience. Are you speaking with colleagues familiar with your work or are you explaining it to the general public? How much detail and information will help your team reach their goals? What will most interest or affect your audience? Answering these questions is an important step to preparing a successful presentation.

outside of and not closely related to the organization; however, they may affect or be affected by the organization. Realizing that effective speakers carry their message to the public in ways that print and digital media cannot match, companies send representatives into the community to deliver speeches in a wide variety of settings.[23] Even people who seem to work in fairly solitary jobs may give speeches to clubs, professional organizations, and community groups.

Because they are not directly affiliated with the organization, external audiences do not share the same level of mastery or knowledge of your topic as internal audiences. As such, presentations to external audiences need to be adapted to provide them with the background information they need in a way that they will understand. Take, for example, the following external audiences and their interests:

- *General Public/Community Members:* The public will be concerned with matters that could affect them and their families or communities in the short- and long-term. Using understandable language and providing supporting information and visual aids will ensure that messages are clear.

- *Customers/Clients:* Potential or existing customers and clients require information that will help them make an informed decision about adopting or upgrading your company's products or services. They expect to learn how the services will provide solutions to problems they may be experiencing. Conversational presentations should include the ability to ask questions and, when appropriate, demonstrate how something works.

- *Media Professionals:* The media has an obligation to investigate newsworthy stories and inform the community of matters of interest to them. Media professionals will expect background information that will help them tell the story, as well as the ability to ask questions. It is important to recognize that, if you do not supply this information, the media will obtain it elsewhere, which may not be to the benefit of your organization.

- *Industry Professionals:* Depending on your line of work, you may also communicate with other professionals working in your industry. This includes competitors, product suppliers, as well as licensing and funding agencies. Because these audiences are familiar with the industry, you can safely assume a moderate level of knowledge. However, background information and supporting data will be necessary when discussing specific problems, projects, or proposals.

Chapter 10 will include further guidance for adapting your presentations to meet your specific audience's needs.

MASTER **the chapter**

review points

- Business professionals use presentations to meet the following general goals: to inform and instruct, to persuade, and to celebrate special occasions.

- Informative presentations include briefings, reports (status and final), webinars, media interviews, podcasts, and training sessions.

- Unlike reports, briefings are short and give the minimum information needed. Status reports review the project's purpose; its current state, its obstacles, and the efforts to overcome them; the next milestone; and the project's future. Final reports require introductions, background information, a description of events, results, and directions to get more information.

- Webinars are lengthier virtual presentations that are used to share information or provide instructions on how to do something. Sessions may be live-streamed or recorded for later viewing. Designing an effective webinar requires clearly conveying outcomes to participants, selecting an engaging speaker and host, and keeping participants engaged and involved during the session.

- Media interviews are used to share important information about an organization with journalists for the purpose of generating media coverage. Media interviews may be planned or unplanned. Press conferences are a specific type of planned media interview.

- Preparing for a press conference requires choosing a newsworthy story, determining a time and location, sending a news release or media advisory to invited journalists, selecting and rehearsing with speakers and hosts, and preparing to answer questions.

- Podcasts may be used to share information and connect with new and existing audiences.

Podcast episodes should be organized as conversations devoted to topics of interest related to the industry, including clear segments that allow users to listen across multiple sessions.

- Training sessions necessitate careful planning that includes defining the desired outcome, scheduling the needed time and resources, involving the audience, and organizing all training elements.

- Many business occasions call for persuasive presentations, such as motivational and goodwill speeches, feasibility reports, proposals, and sales presentations.

- A feasibility report includes an introduction, criteria, methodology, possible solutions and an evaluation of solutions, recommendations, and a conclusion.

- Proposals advocate a specific action and consist of two parts: the problem and the solution. Sales presentations, which are types of proposals, are most successful in the long term when they establish client relationships, consider clients' needs, listen to and welcome clients' participation, focus on benefits rather than features, and use effective closings.

- Business contexts often require special-occasion presentations such as making speeches of welcome and introductions, honoring persons or institutions, making toasts, and presenting and accepting awards. Effective business communicators know the basics of each of these special presentations.

- Presentations should be tailored to the audiences in which they are directed. Two specific types of audiences—internal and external—require special considerations based on their interests.

key terms

activities

1. Invitation to Insight

Interview a professional in a field of study that interests you. Ask the respondent to discuss the types of informative, persuasive, and special occasion presentations they experience most often in the workplace. Talk to them about how they adapt to internal and external audiences when they deliver presentations.

2. Skill Builder

Identify the types of audience members you might encounter when delivering each of the following training sessions. Then, create an approach that will actively involve the audience in the sessions. Demonstrate your technique in class.

a. How to handle social media customer complaints non-defensively.
b. How to use HTML to code a basic website.
c. How to conduct an earthquake preparedness workshop.

3. Invitation to Insight

Increase your understanding of adult learning styles by performing one of the following exercises.

1. Attend a workplace training or explanation session. Analyze the presenter's training goal and use of direct involvement of the learners.
2. Interview a professional who conducts training in the workplace. Ask the respondent to describe successful strategies for involving and adapting messages to the audience.

4. Invitation to Insight

Use a search engine to find a free webinar that covers a topic in your field of study. After viewing the webinar, identify the purpose of the webinar and the goal of the speaker(s). Based on the guidelines for webinars presented in this chapter, would you consider the presentation successful? Explain your answer and provide examples.

5. Skill Builder

Choose a product or service with which you are familiar, or choose one of the following: cloud storage service, mobile phone pricing plan, deli delivery service for employees, company-supported memberships at a health club.

a. Identify an audience to whom you could sell this product.
b. Create a chart with two columns: features and benefits. List and differentiate between the product's features and benefits.

6. Skill Builder

Which type of presentation would be best suited to the message in each of the following situations? Justify your answer.

a. Providing updates on a current construction project.

b. Showing a customer why buying an automobile is a better choice than leasing one.

c. Convincing a charitable foundation to grant money to your job-training program for disadvantaged teenagers.

d. Demonstrating the features of an expensive computer system.

e. Announcing the launch of a new product model design.

f. Describing and dispelling fitness myths.

g. Sharing a university's history and culture with a large group of incoming college students and their families.

h. Introducing local businesspeople to members of a service club to which you belong.

7. Skill Builder

Prepare the following special-occasion speeches using the guidelines shared in this chapter.

a. Welcome: Prepare a speech of welcome for a guest from the community who is visiting your class to better understand your college's opportunities.

b. Introduction: Create an introduction for a guest from a prominent community business who has been invited to speak to your class about job interview strategies.

c. Speech to honor: Construct and present a speech that honors one of your classmates or a person or institution in your community that you believe deserves recognition.

d. Toast: Prepare a toast to your work team that has just met an important project deadline and received rave reviews from your supervisor.

e. Award: Present an award to a classmate (best team member, best listener, best speaker, most improved speaker) that reflects some achievement or activity during the semester.

Mc Graw Hill LearnSmart™

For further review, go to the LearnSmart study module for this chapter.

references

1. Lannon, J. M. (2003). *Technical communication* (9th ed.). New York, NY: Longman.

2. Wright, J. P. (1979). *On a clear day you can see General Motors.* New York, NY: Avon.

3. BeaconLive Marketing Team (n.d.). The 10 types of webinars everyone is doing. *BeaconLive.* Retrieved from https://www.beaconlive.com/blog/types-of-webinars

4. Bednar, M. K., Boivie, S., & Prince, N. R. (2012). Burr under the saddle: How media coverage influences strategic change. *Organization Science, 24*(3), 645–964. https://doi.org/10.1287/orsc.1120.0770

5. Roos, D. (2007, August 29). How press conferences work. *HowStuffWorks.* Retrieved from http://money.howstuffworks.com/business-communications/howpress- conferences-work.htm

6. Misener, D. (2019, December 5). Podcast episodes got shorter in 2019. *Pacific Content.* Retrieved from https://blog.pacific-content.com/podcast-episodes-got-shorter-in-2019-69e1f3b6c82f

7. Misener, D. (2018, October 25). I analyzed 10 million podcast episodes to find the average length. *Pacific Content.* Retrieved from https://blog.pacific-content.com/how-long-is-the-average-podcast-episode-81cd5f8dff47

8. Meister, J. C. (1998). *Corporate universities* (Rev. ed.). New York, NY: McGraw Hill.

9. Lowenstein, M., & Spletzer, J. (1994). *Informal training: A review of existing data and some new evidence,* Report NLS 94–20. Retrieved from http://www.bls.gov/ore/pdf/nL940050.pdf

10. Molenda, M., Pershing, J. A., & Reigluth, C. M. (1996). Designing instructional systems. In R. L. Craig (Ed.), *The ASTD training and development handbook.* New York, NY: McGraw Hill.

11. Blanchard, K. (1987). Managers must learn to teach. *Today's Office, 22,* 8–9.

12. How Lever's 'hands-on' demos ignited rep enthusiasm. (1993). *Business Marketing Digest, 18*(3), 29–32.

13. Adler, R. B., & Rodman, G. (2003). *Understanding human communication* (8th ed.). New York, NY: Oxford University Press.

14. Fisher, A. (1996, November 11). Willy Loman couldn't cut it. *Fortune, 134,* p. 210.

15. Toastmasters. (1992). *Specialty speeches.* Mission Viejo, CA: Toastmasters International.

16. Hans Stennek, quoted in Rackham, N. (1998). *Spin selling.* New York, NY: McGraw Hill.

17. Daly, J. A., & Eisenberg, I. N. (2001). *Presentations in everyday life.* Boston, MA: Houghton Mifflin.

18. Osgood, C. (1988). *Osgood on speaking: How to think on your feet without falling on your face.* New York, NY: Morrow.

19. Gard, G. C. (2008, November). Accepting an award: How to be gracious and effective in 30 seconds. *Toastmaster, 20.*

20. Gonzalez, S. (2017, February 28). It was "Moonlight," not "La La Land": A timeline of a historic Oscars blunder. *CNN.* Retrieved from http://www.cnn.com/2017/02/27/entertainment/academy-awards-mistake-what-happened/

21. Stonehouse, R. (2014, September 15). And the winner is . . . The art of presenting awards: Practical tips & techniques. *LinkedIn.* Retrieved from https://www.linkedin.com/pulse/20140915144547-37280809-and-the-winner-is-the-art-of-presenting-awards-practical-tips-techniques

22. Foley, K. E. (2017, June 6). How to explain anything to anyone, according to Neil deGrasse Tyson. *Quartz.* Retrieved from https://qz.com/998750/how-to-explain-anything-to-anyone-according-to-neil-degrasse-tyson/

23. Conference Board. (1987). *Across the Board,* 24(8), 7.

Chapter Ten

Developing and Organizing the Presentation

chapter outline

chapter objectives

After reading this chapter you should be able to:

1. Develop an effective strategy for a specific presentation based on a complete analysis of the situation.

2. Identify specific goals for a given speaking situation.

3. Construct a clear thesis based on an analysis of a specific speaking situation.

4. Choose and develop an organizational plan for the body of a presentation that best suits its goal and the audience.

5. Create an effective introduction and conclusion for a presentation, following the guidelines in this chapter.

6. Design a presentation that contains effective transitions between the introduction and the body, between points in the body, and between the body and the conclusion.

As discussed in Chapter 9, most people who work in organizations eventually find that their professional success depends, in part, on an ability to organize their ideas and present them effectively. Sometimes a written memo or report will do the job, but presenting ideas orally often has some distinct advantages. For example, if people do not understand a point in a written proposal, they may put the entire proposal aside for weeks or simply veto it. Delivering a message orally before audience members ensures that the speaker obtains immediate feedback that can help to clarify points and answer questions. For example, if the speaker notices that audience members seem confused, they can slow down or repeat key information; if audiences seem disengaged or bored, they can alter their style of address to energize the audience so as not to lose their attention. In practice, organizational members will rarely obtain approval for an important idea without explaining it personally. As one executive explains:

> The people who have the power and responsibility to say yes or no want a chance to consider and question the proposal in the flesh. Documents merely set up a meeting and record what the meeting decided. Anyone serious about an idea welcomes the chance to present it . . . in person. We wisely discount proposals whose authors are unwilling to be present at the launching.[1]

Naturally, the opportunity to give a presentation is just the start of successful communication with an audience. A speaker who presents unclear, unfocused, irrelevant, inappropriate, offensive, or disorganized information is unlikely to inform, persuade, or entertain an audience. Delivering an effective business presentation starts with analyzing the speaking situation, developing clear and specific goals, and carefully organizing your ideas. Additionally, all speakers must recognize that the introduction and conclusion are important opportunities to engage and intrigue the audience—and to ensure they remember the presentation. Of course, successful presenters also carefully and seamlessly move from one point to another, making the entire presentation flow comfortably and easily. We will help you gain confidence in each of these areas in this chapter.

• Analyzing the Situation

Before you plan even one sentence of the actual presentation, you must think about the situation in which you will speak. You can make sure your approach is on target by considering three factors: the occasion, the audience, the speaker (you), and—when speaking as a team—your group.

Analyzing the Occasion

Identifying the speech occasion provides valuable insight into the immediate needs of your audience, as well as opportunities for and limitations to engaging them in your presentation. Several factors contribute to shaping the occasion.

Time   There are at least two considerations related to time when making a presentation. The first is the time of day when you will be speaking. A straightforward, factual speech that would work well with an alert, rested audience at 10:00 a.m. might need to be more entertaining or emphatic to hold everyone's attention if delivered just before quitting time. When speaking to a virtual audience, you should be especially cognizant that participants from multiple time zones may be in attendance. While it is 10 a.m. for those living in the Midwestern portion of the United States, it is 8:30 p.m. for attendees in India.

Second, in addition to taking the hour of day into account, you need to consider the length of time you have to speak. Most business presentations are brief. One director of a Los Angeles shopping mall typically gives prospective vendors 20 minutes to make their pitch: "I automatically x-out anyone who is late or exceeds their time allotment. My experience has shown that people who have trouble adhering to parameters and deadlines are unreliable."[2] Alan Brawn, a principal of Brawn Consulting, reinforces the importance of keeping your remarks within the preset time limit: "Typically, if major points aren't made in about 6 minutes, a person's time in the sun is done."[3]

Sometimes the length of your talk will not be explicitly dictated, but that lack of formal limits does not mean you should speak as long as you like. Usually, factors in the situation suggest how long it is wise for you to speak. Notice, for example, how well speaker Hugh Marsh adapted his remarks to the after-dinner setting when giving a summary business report to a group of association members:

> Good evening, ladies and gentlemen. Whenever I get on a podium this late, after a long day at the office, I remind myself of several immutable laws.
>
> First, there is Marsh's First Law of Oratory—on any platform, any speech will grow in length to fill the time available for its delivery. Well, take heart. I only have fifteen minutes.
>
> Then there is Marsh's Second Law of Oratory—the farthest distance between two points is a speech. Or, as we used to say in Texas, speeches too often are like a Longhorn steer—a point here and a point there and a lot of bull in between. Well, again, take heart. I will try to keep my two points close together.
>
> Another law I remind myself of is Marsh's Third Law of Oratory—no speech ever sounds as good at 7:00 pm as it did at noon.
>
> And, finally, there is Marsh's First Law of Meeting Attendance—everybody's gotta be someplace. As long as we're here, let's be friends. I'll be brief. You be attentive. I'll make my few points and get off so we can get back to the fun part of the meeting—socializing.[4]

Facilities   Figure 10.1 shows how you can adapt the layout of a physical room to suit the speaking situation. Regardless of the arrangement you choose, you need to consider

Consider the strengths and limitations of the following physical room arrangements:

FIGURE 10.1

Room
Arrangement
Options

Source: Morrisey, G. L.,
Sechrest, T. L., & Warman,
W. B. (1997). *Loud and
clear: How to prepare and
deliver effective business
and technical presentations*
(4th ed.). Cambridge,
MA: Perseus Books.

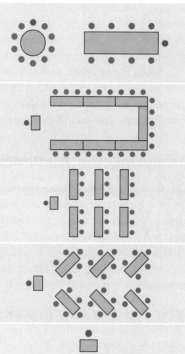

Conference
Accommodates smaller groups (10 or fewer)
Allows audience viewing and writing
Promotes audience interaction and discussion
Allows sharing of materials or viewing models

Horseshoe
Accommodates groups of 10–30
Allows eye contact with all members of the audience
Allows audience viewing and writing
Promotes informal discussion

Classroom
Accommodates formal groups (around 20)
Allows audience viewing and writing
Limits audience interaction
Limits participation to Q & A

Herringbone
Accommodates groups of 20–30
Less formal than classroom
Useful to promote small group discussions
Allows ready switch from lecture to discussion

Auditorium
Accommodates large groups (over 20)
Limits audience writing and interacting
Limits audience participation to Q & A

some important issues. Will there be enough seating for all the listeners? What type of equipment is available for you to use? Will there be distracting background noises?

Answering questions like these is critical, and failure to anticipate facility problems can trip you up at a crucial moment. For example, the absence of an easel to hold your charts can turn your well-rehearsed presentation into a fiasco. Even being unsure of how to work the lighting or where the closest electrical outlet can be found can interrupt the flow of a presentation.

Facilities considerations should also be made for virtual presentations. Although we are not always able to choose the platform we will be using, we should know our way around the digital environment as well as we know our way around a physical room. Facility problems can be especially troublesome in virtual settings. Poor resolution may cause difficulty for iPad or phone participants when sharing visual aids. Lack of video-sharing capabilities can cause an embarrassing blackout.

Prior to the presentation, you proactively investigate the following questions about the virtual presentation platform's capabilities: Can meetings be recorded? Does it have chat capabilities? Can participants edit documents in real-time? Will the presenter(s) and/ or participants be able to share their screens? What engagement features are active?[5]

Most experienced speakers will not settle for others' assurances about facilities; instead, they check out physical rooms and virtual software in advance and come prepared for every possible disaster.

Context   As we discussed in Chapter 1, the context of your message also influences what you say or how you say it. For example, if others are speaking as part of your program, you need to take their presentations into account. ("I had originally planned to discuss the technical aspects of our new express delivery system, but I think Ana has covered them thoroughly. So let me bring your attention to two things.") Preceding speakers may have left your audience feeling bored or stimulated, receptive or angry, thoughtful or jovial. Since that state of affairs will affect how the audience receives your presentation, you should try to adjust to it.

Current events could also affect what you say or how you say it. For example, if you are presenting your new budget proposal just after the company has suffered a major financial loss, you should be prepared to show how your budget will cut costs.

Analyzing the Audience

The saying "Different strokes for different folks" is never more true than when you are delivering a presentation. Having good ideas is not enough—you also have to present those ideas in a way that will connect with your audience. One corporate communication expert declared, "Designing a presentation without an audience in mind is like writing a love letter and addressing it 'To Whom It May Concern.' "[6]

Asking yourself a number of questions about your listeners will help you adapt your presentation material to their interests, needs, and backgrounds.

Who Are the Key Audience Members?   Not all audience members are
equally important. Sometimes one or two listeners have the power to approve or reject your appeal. For example, if you are making a sales pitch for a new database management system to a workgroup, it is important to know who has the final say. Is it the department supervisor? Is it a senior clerk whose judgment the rest of the team trusts? Whoever the decision-makers are, you need to identify their interests, needs, attitudes, and biases, and then direct your appeal toward them.

Sometimes it is easy to identify the key members. You do not have to be a communication expert to figure out that your boss has more power than the interns who are listening to your presentation. At other times, though, you will need to do some pre-speaking investigation to identify the opinion leaders and decision-makers in your audience.

How Much Do They Know?   As you may recall from Chapter 9, an internal
audience does not need the background information that a less informed external audience requires. In fact, these people would probably be bored and offended by your basic explanation. Likewise, people who are familiar with a project do not need to be updated on it—unless they have missed some late-breaking developments.

It is also important to ask yourself what your listeners do *not* know: Uninformed people or nonexperts will be mystified (as well as bored and resentful) unless you give them background information. When speaking to a mixed audience of experts and nonexperts, it is helpful to select a few key points that will help the nonexperts understand the topic without alienating the experts. You might also choose to distribute a resource to uninformed participants prior to your presentation so they can familiarize themselves with the information in advance.

What Do They Want to Know?   People will listen to you if you address *their*
interests, not yours. Your listeners' job titles can give you clues about what they want to know. On the one hand, if your audience members are specialists—in engineering, finance, or marketing, for example—they will probably be interested in the more technical aspects of your talk that pertain to their specialties. On the other hand, an audience of nonexperts would probably be bored by a detailed talk on a subject they do not understand.

Surprisingly, most managers fall into this category. "Just give me a quick description, a schedule, and the dollar figures" is a common managerial attitude.

What Are Their Personal Preferences?

Your listeners' personal idiosyncrasies can make all the difference in how your message is received. Does your audience prefer a presentation to be formal or casual? Humorous or straitlaced? Fast-paced or leisurely? Knowing these preferences can mean the difference between success and failure when you are giving a presentation. One business consultant described how attitudes can vary from one set of listeners to another:

> In the same corporation, engineers giving reports to different department heads were required to go about it in a totally different manner. One department head wanted every detail covered in the report. He wanted analyses of why the report was being done, complete background on the subject under discussion, and a review of the literature, and he expected the report to run twenty or thirty written pages. In addition, he wanted an oral presentation that covered almost every detail of the report. The man who ran the department right down the hall wanted just the opposite. He wanted short, comprehensive reports discussing only the elements that were new. He said he already knew what was going on in his department. He didn't want an analysis of the situation, and he didn't want any young engineer wasting his time . . . Therefore, the first rule for anyone giving a report is to ask those who requested the report what form they would like it to take.[7]

However, audience attitudes can be hard to anticipate. One architect described how their firm disguised the use of cost-saving technology to suit some clients' mistaken assumptions:

> When I [used to] prepare a preliminary design for a client, I often sketch[ed] a floor plan "free-hand," meaning that I quickly [drew] the design idea without a lot of detailed measurements . . . With the advent of computer-aided design (CAD), we can produce the same design on the computer . . . faster, more accurately, and at the same cost as before.[8]

Although this approach seems like a win–win scenario for the architect and the client, experience proved this was not the case.

> Some of our clients have complained that we are spending too much time and money on these preliminaries . . . they want something fast and cheap. They assume that because of how the product looks, we are spending more time (and more of their money) too early in the process. No amount of explanation will appease them.
>
> So, what to do? We just purchased a new software product . . . It takes the very accurate, crisp, straight lines of a computer design and actually makes it look hand-drawn. Now, the clients will look at a computer drawing, but see [a] hand-drawn [floor plan].[9]

Which Demographic Characteristics Are Significant?

A number of your listeners' measurable characteristics might suggest ways to tailor your remarks to that audience. The points you make, the examples you use, and even the language you speak will probably be shaped by your audience's demographic characteristics. At the most basic level, you need to be respectful of your audience. For example, when speaking to people from other countries, avoid ethnocentric remarks like "That's the way we do it back home."[10]

Cultural background is an important audience factor. While anyone can be excluded by language, this especially damaging to traditionally underrepresented groups such as

CULTURE **at work**

Using Inclusive Language

Sometimes we fail to realize the power in our words. Although the way we speak may be influenced by our upbringing and surroundings, it is important to adapt our language to be respectful to others. The following list contains words and phrases that may be used to ensure that your presentation is inclusive of all audience members:

- **Age**: Aging adult/person; elderly person; older adult/person; people over X (age); senior.
- **Class**: Economically disadvantaged; a person experiencing homelessness; a person experiencing poverty; a person living at or below the poverty line.
- **Disability**: Someone living with X; someone diagnosed with X; someone who has X.
- **Gender/Sexuality**: Assigned sex; all assembled; colleagues/workforce/everyone; they/them.
- **Race/Ethnicity**: Bi- or multi-racial individuals; international people; people or person of color.

Source: Rider University. (2021). Using inclusive language: Guidelines and examples. Retrieved from https://online.rider.edu/online-bachelors-degrees/liberal-studies/guide-to-using-inclusive-language/#:~:text=Inclusive%20language%20is%20defined%20as,or%20underprivileged%20groups%2C%20such%20as

racial and ethnic minorities, persons with disabilities, and members of the LGBTQIA+, Deaf and Hard-of-Hearing, and Autistic communities. Thus, it is important to use inclusive language when presenting ideas to an audience. Research has shown that inclusive language use boasts both personal and professional benefits. For example, one study concluded that inclusive language use boosts creativity and performance in multicultural organizations.[11]

A second demographic characteristic to consider is *age*. A life insurance salesperson might emphasize retirement benefits to older customers, but highlight support for dependent children to younger customers with families.

Another demographic factor is your audience's *economic status*. This factor is especially important in sales, where financial resources "qualify" potential customers as prospects for a product or service as well as suggest which features are likely to interest them.

Not every variable is important in planning every speech. For instance, an engineer speaking about recent advances in the field should consider the audience's level of knowledge (about engineering and those advances) and occupations (that is, what those advances have to do with listeners' work); by comparison, characteristics such as age and economic status probably would be less important. Conversely, a representative from Planned Parenthood speaking to a community organization would have to consider listeners' cultural background, age, economic status, religious background, and attitudes toward pregnancy planning and the medical profession when developing the presentation. The first step to good audience analysis is to recognize which dimensions of your listeners' background are important and to profile those dimensions accurately.

What Size Is the Group?   The number of listeners will govern some basic aspects of the presentation plan. Will you be able to see all of them on screen at the same time? How many copies of a handout should you prepare? How much time should you plan for a question-and-answer session? With a large audience, you usually need to take a wider range of audience concerns into account; your delivery and choice of language will tend to be more formal, and your listeners are less likely to interrupt with questions or comments. A progress report on your current assignment would look ridiculous if you delivered it from behind a podium to four or five people. It would be just as foolish to require audience participation during a virtual webinar that has over 100 attendees.

What Are the Listeners' Attitudes? You need to consider two sets of attitudes when planning a presentation. The first is your audience's attitude toward *you as the speaker.* If listeners feel hostile or indifferent ("Charlie is such a bore"), your approach will not be the same as the one you take if they are excited to hear from you ("I'm glad Natasha is going to discuss simplifying the paperwork").

In addition to listeners' feelings about you, the audience's attitude about *your subject* should influence your approach. Do the employees think the new pension plan benefits are too far in the future to be important? Does the sales force think the new product line is exciting or just the same old thing in a new package? Do the workers think the new vice president is a genius or just another figurehead? You should take these kinds of attitudes into account when you plan your approach.

One way to discover your audience's attitudes—and to gain the audience's approval of your idea—is to meet with listeners before your presentation. In addition to speaking directly with audiences, you often can research your audience's attitudes online. With almost instant access to a wealth of sources including news stories, blogs, social networking sites, and comments on company websites, you often can find out what your key listeners think about you and your topic before you speak to them. One trial consultant uses this approach to research potential jurors before a big case: "If a juror has an attitude about something, I want to know what that is. . . . Anyone who doesn't make use of [Internet searches] is bordering on malpractice."[12]

Eric Crama/Shutterstock

Analyzing Yourself as the Speaker

No two presentations are alike. While you can learn to be a better speaker by listening to other speakers, a good presentation is rather like a good hairstyle or a sense of humor: What suits someone else might not work for you. One of the biggest mistakes you can make is to try to be an exact copy of some other effective speaker. When developing your presentation, be sure to consider the following factors.

Your Goals The first question to ask yourself is why you are speaking. Are you especially interested in reaching one person or one subgroup in the audience? What do you want your key listeners to think or do after hearing you? How will you know if you have succeeded?

Your Knowledge It is best to speak on a subject about which you have considerable knowledge. This is usually the case, since you generally speak on a subject precisely because you *are* an authority. Regardless of how well you know your subject, you may need to do some research—sales figures over the past three years, the number of companies that have used the flexible-hours program you are proposing, the actual maintenance costs of the new equipment your company is buying, and so on.

case STUDY

Selling to Seniors

For more than 13 years, entrepreneur Tyrone M. Clark operated "Annuity University." This two-day workshop trained more than 7,000 people to sell annuities to senior citizens. In late 2002, the state of Massachusetts slapped Clark with a cease-and-desist order, alleging Clark's practices tricked seniors into trading in their investments for expensive and complicated annuity policies.

According to *The Wall Street Journal,* here are some of the practices Clark advocated:

- Oversimplifying the nature of the investments being sold. Clark says, "You'll waste time if you think you can impress them with charts, graphs, printouts, or use sophisticated words." Instead, he recommends, "Tell them it's like a CD—it's safe, it's guaranteed."

- Using fear appeals. "[Seniors] thrive on fear, anger, and greed," says Clark. "Show them their

finances are all screwed up so that they think, 'Oh, no, I've done it all wrong.'"

- Enticing retirees to attend sales seminars by offering free meals.

- Learning about investors' concerns. At seminars, seniors note their concerns from a list of topics including taxes, Social Security, insurance, and protection of assets. Salespeople are encouraged to refer to these concerns when they call customers to set up a sales appointment.

Based on the information in this chapter, make an argument about Clark's practices. Consider some ways that Clark could have effectively used audience analysis to accomplish their goals.

Source: Schultz, E. E., & Opdyke, J. D. (2002, July 2), Annuities 101: How to sell to senior citizens. *Wall Street Journal,* C1, C10; Schultz, E. E. (2002, September 26). 'Annuity University' operator is accused of running scam. *Wall Street Journal,* C3.

When leadership author Liz Wiseman was invited to give a presentation on "leadership for the future" at a business forum in Korea, she felt confident in her ability to speak about the topic. Several weeks before the forum, however, she received a briefing document that outlined the topics she was to address—most of which were about national economic policy rather than leadership. Because one of Wiseman's books had raised questions about a few economic issues, she was mistaken for an economist. Wiseman had to quickly research Korean economics and politics to prepare for the presentation.[13]

If you find yourself in a situation where you may need more information, do not lull yourself into a false sense of security by thinking you know enough. It is better to over-prepare now than to look like a fool later. In one painful episode, Kenneth Clarke, who was once Britain's finance minister, was embarrassed due to faulty knowledge. While visiting the town of Consett in northern England, Clarke praised its success as an industrial center, saying it had "one of the best steelworks in Europe." In fact, the steel mill had closed down 15 years earlier, putting 3,000 employees out of work. In an attempt to overcome that gaffe, Clarke cited another Consett factory as a major competitor in the world of disposable diapers—only to discover that the town's diaper plant had closed down two years earlier.[14]

Your Feelings about the Topic   An old sales axiom says you cannot sell a product you do not believe in. Research shows that sincerity is one of the greatest assets a speaker can have.[15] When you are excited about a topic, your delivery improves: Your voice becomes more expressive, your movements are more natural, and your face reflects your enthusiasm. In contrast, if you do not care much about your topic—whether it is a report on your department's sales, a proposal for a new program, a product you are selling, or a new method you are explaining—the audience will know it and think, "If the speaker does not believe in it, why should I?" A good test for your enthusiasm and sincerity is to ask yourself if you really care whether your audience understands or believes

Connecting with Your Audience through Storytelling

The narrative paradigm is a communication theory that contends that humans are more apt to be persuaded by a good story than by a good argument. Researchers interested in the neurobiology of storytelling have discovered that emotionally engaging stories result in an increase in oxytocin, a hormone, in our bodies. The increased oxytocin level often translates into post-narrative actions, such as donating money to a nonprofit organization after watching a particularly heart-tugging public service announcement.

As an example, the athletic wear company Under Armour (UA) was faced with a challenge: Athletic women viewed its brand as overly aggressive and performance-driven. In its #IWillWhatIWant campaign, UA responded to this challenge by telling a story of female athletes overcoming adversity and achieving success on their own terms. As a result, UA connected with women in a way that caused them to see the brand as "a brand for me," which resulted in a 28% increase in sales.

When creating a presentation, think about the message you would like your audience to take from your speech. Can you tell them a story that will sway their emotions and move them toward action?

Source: Droga5. (n.d.). I will what I want. *Jay Chiat Awards 2015*. Retrieved from https://www.aaaa.org/wp-content/uploads/legacy-pdfs/Droga5-WillWhatIWant-Gold2.pdf; Lin, P-Y., Grewal, N. S., Morin, C., Johnson, W. D., & Zak, P. J. (2013). Oxytocin increases the influence of public service announcements. *PLoS ONE, 8*(2), E56934. Retrieved from https://doi.org/10.1371/journal.pone.0056934

what you have to say. If you feel indifferent or only mildly enthusiastic, it is best to search for a new idea for your proposal or a new approach to your subject.

Your Confidence   When the demands of your job include presentational speaking, speech anxiety—or **communication apprehension**, as communication specialists call it—can jeopardize your career success.[16] If you get butterflies in your stomach at the thought of giving a speech, if your hands sweat and your mouth gets dry, if you feel faint or nauseated or have trouble thinking clearly, you might be comforted to know that most people (including famous performers, politicians, and business executives who frequently appear before audiences) experience some degree of nervousness about speaking.

Speech anxiety is common, but it can certainly lead to a lack of confidence. When you are feeling worried or doubtful about your ability to lead a successful presentation, rest assured that your anxiety is not as visible to others as you might fear. In several studies, communicators have been asked to rate their own level of anxiety.[17] At the same time, other people shared their impression of the speaker's level of nervousness. In every case, the speakers rated themselves as looking much more nervous than the observers thought they were. Even when such anxiety is noticeable, it does not result in significantly lower evaluations of the speaker's effectiveness.

More tips for boosting your confidence will be discussed in Chapter 12.

Analyzing Your Group

Group (or team) presentations are common in the business world. Sometimes the members of a group may be asked (or told) to present their information together. At other times team members choose to speak collectively, realizing that several presenters can be more effective than a single person.

Group presentations can be effective for a variety of reasons. Hearing from several speakers can provide the variety that will keep audience members tuned in. In addition, including several people's skills and perspectives can present a more complete message than any single speaker could provide. For example, a sales pitch to a potential client

A Professional Perspective

Kristen Bily

Vice President of Marketing for CoastLife Credit Union

Corpus Christi, TX

Credit: Kristen Bily

I fell in love with public relations and marketing as a college student and have been fortunate to dedicate my professional life to this work across a variety of industries, from nonprofit to entertainment to banking. My job has many different facets (which is part of what keeps life interesting!), one of which is presenting material, both written and oral. Regardless of the medium or the industry, I always ask myself a few questions to get started.

Why am I presenting? Having worked in different fields with different business cultures, my presentations might be an internal status update on the work of a nonprofit, a press conference for HBO Boxing, a launch for Selena Mac Makeup, or a report for a credit union. All these occasions require very different presentations, both in what I present and how I present it.

Related to the first question is the second: To whom am I speaking? When giving a status update at the nonprofit I used to work for, all the attendees were team members within the organization. That means that we had a common language and common reference points. I didn't need to explain certain terms or situations that would have confused someone outside of our team. On the other hand, when giving a press conference or launching a new product, I needed to assume that my audience would have varying levels of familiarity with my topic, so had to make sure I was hitting the main points clearly and not making assumptions about how much people outside the organization knew. In my current position at a large credit union, I give many internal presentations, but the culture is very different from previous jobs. Here the expectation is that I should be very structured and as brief as possible. Falling in step has allowed me to achieve success with my team and the company.

When I began my career, I occasionally worried that I would miss an important aspect of the situation or the audience and therefore would be ineffective. However, the expectation that you can know or plan for every single detail isn't realistic. I do my research, I analyze the situation and my audience, and I consider what I know and need to learn. This gives me the confidence to move forward in my work.

would probably be strengthened by the contributions of experts in marketing, customer support, and product design. Finally, team presentations can boost audience receptivity by providing a balance of gender, ethnicity, age, and other factors. Consider the following as you prepare your group presentation.

Identify Group Goals   Once your group is aware that a presentation is forthcoming, it is important to meet to consider each member's individual goals and work to identify a shared goal. As you will recall from our discussion on Effective Communication in Teams, individual goals are not always in alignment with the group's shared goal. Consider the case of a group representing an advertising agency pitching a campaign idea to a client. One group member may be secretly harboring a goal to stand out enough to land an opportunity to work with a larger account, while another is using the presentation to build a case for a promotion.

Ultimately, the success of the group depends on identifying a shared goal that everyone can support. When groups lack a shared goal, individual members have the tendency to put forth less effort than they would when working alone—a phenomenon known as **social loafing**. Psychologists have found that whether or not social loafing occurs depends on members' value of the group's goal.[18] Thus, if the group is having difficulty identifying a shared goal, it helps to develop a goal that is *audience-centered*. Perhaps, in the aforementioned case of the advertising agency pitch, the group shares a goal to entice the client to dedicate a larger budget to the agency's campaign.

Identify Individual Strengths   When developing a group presentation, it is also a good idea to talk about each other's strengths and limitations upfront. A benefit of presenting in groups is that the responsibility does not all fall on one person. Instead, each individual presenter can excel by taking roles that play to their strengths. For example, dynamic speakers may feel the most comfortable opening and closing the presentation, while logical and data-driven thinkers can tackle the main points and supporting evidence.

As a matter of fact, assigning separate and distinct contributions to each team member encourages accountability and involvement in the group.[19] When group members feel that they are being evaluated individually, they are less likely to participate in social loafing.[20]

• Setting Specific Goals and Developing a Thesis

Two essential steps in planning any presentation are to identify what you want to accomplish and the key message that you want your audience to remember after they listen to you speak. Speaking without a clear goal is a recipe for failure. As speaking coach Sandy Linver put it:

> Giving a presentation without recognizing, focusing on, and remembering your objective is the equivalent of dumping the contents of your briefcase all over your boss's desk. You don't speak to fill time by reeling off fact after unorganized fact, nor to show beautiful pictures that take the breath away, nor to impress the audience with your wit and skill as a dramatic speaker. You don't give speeches to win speech-making awards. You are there to make the best of an opportunity, just as you do in every other aspect of your business activities.[21]

Setting Specific Goals

There are two kinds of goals to consider: general and specific. As we discussed in Chapter 9, a *general goal* (sometimes called a *general purpose*) is a broad indication of what you are trying to accomplish, such as informing, persuading, or celebrating. While one type of goal may be primary, a speaker often attempts to accomplish more than one goal. For example, when commemorating the retirement of a long-time employee, a manager is celebrating the guest of honor, while also entertaining the crowd and informing them about the honoree's many accomplishments.

The **specific goal** (sometimes called the *specific purpose*) of your presentation describes the outcome you are seeking. If you think of a speech as a journey, your specific goal is your destination. Stating the specific goal tells you what you will have accomplished when you have "arrived." A good specific goal statement usually describes *who* you want to influence; *what* you want them to think or do; and *how, when,* and *where* you want them to do it. Your goal statement should combine the answers to these questions into a single statement: "I want (who) to (do what) (how, when, where)." Here are some examples of appropriate goal statements:

> "I want the people who haven't been participating in the United Way campaign to sign up."

> "I want at least five people in the audience to ask me for my business card after my talk and at least one person to schedule an appointment with me to discuss my company's services."

> "I want at least five people in the department to consider transferring to the new Fort Worth office."

> "I want the boss to tell the committee they're in favor of my proposal when they discuss it after my presentation."

Like these examples, your specific goal statements should do three things: describe the reaction or outcome you are seeking, be as specific as possible, and make your goal realistic.

Describe the Reaction You Are Seeking

Your specific goal should be worded in terms of the *desired outcome*—that is, the reaction you want from your audience. You can appreciate the importance of specifying the outcome when you consider a statement that does not meet this criterion: "I want to show each person in this office how to operate the new voicemail system correctly."

What's wrong with this statement? Most importantly, it says nothing about the desired audience response. With a goal such as this, you could give a detailed explanation of the whole system without knowing whether anyone learned a thing! Notice the improvement in the following statement: "I want everyone in this group to show me that they can operate the voicemail system correctly after my talk." With this goal, you can get an idea of how well you have done after delivering your presentation.

Be as Detailed as Possible

A good specific goal statement identifies the *who, what, how, when,* and *where* of your goal as precisely as possible. For instance, your target audience—the *who*—may not include every listener in the audience. Consider one of the specific goal statements mentioned earlier: "I want the boss to tell the committee that they're in favor of my proposal when they discuss it after my presentation." This statement correctly recognizes the boss as the key decision-maker. If you have convinced them, your proposal is as good as approved; if not, winning the support of less influential committee members may not help you. Once you identify your target audience, you can focus your energy on the people who truly count.

The best goal statements describe your goals in *measurable* terms. Consider these examples:

Vague	Measurable
I want to collect some donations in this meeting.	I want to collect **at least $15 from each person** in this meeting.
I want to get my manager's support for my idea.	I want my manager to give me **one day per week and the help of an assistant** to develop my idea.

Knowing exactly what you want to accomplish drastically increases the chances you will reach your goal. Suppose you need to convince a group of subordinates to stay within budget. You already know the following statement is not effective: "I want to talk about the importance of our new budget limitations." (If you are not sure why this goal is not effective, take another look at the preceding section on describing reactions.) A more results-oriented goal would be "I want this group to stay within budget." But even this goal statement has problems. Who are you going to encourage—people who are already holding the line on expenses or those who look like they might overspend? How many people do you hope to persuade? How will you appeal to them? When do you want them to do it, beginning immediately or when they get around to it? The latter occasion may not arise until after the fiscal year ends—too late to save this year's profits in your department.

A comprehensive specific goal statement can take care of these kinds of questions: "I want to convince the four people who had spent more than half their year's budgets by May 1 (who) that the department's solvency depends on their cutting expenses (do what) and have them show me a revised plan (how) by the end of the week (when) that demonstrates how they intend to trim costs for the rest of the year (where)." This statement gives you several ideas about how to plan your presentation. Imagine how much more difficult your task would be if you had settled for the vague goal statement.

Developing a Thesis

The **thesis statement**—sometimes called the *central idea* or *key idea*—is a single sentence that summarizes your message. Some communication coaches even advise boiling down your thesis to two words.[22] Table 10-1 offers some tips for formulating this sort of statement. Once you have a thesis, every other part of your talk should support it. The thesis gives your listeners a clear idea of what you are trying to tell them:

"We're behind schedule, but we can catch up and finish the job on time."

"The credit rating you earn now can help—or hurt—you for decades."

"Investing now in a new system will save us money in the long run."

Presentations without a clear thesis leave the audience asking, "What is this person getting at?" While listeners are trying to figure out the answer, they will be missing much of what you are saying.

The thesis is so important that you should repeat it several times during your presentation. Usually, you state your thesis at least once in the introduction, probably several times during the body, and again in the conclusion; however, there are some exceptions.

Table 10-1	Methods for Defining a Thesis Statement

1. Imagine you have met a member of your audience at the elevator and have only a few seconds to explain your idea before the doors close.

2. Imagine you have to send a one- or two-sentence e-mail that communicates your main ideas.

3. Ask yourself, if my listeners hear only a small portion of my remarks, what is the minimum they should learn?

4. Suppose someone asks one of your listeners what you said in your presentation. What would you want the audience member to tell that person?

For example, if a manager seeking acceptance of changes in staffing thinks the audience will be excited about or supportive of the changes, it makes sense to introduce the thesis early on. If, however, the audience will not be receptive, then it can be better to delay the thesis until the speaker has time to build a case for it.

Beginning speakers often confuse the thesis of a presentation with its specific goal. Whereas a specific goal statement is a note to *yourself* outlining what you hope to accomplish, a thesis statement tells your *audience* your main idea. Consider a few examples:

Specific Goal	Thesis
I want this client to advertise on our website.	Advertising on our website will boost your sales.
Workers will be able to take the steps necessary to ensure on-the-job safety.	Participating in safety training will reduce the likelihood of on-the-job incidents.
I want participating corporations to sign up for our recycling program.	Customers are more likely to do business with companies that recycle, which increases profits.

It may seem unethical to avoid mentioning your specific goal to an audience, but sometimes the omission is a matter of common sense and not deception. Real estate clients know that the listing agent wants to sell the property they are showing, but they are most interested in hearing why it is a good one. Similarly, an after-dinner speaker at a local service club might have the goal of getting the audience to relax, but sharing that goal would probably seem out of place.

Sometimes, however, hiding your goal would clearly be unethical. A speaker who began their presentation by saying, "I don't want to sell you anything; I just want to show you some aspects of home safety that every homeowner should know," and then went on to make a hard-sell pitch for their company's home fire alarms, would clearly be stepping out of bounds. It usually is unnecessary to state your goal as long as you are willing to share it with your audience, if asked. Conversely, it is rare that a speaker does not state the thesis at the beginning of a presentation.

● Organizing the Body

Inexperienced speakers often make the mistake of planning a talk by writing the introduction first. This approach is akin to trying to landscape a piece of property before you have put up a building. The body of the talk is the place to start organizing, even though it does not come first in a presentation. Organizing the body of a talk consists of two steps: identifying the key points that support your thesis and deciding which organizational plan best develops those points.

Brainstorming and Research

Once you have identified your thesis, you are ready to start gathering research to support your presentation. The first step is to pull together a list of all the information you might want to include. You will probably already have some ideas in mind, but finding other possibilities will usually require further research. For example, if your goal is to sell potential customers on your product, you will want to find out which competing products they are using and how they feel about those products. You will also want to discover whether they are familiar with your product and what attitudes they have about it. In other cases, the material you need to include might be obvious. For example, if you are giving a report on last month's sales, the bulk of your remarks might be devoted to those figures. If you are explaining how to use a new piece of equipment, the operating steps would make up the body of your talk.

Your brainstorming and research will produce a list of materials from which you will build your presentation. For example, suppose you have been asked to address a group of employees about why you want them to use Mercury Overnight for letters and packages that need to be delivered quickly. Based on your research on Mercury Overnight, you might make up a list that looks something like the one in Figure 10.2.

- Mercury Overnight will pick up the package at your office instead of you having to go through the mailroom.
- It will also deliver right to your office if the label is marked properly, so you don't have to wait for the mailroom to process and deliver it to you.
- When we experimented with different delivery services, Mercury delivered every single package we gave it within 24 hours.
- Some of the companies we tried took 2 days or more about 25 percent of the time.
- One company we tried got the package in on time about 90 percent of the time.
- Other companies we've tried have held up packages for as much as a week for no good reason.
- Mercury will deliver into the rural areas where many of our customers are, while some of the other companies only deliver in the urban areas.
- Mercury will bill the departmental accounts, saving bookkeeping time.
- Some companies charge a lot of extra money for the odd-sized packages we send sometimes, but Mercury just charges by weight.
- Because we can't always count on overnight delivery with the delivery service we're using now, we often have to take time off to run a package across town.
- Mercury charges less than its competitors for heavy packages.
- If we send several things at once to the same place, Mercury will give us a lower "group rate."
- Mercury will come out at any time to pick up a package.
- Other companies will only make a regular daily stop, which doesn't do you much good if your package isn't ready when they come.
- Mercury will make pickups from 7 in the morning until midnight, which is nice if you're working early or late.
- If you send the package through the post office and don't put enough postage on it, the post office sends it back and the package won't get there in time.
- The packages that we've sent through some other shippers sometimes get so badly damaged that the contents have to be replaced. The shipper will pay for the contents if you insure the package, but that doesn't get it there on time.
- Sometimes you have to ship a one-of-a-kind item, like a prototype for an advertisement, and if it gets lost or damaged it can take weeks to make a new one.
- Mercury's best shipping fee includes insurance.
- It isn't easy to figure out which delivery service is best.
- When the company was smaller, we used to just send things by mail.
- We researched the idea of setting up our own delivery service, but management vetoed it because it cost too much.

FIGURE 10.2 Selling Points Produced by a Brainstorming Session

Notice that this list is just a random assortment of points. In fact, your own collection of ideas does not need to be neatly typed on a single piece of paper. More likely it will be scribbled on an assortment of index cards and note pads, or entered in an app on your phone.

Identifying Main Points and Subpoints

The list of ideas you have compiled through brainstorming and research probably contains more material than you will be able to use in your talk. Thus, the next step is to identify which key points best support your thesis and will help you achieve your specific goal. Your analysis of the speaking situation will also help you to recognize your main points.

On the basis of this analysis, you might decide there are three primary reasons why listeners might sign up to use Mercury Overnight:

1. Mercury Overnight is more reliable.
2. Mercury Overnight is more convenient.
3. Mercury Overnight is more economical.

None of these main points appears on the brainstorming list in Figure 10.2; instead, they emerge as themes from that list. Each of the points that did appear on that list will fit into one of these categories, so the speech can be organized around these three points.

How do you identify your main points? One strategy is to apply the "one-week-later" test: Ask yourself which main points you want the audience to remember one week after the presentation. Since most listeners will recall only a few ideas, logically you should emphasize your one-week-later points during your talk.

The basic ideas that grow out of your audience analysis or brainstorming list might work well as the main points of your talk, but that is not always the case. As with the Mercury Overnight delivery service example, there may be better ways to organize your material. Before you make your final decision about the structure of your talk, you need to think about the different ways the body of a presentation can be organized.

Once you have identified the main points for your presentation, you can fill in your plan with the subpoints that expand on each of them. These subpoints can be added to a standard outline like the one in Figure 10.3.

A more visual way to represent the relationships among the thesis, main points, and subpoints is to draw a logic tree like the one in Figure 10.4.[23]

Rules for Main Points

Your main points should always meet the following criteria.

Main Points Should Be Stated as Claims   A **claim** is a statement asserting a fact or belief. If you state your claims in full, grammatical sentences, they will probably satisfy the one-week-later test and be remembered by your listeners. Notice how describing main points as claims in complete sentences is clearer and far more effective than using simple three- or four-word fragments.

Fragment	Claim
Choosing a physician	It is essential to choose a health care provider from the list of approved doctors.
Sexual and ethnic discrimination	Allowing sexual or ethnic considerations to intrude into our hiring decisions is not just bad judgment, it is also illegal.
Demographic changes in the market	Due to demographic changes, we can expect our market to shrink in the next 10 years.

Purpose: After hearing this talk, the prospective customer will sign up to
            use Mercury as its exclusive overnight delivery service.

Thesis: Mercury is the best service to deliver your high-priority packages
            on time.

INTRODUCTION
   A. Overnight delivery services aren't cheap, but they are worth the expense
      if they do the job of getting important materials into the right hands
      quickly. [*Attention-getter*]
   B. After comparing Mercury with the other delivery services, you'll see
      that it is the best one to do the job. [*Thesis*]
   C. As I'll explain in the next few minutes, Mercury is more reliable,
      convenient, and economical than the competition. [*Preview*]

Transition: Let me start by explaining why Mercury is best with the most
            important feature of any delivery service: reliability.

BODY
   I. Mercury is more reliable than other services.
      A. Mercury's 98 percent trouble-free record beats every other service.
      B. Other services have held up deliveries for as much as 1 week.
      C. Other services have damaged packages.
      D. In some cases, other services have even lost packages.

Transition: Besides being reliable, Mercury is the best service in another
            important way ...
   II. Mercury is more convenient than other services.
      A. Mercury picks up and delivers items to individual offices, not just
         to the mailroom like ABC Overnight.
      B. Mercury picks up or delivers packages any time between 7:00 A.M. and
         midnight, instead of only coming by once a day like International
         Air Freight.
      C. Mercury is the only service that will bill departmental accounts
         separately, saving you bookkeeping time.

Transition: Because it's so convenient and reliable, you might think that
            Mercury is more expensive than other services, but it's not.
   III. Mercury is more economical than other services.
      A. It doesn't charge extra for oddly shaped packages.
      B. It charges less than every other service for heavy packages.
      C. The shipping fee includes insurance.

Transition: By now you can see why it's worth considering Mercury as the
            provider of your overnight mail service ...

CONCLUSION
   A. Mercury is reliable, convenient, and economical. [*Thesis/Review*].
   B. With Mercury you won't just pay for the best service ... you'll get it.

FIGURE 10.3 A Complete Presentation Outline

FIGURE 10.4
A Logic Tree Illustrates the Relationship between the Thesis, Main Points, and Subpoints in a Presentation

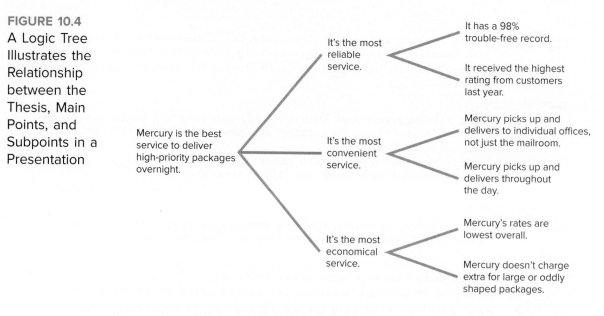

All Points Should Develop the Thesis
Consider the main points supporting the following thesis statement:

Thesis: Allowing employees more latitude in choosing their work hours is good for the company and for the workers.

1. Flexible scheduling can work in several ways.
2. Flexible scheduling improves morale.
3. Flexible scheduling reduces absenteeism.

The first point may be true but does not say anything about flexible scheduling's value (thesis). For this reason, it should be replaced.

A Presentation Should Contain No More Than Five Main Points
Your main points are what you want your listeners to remember, but the reality is that people have difficulty recalling more than five pieces of information presented orally.[24] For that reason, it is imperative that your presentation contain no more than five main points. Adhering to this limit requires some discipline. Consider the advice of David Dempsey, a trial attorney and professor of public speaking at Oglethorpe University in Atlanta, about the need to ruthlessly edit your ideas:

> Make three points that stick, rather than 10 quick points that leave no lasting impression. Constantly ask yourself, "Is this the most important issue, the best example, the most compelling way to illustrate my point?"[25]

Even when you have a large amount of material, it is usually possible to organize it into five or fewer categories. For example, if you were preparing an analysis of ways to lower operating expenses in your organization, your brainstorming list might include these ideas:

- Reduce wattage in lighting fixtures
- Hire an outside data processing firm to handle seasonal billing rather than expand the permanent in-house staff
- Sell surplus equipment
- Reduce nonbusiness use of copying machines

- Reduce the temperature in less-used parts of the building
- Pay overtime rather than add new employees
- Retrofit old equipment instead of buying new machinery

Your outline could consolidate this list into three main points:

Thesis: We can reduce operating costs in three areas: energy, personnel, and equipment.

1. We can reduce our energy costs.
    A. Reduce wattage in lighting fixtures
    B. Reduce the temperature in less-used parts of the building
2. We can reduce money spent on new personnel.
    A. Hire an outside data processing firm for seasonal billing
    B. Encourage overtime instead of adding employees
3. We can reduce our purchase and maintenance costs for equipment.
    A. Retrofit old equipment
    B. Sell surplus equipment
    C. Reduce personal use of copying machines

This outline contains all the items in your list, but organizing them into three broad categories makes your presentation much easier to comprehend than a seven-point presentation.

Main Points Should Be Parallel in Structure Whenever Possible
Parallel wording can be used to dramatize your points and make them more memorable. Consider how the repetition of "We can reduce . . ." in the preceding outline helps drive the point home far more forcefully than does the following, less effective wording of the main points:

1. Managing energy costs can save us money.
2. Careful hiring practices will reduce overhead.
3. Equipment purchase and maintenance are controllable costs.

You will not always be able to state your main points using parallel construction, but a review of many of the examples in this chapter shows that this pattern is often feasible.

Each Main Point Should Contain Only One Idea   Combining ideas or
overlapping them will confuse audiences. Consider this example:

Thesis: Many local businesses boost their effectiveness and serve their communities by seeking a diverse workforce.

1. Employees from diverse ethnic backgrounds can reach multiple audiences.
2. Employees with disabilities can function as effectively as other workers.
3. Age diversity provides a variety of points of view that can help sales, marketing, and operations.

Choosing the Best Organizational Pattern

Once you have developed your main points and identified supporting subpoints, you are ready to organize them in a clear form that will help you achieve your speaking goal. Most people will agree that clarity is important, but few realize precisely how critical it is. A substantial body of research indicates that organizing your remarks clearly can make your messages more understandable, keep your audience happy, and boost your image as a speaker.[26] Despite the benefits of good organization, most presentations suffer from a variety of problems in this area:

- Taking too long to get to the point
- Including irrelevant material
- Leaving out necessary information
- Getting ideas mixed up[27]

Problems such as these can lead to organizational chaos. The key to keeping your talk from turning into a meaningless stream of ideas is to organize your ideas before speaking. No matter what the subject or goal, most effective presentations follow a well-known pattern: First, tell them what you're going to tell them; then, tell them; then, tell them what you told them. More formally, the format looks like this:

Introduction

- Attention-getter
- Thesis
- Preview

Body (two to five main points)

1.
2.
3.
4.
5.

Conclusion

- Review of main point
- Closing statement

Of course, this linear, logical approach to organization is not the only way to structure a presentation. In fact, researchers have found that this strategy works best with Euro-American audiences or listeners who are receptive to Euro-American cultural standards. Listeners from other backgrounds may prefer less linear patterns, which have been given labels including "star," "wave," and "spiral."[28] Despite the value of these patterns in certain situations, the standard format is probably the safest approach with most business audiences who are part of Euro-American culture.

There are many ways to organize the body of a presentation. Some structures work best for fundamentally informative subjects, whereas others are more effective when you want to persuade your listeners. You should choose the organizational pattern that best develops your thesis, thereby helping you achieve your goal.

Chronological   A **chronological pattern** arranges your points according to their sequence in time. You can use this structure to explain a process, such as the steps in putting an order through the order fulfillment and shipping departments or the schedule for developing a new product. One of its most common uses is to give instructions:

Thesis: Downloading the software program is easy.

1. Click *Manual Download.*
2. When the *File Download* box appears, choose a folder location.
3. Close all applications, including your web browser.
4. Double-click on the saved file icon to start the installation process.

Chronological patterns are also useful for discussing events that develop over time:

Thesis: We need to stay on schedule if we are to get the catalog out in time for the holidays.

1. A product list must be ready by March 1.
2. Photography and catalog copy have to be completed by May 6.
3. Page proofs have to be read and corrected by July 30.
4. Final proofs have to be reviewed by department heads by August 30.
5. Catalogs have to be shipped no later than October 5.

In addition, chronological patterns may be used for discussing history:

Thesis: A review of the past five years shows we have been moving toward empowering our entire workforce to make decisions.

1. Five years ago, management introduced the Employee Advisory Council.
2. Four years ago, we started project teams with people from every division.
3. Two years ago, the company started allowing department supervisors to approve purchases.
4. Over the past year, the company has made changes in its billing process.

Spatial   A **spatial pattern** organizes material according to its relationships or physical location. You might use a spatial pattern to show the parts in a model for a new product; the location of various departments in your building; or the safety requirements of a piece of equipment, such as where safety shields should be placed, and so on. A real estate agent might try to persuade potential buyers with a spatially organized presentation like this:

Thesis: This home provides all the space you need.

1. The main floor is spacious, with a large living room, a formal dining room, and an eat-in kitchen.
2. The second floor has enough bedrooms for every member of the family, plus a private study.
3. The basement has a finished playroom for the children and a utility room.
4. The yard has large trees and lots of space for a garden.

You can also show the subject's geographical nature by citing examples from many places:

Thesis: Business is better in some areas than in others.

1. Northeast regional sales are 50% ahead of last year's sales.
2. Mid-Atlantic regional sales are 10% ahead of last year's sales.
3. Southern regional sales are about the same as last year's sales.
4. Midwest regional sales are down about 25% from last year's sales.

Topical

Topical A **topical pattern** groups your ideas around some logical themes or divisions in your subject. For example, you might organize a proposal for simplifying the expense-accounting procedures around the reasons for the change or a sales presentation for photocopiers around the three major types of copiers you think a customer might be interested in. An accountant might organize a proposal for a new inventory system this way:

Thesis: A just-in-time inventory system has three major benefits.

1. It eliminates excess inventory that may result from long-term ordering.
2. It cuts down on waste resulting from supplies becoming outdated or shopworn.
3. It saves on storage and computer records costs.

The topical approach is sometimes termed a *catch-all approach* because people occasionally describe a list of points as "topical" if they cannot think of another pattern that fits the structure. Of course, a jumbled list of ideas does not automatically become organized just because you call it topical. With a genuine topical approach, elements are logically related according to some scheme an audience can easily recognize.

Organizing by topic is especially useful during group presentations where different parts of the material call for special expertise. For example, a press conference in which county department heads announce new approaches to cost-cutting almost demands that each person present their department's information separately. Likewise, a sales presentation would profit from topics such as customer support, engineering, and production being covered by representatives from each of those departments.

Cause–Effect

Cause–Effect A **cause–effect pattern** shows that certain events have happened or will happen as a result of certain circumstances. For example, you might show prospective life insurance customers how certain clauses will provide extra coverage if they are hospitalized or demonstrate how a new advertising program will help a product reach a wider market. You might also use this pattern to demonstrate how certain circumstances are creating a problem:

Thesis: Redecorating the offices before raising salaries *[cause]* will damage morale and affect productivity *[effect]*.

1. When employees see the offices being redecorated and realize they have not received a cost-of-living raise over the past year, they will be discouraged.
2. Discouraged employees are not as likely to give the company their best efforts during the upcoming season.

An alternative form of the cause–effect structure is an *effect–cause* structure. When you use this structure, you focus more on results. In other words, you begin with the result and describe how it came to pass or how you think it can be made to happen. For example, you might use an effect–cause pattern to explain why a company has a strict policy about absenteeism or to explain how you expect to accomplish a sales goal you have set. This pattern may also be used to explain how a problem has been created:

Thesis: The decline in our profits *[effect]* is the result of several problems *[cause]*.

1. Our profits have decreased 15%.
2. Several factors are responsible.
   A. Our competitors are offering better service at lower prices.
   B. Our maintenance costs have nearly doubled.
   C. Our advertising is not effective.

Table 10-2	Presentation Goals and Their Corresponding Organizational Patterns	
	Informative	**Persuasive**
	Chronological	Problem–solution
	Spatial	Criteria satisfaction
	Topical	Comparative advantages
	Cause–effect	Motivated sequence

As Table 10-2 shows, chronological, spatial, topical, and cause-effect plans are best suited to informative presentations.

Problem–Solution   A **problem–solution pattern** is the simplest persuasive scheme. As its name suggests, you begin by showing the audience something is wrong with the present situation and then suggest how to remedy it.

This pattern works especially well when your audience does not feel a strong need to change from the status quo. Because listeners must recognize a problem exists before they will be interested in a solution, showing them that the present situation is not satisfactory is essential before you introduce your idea. For example:

Thesis: Establishing a system of employee incentives can boost productivity.

  1. Our level of productivity has been flat for two years, but the industry-wide rate has climbed steadily in that period. *[problem]*

  2. Establishing an incentive system will give employees a reason to work harder. *[solution]*

A problem-solution pattern might also be used to show how updating a computer system will solve problems with inventory monitoring, why a potential customer needs a personal financial advisor, or why a department needs additional staff.

The problem-solution approach can be effective, but it is not the best strategy for every persuasive situation. If your listeners already recognize a problem exists, you may not need to spend much time proving the obvious. In such circumstances, you might do better to use one of the following three strategies.

Criteria Satisfaction   A **criteria satisfaction** organizational strategy sets up criteria that the audience will accept and then shows how your idea or product meets those criteria.

A venture capitalist used a criteria satisfaction plan when seeking investors for a business project. Notice how they introduced each criterion and then showed how their project would satisfy it:

Thesis: Like any investment, this project needs to be based on the sound foundation of a solid business plan, a talented management team, and adequate financing.

  1. The first criterion is that the business plan must be solid. Extensive market research shows the need for this product.

  2. The second criterion is a talented management team. Let me introduce the key members of this management team and describe their qualifications. . . .

3. The third criterion is a solid, realistic financial plan. The following plan is very conservative, yet shows strong potential for a substantial profit. . . .

A somewhat different approach is to present all the criteria first and then introduce your proposal. The strategy, in this case, is to first gain the audience's acceptance and boost your credibility; then, having accomplished this aim, you show how your plan meets the criteria presented. With this approach, the thesis is deferred—which is especially smart when the audience may not be inclined to accept it without some powerful arguments.

In the next example, a manager used a criteria satisfaction plan with a deferred thesis to announce a wage freeze to employees—hardly a popular idea. If they had announced their thesis first ("A wage freeze is in your best interest"), the employees probably would have been too upset to listen thoughtfully to the arguments. By leading the audience through the reasons leading up to the freeze, the manager increased the chances that the employees would understand the company's reasoning. Notice how the thesis is first presented in the middle of the main points and then restated in the conclusion:

1. There are three important criteria for selecting a policy. *[introduces criteria first]*

   A. It should be fair.

   B. It should cause the least harm to employees.

   C. It should allow the company to survive this difficult period without suffering permanent damage.

2. A wage freeze is the best plan to satisfy these criteria. *[satisfaction of criteria; thesis]*

   A. It is fair.

   B. It causes minimal harm to employees.

   C. It will enable the company to survive.

Conclusion/Thesis: A wage freeze is the best plan at this difficult time.

Comparative Advantages

A **comparative advantages** organizational plan puts several alternatives side by side and then shows why your preferred option is the best. This strategy is especially useful when the audience is considering an idea that competes with the one you are advocating. In many such cases, offering a head-on comparison that supports your case is far more effective than ignoring alternative plans. In the next example, a purchasing agent made a case to their boss for leasing office equipment instead of borrowing to buy it outright:

Thesis: When we remodel the offices, we can use our budget far more efficiently by leasing equipment and furnishings instead of buying them.

1. Our up-front costs will be dramatically lower because there is no down payment.

2. The application process will be easier. To qualify for a loan, we have to give the bank two to three years of financial records. A lease requires us to furnish only six months of records.

3. We can keep pace with technology. Short-term leases will cost us less than buying new equipment every few years. We could not afford to do that if we buy equipment outright.

4. We can buy more. Because lease costs are lower, we can get better-quality equipment that will improve our productivity.

Motivated Sequence   The **motivated sequence** organizational plan is a five-step scheme designed to boost the audience's involvement and interest.[29] Regardless of the topic, the sequence of steps in this structure is the same:

1. *Attention.* Capture the audience's attention by introducing the problem in an interesting manner. (This attention-getter functions as an introduction.)

2. *Need.* Explain the problem clearly and completely. Use a variety of supporting materials to back up your claim, proving the problem is serious. Ideally, make your listeners feel the problem affects them in some way. Make them eager to hear a solution.

3. *Satisfaction.* Present your solution to the problem. Provide enough support to prove that the solution is workable and that it will, indeed, solve the problem.

4. *Visualization.* Describe clearly what will happen if your proposal is adopted so the audience has a clear mental picture of how your proposal will solve the problem. You might also describe what will happen if your proposal is *not* adopted. In either case, the key to success in this step is to paint a vivid picture of the outcomes, showing how your proposal will make a real difference.

5. *Action.* Call for a response from your audience. Explain what listeners can do to solve the problem. (This call to action functions as the conclusion.)

The motivated sequence plan provides a step-by-step approach for organizing a speech. It builds on the basic problem–solution plan: Step 1 arouses listeners' interest so they will be more receptive to the topic. Step 4 goes beyond simply providing a solution and helps the audience picture what kind of a difference it will make. Step 5 guides the audience on how to bring the solution to fruition, making it easier for listeners to take the necessary steps and rousing them to act.

Unlike most presentation patterns, the motivated sequence plan usually does not require a preview in the opening of your remarks. At first glance, this approach seems to depart from the basic introduction–body–conclusion pattern of organizing a presentation. A closer look, however, reveals that the plan does follow the same pattern:

Introduction

- Attention

Body

1. Need
2. Satisfaction
3. Visualization

Conclusion

- Action

The motivated sequence approach works best when the problem you present and the solution you propose are easy to visualize. If your listeners can imagine the problem and see themselves solving it by following your plan, then they will be motivated to accept your reasoning. Because the motivated sequence approach closes with an appeal to action, it is especially well suited to achieving an immediate response to your proposal. Recognizing this fact, a fund-raiser used it to generate pledges for an urgent appeal:

[Attention]   Here's a picture of the Myer family. Ted, the dad, is a trained stonemason and proud of it. Anne, the mom, is a registered nurse. Little Chris loves baseball and pizza. His teachers say he has a gift for math and languages.

[Need]   Since this photo was taken, the Myers have had a run of terrible luck. Last year, Ted fell at work and wrenched his back. He's been unable to work ever since, and his disability insurance has almost run out. Three months after Ted's accident, Anne was diagnosed with leukemia. She's undergoing treatment, and the doctors are optimistic. But she can't work now, and there's no telling when she will be able to return to her job. The Myers lived on their savings for six months, but now all the money is gone. Last week they had to move out of their apartment, and they have nowhere else to go. Nowhere, that is, except Transition House.

[Satisfaction]   You can help provide temporary housing for the Myers and other neighbors who are in trouble by contributing to Transition House. Your donations will give them a safe place to stay while they get back on their feet.

[Visualization]   We're hoping to raise enough money tonight to give the Myer family a month at Transition House. During that time, Ted can finish training for a new career as a bookkeeper and get back to work. He hopes to become a CPA. Once he's on the job, the Myers will be able to find a new apartment so Anne can fight for her health and Chris can stay in his same school, where he's doing so well.

[Action]   What we need from you tonight is a donation. We're asking for anything you can afford: the price of an evening on the town or maybe a postponement of that new outfit you were thinking of buying. In just a moment, I'll be passing out pledge cards. . . .

• Developing Introductions, Conclusions, and Transitions

The body of a presentation is important, but the introduction that precedes it needs just as much attention, as does your conclusion and the transitions that carry you smoothly between speech sections and main points. These topics are discussed next.

Functions of Introductions

Your introduction should take between 10% and 15% of the speaking time. During this short time—less than 1 minute of a 5-minute talk—your listeners form their initial impression of you and your topic. That impression, favorable or not, will affect how they react to the rest of your remarks. That is why, in group presentation situations, introductions are often delegated to a single member with a dynamic speaking style.

Whether a talk is delivered by an individual presenter or a group, its introduction should have three parts: an opening statement, a thesis statement, and a preview of the main points of your presentation. These three parts should accomplish five things.

Capture the Listeners' Attention
As you learned in Chapter 3, audiences do not always approach a presentation in a state where they are ready to listen. Sometimes the topic may not seem important or interesting to them. Sometimes the listeners may have been required to attend your presentation, rather than coming willingly. Even when the presentation is obviously important, your listeners will usually have other matters on

their minds. If there is any chance the listeners' minds are elsewhere, it is vital to begin by focusing their attention on you and your topic.

Give Your Audience a Reason to Listen

The best way to grasp and hold your listeners' attention is to convince them that your message will be important or interesting to them. For example, if company employees are generally satisfied with the insurance program the company has been using, they will not be interested in hearing about a new health plan that will be cheaper for the company unless you begin by enumerating its advantages to them—for instance, by explaining that the new plan will provide them with better emergency services. Similarly, management will be more interested in hearing your new ideas if you first say that the plans you are proposing will yield higher profits.

Set the Proper Tone for the Topic and Setting

If you want potential customers to buy more fire insurance, your opening remarks should prepare them to think seriously about the problems they would encounter if they had a fire in their home. If you want to congratulate your subordinates on their recent performance and encourage them to perform even better on the next assignment, your opening remarks should put them in a good mood—not focus on the problems you must face. In any case, your introduction should establish rapport with your listeners.

Establish Your Qualifications

If the audience already knows you are an expert on the subject, if a previous speaker has given you an impressive introduction, or if your authority makes it clear you are qualified to talk, establishing credibility is not necessary. In other cases, however, you need to demonstrate your competence quickly so the listeners will take your remarks seriously. Nonverbal behaviors can also help boost (or diminish) your credibility. Recall the information on nonverbal communication provided in Chapter 4, and see additional advice on building credibility through nonverbal behavior in Chapters 11 and 12.

Introduce Your Thesis and Preview Your Presentation

In most cases, you need to state your main idea clearly at the beginning of your remarks so your listeners will know exactly what you are trying to say. In addition to giving your thesis statement, a preview of your main points tells your listeners where you are headed.

Accomplishing these five goals in less than 1 minute is not as difficult as it might seem, because you can accomplish several functions at the same time. For example, notice how an insurance agent introduced a 30-minute talk on an admittedly difficult topic:

> Being an insurance agent gives me a lot of sympathy for tax collectors and dog catchers. None of us has an especially popular job. After all, it seems that with life insurance you lose either way: On the one hand, if the policy pays off, you won't be around to enjoy the money. On the other hand, if you don't need the policy, you've spent your hard-earned savings for nothing. Besides, insurance isn't cheap. I'm sure you have plenty of other things you could use your money for: catching up on bills, fixing up your house, buying a new car, or even taking a vacation.
>
> With all those negatives, why should you care about insurance? For that matter, why am I devoting my career to it? For me, the answer is easy: Over the years, I've seen literally hundreds of people—people just like you and me—learn what a difference the right kind of insurance coverage can make. And I've seen hundreds more suffer from learning too late that insurance is necessary.

Well, tonight I want to give you some good news. I'll show you that you can win by buying insurance. You can win by gaining peace of mind, and you can even win by buying insurance that works like an investment, paying dividends that you can use here and now.

Types of Opening Statements

Of all parts of a presentation, the opening words—which typically function to capture the attention of your audience—are the hardest to choose for many speakers. To gain your audience's attention, you have to be interesting, you have to establish the right tone, and your remarks have to relate to the topic at hand. At the same time, the opening statement has to feel right for you—it has to match your own personal style.

The type of opening you choose will depend on your analysis of the speaking situation. With familiar topics and audiences, you may even decide to skip the preliminaries and give just a brief bit of background before launching into the thesis and preview:

"We've made good progress on Mr. Boynton's request to look into cost-cutting steps. We've found it is possible to reduce operating expenses by almost 10% without cutting efficiency. We'll be introducing six steps to accomplish that goal this morning."

In most cases, you will want to preface your remarks with an opening statement. Following are seven of the most common and effective ways to begin a presentation.

Ask a Question   Asking a question that is relevant to your topic is a good way to involve your listeners and establish its importance to them.

Many speakers try to capture attention by asking the audience a **rhetorical question**—one that requires listeners to think but does not call for a verbal response. For example, the head of a team of video console developers might ask, "Why do you think the competition is appealing to our customers?" Rhetorical questions work well when the questioner already knows the answer to the question and can expect the audience to know the answer, too.

When used poorly, rhetorical questions can be risky. Beware of asking questions that listeners will not care about: "Have you ever wondered what the Sherman Antitrust Act means to you?" Other rhetorical questions can be so thought-provoking that your audience will stop listening to you: "If you had to fire three of the people who report to you, how would you decide which ones to let go?" When you decide to begin with a rhetorical question, be sure to avoid mistakes like these.

Other questions call for an overt response: "How many people here are from out of state?" "Who has had trouble meeting deadlines for sales reports?" "What do you see as the biggest threat facing the company?" If you *are* seeking an overt reaction from your listeners, be sure to let them know: "Let me see a show of hands by the people who . . ." "Hold up your program if you're among those who . . ." If you want them to respond mentally, let them know: "Answer this question for yourself: Are you sure all of your expense reports would pass an Internal Revenue Service audit?"

Tell a Story   Because most people enjoy a good story, beginning with one can be an effective way to get the audience's attention, set the tone, and lead into the topic. When opening with a story, two important guidelines should be followed.

First, *keep it brief.* Remember, an introduction should take no more than 15% of your total speaking time—which means the story has to be even shorter. Second, *establish a clear connection between the story and your topic.* Even though the connection may be clear to you, make sure you explain to your listeners why your story is relevant.

Africa Studio/Shutterstock

Present a Quotation
Quotations have two advantages: First, someone else has probably already said what you want to say in a clever way. Second, quotations let you use a source with high credibility to back up your message.

Not every quotation has to come from a distinguished person. As long as the individual whom you quote is appropriate for the audience and the topic, they can be almost anyone—even a fictional character:

> "The comic strip character Pogo once said, 'We have met the enemy, and he is us.' If you think about all the paperwork that keeps us from being more productive, that comment could describe us."

Make a Startling Statement
An excellent way to get listeners' attention is to surprise them. Sales presentations often include startling facts in their openings: "Do you know that half of all business calls never reach the intended party?" This approach will work only if your startling statement bears a clear relationship to your topic. Social networking executive Pamela Meyer used this approach in a speech about the prevalence of deception in everyday life:

> It's just come to my attention that the person to your right is a liar. Also, the person to your left is a liar. Also, the person sitting in your very seat is a liar. We're all liars.[30]

Refer to the Audience
Mentioning your listeners' needs, concerns, or interests clarifies the relevance of your topic immediately and shows you understand your listeners. Consider this example: "I know you're all worried by rumors of cutbacks in staff. I called you here today to explain just what the budget cuts will mean to this department."

Former California governor George Deukmejian used the technique of referring to the audience in a talk to the Los Angeles Rotary Club. Deukmejian acknowledged the fact that people who listen to after-lunch speakers—even famous ones—appreciate brevity:

> I promise not to speak for too long this afternoon. It's worth noting that the Lord's Prayer is only 56 words long. The Gettysburg Address is 226. The Ten Commandments are 297. But the U.S. Department of Agriculture's order on the price of cabbage is 15,269 words. I'll try to finish somewhere in between.[31]

Refer to the Occasion
Sometimes the event itself provides a good starting point: "We're here today to recognize some very important people." At other times you can begin by referring to some other aspect of the situation—for example, by relating your remarks to those of a previous speaker: "I was interested in what Larry had to say about the way our expenses will rise in the next couple of years. Let's look at one way we can keep that increase as small as possible."

In a speech to employees at the U.S. Department of Justice, former U.S. attorney general Eric Holder referred to the occasion that prompted his remarks: "Every year, in

February, we attempt to recognize and to appreciate Black history. It is a worthwhile endeavor, for the contributions of African Americans to this great nation are numerous and significant."[32]

By referring to the occasion of Black History Month, Holder prepared his audience for the message that Americans reach out to those from different racial backgrounds:

> Black History Month is a perfect vehicle for the beginnings of such a dialogue. And so I urge all of you to use the opportunity of this month to talk with your friends and coworkers on the other side of the divide about racial matters. In this way we can hasten the day when we truly become one America.[33]

Use Humor   A joke can be an effective way to get attention, make a point, and increase your audience's liking for you. However, jokes are not the only kind of humorous opener. Sometimes you can make an amusing remark that will set the tone perfectly for your message. For instance:

> Some people say that problems are not problems, but rather . . . are opportunities. If that's the case, then given the present situation, we are faced with a hell of a lot of opportunities.[34]

Any humor you use should be appropriate to your topic and to the occasion. Telling a few knock-knock jokes before you launch into your financial report will draw attention—but not to your topic. The tone of your presentation could be ruined by a joke. For instance, you probably should not tell a few jokes about smog and then say, "But seriously, folks, I want to talk about what we're doing to curb air pollution from our own factories."

Your jokes should also be appropriate for your audience. The inside jokes that work well with your office staff, for example, are likely to alienate clients at a contract negotiation because outsiders will not understand them. Jokes that are crude or in any way make light of sexism, racism, or disabilities are likely to offend or embarrass someone in your audience. The risks of telling such jokes are not worth the laughs they might generate.

Think twice about using humor cross-culturally, because jokes rarely translate well. Not everyone will have the advantage that former U.S. president Carter recounted about telling a joke during a speech in Japan: "I told my joke, and then the interpreter gave it and the audience collapsed in laughter. It was the best response I have ever had to a joke in my life."

When Carter asked his translator to explain the words he used when repeating the joke in Japanese, he got an evasive response. When the president insisted on knowing, the translator explained: "I told the audience, 'President Carter told a funny story. Everyone must laugh.'"[35]

Functions of Conclusions

With the end of your presentation in sight, it can be tempting to wrap things up with a vague comment such as "That's about it." Resist this temptation to close quickly and weakly: Experts agree your final words may create a lasting impression.[36] The conclusion of your presentation should be even shorter than the introduction—not much more than 5% of your total speaking time.

When speaking as a group, the group's spokesperson or the final speaker may deliver the conclusion; however, they must be careful not to simply review the most recent remarks.

Rather, within those last few moments, two important things must be accomplished by individual and group presenters: review and close.

The Review Your review should contain a restatement of your thesis and a summary of your main points. Sometimes these two elements will be presented almost exactly as they appear on your outline:

PeopleImages.com/Digital Vision/Getty Images

> "This afternoon, I've suggested that our merchandising approach needs changing to become more profitable. I've suggested three such changes: first, to increase our social media advertising; second, to feature higher-quality merchandise; and third, to expand our product line in all areas."

Your review can also be a subtler rewording of the same information:

> "By now I hope you agree with me that some basic merchandising changes can improve our balance sheet. When people find out we have a broad range of high-quality products, I'm convinced we'll have more customers who will spend more money."

The Closing Statement A strong closing will help your listeners to remember you favorably; conversely, a weak ending can nullify many of your previous gains. In addition to creating a favorable impression, the closing statement should give your remarks a sense of completion. You should not leave your audience wondering whether you have finished. Finally, a closing statement ought to incite your listeners, encouraging them to act or think in a way that accomplishes your purpose. Several varieties of closing statements are discussed in the following section.

Types of Closing Statements

Several of the techniques used to capture your audience's attention in the introduction will also work well as closing statements: ask a question, tell a story, give a quotation, make a startling statement, refer to the audience, refer to the occasion, or use humor. In addition, you might use several other types of closing statements.

Return to the Theme of Your Opening Statement Coming back to where you started gives a sense of completeness to your presentation. With this approach, you should refer to your opening statement but add new insight, further details, or a different ending:

> "At the beginning of my talk, I asked whether you might not be paying more tax than you need to. I suspect you discovered you've been overly generous with Uncle Sam. I hope I have helped you to understand your real liability and to take advantage of some of the tax shelters available to you."

Another way to capture your audience's attention is to split your story. Start but do not finish it in your introduction. Cut off your narrative at a key point, perhaps just before the climactic finish, promising your audience you will wrap it up in the course of your remarks. Then, follow up with the ending to the story in the closing statement.

Appeal for Action

When your goal involves getting the audience members to act in a certain way, you can sometimes close your presentation by asking for your desired result:

> "So now that you know what these workshops can do, the only question is when you ought to enroll. We have openings on August 19 and on September 23. I'll be available in a moment to sign you up for either date. I'm looking forward to seeing you soon."

End with a Challenge

Whereas an appeal asks for some action, a challenge almost demands it:

> "You can go on as before, not failing completely but not doing the best possible job. Or you can use the ideas you've heard this morning to become more creative, more productive, and more successful. Why be average when you can be superior? Why settle for a few hopes when you can reach your dreams? It's up to you."

Functions of Transitions

Transitions are words or sentences that connect the segments of a presentation. They work like bridges between the major parts of your remarks and tell your listeners how these parts are related. Transitions should occur between the introduction and the body, between the main points within the body, and between the body and the conclusion.

The following examples illustrate each of these instances:

> "Those are big promises. Let me talk about how we can deliver on them."
>
> "Not all the news is bad, however. Let me tell you about some good things that happened at the conference."
>
> "After hearing about so many features, you may have trouble remembering them all. Let's review them briefly."

Transitions like those in the preceding examples serve three important purposes.

Transitions Promote Clarity

Clarity in speech—especially in one-way, speech-like presentations—is more difficult to achieve than clarity in writing. The format of a letter, memo, book, or report makes its organization of ideas clear. Paragraphs, headings, numbered and bulleted lists, different typefaces, and underlining can all emphasize how ideas are related to one another. In a presentation, however, listeners do not have the benefit of any of these visual aids to figure out how your ideas are put together. They have only what the verbal cues—transitional words and phrases—provide.

Transitions are an especially important way to help listeners follow the structure of a group presentation. Clear transitions help smooth the adjustments that listeners need to make as they shift their attention from one speaker to another.

When delivering group presentations, each speaker should provide internal previews and summary statements within their own segment. These statements enhance clarity by helping listeners follow the overall plan. The following internal preview was part of a group presentation by members of an architectural firm seeking to make the short list of candidates for a corporate design job:

> Good morning, everybody. As David told you in his introduction, I'm Diana Salazar. I think you'll agree my colleagues have shown you a beautiful design. But beauty alone isn't enough: You need a building that can be constructed on time

and on budget. That's why I want to spend a few minutes showing you how we can deliver just that.

Transitions Emphasize Important Ideas
Transitions within presentations highlight important information, just as italics and bold type emphasize key points in print:

> "Now let's turn to a third reason—perhaps the most important of all—for equipping your field representatives with tablets."

> "That's what company policy says about the use of expense accounts. Now let's take a look at how things *really* work."

Transitions Keep Listeners
Interested Transitions give momentum to a presentation. They make listeners want to find out what comes next:

> "So we gave them the best dog-and-pony show you've ever seen. And it was perfect—just like we planned. What do you think they said when we were finished?"

> "By now you're probably asking yourself what a product like this will cost. And that's the best news of all. . . ."

Characteristics of Effective Transitions

Transitions that promote clarity, emphasize important ideas, and keep listeners interested possess two characteristics. First, successful transitions refer to both preceding and upcoming ideas. A transition is like a bridge: To get listeners from one point to another, it must be anchored at both ends. By referring to what you just said and to what you will say next, you show the logical relationships among your ideas. Notice the smooth connections between the ideas in these transitions:

> "Those are the problems. Now let's see what can be done about solving them."

> "Now you see that the change makes sense financially. But how will it be received by the people who have to live with it?"

If you have trouble planning a transition that links the preceding and upcoming material smoothly, the difficulty may indicate that the ideas are not logically related or that the organizational plan you have chosen is flawed. Review the guidelines for choosing an organizational pattern and identifying main points to be sure that the structure of your presentation's body is logically suited to the topic.

Second, effective transitions call attention to themselves. You should let listeners know when you are moving from one point to another so they will be able to follow the structure of your ideas easily. Notice how the examples provided so far have all made it clear that the presentation is shifting gears. The use of keywords can highlight the transition:

> "The *next* important idea is . . ."

> "*Another* reason we want to make the change . . ."

> "*Finally,* we need to consider . . ."

> "To *wrap things up* . . ."

When used as part of a transition that refers to previous and upcoming material, these phrases signal your listeners that you are moving to a new part of your presentation.

Finally, there are two ways to handle transitions in group presentations: A single group spokesperson (probably the person who introduced the presentation) can make them, or each speaker can introduce the next person after providing an internal summary of their own section. Whichever method you choose, make sure the relationship between the preceding and following sections is clear.

A presentation checklist, covering transitions and the other organizational concepts discussed in this chapter, is presented in this chapter's Self-Assessment.

Self-Assessment   Checklist for Organizing a Presentation

Use this list to check how well your presentation is organized.

Does the **introduction**

_____ 1. Capture the attention of your audience?

_____ 2. Give your audience reasons to listen?

_____ 3. Set an appropriate tone?

_____ 4. Establish your qualifications, if necessary?

_____ 5. Introduce your thesis and preview the content?

Does the **body**

_____ 1. Use the most effective organizational pattern?
      A. Chronological
      B. Spatial
      C. Topical
      D. Cause–effect
      E. Problem–solution
      F. Criteria satisfaction
      G. Comparative advantages
      H. Motivated sequence

_____ 2. State your main points in complete sentences?

_____ 3. Use your main points to develop your thesis?

_____ 4. Contain no more than five main points?

_____ 5. Express only one idea in each main point?

_____ 6. State your main points in parallel structure if possible?

Do you have **transitions** that

_____ 1. Refer to both recent and upcoming material, showing the relationships between the two?

_____ 2. Emphasize your important ideas?

_____ 3. Clarify the structure of your ideas?

_____ 4. Link all necessary parts of the presentation?
      A. Between the introduction and the body
      B. Between the main points within the body
      C. Between the body and the conclusion

Does the **conclusion**

_____ 1. Review your thesis and your main points?

_____ 2. Conclude with an effective closing statement?

MASTER **the chapter**

review points

- Speakers should use a four-part analysis when planning a presentation:

  - First, speakers should analyze the speaking occasion by considering the time of day and length of time they will speak, the facility, and the context in which these remarks will occur.

  - Second, speakers should analyze the audience: Who are the key listeners; what do they already know; what do they want to know; and what are their preferences, significant demographics, size, and attitudes?

  - Third, speakers should analyze themselves by considering their goal for speaking, their knowledge of the subject and feelings about the topic, as well as their confidence in speaking.

  - When presenting as a group, speakers should analyze the group by identifying the group's goals, as well as the individual strengths of each speaker.

- A speaker's next steps are to define general and specific goals and to create the thesis. Is the general goal to inform, persuade, or celebrate? The specific goal identifies who the speaker wants to reach; what the speaker wants them to do; and how, when, and where the speaker wants them to act. Clear goal statements define the desired audience reaction in a specific and attainable manner.

- After defining the goal, the speaker must clearly structure the thesis as a single sentence. The thesis is the central idea that will be repeated throughout the presentation, so it is essential to design it carefully.

- While brainstorming and researching ideas, the goal statement and audience analysis serve as guidelines for choosing items that are appropriate for this specific presentation. These items are then arranged into main points and subpoints, and into the most appropriate organizational pattern.

- Clearly organized presentations increase audience comprehension and speaker credibility by following a basic structure of introduction, body, and conclusion.

- Commonly used organizational patterns for presentations are chronological, spatial, topical, cause-effect, problem-solution, criteria satisfaction, comparative advantages, and motivated sequence.

- After the body of the presentation has been developed, an introduction is created to capture the attention of the audience, give them a reason to listen, and state the thesis. The conclusion reviews the thesis and main points, then closes with a strong statement.

- Transitions connect the introduction to the body, the main points of the body, and the body to the conclusion. They call attention to themselves to keep listeners oriented and highlight both the preceding and the following material.

key terms

cause-effect pattern   322
chronological pattern   320
claim   316
communication apprehension   309
comparative advantages pattern   324
criteria satisfaction pattern   323
motivated sequence pattern   325
problem-solution pattern   323

rhetorical question   328
social loafing   311
spatial pattern   321
specific goal   312
thesis statement   313
topical pattern   322
transition   332

activities

1. Invitation to Insight

Gain insights about analyzing occasions and audiences by interviewing a professional who frequently delivers presentations to a variety of listeners in the workplace. Ask your respondent questions such as the following:

a. How do you gather information about your potential audience? About the expectations of the occasion?
b. Compare the expectations of some of the various audiences you address.
c. How do you adjust your presentations for these audiences?
d. What do you do if you discover your audience members' knowledge level about your topic will vary widely?
e. How do you appeal to an audience who will probably be bored by or opposed to your topic?
f. What are some strategies for tweaking your presentation so it is more appropriate to the occasion?

In class, share the answers gleaned from various interviews.

2. Skill Builder

Identify the most important factors related to your audience, the occasion, and yourself as a speaker that you should consider when planning a presentation to meet the following goals:

a. Explain what "TikTok" is to a group of senior citizens.
b. Give instructions to a group of trainees.
c. Encourage high school seniors to attend your college.
d. Announce a cost increase in employee health care benefits (assume you are a human relations representative at your company).
e. Honor a beloved ecology professor during a public ceremony on your college commons, where a tree will be planted in their name.

3. Skill Builder

With your group, imagine you have been asked to speak to one of the audiences described in this activity. Your task is to present a 15-minute

description of your workplace department's functions. With this audience in mind, answer each of the seven questions listed in the Analyzing the Audience section. Because this is a hypothetical scenario, you will need to make your best estimate of the answers to the questions rather than conducting real audience research. Then, describe how you could use that information to create an interesting and informative presentation tailored to this specific audience.

a. A group of new employees from all over the company.
b. New employees within the department.
c. A group of managers from other departments.
d. Several of your superiors.
e. A supplier whose representative is helping you update equipment.
f. A group of customers touring the company.

Each group should share and compare its analyses. Before sharing with the class, follow the guidelines for Analyzing Your Group discussed in the chapter.

4. Skill Builder

Write a specific goal statement for four of the following situations. Then translate your goal into an effective thesis:

a. A farewell speech honoring an unpopular manager at their retirement dinner.
b. A training session introducing a new emergency evacuation plan.
c. A kick-off speech for the United Way payroll deduction campaign.
d. An appeal to your boss to hire an additional employee in your department.
e. A proposal to your department head to change the course requirements for your major.
f. A banker's speech to an economics class on the topic "The Changing Banking Industry."
g. A request to your landlord for new office carpeting.

5. Skill Builder

Write a specific goal and thesis statement for a presentation on the value of learning the communication skills introduced in this book. Imagine you will

336

be addressing an organization you work for or the members of a college class you are taking. Which demographic information would be important to know about your audience? Which demographic information would not be relevant to your presentation? Identify three to five key points you would cover in your presentation.

6. Invitation to Insight

How could you enhance your credibility if you were delivering a presentation to various businesses in your community, asking them to establish internships for communication students?

7. Skill Builder

What kinds of material would you gather for a presentation on each of the following topics? Where would you find your information?

a. How changes in the cellular telephone industry will affect consumers.
b. How to begin an investment program.
c. Changing trends in the popularity of various academic courses over the last 10 years.
d. Why students should (or should not) buy an e-book reader.
e. Career opportunities for women in the field of your choice.

8. Skill Builder

With your group, determine which organizational pattern (chronological, spatial, and so on) you would recommend for each of the following presentations. Explain your rationale.

a. Instructions on how to file a health insurance claim form.
b. A request for time and money to attend an important convention in your field.
c. A comparison of products or services offered by your organization and by a competitor.

d. A report on an industrial accident.
e. Suggestions on reducing employee turnover.

9. Skill Builder

Select two of the following topics (or other topics that you are knowledgeable about). For each topic, first create a thesis statement. Then, while applying the rules for main points from this chapter, write two to five main points you would cover in delivering a presentation relevant to your thesis. Express each main point in a complete sentence.

a. When to use small claims court.
b. The importance of creativity in advertising.
c. Renting versus leasing a car.
d. The proper format for a business letter.
e. Types of sexual harassment.
f. The fastest-growing jobs in the twenty-first century.

10. Skill Builder

Prepare an introduction and a conclusion for the topics you developed in Activity 9, or choose two of the following presentations. Exchange your ideas with a classmate. Use the checklists for the introduction and the conclusion found in the Self-Assessment: Checklist for Organizing a Presentation to review each other's introductions and conclusions.

a. A talk to employees announcing personnel layoffs.
b. The last in a day-long series of talks to a tired audience on maintaining and operating equipment.
c. An appeal to coworkers for donations to the Community Holiday Relief Fund.
d. A talk on "What Employers Look for in a College Graduate," to be delivered to your class by the president of the local chamber of commerce.

McGraw Hill LearnSmart™

For further review, go to the LearnSmart study module for this chapter.

references

1. Boettinger, H. M. (1969). *Moving mountains, or the art of letting others see things your way.* New York, NY: Collier.
2. Meilach, D. Z. (1994). Even the odds with visual presentations. *Presentations, 8*(11), SS1–SS6.
3. "The gray flannel sideshow." (1983). *Presentations, 7*(11), 50.
4. Marsh, H. L. (1983, May). Summary membership remarks. Presentation at New York Chapter of the Institute of Internal Auditors Meeting, New York, NY.
5. Linthicum, A. (2021, January 12). Virtual meetings in 2021: Tips, ideas & tools. *Cvent.* Retrieved from https://www.cvent.com/en/blog/events/virtual-meetings
6. Zelazny, G. (2006). *Say it with presentations.* New York, NY: McGraw Hill.
7. Molloy, J. T. (1985). *Molloy's live for success.* New York, NY: Bantam.
8. Vasilion, S., Personal communication, September 24, 1997.
9. Vasilion, S., Personal communication, September 24, 1997.
10. Naguib, R. (2009). International audience. Retrieved from http://www.toastmasters.org/MainMenuCategories/FreeResources/NeedHelpGivingaSpeech/BusinessPresentations/SpeakingGlobally_1/InternationalAudiences.aspx
11. Lauring, J., & Klitmøller, A. (2017). Inclusive language use in multicultural business organizations: The effect on creativity and performance. *International Journal of Business Communication, 54*(3), 306–324. Retrieved from https://doi.org/10.1177/2329488415572779
12. Williams, C. J. (2008, September 29). Jury duty? You may want to edit your online profile. *Los Angeles Times*, p. A6.
13. Wiseman, L. (2016, August 20). What giving a presentation I knew nothing about taught me about true confidence. *Fortune.* Retrieved from http://fortune.com/author/liz-wiseman/
14. "Thud and blunder in the news rooms." (1995, March 5). *The Independent.* Retrieved from http://www.independent.co.uk/opinion/thud-and-blunder-in-the-news-rooms-1610069.html
15. Bradley, B. E. (1991). *Fundamentals of speech communication: The credibility of ideas* (6th ed.). Dubuque, IA: Wm. C. Brown.
16. Watson, A. K. (1995). Taking the sweat out of communication anxiety. *Personnel Journal, 74,* 111–117.
17. Behnke, R. R., Sawyer, C. R., & King, P. E. (1987). The communication of public speaking anxiety. *Communication Education, 36,* 138–141; Burgoon, J.,

Pfau, M., Birk, T., & Manusov, V. (1987). Nonverbal communication performance and perceptions associated with reticence. *Communication Education, 36,* 119–130; McEwan, K. L., & Devins, G. (1983). Increased arousal in emotional anxiety noticed by others. *Journal of Abnormal Psychology, 92,* 417–421.
18. Karau, S. J., & Williams, K. D. (1993). Social loafing: A meta-analytic review and theoretical integration. *Journal of Personality and Social Psychology, 65*(4), 681–706. Retrieved from https://doi.org/10.1037/0022-3514.65.4.681
19. Harkins, S. G., & Szymanski, K. (1989). Social loafing and group evaluation. *Journal of Personality and Social Psychology, 56*(6), 934–941. Retrieved from https://doi.org/10.1037/0022-3514.56.6.934
20. Hardy, C., & Latané, B. (1986). Social loafing on a cheering task. *Social Science, 71*(2-3), 165–172. Retrieved from https://psycnet.apa.org/record/1988-07385-001
21. Linver, S. & Mengert, J. (1994). *Speak and get results: The complete guide to speeches and presentations that work in any business situation* (Rev. ed.). New York, NY: Fireside.
22. Windsor, J. (2010, July 31). Smart presentations: Will you pass the two-word test for ultimate presentations? *Sales and Marketing Management.* Retrieved from http://www.salesandmarketing.com/article/smart-presentations-will-you-pass-two-word-test-ultimate-presentations
23. "Presentation planning: Draw a logic tree." (1993). *Meeting Management News, 1,* 1–2.
24. Katt, J., Murdock, J., Butler, J., & Pryor, B. (2008). Establishing best practices for the use of PowerPointTM as a presentation aid. *Human Communication, 11,* 193–200.
25. Zielinski, D. (2003, June 4). Perfect practice. *Presentations.*
26. Lucas, S. E. (2009). *The art of public speaking* (10th ed.). New York, NY: McGraw Hill; Faylor, N. R., Beebe, S. A., Houser, M. L., & Mottet, T. P. (2008). Perceived differences in instructional communication behaviors between effective and ineffective corporate trainers. *Human Communication, 11,* 145–156.
27. Bovée, C. L., & Thill, J. T. (1989). *Business communication today* (2nd ed.). New York, NY: Random House; DeVito, J. A. (2000). *The elements of public speaking* (7th ed.). New York, NY: Longman.
28. Jaffe, C. (2001). *Public speaking: Concepts and skills for a diverse society* (3rd ed.). Belmont, CA: Wadsworth; Lustig, M. W., & Koester, J. (2003). *Intercultural competence: Interpersonal communication across culture* (4th ed.). New York, NY: Allyn & Bacon.

29. Hybels, S., & Weaver, R. L., Jr. (2001). *Communicating effectively* (6th ed.). Boston, MA: McGraw Hill; Osborn, M., & Osborn, S. (2000). *Public speaking* (5th ed.). Boston, MA: Houghton Mifflin.

30. Meyer, P. (2011, July). *How to spot a liar* [Video]. TED Global Conference. Retrieved from http://www.ted.com/talks/pamela_meyer_how_to_spot_a_liar.html

31. Robinson, J. W. (1987). *Winning them over.* Rocklin, CA: Prima.

32. U.S. Department of Justice. (2009). Remarks as prepared for delivery by U.S. Attorney General Eric Holder at the Department of Justice African American History Month Program.

33. U.S. Department of Justice. (2009). Remarks as prepared for delivery by U.S. Attorney General Eric Holder at the Department of Justice African American History Month Program.

34. Unknown. (1993). *Executive Speechwriter Newsletter, 8,* 3.

35. Carter, J. (2003). *Camp David 25th Anniversary Forum special conference series.* Washington, DC: Woodrow Wilson International Center for Scholars.

36. Advanced Public Speaking Institute. (2003). *How to close a speech.* Retrieved from http://www.public-speaking.org/public-speaking-closings-article.htm

Chapter Eleven
Supporting the Presentation

chapter outline

chapter objectives

After reading this chapter you should be able to:

1. Define and describe guidelines for each type of verbal support, and develop and use each type of verbal support as suitable to add interest, clarity, or proof to a main point.

2. Discuss additional types of supporting information for persuasive speeches.

3. Discuss whether there is a need for visual support in various situations; determine the advantages and disadvantages of various types of visual support for those contexts; and design a visual aid appropriate for a given context.

4. Choose the most effective medium for presenting visual support in specific contexts.

5. Design a presentation that properly cites and uses support sources responsibly, and incorporates inclusive and accessible language and visuals.

Tom Sutcliffe was frustrated. "I know I deserve that raise," Tom said firmly to his friend and coworker Tina Agapito. "I laid out all the reasons to the boss as clear as day. I've been doing the work of two people ever since Van left. My productivity is higher than anybody else's in the place. My salary is way below the industry average, and all my clients are happy. What else do they want?"

Tina tried to be supportive. "I know you deserve the raise, Tom, and I just can't believe the boss doesn't see that, too. Did you back up your claims?"

"What do you mean?" Tom asked.

"Did you provide evidence about your productivity or about how your salary compares with the industry average? Did you show some proof about all your happy clients?"

"I guess not," said Tom. "But I shouldn't have to sell myself around here. The boss ought to appreciate a good employee when they have one!"

"Maybe so," Tina answered. "But the boss hears a lot of requests for money and resources and is really busy. Maybe if you can make your case clearer and more interesting, you would have a stronger chance."

Tina's advice to Tom was right on the mark. Solid ideas will not always impress an audience. Most listeners are busy and preoccupied, and they usually do not care nearly as much about your message as you do. Using the clear organization described in Chapter 10 will help make your presentations successful, but you need to back up your well-organized points in a way that will make your audience take notice, understand you, and accept your message. In other words, you need to use plenty of supporting material.

• Functions of Supporting Material

Supporting material helps speakers back up the claims they are making in a presentation. Several types of verbal and visual supporting material, including examples, stories, statistics, infographics, and interactive polls, are discussed in this chapter. In the following examples, you can see the relationship between claims and supporting material:

Claim	Support
We could increase sales by staying open until 10 p.m. on weekday evenings.	An article in *Modern Retailing* cites statistics showing that stores with extended evening hours boost their profits by more than 20% of the direct overhead involved with the longer business day.
Configuring a wireless network is not as hard as it might seem.	Here's a video that shows how easy it can be.
Taking the time to help customers will boost their loyalty and increase your commissions.	Let me read you a letter written just last week by one satisfied customer.

As these examples show, a presentation without supporting material would still be logical if it followed the organizational guidelines in Chapter 10. Nevertheless, the speakers probably would not achieve their goals because their presentations would lack the information necessary to develop their ideas in a way the audience would understand or appreciate. Listeners are likely to understand and remember a message when you use verbal and visual support to present it.

You can show a diagram, for example, while you describe it. If you are discussing a physical object, you might display photos of it on slides or even bring the object itself to show your listeners. If you are illustrating a process, you might play a brief video showing the process in action. Talking about the flavors of a new food product is not nearly as effective as giving your audience a taste. Likewise, telling listeners in a training session how to deal with customer objections is less effective than demonstrating the procedure for them or letting them handle a situation themselves. As illustrated by these examples, carefully selected supporting material can make a presentation more effective by adding three things: clarity, interest, and proof.

Clarity

Supporting material can make abstract or complicated ideas more understandable. Notice how the presenter uses the following analogy to clarify how computers with point-and-click user interfaces were such a revolutionary improvement over earlier generations that relied on keyboard commands:

> Imagine driving a car that has no steering wheel, accelerator, brake pedal, turn signal lever, or gear selector. In place of all the familiar manual controls, you have only a typewriter keyboard.
>
> Whenever you want to turn a corner, change lanes, slow down, speed up, honk your horn, or back up, you have to type a command sequence on the keyboard. Unfortunately, the car can't understand English sentences. Instead, you must hold down a special key with one finger and type in some letters and numbers, such as "S20:TL:A35," which means, "Slow to 20, turn left, and accelerate to 35."
>
> If you make a typing mistake, one of three things will happen. First, if you type an unknown command, the car radio will bleat and you will have to type the command again. Second, if you type something that is wrong but still a valid command, the car will blindly obey. (Imagine typing A95—the command to accelerate

to 95—instead of A35—the command to accelerate to 35.) Third, if you type something the manufacturer didn't anticipate, the car will screech to a halt and shut itself off.[1]

Well-designed graphics are easier to understand than words alone. The computer analogy described may be combined with the use of a photograph or a video simulation of the keyboard commands to enhance clarity.

Interest

Supporting material can enliven a presentation by making your main points more vivid or meaningful to the audience. Notice how one attorney used a story to add interest to a summary aimed at discrediting his opponent's restatement of evidence:

> It seems that when Abe Lincoln was a young trial lawyer in Sangamon County, Illinois, he was arguing a case with a lawyer whose version of the facts came more from his imagination than the testimony. Lincoln, in his argument, turned on him and said:
>
> "Tell me, sir, how many legs has a sheep got?" "Why, four, of course," the fellow answered. "And if I called his tail a leg, then how many legs would that sheep have?" Lincoln asked. The answer came, "Then he'd have five." "No!" Lincoln roared, pounding the jury rail, "he'd still have just four legs. Calling his tail a leg won't make it a leg. Now let's look at the actual testimony and see how many tails you've been calling legs."[2]

Proof

Besides adding clarity and interest, supporting material can provide evidence for your claims and make your presentation more convincing. For example, a speaker might display an infographic on employee absenteeism and employer-sponsored daycare while discussing statistics to back up the claim, "Employer-sponsored daycare can boost productivity as well as help parents":

> According to the Early Care & Learning Council, U.S. businesses lose $3 billion annually due to child-care-related employee absenteeism. Employer-sponsored care can decrease employee absences by up to 30% and job turnover as much as 60%.[3]

Whenever you use others' work to back up your claims, be sure to cite the source. Some sources, of course, are more credible than others. In the preceding paragraph, for example, the claim that employer-sponsored daycare is good for employers is strengthened by citing a survey done by a respected bank. The same claim would not be as persuasive if it relied on a survey of employees who were seeking daycare, because those respondents' motives would be more self-serving.

• Verbal Support

Many types of verbal supporting material can be used to add clarity, interest, or proof to a presentation. Definitions, examples, stories, statistics, comparisons, and quotations are the most common types of verbal support used in business and professional presentations. The use of verbal support is especially important when your goal is to persuade an audience. Research demonstrates that when an audience hears evidence backing up a persuasive claim, the chances increase that the influence of the message will last long after the presentation has concluded.[4] Furthermore, hearing evidence supporting a claim makes listeners less likely to accept opposing viewpoints they may hear after you have finished speaking.

Table 11-1	Types of Verbal Support

Type	Definition	Use	Audience
Definition	Explains the meaning of a term	Clarify	Use when terms are unfamiliar to an audience or used in an uncommon way
Example	Illustrates a point using a brief reference	Clarify Add interest (if a sufficient number are given)	Utilize when presenting a novel or technical idea or delivering instructions to an audience
Story	Provides a detailed account of an incident	Clarify Add interest Prove (factual story only)	Adapt to the audience's attitudes, demographics, and knowledge level
Statistics	Numerical representations of a point	Clarify Add interest (when combined with other forms of support) Prove	Link to the audience's frame of reference
Comparisons	Examinations or processes that show how one idea resembles another	Clarify Add interest (figurative) Prove (literal)	Tailor a familiar item to the audience, making sure the comparison is valid
Quotations	Opinion of an expert or articulate source	Clarify Add interest (sometimes) Prove	Use sources that will be credible to the audience

As Table 11-1 shows, regardless of the general purpose of your presentation, your use of verbal support should always be audience-centered. Tailoring supporting materials to your audience's needs and preferences will aid in their understanding and interest in your presentation. This table also introduces some common types of verbal support which will be detailed in the next sections.

When giving a presentation, you will undoubtedly find yourself supporting your presentation with a variety of verbal strategies, including the following.

Definitions

You can appreciate a speaker's need to define unclear terms by recalling times when someone began using unfamiliar language, leaving you confused and unable to understand:

> "SQLite is a software library that implements a self-contained, serverless, zero-configuration, transactional SQL database engine. Content can be stored as INTEGER, REAL, TEXT, BLOB, or as NULL."

Definitions remove this sort of confusion by explaining the meaning of terms that are unfamiliar to an audience or used in a specialized or uncommon way. Words can be defined by denotation (specific or literal meaning), connotation (associated or suggestive meanings), etymology (history or origin of the word), or negation (stating what it is not):

A *smart electrical meter* doesn't just measure how much energy a customer uses; it also identifies when you used it and sends that information back to the local utility for monitoring and billing purposes. (denotation)

We prefer not to refer to our peer groups as *cliques* because people tend to associate cliques with the act of excluding others. (connotation)

Bollywood is the informal name of the Hindi-language film industry based in Mumbai, India. The term is a combination of the words "Bombay"—the old name for Mumbai—and "Hollywood." (etymology)

In the tax code, *a capital gain* is not the same as ordinary income. It is the profit that results when you sell assets like real estate or shares of stock for more than you paid for them. The *capital gains tax* is the amount of that profit the government takes. (negation)

Examples

Speakers often require brief illustrations to back up or explain a point. A speaker arguing for an enhanced package of employee benefits could share **examples** of companies that already provide a variety of perks:

- The Microsoft campus includes a space known as "The Commons" that includes a variety of shops and restaurants, including a credit union, hair salon, auto-body shop, coffee shop, gastropub, and vegan bar.[5]
- Umpqua Bank employees get 40 hours of paid time off every year to do volunteer work.[6]
- Netflix allows employees to choose how many vacation days they take each year.[7]

Likewise, a marketing consultant explaining how the name of a business can attract customers could back up the claim by citing examples of clever names:

- Totally Twisted, a Pennsylvania pretzel company[8]
- Now Showing, a movie theater turned lingerie shop
- accessAbilities, a nonprofit organization that provides support services to persons with disabilities.[9]

In many cases, you do not need to look outside your own experience for examples to back up a point. Union members claiming that "management cares more about buildings and grounds than employees" might back up their claim by offering the following examples:

We keep hearing that "employees are our most important asset," yet we don't see dollars reflecting that philosophy. In the two and a half years since our last pay raise, we have seen the following physical improvements at this site alone: a new irrigation system for the landscaping, renovation of the corporate offices, expansion of the data processing wing, resurfacing of all the parking lots, and a new entrance to the building. Now all those improvements are helpful, but they show that buildings and grounds are more important than people.

When they are used to prove a point, examples are most effective when several are given together. If you are supporting the claim that you are capable of taking on a more challenging job, it is best to remind your boss of several tasks you have handled well. After all, a single example could be an isolated instance or a lucky fluke.

Stories

Almost everyone loves to hear a good story. **Stories** illustrate a point by describing an incident in some detail. A well-told story adds interest and, when well-chosen, can drive home a point better than logic and reasoning alone.[10]

This account of a farmer and their children shows how stories can make a powerful point. In this case, the farmer's story contrasts conventional agriculture practices and an organic approach:

> When I worked for a conventional farm, I would come home and my kids would want to hug me. They couldn't because I had to shower first and my clothes had to be removed and disinfected. Today, I can walk right off the field into the waiting arms of my kids because there's nothing toxic on my body to harm them.[11]

As the consultant who retold this story explained, "While data are obviously important and must support your story, you have to touch hearts before you can influence minds."[12]

Research bears out the power of stories to reach an audience. In a study exploring effective ways to persuade listeners, one group of subjects was presented with statistical information such as "Food shortages in Malawi are affecting more than 3 million children." A second group was shown the photo of a 7-year-old girl from Malawi named Rokia and told that she was desperately poor and that "her life will be changed for the better by your gift." People in the second group gave significantly more.[13]

Three types of stories may be used in presentations: fictional, hypothetical, and factual. *Fictional stories* allow you to create material that perfectly illustrates the point you want to make. This fictional story uses humor to help listeners understand the importance of being proactive in business:

> In Greece there is an old monastery perched on top of a high mountain, with steep cliffs on every side. The only way to visit it is to get in a wicker basket and have a monk pull you up by ropes.
>
> One visitor noticed that this rope—the one his life depended on—was old and quite frayed. He asked the monk, "When do you change the rope?" The monk replied, "Whenever it breaks."

After the laughter died down, the speaker used this story to make his point:

> In this company we don't wait until the rope breaks. We don't even let it fray. We fix things before they become hazards.[14]

Other stories are *hypothetical:* "Imagine yourself . . . ," "Think about a typical customer . . . ," and "What would you do if . . ." Besides being involving, hypothetical stories allow you to create a situation that illustrates exactly the point you are trying to make. You can adjust details, create dialogue, and use figures that support your case. Note, however, that your account will be effective only if it is believable.

A representative explaining the concept of "guaranteed account value" in a variable annuity investment might use a hypothetical example like this:

> Suppose you were unlucky enough to have a nasty accident that kept you from working for six months. Imagine dealing with the pain and inconvenience of your injuries. Then imagine yourself trying to cope with your loss of income. Would you have enough money saved to support yourself and the people who are counting on you? Would you have enough insurance coverage to make up for your lost income?

Factual stories can also add interest and clarity. The following story, from a frustrated consumer, illustrates the thesis that many businesses are more interested in making a sale

Culture Shapes Support Preferences

Most native English speakers are raised to value arguments in which a clear thesis is backed up by supporting material. But this style is not preferred in every culture. For example, in Latin America, an inductive approach that begins with multiple pieces of support can be more compelling. Hispanic marketing consultant Miguel Gomez Winebrenner explains:

> When asked a question like "What is your favorite color?" most Americans tend to work down from that question and explain the reasoning behind the answer. So, a typical answer would be "My favorite color is blue, and this is why. . . ."
>
> When asked the same question, many Latin Americans would answer something along the lines of "When I was a kid I preferred yellow because the flag of my favorite sports team was yellow, but then I started to like black because of the color of my first girlfriend's eyes . . . ," until after a rather long [and] personal dialogue they would answer, "So my favorite color is blue."
>
> Neither is right nor wrong—they are just different. U.S. Americans expect an answer up front, followed by supporting arguments. Latin Americans might first give the supporting arguments that lead to the answer.

Even the most persuasive type of support can depend on the audience's cultural background. In Latin America, examples and stories that evoke an emotional reaction can be more compelling than data-based arguments.

Culture is not the only factor that shapes an audience's preferences. Educational background, career focus, and socioeconomic status can also be powerful influences. An effective speaker will consider all these variables when choosing how to support arguments.

Source: Jaffee, C. I. (2013). *Public speaking: Concepts and skills for a diverse society* (7th ed.). Boston, MA: Wadsworth; Moran, R. T., Harris, P. R., & Moran, S. V. (2007). *Managing cultural differences: Global leadership strategies for the 21st century* (7th ed.). Amsterdam, NL: Elsevier; Weinbrenner, M. G. (2007, June 13). Building an effective case to Latin American and Hispanic dominant consumers: The inverted triangle dilemma, *Hispanic Marketing and Public Relations.* Retrieved from https://hispanicmpr.com/2007/06/20/building-an-effective-case-to-latin-american-and-hispanic-dominant-consumers-the-inverted-triangle-dilemma/

than in supporting their products after the deal is closed. Notice how the last sentence restates the main idea so the point of the story is clear:

> Last Tuesday I decided to call the automobile dealership. There were two numbers listed in the phone book, one for "Sales" and one for "Service." I asked the service manager if I could bring my car in the following Saturday. Service managers always have a way of making you feel unwanted, and he seemed pleased to be able to tell me that they were closed Saturday and wouldn't be able to take me until a week from Thursday.
>
> I didn't make a date. Instead, I called the other number, under "Sales." "Are you open Saturday?" I asked. "Yes, sir," the cheery voice said at the other end of the phone. "We're here Saturdays from eight in the morning till nine in the evening, and Sundays from noon until six."
>
> Now, if I can buy a car on Saturday, why can't I get one fixed on Saturday? What's going on here, anyway? I think I know what's going on, of course. We're selling things better than we're making them, that's what's going on.[15]

While both factual and fictional stories can make a presentation clearer and more interesting, only the factual type can prove a point:

> "Cutting the payroll by using temporary employees sounds like a good idea, but it has problems. Listen to what happened when we tried it at the place I used to work . . ."
>
> "I'm sure Kyle can handle the job. Let me tell you what happened last year when we assigned Kyle to manage the Westco account . . ."
>
> "You might think life insurance isn't necessary for a young, healthy person like you, but remember Vince Kendall, the linebacker from State who was about as healthy as they come, but . . ."

Whether they are fictional or factual, effective stories share several characteristics.[16] First, they are relatively brief: You should not spin out a 5-minute yarn to make a minor point. Second, they are interesting and appropriate for your audience: A story that offends your listeners will be memorable but not in the desired way. Finally, and most important, an effective story supports the point you are trying to make. An amusing story that does not support your thesis will just distract your listeners.[17]

Statistics

Numeric data, or **statistics** can be used to help your audience visualize the information you are presenting. If you were arguing that there is a serious manufacturing problem with a new product line, for example, describing one or two dissatisfied customers would not drive home the point that the problem goes beyond the usual "acceptable" rate of error in manufacturing. The following statement, however, would constitute proof: "Our return rate on the new line is little more 40%—as opposed to the usual rate of 5%—and of all those returns, four-fifths are related to a flaw in the gear assembly."

Statistics are a commonly cited form of support in business presentations. They are used to quantify the size of market segments, sales trends, decreasing or increasing profits, changes in costs, and many other aspects of business. When handled well, statistics are especially strong proof because they are firmly grounded in fact and show that the speaker is well informed.[18] Consider this example:

> The U.S. Census Bureau reports that people with a bachelor's degree earn an average of 62% more than those with only a high school diploma. Over a lifetime, the gap in earning potential between a high school graduate and someone with a B.A. is more than $1 million. These figures show that whatever sacrifices you make for a college education in the short term are worth it in the long term.

Despite their potential effectiveness, poorly used statistics can spoil a presentation. One common mistake is to bury an audience under an avalanche of numbers, as this speaker did at an annual stockholders' meeting:

> Last year was an exciting one for our company. We earned $6.02 per share on a net income of $450 million, up from $4.63 per share on income of $412 million in the preceding year. This increase came in part from a one-time gain of $13 million from the sale of common stock to New Ventures group, our research and development subsidiary. Excluding this one-time gain, we increased our earnings per share 5.8% in the last year, and we increased our net income 6.5%.

This collection of numbers would be appropriate in a printed annual report, but when a speaker rattles them off one after another, there is little chance that audience members will follow them. Rather than smothering your listeners with detail, you should provide a few key numbers in your presentation, backed up by accompanying written materials if necessary.

> As the report you're holding details, last year was a good one for us. Earnings per share was up almost 6%, and our net income grew by 6.5%, on top of a $13 million one-time gain.

As this example shows, it is usually best to simplify information by rounding off numbers. For example, it is easier to understand "almost two-thirds" than it is to absorb "64.3%"; likewise, "approximately twice the cost" is easier to grasp than "Item A costs $65.18, while Item B runs $127.15." In a speech to United Nations officials, Hollywood star Angelina Jolie used "over" and "almost" to maximize the comprehensibility of the statistics she cited:

> Of the over 400,000 Somali refugees [in the Dadaab Refugee Camp in Northeast Kenya], almost 100,000 arrived in the past nine months, fleeing drought, insecurity, and famine conditions.[19]

Besides containing too many numbers, statistics-laden presentations are too dry for all but the most dedicated and involved audiences to handle. When you are speaking to a group of nonspecialists, it is important to link your figures to a frame of reference that the group will understand. Notice how the following statistics (presented in the form of examples) give new impact to the old principle that "time is money":

> For a manager who is earning $30,000 a year, wasting 1 hour a day costs the company $3,750 a year. . . . And for a $100,000-a-year executive, a 2-hour lunch costs the company an extra $12,500 annually.[20]

The late Swedish statistician Hans Rosling, whose TED Talk about statistics has been viewed almost 4 million times, said: "I know having the data is not enough. I have to show it in ways people both enjoy and understand."[21] When a presentation contains more than a few statistics, you will probably need to use visual aids to explain them: Numbers alone are simply too confusing to understand. Later in this chapter, we offer guidelines about how to present statistical data graphically.

Comparisons

Speakers often make a point by using a **comparison** that shows how one idea resembles another. Some comparisons—called analogies—are *figurative.* If you are speaking to an audience about an idea they may be unfamiliar with, you could compare it to an idea that

Morsa Images/Getty Images

is familiar to them. By considering the following example, you can appreciate the value of using figurative comparisons to add clarity and interest to a presentation:

> The cheap special fares advertised by some airlines are misleading since the "mouse print" at the bottom of the page lists so many restrictions. No food chain could get away with advertising prime rib at $3 a pound, limited to six roasts per store, available only when bought in pairs Tuesday through Thursday afternoons.[22]

U.S. Senator Mitch McConnell used a comparison to illustrate the magnitude of spending in a multitrillion-dollar bill before Congress: "If you had spent a million dollars every day since Jesus was born, you still wouldn't have spent a trillion."[23]

By linking the familiar with the unfamiliar, figurative analogies can also help listeners understand concepts that would otherwise be mystifying. One speaker used a figurative comparison to explain a limitation of cable modem Internet connections in terms that are easily understandable by non-experts:

> Remember what happens when you're taking a shower and someone turns on another faucet or flushes the toilet? The flow of water drops for everybody. A similar thing happens with the flow of data over an Internet connection: When more people are using the system, the speed at which data flows is slower.

Other comparisons are *literal,* linking similar items from two categories. An account executive might use this sort of comparison to argue, "We need to spend more of our advertising budget on direct mail. That approach worked wonders on the NBT campaign, and I think it can do the same for us here."

After an explosion killed 12 people in a West Virginia coal mine, some observers used a comparison to argue that weak federal laws make it financially worthwhile for mine owners to break safety rules:

> Driving solo in a California carpool lane carries a bigger fine than allowing combustible materials to accumulate in a coal mine.[24]

Whenever you propose adopting a policy or using an idea because it worked well somewhere else, you are intrinsically using comparisons as proof. The strength of this proof will depend on how clearly you can establish the similarity between the items you are comparing. Microsoft founder and philanthropist Bill Gates used a vivid statistical comparison to demonstrate misplaced priorities in drug research:

> Ten times as much funding is devoted to research on the prevention of male baldness as malaria, a disease that kills more than 1 million people each year.[25]

Whether their purpose is to add clarity, interest, or proof, comparisons should possess two characteristics. First, the familiar part of comparisons should be well-known to the audience. For instance, it would be a mistake to say, "Jumbo certificates of deposit are similar to Treasury bills in several ways" if your listeners do not know anything about Treasury bills. Second, your comparisons should be valid. You would be stretching a point if you tried to discourage employee abuse of the copying machine by claiming, "Using the machine for copying personal papers is a crime, just as much as committing robbery or assault." A closer match between the concepts would be both more valid and more effective: "You wouldn't help yourself to spare change from a cash register; everyone with a conscience knows that would be a case of petty theft. But using the copying machine for copying personal papers costs the company, just as surely as if the money had come out of a cash register."

A Too-Close Paraphrase

During a speech to the National Press Club of Australia, Anthony Albanese, leader of the Australian House of Representatives, provided the following criticism of fellow politician, Tony Abbott:

> In Australia we have serious challenges to solve and we need serious people to solve them. Unfortunately, Tony Abbott is not the least bit interested in fixing anything. He is only interested in two things: making Australians afraid of it and telling them who's to blame for it.

It did not take long for Australian media outlets to report the striking similarities between Albanese's words and a passage from a speech given by Michael Douglas in the 1995 film, *The American President:*

> We have serious problems to solve and we need serious people to solve them. And whatever your particular problem is, I promise you, Bob Rumson is not the least bit interested in solving it. He is interested in two things and two things only: making you afraid of it and telling you who's to blame for it.

This case highlights two common errors made when paraphrasing others' quotes: (1) Using too much of the original author's language (referred to as a *too-close paraphrase*), and (2) Failing to cite the source of the original material.

Source: The Deadline Team (2012, January 26). Aussie politician plagiarizes Michael Douglas speech in 'American President.' *Deadline.* Retrieved from https://deadline.com/2012/01/aussie-politician-plagiarizes-michael-douglas-speech-from-the-american-president-220681/; Yale Poorvu Center for Teaching and Learning (n.d.). Too-close paraphrase. Retrieved from https://poorvucenter.yale.edu/too-close-paraphrase

Quotations

Sometimes speakers need to use the words of others who are authoritative or articulate to help them make a point more effectively than they could on their own. Some **quotations** add clarity and impact. You might, for example, add punch to a talk on the importance of listening to customer complaints by citing a successful businessperson like Bill Gates, founder of Microsoft: "Your most unhappy customers are your greatest source of learning." Likewise, you could emphasize the importance of getting agreements in writing by quoting movie producer Sam Goldwyn: "A verbal contract isn't worth the paper it's written on." Or you might repeat former President Barack Obama's words about taking responsibility for your own success:

> Change will not come if we wait for some other person or for some other time. We are the ones we've been waiting for. We are the change that we seek.[26]

A few important guidelines must be followed to ensure that you are using quotations effectively and honestly. While short quotes can be read verbatim, speakers should paraphrase lengthy quotes. Paraphrasing enables you to take the original speaker's general idea and put it into your own words. The value of the quote remains without the possibility of losing your audience's attention by what may seem like rambling. Additionally, quotes should be followed by a restatement or explanation of the main point to show the audience how the quote reinforces your claim. Finally, you should always cite the source of the quoted or paraphrased material. More information on appropriately citing sources appears later in this chapter.

● Persuasive Support

In addition to the types of verbal support described in the previous section, persuasive speeches utilize a unique set of supporting information in the form of credibility, logical arguments, and psychological appeals. This particular type of support must be embedded in the key points of presentations to earn the audience's trust and endorsement.

Maximize Your Credibility

Winston Churchill once said that when it comes to public speaking, what matters most is who you are, then how you say what you want to say, and, finally, what you say. Even without taking this assertion literally, it is true that credibility is a powerful factor in persuasion. **Credibility**, also referred to as *ethos*, is the persuasive force that comes from the audience's belief in and respect for the speaker. When your audience has little time or inclination to examine your evidence and reasoning in detail, it will rely almost exclusively on your credibility to decide whether to accept your claims.[27] Research shows that you can enhance your credibility in a variety of ways.[28]

Demonstrate Your Competence   Listeners will be most influenced by a speaker whom they believe is qualified to present material on the subject. For example, a department's staff is more likely to accept the direction of a new manager who seems knowledgeable about that department's specific work. Management is more likely to take a risk on a new manufacturing material if the product manager seems to know the market well. In both of these examples, the level of trust in the speaker's competence is a key factor in determining the credibility of the presentation.

There are three ways to boost your credibility:

- *Demonstrate your knowledge of the subject.* For example, the product manager might enhance their credibility by citing statistics ("Our market research showed 85% of the potential market is more concerned with maintenance costs than the initial cost of the product"). They could also remember facts ("Dorwald Associates tried something like this, although only in government markets, and it was pretty successful") and recent appropriate examples ("I was checking the records last week, and I realized we could afford to replace the machines every five years based on what we'd save on maintenance if we used plastic instead of metal").

- *Make your credentials known.* These credentials could be academic degrees, awards and honors, or successful experiences ("I helped set up Hinkley's profitable system a few years ago, and I think the same approach we took there could help us now"). To avoid the appearance of egotism, it can be best to have others talk about your credentials ("Clara has a degree in accounting, so her ideas have special value here").

- *Demonstrate your ability.* This means speaking effectively during your presentation, of course. With an audience who already knows you, the reputation you have acquired over time will have even more powerful effects during your presentation. If you have a reputation for being talented and hardworking, listeners will be disposed to accept what you have to say. Conversely, if they regard you as incompetent, you will have a hard time persuading them to accept the ideas in your presentation. Tips for effective delivery are discussed in the next chapter.

If your credibility on the subject is not high, be sure to cite others whose expertise and impartiality your listeners respect. For example, a prospective customer would expect a sales representative to praise a product they are trying to sell. But if the salesperson cites others who know the product and do not have an interest in its sale, the message ("This product is excellent") becomes more persuasive. In such a case, the testimony of other customers or the findings of an independent testing service such as Consumers Union would be excellent evidence.

Earn the Trust of Your Audience   The most important ingredient of trustworthiness is *honesty.* If listeners suspect you are not telling the truth, even the most impressive credentials or verbal support will mean little to them. For instance, a union leader will draw little support from union members if they think that official has made a private agreement with management. If your motives might be considered suspect, confess them before others can raise doubts about your honesty ("I know the compensation plan in this proposal will benefit me, but I hope you can see how it will boost productivity and cut turnover"). Of course, you should never say *anything* that can be considered dishonest.

Impartiality is the second element of trustworthiness. We are more likely to accept the beliefs of impartial speakers than the beliefs of those speakers who have a vested interest in persuading us. If you have a vested interest in the position you are presenting (e.g., asking for a pay raise or a desired assignment), you can boost your credibility by citing impartial third parties who support your position. With the pay raise proposal, for example, you might cite salary surveys showing the compensation you are seeking is in line with industry standards. If you are asking for a promotion, you could get the people with whom you would be working to endorse your request.

Emphasize Your Similarity to the Audience

Audiences are most willing to accept the ideas of a speaker whose attitudes and behaviors are similar to their own. This relationship supports the strategy of establishing *common ground* between speaker and listeners early in a presentation. A speaker who shows they and the audience have similar beliefs will create goodwill that can make listeners willing to consider more controversial ideas later on. Notice how the following business owner, when seeking a zoning variance, based their appeal to the local architectural review board on common ground:

> Like you, I'm a strong believer in preserving the character of our town. As a businesswoman and a long-time resident, I realize beauty and lack of crowding are our greatest assets. Without them, our hometown would become just another overgrown collection of shopping malls and condominiums.
>
> Also, like you, I believe change isn't always bad. Thanks to your efforts, our downtown is a more interesting and beautiful place now than it was even a few years ago. I think we share the philosophy that we ought to preserve what is worth saving and improve the town in whatever ways we can. I appreciate the chance to show you how this project will make the kind of positive change we all seek.

This speaker's demonstrated support for the principles advocated by the review board increased their chances of gaining acceptance for the proposal. Of course, the board has to believe the speaker is sincere. If members suspect the speaker is just telling them what they want to hear, their credibility will shrink, not grow.

Use Logical Reasoning

Many arguments that sound logical at first are later revealed to have errors in reasoning, or **fallacies**.[29] Fallacious reasoning is not always intentional: The person making the case might not be aware that their thinking is flawed. Whether or not they are deliberate, fallacies can weaken your case by casting doubt on the merits of your position. The following are descriptions of the most common fallacies (by both English and Latin names), so you can avoid using them.[30]

- *Personal attack (ad hominem)* An ad hominem fallacy attacks a person's integrity to weaken the argument they are making. Some ad hominem arguments are easy to spot: Clearly, calling someone an "idiot" is not persuasive. Other ad hominem arguments are not as obvious.

- *Reduction to the absurd (reductio ad absurdum)* A reductio ad absurdum fallacy attacks an argument by extending it to such extreme lengths that it looks ridiculous: "If we allow developers to build homes in one section of this area, soon we will have no open spaces left" or "If we have our after-hours customer service handled by an offshore company, pretty soon we won't have any employees here at home." Far-fetched projections like these call for a closer look: Developing one area does not nec-essarily mean that other areas have to be developed, and hiring some employees from overseas will not necessarily lead to widespread layoffs at home. Either of these poli-cies might be unwise, but the ad absurdum reasoning does not prove it.

- *Either-or* An either–or fallacy sets up false alternatives, suggesting that if the infe-rior choice must be rejected, then the other option must be accepted. "If you believe the arts in this community are important, you'll contribute to our fundrais-ing campaign." This sort of argument ignores the fact that it is possible to support the arts in other ways besides donating to a particular cause.

- *False cause (post hoc ergo propter hoc)* A post hoc fallacy mistakenly assumes that one event causes another because those events occur sequentially. Post hoc fallacies are not always easy to detect without careful research. For example, a critic might blame a drop in productivity on the policy of letting some employees work from home, noting that output began to drop shortly after the start of COVID-19. A causal link *may* exist in this case, but other reasons might also explain the decline—a change in the nature of work, for example.

- *Bandwagon appeal (argumentum ad populum)* An argumentum ad populum fallacy is based on the often dubious notion that just because many people favor an idea, you should, too. Sometimes, of course, the mass appeal of an idea can be a sign of its merit. If leading companies have adopted a product, for instance, there is a good chance it will work for your organization. In other cases, widespread accep-tance of an idea is no guarantee of its validity. The majority of employees in your company might invest the bulk of their retirement plan dollars in the company's stock, but almost every financial advisor will tell you this is a dangerous strategy. The lesson here is simple to comprehend but often difficult to follow: Do not just follow the crowd; consider the facts carefully and make up your own mind.

The types of logical support regarded as most persuasive differ from one culture to another. Euro-American culture places a high value on data that can be observed and counted. Statistical data and eyewitness testimony are considered strong evidence. Com-municators from other backgrounds are less impressed by these sorts of proofs. Arab speakers commonly rely on religious and national identification. They are more likely to use elaborate language, which would be considered flowery by other cultural standards. For example, in some parts of Africa, the words of a witness would be regarded with suspicion because members of that culture believe people who speak out about a topic have a particular agenda in mind.

Use Psychological Appeals

Logical arguments, also referred to as *logos*, and your own credibility are both strong assets when you are trying to persuade others. Using the following strategies for appealing to the audience's emotions (known as *pathos)* will boost the odds you can achieve your goal through your persuasive presentation.

Appeal to the Needs of Your Audience   Perhaps the most important aspect of effective selling is identifying the prospective buyer's needs and showing how the prod-uct can satisfy them. Even if the audience is not interested in or is unsympathetic to an idea, there is usually some way to link a proposal to the listeners' needs or values. A representative of an oil company speaking to residents of a coastal town where offshore drilling is being proposed could defend the move by showing how the local economy would benefit and how drilling platforms increase the abundance of marine life in the oceans which, in turn, improves fishing.

Whenever possible, base your appeal on several needs. Listeners who are not reached by one appeal might potentially be persuaded by another. If you are trying to persuade your fellow workers to use public transportation instead of driving their own cars to work, for example, you could identify several needs and show how your proposal would satisfy each one:

Need	Satisfaction
Save money	Getting out of your car, even for a few days each week, means you will spend less on gas, parking, and auto maintenance.
More time	You can read and/or work on the bus or train instead of having to drive yourself and work later.
Less stress	You will not have to deal with the aggravation of traffic congestion and annoying drivers.

Make Your Goal Realistic Presentational speaking is like most other aspects of life: You usually do not get everything you want. Asking audience members to accept an idea they strongly oppose can backfire. Persuasion experts have refined this commonsense principle into *social judgment theory.*[31]

Social judgment theory helps speakers decide how to craft their arguments by identifying the range of possible opinions listeners might have about a speaker's arguments (Figure 11.1). A listener's preexisting position is termed an **anchor**. All the arguments a persuader might use to change the listener's mind cluster around this anchor point in three zones. The first area is the listener's **latitude of acceptance**. As its name implies, this zone contains positions the listener would accept with little or no persuasion. By contrast, the **latitude of rejection** contains arguments the listener opposes. Between these areas lies the **latitude of noncommitment**, which contains arguments the listener neither accepts nor rejects.

Social judgment theory teaches a practical lesson about how much to ask from your audience. Arguments in the listeners' latitude of noncommitment may not impress them, and those in the latitude of rejection will just strengthen their opposition. The best chance for success comes when your plea touches the outer edge of the audience's latitude of acceptance. Communication scholar Em Griffin offers a perfect example of this principle:

> A striking story of social judgment theory in action comes from a university development director I know who was making a call on a rich alumnus. He anticipated that the prospective donor would give as much as $10,000. He made his pitch and asked what the wealthy businessman would do. The man protested that it

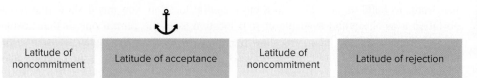

FIGURE 11.1
Range of Responses to a Persuasive Appeal

had been a lean year and that times were tough—he couldn't possibly contribute more than $20,000.

The fund-raiser figured that he had seriously underestimated the giver's latitude of acceptance and that $20,000 was on the low end of that range. Without missing a beat he replied, "Trevor, do you really think that's enough?" The alumnus wrote a check for $25,000.[32]

Social judgment theory teaches that persuasion is not a one-shot affair. In many cases, your persuasive campaign will consist of many messages delivered over time, each one aimed at expanding your listeners' latitude of acceptance. A human resources assistant at a medium-sized company used the lessons of social judgment theory to choose a realistic goal in their campaign to persuade the corporation to set up a daycare center for the preschool children of employees. Rather than ask the boss to authorize funds for the center—an unrealistic outcome—they requested approval to conduct a feasibility study to explore the ways that similar companies supported child care. If the boss responded favorably to the center after seeing the results of this survey, they would present a full-blown proposal. If the boss still had doubts, the backup proposal would suggest the company subsidize tuition at a nearby child care center—a plan closer to the boss's anchor point.

Consider Citing Opposing Ideas
Well-informed listeners, even if they have not made up their minds about an issue, will find a one-sided appeal less persuasive than a presentation that considers the opposing arguments. Discussing these ideas shows you are not trying to avoid the opposition. Even if you refute the competing ideas, considering them at all is more evenhanded than focusing exclusively on your plan and never acknowledging the existence of alternatives.

An account executive at a full-service stock brokerage showed they respected their listeners' knowledge and judgment at an investment seminar when they discussed the alternatives to using their firm's services:

> I know most of you are familiar enough with the financial marketplace to be asking yourself, "Why don't I save money and use a discount brokerage?" And that's a fair question. After all, discount firms charge you a much smaller commission for each transaction than full-service houses like mine. I'd like to suggest that the answer to the question of which kind of brokerage to use lies in the old saying, "You get what you pay for." If you use a discount firm, you'll get limited service. Now, that may be all you want and all you need. But if you're looking for a source of financial support and attention, you'll get it at a full-service brokerage. Let me explain.

Similarly, with hostile listeners, it is wise to compare their position and yours, showing the desirability of your thesis. If management has previously opposed products similar to the one whose launch you are about to propose, for instance, you will need to bring up the managers' objections ("It's too risky, the capital outlay is too big, and the sales force can't sell it") and show how your proposal will meet their objections ("We can minimize the risk and the initial costs by limiting the first production run; if we put extra emphasis on advertising and show the salespeople how other companies have sold similar products very successfully in the last few years, they'll be more enthusiastic and more effective"). Similarly, if you are trying to sell an out-of-the-way plant location to a company that wants to build its new plant in a more central location, you might show that transportation is as cheap and available in your location as in the central one or that savings on real estate taxes and labor will allow the company to cover the higher transportation costs. If you do not mention the arguments already on their minds, your listeners may consider you uninformed.

Self-Assessment   Persuasive Support Strategies

Rate your presentation on the following items using this scale: 3 = accomplished excellently, 2 = accomplished competently, 1 = needs improvement.

1. I maximized my credibility by:
   - Demonstrating my competence with my knowledge of the topic and by sharing   1   2   3
     my credentials.
   - Earning the trust of my audience via honesty and impartiality.   1   2   3
   - Establishing common ground with the audience   1   2   3

2. I structured my arguments logically by:
   - Avoiding the use of logical fallacies (e.g., *ad hominem, post hoc*).   1   2   3

3. I used appropriate psychological strategies such as
   - Appealing to my audience's needs.   1   2   3
   - Setting a realistic goal.   1   2   3
   - Citing opposing ideas when appropriate   1   2   3
   - Adapting to the cultural style of my audience   1   2   3

You should also follow this guideline when the audience will soon hear your viewpoint criticized or another one promoted. You will be better off defusing the opponents' thesis by bringing up and refuting their arguments than letting them attack your position and build up their own in its place.

Adapt to the Cultural Background of Your Audience   Your listeners' cultural background may affect the way they respond to various types of persuasive appeals.[33] The traditional Euro-American ideal is to communicate without becoming too excited. By contrast, cultures in Latin America and the Middle East are generally more expressive, and their members respond more favorably to displays of emotion. An approach that would seem logical and calm to an audience in Seattle or Toronto might seem cold and lifeless to a group in Mexico City or Istanbul. Conversely, a Mexican or Turkish speaker might seem overly excitable to a group in the United States or Canada. A review of the tips for analyzing your audience in Chapter 10 will be useful in identifying the supporting materials that will most effectively appeal to your audience.

• Visual Support

The old cliché is true: A picture often *is* worth a thousand words. That is why charts, diagrams, and other graphic aids are part of most business presentations.

Researchers have verified what good speakers have always known intuitively: Using visual aids makes a presentation more effective. In one study, two groups of business students watched videotaped presentations describing upcoming time-management seminars. One group saw a version of the talk with no visual support, while the other saw the same talk with a number of high-quality visuals. After the presentation, audience members were asked about their willingness to enroll in the time-management course and about their opinion of the speaker they had just viewed.

Audience members who saw the presentation with visuals were clearly more impressed than those who saw the same talk with no visual support. They planned to spend 16.4% more time and 26.4% more money on the time-management seminar being promoted. They also viewed the speaker as more clear, concise, professional, persuasive, and interesting.[34]

Visuals can also boost your image in ways that extend beyond the presentation itself. A professional display of visual aids labels you as a professional person—a candidate for recognition in the future by superiors and the public. Finally, visual aids can make your information more memorable. Researchers have discovered that audiences recall far more information when it is presented both verbally and visually than when it is presented in only one way.[35]

Visual aids add clarity, interest, and proof by performing the following functions:

- *Showing how things look.* An architect might use a model or an artist's sketch to describe a project to potential clients; an advertising director could use photographs of a new product as part of a campaign.

- *Showing how things work.* An engineer might include diagrams as part of the instructions for a piece of equipment; a sales representative could use a model to show how a boat is designed for speed and safety.

- *Showing how things relate to one another.* An organizational chart provides a clear picture of the reporting relationships in a company; a flowchart depicts the steps necessary to get a job done.

- *Emphasizing important points.* An account representative might use a chart to show customers the features of a new product; an investment consultant could use a graph to highlight the performance of a stock.

Types of Visual Support

As a speaker, you may choose from a wide array of visual support, or *visual aids*, to make your presentations more effective. Of course, you will not use all of these graphics every time you speak. Sooner or later, though, you will likely use almost every type described in the following sections.

Objects and Models
Sometimes objects can add interest, increase clarity, and provide proof to your presentation. This is certainly true in training sessions and in some types of selling, where hands-on experience is essential. It is difficult to imagine learning how to operate a piece of equipment without actually giving it a try, and few customers would buy an expensive, unfamiliar piece of merchandise without seeing it in person.

When you do use an object or model for instructional purposes, make sure the item is large enough for everyone to see. Small objects such as a microchip or a piece of jewelry can work as visual aids in a one-on-one presentation, but this same approach will merely frustrate a larger group of listeners. In the latter case, it may be best to show the audience a photograph or video of the item. Furthermore, it is almost always a bad idea to pass an object around for the audience to examine during face-to-face presentations. Doing so will likely distract the person who has the object at a given moment as well as the other people who are craning their necks to get a preview.

It is important to practice using your model or object to avoid unpleasant surprises during the actual presentation. One accountant, for example, hoped to illustrate the point that people's money can go up in smoke if they do not consider the tax consequences of their financial decisions. The speaker attempted to ignite a piece of paper; unfortunately, the demonstration ended with an audience member having to put out a fire.[36]

Photographs   One of the most effective means of illustrating a variety of images that need literal representation—an architectural firm's best work, a corporation's management team, or a stylish new product—photographs also provide an excellent form of proof. For instance, an insurance investigator's picture of a wrecked automobile may be all that exists of the car months later when a claim is argued in court. Additionally, a screenshot of negative reviews about a brand on social media can be used during a crisis communication training workshop. When using a photograph as a visual aid, ensure that the photo is clear and does not appear pixelated from being resized. You should also consider whether the image is large enough for everyone in your audience to see. This is especially crucial in virtual presentations where images are being transmitted to many people with varying Internet speeds. To ensure that your photograph loads properly, you should optimize them by lowering the size and compressing them as much as possible without sacrificing quality.[37] An online search will help you locate free tools for optimizing photos.

Infographics   The use of infographics (see Figure 11.2) is increasing as a means to visually represent information or data. These types of graphics are especially useful when complex information (e.g., statistics, relationships, trends) needs to be presented in a

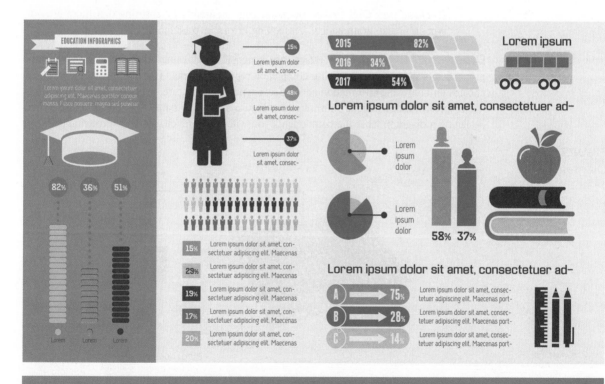

FIGURE 11.2 Infographic

Visual Generation/Shutterstock

manner that is clear and easy for a wide audience to understand. Follow these steps to create an effective infographic:

1. *Identify the story that you want to tell.* Think about the goal of your infographic: What do you want your audience to learn?

2. *Locate credible statistical data.* Break your story into one to six main points, and utilize the data to help you tell the story.

3. *Create a **wireframe**, or outline of where your text and images will be placed.* This layout will help you decide how your information needs to be structured.

4. *Ensure that the design of your infographic matches the tone of the information being presented.* An infographic that seeks to raise awareness of human trafficking, for example, should not rely on pastel colors and playful icons.

5. *Use a variety of icons, illustrations, and charts to present your data.* Get creative and include several types of visualizations in the infographic.

6. *Choose a color palette.* Limit your graphic's palette to three colors and corresponding shades of those colors. If your company uses specific colors as part of its branding, be sure to obtain the hexadecimal (representing the colors red, green, and blue #RRGGBB), or *hex*, color codes to locate the exact shades of each color.

7. *Become comfortable with whitespace.* Including too much information creates clutter, which reduces your audience's ability to process the information quickly.

8. *Proofread your final version.* Maintain your credibility by ensuring that there are no typographical, grammatical, or spelling errors in your infographic.

Diagrams   Diagrams are abstract, two-dimensional drawings that show the important properties of objects without being completely representational. These graphics are excellent choices for conveying information about size, shape, and structure. Types of diagrams you may use in presentations include drawings (see Figure 11.3) and maps (see Figure 11.4). When designing a diagram, label the components you will be referencing in your presentation.

FIGURE 11.3
Diagram

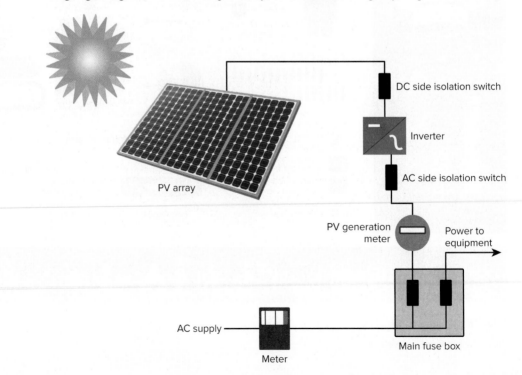

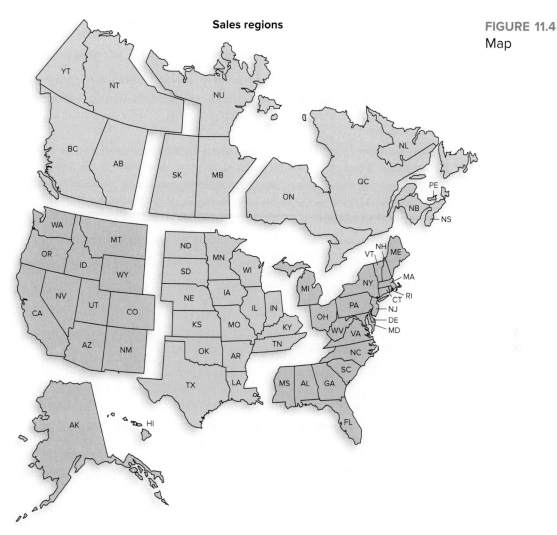

Sales regions

FIGURE 11.4
Map

Lists and Tables   Lists and tables are effective means of highlighting key facts and figures. Lists are especially effective to illustrate steps, call attention to features, or reinforce main points. Tables are useful when you would like to compare related facts, such as advantages and disadvantages, current and past performance, and your product versus a competitor's product. For example, the table in Figure 11.5 shows how the cost of a college education has increased over time. A sales manager might use a similar table to compare this year's sales performance and last year's sales performance in several regions.

Unpolished speakers often assume they just need to enlarge tables from a written report to include them in an oral presentation. In practice, this simple approach rarely

College costs, 2008–2017

FIGURE 11.5
Table

Year	Private 4-year	Public 4-year	Public 2-year
2008–2009	$25,143	$6,585	$2,402
2011–2012	$28,500	$8,244	$2,963
2016–2017	$33,480	$9,650	$3,520

works as intended. Most written tables are far too detailed and difficult to understand to be useful to a group of listeners.

As you design lists and tables for presentation, remember the following points:

- *Keep the visual aid simple.* Use only keywords or phrases, never full sentences.
- *Use numbered and/or bulleted lists to emphasize key points.* Numbered lists suggest ranking or steps in a process, while bulleted lists work best for items that are equally important.
- *Use text sparingly.* If you need more than seven lines of text, create two or more lists or tables. Lines of text should never show more than seven words across the page.
- *Use large type.* Make sure the words and numbers are large enough to be read by everyone in the audience.
- *Enhance the list's or table's readability.* Careful layout and generous use of whitespace will make it easy to read.

Pie Charts   **Pie charts**, like the one in Figure 11.6, illustrate component percentages of a single item. They are often used to show how money is spent, but they can also illustrate the allocation of resources. For example, a personnel director might use a pie chart to show the percentage of employees who work in each division of the company.

Follow these guidelines when constructing pie charts:

- *Place the segment you want to emphasize at the top center* (12 o'clock) *position* on the circle. When you are not emphasizing any segments, organize the wedges from largest to smallest, beginning at 12 o'clock with the largest one.
- *Label each segment,* either inside or outside the figure.
- *List the percentage for each segment* along with its label.

Bar and Column Charts   **Bar charts**, like the one shown in Figure 11.7, compare the value of several items: the productivity of several employees, the relative amounts of advertising money spent on different media, and so on. Simple **column charts** reflect changes in a single item over time. Multiple-column charts, like the one in Figure 11.8, compare several items over time.

FIGURE 11.6
Pie Chart

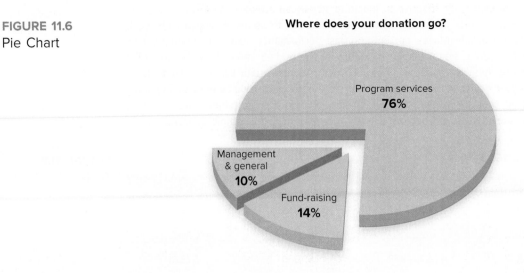

Where does your donation go?

Program services
76%

Management
& general
10%

Fund-raising
14%

Global download speed (MBps)

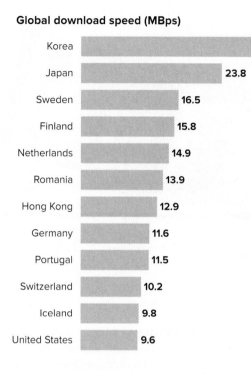

Korea	33.5
Japan	23.8
Sweden	16.5
Finland	15.8
Netherlands	14.9
Romania	13.9
Hong Kong	12.9
Germany	11.6
Portugal	11.5
Switzerland	10.2
Iceland	9.8
United States	9.6

FIGURE 11.7
Bar Chart

Follow these tips to design effective bar and column charts:

- *Always represent time on the horizontal axis* of your chart, running from left to right.
- *Arrange the bars in the sequence* that best suits your purpose. You might choose to order them from high to low, from low to high, in alphabetical order, or in order of importance.
- *Make sure the numerical values represented are clear.* This may mean putting the numbers next to bars or columns, as illustrated in Figure 11.7. In other cases, the figures may fit inside the bars. In a few instances, such as in the chart in Figure 11.8, the scale on the axes will make numbering each bar unnecessary.

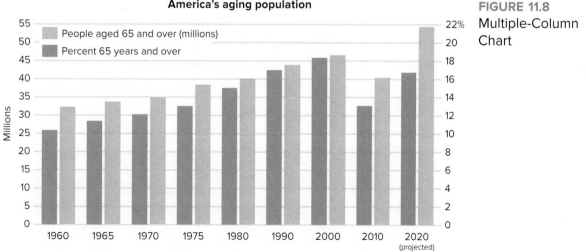

FIGURE 11.8
Multiple-Column Chart

FIGURE 11.9
Pictogram

Ken Cavanagh/McGraw
Hill

Where your textbook dollar goes

53.2¢
Publishing
expenses

19¢
Bookstore
overhead

12.2¢
Author's
royalty

8¢
Taxes

6.6¢
Publisher's
profit

1¢
Bookstore
profit

Pictograms   **Pictograms** are artistic variations of bar, column, or pie charts. As Figure 11.9 shows, pictograms are more interesting than ordinary bar charts. Their attention-getting properties make them especially useful in presentations aimed at lay audiences, such as the general public. Pictograms are often not mathematically exact, however, which makes them less suited for reports that require precise data.

Graphs   **Graphs** show the correlation between two quantities. They are ideally suited for showing trends, such as growth or decline in sales over time. They can also represent a large amount of data without becoming cluttered. Graphs can chart a single trend, or they can show relationships among two or more trends, as in the graph in Figure 11.10. Notice in Figure 11.11 how identical data can be manipulated by adjusting the horizontal and vertical axes.

Videos   Some presentations may benefit from video support. If you are illustrating some sort of action—the performance of an athletic team or the gestures of a speaker, for example—video may do the job better than any other medium.

Despite the benefits of video, including clips you pull off websites or apps YouTube or TikTok or footage you create yourself in a presentation can be risky. Notable problems

FIGURE 11.10
Multiple-Line
Graph

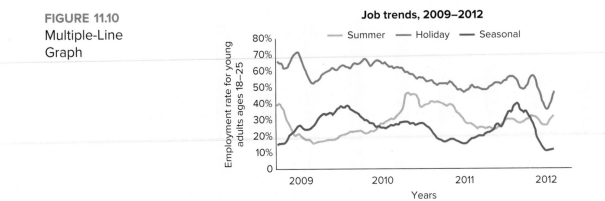

Job trends, 2009–2012

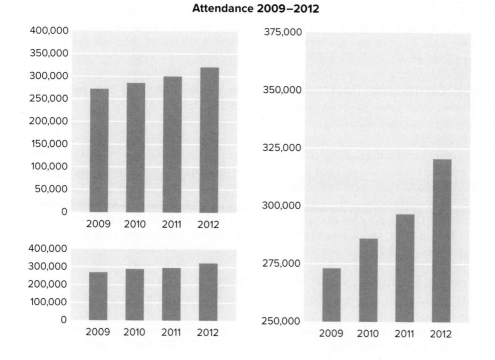

Attendance 2009–2012

FIGURE 11.11

Graphs with Identical Data

The same data can be distorted by varying the horizontal and vertical size and axes of a graph. These graphs were created using Microsoft PowerPoint.

with amateur work include segments that last too long and segments that lack continuity; these shortcomings may then cause the audience to see the rest of your message as equally unprofessional.

Polls Virtual presentations provide speakers with an opportunity to use interactive elements that serve a dual purpose of visually supporting main points and maintaining the audience's interest. In a poll, participants are prompted with a multiple-choice, true/false, or yes/no question, and the results are shown to everyone after the poll has ended. This may be used to gauge your audience's opinion on an issue or reinforce an important point ("Consistent with other organizational research, over 85% of you feel that you don't have enough work–life balance, and you all unanimously feel that this is important to achieve. The strategies I'm going to share with you today will help you find ways to lead a more balanced life.").

Display Media

Choosing the most advantageous way to present your visual aids is just as important as picking the right type of visuals. Even the best photograph, chart, or diagram will flop if it is not displayed effectively.

Whiteboards When whiteboards are available in a presentation room—physical or virtual—they can be useful for recording information that comes up on the spot, such as brainstorming ideas or a tally of audience responses to your questions. Most virtual meeting platforms, like Zoom, include a whiteboard feature that allows for text entry, drawing, highlighting, and saving your work.

However, when you are presenting preplanned visuals in face-to-face settings, it is generally best to use a medium that does not require you to turn your back on the audience and write or draw freehand. Instead of using a whiteboard in these cases, consider using a Post-it self-stick wall pad. This large version of a Post-it note makes it easy for you (or other participants) to recategorize ideas without having to erase and rewrite them. Also, you can take the sticky notes with you at the end of your talk as a record of the points made.

Flip Charts and Poster Boards

Flip charts consist of a large pad of paper attached to an easel. You reveal visuals on a flip chart one at a time by turning the pages. You can also place visuals on a rigid poster board, which you can display on the same sort of easel.

A major advantage of flip charts and poster displays is that they are relatively simple to prepare and easy to use. Their low-tech nature eliminates the risk of equipment problems. You can create them with familiar materials—pens, rulers, and so on—and most copy shops can turn computer-generated files into high-quality posters. Flip charts and poster boards are also relatively portable (most easels collapse into a carrying case) and easy to set up.

Despite these advantages, the size of flip charts and poster boards is a problem: They may be too small for easy viewing and too large to transport easily.

Computer Displays and Virtual Meeting Platforms

With a computer, data projector, or meeting software, you can present a wealth of material during your presentation—for example, text, photos, charts, graphs, and video. You can use a computer to create visuals *during* your presentation: a website demonstration, for example, or an audience poll. Furthermore, with the screen-sharing capabilities available with virtual meeting platforms, speakers and attendees can share screens and access annotation tools to markup the screen. With the right setup, you can integrate visuals into the speaker's screen. For example, in lieu of sharing your screen, Prezi Video allows your slide show and other visual aids to appear on-screen simultaneously with the speaker.[38]

With all computer-supported presentations, you must keep Murphy's Law in mind: Whatever can go wrong with the system probably will. Do not count on having a fast, stable Internet connection. Beware of compatibility problems. Test all parts of the system together, just as you plan to use it, ideally in the place where you will speak. A sophisticated display is useless if it does not work when you are in front of an expectant audience.

Handouts

Speakers can use **handouts** to provide audiences with a permanent record of their ideas. Intricate features of a product, names and phone numbers, and "do's and don'ts" are all easier to recall when your listeners have a printed record of them. Handouts also enable you to give your audience more details than you want to discuss in your presentation. You might, for instance, mention the highlights of a sales period or briefly outline a new product's technical features during your talk, and then refer your listeners to a handout for further information.[39]

Handouts may also reduce or eliminate your listeners' need to take notes. If you include key ideas and figures in a handout, listeners' attention will stay focused on you during your talk, instead of on their notebooks—and you will be sure their notes are accurate.

Some speakers use an "electronic blackboard"—a plastic write-and-wipe board that can produce handout-sized copies of what the speaker writes on the board. Environmentally astute presenters may save paper and boost portability by e-mailing handouts after the presentation or posting them online.

The biggest problem with handouts is that they can be distracting. The act of passing around papers during a face-to-face presentation or making attendees wait while you load your files for screen sharing may interrupt the flow of your presentation. Once the handout is distributed, you will have to compete with it for your audience's attention; sharing a handout may turn listeners into readers. For this reason, it is best to share handouts *after* you have finished speaking. If you must introduce such material during your presentation, tell your listeners when to begin referring to it and when to stop: "Let's take a look at the budget. . . . Now that we've examined the budget, let me direct your attention to the chart up here."

Presentation Software/Apps

Presentation software/apps, such as Microsoft PowerPoint, Apple Keynote, Prezi, Pitch, and Canva, allows anyone with a computer to create and deliver a professional-looking presentation with text and visuals. Presentation software enables speakers to generate customized materials on an as-needed basis. Among the things you can do with a good software program are the following tasks:

- Deliver an onscreen show with special effects such as smooth transitions between screens, animation, and synchronized timing that reveals each point as you raise it.
- Organize a set of speaker's notes for yourself.
- Prepare a variety of handouts for your audience, based on your speaking notes or displays.
- Create "run-time" versions of your displays so you can distribute copies of your presentation to people who may not have seen you speak.
- Create charts, graphs, and tables.

Every competent speaker should be able to use presentation software when the need arises. But, like any form of technology, presentation software programs can cause new problems at the same time as they solve old ones.[40] You should take care to avoid several pitfalls of computerized design programs, which can inadvertently diminish the effectiveness of your presentation.

Poorly conceived messages   Presentation software makes it relatively easy to create charts and graphs, import images, integrate animation, and wrap all of these elements up in an attractive design. Even so, if the structure of your presentation is not clear, listeners will not understand your message or believe what you say. For this reason, it is essential that you organize your points clearly and back up your claims before you begin inputting your message in a software program. Resist the temptation to format your ideas with presentation software before you have a structure for your talk that follows one of the organizational plans in Chapter 10, and make sure your points are backed up with the kinds of supporting material described earlier in this chapter.

Design over content   An all-too-common mistake is to spend more time on the design of a presentation than on its content. Even the most sophisticated designs will not make up for weak ideas. Design expert Edward Tufte says:

> If your numbers are boring, then you've got the wrong numbers. If your words or images are not on point, making them dance in color won't make them relevant. Audience boredom is usually a content failure, not a decoration failure.[41]

There is something seductive about the ease with which you can tinker with fonts, backgrounds, and transitions. Before you know it, you may have devoted far too much time to prettifying your graphics without much additional return. As one expert put it:

> We've got highly paid people sitting there formatting slides—spending hours formatting slides—because it's more fun to do that than concentrate on what you're going to say. . . . Millions of executives around the world are sitting there going "Arial? Times Roman? Twenty-four point? Eighteen point?"[42]

Again, the best way to avoid the seduction of favoring form over content is to create at least a rough outline of your material before you start using presentation software to construct your visual aids.

Overly complex presentations   It is important to resist the temptation to overuse presentation software. In most presentations, simplicity is a virtue. Just because it is *possible* to produce an elaborate visual full of detail, that does not mean this sort of display will always communicate your message effectively. A digital display may dazzle your audience, but the spectacle might actually draw their attention away from you and your message. A presentation is hardly a success if listeners remember your terrific graphics and elaborate animation but cannot recall the points you made.

Another danger of overly elaborate presentations is the possibility they will make material more confusing than it would have been if presented in a simpler way. This has been a problem in the U.S. Armed Forces, where overzealous presenters are known as "PowerPoint Rangers." Former Secretary of the Army Louis Caldera acknowledged that some military brass have alienated lawmakers by staging overly elaborate presentations. "People are not listening to us because they are spending so much time trying to understand these incredibly complex slides," Caldera says.[43] Figure 11.12 shows an example of an overly complex visual aid.

Detailed visuals may be appropriate for written reports but in oral talks, simplicity is usually the best approach.

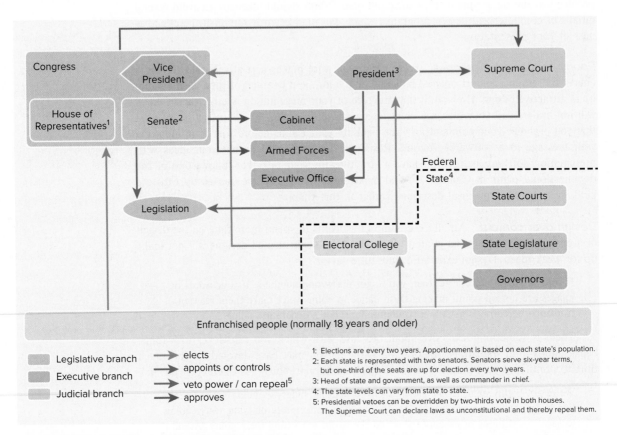

FIGURE 11.12 An Overly Complex Visual Aid

Avoiding Computer Catastrophes in Presentations

When you use computers and virtual presentation platforms, you can count on an equipment failure happening sooner or later. Following these tips will minimize the chances that hardware or software glitches will scuttle your performance:

- *Set up in advance.* Give yourself lots of time to set up and test your equipment before the presentation is scheduled to begin. The last thing you want your audience to see is you frantically rebooting the computer, swapping cables, and trying to troubleshoot software.

- *Always bring two of everything.* Assume your equipment will fail—because it certainly will at some point. Borrow backups for laptop computers, display panels or projectors, modems, and any other hardware you plan to use.

- *Back up your programs.* Having your work saved on a CD, flash drive, the cloud, or some other storage medium can salvage a catastrophe. You might also want to e-mail a copy of your files to yourself as another form of backup.

- *Have backup technical support available.* Line up an expert you can call if something does not work.

- *Beware of the Internet.* Real-time use of the Internet to cue up visual aids is an invitation to disaster. Connections can be slow, and websites can go down without notice. Whenever possible, it is best to store images of sites you will use on your hard drive and/or on a backup medium.

- *Have a contingency plan.* Be prepared for the possibility that your equipment might fail. Have copies of key exhibits prepared as handouts. Handouts may not be as glamorous as high-tech displays, but they are far better than nothing.

Guidelines for Using Visual Aids

Regardless of the display media you choose to use for your presentations, be sure to follow the basic rules discussed in this section.[44]

Selection   Like any part of your presentation, visual exhibits must be chosen carefully. Use a visual only when it enables you to make a point better than you could with words alone.

Be sure you have a reason for using a visual aid   If your image does not explain a point better than words alone, do not use it. One professional described the common mistake of using too many visuals:

> The biggest mistake people make is in expecting the visuals to be the presentation when, in reality, you should be the presentation. If the audience is too involved in looking at the screen, they're not looking at you, so your words have less of an impact. The goal of any visual presentation should be to enhance what the speaker says, not distract from it.[45]

Visuals used for their own sake will distract your audience from the point you are trying to make.

Keep your slide shows brief   Keep in mind the "less is more" rule. The chances of listeners recalling your points is inversely proportional to the number of slides you show.

Match the sophistication of your visuals to the audience   Presentations to important audiences—top management, bosses, key customers, and so on—usually require polished graphics. There are exceptions, however. For example, financial and scientific professionals are usually receptive to a no-frills approach.

A Professional Perspective

Stephanie Russell

Digital Content, Marketing Strategy, and Analytics Specialist at Avid Design

Vail, CO

Credit: Stephanie Russell

As a digital marketing director, it is my responsibility to plan, pitch, and activate advertising campaigns with ethical tracking parameters that show proven and transparent results. When presenting results or new strategies, I must cater to audiences that span age ranges and industries. To accomplish this and build trust, I rely on thoughtful presentations that incorporate inclusive language and straightforward visuals.

Inclusive language that avoids jargon or abbreviations helps me clearly define metrics and explain their implications. I also explain the tracking strategies so everyone knows exactly how I collected this data. Using such forthright language levels the playing field and builds trust, helping everyone understand the meaning of the information presented and paving the way for a mutually beneficial decision-making process. My strategy for persuasive pitches is to engage the client using open-ended questions, then present solutions that meet business goals with respect for both the client's needs and their patrons' expectations.

I use visuals that are easily digestible upon first glance, such as line charts, uncluttered presentation slides with concise labeling, and mockups. Metrics are transparent and always cited by both source and settings. Charts feature comprehensive data, including any failures. This not only shows the client the full picture, but also ensures that metrics provided, especially with comparisons, are never skewed and always "apples-to-apples." I supplement these slides with printed detailed reports that I can refer to while navigating the more concise presentation slides. Every presentation is tested beforehand to mitigate technical issues and ensure clarity.

For routine talks, you can probably produce perfectly adequate exhibits on your own. In any case, you should not mix informal images with more formal ones.

Design   Confusing or sloppy exhibits will be counterproductive. Following a few simple guidelines will help you create clear, neat images.[46]

Make sure the visual is large enough to see   The visual that looks so clear on the desktop in front of you might appear almost microscopic to your listeners, especially if they are tuning into your presentation from their mobile phones or tablets. Avoid using items, drawings, or photographs that are so small you have to describe them or pass them around. Remember, a distracting or unclear visual aid is worse than no support at all.

Keep the design of your visuals simple   Show only one idea per exhibit and avoid unnecessary details. Use simple typefaces.[47]

Use only a few words   Most exhibits are visual images, so you should avoid excessive text. Captions should contain only keywords or phrases, not sentences. Omit subtitles. Follow the "Rule of Seven": Each slide should contain no more than seven lines, and each line should have no more than seven words. If an exhibit needs further explanation, supply it verbally. Remember, you are giving an oral presentation, not showing your audience a written report.

Use only horizontal printing   Avoid vertical or diagonal wording. If necessary, place captions in the margins so that you can use a horizontal format.

Label all items clearly   Make sure each exhibit has a descriptive title. Label each axis of a chart, each part of a diagram, and so on to ensure its clear identification.

Display a visual only while you are discussing it   Both putting up a graphic before discussing it and leaving a graphic up after you have finished talking about it are confusing and distracting. In PowerPoint, for example, you can blank out the screen by pushing either the "B" or period (".") key. Pushing the key a second time makes the screen visible again.

Make sure your visuals will work in the meeting room   Double-check the availability of easels, screens, screen-sharing capabilities, and other equipment you will need. For face-to-face presentations, also make sure electrical outlets are in the needed locations and extension cords are available if you will need them. Check sight lines from all audience seats. Be sure you can easily control lighting levels as necessary.

Practice using your visuals   Rehearse setting up and removing visuals smoothly and quickly. Review the comments you will make with each one. Be sure exhibits are arranged in the correct order and lined up properly so you can avoid the embarrassment of mixed-up charts or upside-down slides.

• Using Support Ethically

You have done your research and found solid, interesting verbal support to enhance your presentation. You spent time carefully thinking through the guidelines for visual support to ensure that your visual aids enhance your presentation and do not distract from it. If you are attempting to persuade your audience, you have likely also considered how to best incorporate competence, logic, and emotional appeals. Before you are ready to present, however, you must ensure that your support—in all of its forms—is **ethical**. This section will help ensure that your presentations meet the standards of behavior expected by your audiences and professional colleagues.

Cite Your Sources

Whether you are quoting someone, giving a statistic, or using a photo from the Internet, it is both proper and effective to cite the source of the information.

Showing your verbal ideas are based on authoritative sources boosts your credibility and helps you avoid potentially embarrassing situations like the one in the Case Study in this chapter. When citing sources, follow these simple guidelines:

- *Cite the source in a way that adds to the credibility of your presentation.* If necessary, explain why the source is credible: "Here's what the nonpartisan, independent Congressional Budget Office said . . ."

- *Cite sources that have credibility with your audience.* Citing socialist Karl Marx about the abuse of workers will not impress an audience consisting of Republican manufacturers, whereas a similar message from an article in the *Wall Street Journal* might be effective.

To cite sources without interrupting the flow of your presentation, the following four-step method can be used:

1. *State your point:*	"The trend of working from home is growing."
2. *Identify the source of your citation:*	"In the March 12 edition of *USA Today,* columnist Stephanie Armour states . . ."
3. *State the content of your citation:*	"Just about anyone with a high-speed Internet connection and a telephone can become a virtual free agent, handling customer service calls for major corporations."
4. *Explain how and why the material is important for members of your audience:*	"That means almost everyone in this room has the potential to work from home, whether you are going to school, raising a child, or have limited mobility."

It is also important to cite the sources of the visual support that you incorporate in your presentation. At times, it is appropriate to orally cite the source while you are showing the visual aid ("As you can see from the results of this survey conducted by Gallup in 2021....."). Other times, it is acceptable to have a text-based list of your sources adjacent to the images or at the end of your presentation slide deck.

Strive to Be Inclusive

When making a business presentation, one of your goals should be to make your presentation welcoming and accessible to everyone in your audience. To achieve this goal, it is important to recognize that unintentional or unconscious bias is often present in the stories, examples, language, and visuals used by speakers. When creating a hypothetical example or a fictional story, consider how you might promote the representation of underserved groups and combat stereotypes. Using cross-cultural names, or positioning persons of various cultural groups in high-ranking positions are two ways to ensure that your presentation is relatable to a variety of audience members. For example, when displaying a photo of a surgeon, you might consider using a photo of a physician with visible tattoos. Similarly, placing members of different ethnicities and gender identities in roles they are not stereotypically associated with will demonstrate inclusivity. Additionally, you should avoid using language like "as you can see," which may single out members of the audience with vision challenges.

Furthermore, it is important that speakers take accessibility seriously. The term *universal design*, coined by architect Ronald L. Mace, refers to designing environments that are accessible to everyone, regardless of their language, race, age, sexual orientation, learning style, and ability. Globally, with over 2.2 billion people suffering from visual impairment[48] and over 477 million with hearing loss,[49] there is an important need for visual accessibility. Two common accessibility issues with computer-based visual aids include[50]:

- *Low contrast on text.* Low color contrast can pose challenges to audience members with low vision or color blindness. A color contrast checker can be used to make sure there is enough contrast between your text and highlighting or backgrounds.

Cherry-Picking Support?

Imagine you are planning a sales presentation to a prospective client. To back up your claims that the product or service you are offering is outstanding, you know you need to provide examples of outstanding service and testimonials of satisfied customers. You do have a few good examples of each, but sadly they are not representative of the kind of feedback your organization usually receives. In fact, it would be much easier to come up with examples and complaints that reflect unhappy clients.

How can you reconcile the need to be honest with the desire to sign up a new customer?

- *Missing alt-text on images.* Screen reading programs allow persons with visual impairments to listen to descriptions of the content on the screen. If alt-text descriptions are not provided for visuals, however, the program is unable to accurately describe the image. For each image, you should identify who is in the image, the who/what/when/where/why of the image, and any descriptions of mood, atmosphere, or tone. When crafting image descriptors, be sure to use appropriate language for your audience's knowledge level.

Additionally, speakers can take the following steps to make visual aids accessible for all[51]:

- Make sure that any videos used in the presentation are captioned or have a text transcription available.
- Have a few handouts available in larger print, and black and white.
- If appropriate, provide materials ahead of time for sign language interpreters so they can prepare.

Use Sources Responsibly

Your credibility as a speaker is tied to the sources that you use to verbally and visually support your ideas. While it is natural to seek out information to support your position, it is never acceptable to manipulate or fabricate supporting material to trick the audience into thinking or acting a certain way. Deceptive practices, such as cutting axes, changing data from positive to negative, or taking information out of context, are all unethical forms of persuasion. David Spiegelhalter, Winton professor for the public understanding of risk at the University of Cambridge, shares a memorable example:

> I got very grumpy at an official graph of British teenage pregnancy rates that apparently showed they had declined to nearly zero. Until I realized that the bottom part of the axis had been cut off, which made it impossible to visualize the (very impressive) 50% reduction since 2000.[52]

Deception is dangerous—if it is detected, the influenced parties may feel betrayed, leading to a "boomerang effect" in which people change their attitudes to the opposite of the one a speaker advocated.[53] Moreover, some forms of manipulation are downright illegal. For example, a financial advisor cannot promise that a stock or mutual fund will have the same stellar performance in the future as it has demonstrated in the past.

By being honest, ethical communicators can feel good about themselves and their presentations. They will also build a solid reputation in their workplace and the larger community.

MASTER the chapter

review points

- Supporting materials are vital in any presentation and serve three purposes: to clarify ideas, to make content more interesting, and to offer proof.

- Definitions, examples, stories (fictional, hypothetical, and factual), statistics, comparisons (figurative and literal), and quotations all serve as verbal supports.

- In addition to traditional types of verbal support, persuasive speeches require additional forms of verbal support: maximizing credibility, using logical reasoning, and using psychological appeals.

- Persuasive speakers must consider their audiences' possible opinions when crafting arguments. The best chance for success happens when a speaker appeals to an audience member's latitude of acceptance.

- In business presentations, well-designed visual aids can make a point more quickly and clearly than words alone, add variety and interest, and boost a speaker's professional image.

- Visuals serve several functions: They highlight important information and show how things look, how they work, or how they relate to one another.

- Speakers can use several types of visual aids: objects, models, photographs, infographics, diagrams, lists and tables, pie charts, bar and column charts, pictograms, graphs, videos, and polls.

- Visuals can be presented via a number of media: whiteboards, flip charts and poster boards, computer displays, virtual meeting platforms, handouts, and presentation software/apps.

- Presentation software allows presenters to develop professional-looking visual exhibits. Take care not to overuse features that result in cluttered and overstimulating, but unclear, visuals.

- Whatever the medium used, all visual aids should meet some basic selection and design standards: they should be easy to understand, purposeful, suited to the point they illustrate and to the audience, and workable in the presentation's setting.

- Successful speakers plan their messages carefully, emphasize content over design, and strive for simplicity and clarity.

- Speakers need to be familiar with their visual aids to avoid unpleasant surprises during the delivery of the presentation.

- Speakers can create ethical and credible presentations by knowing when and how to cite verbal and visual sources, striving to be inclusive and enhancing visual accessibility, and using sources responsibly to avoid manipulating the audience.

key terms

anchor   355
bar chart   362
column chart   362
comparison   349
credibility   352
definition   344
ethics   370
example   345
fallacies   353
flip chart   366
graph   364
handout   366

latitude of acceptance   355
latitude of noncommitment   355
latitude of rejection   355
pictogram   364
pie chart   362
presentation software/apps   367
quotation   351
statistics   348
stories   346
supporting material   341
wireframe   360

activities

1. Invitation to Insight

Read a printed version of a speech. You can find sample speeches in your college library or at an online site such as American Rhetoric.

Find examples of at least three types of supporting materials. For each item, categorize which type of support it is. How well does it follow the guidelines in the text? For example, if it is a citation, does it follow the four-step method? Analyze whether the supporting material provides clarity, interest, and/or proof of the thesis. In your analysis, consider the interests and knowledge level of the intended audience.

2. Skill Builder

Which types of support introduced in this chapter would you use to add interest, clarity, and proof to the following points? Provide specific examples.

a. Tuition costs are keeping promising students out of college.
b. Textbooks are (are not) overpriced.
c. Timely payment of bills is in the customer's best interest.
d. Companies help themselves as well as their employees when they sponsor and subsidize exercise programs during work hours.
e. A liberal arts education can benefit one's career more effectively in many ways than technical training.

3. Skill Builder

Practice paraphrasing definitions into your own words by selecting several detailed definitions from an encyclopedia or from an online dictionary. First, read the definition to the class word for word. Then restate the definition in your own words. Ask your classmates which version of the definition was easier to follow.

4. Invitation to Insight

Public service announcements (PSAs) are short pieces aimed at persuading audiences to support nonprofit organizations, issues, or causes. Locate and view a PSA online.

Which strategies are used to motivate the audience in the PSA you viewed? Why are these strategies successful? Are these strategies ethical? Explain your answers.

5. Skill Builder

Well-chosen and well-told stories can help you make a point in an interesting and compelling way. In a brief presentation of 1 minute or less, use a story to illustrate an important lesson about professional communication. The story you tell may be based on your personal experience, something you observed, or something you read or heard about from others.

Organize your presentation in one of two ways: (1) State your thesis first and then show how the story supports it, or (2) tell the story first, and then show how it illustrates your thesis. In either case, conclude by showing audience members how your thesis and the story that illustrates it relates to their professional lives.

6. Skill Builder

Practice citing references aloud. Locate interesting facts in a variety of types of sources (e.g., newspapers, credible magazines, books, Internet sites, interviews with a professional). In class, cite the facts and references aloud, using the four-step method for citing sources found in this chapter.

7. Skill Builder

Suggest an ethical persuasive approach to providing verbal and visual support for each of the following situations:

a. A boss tries to get volunteers to work weekend hours.
b. A union representative encourages new employees to join the union.
c. An insurance agent tries to persuade a child-free young professional couple to buy life and income protection policies.
d. The representative for a waste disposal company tries to persuade residents of a town that locating a regional recycling center nearby would be good for the community.
e. A sales representative needs one more sale to meet their monthly quota and knows a competitor's product better meets this client's needs.

8. Skill Builder

Practice your skill at developing visual aids by doing one of the following activities:

a. Develop a chart or graph showing the overall changes in the demographic characteristics (age, sex, and so on) of your school's student body over the past 10 years.

b. Suppose the local chamber of commerce has hired you to compile graphic exhibits that will be used in presentations to encourage people to visit and settle in your area. Design materials reflecting the following information:

   1. Average salaries for typical types of jobs.
   2. Types of recreational activities available.
   3. Average days per month with sunshine.

   If you believe that these figures would *discourage* an audience, choose other data that paint an appealing picture of your area.

c. Develop three visual aids that could be used to introduce new employees to the benefits offered by your company.

9. Skill Builder

Choose a fact or statistic you can illustrate with visual aids. Develop two different versions of your visual aid that would be effective for two different audiences or occasions (e.g., a group of interns, a workshop at a scientific conference, a formal company dinner, a weekly staff meeting). Share your visual aids with a group of classmates and offer a critique based on the guidelines discussed in this chapter.

10. Invitation to Insight

You can get a sense of how visual aids are used, ignored, overused, misused, or lack inclusivity by attending a presentation of your choice in the community. Identify the visual supports the speaker uses, and evaluate their effectiveness for the intended audience and occasion. If you had been hired as a consultant, what advice would you give the speaker about the effectiveness of their visual exhibits?

Mc Graw Hill **LearnSmart**™

For further review, go to the LearnSmart study module for this chapter.

references

1. Poole, L. (1984, February). A tour of the Mac desktop. *Mac World, 1*(2), 16–27.
2. Spangenberg, C. (1977). Basic values and the techniques of persuasion. *Litigation, 3*(3), 13–18. Retrieved from https://www.jstor.org/stable/29758340
3. Primrose on Premise (n.d.). Understanding the benefits of employer-sponsored child care. Retrieved from https://franchise.primroseschools.com/onpremise /insights/understanding-the-benefits-of-employer -sponsored-child-care/
4. Burgoon, M., & Burgoon, J. K. (1975). Message strategies in influence attempts. In G. J. Hanneman & W. J. McEwen (Eds.), *Communication and behavior.* Reading, MA: Addison-Wesley.
5. Schroer, A. (2018, November 12). Life at headquarters: A guide to Microsoft's Redmond campus. *Built in Seattle.* Retrieved from https://www.builtinseattle .com/2018/11/12/microsoft-redmond-campus-head quarters
6. Umpqua Bank (n.d.). Corporate responsibility: Community partnerships. Retrieved from https:// www.umpquabank.com/corporate-responsibility /partnerships/
7. Kramer, H. (2017, October 10). 13 Unusual but awesome perks at companies hiring now. *Glassdoor.* Retrieved from https://www.glassdoor.com/blog /unusual-awesome-perks/
8. Totally Twisted Pretzel. (2020). Retrieved from https://www.totallytwistedpretzel.com/
9. accessAbilities. (n.d.). Retrieved from https:// accessabilities.org/
10. Poundsford, M. (2007). Using storytelling, conversation and coaching to engage. *Strategic Communication Management, 11,* 32–35.
11. Gallo, C. (2008, September 12). Use storytelling to strengthen your presentations. *BusinessWeek.* Retrieved from http://www.businessweek.com/small- biz/content/sep2008/sb20080912_141650.htm

12. Gallo, C. (2008, September 12). Use storytelling to strengthen your presentations. *BusinessWeek*. Retrieved from http://www.businessweek.com /smallbiz/content/sep2008/sb20080912_141650.htm

13. Small, D. A., Loewenstein, G., & Slovic, P. (2007). Sympathy and callousness: The impact of deliberative thought on donations to identifiable and statistical victims. *Organizational Behavior and Human Decision Processes, 102,* 143–153. Retrieved from https://doi.org/10.1016/j.obhdp.2006.01.005

14. Daly, J. A., & Englebert, I. N. (2011). *Presentations in everyday life*. Boston, MA: Houghton Mifflin.

15. Rooney, A. (1989). Sales vs. service. *Executive Speechwriter Newsletter, 14,* 5.

16. Slan, J. (1998). *Using stories and humor: Grab your audience!* Boston, MA: Allyn & Bacon.

17. Lukaszewski, J. E. (1997). You can become a verbal visionary. *Executive Speeches, 12*(1), 23–30.

18. Lindsey, L. L., & Yun, K. A. (2003). Examining the persuasive effect of statistical messages: A test of mediating relationships. *Communication Studies, 54,* 306–321. Retrieved from https://doi.org/10.1080 /10510970309363288

19. Jolie, A. (2012). Remember the refugees . . . who are dying at this very moment. *Vital Speeches International, 4*(2), 38–39.

20. "Small business report: Making time and money real." (1987, March). *Executive Communication Report, 3.*

21. Rosling, H. (2010, May 22). The best stats you've ever seen. [Video file]. Retrieved from https://www. ted.com/talks/hans_rosling_shows_the_best_stats_ you_ve_ever_seen/transcript?language=en

22. Diamond, S. J. (1991, June 13). Some airlines' ads mislead without lying. *Los Angeles Times*, p. E1.

23. Romans, C. (2009, February 4). Numb and number: Is trillion the new billion? *CNN*. Retrieved from http://www.cnn.com/2009/LIVING/02/04/trillion.dol-lars/index.html?eref=rss_topstories

24. "Miners deserve better." (2006, January 5). *Los Angeles Times*, p. B12.

25. Anderson, K. (2011, December 29). Craft an attention-grabbing message. *Harvard Business Review Blog*. Retrieved from http://blogs.hbr.org/cs/2011/12/ craft_an_attention-grabbing_me.html

26. Woopidoo Quotations. (n.d.). Business quotes by business leaders. Retrieved from http://www.woop idoo.com/business_quotes

27. Petty, R. E., & Cacioppo, J. T. (1990). Involvement and persuasion: Tradition versus integration. *Psychological Bulletin, 107,* 367–374.

28. Gass, R. H., & Seiter, J. S. (1999). *Persuasion, social influence and compliance-gaining*. Boston, MA: Allyn & Bacon; Lucas, S. E. (2009). *The art of public speaking* (10th ed.). New York, NY: McGraw Hill.

29. Adler, R. B., & Rodman, G. (2009). *Understanding human communication* (10th ed.). New York, NY: Oxford University Press.

30. Sprague, J., Stuart, D., & Bodary, D. (2012). *The speaker's handbook* (10th ed.). Boston, MA: Cengage.

31. O'Keefe, D. J. (1990). *Persuasion: Theory and research*. Newbury Park, CA: Sage; Griffin, E. M. (2009). *A first look at communication theory* (7th ed.). New York, NY: McGraw Hill.

32. Griffin, E. M. (2009). *A first look at communication theory* (7th ed.). New York, NY: McGraw Hill.

33. Lustig, M. L., & Koester, J. (2006). *Intercultural competence: Interpersonal communication across cultures* (5th ed.). Boston, MA: Pearson Education; Lieberman, D. A. (1994). *Public speaking in the multicultural environment*. Englewood Cliffs, NJ: Prentice-Hall.

34. "Paper work is avoidable (if you call the shots)." (1977, June 17). *Wall Street Journal*, p. 24.

35. Vogel, D. R., Dickson, G. W., & Lehman, J. A. (1986). Driving the audience action response. *Computer Graphics World, 5*(6), 25–28.

36. Molina, D. (2011, October 2). Conquering my fear of speaking in public. *New York Times*, p. B8.

37. Eggleston, A. (2018, February 27). Types of visual aids that work best for webinars. *Worktank*. Retrieved from https://worktankwebcasts.com/types-of-visual -aids-that-work-best-for-webinars/

38. Staneart, D. (n.d.). Visual aid examples for both in-person and virtual presentations. *Fearless Presentations*. Retrieved from https://www.fearless presentations.com/visual-aid-examples-for-both-in -person-and-virtual-presentations/

39. Pike, R. W. (1994). Handouts: A little charity to your audience goes a long way. *Presentations, 8*(5), 31–35.

40. Ganzel, R. (2000). Power pointless. *Presentations, 14*(2), 54–57.

41. Tufte, E. R. (2003). *The cognitive style of PowerPoint*. Cheshire, CT: Graphics Press.

42. Parker, I. (2001, May 28). Absolute PowerPoint. *The New Yorker*, pp. 76–87.

43. Jaffe, G. (2000, April 26). What's your point, Lieutenant? Just cut to the pie charts. *Wall Street Journal*, p. A1.

44. Kosslyn, S. M., & Chabris, C. (1993). The mind is not a camera, the brain is not a VCR: Some psychological guidelines for designing charts and graphs. *Aldus Magazine, 4*(6), 33–36.

45. Medaris, K. (2008, October 6). Purdue expert gives do's and don'ts of visual presentations. *Purdue University News*. Retrieved from http://news.uns.pur-due.edu/x/2008b/081006T-SmithPower.html

46. Tuck, L. (1994). Using type intelligently. *Presentations, 8*(4), 30–32; Hinkin, S. (1995). Not

just another pretty face: 10 tips for the most effective use of type. *Presentations*, *9*(1), 34–36.

47. Terberg, J. (2005). Font choices play a crucial role in presentation design. *Presentations*, *19*(4). Retrieved from www.presentations.com/presentations/creation /article_display.jsp?vnu_content_id=1000875169

48. World Health Organization (2021, February 26). Blindness and vision impairment. Retrieved from https://www.who.int/news-room/fact-sheets/ detail/blindness-and-visual-impairment

49. Hearing Health Foundation (n.d.). Hearing Loss & Tinnitus Statistics. Retrieved from https://hear-inghealthfoundation.org/hearing-loss-tinnitus-statis-tics#:˜:text=48%20million%20people%20in%20 the,worldwide%20live%20with%20hearing%20 loss.&text=Nearly%20half%20of%20people%20old-er,health%20condition%20facing%20older%20 adults.

50. Accessible Metrics. (2019, July 16). Top 8 most common accessibility issues to avoid and solve. Retrieved from https://www.accessiblemetrics.com/blog/top -8-most-common-accessibility-issues-to-avoid-and-solve/

51. Bugstahler, S. (2015). Equal access: Universal design of your presentation. Retrieved from http://www .washington.edu/doit/ equal-access-universal-design-your-presentation

52. Akshat, R. (2016, March 26). A Cambridge professor on how to stop being so easily manipulated by misleading statistics. *Quartz*. Retrieved from https:// qz.com/643234/cambridge-professor-on-how-to -stop-being-so-easily-manipulated-by-misleading -statistics/

53. Burgoon, M., & Miller, M.D. (1990). Communication and influence. In G. L. Dahnke & G. W. Clatterbuck (Eds.), *Human communication: Theory and research*. Belmont, CA: Wadsworth.

Chapter Twelve
Delivering the Presentation

chapter objectives

After reading this chapter you should be able to:

1. Evaluate delivery styles and select and use the style best suited to a specific presentation.

2. Create and deliver effective extemporaneous and impromptu presentations.

3. Apply confidence-building strategies to reduce communication apprehension and improve effectiveness.

4. Deliver a presentation that follows the guidelines for effective visual, verbal, and vocal delivery.

5. Conduct effective question-and-answer sessions and solicit feedback following recommended guidelines.

After reading this far, you know how to design an effective presentation. The information in Chapters 9 through 11 will serve you well, but specific situations call for specific approaches. This chapter builds on the skills you have already learned, helping you gain an extra margin of confidence and polish that can make your presentations interesting and effective—even outstanding.

No matter how well designed, a presentation must be well delivered if it is to succeed. If you look sloppy, speak in a way that is hard to understand, or seem unenthusiastic, listeners are likely to doubt or even reject your ideas.

In this chapter, we offer a description of the various styles of delivery, tips for building your confidence, guidelines for visual and vocal delivery, and how to deal with questions and solicit feedback from the audience. These suggestions will help you deliver your remarks in a way that makes your message clearer, more interesting, and more persuasive.

• Delivery Styles

Although people typically think of presentations consisting of a speaker standing behind a lectern delivering information to a passive audience, many business and professional presentations are far more interactive. Regardless of whether you must deliver a long lecture, guide a discussion, or engage in an interactive presentation,[1] you may choose from four styles: manuscript, memorized, extemporaneous, and impromptu. However, two of them—extemporaneous and impromptu—will serve you best in most professional situations.

Manuscript Presentations

In **manuscript presentations**, speakers read their remarks word for word from a prepared statement. Manuscript speaking is common at annual company meetings, conventions, and press conferences. Unfortunately, few experiences are as boring as the average manuscript presentation.

Novice speakers often try to conceal their nervousness about facing a large audience by reading from a script—and often delivering lifeless presentations as a consequence. Because most speakers are not trained at reading aloud, their delivery is halting and jerky. Even worse, a nervous speaker who relies too heavily on a manuscript can make serious mistakes without even

381

Using a Virtual Teleprompter

When virtually delivering a manuscript presentation is necessary, a teleprompter may be used to help you maintain eye contact with the audience, rather than looking down at your notes.

Free online software like Teleprompter Mirror allows speakers to paste their script into a teleprompter that then projects the script in a browser window over your video conferencing software. Speakers can choose between automatic and voice-activated scrolling, adjust the speed to the presentation style, and pause the script to answer audience questions.

Source: The Democracy Labs. (2020, September 22). Communicate better on Zoom: Keep eye contact with an on-screen teleprompter. *DemLabs Blog.* Retrieved from https://thedemlabs.org/2020/09/22/teleprompter-compatible-with-zoom/#

knowing it. Marilyn Landis, president and CEO of a management consulting firm, describes one such disaster:

> I remember the president of a large corporation who followed his usual pattern of asking his public relations director to write a speech for him. Due to a collating error, the script contained two copies of page five. You guessed it. The president read page five twice—and didn't even realize it.[2]

In legal or legislative testimony, diplomatic speeches, or other situations in which a slight misstatement could have serious consequences, manuscript speaking may be your best means of delivery. Most presentations, however, do not fall into this category. A simple but important rule for most cases, then, is *do not read your presentation.*

Memorized Presentations

As with speaking from a manuscript, speaking from memory poses unique challenges. You have probably been subjected to a memorized sales pitch from a telemarketer or door-to-door salesperson. If so, you know that the biggest problem of a **memorized presentation**—one recited word for word from memory—is that it *sounds* memorized. Speakers who recite their presentations from memory often fail to incorporate natural nonverbal expressions or demonstrations of emotion in their delivery. As a result, their speeches sound rehearsed to the point of almost being robotic.

It might seem that memorizing a presentation would help alleviate your nervousness, but, in fact, memorization increases the odds that a speaker will experience stage fright. During the presentation, they must focus on remembering what comes next instead of getting involved in the meaning of their remarks. It is difficult to recover from forgetting a portion of a memorized speech without the mistake being obvious to the audience.

Sometimes it is necessary to memorize parts of a presentation because referring to notes at a critical moment can diminish your credibility. A salesperson is usually expected to know a product's major features: how much horsepower it has, how much it costs, or the Bluetooth range it delivers. A personnel manager might be expected to know, without referring to a brochure, the value of employee life insurance (if each employee's benefit is the same) and how much employees contribute to the premium. A coworker would look foolish at a retirement dinner if they said, "Everyone knows about Charlie's contributions . . ." and then had to pause to refer to their notes. In such situations, it is recommended to memorize only the essential *parts* of a presentation.

Extemporaneous Presentations

An **extemporaneous presentation** is planned and rehearsed but not memorized word for word. When you speak extemporaneously, you learn your key points and become familiar with the support you will use to back them up. In other words, you practice the big picture but let the specific words come naturally during your delivery. If you prepare carefully and practice your presentation several times with a friend, family member, or even a group of coworkers or subordinates, you will have a good chance of delivering an extemporaneous talk that seems spontaneous—and maybe even effortless. Almost every presentation you plan—a sales presentation, a talk at the local high school, a progress report to a management review board, a training lecture, an annual report to employees or the board of directors—should be delivered extemporaneously.

Juice Images/Cultura/Getty Images

A good extemporaneous presentation should be carefully rehearsed, but it will never be exactly the same twice because you will be speaking *with* the audience, not *at* them. One speaking coach explained:

> I tell presenters to strive for dialogue behavior in a monologue setting. Dialogue behavior is two people talking across a kitchen table—it's comfortable and natural, and you don't have to think much about it. Monologue behavior is a presenter talking stiffly to [their] slides.[3]

Extemporaneous speakers use notes for reminders of the order and content of ideas. There is no single best format for these notes. Some speakers prefer abbreviated outlines, while others find that index cards with keywords or phrases work best. One hint if you use note cards: It is a good idea to have them hole-punched and clipped on a ring, so they do not scatter if dropped. If you do not want to put them on a ring, you can number the back of each card, so you can quickly put them in the correct order.

Whatever form you use, your speaking notes should have the following characteristics.

Notes Should Be Brief   Overly detailed notes tempt a speaker to read them. Inexperienced salespeople who rely on a brochure, for instance, often wind up reading to their prospective customers. More experienced salespeople might be able to use the brochure's boldface headings as a guide. If you are using presentation software, the points on your slides may be all you need to guide you.

Notes Should Be Legible   Your words should not turn into meaningless scribbles when you need them. The writing on your notes should be neat and large enough to be read at a glance. Better yet, print your notes out in an easy-to-read typeface and size. When doing so, you should double-space the text and use a font size large enough that you can read it at a quick glance.

Notes Should Be Unobtrusive   Most audiences will not be offended if you speak from notes, as long as those notes are not distracting. Flapping a sheet of paper in your hand or shuffling several sheets of paper on a lectern can become a noisy irritation. Some speakers avoid such problems by providing their listeners with a printed handout, which they also use for their own notes. That can be a fine idea as long as the handout is brief enough that it does not tempt the audience to read instead of listening.

Impromptu Presentations

Sooner or later you will be asked to give an **impromptu presentation**—an unexpected, off-the-cuff talk. A customer might stop in your office and ask you to describe the new model you will have next spring. At a celebration dinner, you might be asked to "say a few words." A manager might ask you to "give us some background on the problem" or to "fill us in on your progress." You may suddenly discover at a weekly virtual meeting that your subordinates are unaware of a process they need to know about to understand the project you are preparing to explain. In fact, the *Wall Street Journal* reported that impromptu presentations far outnumber planned speeches in the workplace.[4]

The good news is that giving an impromptu talk need not be as threatening as it seems. Most of the time, you will be asked to speak about a subject within your expertise—such as a current project, a problem you have solved, or a technical aspect of your training—which means you have thought about the topic before. Another reassuring fact is that most listeners will not expect perfection in unrehearsed remarks.

Your impromptu presentations will be most effective if you adhere to the following guidelines.[5]

Anticipate When You May Be Asked to Speak

Most impromptu speaking situations will not come as a complete surprise. You may be an "expert" on the subject under discussion or one of the people most involved in a situation. Or perhaps your knowledge of the person in charge suggests impromptu remarks are to be expected. Just in case you are asked to speak, your remarks will be better planned and delivered if you prepare yourself.

Focus on Your Audience and the Situation

Think about your audience and the situation in which you will be speaking. What is on your listeners' minds? What are their attitudes? What are the circumstances in which you are speaking? The more you can ground your remarks in the context, the better.

Accept the Invitation with Assurance

Try to look confident, even if you are less than delighted about speaking. If you stammer, stall, or look unhappy, your audience will doubt the value of your remarks before you say a word. Once asked, you will have to speak even if you do not want to. You might as well handle the situation with panache.

Organize Your Thoughts

To avoid rambling, use the few moments before you speak to sketch an outline—jotted down if possible. The outline might, for example, follow the introduction–body–conclusion format described in Chapter 10. When you speak, state your thesis in the first moments you are addressing the audience: "I see several problems with that idea," or "From my experience with the Digitech project, I think our cost projections are low." If you are not sure what your opinion is, present that thesis: "I'm not sure which approach we ought to take. I think we need to look at both options closely before we decide."

Label each of your main points as you cover it in the body of your remarks: "My first point is. . . ." Then conclude by restating your thesis.

Present Reasons, Logic, or Facts to Support Your Viewpoint

As with any presentation, your points will be clearer and more persuasive when you back them up with supporting material: statistics, examples, comparisons, and so forth. Of course, this information will not be as detailed as it would be if you had been able to prepare it in advance, but you should still provide some evidence or explanation to support your points: "As I recall, the Digitech job ran 10% over the estimate on materials and 15% over on labor."

Do Not Apologize   No one expects a set of impromptu remarks to be perfectly polished, so it is a mistake to highlight your lack of knowledge or preparation. Remarks like "You caught me off guard" and "I'm not sure whether this is right" are unnecessary. If you really do not have anything to contribute, say so.

Do Not Ramble   Many novice speakers make the mistake of delivering their message and then continuing to talk: "So that's my point: I think the potential gains make the risk worthwhile. Sure, we'll be taking a chance, but look what we stand to win. That's why I think it's not just a matter of chance, but a calculated risk, and one that makes sense. We'll never know unless we try, and. . . ." In reality, this speaker needed only one sentence to conclude the remarks: "I think the risk is worth taking."

• Building Your Confidence

If the thought of delivering a presentation leaves you feeling anxious, you are in good company. According to Irving Wallace and David Wallechinsky's *Book of Lists,* a sample of 3,000 Americans identified "speaking before a group" as their greatest fear, greater even than death.[6] This does not mean most people would rather die than give a speech, but it does underscore the fact that public speaking can be a nerve-wracking experience.

Communication apprehension is just as much a problem for businesspeople as it is for the general population. Communispond, a New York communications consulting firm, surveyed 500 executives and found that nearly 80% listed stage fright as their greatest problem in speaking before a group, putting it ahead of such items as "handling hostile interrogators."[7] Another survey found that roughly one-third of a city's population suffered from more-than-normal anxiety about speaking to an audience.[8]

Although it is common, communication apprehension does not have to present a serious problem. Some speakers feel apprehensive because of the way they *think* about the speech rather than because of the act of speaking.[9] The following sections contain advice for managing uncertainty about your effectiveness as a speaker.

Accept a Moderate Amount of Nervousness

A certain amount of anxiety is not just normal—it is actually desirable. One consultant says, "If I had a way to remove all fear of speaking for you, I wouldn't do it. The day you become casual about speaking is the day you risk falling on your face."[10] The threat of botching your presentation can lead to what Edward R. Murrow once called "the sweat of perfection," spurring you to do your best. The adrenaline rush that comes as you stand up—your body's response to a threatening situation—can make you appear more energetic, enthusiastic, and forceful than if you were more relaxed and casual. The proper goal is, therefore, not to eliminate nervousness, but rather to control it.

Most speakers' time of greatest nervousness is before they even begin speaking—when they are thinking about an upcoming presentation.[11] Researchers have identified a number of irrational

Blend Images/Hill Street Studios/Getty Images

but powerful beliefs that lead to unnecessary apprehension.[12] Among these mistaken beliefs are the following myths:

Myth: A Presentation Must Be Perfect

Whether you are addressing a meeting of potential clients worth millions of dollars to your company or a small group of trainees, your presentation must be clearly organized, well documented, and effectively delivered. Expecting it to be perfect, though, is a surefire prescription for nervousness. According to Otis Williams Jr., founder of a professional development and training firm in Cincinnati, "Practice only makes you better, but perfection doesn't exist. The goal is to become so comfortable with what you're saying, it'll roll off your tongue with minimum effort."[13] A talk can be effective without being flawless. The same principle holds for other types of speaking errors. Most listeners will not notice if you omit a point or rearrange an idea or two.

Myth: It Is Possible to Persuade the Entire Audience

Even the best products do not appeal to everyone, and even the most talented people do not always win the full support of their audiences. It is unrealistic to expect a single presentation to achieve everything you are seeking. If you think of your remarks as one step in a larger campaign to achieve your long-term goals, you will feel less pressure.

Myth: The Worst Will Probably Happen

Some pessimistic speakers make themselves unnecessarily nervous by dwelling on the worst-case scenarios. They imagine themselves tripping on the way to the podium, going blank, or mixing up their ideas. They picture the audience asking unanswerable questions, responding with hostility, or even laughing. Even though such disasters are unlikely, these daydreams take on a life of their own and may create a self-fulfilling prophecy: The fearful thoughts themselves can cause the speaker to bungle a presentation.

Replacing this type of self-defeating thinking with more rational, positive beliefs can result in dramatically increased confidence when you face an audience.[14] It is more helpful to consider the possibility that you will encounter minor problems, such as being interrupted or experiencing a technology glitch, and to prepare for those issues, than it is to become stressed about the worst-case scenario.

Myth: The Audience Knows I'm Afraid

It is completely normal to feel nervous when speaking to an audience. Even after many years of teaching, we still get jitters while standing in front of the class on the first day of each semester. However, it is reassuring to know that, even if you are frightened, your listeners are unlikely to recognize that fact or find it distracting. It may seem like the audience knows that you're afraid because you sense that you are shaking, sweating excessively, turning flush, or forgetting your speech; however, these are only signs that tell *you* that you're nervous.[15] As international public speaking coach and best-selling author, Jason Teteak explains, your audience sees your nervousness based on different signs: shifting your weight, crossing your arms, looking away from the audience, putting your hands in your pockets, or touching your face, among others.[16] The good news, however, is that these behaviors can be managed with awareness and practice. The guidelines presented in this chapter will help you gain confidence and learn how to implement effective visual, verbal, and vocal behaviors.

Focus on the Positive

Brain imaging research shows that imagining a perceived threat causes your brain and body to respond as if you were actually experiencing the threat.[17] Imagining that you are going to forget your words or that the audience is going to judge you will only result in heightened anxiety. However, just as these negative imagined scenarios can have damaging effects, there is evidence to support that positive visualization and verbal thoughts can significantly reduce anxiety.[18]

One way to use this technique to your advantage is to reflect on the positive experiences you have had with speaking. Perhaps you were able to use a personal story to connect with a prospect during a sales pitch that resulted in securing a major account. Maybe you delivered a lighthearted toast at your best friend's wedding that made everyone laugh until they cried. At the least, you might recall that you always feel more at ease once you get underway. Keeping this fact in mind ("It will get better once I start speaking") may even help reduce your pre-speech nervousness.

Draw from Negative Experiences

Even the most effective speakers will deliver a less-than-stellar presentation on occasion. While you should not dwell on negative experiences, it is important to reflect on those moments and use them as learning opportunities. Recalling "the worst presentation [they] ever gave," keynote speaker and consultant Rob Biesenbach cites one of the lessons they took away from the negative experience:

> "Prepare adequately? Hell, I barely prepared at all! I pretty much winged it, which should really be a capital crime in the presentation world. Believe me, nobody wants to see you wing it. The lesson? Practice, practice, practice. Practice your message, refine your content, work on your delivery technique, get feedback from others. There really is no such thing as over-rehearsal."[19]

If you view each presentation as an opportunity to refine your preparation and delivery based on the previous experience, then you will continue to grow as a speaker.

Seek Opportunities to Speak

Like many unfamiliar activities—ice skating, learning to drive a car, and interviewing for a job, to mention a few—the first attempts at speaking before a group can be unnerving. One source of anxiety is a lack of skill and experience. In other words, the very newness of the act is frightening.[20]

One way to become a more confident speaker is to speak more. As with other skills, your first attempts should involve modest challenges with relatively low stakes. Speech courses and workshops taught in colleges, corporations, and community organizations provide opportunities for a group of novices to practice before one another and a supportive instructor. Once you are on the job, it is helpful to make several beginning presentations to small, familiar audiences about noncritical matters.

Rehearse Your Presentation

Many presentation-related catastrophes stem from inadequate rehearsal. Problems with missing note cards, excessive length, clumsy wording, and screen sharing or virtual breakout room confusion can all be remedied if you practice in advance. As you add more and more technological aids to your presentation, the need for complete and careful rehearsal increases dramatically. Projector bulbs can burn out, extension cords can be too short, Internet connections and presentation files can crash, and microphones can fail. It is important to prepare a backup plan that accounts for all of these scenarios and rehearse before facing a real audience. As you practice your talk, follow these guidelines.

Pay Special Attention to Your Introduction and Conclusion   Audiences remember the opening and the closing of a talk most clearly. The first and last moments of your presentation have special importance, so make sure you deliver them effectively in a way that makes every word count.

Rehearse in Front of an Audience   Mental rehearsal has its place, but you will not know if your ideas sound good or if they fit into the available time until you say them aloud. Perform a formal rehearsal several times in front of live listeners. In fact, the more closely the size of your practice audience resembles the number of people you will face in your real presentation, the more confident you will feel.[21]

Rehearse in a Real Setting   If possible, rehearse in the physical room or on the virtual meeting platform where you will actually speak. Make sure you have all the equipment you will need, that you know how to use it, and that it all works correctly.

Rehearse with your Group   The potential for mix-ups and mistakes is especially great in group presentations. The key to minimizing problems is extensive rehearsal. Consider issues such as the setup, position, and order of speakers in advance to avoid last-minute bumbling. In a physical presentation: Will members speak while seated around a table? Will they sit in a row until it is each one's turn? Or will they come up from the audience? For a virtual presentation: Who will be the room host? Who will be able to share their screens?

Choose the format that helps you make the best possible impression and avoid delays. Waiting for speakers to get from their chairs to the lectern or to hand over screen-sharing privileges greatly increases lag time. Sitting together at a table in a physical room, or selecting a team member or facilitator to be in charge of screen sharing or compiling questions from the chat box, may provide a better and more cohesive look, as well as minimize delays. However you set up the presentation, make sure speakers can perform the necessary tasks without distraction or confusion.

Additionally, it may make sense to assign speakers separate roles within the discussion of a topic. One role might be that of the "spokesperson," who introduces the main points. Other members might take the roles of "example-givers," offering details to support the spokesperson's claims.

Remember, group members will make an impression even when they are not the principal focus of attention. When it is your turn to speak, be sure to talk to the audience, not your teammates. When you are not speaking, look at the speaker and listen with undivided attention. Even if you are bored because you have heard the remarks so often during rehearsal, or if you are nervous about your upcoming turn, act like the ideas are fresh or interesting.

Assess Your Delivery with Technology

Seeing yourself from the audience's point of view can be an effective way to analyze and improve your delivery in presentations. While gaining experience by speaking and reflecting on past presentations is helpful, it is only part of the work that is needed to become an effective speaker. In the words of career coach Shweta Khare,

> ". . . none of these methods will be effective if you do not ensure a proper feedback process, either by recording (video/audio) and self-evaluation, or through a feedback process where you actually get to see or hear your audience's response."[22]

Video will help you identify nonverbal behaviors that allow audiences to see your nervousness so you can work to eliminate them. For example, one of the authors of this

Preventing Videoconference Hacking

For many business professionals around the world, videoconferencing has become a primary presentation format due to COVID-19. This has led to some unexpected challenges, including the occurrence of disruptive and often offensive intrusions, referred to as *zoombombing*.

In May 2021, during a guest presentation about racism in health care sponsored by the Yale School of Nursing's Office of Student Life, an unknown person entered the Q&A session, scrawling deeply offensive racial epithets in all-caps in the chat and unmuting themselves to utter the slurs aloud.

While not all zoombombings include harassment, they are a distraction from the presenters. To avoid this experience, virtual meeting hosts should:

- Set a unique password for the room
- Avoid using meeting IDs that reveal the presentation topic
- Share meeting IDs and links using private messaging
- Enable the waiting room feature
- Ensure that only the host has screen-sharing privileges
- Disable the ability to initiate a file transfer, as well as the feature that allows removed participants to rejoin the session

Source: Hamilton, E. (2020, May 12). Zoom hacking is on the rise: Here's what you need to do to be secure. *Tech Times*. Retrieved from https://www.techtimes.com/articles/249572/20200512/zoom-hacking-is-on-the-rise-heres-what-you-need-to-do-to-be-secure.htm#:~:text=Cybercriminals%20have%20been%20targeting%20Zoom,platform's%20new%20interface%20and%20functions.; Mangla, A. (2021, May 7). Racist Zoom-bombing occurs during YSN event. *Yale News*. Retrieved from https://yaledailynews.com/blog/2021/05/07/racist-zoom-bombing-occurs-during-ysn-event/

book recalls the first time she watched a video of herself presenting a speech. Prior to watching the video, she had no idea that she would sway from side to side when nervous. Upon gaining awareness of the behavior, she focused on learning to channel that nervousness into effective movements, such as walking from one side of the stage at a few points during the presentation. Over time, this became second nature and no longer needs to be maintained with conscious effort.

Audio is also useful for critiquing verbal, vocal, and visual cues. You will be able to decipher whether you spoke loudly or slowly enough, if your visual aid was large enough for the audience to see, or whether you effectively transitioned from one main point to the next.

After recording your presentation, view it carefully, taking notes along the way. Make two columns labeled "Strengths" and "Weaknesses." Then jot down a list of things you did well and areas to improve as you watch the video four times:

- *As is:* Replay the video in its original form, just as it would appear to an audience.
- *Muted:* Now watch yourself with no audio. Pay attention to your physical presence: posture, gestures, facial expressions, and so on.
- *Audio only:* Listen to your voice without any video. Are you easy to understand? Fluent? Enthusiastic? Are you pronouncing words correctly and enunciating clearly?
- *Fast forward:* Speed up the video and see whether any important expressions, mannerisms, or other movements become apparent.

This simple exercise will give you both a sense of your delivery strengths and a list of areas that need improvement. You may also choose to record and evaluate your practice sessions or share them with colleagues, friends, and family members with a request for constructive feedback.

• Guidelines for Delivery

In addition to choosing an appropriate delivery style and finding ways to build your confidence, you should also consider the visual, verbal, and vocal elements of delivery: how you look, which words you use, and how you sound.

Visual Elements

A major part of good delivery is how a speaker looks. You can improve your visual effectiveness by following several guidelines.

Dress Effectively   Appearance is important in any setting, but your attire is even more important when you are speaking to an audience. It may be particularly tempting to wear a wrinkled t-shirt or oversized sweatshirt while presenting a session via videoconference but, generally speaking, you should follow the norms of professional dress for your organization and the tips in Chapter 4.

Dressing effectively does not always mean dressing up. If the occasion calls for casual attire, an overly formal appearance can be just as harmful as being under-dressed. Automotive consultant Barry Isenberg found an informal appearance contributed to his success as a leading speaker. While waiting to speak to an audience of hundreds of auto wreckers at a day-long seminar, Isenberg looked on as an attorney who was dressed impeccably in a three-piece suit gave an organized talk on warranties. Despite the importance of the topic, the audience was obviously bored silly. Isenberg rushed upstairs to his hotel room and changed out of his business suit and into the attire of his listeners—casual pants and an open-neck shirt. When his turn to speak arrived, Isenberg moved out from behind the lectern and adopted a casual speaking style that matched his outfit. Afterward, a number of listeners told Isenberg that he was the first speaker who seemed to understand their business.[23]

Get Set before Speaking   It is important to set up the aspects of your presentation that you can control—such as the arrangement of the room or your visual support—before you begin your speech. If you need an easel or projection screen, or if a lectern needs repositioning, move it into position before you begin. If you need to cue up a video or open a few files on your computer so they are ready to be shared, take care of that task before you begin your talk. The same goes for the other details that need to be addressed with so many presentations: Adjust the microphone, close the door, reset the air conditioner, rearrange the seating, admit participants into the room, or lock the virtual session.

Just as important, be sure to position yourself physically before beginning. Some speakers blurt out their opening remarks, usually out of nervousness, before they are set in their speaking position. Once you are in the position from which you will talk, a far better approach is to get set, wait a brief moment (a "power pause") while you connect with your audience, and then begin speaking.

Begin with Confidence and Authority   Your presentation begins the moment you come into your listeners' view. For a virtual presentation, this means you are "on stage" from the moment your video is turned on. Act as if you are a person whose remarks are worth listening to. Employees are often surprised to discover that their forceful, personable superiors completely lose their effectiveness when they have to address a group of people—and that they show their lack of confidence before they say a word. Speakers who fidget with their hands or their clothing while waiting to speak, approach the podium as if they were about to face a firing squad, and then fumble with their notes or the microphone and webcam positioning send a clear nonverbal message: "I'm not sure about myself or what I have to say." An audience will discount even the best remarks with such a powerful nonverbal preface.

Begin without Looking at Your Notes Make contact with the audience as you begin speaking. You cannot establish a connection if you are reading from notes. You can memorize the precise wording of your opening statement, but that step is not really necessary. Whether you say, "I have a new process that will give you more reliable results at a lower cost," or "My new process is more reliable and costs less," is not critical: The important thing is to make your point while speaking directly to your listeners.

Establish and Maintain Eye Contact A speaker who talks directly to an audience will be seen as more involved and sincere, regardless of the speaking occasion. This type of immediacy largely reflects the degree of eye contact between speaker and listeners. Use the moment before you speak to establish a relationship with your audience. Look around the room. Get in touch with the fact that you are talking to real human beings: people you work with, potential customers who have real problems and concerns you can help address, and so on. Let them know through your eye contact that you are interested in them. Be sure your glance covers everyone in the room. In a physical room, look about randomly: A mechanical right-to-left sweep of the group will make you look like a robot. Many speech consultants recommend taking in the whole room as you speak. If the audience is too large for you to make eye contact with each person, choose a few people in different parts of the room, making eye contact with each one for a few seconds. In a virtual setting, maintain eye contact by looking directly into the camera. It can be difficult for speakers to break the habit of looking at the audience's faces on the screen instead of at the camera—to get the best of both worlds, move the video app window to the area of the screen (typically top and center) closest to your camera.

Move Effectively Table 12-1 describes some effective and ineffective ways to move when you are speaking. The best stance for delivering a presentation is relaxed but firm. In such a stance, the speaker's feet are planted firmly on the ground and spaced at shoulder width. The body faces the audience. The head is upright, turning naturally to look at the audience.

Having good posture does not mean staying rooted in one position. Indeed, moving about can add life to your presentation and help release nervous energy. You can approach and refer to your visual support, move away from and return to your original position, and approach the audience.

If you are addressing a small group, such as four or five employees or potential customers, it may be more appropriate to sit at an equal level to them when you are delivering a presentation. Generally, the rules for virtual speaking apply in such cases. You should sit up straight and lean forward—lounging back in your chair or putting a foot up on the desk indicates indifference or even contempt. Sit naturally. Your behavior while in a seated position should be as direct and animated as it would be if you were conversing with these people—which, in a way, you are.

Do Not Pack Up Early Gathering your notes, turning off your camera, or removing yourself from your speaking position before concluding sends the message that you are anxious to finish your presentation. Even if you are, advertising the fact will just make your audience see the presentation as less valuable. Keep your attention focused on your topic and the audience until you are actually finished.

Pause, Then Move Out Confidently Be certain you drop your vocal pitch to end your remarks so you clearly indicate you are finished. A raised pitch sounds questioning and unsure, and it leaves the audience wondering whether you are finished. When you end your remarks (or finish answering questions and recapping your thesis), pause, then move out smartly. Even if you are unhappy with your performance, do not shuffle

Table 12-1	Common Interpretations of a Speaker's Body Language

Viewed as dictatorial or arrogant:
- Crossed arms
- Pounding fists
- Hands on hips
- Pointing index finger
- Hands behind back
- Hands in "steeple" position
- Hands on lapel or hem of jacket
- Preening gestures

Viewed as insecure or nervous:
- Gripping the lectern
- Chewing on objects, cuticles, fingernails, or lips
- Constant throat clearing
- Playing with hair, beard, or jewelry
- Rocking back and forth
- Rubbing or picking at clothes or body
- Clenched fists
- Jingling coins or keys in pockets or hands
- Repeatedly putting glasses on and taking them off
- Slouching
- Standing extremely rigidly

Viewed as open and confident:
- Open hands
- Expansive gestures
- Moving out from behind the lectern
- Moving toward and into the audience
- Animated facial expressions
- Dramatic pauses
- Confident and consistent eye contact

Source: Bocher, D. (2003). *Speak with confidence: Powerful presentations that inform, inspire and persuade.* New York, NY: McGraw Hill

off dejectedly, stomp away angrily, or leave the presentation room. Most speakers are their own harshest critics, and there is a good chance the audience rated you more favorably than you did. If you highlight your disappointment, however, you might persuade them you really were a flop.

Verbal Elements

The words you choose are an important part of your delivery. As you practice your presentation, keep the following points in mind.

Use an Oral-Speaking Style   Spoken ideas differ in structure and content from written messages. The difference helps explain why speakers who read from a manuscript may sound so stuffy and artificial. When addressing your audience, your speech will sound normal and pleasing if it follows these simple guidelines:

- *Use short sentences.* Long, complicated sentences may be fine in a written document, where readers can study them until the meaning is clear. In contrast, in an oral presentation, your ideas will be easier to understand if they are phrased in brief statements. Complicated sentences can leave your listeners confused: "Members of field staff, who are isolated from one another and work alone most of the time, need better technology for keeping in touch with one another while in the field as well as while working from a home office." Ideas are much clearer in a presentation when delivered in briefer chunks: "Members of the field staff work alone most of the time. This makes it hard for them to keep in touch with one another and with the home office. They need better means of technology to stay in contact."

- *Use personal pronouns freely.* Speech that contains first-person and second-person pronouns sounds more personal and immediate. Instead of saying, "People often ask . . . ," say, "You might ask. . . ." Likewise, say, "*Our* sales staff found . . . ," not "The sales staff found. . . ."

- *Use the active voice.* The active voice sounds more personal and less stuffy than the passive use of verbs. Saying, "It was decided . . ." is not as effective as saying, "We decided. . . ." Do not say, "The meeting was attended by 10 people"; say, "Ten people attended the meeting."

- *Use contractions.* Unless you need the complete word for emphasis, contractions sound much more natural. Rather than saying. "I do not know; I will find out and give you an answer as soon as possible," say "I don't know; I'll find out and give you an answer as soon as possible."

- *Use number items.* Emphasize the organization of your material by numbering it: "The first advantage of the new plan is . . ." or "A second benefit of the plan is. . . ."

- *Use signposts.* Help listeners understand the structure of your material: "We've talked about the benefits of our new health care plan. Now let's talk about who will provide them"; "Another important cost to consider is our overhead"; "Next, let's look at the production figures"; and "Finally, we need to consider changes in customer demand."

- *Use interjections.* Emphasize important points: "So what we've learned—and this is important—is that it's impossible to control personal use of office telephones."

- *Use repetition and redundancy.* Make sure the audience remembers key information: "Under the old system it took three weeks—that's 15 working days—to get the monthly sales figures. Now we can get the numbers in just two days. That's right—two days."

- *Use internal summaries and previews.* Ensure that your audience can easily follow along as you move between points: "You can see we've made great progress in switching to the new inventory system. As I've said, the costs were about 10% more than we anticipated, but we see those costs as a one-time expense. I wish I could be as positive about the next item on the agenda—the customer service problems we've been having. Complaints have increased. We do believe we've finally identified the problem, so let me explain it and show you how we plan to deal with it."

- *Address your listeners by name.* Using direct forms of address makes it clear you are really speaking to your listeners and not just reading from a set of notes.

CULTURE **at work**

Speaking to International Audiences

Developing a presentation for any audience takes careful planning. When your listeners come from a background different from yours, extra thought is required. The following tips will boost the odds of achieving your goal with a diverse audience.

1. *If in doubt, address listeners more formally than usual.* As a rule, business is conducted more informally in the United States and Canada than in many other parts of the world. What seems friendly in much of North America may be perceived as disrespectful elsewhere.

2. *Make your presentation highly structured.* Be sure to follow the guidelines for organizing a presentation in Chapter 10. Have a clear introduction in which you identify your thesis and preview your remarks. Highlight key points during the body of your presentation, using a clear organizational pattern. Conclude with a summary of your main ideas.

3. *Use standard English.* Most non-native speakers learned English in school, so avoid idioms and jargon that may be unfamiliar. Whenever possible, use simple words and sentences. Also, use nouns instead of pronouns whenever possible to minimize confusion.

4. *Speak slightly more slowly than usual.* Don't raise the volume of your voice, though: Shouting won't make you easier to understand.

5. *Use handouts.* Most non-native audience members will have higher reading comprehension than listening comprehension, so printed supporting materials will help them understand and remember your points. Providing listeners with printed information in advance of your presentation will make it easier for them to follow your remarks.

6. *Consult with a local coach.* Share your remarks with someone who is familiar with your audience before making the presentation, so as to make sure your ideas are clear and free of blunders that might otherwise undermine your credibility.

Source: Adapted from Pearson, L. (1996). Think globally, present locally. *Presentations, 68,* 20–27; Schmidt, K. (1999). How to speak so you're open to interpretation. *Presentations, 68,* 126–127.

Personalized statements will help build rapport and keep an audience listening: "Frank, you and your colleagues in the payroll office are probably wondering how these changes will affect you"; "Ms. Diaz, it's a pleasure to have the chance to describe our ideas to you this morning."

Do Not Emphasize Mistakes Even the best speakers forget or bungle a line occasionally. The difference between professionals and amateurs is the way they handle such mistakes. The experts simply go on, adjusting their remarks to make the error.less noticeable.

Usually, an audience is unaware of mistakes. If listeners do not have a copy of your speaking outline, they will not know about the missing parts. Even if they notice you have skipped a section in a brochure you are reviewing with them or in a prepared outline you have distributed after your speech for their reference, they will assume you did it on purpose, perhaps to save time. If you lose your place in your notes, a brief pause will be almost unnoticeable—as long as you do not emphasize that gap in the presentation by frantically pawing through your notes.

What about obvious mistakes, such as citing the wrong figures, mispronouncing a name, or trying to use equipment that does not work? The best response here is once again the least noticeable. "Let me correct that. The totals are for the first quarter of the year, not just for March," you might say and then move on. When technology fails, adapt and move on: "The chart with those figures seems to be missing. Let me summarize it for you."

Finally, emphasize what you *did* ("I researched the sales figures for the past five years") rather than what you *did not* do ("I didn't have time to create a chart like I wanted to").

Use Proper Vocabulary, Enunciation, and Pronunciation
The language of a board of directors' meeting or a formal press conference is different from that of an informal gathering of sales representatives at a resort. Each situation will call for varying amounts of formality in terms of address, jargon, slang, contractions, and so forth. When making any presentation, it is important to choose the language that is appropriate to the particular setting.

It is also important to pronounce your words correctly. Few mistakes will erode your credibility or irritate an audience as quickly as mispronouncing a term or name. Bryce Harper, Major League Baseball player and National League MVP, learned this lesson the hard way when he mispronounced *meme* during an interview on ESPN's *SportsCenter*. "I don't even want to answer that right now, because I know how many *meh-mays* are going to be out there of me with a bald head." Ironically, his pronunciation became a viral meme of its own.[24]

Enunciation—articulating words clearly and distinctly—is also important. "We are comin' out with a new data processin' system" makes the speaker sound unprofessional to many people, even if the idea was a good one.

Vocal Elements

During a presentation, how you sound is just as important as what you say and how you look. Speakers' voices are especially effective at communicating their attitudes about themselves, their topics, and their listeners: enthusiasm or disinterest, confidence or nervousness, friendliness or hostility, respect or disdain. The following guidelines are important elements for effective communication.

Speak with Enthusiasm and Sincerity
If you do not appear to feel strongly about the importance of your topic, there is little chance your audience will. Yet professionals often seem indifferent when they present ideas to which they are deeply committed.[25] The best way to generate enthusiasm is to think of your presentation as sharing ideas you truly believe in and speak with conviction, in your own style. As slam poet Taylor Mali emphatically expressed in the poem, *Totally like whatever, you know*:

> . . . I challenge you: To speak with conviction.
> To say what you believe in a manner that bespeaks
> the determination with which you believe it.
> Because contrary to the wisdom of the bumper sticker,
> it is not enough these days to simply QUESTION AUTHORITY.
> You have to speak with it, too.[26]

In the stress of making a presentation, you might forget how important your remarks are. Remind yourself of why you are speaking in the moments before you speak. Thinking about what you want to say can put life back into your delivery.

Speak Loudly Enough to Be Heard
Speaking in a quiet voice makes it likely that listeners will not hear important information. In addition, listeners often interpret an overly soft voice as a sign of timidity or lack of conviction ("The team members just didn't sound very sure of themselves."). Shouting is offensive, too ("Do they really think they can force their product down our throats?"). A happy medium is the goal: A speaker ought to project enough to be heard clearly and to sound confident.

A Professional Perspective

Curtis Falkner

Supply Chain Account Specialist

Rehrig Pacific Company

Shawnee, KS

Credit: Curtis Falkner

As COVID-19 plagued 2020, many businesses recognized the need to transition from formal face-to-face meetings to virtual meetings using a variety of online platforms. Thankfully, these options for virtual meetings allowed my organization's sales and customer service teams to maintain and deepen relationships with our customers during what was otherwise an extremely isolating time. We had the ability to be in front of an audience at a moment's notice.

In order to adjust to this virtual environment, I needed to analyze myself as a speaker because speaking in front of a virtual audience is not the same as speaking to a group and in-person setting. In order to ensure that my meetings were successful, I found the following self-reflective questions to be enormously helpful:

- How do my customers see me? It's not enough that people see my face on the screen. My surrounding environment (such as lighting, sound, and background) needed to communicate that I am organized and professional. I found it helpful to set up a faux call with a teammate and get feedback on how my environment was coming across.

- How is my eye contact? Sure, this is always a concern for public speaking. During face-to-face meetings it is natural to look someone in the eye and communicate directly. This is not the case virtually. I had to adjust to keeping my eyes focused on the camera as the presentation unfolds— and this takes some getting used to!

- How do I sound? At this point, I've sat through my fair share of meetings with crackling micro-phones, distracting background noises, and inaudible speakers. To avoid putting my customers through this experience, I needed to be aware of technological challenges related to sound. I also needed to be more aware of my personal tone, volume, and speaking rate as I often lacked visual feedback from my virtual audience which would indicate confusion.

Even after COVID-19 subsides, I know that virtual meetings will remain a part of my professional life and I am grateful for the crash course in these essential communication skills.

Avoid Disfluencies   As you learned in Chapter 4, disfluencies are those stammers and stutters ("eh," "um," and so forth) that creep into everyone's language at times. Other "filler words" or phrases include "ya know what I mean," "like," "so," "OK," and so on. A few disfluencies will go largely unnoticed in a presentation; in fact, without them, the talk might seem overly rehearsed and stilted. An excess of stumbles and fillers, however, makes a speaker sound disorganized, nervous, and uncertain. In cases where disfluencies are extreme, listeners may stop listening to the content of your ideas and instead start counting the number of times you say "like" or "you know."

Vary Your Speech   Just as in your best everyday speaking style, the rate, pitch, and volume of your speech in a presentation should vary. Let your genuine enthusiasm for the topic and situation drive your speaking style, just as it does in your everyday conversations. Slow down and speak slightly louder when you are stating your thesis and your main points, however. Your audience will interpret such cues as meaning "This is important."

Use Pauses Effectively   Do not be afraid of silence; it can be used for emphasis, to give your audience time to consider what you have presented, to formulate an answer to a question you have posed, or to indicate the importance of what you have just said. Pausing gives you time to think, which can help curtail your use of disfluencies. Being comfortable with pauses also indicates you are comfortable in the role of speaker; every second does not have to be filled in with words.

• Managing Questions and Feedback

Audience questions are a part of almost every business and professional talk, from sales presentations and training sessions to boardroom meetings and press conferences. Sometimes question-and-answer sessions are a separate part of the presentation. At other times, they are mingled with the speaker's remarks. In any case, responding skillfully to questions is essential.

The chance to answer questions on the spot is one of the biggest advantages of oral presentations. Whereas a written report might leave readers confused or unimpressed, your on-the-spot response to questions and concerns can win over an audience. Speakers should also seek audience feedback after the presentation. Guidelines for managing questions and feedback are presented in the following sections.

When to Answer Questions

The first issue to consider is whether you should entertain questions at all. Sometimes you have no choice, of course. If the boss interrupts your talk to ask for some facts or figures, you are not likely to rule the question out of order. In other cases, the time allotted for your talk or the risk of being distracted will lead you to say something like, "Because we have only 10 minutes on the agenda, I won't have time for questions. If any of you do have questions, see me after my presentation or during the break or lunch."[27] In the case of webinars, it is the responsibility of the speaker and the host to determine if and when questions will be solicited. If your presentation calls for questions from the audience, you can control when they are asked. It is good practice to set the tone for the presentation by letting the audience know when questions will be addressed.

During the Presentation   Speakers often encourage their listeners to ask questions during a talk. Time slots may be assigned within the body of the presentation for questions and discussions. This approach lets you respond immediately to your listeners'

CAREER **tip**

Minimizing Audience Interruptions

A few kinds of interruptions can rattle even the most confident speakers. The following tips can help minimize the chances that deliberate or unintentional interruptions will throw you off:

- Post a sign outside the room warning that a presentation is in progress, and close the doors to the room before you begin speaking. In virtual meetings, enable the waiting room feature that requires the host to admit attendees to the session.

- Program telephones in the room to ring elsewhere, flip them to silent mode, or activate voice mail to prevent them from ringing during your talk.

- Ask your audience to silence their mobile phones and mute the audio on their devices for the duration of the presentation.

- Ask that questions and comments be held until the end of your presentation (if you are not comfortable responding to them during your talk).

- Let the audience know when there will be a break in the presentation.

- If presenting in a physical location, check with service personnel or post notices outside the room to ensure that refreshments are not delivered in the middle of your presentation.

- Be certain that setup for another event is not about to begin in your room before you are finished. (This consideration is especially important if you are the last speaker in a program.)

vitranc/iStock/Getty Images

concerns. If people are confused, you can set them straight by expanding on a point; if they have objections, you can respond to them on the spot.

Dealing with your listeners' questions during a talk does have its drawbacks. Some questions are premature, raising points that you plan to discuss later in your talk. Others are irrelevant and waste both your time and other listeners' time. If you decide to handle questions during a talk, follow these guidelines.

Allow for extra time Answering questions sometimes occupies as much time as your planned talk. A 15-minute report can run 30 minutes or longer with questions. If your time is limited, keep your remarks brief enough to leave time for the audience to respond.

Promise to answer premature questions later You should not feel obligated to give detailed responses to every question. If you plan to discuss the information requested by a questioner later in your talk, say, "That's a good question; I'll get to that in a moment."

After the Presentation Postponing questions until after you finish your prepared remarks lets you control the way your information is revealed. Webinar or virtual session hosts may collect audience questions via the chat or messenger mechanism of the presentation software and then ask these questions on behalf of the audience members at the appropriate time.[28] With this approach, you will not have to worry about someone distracting you with an irrelevant remark or raising an objection you plan to address. You will also have much better control over the length of your talk, lessening the risk that you will run out of time before you run out of information.

Sometimes, however, when you deny listeners the chance to speak up, they may be so preoccupied with questions or concerns that they miss much of what you say. For

Anticipating Customers' Questions

When creating a sales presentation, it is important to anticipate the types of questions that prospective customers will ask. Following are a few of the many questions that best-selling author Jeffrey Gitomer suggests preparing for:

- What do you offer that no one else has?
- How does your product compare to others?
- Will the product work in our environment?
- How will the product impact our people? Our success?
- How will we profit as a result of purchasing your product?
- How do we buy it?
- Will you/your company keep its promises?
- Will you be my main contact after purchase?
- Are you being truthful?

Keeping in mind customers' goals—such as profiting from the product and being able to trust and develop a long-term relationship with the companies and salespersons they do business with—will help you craft a more effective sales pitch.

Source: Gitomer, J. (2015). The questions that matter most in a sales presentation. *Grand Rapids Business Journal, 33*(11), 9. Retrieved from https://grbj.com/opinion/the-questions-that-matter-most-in-a-sales-presentation/

instance, you might spend half your time talking about a product's benefits while your listeners keep wondering whether they can afford it. In addition, because most of the information people recall is from the beginning and the end of presentations, you risk having your audience remember the high price you mentioned during the question-and-answer session or the tricky question you were unable to answer rather than the high quality you emphasized in the body of your presentation.

How to Manage Questions

Whether you handle them during or after a presentation, questions from the audience can be a challenge. Some questions may be confusing. Others may be thinly veiled attacks on your position. Still other questions may not be related to the topic you are discussing.

No matter what the audience member's question, it is important to respond to it carefully. Researchers have found that how presenters respond to questions and objections affects the audience's perceptions more than the quality of the presentation delivery itself. A speaker who delivers a good presentation but handles questions poorly is typically rated lower than speakers who deliver a good speech with no questions.[29] Furthermore, speakers who deliver a poor presentation and also handle questions poorly may be rated lower than speakers who just give a poor speech.[30]

You can handle questions most effectively by following these suggestions.

Start the Ball Rolling   Sometimes listeners may be reluctant to ask the first question. Rather than asking them "Do you have any questions?," you can get a question-and-answer session rolling with your own remarks: "One question you might have is . . ." or "The other day someone asked whether . . ." You can also encourage questions nonverbally by leaning forward as you invite the audience to speak up. You might even raise your hand as you ask for questions.

Anticipate Likely Questions   Put yourself in your listeners' position. What questions are they likely to ask? Is there a chance they will find parts of your topic difficult to understand? Might some points antagonize them? Just as you prepare for an important exam by anticipating the questions that the professor is likely to ask, so you should prepare responses to the inquiries that you are likely to receive in relation to your presentation.

Clarify Complicated or Confusing Questions
Make sure you understand the question by rephrasing it in your own words: "If I understand you correctly, Eddie, you're asking why we can't handle this problem with our present staff. Is that right?" Besides helping you understand what a questioner wants, clarification gives you a few precious moments to frame an answer. In addition, it helps other audience members to understand the question. If the audience is large, rephrase every question to make sure it has been heard: "They just asked whether we have financing terms for the equipment."

Treat Questioners with Respect
There is little to gain by antagonizing or embarrassing even the most hostile questioner. You can keep your dignity and gain the other listeners' support by taking every question seriously or even complimenting the person who asks it: "I don't blame you for thinking the plan is far-fetched, Julieta. We thought it was strange at first, too, but the more we examined it, the better it looked."

Even when you are certain you are right, it does not pay to argue with audience members. A "yes-but" reply ("Yes, we did exceed the budget, but it wasn't our fault.") is likely to make you sound argumentative or defensive and antagonize the questioner. Instead, you can use a "yes-and" response: "Yes, we did exceed the budget, and that bothers us, too. That's why we included an explanation of the problems in our report."[31]

Keep Answers Focused on Your Goal
Do not allow questions to drag you off track. Try to frame answers in ways that promote your goal: "This certainly is different from the way we did things back when you and I started out, Tremaine. For instance, the computerized system we have now will cut both our costs and our errors. Let me review the figures once more."

You can avoid offending questioners by promising to discuss the matter with them in detail after your presentation or to send them further information: "I'd be happy to show you the electrical plans. Let's get together this afternoon and go over them."

Buy Time When Necessary
Sometimes you need a few moments to plan an answer to a surprise question. You can buy time in several ways. First, *wait for the questioner to finish speaking.* Besides being courteous, this gives you time to mentally compose an answer. Next, *reflect the question back to the person who asked it:* "How would you deal with the situation and still go ahead with the project, Olivia?" You can also *turn the question to another audience member:* "Jayron, you're the best technical person we have. What's the best way to save energy costs?"

Address Your Answer to the Entire Audience
Make eye contact with the person asking the question while they are asking it, but address your answer to everyone in the audience. This approach is effective for two reasons. First, it keeps all the audience members involved instead of making them feel like bystanders to a private conversation. Second, it can save you from getting trapped into a debate with hostile questioners. Most critics are likely to keep quiet if you address your response to the entire group. You may not persuade the person who has made a critical remark, but you can use your answer to gain credibility with everyone else.

Be Open to Anonymous Questions
When it comes to some sensitive or important topics, audience members may be more likely to ask questions if their names are not attached to the questions. Consider implementing a mechanism for collecting

anonymous questions, such as a question box or directing remarks to a moderator instead of the speaker themself.

Follow the Last Question with a Summary
Because listeners are likely to remember especially well the last words they hear you speak, always follow the question-and-answer session with a brief restatement of your thesis and perhaps a call for your audience to act in a way that accomplishes your purpose for speaking. A typical summary might sound like this:

> I'm grateful for the chance to answer your questions. Now that we've gone over the cost projections, I think you can see why we're convinced this proposal can help boost productivity and cut overhead by almost 10% overnight. We're ready to make these changes immediately. The sooner we hear from you, the sooner we can get started.

Seeking Feedback

Effective speakers understand the value of feedback when it comes to improving their presentation skills. **Audience feedback** includes non-verbal, verbal, spoken, or written information from your audience that helps you improve your presentation skills.[32] The following are a few ways to solicit helpful feedback during and after your presentation.

Read the Audiences' Nonverbal Communication
As you learned in Chapter 4, nonverbal communication always has value. In a speaking situation, the audience primarily expresses their attitudes using nonverbal facial expressions and body positioning. While you are speaking, keep an eye on the faces of the audience members. If they look confused or bored, try increasing your eye contact, moving on to the next main point, or interjecting with an element of audience interaction. On the other hand, if audience members look excited, are smiling, or are nodding their heads in agreement, keep doing what you are doing.[33]

Use Interactive Polling
Another great way to collect feedback before the audience has left the room is to implement interactive live polling during your presentation. The results of anonymous polling will be available immediately and can be used to make adjustments, such as clarifying points of confusion or adding depth to topics of interest, before the opportunity has passed.[34]

Encourage Social Media Interaction
The creation and use of a unique hashtag associated with your presentation is a helpful tool for gathering audience feedback.[35] Audience members may be encouraged to use the hashtag on platforms such as Twitter and LinkedIn to begin or join a conversation about the presentation. You may also prompt them to post comments or questions. If you do welcome questions, however, be sure to regularly check the hashtag and reply within a timely manner.

Provide Feedback Forms
After your presentation has concluded, provide your audience with either a hard copy or an online feedback form. To receive the most honest feedback, do not collect identifying information on the form. Ask open-ended questions aimed to solicit useful feedback, such as "What is the most valuable thing you learned today? How could this session have been more valuable? What recommendations do you have?"[36]

Remember, each presentation is a learning experience. Use any feedback that you receive to adjust your approach for the next opportunity.

MASTER the chapter

review points

- An extemporaneous style of delivery is usually the most effective of the four approaches to presentations (manuscript, memorized, extemporaneous, impromptu), as it combines the enthusiasm of spontaneity with the accuracy of rehearsal. Sometimes, however, manuscript delivery may be necessary for legal or diplomatic reasons.

- A speaker's notes should be brief, legible, and inconspicuous.

- To prepare for impromptu talks, speakers should anticipate when they may be asked to speak, focus on the audience and situation, and accept the invitation with assurance.

- When an impromptu talk is necessary, it is most effective if the speaker presents organized thoughts; supports their thesis with reasons, logic, or facts; speaks without apologizing; and does not ramble.

- Keep anxiety within tolerable limits and build your confidence by accepting it as normal, focusing on the positive, drawing from negative experiences, speaking often, rehearsing, and assessing your delivery with technology.

- Good delivery involves visual, verbal, and vocal elements.
  - Visually, a speaker needs to look professional and convey a sense of confidence and authority by getting set physically and making eye contact before beginning, maintaining eye contact and moving naturally, and ending without rushing away.
  - Verbally, a speaker should use an oral style, avoid calling attention to mistakes, and use appropriate vocabulary, enunciation, and pronunciation.
  - Vocally, a speaker sounds committed to both the topic and the audience when speaking enthusiastically and sincerely, and using enough volume, variety, and pauses without disfluencies.

- Question-and-answer sessions are part of almost every presentation, allowing speakers to respond to audiences quickly.

- Speakers should set the tone for the presentation at the start by letting audience members know if and when the floor will be open for questions.

- Speakers should decide whether to invite questions during or after the prepared presentation. Handling questions during a talk permits the speaker to clarify points as they arise, although there is a risk of getting sidetracked. Responding to questions after the talk lets the speaker control the timing of the information.

- Speakers can improve question-and-answer sessions by asking a question if no one else does, anticipating potential questions, clarifying complex questions, addressing the audience with focus and respect, being open to anonymous questions, and providing a summary.

- Audience feedback is useful for improving presentational skills. Feedback may be solicited during and after the presentation by analyzing the audiences' nonverbal communication, and with the use of interactive polling, social media hashtags, and feedback forms.

key terms

audience feedback   401
extemporaneous presentation   383
impromptu presentation   384

manuscript presentation   381
memorized presentation   382

activities

1. Invitation to Insight

With two or more classmates, try the various styles of delivery for yourself. Follow these steps:

a. Begin by choosing a paragraph of text on an appropriate business or professional topic. You can write the copy yourself or select an article from a news article, magazine, or some other publication.

b. Read the text to your listeners verbatim. Pay attention to your feelings as you deliver the comments. Do you feel comfortable and enthusiastic? How do your listeners describe your delivery?

c. Try to memorize and then deliver the segment. How difficult is it to recall the remarks? How effective is your delivery? What do you do if you get stuck and cannot remember the rest of the passage?

d. Deliver the same remarks extemporaneously, rephrasing them in your own words. Create a brief set of speaking notes, written as key phrases rather than as complete sentences. Arrange your notes in outline format with an introduction (attention-getter, thesis, and preview), a body (organized according to the main points and supporting points), and a conclusion. See whether this approach leaves you more comfortable and your listeners more favorably impressed.

2. Skill Builder

Practice your ability to speak off the cuff by delivering a brief (approximately 1 minute) talk to your group on a topic your instructor has just presented to you or that you have just drawn out of a hat. Follow the guidelines for impromptu speaking in this chapter as you plan and deliver your remarks. Take a few minutes to organize your thoughts into an identifiable plan: topical, chronological, problem–solution, and so on. Move to your speaking position with confidence, pause, then begin to present your talk to your classmates. Make sure both your introduction and your conclusion contain a clear statement of your thesis.

3. Skill Builder

Follow these steps:

a. On a sheet of paper, write a phrase that represents an interesting piece of information about yourself you would like to share with the class.

b. Taking turns with your classmates, share this information with the class. Heed the guidelines for delivery (e.g., arrange your notes before you speak, establish eye contact and a confident posture before you begin speaking) presented in this chapter.

c. After you finish speaking, encourage and manage audience questions. Once the question-and-answer session concludes, maintain eye contact while the audience applauds.

d. Solicit feedback from your audience and make note of strengths and areas for improvement.

4. Invitation to Insight

Using a current television guide or streaming device, choose a movie, series, or program in which a speaker is making an oral presentation. The subject matter is not important: The show can be educational, religious, political, or news-related. Follow these steps:

a. Turn down the volume, and observe the speaker's visual delivery. Notice the effects of dress, posture, gesture, facial expression, and eye contact. What do these aspects of delivery suggest about the speaker's status, enthusiasm, sincerity, and competence?

b. Use the Guidelines for Delivery presented in this chapter to evaluate the quality of delivery. What lessons can you apply to your own speaking based on your analysis of this speaker?

5. Skill Builder

Practice using an oral-speaking style. Fill in the empty boxes in the table on page 404 with examples of effective oral language. A few examples have been completed for you.

6. Skill Builder

Use an Internet search engine to locate a transcript of a speech. Read the transcript and highlight instances where the speaker uses number items, signposts, interjections, repetition and redundancy, and internal previews and summaries. Assess how well the speaker used these aspects of oral-speaking style, then share examples of the appropriate use of these elements with the class.

Advice	Poor	Better
Keep sentences short	"Members of field staff, who are isolated from one another and work alone most of the time, need better technology for keeping in touch with one another while in the field as well as with the home office."	"Members of the field staff work alone most of the time. This makes it hard for them to keep in touch with one another and with the home office. They need better means of technology to stay in contact."
	"The idea I'd like to explain to you is that, although avoiding and accommodating seem like polite ways of interacting, it can sometimes be preferable to employ an assertive linguistic style."	
	"A substantial body of research indicates that organizing your remarks clearly can make your messages more understandable, keep your audience happy, and boost your image as a speaker."	
Use personal pronouns	"People often ask . . ."	"You might ask . . ."
	"Those who attempt to use this strategy don't always succeed at first."	
	"Students would be well advised to learn strategies of effective communication."	
	"Members of the audience might like to try this idea."	
Use the active voice	"It was decided that . . ."	"We decided that . . ."
	"It has been pointed out that . . ."	
	"Memorization was tried by some of the most apprehensive student speakers in the class."	
Use contractions	"We do not expect many changes."	"We don't expect many changes."
	"I will describe the strategies that I have found to be most effective in conducting interviews."	
	"It is important to ponder how often you have been in this situation."	
Address listeners by name	"We're pleased to present our ideas this morning."	"Ms. Diaz, it's a pleasure to describe our ideas to you this morning."
	"Last week someone gave a speech about wearing seat belts. Tonight I'll build on that theme."	

7. Invitation to Insight

Gain useful insights about managing communication apprehension by interviewing several professionals who frequently deliver presentations. Ask the interviewees whether they have ever felt anxiety about speaking in front of others. If so, how have they managed their stage fright?

Mc Graw Hill **LearnSmart**™

For further review, go to the LearnSmart study module for this chapter.

references

1. Locker, K. O. (2000). *Business and administrative communication* (5th ed.). Boston, MA: McGraw Hill/Irwin.

2. Landis, M. (1980, Spring). Taking the butterflies out of speechmaking. *Creative Living, 9*, 19.

3. Zielinski, D. (2003, June 4). Perfect practice. *Presentations*.

4. Shellenbarger, S. (2018, December 3). How to overcome your terror of making an off-the-cuff speech. *The Wall Street Journal*. Retrieved from https://www.wsj.com/articles/how-to-overcome-your-terror-of-making-an-off-the-cuff-speech-1543851913

5. Fletcher, L. (1990). *How to design and deliver a speech* (4th ed.). New York, NY: Harper & Row.

6. Wallace, I., & Wallechinsky, D. (1977). *Book of lists*. New York, NY: Bantam.

7. "The speaker may look calm but survey confirms jitters." (1981, September 13). *Los Angeles Times*, p. 13.

8. Stein, M. B., Walker, J. R., Jr., & Forde, D. R. (1996). Public-speaking fears in a community sample: Prevalence, impact on functioning, and diagnostic classification. *Archives of General Psychiatry, 53*, 169–174. doi:10.1001/archpsyc.1996.01830020087010; Addressing fears. (1996, May/June). *Psychology Today, 29*(3), 11.

9. Daly, J. A., Vangelisti, A. L., & Weber, D. J. (1995). Speech anxiety affects how people prepare speeches: A protocol analysis of the preparation processes of speakers. *Communication Monographs, 62*, 383–397. doi:10.1080/03637759509376368

10. Humes, J. C. (1980). *Talk your way to the top*. New York, NY: McGraw Hill.

11. Sawyer, C. R., & Behnke, R. R. (1999). State anxiety patterns for public speaking and the behavior inhibition system. *Communication Reports, 12*, 33–41. doi:10.1080/08934219909367706

12. Ellis, A. (1977). *A new guide to rational living*. North Hollywood, CA: Wilshire Books; Beck, A. (1976). *Cognitive therapy and the emotional disorders*. New York, NY: International Universities Press.

13. Baskerville, D. (1994, May). Public speaking rule #1: Have no fear. *Black Enterprise, 24*(10), 76–81.

14. Ayres, J., Hopf, T., & Peterson, E. (2000). A test of communication orientation motivation (COM) therapy. *Communication Reports, 13*, 35–44. doi:10.1080/08934210009367721

15. Teteak, J. (2021, March 9). Top 10 fears of public speaking. *Rule the Room: Public Speaking*. Retrieved from https://ruletheroompublicspeaking.com/top-10-fears-public-speaking/

16. Teteak, J. (2021, March 9). Top 10 fears of public speaking. *Rule the Room: Public Speaking*. Retrieved from https://ruletheroompublicspeaking.com/top-10-fears-public-speaking/

17. Reddan, M. C., Wager, T. D., & Schiller, D. (2018). Attenuating neural threat expression with imagination. *Neuron, 100*(4), 994–1005. doi:10.1016/j.neuron.2018.10.047

18. Eagleson, C., Hayes, S., Mathews, A., Perman, G., & Hirsch, C. R. (2016). The power of positive thinking: Pathological worry is reduced by thought replacement in generalized anxiety disorder. *Behaviour Research and Therapy, 78*, 13–18. Retrieved from https://doi.org/10.1016/j.brat.2015.12.017

19. Biesenbach, R., (n.d.). The worst presentation I ever gave. Retrieved from https://robbiesenbach.com/worst-presentation-ever-gave/

20. Finn, A. N., Sawyer, C. R., & Schrodt, P. (2009). Examining the effect of exposure therapy on public speaking state anxiety. *Communication Education, 58*, 92–109. doi:10.1080/03634520802450549

21. Smith, T. E., & Bainbridge, A. (2006). Get real: Does practicing speeches before an audience improve performance? *Communication Quarterly, 54*, 111–125. doi:10.1080/01463370500270538

22. Khare, S. (2010, August 2). Improve your presentation skills. *Forbes*. Retrieved from https://www.forbes.com/2010/08/02/presentation-skills-public-speaking-communication-forbes-woman-leadership-career.html?sh=290841231220

23. Grossman, J. (1983, March). Resurrecting auto graveyards. *Inc., 5*(3), 73–80.

24. Lehman, J. (2015, November 20). Bryce Harper mispronounces meme, instantly becomes one. *New York Post*. Retrieved from http://nypost.com/2015/11/20/bryce-harper-mispronounces-meme-instantlybecomes-one/

25. Haynes, W. L. (1990). Public speaking pedagogy in the media age. *Communication Education, 38*, 89–102. doi:10.1080/03634529009378792

26. Taylor, M. (2002). Totally like whatever, you know? In *What Learning Leaves*. New York, NY: Hanover Press.

27. Stella, P. J. (1994, November). Are there any questions? *Presentations, 8*(11), 12–13

28. Majumdar, A. (2014, February 20). 4 tips to create and present a highly effective webinar. *eLearning Industry*. Retrieved from https://elearningindustry.com/14-tips-to-create-and-present-a-highly-effective-webinar

29. Daly, J. A., & Redlick, M. H. (2016). Handling questions and objections affects audience judgments of speakers. *Communication Education*, *65*(2), 164–181. doi:10.1080/03634523.2015.1081958

30. Daly, J. A., & Redlick, M. H. (2016). Handling questions and objections affects audience judgments of speakers. *Communication Education*, *65*(2), 164–181. doi:10.1080/03634523.2015.1081958

31. Cleveland, K. E. (2003). Agree for maximum impact. *Pertinent.com*. Retrieved from http://www.pertinent.com/articles/persuasion/kenrickP2.asp

32. Dlugan, A. (2015, August 18). How to get useful feedback: A speaker's guide. *Six Minutes*. Retrieved from http://sixminutes.dlugan.com/feedback-speaker/

33. Dlugan, A. (2015, August 18). How to get useful feedback: A speaker's guide. *Six Minutes*. Retrieved from http://sixminutes.dlugan.com/feedback-speaker/

34. Presentation Training Institute. (2019, June 28). Asking for feedback after your presentation. Retrieved from https://www.presentationtraininginstitute.com/asking-for-feedback-after-your-presentation/#:~:text=It's%20always%20a%20good%20idea,there%20is%20room%20for%20improvement.

35. Presentation Training Institute. (2019, June 28). Asking for feedback after your presentation. Retrieved from https://www.presentationtraininginstitute.com/asking-for-feedback-after-your-presentation/#:~:text=It's%20always%20a%20good%20idea,there%20is%20room%20for%20improvement.

36. Presentation Training Institute. (2019, June 28). Asking for feedback after your presentation. Retrieved from https://www.presentationtraininginstitute.com/asking-for-feedback-after-your-presentation/#:~:text=It's%20always%20a%20good%20idea,there%20is%20room%20for%20improvement.

• Sample Plan for an Informational Interview

The following plan shows the kind of work that should occur before an interviewer and a respondent sit down together. Every important interview requires the type of planning exhibited here to achieve its goals. As you read this account, notice that it follows the advice outlined in Chapter 6.

Analysis and research

I know I'll never build the kind of financial security I'm seeking by relying only on the income I earn from my job. Investing successfully will be the path to financial success. I also know I'm very unsophisticated when it comes to investing, so I want to get a financial advisor who can teach me about the world of finance and help me set up and follow a plan.

Picking a financial advisor is like choosing a doctor. Skill is important, but it's not the only thing that matters. I need to find someone who has a personal style I'm comfortable with and whose philosophy matches mine. I also need to find someone who is willing to devote time to me even though I don't have a great deal of money to invest . . . yet!

I've compiled a list of possible advisors from friends, Google and Facebook reviews, news articles, and online phone listings. I will call several of the people in this list to set up appointments for interviews.

Goal

To identify a financial planner with expertise in the field, whose investment philosophy matches mine, and who has a personal style I'm comfortable with.

Interview strategy

If possible, I'll conduct interviews in the physical offices of each financial planner or by videoconference. Seeing where and how they do business will give me a good idea of my comfort level before asking any questions. On the one hand, seeing a shabby or disorganized office would cause me to doubt an advisor's competence. On the other hand, a very plush office might make me wonder if I would be charged too much just to support a lavish lifestyle.

I'm also interested in seeing how much time each person gives me for the interview. If the person is rushed when trying to get a new client, this could mean I won't get the time or attention I need once my money is in the planner's hands.

I want to see how much each person lets me explain my concerns and how much each controls the conversation. I'm no financial expert, but I don't like the attitude, "I'm the expert, so don't waste time asking too many questions." Because I would like someone who is willing to explain investing to me in a way I can understand, I'll be looking for a good teacher.

Topics and questions   The following list shows the questions I'm planning to ask in each topic area, as well as follow-up questions I can anticipate asking. I'm sure there will be a need for other secondary questions, but I can't predict all of them. I'll have to think of them on the spot.

Topic A: Expertise in Investments and Financial Planning

[This series of open questions explores the financial planner's qualifications and provides an opportunity for them to talk about themselves.]

1. What credentials do you have that qualify you as a financial planner? How important are credentials? If they aren't important, what is the best measure of a financial planner's qualifications?

[These questions move from a narrow to a broader focus.]

2. Do you have any areas of specialization? How and why did you specialize in this area?

[These indirect questions are a way of finding out whether the advisor's performance has been satisfactory.]

3. How many clients have you served in the last five years? What is the length of the relationship with your clients? How many have you retained, and how many are no longer with you?

[The average portfolio size is one measure of the advisor's expertise.]

4. What's the average amount of money you have managed for your clients?

[A closed question, designed to give the interviewer references.]

5. May I see a list of your past and current clients and call some of them for references?

[The first question is a broad, open one. The second, closed question will produce a specific answer that can be compared with those of other potential advisors.]

6. How would you describe your track record in terms of investment advice? Specifically, what has been the ratio of successful to unsuccessful advice?

Topic B: Investment Philosophy

[This broad, open question gives the advisor a chance to describe their approach.]

1. How would you describe your investment philosophy?

[This hypothetical question provides specific information about how a client–advisor relationship might operate.]

2. If I became your client, what steps would you recommend to start and maintain a financial program?

[This sequence of questions moves from broad to specific topics in a logical order.]

[This two-question sequence moves from a broad to a narrow focus. The most important information for the client is contained in the second question.]

3. What kinds of products do you like to deal in? Which specific ones might you recommend for me? Why?

4. I've read that some financial advisors make their income from commissions earned when their clients buy and sell investments. Other advisors charge a fee for their time. Which approach do you take? Can you explain how this approach is in my best interest as well as yours?

[Although this sounds like a closed question, it is likely to generate a long answer.]

5. How much should I expect to pay for your advice?

Topic C: Personal Style

[This indirect question really asks, "Would we work well together?"]

1. What kinds of clients do you work well with? What kinds don't you work well with?

[The first question here is really an indirect way of discovering how much attention the advisor has paid to the potential client.]

2. Have you looked over the papers I sent you about my financial condition? What did you think of them?

[This clever hypothetical question has a better chance of generating a useful answer than the more direct "What can you tell me about the kind of service I can expect?"]

3. If I were to call one of your clients at random, what would they tell me about the type of service and frequency of communication I can expect with you?

[This is a straightforward, open question.]

4. If we were to develop a relationship, what would you expect of me?

[This hypothetical question anticipates an important issue.]

5. Suppose I were to disagree with your advice. What would you say and do?

• Sample Employment Interview

The following transcript is based on a real interview. As you read it, pay attention to both the interviewer's questions and the respondent's replies. In both cases, notice the strengths and the areas needing improvement. Which parts of this interview would you like to incorporate into your interviewing style? Which parts would you handle differently?

[The interview begins with an exchange of pleasantries . . .]

Interviewer: Alfonso Capossela? I'm Sandra Alaniz. Welcome.

Respondent: It's good to meet you.

[. . . and small talk.]	**Interviewer:**	Did you have any trouble finding us?
	Respondent:	The directions were perfect. Thanks for the parking pass.
[The interviewer briefly previews the approach of the interview and the anticipated amount of time.]	**Interviewer:**	Oh, yes. That's a necessity. The garage costs $12 per day if you don't have one. We'll have about a half-hour this morning to talk about the personnel administrator's position you've applied for. I'd like to learn about you and, of course, I want to answer any questions you have about us.
	Respondent:	Great. I'm looking forward to it.
[Body of interview begins with an open question about employment history.]	**Interviewer:**	Good. Let's begin by having you tell me about your most recent position. Your résumé says you were at ITC in Springfield. Is that right?
[Respondent uses answer to showcase the skills acquired in past job that could help in the one being offered here.]	**Respondent:**	That's right. My official job title was personnel assistant, but that really doesn't describe very well the work I did. I recruited nonexempt employees, processed the payroll, oriented new employees, and maintained the files.
[Follow-up questions explore areas of interest in the new job.]	**Interviewer:**	Were you involved with insurance?
[The respondent uses this answer to point out another skill that they bring to the job.]	**Respondent:**	Yes. I processed workers' compensation claims and maintained the insurance reports for our health care plans. I learned a lot about dealing with government regulations.
	Interviewer:	And you said you were involved in hiring?
	Respondent:	Yes. I was responsible for recruiting and interviewing all clerical and administrative support staff.
[Another open question, this time exploring the respondent's ability to analyze their own performance.]	**Interviewer:**	How did that go?
[The respondent fails to use this answer to showcase their abilities . . .]	**Respondent:**	It was tough in Springfield. There's actually a shortage of talented support people there. It's an expensive town to live in, and there aren't a lot of people who can afford living there on an administrative assistant's salary. It's not like Atlanta, where there's plenty of good help.

[. . . so the interviewer follows up with another question.]

Interviewer: What did you learn about hiring from your experiences at ITC?

[This answer is better because it describes insights and skills the respondent brings to this job.]

Respondent: I learned to look further than the résumé. Some people seem great on paper, but you find there's something wrong when you hire them. Other people don't have much experience on paper, but they have a lot of potential.

Interviewer: How did you get beyond paper screening?

Respondent: Well, if someone looked at all promising, I would phone the former employers and talk to the people the applicant actually worked for. Of course, a lot of former employers are pretty noncommittal, but they usually would give clues about what they really thought about the person I was investigating—giving an indirect opinion without saying it outright.

Interviewer: What would you do if this was the person's first job?

[The respondent demonstrates resourcefulness here, spelling out their skill in the last sentence of the answer.]

Respondent: I found that almost everyone had done some kind of work—part-time or volunteer and I could check up on that. Or I would even ask for the names of a few teachers and phone them if the person was just graduating. I learned there's almost always a way to find what you're looking for if you get creative.

Interviewer: Didn't that take a lot of time?

[This is a subtle way of saying, "I have good judgment."]

Respondent: Yes, it did. But it was worth it in the long run because we got much better employees that way. We almost never had to dismiss someone whom we'd done a phone check on.

Interviewer: You were promoted after a year. Why?

[Again, the respondent's answer introduces a trait that would be valuable in the new job: the desire for self-improvement.]

Respondent I was lucky to be in the right place. The company was growing, and we were very busy. I tried to take advantage of the situation by offering to do more and by taking classes at night.

Interviewer: Which classes did you take?

[Presumably, the skills acquired in these courses would be useful if the respondent is hired. In any case, they demonstrate the desire to learn skills useful in the business world.]	**Respondent:**	I took an applied human relations class last spring and, before that, a couple of computer classes: one in database management and one in desktop publishing. Our department was thinking about starting an employee newsletter, and I wanted to see if we could produce it in-house.
	Interviewer:	It sounds like you've done very well at ITC. Why do you want to leave?
[The response begins with a provocative statement and then goes on to supply a solid reason for seeking a new job.]	**Respondent:**	In some ways, I *don't* want to leave. The people are great—most of them—and I've enjoyed the work. But I'm looking for more challenges, and there isn't much chance for me to take on more responsibility there.
	Interviewer:	Why not?
	Respondent:	Well, my boss, the personnel director, is very happy in her job and has no plans to leave. She's young, and there's very little chance I'll be able to advance.
[The interviewer seeks specifics to elaborate on the broad statement "I'm looking for more challenges" . . .]	**Interviewer:**	I see. Well, that is a problem. What kind of responsibilities are you looking for?
[. . . and the respondent supplies answers.]	**Respondent:**	I'd say the biggest one is the chance to help make policy. In my past jobs, I've been carrying out policies that other people—management—have made. That's been fine, but I'd like to be involved in setting some policies myself.
[Again, the interviewer follows up by seeking more specifics . . .]	**Interviewer:**	What kinds of policies?
[. . . and the respondent is prepared with detailed responses.]	**Respondent:**	Oh, there are several. Designing benefits packages. Coming up with a performance review system that people will take seriously. Teaching our supervisors how to interview and hire more systematically.
[The interviewer makes a smooth transition to a new topic.]	**Interviewer:**	I see. Well, the position you've applied for certainly does have those sorts of responsibilities. Let me ask you another question: What do you enjoy most about personnel work?

[The stock answer "I like to work with people" is so broad that it has little meaning . . .]	**Respondent:**	Well, I really enjoy the chance to work so much with people. Of course, there's a lot of paperwork, too, but I especially like the chance to work with people.
[. . . so the interviewer seeks clarification.]	**Interviewer:**	When you say "people," what kinds of work are you thinking of?
	Respondent:	I guess the common denominator is making people happy. Lots of employees get involved with the personnel department—once they've been hired, that is—because they have problems. Maybe it's an insurance claim or a problem with their performance review. It makes me feel good to see them leave feeling satisfied, or at least feeling better after they've come in so upset.
	Interviewer:	Are you always able to help them?
	Respondent:	No, of course not. Sometimes a person will want the impossible, and sometimes there just won't be any answer.
[Again, the interviewer uses a situational approach, seeking specifics.]	**Interviewer:**	Can you give examples of these times?
[The respondent does a good job of describing a situation that illustrates their previous answer.]	**Respondent:**	Well, one example of an impossible request comes up a lot with health insurance. At ITC, we could choose from two plans. With one plan, you could use any doctor you wanted. You had to make a co-payment with that one. With the other plan, you had to choose a doctor from a list of preferred providers, but there was no co-payment. If an employee chose the preferred-provider plan and later decided they wanted to use a doctor who wasn't on the list, we just couldn't do anything about it.
	Interviewer:	We've had that problem here, too. How did you handle it?

Respondent: Being sympathetic helped a little. Even if I couldn't give them what they wanted, at least saying I was sorry might have made it seem less like a total rejection. I also pointed out that they *could* switch plans during the open-enrollment period, which comes every year. I've also suggested to my supervisor that we do a better job of informing people about the restrictions of the preferred-provider plan before they sign up and maybe even get them to sign a statement that says they understand them. I think that would reduce the surprises that come up later.

[With this new topic, the interviewer shifts from fact to opinion questions.]

Interviewer: That's a good idea. Alfonso, what qualities do you think are important for a personnel officer?

Respondent: Knowing the job is definitely important, but I'd say getting along with people might be even more important.

Interviewer: And how would you describe your ability to get along?

Respondent: Sometimes I think I deserve an Academy Award for acting the opposite of the way I feel.

Interviewer: Really? Tell me about it.

[The respondent offers a specific example to illustrate their provocative statement about acting the opposite of the way they feel.]

Respondent: Every so often people will come in with an attitude problem, and I try to calm them down by acting more pleasantly than I feel. For example, we've had people who think they're entitled to take six months off for a worker's compensation claim, when the doctor has said they're ready to come back after a few weeks. They come in and yell at us, and it's tough to be pleasant at times like those. But I don't think there's any point in being blunt or rude. It just makes them more angry.

[This indirect question really asks, "What kind of manager might you be?"]

Interviewer: I see what you mean. Let's shift gears, Alfonso. If you were to pick a boss, what are the important traits that they should have?

	Respondent:	Let me see . . . certainly lots of follow-up—letting people know where they stand. The ability to give criticism constructively and to compliment good work. Giving people a task and then leaving them alone, without nagging.
	Interviewer:	But still being there to help if it's needed, right?
	Respondent:	Sure. But also giving me the space to finish a job without staying *too* close.
	Interviewer:	Anything else?
	Respondent:	Being available for help, as you said. Being consistent and being willing to train employees in new jobs, letting them grow. Considering employees' personal goals is also important.
[The interviewer turns to a new topic area.]	**Interviewer:**	In personnel work, there's a need for confidentiality. What does that mean to you?
	Respondent:	That's an important area. You see lots of personal information, and it's easy to make offhand remarks that could upset someone.
	Interviewer:	What kinds of things do you have to be careful about?
	Respondent:	Oh, even something as simple as a person's birthday. Most people wouldn't care, but some people might be offended if their birthdays got out. I've learned to be constantly on guard, to watch what I say. I'm a private person anyway, so that helps.
[This question explores the respondent's personal attitudes.]	**Interviewer:**	Alfonso, I've been asking you a lot of questions. Let me ask just one more; then it can be your turn. What are the factors that motivate you?
	Respondent:	Well, I like to be busy. If things aren't busy, I still work, but I like to be stimulated. I seem to get more work done when I'm busy than when there's plenty of time. It's crazy, but true. I'm also motivated by the chance to grow and take on as much responsibility as I can handle.

[Almost every employment interview includes a chance for the respondent to ask questions.]	**Interviewer:**	Alfonso, what questions do you have for me? What can I tell you about the job or the company?
[The respondent wisely begins by asking about the company, not focusing on personal questions such as compensation.]	**Respondent:**	What kind of growth do you see for the company?
	Interviewer:	Well, we have 155 employees now. As I think you know, we're five years old, and we started with 5 employees. Our sales were up 14% last year, and it looks like we'll be expanding more.
	Respondent:	How many employees do you think will be added?
	Interviewer:	Well, we hired 20 new people last year, and we expect to hire almost the same number this year.
	Respondent:	What's the turnover like?
	Interviewer:	That's a good question for a personnel person to ask! We've been growing so much, and people have been able to move into more responsible jobs, so they've been satisfied for the most part. Our turnover has been pretty low—about 15% annually.
[This question focuses on the responsibilities of the job.]	**Respondent:**	Will the person you hire be involved in making policy?
	Interviewer:	Yes, definitely. We're still trying to catch up with ourselves after growing so fast. A big project for this year is to put together an employee handbook. Too many of our policies are verbal now, and that's not good. Developing that handbook would mean working directly with the president of the company, and that definitely involves developing policy.
[Finally, the respondent asks about compensation and benefits.]	**Respondent:**	Of course, I'm interested in learning about the benefits and salary.
[The interviewer appropriately defers a complete answer until the company has a clearer idea of the candidate's desirability.]	**Interviewer:**	Of course. Here's a copy of our benefits summary for you to study. We can talk about salary later. Right now, I'd like you to meet a couple of our managers. After you've spoken with them, we can get back together to discuss salary and other matters.

[The interviewer wraps up the conversation by describing when the hiring decision will be made.]

We will definitely be making our decision within the next 10 days, so I promise you'll have an answer before the first of next month. It's been a real pleasure talking to you, Alfonso. You certainly express yourself well. I'll talk with you again soon.

Respondent: Thanks. I've enjoyed the talk, too. I'll look forward to hearing from you.

appendix II
Business Writing

Entire books and academic courses are devoted to the study of business writing. This appendix is no substitute for a thorough study of *this* important topic. It does, however, provide some guidelines about creating the most common types of written business messages. Many organizations have their own styles, which may vary in one or more ways from these basic rules. When you are writing on behalf of an organization, you will want to learn and follow its conventions.

• Writing Well

Just as your appearance creates the first impression when you meet others in person, the quality of your written messages makes a powerful statement to readers, who are likely to consider them a reflection of your capabilities. Besides creating a good impression of yourself and the company, well-designed and well-executed business writing makes your message easier to understand and more likely to be viewed favorably by audiences. As business writing coach Jodi Torpey explains, being unable to write well can have negative consequences:

> If you have a reputation as a bad communicator, a bad writer, when emails come in and they see it's from a certain person, a lot of people might just delete it before reading it. Like "Oh, I know this never has anything important in it."[1]

The following guidelines will help you construct effective written messages.

Adapt to Your Audience

Put yourself in the shoes of the person or people who will read your message, and write in a way that addresses their concerns, knowledge, and interests. Just as you would when developing and organizing a presentation, ask yourself: What do they want or need to know? How much detail is necessary? Why should they care about my topic? What will motivate them to do what I'm asking?

Once you have identified what your readers care about, write in a way that demonstrates your concern. Make the receiver's needs the subject of your first sentences. Instead of writing "We received your request for a refund and will begin working on it," write "You should receive your refund within 4 days." When responding to a complaint, do not say, "The long wait you experienced was due to a temporary staffing shortage." (The reader is not likely to care about your staffing problems.) Instead, say, "You are absolutely right: Customers shouldn't have to wait for service."

To find the right tone that will resonate with your audience, writing consultant and author Natalie Canavor suggests writers "take a minute to see them in your head, look at their office, hear their voice in your head."[2] Seeing the audience as real people will help remind you that you are communicating with real people, even if they do not appear in front of you.

Build Goodwill

The best way to build goodwill is to demonstrate you have the reader's best interests in mind.

- *Emphasize positive concepts rather than negative ones.* State what can be done, rather than what cannot be or has not been done. For example, when proposing a meeting, instead of saying you are busy next Tuesday, say, "I can meet anytime next Monday, Wednesday, Thursday, or Friday."

- *Adopt a helpful and respectful approach.* Blaming others and using "you" statements often create defensiveness. "You didn't turn in your time sheet before the June 1 deadline" is an accusatory "you" statement that blames the reader. You minimize the chance of a defensive reaction by saying the same thing just as clearly and less aggressively: "Because we received your time sheet on June 4, your check will be processed with others submitted that week and will be ready June 15."

Organize Carefully

Perhaps most importantly, business writing must be organized. Start by listing all of the items you need to cover and then group them into logical categories. Then, arrange the categories into a clear organizational pattern according to your purpose. One general rule is to list items from most to least important.

A common flaw in business writing is taking too long to state the point. To avoid this error, be sure to state your purpose at the beginning of the communication and then provide supporting details.[3] Another guideline is to consider what the reader needs to know first to understand what comes next. The organizational patterns in Chapter 10 can also be used in many written messages.

Writing experts also recommend putting good news first whenever possible: "Your order will be shipped today." If you are delivering bad news, begin by expressing agreement, appreciation, or explanation: "I was pleased with the quality of your crew's work on the recent job. The only question I have is about the $250 listed as 'extra charges.'"

Your message will be clearest if you build coherence into each paragraph as well as into the overall design by using parallel structure and transitions, as demonstrated in Chapter 10.

Be Accurate, Clear, and Professional

Whenever possible, use precise terms, describe in detail, and quantify facts rather than give opinions or evaluations. Use concrete statements rather than abstract ones, and avoid jargon, slang, clichés, and idioms. The use of proper grammar is also important. Consider downloading a writing assistance tool. Grammarly, for example, is a free Google Chrome extension and desktop app that reviews documents while you are writing and highlights errors. Suggestions are then provided for improving spelling, grammar, and punctuation, enhancing clarity, making your writing more interesting, and adjusting the tone and level of formality.

Follow these additional guidelines for ensuring the accuracy, clarity, and professionalism of your writing:

- *Proofread carefully.* Do not rely on your spell-checker to catch a misspelling of *principle* when you meant *principal* or *it's* when you meant *its*. Spell-checking is no help with most names, so you will have to be sure the letter to Ms. MacGregor does not leave your desk addressed to Ms. McGregor.

- *Use precise terms that give specific details.* "We will contact you soon" leaves the reader asking, Who will contact me? How will contact be made? A letter, phone, in person? When will I be contacted? Next week? Next month? Instead, write "Our sales manager, Nahid Ravi, will phone you by June 6."

- *Use the active voice for livelier and more direct writing.* "The memo was sent by the director" is written in the passive voice. "The director sent the memo" is written in the active voice.

- *Use names and titles consistently.* If you are referring to everyone in a group by first and last names, do not add a title ("Ms." or "Dr.") to only one person's name. Use titles and first and last names for *all* parties. Stay fair and consistent. If you do not know the gender of the recipient and their preferred pronouns, use "Dear First Name, Last Name."

- *Refer to an individual's age, race, or different ability only if necessary.* If you need to refer to ethnicity or race, use the term the group or the individual prefers (see the discussion of ethnicities and disabilities in Chapter 2). Always refer to a person before a condition. Use "persons with HIV," not "HIV patients or victims." Use "persons who use wheelchairs," not "handicapped persons" nor "persons *confined* to wheelchairs." Do not label groups of people by a condition (epileptics, amputees).

- *Avoid jargon.* When writing for external audiences, avoid jargon and acronyms that your readers may not understand.

- *Avoid slang and pop culture terms.* Using slang ("shook," "sus," "yeet!") will make you seem more adolescent than professional. Save informality for nonbusiness messages.

Be Concise

Time is precious for most businesspeople. There are several ways to tighten up your writing so your message can be read and understood quickly.

- *Omit needless words and phrases.* If one word will do, use it and eliminate the others. Some phrases are too cumbersome for business writing. For instance, "at the present time" can more succinctly be stated as "now." Other common phrases can be shortened[4]:

Lengthy Phrase	Shortened Version
The question as to whether	Whether
In the month of May	In May
We are in receipt of	We received
Please do not hesitate to call	Please call
Please be advised that I will arrive at 8:00.	I will arrive at 8:00.
A distance of 3 feet	3 feet

- *Eliminate "who is" and "that are."*[5] The sentence "Jeannette, who is the paralegal, declined to comment on the case" could be stated more simply: "Jeanette, the paralegal, declined to comment on the case."

- *Do not overuse intensifiers* ("really," "very," "so") *and superlatives* ("fantastic," "best"). Avoid excessive and unnecessary adverbs ("absolutely," "positively").

- *Avoid "fumblers."* Phrases like "what I mean is" and "what I'm trying to get at is" imply "I don't think I'm being clear" or "I don't think you can understand what I mean from what I wrote."[6]

Pay Attention to Appearance

The appearance of your message will determine the reaction it creates as much as its content. One consultant put it this way: "In memos and reports, intonation and body language are not available to you. That is what formatting is for—to substitute for them."[7]

The first decision when formatting a business document is whether to type it or write it longhand. The culture of an organization usually offers clues about when handwritten notes are acceptable, so pay attention to how the successful people around you communicate.

Three occasions when handwritten notes are definitely appropriate—even preferable—are for thank you notes and personal messages of congratulations or condolence. In addition, it may be acceptable to jot a quick note to a colleague or boss in longhand. In virtually every other situation, though, it is professional to type.

Documents should be laid out on the page or screen so they are easy to read and understand. One trick for making documents look professional is using "whitespace"—a term that refers to blank space on a page or screen. For instance, margins should be wide enough to keep the document from looking cramped—at least 1 inch all around on a printed page. Blank lines should be inserted between single-spaced paragraphs or between sections. Another trick for increasing readability is to left-align your documents. A ragged right edge is easier to read than a justified document that has a straight right margin.

For most documents, choose a font size between 10 and 12 points. The font you use also sends a message. In business documents, avoid shadow, script, outline, or radically different fonts because they can be difficult to read and may call more attention to the medium than the message. Keep fonts consistent for easier reading.

• Routine Business Messages

Along with the writing practices described so far, some forms of business writing call for specific considerations.

E-mail Messages and Memos

E-mail is one of the most widely used communication tools in the workplace. Professional e-mails may be used to exchange information, schedule meetings, ask quick questions, share updates, or send memos.

Memos (or memorandums)—e-mail and the printed variety—are a common form of written business correspondence. They range from short messages to longer documents and bear much resemblance to e-mail messages.

The shared guidelines for formatting e-mail messages and memos are discussed in the sections that follow. However, despite these similarities, memos are more formal than e-mail and are only used for internal communication. As such, one must determine whether to deliver a memo electronically, in hard copy, or both. Here are some factors to consider when deciding which format is most appropriate.

Choose e-mail when:

- The message is informal.
- You want the message delivered immediately.
- There are multiple recipients, especially when they are distributed over different geographic locations.
- You want a record that can be stored electronically and circulated easily.

Use paper when:

- You want to make a formal impression.
- Legal requirements demand a printed format.
- You want your message to stand out from a flood of e-mails.
- The recipient prefers hard copies.

The proper format for printed memos (like the one in Figure A2.1) differs slightly from the format for memos sent as e-mails (see Figure 6.1).

MEMO

Date: June 17, 2022
To: Halim Eby, Director of Human Resources
From: Daniel Goldstein *DG*
Re: Notification of FMLA

Per our conversation earlier this week, I am requesting Family Medical Leave in conjunction with the upcoming adoption of my child. I am requesting that my leave begin August 1 and extend 12 weeks through October 24. I plan to return to Miller Industries full-time at the end of the leave. I have attached a completed leave request form to this memo. Please let me know if you need me to provide any additional information or documentation to finalize this request.

Thank you, again, for your willingness to work with me as I welcome our newest addition into our family.

FIGURE A2.1 Memo Format

Additional tips specific to writing appropriate and effective memos include the following:

- Do not include a salutation ("Dear Joe") or a complimentary close ("Sincerely,").
- Do not sign the memo at the bottom. You may write your initials next to your name on the "FROM" line.

Shared Style Guidelines for E-mail Messages and Memos   As the example in Figure A2.1 shows, how you express an e-mail message can be as important as the ideas behind it. Keep these factors in mind as you compose your thoughts.

- *Keep it short.* The most important stylistic guideline in crafting a useful e-mail is to make it as concise as you can. Whenever possible, limit your message to two or three paragraphs—one screenful of text.
- *Make the essence of your message clear in the opening paragraph.* For example, you might state, "We need to decide on a logo for the new product within the next week" or "I'm writing to see whether you would be interested in serving on a community outreach committee."
- *Use formatting to make your points clear.* Single-space your message, with a double space separating paragraphs. Use bullets and numbered lists to make information more readable and accessible.
- *Limit the use of exclamation points.* Reserve your use of exclamation points for times when you truly wish to express excitement ("Congratulations on being named Employee of the Year!") or support ("I appreciate all of your hard work on this, Santiago!"). Before pressing "send" on an e-mail, review your message and replace excessive exclamation points with periods. A good rule of thumb is to limit your use of exclamation points to one per e-mail.[8]
- *Be mindful about using special formatting.* The fancy fonts and images you use may appear differently on your recipient's computer screen or portable device.
- *Be wary of using the informal style you might use outside of work.* Shortcuts ("wanna," "sorta"), emojis, text abbreviations ("rn," "lmk"), and chat acronyms

(LOL for "laughing out loud") can create problems, especially with strangers. Avoid using all capital letters, as this practice creates the effect of shouting. All-lowercase letters are unprofessional and inappropriate, too. Capitalization, grammar, and spelling are important. Profanity, crude remarks, and gossip never belong in company e-mail.

Shared Elements of E-mail Messages and Memos

Every e-mail and memo should include the date, your name, other people receiving the message (usually labeled "cc"), and a subject line. Beyond these basics, consider the following:

- Double-check your addressee list. A misaddressed message can lead to embarrassment and humiliation.

- Use "cc" when others need and expect copies and when you want the recipient to know you are sending them. In reply to a customer's complaint, you might want that customer to see you are sending your response regarding safety to all technicians who were part of the problem.

- Consider sending a blind carbon copy ("bcc") if you do not want the primary recipients to know that others are seeing the correspondence. This approach is not necessarily devious. For example, you might include your boss on a bcc of your e-mail to an irate customer, as if saying, "This is how I resolved the problem we discussed last week."

- Make your subject line brief and descriptive (e.g., "Agenda change for Friday's meeting") to help the receiver identify your topic. Messages with vague subject lines (e.g., "Update" or "Hi") run the risk of being ignored, misfiled, or deleted.

- If you need to correspond about several topics, consider separate messages for each one. This makes it easier for the recipient to keep track of and respond to each message.

Additional Practices for E-mail Messages

When composing and sending e-mail messages, follow this advice:

- *Do not use company channels for personal business.* Use your own personal e-mail account for private correspondence, chatting with friends, and other nonbusiness exchanges. One expert advised thinking of e-mails as "giant, moving billboards, exposing our every thought to the cyberworld."[9] Your personal e-mails most likely would not be the best advertising for your company.

- *Do not impose on others.* Most professionals are already overwhelmed with e-mail and paperwork, so send messages only on a "need-to-know" basis. Avoid the temptation to send unnecessary messages to others or forward ones the recipient will not appreciate.

- *Be cautious about putting delicate topics in writing.* Do not write about topics that would better be handled by phone or in person. Written channels usually are not the best way to send difficult messages such as negative appraisals, firings, and resignations. An e-mail has the potential to be misunderstood, so avoid using it in a hurry or to convey sarcasm or humor if the receiver is likely to misunderstand the message.

- *Think before sending problematic messages.* Stop, think, and wait *before* you send a message if you are angry or frustrated. The scathing note you wrote in anger to one person may be forwarded to many colleagues. Once a message is sent, it is irretrievable and the impact on your career could be disastrous. Never send information you are not sure is accurate (e.g., canceled meetings, changed deadlines, budget figures).

- *Treat every message as a public, permanent document.* Despite what you might assume, e-mail is not private: It has the potential to be forwarded (purposely or accidentally) without your permission or knowledge. Even if you delete a message, it can remain available to employers, other businesses, and courts for years. In fact, e-mail has the same weight as a letter or memo sent on company letterhead.[10]

- *Honor the chain of command.* E-mail can be a way to level hierarchies and reach important people, expedite projects, and reduce time otherwise spent in meetings. Despite these advantages, it is often important to follow the regular chain of command. Pay attention to your organization's culture and your communication goals. Sending an e-mail to your CEO suggesting a new procedure for your division without first checking with your immediate supervisor could spell disaster for your career.

- *Include relevant copy from earlier messages when you forward them or reply to the sender.* This practice provides all the relevant information in a single document.

- *Consider using salutations.* Salutations ("Dear Dr. Nakayama," "Hi Gina") are an optional, but often useful, element of e-mail messages. As one expert pointed out, "Blunt is not businesslike."[11] (Salutations typically are not used in printed memos.) Bulk or group e-mails can begin with salutations like "Good morning" or "Dear Computer Policy Committee Members."

- *Include a closing line that expresses gratitude to the recipient and serves as a call-to-action (CTA).* The CTA is used to motivate the recipient to respond ("Thank you for taking time to attend the virtual grant training seminar. I look forward to receiving your project proposal.").

- *Append a signature block.* You can set your e-mail program to append a signature block to the end of each e-mail message. The signature block should list your name, job title, organization, phone number, fax (if applicable), e-mail and physical addresses, and website link. You may also opt to include your LinkedIn handle to encourage professional networking. This information allows others to reach you easily, regardless of where they are picking up your message. Cute quotations and graphics in your signature are not advisable for business unless it is your company logo, slogan, or tagline indicating the work you do.

- *Think twice before using reply-all.* Use of the reply-all feature is only appropriate when your reply is relevant to every recipient of the original e-mail message. Before clicking reply-all, ask yourself whether everyone in the previous message needs to see your response, or if only the sender or certain individuals need to see it. Reply-all may be necessary if the sender requests a group discussion, if there are compliance or legal requirements to track conversations, or if the group needs to see your input on a topic.[12] Other than these few situations, it is rare that the use of reply-all is warranted; rather, it may set off a barrage of notifications that frustrate all recipients of the e-mail.

Letters

Even in an age of digital communication, there is still a place for traditional letters. Letters are appropriate for formal occasions, when the correspondence may be displayed, when a signature on paper is a legal requirement, or when the recipient prefers to have a paper version.

Perhaps the most common layout for business letters is the block format. For an example, see Figure A2.2. As this name suggests, each element and paragraph is set flush with the left margin. As you will notice in the example, professional etiquette prescribes the use of a courtesy title, such as Mr, Ms, or Mrs, when addressing the recipient of your

Heading	**TAMARA J. BUTTON** **1111 W. Stanton Rd.** **Andover, KS 67002** **(241) 264-1411 tjb@teacom.com**
Date *Don't abbreviate.*	March 11, 2022
Addressee *Unless writing a friend,* *include courtesy title* *(Mr., Ms., Dr., etc.).*	Mr. Jacob Bruneau Franco-American Electrical Specialists 300 W. Burton Street Wichita, KS 67202
Salutation	Dear Mr. Bruneau:
Body of letter	
Set paragraphs flush *with left margin.*	After six years as an electrician in the U.S. Air Force, I am prepared to take the skills I developed in the military into the civilian sector. I hope you will find that the wide range of abilities and the work habits I developed in the military provide strong qualifications for the position of field manager that is currently posted on the Franco-American website.
Separate paragraphs *with a single* *vertical space.*	As the enclosed résumé indicates, I bring to the field manager's job a wide range of skills. I have worked on commercial, industrial, and residential projects. I learned the trade from the bottom up, starting as an apprentice and progressing until I supervised a crew of 40 subordinates on complex multimillion-dollar projects, both in the United States and abroad.
	My experience in the Air Force has also helped to develop the personal skills necessary to work in this demanding field. I have worked successfully with a wide range of "customers," including military commanders and civilian contractors. As I gained more responsibilities, I learned how to manage subordinates to get jobs done error-free and on schedule. I'm proud to say that, in my final assignment with the Air Force, I was recognized as "Noncommissioned Officer of the Year."
	I also bring to Franco-American a strong work ethic. I have tackled jobs under a variety of demanding conditions, ranging from the frozen arctic cold to triple-digit desert heat. Many of the jobs for which I was responsible required 24-hour availability.
	I would welcome the chance to meet with you in person to explore how I might help Franco-American Electric as a field manager. Thank you in advance for your time and consideration.
Complimentary close	Sincerely,
Signature	*Tamara J. Button*
Enclosure line	Enclosure: Résumé

FIGURE A2.2 Letter Format

correspondence. In cases where you know the recipient identifies with the masculine or feminine gender, you can rely on these courtesy titles. However, in cases where you do not know the recipient's preferred pronoun, it is important to use inclusive language. For example, it may be acceptable to simply address the recipient by name ("Dear Jacob Bruneau") or with a general salutation ("Dear Policyholder" or "Dear Colleague").[13]

Beyond the elements in Figure A2.2, some letters need to contain additional information. This information might include a status (e.g., Urgent, Confidential), attention line, list of recipients receiving copies, postscript, and second page headers.

Text and Group Text Messages

Regular communication with your supervisors and coworkers is expected and appreciated in the workplace. Technology advances have made it easier to communicate with each other, but have also increased the possibility for violated expectations and frustrations. Text messaging is one form of communication that can be particularly troublesome, especially among professionals that have generational differences.

The etiquette for workplace texting differs from what you may be used to in your personal life. Some professionals may welcome quick interactions to avoid a barrage of e-mail exchanges, while others may find texting to be an invasive violation of work–life balance. Group text messaging further complicates the scenario as individuals are bombarded by constant replies and reactions to notifications that may not be pertinent to them–much like a reply-all e-mail.

Additionally, of those Americans who own a mobile phone, roughly 11% do not have smartphones.[14] The limitations of texting on these phones create additional ambiguity for recipients. For example, individuals may not be able to view a laughing emoji that would enable them to properly decipher the tone of a message.

The following guidelines[15] will help you avoid a potential faux pas:

- *Ask if your company has an official policy on text messaging.* If a policy does not exist, it is wise to ask your supervisors and coworkers for their permission and expectations for communicating using texts. Despite official policy or unstated company norms, it is crucial to ask permission before starting a text messaging group.

- *Clearly label your contacts.* To avoid the potentially embarrassing situation of sending a message to the wrong person, you should use full names when adding contacts to your phone. If appropriate, you may also include a title like "Supervisor Chris Gomez." One of the authors of your textbook recalls an acquaintance who was fired from their job because of an inappropriate late-night text sent to a colleague that was meant for a different contact with the same name.

- *Send messages during regular business hours.* To respect individuals' boundaries, it is good practice to send text messages only during regular business hours. Always seek permission before texting outside of business hours or on the weekends.

- *Keep your text messages short and to the point.* While sending a text to your boss to let them know that you are running late to work may be permissible, a long-winded explanation about the reasons you are late is not necessary. Messages should always be brief and have a clear call-to-action: "The clients would like to reschedule their proposal meeting to 3 p.m., how would you like for me to respond to them?" "Please call the office when you have a chance." "Becky, I am running late to the office. Can you unlock the door for our first patient and get their paperwork started?"

- *Avoid double-texting.* We have likely all experienced a texting interaction where someone sends a long thought as several individual messages. Hearing the notification sounds of multiple incoming messages can be stressful and annoying for receivers. Instead, only press "send" after you have gathered all of your thoughts and compiled them into a single message.

- *Move complex or sensitive conversations to a more appropriate medium.* Text messaging should be used for quick communications and should never be used to discuss significant matters. Asking for a raise or promotion, sharing negative news such as impending layoffs or furloughs, delivering a resignation, offering criticisms, and raising concerns should be saved for a face-to-face meeting or e-mail conversation.

- *Use a professional writing style.* While the use of shorthand ("rn" "wyd") may be the norm when communicating with your friends and family, professional text conversations are not the place for lazy writing. Be sure to proofread your messages for spelling, grammar, and improper autocorrects, before sending them. Furthermore, avoid excessive use of emojis or GIF images in your messages, especially when communicating with supervisors.

- *Think twice before using group texts.* Just like the case of a reply-all e-mail, the use of group text messaging is only appropriate when every group members' reply will be relevant to every recipient of the text message. While congratulating someone on their promotion is a kind gesture, this can be accomplished with a private text message to the honoree. Other recipients will likely be distracted by a multitude of "Congrats!" messages that do not pertain to them.

News Releases and Media Advisories

In Chapter 9, we discussed the use of news releases and media advisories to invite journalists to a press conference. A **news release** (or **press release**) is a form of written communication released to the media with the purpose of turning an announcement into a news story. Oftentimes, a news release is edited only slightly before being published as a story in the newspaper or read on air during a news program. For this reason, it is important to make sure that your news release is free from spelling, grammatical, and typographical errors; includes a catchy headline and photos; and meets the Associated Press (AP) Stylebook guidelines.

A news release contains the following elements, as demonstrated in Figure A2.3:

- Contact information for the company's designated spokesperson: Company name, physical address, contact name, phone number, e-mail address. You may also opt to include the spokesperson's social media handle.

- Header: When the story should be published—either immediately ("FOR IMMEDIATE RELEASE") or on a specific date ("FOR RELEASE ON SEPTEMBER 15, 2021").

- Headline: A 60- to 80-character title previewing the content of your story. The headline should clearly convey who and what is covered in the story.

- Dateline: Information regarding the origin (city/state) of the news release.

- Lead: Written in the third person, the opening sentence answers the five W's: who, what, when, where, and why.

- Body: Written in the third person, it tells the story and incorporates at least two quotes from company spokespersons or other relevant individuals.

- Search engine optimized (SEO) keywords: The body of the news release should contain hyperlinks to content that allows the journalist to seek more information.

- Videos, photos, infographics, logos, and other graphics should be included, as appropriate, to aid the journalist in developing their story.

- Boilerplate: The final paragraph should include a description of the organization, usually including its mission statement and where to get more information, followed by a close symbol ("###"). Since news releases are typically sent via

[Contact information]	Faux Literally Bookstore 1234 Townsquare Blvd. Casterfield, Texas 77777 Contact: Martin Mendez 555-555-5555 mmendez@fauxliterallybooks.com @flbsocial
[Release header]	**FOR RELEASE ON MAY 13, 2022**
[Headline]	**Faux Literally Bookstore to Host Book Festival Celebrating AAPI Heritage Month**
[AP Formatted Dateline; Lead; Underlined SEO keywords that link to an article containing more information about the underlined topic]	CASTERFIELD, Texas—Faux Literally Bookstore announces its inaugural book festival celebrating <u>Asian American and Pacific Islander (AAPI) heritage month</u> on May 14, 2022 from 8 a.m. to 5 p.m. at 1234 Townsquare Blvd. Community members are encouraged to attend the free festival, which highlights and provides access to the works of multiple AAPI authors. A variety of genres, including historical and contemporary fiction, graphic novels, young adult and children's books and memoirs and autobiographies will be featured. Book club-style sessions will be held throughout the day featuring open discussions about the issues and cultural significance of the featured book topics.
[Spokesperson quote]	"As a bookstore, we are proud to assist in the preservation and promotion of the culture and contributions of Asian American and Pacific Islander authors," says Faux Literally Bookstore manager Mele Leota. "We are excited to have the opportunity to initiate conversations and raise awareness of the important topics and themes found in these works."
[Boilerplate]	**About Faux Literally Bookstore** Faux Literally Bookstore is a local bookstore dedicated to promoting literacy and intercultural understanding since its opening in 2000. The bookstore gives back to the community by supporting a variety of educational and cultural preservation initiatives. To learn more, visit fauxliterallybookstore.com or call 555-555-5555.
[Close symbol]	###

FIGURE A2.3   News Release Format

e-mail, the close symbol tells the journalist that any information after the symbol–for example, a signature block–is not part of the official news release.

A media advisory alerts the media to an upcoming news event in hopes that journalists will attend. This type of document is usually one page in length and contains the following elements, as illustrated in Figure A2.4:

- Contact information
- Header
- Headline
- A description of the five W's (who, what, when, where, why) in outline format
- A description of the availability of individuals for interviews and/or photo ops
- Close symbol

[Contact information]	Faux Literally Bookstore 1234 Townsquare Blvd. Casterfield, Texas 77777 Contact: Martin Mendez 555-555-5555 mmendez@fauxliterallybooks.com @flbsocial
[Release header]	**FOR IMMEDIATE RELEASE**
[Headline]	**Faux Literally Bookstore to Host Book Festival Celebrating AAPI Heritage Month**

[5 W's]	**WHO:** Faux Literally Bookstore
	
	WHAT: A one-day book festival, free and open to the public. Book club-style sessions will be held throughout the day, featuring open discussions about the issues and cultural significance of featured books from the following genres:
	  • Historical fiction
	  • Contemporary fiction
	  • Graphic novel
	  • Young adult
	  • Children's
	  • Memoir and autobiography
	
	WHEN: May 14, 2022, 8 a.m. - 5 p.m.
	
	WHERE: Faux Literally Bookstore, 1234 Townsquare Blvd., Casterfield, Texas 77777
	
	WHY: To highlight and provide access to literary works authored by members of the Asian American and Pacific Islander community.

[Availability]	Faux Literally Bookstore Manager Mele Leota will be available for media interviews and photographs from 8 a.m. - 12 p.m. For more information or to schedule an interview, contact Martin Mendez, director of public relations, at 555-555-5555 or mmendez@fauxliterallybooks.com
[Close symbol]	###

FIGURE A2.4 Media Advisory Format

• Writing for Employment

Chapter 6 describes several paths to seeking employment. At some point, most job seekers will send out an employment-seeking letter and a résumé. The résumé remains a mainstay of the employment process, and now Internet options can enhance both the résumé creation process and the final product.

Résumés

A résumé is a marketing document—an advertisement in which you sell your skills to potential employers. A résumé summarizes your background and qualifications for employment. Résumés serve as a screening device, helping prospective employers decide which candidates' applications are worth further consideration.

A résumé will not automatically get you hired, but it can put you on the shortlist of candidates to be considered or cause you to be dropped from the running. As you read in Chapter 6, in competitive hiring situations, screening candidates is a process of elimination as much as selection. The people doing the hiring likely have more applications than they can handle, so they naturally look for ways of narrowing down the pool of candidates to a manageable number. A good résumé can also be useful for presenting yourself to potential employers who might hire you for a job that has not yet been announced or even created.

Besides listing your qualifications, a résumé offers tangible clues about the type of person you are. Are you organized and thorough? How well can you present your ideas? Is your work accurate? Are you attentive to detail? After you have left the interview, your résumé will remain behind as a reminder of the way you tackle a job and of the kind of employee you are likely to be.

Résumé Fundamentals   No matter what the job or the field, all good résumés incorporate the same fundamental principles.

Customize to fit a particular position   You may keep a generic résumé on hand when a new networking contact unexpectedly asks for your résumé or to use as a template to adapt when specific openings occur, but the most effective résumés are tailored to the interests and needs of a particular position and employer. For example, a medical technician should stress laboratory skills when applying for a job in a lab; conversely, when a job opening is in a clinic, the same technician should emphasize experiences that involve working with people. A résumé that encourages job offers focuses on how you can fulfill the employer's needs.

Be sure your résumé looks professional   Like every important business document, your résumé should be impeccable. Any mistakes or sloppiness could cost you the job by raising doubts in an employer's mind. Even small errors can be fatal: According to the Society for Human Resource Management, more than 75% of employers reject applicants whose résumés contain spelling errors or are grammatically sloppy.[16]

Because the design of résumés can be complicated and the stakes are high, many candidates hire professional services to create them. Whether you create the résumé yourself or have it professionally done, the final product should reflect the professional image you want to create. This is especially important if you are using a design template from a service like Canva. The style of the design should match the sophistication of the company to which you are applying.

Although you want to make yourself stand out from the crowd, be cautious about using unusual fonts, bright colors, or special paper. A novel approach might capture the fancy of a prospective boss, but it might also be a complete turn-off. The more you know about the field and the organization itself, the better your decisions will be about the best approach.

In companies and positions looking for creativity, some novel ideas may work. A third-place winner of an Enterprise Rent-A-Car creative résumé contest submitted a pizza box résumé to a pizza corporation and their photo on a milk carton (to alert the company of its "missing" worker) to another.[17] One job applicant even supplied a prospective employer with a Lego figurine of herself attached to a flash drive containing her résumé and portfolio. The creativity landed her the job, which is unsurprisingly in the visual design field.[18]

Although you may be remembered because of your creative and unusual résumé, these gimmicks will not work in most traditional employment situations. The résumé is a business document and needs to look professional.

Be positive, dynamic, and specific   Figures A2.5 and A2.6 illustrate several characteristics of effective résumés. Use the word "I" sparingly. The words "fired" and "unemployed" do not belong on your résumé.[19] You should also avoid using vague or cliché phrases (*A proven track record of . . ., With a passion for . . ., Goal-oriented, Team player, Detail-oriented, Excellent communication skills*). It can be assumed that a candidate applying for a job as a sports team manager will be passionate about sports. Furthermore, skills-based descriptions, such as being detail-oriented, should instead be demonstrated in your work samples and application materials.[20]

ANTHONY TOLIVAR

e-mail: a.tolivar@connectnet.org   phone: 223-705-6596

Home address   University address
1716 S. Hacienda Rd.   3211 Coit Rd.
La Habra, CA 90631   Dallas, TX 75254

SUMMARY OF QUALIFICATIONS

- Academic background in political and economic dimensions of food policy
- Experience working in commercial and nonprofit organizations related to international food security
- Strong work ethic and ability to work independently as necessary

EDUCATION

Current: University of Texas at Dallas
Graduating (Bachelor of Science degree) in May 2020
Major in International Relations, Asian Studies emphasis

Fall 2017: Shanghai International Studies University (Rotary International Ambassadorial Scholar)
Mandarin language program, ethnographic study of contemporary Chinese culture.

RELATED EXPERIENCE

September 2016–present: Assistant Coordinator, International Food Security Treaty, Southwest Division
Assisted in coordinating media and fundraising events to educate public and recruited volunteers for this campaign to guarantee nutrition rights around the world.

September 2018–February 2019: Correspondent, Food Policy blog (http://foodpolicy.org)
Published dispatches on insights gained from travels in East Asia for the award-winning Web site.

August 2018–January 2019: Undergraduate Research Fellow, University of Texas at Dallas
In Asia, analyzed the effectiveness of Rotary International programs in promoting international trade. Interviewed officials from municipal government, business, and nonprofit sectors in Philippines, Taiwan, Japan and China.

May 2018–August 2019: International Trade Research Intern, Southern California World Trade Center
Conducted individualized, in-depth sales and marketing research for the Trade Center's members.

Fall 2017: Intern, The American Chamber of Commerce, Shanghai
Developed marketing materials, publications, and grant proposals to promote U.S. economic interests in China.

Summer 2016: Intern, Center for Food Safety, San Francisco, California
Conducted research to identify and remediate threats to food safety; helped develop funding proposals for major donors.

LANGUAGES

Fluency in Spanish
Competence in *biao zhun* (standard pronunciation) Mandarin Chinese

---

FIGURE A2.5 Chronological Résumé Featuring Education and Work Experience

Amy Matthews

Box C-23123
Cambridge, MA 02138
617-555-0392
amatthews@harvard.edu

OBJECTIVE	To contribute my education and health management skills in a position with a growing and dynamic firm.
EDUCATION	**BACHELOR OF SCIENCE** **Harvard University**, Cambridge, Massachusetts, May 2019 Major: Health Sciences Minor: Management
RELEVANT COURSES	• Human Anatomy & Physiology I • Human Anatomy & Physiology II • Health Policy • Organizational Analysis and Health Care • Health Care Management • Human Resource Management
Health Management Skills	• Served as Assistant to the Director of the Stacey G. Houndly Breast Cancer Foundation. • Functioned as Public Health Representative for the Cambridge Area Public Health Administration. • Coordinated, Harvard University Public Health Awareness Week, 2017, 2018.
Communications Skills	• Served as a phone-a-thon caller on several occasions, soliciting donations from Harvard alumni and parents for Harvard University. • Volunteered for a political campaign, distributing literature door to door, fielding questions and making phone calls to local constituents.
Management Skills	• Handled all back-office management functions, including employee relations and accounting. • Oversaw client relations, order processing and routine upkeep of the business. • Coordinated efforts between customer needs and group personnel. • Designed all market research analysis and projects for our client. • Delegated suggestions and duties to other team members. • Presented market research results to client with suggestions of implementation. • Participated in Youth Leadership Boston, a group dedicated to developing leadership skills through diverse programming.
Leadership Skills	• Served as formal/social coordinator for my sorority program council. • Elected Vice President of Risk Management for Panhellenic, a group that oversees and coordinates educational programming for Harvard's Greek system.
Systems Abilities	• Windows 8, Macintosh OS, and Linux operating systems • Microsoft Office (all applications and versions) • HTML/XML Web Publishing: Multiple authoring tools. Microsoft SQL, Oracle, and FileMaker Pro database management systems

FIGURE A2.6   Functional Résumé Focusing on Demonstrated Skills

Source: Adapted from Quintessential Careers. (n.d.). Quintessential Careers functional resume sample. Retrieved from http://www .quintcareers.com/resume_sample_1.html

Table A2-1	Dynamic Verbs in Résumés Demonstrate Accomplishments

Communication/People Skills	Technical Skills	Organizational Skills
Collaborated	Assembled	Arranged
Communicated	Calculated	Compiled
Consulted	Constructed	Executed
Directed	Engineered	Maintained
Drafted	Fabricated	Monitored
Interviewed	Installed	Processed
Marketed	Maintained	Purchased
Moderated	Operated	Screened
Negotiated	Overhauled	Standardized
Presented	Programmed	Systematized
Publicized	Solved	Updated
Translated	Upgraded	Verified

Source: Sampled from Quintessential Careers. (n.d.). "Action Verbs By Skills Categories." Retrieved from http://www.quintcareers.com/action_skills.html. This website also lists action verbs to describe skills in each of these areas: creative, data/financial, helping, management/leadership, research, and teaching.

Begin sentences with positive verbs (*created, developed, analyzed*), as in Table A2-1. Most importantly, be absolutely honest about everything you include. The results of a survey conducted by ResumeLab found that employers do not usually forgive candidates who are caught with fabricated résumés; of the candidates who were caught lying on their résumés, 65% were either fired or not hired at all.[21]

Be specific about accomplishments, including numbers whenever possible. For example, replace "Designed training for large groups" with "Designed training for groups of more than 100 employees." It is less effective to say "Helped cut costs" than to say "Reduced costs by 21% in 3 years."

Your résumé should almost never exceed two pages in length, and one page is usually better. Employers are often unimpressed with longer résumés, which are hard to read and can seem padded, especially when they come from people with comparatively little job experience.

Résumé Elements   While résumés can be organized in more than one way, they almost always contain the same basic information. Résumés are not autobiographies: The purpose is to get an interview, not tell your life history. Personal information such as age, height, weight, religion, race, marital status, and children does not belong in a résumé. The following elements appear in most, if not all, résumés.

Name and contact information   This information usually includes your name, phone number, e-mail address, and professional portfolio website. Make sure the information allows an interested employer to reach you easily. Listing a personal e-mail address and home or cell phone number is preferable to listing a current employer's address and phone number. Be certain to check for messages frequently and respond speedily. Be certain your voice mail message and e-mail address are not offensive or do not create an impression you would not want. A screen name like "partyfan" does not convey the impression of a serious job candidate, so you might set up a separate e-mail account expressly for seeking employment.

Summary of qualifications   An effective strategy is to begin your résumé with a summary of the assets you bring to a job. For example:

- Demonstrated skills as a self-starter who builds strong relationships with clients.
- Consistently met sales goals while working independently in satellite office.
- Had highest client retention rate of all sales representatives in Western Division.
- Earned "Certificate of Mastery" from TCE Institute while working full-time.

Although you will probably describe this information in the body of your résumé, leading with your strengths, presented in summary form, highlights them and motivates a prospective employer to examine the rest of your application more carefully.

Education   Employers are usually interested in learning about your post–high school education and training, degrees earned, major and minor fields of study, and dates of attendance and/or graduation. If you attended college, it is unnecessary to include high school. Begin with your most recent education and work backward. If the information is helpful and space permits, list notable courses you have taken. If your grade-point average is impressive, include it along with the scale in which it is calculated "3.95 on a 4.0 scale." Finally, note any honors or awards you have earned. If they are numerous, list them in a separate "Awards and Honors" section.

Experience   Every employer wants to know which types of work you have performed. By using the general title "Work Experience" instead of the more limited "Employment History," you can highlight a summer internship, delete a dishwashing job, group minor or similar jobs together, and include volunteer work, service-learning class projects, or club activities that taught you marketable skills.

Employers are more interested in the duties you performed than in job titles. They search for the answers to two questions: What can you do? What are your attributes as an employee? You can provide answers to these questions by accompanying your job title, name of employer, and city/state with a list of the duties you performed. There is no need to use complete sentences—phrases presented in a list of bullet points will do. Be sure to use concrete language, including technical terminology, to describe the work you performed. Place this section either before or following the section on education, depending on which you have more of or which will be most important to an employer.

Special interests and aptitudes   This is the place to showcase any unique talents or experiences you bring to the job. This section might include community service activities (cite offices you have held), languages you can write or speak, special equipment you can operate, relevant hobbies, and so on. The key here is to include only information the employer will find useful and that casts you in a favorable light.

Memberships   Include this section only if you belong to organizations related to the career field or position you are seeking. Include any offices or significant committee appointments you have held. Membership in service and civic groups is usually less important, so include it only if you have held a major office.

Certifications   If you are certified or licensed in any occupational field, either create a category in which to display that fact, or include it in the "Special Interests and Aptitudes" section described earlier. For instance, if you are a Microsoft Certified Systems Engineer, list your MCSE certification. If your Notary Public or CPR certification could benefit an employer, include it.

References   List references on a résumé only if they are specifically requested. Instead, create a references list separate from your résumé and bring it to an interview. This list can include three to five professional contacts (not family members) who know your work and character. Be certain you ask each potential reference in advance for permission to use their name.

Give each reference a copy of your résumé and keep each person informed of the places and positions to which you are applying. You might remind a college professor of the term project you completed or remind a past employer of an accomplishment you would like mentioned.

Types of Résumés

There are two common approaches to organizing a résumé: chronological and functional. Each has its own advantages; the one you choose will probably depend on the specific job you are applying for and your past accomplishments.

Chronological résumés emphasize your education and work experience and are most effective when such experience clearly relates to the job you are seeking, such as when you have worked within the field. Within the categories "Education," "Work Experience," and "Related Experience" (if you have such a section), list entries in reverse order, beginning with your most recent experience. Under each position, describe your responsibilities and accomplishments, emphasizing ways in which they prepared you for the job you are now seeking. If you are a recent graduate, you may want to list your education first. (See Figure A2.5.)

Functional résumés feature the skills you bring to the job (e.g., organizer, researcher, manager). As Figure A2.6 illustrates, they provide examples of the most significant experiences that demonstrate these abilities. This approach is especially appropriate in the following instances:

- When you are first entering the job market or reentering it after an absence
- When you have held a variety of apparently unrelated jobs
- When you are changing careers or specialties
- When your work history has been interrupted
- When your past job titles do not clearly show how you are qualified for the position you are seeking

When you create a functional résumé, follow the "Skills" category immediately with a chronological "Work History" and a scaled-down "Education" section that lists only institutions, degrees, and dates. Either of the latter two categories may come first, depending on whether you gained most of your skills and experience in school or on the job.

Whatever format you choose, experts agree that strong résumés possess the same qualities:

- *They focus on the employer's needs.* If you understand which qualities (perseverance, innovation, ability to learn quickly) and skills (mastery of software, selling) an employer needs, you can tailor your résumé to show how you fit the job.
- *They are concise.* A long-winded résumé sends the wrong message in a business environment where time is money and clarity is essential. Use simple, brief statements to describe yourself, and avoid verbose language.

- *They are honest.* Outright lies are obvious grounds for disqualification, of course. But getting caught exaggerating your qualifications will raise serious doubts about your honesty in other areas. As one expert put it, "Be aggressive, be bold, but be honest."[22]

Electronic Résumés

Electronic résumés have become a standard requirement in comparison to the paper-and-ink alternative. Since many employers require applicants to submit information electronically, it is important to know how this part of the hiring system operates.

Strategies for electronic résumés   Résumé preparation and delivery may evolve over the years, but a basic principle holds: Adapt to your audience. Customize the content and method of transmission of your résumé for individual companies, positions, and, when possible, the people who will read it.

Electronic résumés have both advantages and drawbacks. When you send a paper résumé, the recipient sees exactly what you created, although receiving and forwarding it to others may take time. With electronic résumés, there is a greater risk that your reader may not be able to view the document for technical reasons or may not want to open the file because of the additional time it takes and the risk of its infection with a virus. Furthermore, some companies automatically delete unsolicited e-mails with attachments, so find out before you attach your résumé to your original message.

When you do submit a résumé electronically, follow these guidelines[23]:

- Do not bombard employers with résumés for positions that do not exist or for which you are not qualified.

- Do include a cover letter that tells the employer which position you are applying for. See the next section for more details on how to compose a cover letter.

- Do include key buzzwords. Many résumés are no longer read by a human. Instead, computers scan résumés for keywords related to specific jobs. For examples of skill keywords (by job categories) and personal trait keywords specific to your career field, consult the Bureau of Labor Statistics' *Occupational Outlook Handbook* and other online resources.

- Do consider the channels for submitting your résumé. The most common ways to submit electronic résumés are through e-mail attachments and web-based interfaces.[24]

E-mail attachments   You will probably create your résumé in a word processing format or using an online design service like Canva, but it is wise to convert and submit it in PDF format so it will have the desired appearance on any computer, and so it cannot be modified. A résumé might also consist of a web page (HTML) file or, in some cases, even an audio or video format. The most important consideration when crafting a résumé you plan to submit as an e-mail attachment is to be sure the recipient will be able to open and read it after downloading.

Web-based interfaces   Web-based job banks are services where job seekers can post information about themselves for potential employers to review. Résumés posted on some job banks are open to anyone who wants to see them, whereas other banks allow you to store a résumé and send it to employers that you select.

Web-based résumés have several advantages. Literally thousands of employers worldwide can access your materials as quickly as you post them. You can also readily update and change your résumé. In addition, you can include portfolios with accessible graphics and sound that demonstrate your experience and showcase your expertise.[25]

Despite these advantages, online résumés have a unique set of drawbacks. Once your résumé is posted on the web, you may have no control over who sees it and where it is transferred. Many currently employed job-seekers have been chagrined to learn that their current bosses found their postings in job banks. Check the privacy policies of sites before posting, but be aware that those policies may change in the future. The bottom line is that privacy is not assured once a résumé is posted publicly.

Be sure to date your résumé in case it becomes a permanent irretrievable fixture in cyberspace. For résumés posted online, you may choose to protect at least some of your privacy by listing only an e-mail address for contact. Before posting a résumé for a specific employer, check the employer's existence and legitimacy. You may want to leave out your current employer, listing only the type of position or the industry in which you are currently employed so unscrupulous headhunters do not contact you at your present job.

Employment-Seeking Letters

Letters give you the chance to present yourself to prospective employers in a favorable manner. As with all business correspondence, it is important to always check your spelling and grammar. A helpful suggestion is to read your letter out loud to catch any mistakes. The following advice suggests how you can use this correspondence to your best advantage.

Cover Letters   Whenever you provide your résumé to a prospective employer, accompany it with a cover letter that is personalized for the particular job you are applying for and the organization to which you are applying. As one expert put it, a cover letter is "an introduction, a sales pitch, and a proposal for further action all in one."[26]

Cover letters should be sent to a specific individual. If you do not know the appropriate person, call the company and ask for the individual's name, being certain that you get the spelling, title, and pronoun correct. If it is not possible to contact the company, you may instead use a greeting like "To Whom It May Concern" or "Dear Hiring Manager."

As Figure A2.7 illustrates, cover letters include the following information:

- In the first paragraph, introduce yourself to the reader. Clearly reference the job you are applying for and state your purpose for writing (e.g., in response to an advertisement, at the suggestion of a mutual acquaintance, as a result of your research). When appropriate, mention any mutual acquaintances the addressee will recognize. If you have a connection with the person you are writing to (as discussed in the Personal Networking section in Chapter 2), mention that. If you are writing to the human resources department of a medium- or large-size organization, be sure to give the job number if there is one; a company that has many job openings will not know which position you are applying for unless you identify it. You should also describe your ability to meet the company's needs and make it clear that you are eager to work there. These steps ensure that the company knows your letter was designed for them. Otherwise—as Nisha Chittal, editor at fashion-and-beauty website Racked, explains—the letter "could have been copied, pasted, and sent to 1,000 random companies."[27]

- In the next paragraph or two, highlight one or two of your most impressive accomplishments that are *relevant to the job at hand*. Rather than simply saying that you can help the organization, offer some objective evidence that backs up your claim. It is good practice to use exact words from the job listing when explaining how your skills match the job duties.

- In the closing paragraph, describe the next step you hope to take—usually requesting an interview. Detail any information about limits on your availability (though

From: Krista Dudley [krista.dudley@rockycast.net]
Sent: Friday, April 15, 2022 5:41 PM
To: John Waldmann [john.waldmann@boulderarts.org]
Subject: Events Coordinator application

Attached: 📎 K Dudley Resume.doc

Dear Mr. Waldmann:

Our mutual friend Marcia Sherwood recently alerted me to the open position of Events Coordinator for the Boulder Arts Council, and I am writing to express my interest in that position.

I would welcome the chance to use skills acquired over the past 12 years planning events for a variety of community organizations in the Denver area to help the Council extend its reach in the community. The attached résumé will help you gain a sense of my experience.

As a person who has coordinated a wide range of community events for nonprofit organizations, I can bring the Arts Council demonstrated ability to motivate and coordinate the work of volunteers and to generate widespread publicity for events on a limited budget. Most recently, I was chairperson for Aurora's Earth Day festival, and I was the public information coordinator for last year's Halloween auction and dance to benefit Denver's Shelter Services for Women. The enclosed résumé details a variety of other activities that have helped prepare me for the position of Events Coordinator.

I would welcome the chance to discuss how I might help the Boulder Arts Council. I will be available any time in the next month, except for the weekend of April 23–24.

I look forward to hearing from you soon.

Sincerely,
Krista Dudley
387 Blythe St.
Aurora, CO 80017
(303) 654-7909

FIGURE A2.7 Sample Message Requesting Employment Interview

you should keep these to an absolute minimum). Supply any other information the prospective employer may have requested. Finally, close with a cordial expression of gratitude and your signature. Print and sign your name using blue or black ink for paper cover letters; if sending an electronic letter, scan your signature, save it as a .jpg file and insert it in the letter above your typed name.

Follow-up Letters   Always follow up an interview by sending a thank you note to the interviewer(s). As with other correspondence, the decision about whether to convey this message in print or via e-mail depends on the preferences of the person to whom you will be writing. In any case, make sure your thank you message arrives within a day or two following your interview. Besides showing your good manners, a follow-up letter is an opportunity to remind the interviewer of your uniqueness and the strengths you will bring to the company.

Your follow-up letter should thank the interviewer for the opportunity to meet and the chance to have learned more about the position and the company. Also, offer thanks for the chance to have met any other people to whom you were introduced. Use the letter to assert why you believe you are well qualified for the job, and how you can serve the company's needs. Address any concerns the interviewer may have had, and add information about yourself you did not have an opportunity to state during the interview. Be certain the letter concludes on a positive note and expresses goodwill. Be absolutely positive you have correctly spelled every name you use and that your letter is free of any other mistakes. Any errors in this letter are likely to raise doubts about the quality of work you might do after you are hired.

Thank you letters are also appropriate for someone who has referred you to an employer, given a recommendation (phone or written) for you, or given job search information to you.

● Reports

Once you get the job, you will likely have a lot of writing to do as part of your duties. Reports are a routine part of business life. They vary in size and frequency, from a half-page weekly memo on the number of new hires to a 20-page report complete with graphs, analysis, and recommendations on the feasibility of some new office space. The readers' needs and the corporate culture will determine the size, format, and frequency of reports.

Types of Reports

Reports, like presentations, may be informative or persuasive. Some reports present information, others may propose solutions to problems, or analyze a problem and propose a course of action. Common types of reports include trip, progress, incident, and feasibility.

Trip Reports   Trip reports often justify the money organizations spend on trips taken by their employees. Know why the report is being written and for whom. Is it for your manager to justify the type of workshop you attended or for accounting to withstand an audit? Usually, trip reports answer these questions: Where did you go? With whom? Why? When? What did you learn? Whom did you meet? State the name of the conference or meeting, city and location, and your purpose for attending.

In the body of your narrative, emphasize two or three key points. If your job is to report to all employees, select information that employees need and will find interesting on safety, legal issues, or changes in policies. If the conference you attended introduced new products or new prices for old products, you may want to detail those. If your report goes only to your supervisor, you may want to include a section on needs or ideas for change that you learned on the trip.

Progress Reports   Progress reports (also called periodic operating reports) occur at fixed intervals: weekly sales reports, monthly customer complaints, yearly safety reports. These reports may be largely statistical, but most will require some description of regular events and any unusual events (special sales, emergency closures, power outages). In such a report, you must answer the key question: What is our status? If appropriate, indicate any hurdles you have overcome or have yet to overcome, and then describe the next objective.

Incident Reports   Incident reports (also called situational reports) report on nonroutine occurrences such as accidents or special events. They may be formatted as memos, or the organization may have special forms for these reports with very precise requirements that address legal or human resources concerns. Before beginning an incident report, make sure you know who is asking for the report and which level of detail is required. Always ask for guidance on creating the report if you are unsure about this process. When describing the incident, use precise facts such as numbers, dates, times, and quotations. Rather than report, "An employee fell on a staircase," write "Jane Winthrop, an employee in the Claims Department, reported that she fell on the north staircase inside the building at 4:00 p.m., Monday, June 21, 2021."

Feasibility Reports   Feasibility reports address the questions of whether projects are possible, practical, advantageous, safe, or advisable. They use data to analyze the advantages and disadvantages of a particular project or to determine whether something can or should be done.

Begin by knowing what the main question is: How can we improve employee accessibility to supplies without incurring any loss of supplies? How can we improve training on new equipment in a timely manner to minimize repairs caused by improper use of new equipment? Then describe the problem or need, the criteria for comparing solutions, the possible solutions, and how well each solution meets the criteria. Tables, graphs, and other visual aids are effective ways to enhance this analysis section. Be certain you understand whether your assignment is to report information only or to draw conclusions and make recommendations. If the latter is part of your assignment, you will want a section in which you give your recommendations.

Report Basics

Regardless of the report's contents and size, the following guidelines will help you produce a top-quality document and complete it on schedule.

Understand the Purpose   Begin by identifying the purpose of the report. A specific goal statement for reports should follow the same format for presentations described in Chapter 10:

> "After reviewing this report, the Operations Manager will have a clear idea of how the cost of electricity has changed over the past three years, and how costs are likely to change in the next two years."
>
> "After reading this report, my boss will see that giving traveling staff laptop computers will increase their productivity enough to pay for the equipment."

You can define the purpose of a report by asking yourself what it will be used for, who will read it, and what amount of detail is required. A routine one-page expense report is not the place to present your ideas for reforming the company's accounting policy. By contrast, if you have been asked to analyze a problem of high employee turnover, simply presenting data without including your analysis of causes and proposing solutions would make the report incomplete. If you have any doubts about the purpose of the report, ask the person or people who have requested it for clarification.

Create a Schedule for a Longer Report   Once you understand the purpose of the report, list all of the tasks necessary to complete the report and devise a workable schedule. Allot time for researching (Internet, library visits, studies, surveys, interviews), outlining, writing a draft, getting any preliminary approvals needed, creating exhibits, and writing and editing the final copy.

Organize for Comprehension   Determine which organizational pattern will best help readers understand your report. The organizational patterns discussed in Chapter 10 can also be used for written reports. Chronological patterns are often appropriate for progress reports, whereas topical patterns work well for reports that need to cover several areas. For example, a report on a possible location for a new factory might be organized by topics such as natural resources, transportation, workforce availability, and tax base. Another common organizational pattern for reports is by the level of importance. A report on the growing loss of quality personnel, for example, might focus on the most important features first and then move on to discuss less important ones. Create an outline for the report and use it as a basis for developing the content of the report; it will help you clarify the organizational pattern.

Format for Readability   Break your report into logical divisions, which you then indicate with formatting, such as boldface, boxes, horizontal lines, headings, bullets, numbers, and whitespace. All of these formatting elements can help the reader see what goes together and which are the important features. If it is permissible in your organization, use the templates for reports that are included in most word processing programs.

Document Carefully   The purpose of documentation is to give credit to your sources and allow the reader to identify and find the source if more information is needed. Citing your sources avoids plagiarism. In longer reports to scientific and academic organizations, use MLA or APA style. In business, use the style of documentation that is accepted within your organization or industry.

Determine the Preferred Medium   Some organizations prefer reports to be submitted electronically, while others expect printed documents. Follow the protocol of the organization to which you will be presenting the report.

Report Elements

Not every report should include all of the following elements. The amount of information covered, its nature, the conventions of the organization, and the needs of your readers will help you decide which parts to include.

Title Page   Every report needs a descriptive title. If the document is a long one, the first page should include the title; "Submitted by . . ." or "Prepared by . . ." with the author(s) name(s); and "Submitted to . . ." or "Prepared for . . ." with the name of the intended audience or person requesting the report. The last item on the page is the date of submission.

Letter of Transmittal   If the report is presented to persons inside the company, use a memo (instead of a letter) of transmittal. This letter or memo should include a short history of the report (who assigned or authorized it and why), a brief summary of significant findings, conclusions, expression of thanks and acknowledgment of assistance from others, and clear instructions regarding how the reader is to respond. It is also appropriate to offer to answer questions and indicate how best to contact you.

Table of Contents   If the report is a long one with several sections, a table of contents will help readers locate material. In this section, identify the major sections of the report and list the page on which each section begins.

Abstract or Executive Summary   This section provides readers with a quick overview of the report's key sections. In most cases, the summary should be no longer than one page or 10 percent of the length of the full report.

Exhibits and Appendixes   Many reports include tables, charts, graphs, and other visual elements that illustrate points made in the body of the document. If the report includes several visual aids, a list of the exhibits and the page numbers on which they appear will help readers locate them. Depending on the accepted style in your field, these items can be listed as exhibits either within the body of the report or in appendixes at the back of the document.

Bibliography or References   Depending on the accepted practices in your occupation and the formality of the report, you might include only sources that you cited or sources that you cited plus others you used but did not cite. Some reports will include those sources cited and used, as well as additional sources of information.

references

1. Moran, G. (2018, December 14). Are you making one of these 4 common business writing mistakes? *Fast Company*. Retrieved from https://www.fastcompany.com/90278739/4 -common-business-writing-mistakes
2. Moran, G. (2018, December 14). Are you making one of these 4 common business writing mistakes? *Fast Company*. Retrieved from https://www.fastcompany.com/90278739/4-common -business-writing-mistakes
3. "Avoid these writing mistakes." (2019, February). *Strategies and Tactics*.
4. "The economy of plain English." (1995, January). *American Salesman, 40*(1), 15; "Five phrases to eliminate from your business writing." (2000, September). *Manager's Intelligence Report,* p. 1.
5. "Trim the fat from your business writing with these ideas." (2000, January). *Manager's Intelligence Report,* p. 4.
6. "Trim the fat from your business writing with these ideas." (2000, January). *Manager's Intelligence Report,* p. 4.
7. Lewis, B. (1999, November 22). Make sure you actually communicate rather than simply offer information. *InfoWorld,* p. 80.
8. Boogaard, K. (n.d.). A friendly person's guide to using exclamation marks correctly! And incorrectly! *The Muse*. Retrieved from https://www.themuse.com/advice/a-friendly-persons-guide -to-using-exclamation-marks-correctly-and-incorrectly
9. Baldrige, L., & O'Brien, G. (2000). Netiquette. *Kinko's Impress,* 1, 20–21.
10. Lucrezio, P. (2000, February 2). Companies must develop, enforce email usage policies. *Capital District Business Review,* p. 37.
11. Humphries, A. (2000, September 29). Email for careerists: Care enough to send the very best. *CNN*. Retrieved from http://archives.cnn.com/2000/CAREER/corporateclass/09/29 /email.protocol/index.html
12. Arden (2019, October 22). The dreaded "reply all" email response. *Clise Etiquette*. Retrieved from https://www.cliseetiquette.com/dreaded-reply-email-response/
13. Versace, J. (2018, February 5). Making letters and emails gender-inclusive. *Government of Canada*. Retrieved from https://www.noslangues-ourlanguages.gc.ca/en/blogue-blog/inclu-sifs-gender-inclusive-eng?wbdisable=true
14. Pew Research Center (2019, June 12). Mobile fact sheet. Retrieved from https://www .pewresearch.org/internet/fact-sheet/mobile/
15. SnapDesk (2021, February 15). Texting etiquette | Text message etiquette for business. Retrieved from https://snapdesk.app/text-message-etiquette/
16. Hsu, T. (2009, March 29). Crafting a resume that will grab recruiters. *Los Angeles Times*. Retrieved from http://www.latimes.com/business/la-fi–cover29-2009mar29,0,4601180 .story?page=3
17. Bass, C. D. (2000, June 18). Unusual résumé may net that job. *Albuquerque Journal,* p. I-1.
18. Ward, M. (2017, March 1). 7 of the most creative resumes we've ever seen. *CNBC*. Retrieved from https://www.cnbc.com/2017/03/01/7-of-the-most-creative-resumes -weve-ever-seen.html

19. Bureau of Economic Research and Analysis. (2000). *The job hunters guide*. Albuquerque, NM: New Mexico Department of Labor.

20. Una Dabiero via Fairygodboss (2019, October 14). 8 cringeworthy phrases that are ruining your resume. *Ladders*. Retrieved from https://www.theladders.com/career-advice/8-cringeworthy -phrases-that-are-ruining-your-resume

21. Turczynski, B. (2021, March 18). Lying on a resume (2020 study). *ResumeLab*. Retrieved from https://resumelab.com/resume/lying

22. Enelow, W. S. (n.d.). What do employers really want in a résumé? *Jobweb.com*. Retrieved from http://www.jobweb.com/catapult/enelow-r.html

23. Hansen, K. (n.d.). Common sense steps can prevent employer backlash against online resumes. *Quintessential Careers*. Retrieved from http://www.quintcareers.com/online_resume _guide.html

24. Smith, R. (2001). *eResumes 101: Choosing your best electronic resume format*. Retrieved from http://www.eresumes.com/tut_eresume.html

25. Gerson, S. J., & Gerson, S. M. (2000). *Technical writing: Process and product* (3rd ed.) Upper Saddle River, NJ: Prentice-Hall.

26. Tullier, M. (2002). The art and science of writing cover letters: The best way to make a first impression. *Monster.com*. Retrieved from http://resume.monster.com/coverletter/coverletters

27. Public Relations Society of America (2018, February 1). Cover letter mistakes that could cost you a job. *Strategies & Tactics*. Retrieved from https://apps.prsa.org/StrategiesTactics /Articles/view/12177/1154/Storytelling_Briefs_Online_Reviews_Mobile_Emails_a# .YG4RwxRudAc

appendix III
Problem-Solving Communication

Most of the communication aimed at solving problems and making decisions occurs in meetings. In the past decades, researchers have developed several methods for accomplishing these goals. Each decision-making method has its advantages and disadvantages. The choice of which one to use depends on several factors:

What type of decision is being made? If the decision can best be made by one or more experts, or if it needs to be made by the authorities in charge, then involving other group members is not appropriate. If, however, the task at hand calls for creativity or requires a large amount of information from many sources, then input from the entire team can make a big difference.

How important is the decision? Trivial decisions do not require the entire team's involvement. It is a waste of time and money to bring everyone together to make a decision that can easily be made by one or two people.

How much time is available? If time is short, it simply may not be possible to consult everyone in the team. This is especially true if the members are not all available—if some are away from the office, working remotely, or out of town, for example. Even if everyone is available, the time-consuming deliberations that come with a team discussion may be a luxury you cannot afford.

What are the personal relationships among members? Even important decisions might best be made without convening the whole team if members are on bad terms. If talking things out will improve matters, then a meeting may be worth the emotional wear and tear it will generate. Conversely, if a face-to-face discussion will just make matters worse, then the decision might best be made in some other way.

You will participate in many decision-making meetings throughout your professional life. Understanding the stages and process of group problem solving will help you produce high-quality work.

• Stages of Group Problem Solving

When it comes to solving problems and making decisions, groups move more or less regularly through several phases characterized by different types of communication. Aubrey Fisher identified four of these stages: orientation, conflict, emergence, and reinforcement.[1]

The first stage in a group's development is the **orientation phase**, sometimes called **forming**.[2] This is a time of testing the waters. Members may not know one another well so they may be cautious about making statements that might offend other members. For this reason, during the orientation stage, group members are not likely to take strong positions even on issues they regard as important. It is easy to mistake the lack of conflict during this phase for harmony and to assume the task will proceed smoothly. Peace and quiet are often a sign of caution, not agreement, especially in high context cultures where individuals must prioritize the group and think carefully before expressing their opinions. Despite the tentative nature of communication, the orientation stage is important because the norms that can govern the group's communication throughout its life are often established at this time.

After the group members understand the problem and have a feel for one another, the group typically moves to the **conflict phase**, which has also been called **storming**.

During this phase, members take strong stands on the issue and defend their positions against others. Disagreement is likely to be greatest during this phase, and the potential for bruised egos is strongest. It is important to recognize the role that culture plays during storming. For example, persons from low context cultures might use strong words when openly expressing criticisms that could be deemed offensive by members of other cultures. Whereas indirect and subtle statements are often used during disagreements in high context cultures. Imagine the difference between "This is an absolutely ridiculous idea!" versus "This idea might still need a little bit of work."

The norms of politeness formed during orientation, along with those inherent in one's culture, may weaken as members debate with one another and there is a real risk that their personal feelings will interfere with the kind of rational decision-making described in the preceding section. Conflict does not have to be negative, however. If members adopt the types of constructive approaches outlined in Chapter 5, they can come up with higher-quality solutions than groups that make harmony a top priority.[3]

Some groups never escape from the conflict stage. Their interaction—at least about the problem at hand—may end when time pressures force a solution that almost no one finds satisfactory. The boss may impose a decision from above, or a majority might overrule the minority. Time may even run out without any decision being made.

Not all groups suffer from such unhappy outcomes, however. Productive teams manage to work through the conflict phase and move on to the next stage of development.

The **emergence phase** of problem-solving, sometimes called **norming**, occurs when the members end their disagreement and solve the problem. Every member may enthusiastically support the final decision. In some cases, though, members may compromise or settle for a proposal they did not originally prefer. In any case, the key to emergence is acceptance of a decision that members can support (even if reluctantly). Communication during the emergence phase is less polarized. Members back off from their previously held firm positions. Comments like "I can live with that" and "Let's give it a try" are common at this point. Even if some people have doubts about the decision, there is a greater likelihood they will keep their concerns to themselves. Harmony is the theme.[4]

The fourth stage of discussion is the **reinforcement phase**. This stage has also been called **performing** because members not just accept the decision but actively endorse it. Members who made arguments against the decision during the conflict stage now present evidence to support it. In school, the reinforcement stage is apparent when students presenting a team project defend it against any complaints the instructor might have. In the workplace, the same principle applies: If the boss finds fault with a team's proposals, the tendency is to band together to support them.

In real life, groups do not necessarily follow this four-step process (summarized in Table A3-1) neatly. In an ongoing group, the patterns of communication in the past can influence present and future communication.[5] Teams with a high degree of conflict may have trouble reaching emergence, for example, whereas teams that are highly cohesive might experience little disagreement.

Sometimes a group can become stuck in one phase, never progressing to the phases that follow. For example, members may never get beyond the superficial, polite interaction of orientation. If they do, they may become mired in conflict. Ongoing groups might move through some or all of the stages each time they tackle a new problem, as depicted in Figure A3.1. In fact, a group that deals with several issues at one time might be in different stages for each problem.

Knowing that the team to which you belong is likely to pass through these stages can be reassuring. Your urge to get down to business and quit wasting time during the orientation phase might be tempered if you realize the cautious communication is probably temporary. Likewise, you might be less distressed about conflict if you know that the emergence phase may be just around the corner.

Table A3-1	Characteristics and Guidelines for Problem-Solving Stages		
	Member Behaviors	**Member Concerns**	**For Higher Performance**
Forming	Most comments directed to designated leader Direction and clarification frequently sought Status accorded to members based on their roles outside the group Issues discussed superficially	Why am I in this group? Why are the others here? Will I be accepted? What is my role? Which jobs will I have? Will I be able to handle them? Who is the leader? Are they competent?	Clarify tasks, roles, and responsibilities Provide structure Encourage balanced participation Identify one another's expertise, needs, values, and preferences
Storming	Some members try to gain a disproportionate share of influence Subgroups and coalitions form The designated leader may be challenged Members overzealously judge one another's ideas and personalities	How much autonomy will I have? Will I be able to influence others? What is my place in the pecking order? Who are my friends and allies? Who are my enemies? Do my ideas get any support here? Why don't some of the others see things my way? Is this aggravation worth the effort?	Use joint problem-solving Discuss the group's problem-solving ideas Have members explain how others' ideas are useful and how to improve them Establish a norm supporting expression of different viewpoints Discourage domination by a single person or subgroup
Norming	The group establishes and follows rules and procedures Members sometimes openly disagree The group laughs together, has fun Members have a sense of "we-ness" The group feels superior to other groups Groupthink may be a risk	How can we get organized well enough to stay on top of our tasks? How close should I get to other members? How can we work in harmony? How do we compare to other groups? What is my relationship to the leader? How do we keep conflicts and differences under control? How can we structure things to run smoothly?	Challenge the group, fight complacency Establish norms of high performance Request and provide both positive and constructive feedback on individual and group actions Encourage open discussions about individual ideas and concerns
High Performing	Members seek honest feedback from one another Roles are clear, yet members cover for one another as needed Members openly discuss and accept differences Members encourage one another to do better	How can we continue at this pace? How might we share our learnings with one another? What will I do when this process is over? How will I find another group as good as this one?	Jointly set challenging goals Look for opportunities to increase the group's scope Question assumptions, norms, and traditional approaches Develop a mechanism for ongoing self-assessment and group assessment

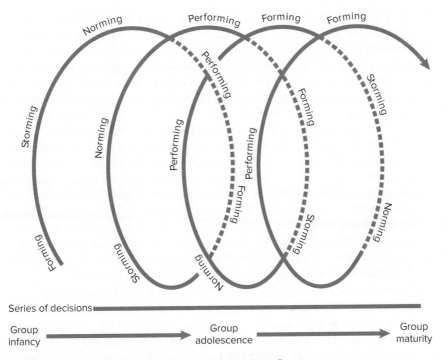

FIGURE A3.1   Cyclical Stages in an Ongoing Group
Source: Galanes, G. J., Adams, K., & Brilhart, J. K. (2004). *Effective Group Discussion* (11th ed.).
New York, NY: McGraw Hill.

● Systematic Problem Solving

The range of problems that groups face on the job is almost endless. How can we cut expenses? Increase market share? Reduce customer complaints? Offer a better employee benefits program? Not all groups approach problems like these systematically,[6] but most researchers agree that groups have the best chance of developing high-quality solutions to such problems when they follow a systematic method for solving problems.[7]

The best known problem-solving approach is the **reflective-thinking sequence**, developed more than 100 years ago by John Dewey and used in many forms since then.[8] In its most useful form, the reflective-thinking sequence is a seven-step process.

1. *Define the problem.* A group that does not understand the problem will have trouble finding a solution. Sometimes the problem facing a group is clear. It does not take much deliberation to understand what is necessary when the boss tells you to work out a vacation schedule for the next six months. In contrast, some problems need rewording because they are too broad as originally presented. The best problem statements are phrased as probative questions that encourage exploratory thinking:

Too Broad	Better
How can we reduce employee turnover?	How can we reduce turnover among new employees? (This suggests where to look for the nature of the problem and solutions.)
How can we boost the office staff's morale?	How can we reduce the complaints about too much work?

2. *Analyze the problem*. At this stage, the group tries to discover the causes and extent of the problem, probably by doing some research between meetings. The following queries are examples of questions that are usually appropriate in this stage: (a) How bad is the problem? (b) Why does it need to be resolved? and (c) What are its causes? It can be just as useful to focus on the positive aspects of the situation during this phase to consider how they can be strengthened. In this stage, the following questions might be asked: (a) Which forces are on our side? (b) How do they help us? and (c) How can we strengthen them? A team analyzing the question "How can we reduce the office staff's complaints about too much work?" might find the problem is especially bad for certain staffers. They may discover the problem is worst when staffers have to do a slew of web-site updates at the last minute. They may learn the major complaint does not involve hard work as much as it does resentment at seeing other people apparently having a lighter load. Positive research findings might be that the staffers understand the importance of their role, that they view being chosen to do important jobs as a sign of respect for the quality of their work, and that they do not mind occasional periods of scrambling to meet a deadline.

3. *Establish criteria for a solution*. Rather than rushing to solve the problem, it is best to spend some time identifying criteria—that is, the characteristics of a good solution and the standards you will use to evaluate your proposed solutions. For example, who must approve your solution? What are the cost constraints? What schedule needs to be met? Sometimes criteria like these are imposed from outside the group. Other requirements may come from the members themselves. Regardless of the source of the requirements, the team needs to make them clear before considering possible solutions. If it fails to define the criteria for a satisfactory solution, the team may waste time arguing over proposals that have no chance of being accepted.

4. *Generate possible solutions to the problem*. This is the time for using creative thinking techniques, such as brainstorming. A major hazard of group problem solving is that this process may get bogged down as team members argue over the merits of one or two proposals without considering other solutions that might exist. Besides limiting the quality of the solution, such squabbling leads to personal battles among members.[9] The most valuable feature of brainstorming is the emphasis on generating many ideas before judging any of them. This sort of criticism-free atmosphere encourages people to volunteer solutions that, in turn, lead to other ideas. A brainstorming list for the overworked staffers might include the following items:

- Cut down on the number of jobs that must be redone; create a company style book that shows how letters are to be set up, how contract clauses should be phrased, and so on.

- Have staffers help one another out—someone with too much work to do can ask someone else to take over a project.

- Invest in scanning technology that digitizes documents so they do not need to be retyped from scratch.

5. *Decide on a solution*. Once the group has considered all possible solutions to a problem, it can revisit these possibilities and find the best answer to the problem. This is done by evaluating each idea against the list of criteria developed earlier by the team. In addition to measuring the solution against its own criteria, team members should judge any potential solutions by asking three

questions: First, will the proposal bring about all the desired changes? If it solves only part of the problem, it is inadequate unless some changes are made. Second, is the solution feasible? If the idea is good but beyond the power of this group to achieve, it needs to be modified or discarded. Third, does the idea have any serious disadvantages? A plan that solves one set of problems while generating a whole new set of problems is probably not worth adopting.

6. *Implement the solution.* Inventing a solution is not enough; the group also has to put the plan into action. This implementation process involves several steps. First, the group must identify the specific tasks to be accomplished. Second, the group must identify the resources necessary to make the plan work. Third, individual responsibilities must be defined: Who will do what, and when? Finally, the group should plan for emergencies: What will happen if someone is sick? If the project runs over budget? If a job takes longer than expected? Anticipating problems early is far better than being caught by surprise.

7. *Follow up on the solution.* Even the best ideas do not always work out perfectly in practice. For this reason, the group should check up on the implementation of the solution to see whether any adjustments are needed.

references

1. Fisher, B. A. (1970). Decision emergence: Phases in group decision making. *Speech Monographs, 37,* 53–66; Poole, M. S., & Roth, J. (1989). Decision development in small groups, IV: A typology of group decision paths. *Human Communication Research, 15,* 232–256.

2. Tuckman, B. W. (1965). Developmental sequence in small groups. *Psychological Bulletin, 63,* 384–399.

3. Kuhn, T. (2000). Do conflict management styles affect group decision making? *Human Communication Research, 26,* 558–590; Nemeth, C. J., & Nemeth-Brown, B. (2003). Better than individuals? The potential benefits of dissent and diversity for group creativity. In P. Paulus & B. Nijstad (Eds.), *Group creativity.* Oxford, UK: Oxford University Press; Nemeth, C. J., & Ormiston, M. (2007). Creative idea generation: Harmony versus stimulation. *European Journal of Experimental Social Psychology, 37,* 524–535.

4. Buzaglo, G., & Wheelan, S. A. (1999). Facilitating work team effectiveness. *Small Group Research, 30,* 108–129.

5. Poole, M. S., & Roth, J. (1989). Decision development in small groups, V: Test of a contingency model. *Human Communication Research, 15,* 549–589.

6. Zey, M. (Ed.). (1992). *Decision making: Alternatives to rational choice models.* Newbury Park, CA: Sage.

7. Hirokawa, R. Y. (1983). Group communication and problem-solving effectiveness: An investigation of group phases. *Human Communication Research, 9,* 291–305; Marby, E. R., & Barnes, R. E. (1980). *The dynamics of small group communication.* Englewood Cliffs, NJ: Prentice-Hall; Maier, N. R. F., & Maier, R. A. (1957). An experimental test of the effects of 'developmental' vs. 'free' discussions on the quality of group decisions. *Journal of Applied Psychology, 41,* 320–323; Bayless, O. L. (1967). An alternative model for problem-solving discussion. *Journal of Communication, 17,* 188–197.

8. Gouran, D., Hirokawa, R., Julian, K., & Leatham, G. (1993). The evolution and current status of the functional perspective on communication decision-making and problem-solving groups. In S. A. Deetz (Ed.), *Communication yearbook 16.* Newbury Park, CA: Sage.

9. Mayer, M. E. (1998). Behaviors leading to more effective decisions in small groups embedded in organizations. *Communication Reports, 11,* 123–132.

appendix IV
Sample Presentations

• To Inform and Instruct
Briefing

The following is a sample briefing for a group of representatives who are preparing to staff a start-up company's exhibit booth at a trade show. Notice that the remarks are concise and well organized. They briefly state a thesis ("How we handle ourselves will make a huge difference") and then provide clear instructions for the sales team.

> This is our first chance to show the public what we've got. The way we handle ourselves over the next three days can make a huge difference in our initial year. [*Thesis.*] I know you're up to the job. Here are a couple of last-minute items before we get going. [*Instructions.*]
>
> First, about the brochures: They were supposed to show up today via overnight mail, but they haven't arrived yet. Casey will keep checking with the mail room, and if they aren't here by 9:00 a.m., he will head over to the copy shop across the street and print 500 fact sheets we can use until the brochures arrive. So if the brochures are here, we'll use them. If they're not here, we'll hand out the fact sheets.
>
> It's going to get very busy, especially midmorning and midafternoon. You may not have as much time as you'd like to chat with visitors. At the very least, be sure to do three things.
>
> First, sign up each person for the drawing for our free Caribbean vacation. The information people give us on the sign-up sheets will help us track who visited our booth.
>
> Second, invite each person to the reception we're giving tomorrow night. Give them one of our printed invitations so they know where and when it is.
>
> Finally—and this is the most important thing—ask them which product they're using and how they like it. If they are happy with their current product, find out what they like about it and show them how they might find ours even easier to use. If they don't like the product they're using, show them the features of ours.
>
> Remember—stay upbeat, and never criticize our competitors. Listen to the customers, and show them how our product can meet their needs. Any questions?

Status Report

A brief status report would sound something like this:

> On February 3, we were told to come up with an improved website for the company. [*Reviews the project's purpose.*] Paul and I have been exploring the sites of other companies in the field, and we've developed a list of features our site should have. We'll be happy to share it with anybody who is interested. [*Describes the current status of the project. In a longer progress report, the speaker might identify the features and even give examples of them.*]
>
> We know we'll need a website designer soon, but we haven't found anyone locally whose work we like. [*Identifies issues and problems. In a longer report, the speaker might list the shortcomings.*] We would welcome any suggestions you might have. If you have some names and contact information, please e-mail them to me.
>
> We plan to pick a designer and have sketches ready by the end of next month. [*Describes next milestone.*] If we can do that, we should be able to have the new website up by the end of March, right on schedule. [*Forecasts the future of the project.*]

Final Report

An abbreviated final report might sound like this:

> Hi, everybody. My name is Betsy Lane, and I'm the chair of our county's United Way campaign. *[Self-introduction.]*
>
> As you know, United Way is dedicated to helping people in our community help themselves by developing healthier, more productive lives. We support more than 50 agencies that provide a multitude of services: promoting wellness for all ages and abilities, making sure all children enter school ready to learn, helping people toward lifetime independence, sustaining safe neighborhoods, and educating young people for responsible adulthood. The need and the opportunities are great, and we set the fund-raising bar high this year: $3 million. *[Provides necessary background.]*
>
> This has been an especially challenging year for local nonprofits: The economy has been on the weak side, and there are more deserving causes and people needing support than ever before. Rather than letting this situation discourage us, it energized the United Way team. This year our work was fueled by the efforts of almost 2,500 volunteers at more than 400 organizations, large and small. Every one of them gave generously of their time and talents. *[Describes what happened.]*
>
> I am delighted to tell you that, as of last Friday, we met our goal. The campaign has raised more than $3 million in donations and pledges for the coming year. This means we won't have to say no to a single organization that asks us for help. *[Describes results.]*
>
> There is so much to tell you about this campaign and the work of so many terrific people. We do hope you'll read more about the effort that led to this year's success. Our report will be available in about three weeks and, in the meantime, you can read the highlights on the United Way website. *[Tells listeners how to get more information.]*

General Informative Presentation

The following presentation is typical of informative talks given every business day. In this scenario, the personnel specialist in a medium-sized company has gathered a group of staff members together to describe the features of a tax-reduction plan as part of the employee benefits. Notice how the speaker uses most of the strategies covered in Chapters 9–12 to make the ideas clearer and to increase the attention of the audience.

The speaker's goal is to help listeners decide whether they are interested enough in the benefits plan to attend a much longer meeting on the subject. This approach allows the speaker to avoid going into detail about the plan when some people might not be interested, thereby showing that the speaker understands the type of audience listening to the presentation. By giving a short description of how the plan works, the presenter can keep this introductory talk brief and simple.

[The promise of increasing take-home pay is a guaranteed attention-getter.]	I know you're busy, but I don't think you'll mind taking a few minutes away from work this morning. You see, I'm here today to show you a way that you can increase the amount of money you take home each month.
[This opening illustrates the persuasive element that is called for in many informative presentations.]	No, I'm not going to announce an across-the-board raise. But increasing your salary isn't the only way to boost your income. Another way that works just as well is to reduce your taxes. After all, every dollar less you pay in taxes is like having a dollar more in your pocket.

[An overall view of the plan is presented here.]

In the next few minutes, I'll explain the company's flexible benefits plan. It's a perfectly legal option that lets you increase your real income by cutting the amount of taxes you pay, so that your income will grow even without a raise. I know this sounds too good to be true, but it really works! I've already signed up, and I figure it will save me almost $2,000 a year. It can probably save you a lot, too.

[A brief transition alerts listeners to the first main point in the body of the presentation: the difference between before- and after-tax dollars.]

Before you can appreciate how the flexible benefits plan works, you have to understand the difference between before-tax and after-tax dollars. *[The speaker shows Exhibit 1 here.]* Before-tax dollars are the amount that shows up every month in the "Gross Amount" box on our paychecks, but we don't get to spend our full salaries. There are several deductions: federal income tax withholding, Social Security (the amount in the "F.I.C.A." box), state tax withholding, and disability insurance premiums (the amount in the "S.D.I." box). What's left in the "Net Amount" box is our pay in after-tax dollars.

[The enlarged display of a familiar paycheck stub clarifies the unfamiliar concepts of before- and after-tax dollars.]

										90-2176 1222 **7209**
PAY			One thousand four hundred twenty nine and 60/100							DOLLARS

TIME WK'D	DATE	TO THE ORDER OF	GROSS AMOUNT		FED. W/H	F.I.C.A.	STATE W/H	S.D.I.		CREDIT UNION	NET AMOUNT
	7/31/22	J. Doe	1958.33		293.74	78.33	68.54	88.12			1429.60
						DESCRIPTION					

GU. Horton

EXHIBIT 1 Paycheck Stub

[The speaker wisely avoids a complicated discussion of before- and after-tax dollars in different tax brackets.]

Once all those deductions are taken away from our pay, every before-tax dollar shrinks in value to about 73 cents *[The speaker shows Exhibit 2 here.]*, and that's in a low tax bracket. If your income is higher, then the difference between before- and after-tax dollars is even bigger. This means that it takes at least $136.33 in after-tax dollars to buy something that costs $100 in before-tax dollars.

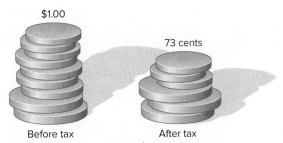

$1.00

73 cents

Before tax   After tax

EXHIBIT 2   Value of Before- and After-Tax Dollars

[The visual display increases the clarity and impact of the difference between before- and after-tax dollars.]

[The transition here makes the movement to the second part of the body clear.]

You can probably see now that it's better to buy things in before-tax dollars whenever you can, and that's what the flexible benefits plan lets you do. Let me explain how it works.

[An internal preview orients the audience to the next two points.]

The flexible benefits plan is great because it allows you to pay for some important items in before-tax dollars. The plan lets you set aside pay in two categories: medical costs and dependent care. Let's cover each of these in detail so you can see which expenses are covered.

[The speaker generates audience involvement by inviting listeners to consider their own expenses in the following areas.]

A look at the chart entitled "Allowable Medical Expenses" shows which items you can use under the flexible benefits plan. *[The speaker points to each item in Exhibit 3 as they discuss it.]* As I cover these expenses, think about how much you spend in each area.

[The chart helps listeners understand which expenses are covered.]

- Health insurance deductibles
- Health insurance co-payments
- Drugs and prescriptions
- Vision care and equipment
- Psychologists and psychiatrists
- Dental care and orthodontia

EXHIBIT 3   Allowable Medical Expenses

[The hypothetical example helps listeners understand how the plan works in real life.]

First we'll talk about health-insurance deductibles and co-payments. Under our company's policy, you pay the first $300 of expenses for yourself and each dependent. You also make a $10 co-payment for each visit to a doctor. Let's say that you and one dependent have to pay the $300 deductible each year, and that you made five visits to the doctor. That's a total of $650 per year you could have covered under the plan.

[A citation helps prove that the cost of medicines is considerable.]

Drugs and prescriptions include various types of medication you buy, even many that you buy over the counter without a prescription. Don't forget that the plan also covers payments you make for everyone you claim as a dependent: your kids, maybe your spouse, and maybe even an older parent whom you're caring for.

An article from *Changing Times* magazine says a family of three spends an average of $240 per year on drugs. Maybe you spend even more. Whatever you do spend on medicine can be included in the plan, which means you will pay less for it than if you used after-tax dollars.

[Examples of typical vision-care fees illustrate the potential costs in this area.]

Vision care and equipment include eyeglasses and contact lenses as well as any fees you or your dependents pay to optometrists or ophthalmologists. With a pair of reading glasses costing at least $45 and a new set of contact lenses costing more than $80, those expenses can really mount up.

Psychologists and psychiatrists are also covered, which means that any counseling you receive will cost a lot less.

Dental care and orthodontia are covered, too. If you or your dependents need major dental work, this difference can amount to a lot of money. If you're paying for your kids' braces, you can really save a bundle. We did some checking, and the average orthodontic treatment today runs about $3,500 over 3 years—or more than $1,000 per year.

[Comparing the unfamiliar benefits plan to the familiar notion of a discount helps make the advantages clear.]

Nobody likes to spend money for medical expenses like these, but paying for them with before-tax dollars under the flexible benefits plan is like getting a discount of 20% or more—clearly, a great deal.

[The transition here uses signposts to mark a shift to the second type of expense covered by the plan.]

Medical costs aren't the only expenses you can include in the flexible benefits plan. There's a second way you can boost your take-home pay: by including dependent care in the plan.

[The example of potential savings under the plan is a guaranteed attention-getter for working parents.]

For most people, dependents are children. Any costs of caring for your kids can be paid for in before-tax dollars, meaning you'll pay a lot less. You can include daycare services, preschool fees, even in-home care for your child. We did some checking and found that the cost of keeping a child in preschool or daycare in this area from 8:30 a.m. until 5 p.m. averages about $5,000 per year. By shifting this amount into the flexible benefits plan, the real cost drops by more than $1,000. Not bad for filling out a few forms!

[A restatement of the thesis is combined with the introduction of an example to support its claim.]

When you combine the savings on health care and dependents, the potential savings that come from joining the flexible benefits plan are impressive. Let's take a look at a typical example of just how much money the flexible benefits plan can save. Your personal situation probably won't be exactly like this one, but you can still get a feeling for how good the plan is. *[The speaker shows Exhibit 4.]*

	WITHOUT PLAN	WITH PLAN
GROSS SALARY	$23,500	$23,500
SALARY REDUCTIONS		
Health Care	0	650
Prescriptions and Drugs	0	240
Vision Care	0	60
Dental Care	0	180
Dependent Care	0	1,800
	$23,500	$20,570
TAXES		
Federal Income Tax @ 15%	3,525	3,085
State Income Tax @ 3.5%	764	720
FICA and SDI @ 8.15%	1,915	1,676
	$6,204	$5,481
AFTER-TAX EXPENSES		
Health Care	650	0
Prescriptions and Drugs	240	0
Vision Care	60	0
Dental Care	180	0
Dependent Care	1,800	0
Net Pay	$14,366	$15,089
ANNUAL SAVINGS $723		

EXHIBIT 4   Savings with Flexible Benefits Plan

[The chart provides a visual outline of the example. Without the exhibit, the dollar amounts would be too confusing to follow.]

Suppose your salary is $23,500 and you have a spouse and one child. Let's say that your health and dependent expenses are pretty much like the ones we've been discussing here today. *[The speaker points to the "Salary Reductions" section of chart.]* Your health insurance deductibles and co-payments amount to $650, and you spend $240 over the year on prescriptions and drugs. Let's say that one person in your family needs one set of eyeglasses. You all get dental checkups, and you don't even have cavities! You spend $1,800 on child care—not bad these days.

   If we look at the top third of the chart, it might seem that enrolling in the flexible benefits plan will cost you more. After all, your salary would be $23,500 without the plan but only $20,570 with your expenses deducted from the plan.

[As the speaker points to the "Annual Savings" line on the chart, the audience sees in real dollars the potential advantage of the plan.]

However, look what happens once we add taxes into the equation. *[The speaker points to "Taxes" section of chart.]* Since your pay with the plan is less, you pay less in taxes. A little subtraction shows that the difference between the $6,204 you'd pay without the plan and the $5,481 you'd pay with it amounts to a savings of $723.

This is just a small example of how much you can save. If your expenses are higher—if you have more medical costs, for example—the advantage is even greater. As your salary goes up and you move into a higher tax bracket, the advantages grow, too. And don't forget that the savings I've been talking about are just for one year. As time goes by, your earning power will grow even more.

[In a restatement of the thesis, the speaker returns to the main advantage of the plan.]

Now you can see why we're so glad to offer the flexible benefits plan. It can boost your take-home pay even before you get a raise. It costs you nothing.

[Listeners are told what to do next if they are interested in the plan.]

If you're interested in learning more, we encourage you to read the booklet I'll hand out in a moment. It contains a worksheet that will help you estimate how much you stand to save under the plan. If the idea still interests you, please attend the workshop we'll be holding next Friday during the lunch hour in the third-floor meeting room. At that time, we can answer your questions and make an appointment for each of you to sign up at the personnel office. In the meantime, I'll be happy to answer any questions you have now.

• To Persuade

The following sales presentation (outlined in Figure A4.1) demonstrates the general guidelines about speaking to an audience introduced in Chapters 9 through 12. The purpose and approach are based on sound audience analysis. As you will see, the talk has a clear thesis and a logical organizational structure. A variety of verbal and visual supports add interest, clarity, and proof.

The speaker's company, Ablex Technologies, manufactures sophisticated electronic components. One of its best customers is BioMedical Instruments (BMI), which produces a wide variety of sophisticated medical diagnostic instruments. The company's biggest contracts with BMI are for kidney-dialysis and blood-analyzer parts, which total almost $1 million per year.

Under a much smaller and older contract, Ablex also supplies BMI with parts for an X-ray unit. BMI no longer makes the unit, but is committed to furnishing current users with replacement parts until the machines drop out of use, and Ablex is obliged to supply BMI with these parts. Producing these X-ray unit parts is usually a problem: Orders are small and sporadic, leading to delays and headaches for everyone concerned. The speaker is presenting a plan that offers a better way to handle replenishment of the X-ray unit parts.

Thesis: The proposed forecasting and purchasing agreement will allow both BMI and Ablex to better supply X-ray parts in a timely, affordable, and trouble-free manner.

Introduction
I. Our basically positive relationship with BMI has only one problem: the X-ray parts.
II. While a problem does exist,there is a solution.
    A. The problem involves erratic orders for X-ray parts.
    B. Our solution has several benefits.

Body
I. Supplying X-ray parts has been a continuing headache.
    A. Orders for X-ray parts are irregular and unpredictable.
    [*line graph*]
    B. These irregular orders make it tough to ship orders to BMI in a timely way. [*example*]
II. Fortunately, there is a solution to the X-ray problem.
    A. Here's an outline of our plan.
    B. The plan has several advantages.
        1. Orders can be delivered more quickly.
        [*comparison chart*]
        2. Ordering is more flexible. [*examples*]
        3. Time can be saved in ordering and follow-up.
        [*example*]
        4. The unit cost is less than under current plan.
        [*column chart, comparison chart*]

Conclusion: By now you can see that there's a solution to the X-ray problem.
I. The plan has advantages for everyone involved.
II. We look forward to putting it into action soon.

FIGURE A4.1   Outline of Sample Presentation

The audience includes Mary Ann Hirsch—the buyer at BMI—and two production engineers. Although the purchasing director and the chief project engineer are not attending the presentation, they will rely on the information gathered by their subordinates and, ultimately, will be the ones to approve or reject this idea—so in a way, they are part of the audience, too.

[The introduction emphasizes the positive aspects of the relationship with the customer. A brief sketch of the problem establishes common ground. "We're in this together, and it's no good for either of us."]

We've been involved in a long, positive relationship with BMI. The only troubles we've ever encountered have come from the X-ray parts. Even though they are just a small part of our business with you, they seem to involve the greatest headaches for both you and us. The timing of these orders is impossible for you to predict, which makes it hard for us to get parts from our suppliers and deliver the product to you quickly. This leads to all sorts of problems: unhappy customers who have to wait for the equipment they ordered and time spent by people at both of our companies keeping in touch.

[The preview lists the main advantages of the plan that will be proposed.]

We think there's a better way to handle the X-ray problem. It'll reduce frustration, cut costs, and let all of us spend our time on more productive parts of our jobs. Before we talk about this new plan, let me review why the present arrangement for handling X-ray orders is such a headache.

[A transition leads to the "problem" section of the presentation.]

The main problem we face is irregular orders. A look at the order history for the last year shows that there's no pattern—and no way to predict when customers will order replacement parts for their X-ray units. *[The speaker shows Exhibit 5 here.]*

[The visual exhibit clearly demonstrates the unpredictable nature of customer orders.]

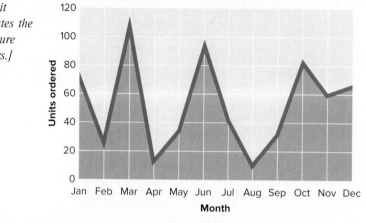

EXHIBIT 5   X-Ray Parts Ordering Pattern

[An example shows the problems flowing from irregular orders.]

This unpredictable pattern makes it tough for us to serve you quickly. We have to order parts from our suppliers, which often can take a long time. For instance, with the February 17 order, it took 6 weeks for our suppliers to get us the parts we needed to manufacture the X-ray components you needed. Once we had the parts, it took us the usual 4 weeks to assemble them. As you said at the time, this delay kept your customer waiting almost 3 months for the components needed to get its equipment up and running, and that's poison for customer relations.

[An example highlights amount of time wasted.]

Delays like this aren't just bad for your relationship with customers; they also waste time—yours and ours. Mary Ann, do you remember how many phone calls and letters it took to keep track of that February order? In fact, every year we spend more time on these X-ray orders that involve a few thousand dollars than we do on the dialysis and blood-analyzer parts that involve around a million dollars annually. That's just not a good use of time.

[A transition leads to the second consequence of irregular orders: wasted time. "Solution" part of the presentation then introduced.]

So we clearly have a situation that's bad for everybody. Fortunately, we believe there's a better way—better for you, for us, and for your customers. This plan involves your giving us an annual purchasing forecast for X-ray parts. Instead of waiting for your customers to place individual orders, you would estimate the total sales likely to occur in a year. Then we would acquire enough parts from our suppliers to assemble those items so that we could have them ready quickly as your customers place orders.

[The advantages of the solution are previewed in the chart.]

This simple plan has several advantages. They're summarized on this chart, but let me explain them in a little more detail. *[The speaker shows Exhibit 6 here.]*

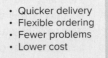

- Quicker delivery
- Flexible ordering
- Fewer problems
- Lower cost

EXHIBIT 6   Advantages of Annual Forecasting
for X-Ray Parts

[The strongest advantage to the listeners is introduced first to develop a positive impression early.]

The first advantage is that advance purchasing will speed up delivery of your orders. Instead of waiting for our suppliers to ship parts, we can begin to assemble your order as soon as you send it. You can get an idea of the time savings by looking at how much time this plan would have saved on the order you placed in February. *[The speaker shows Exhibit 7.]*

[A bar chart graphically demonstrates the amount of time saved.]

WITH ANNUAL FORECASTING SYSTEM | PARTS FABRICATED | 4 WEEKS

CURRENT SYSTEM | PARTS ON ORDER FROM SUPPLIER | PARTS FABRICATED | 10 WEEKS

17   24   3   10   17   24   31   7   14   21   28

FEB.   MARCH   APRIL

EXHIBIT 7   Annual Forecasting Speeds Delivery Time

[A transition leads to the second advantage of the plan: flexibility. A hypothetical example helps the audience visualize this advantage.]

Besides being quick, the plan is flexible. If you wind up receiving more orders than you anticipated when you made your original forecast, you can update the plan every six months. That means we'll never run out of parts for the X-ray units. Suppose you projected 1,400 units in your original forecast. If you've already ordered 1,000 units six months later, you could update your forecast at that point to 2,000 units and we'd have the parts on hand when you needed them.

[A transition leads to anticipation of a possible listener objection: What if orders decrease? Credible authority is cited to support this point.]

This semiannual revision of the forecast takes care of increases in the number of orders, but you might be wondering about the opposite situation—what would happen if there are fewer orders than you expected. The plan anticipates that possibility, too. We're willing to extend the date by which you're obliged to use your annual estimate of parts to 18 months. In other words, with this plan you'd have 18 months to use the parts you expected to use in 12 months. That's pretty safe, because Ted Forester [BMI's vice president of sales and marketing] predicts that the existing X-ray machines will be in use for at least the next six or seven years before they're replaced with newer models.

[An internal review reminds listeners of the previously introduced advantages and leads to identification of a third benefit: less wasted time.]

Flexibility and speed are two good advantages, but there are other benefits of this plan as well. It can save time for both you and us. You know how much time we spend on the phone every time there's a surprise X-ray order, and I imagine you have to deal with impatient customers, too. Talking about delays is certainly no fun, and with this annual purchasing plan it won't be necessary because we can guarantee delivery within 4 weeks of receiving your order. Think of the aggravation that will avoid!

[The second most important advantage is introduced last, where it is likely to be remembered by listeners.]

By now, you can see why we're excited about this plan. But there's one final benefit as well: The plan will save you money. When we order our parts in larger quantities, the unit price is less than the one we're charged with smaller orders. We're willing to pass along the savings to you, which means that you'll be paying less under this plan than you are now. Notice how ordering a year's supply of parts drops the unit price considerably. *[The speaker shows Exhibit 8.]*

[The chart provides an easy-to-follow visual representation of how the cost per unit changes based on the quantity ordered.]

EXHIBIT 8 Annual Forecasting Reduces Unit Price

[Providing a visual calculation of savings reinforces the point that the cost of the plan would be significantly reduced.]

You can see that this plan is a real money saver. Compare the savings you could have realized on last year's order of 597 units if this plan had been in effect. *[The speaker shows Exhibit 9.]*

597 units at higher unit price	$55,506
597 units at volume unit price	45,969
First year savings	$ 9,537

EXHIBIT 9 One Year's Saving with Annual Forecasting Plan

[The conclusion reviews the plan's advantages and makes an appeal to the listeners to adopt it.]

So that's the plan. It's simple. It's risk-free. It's convenient. It's flexible. Along with all these advantages, it can cut your costs. We're prepared to start working with you immediately to put this plan into action. If we start soon, we'll never have to deal with X-ray headaches again. Then we can put our energy into the larger, more satisfying projects that are more rewarding for both of us.

• To Celebrate

Welcoming a Guest or Group

The following example illustrates how the guidelines discussed in Chapter 9 can be used to produce effective welcoming remarks:

> All of us at Siztec USA *[Mentions whose behalf they are speaking]* welcome members of our Japanese plant's team to the ribbon-cutting of our new facility *[Identifies the people that are being welcomed]*. We are honored you took the time to travel so far to be with us today *[Expresses gratitude to the guest for coming]*. We have a great deal to learn from one another, and your visit will help all of us make Sizetec an industry leader *[Explains why the occasion is important or significant]*. This is an exciting day for us, and we extend a warm welcome to you. *[Turn to the audience.]* Please join me in a round of applause to welcome our guests.

Introducing a Speaker

Notice how the guidelines discussed in Chapter 9 have been incorporated in this informative introduction:

> For the last nine months, you've heard a great deal about how we will be expanding operations into Mexico *[Previews the topic about which the person will speak]*. Today I'm pleased to introduce you to Mr. Dante Gutierrez, who will be managing our Mexico operations. Mr. Gutierrez comes to us with a great amount of experience on both sides of the border. After founding and operating one of northern Mexico's foremost import–export firms, Mr. Gutierrez became executive director of Baja California's Asociación de la Industria, a leading business group. He has lived and worked in both Mexico and the United States. His experience in manufacturing and cross-border trade will be a tremendous help as we expand our operation in Mexico and Central America *[Establishes the credibility of the person being introduced]*.
>
> Along with his professional credentials, you'll find that Mr. Gutierrez is a great person. He's friendly and helpful, and very approachable. I'm sure you will find that Mr. Gutierrez is a terrific resource as we learn more about our new market and its customers *[Gives the audience reasons to listen to the person being introduced]*.
>
> Please join me in giving Mr. Gutierrez a warm welcome!

Delivering a Tribute

An example tribute to an accountant who is leaving a firm is presented here. Of course, if the speaker had more time, each of the traits selected could be illustrated with more anecdotes with which the audience would be familiar:

> Today is a day of celebration as we pay tribute to Joseph Begay. It is a privilege to speak for the management team here at Contrast Accounts and to honor Joe.
>
> In thinking about Joe's accomplishments here, two words come to mind: commitment and community. Joseph is committed to doing a job well. He commands a tremendous measure of respect and esteem from colleagues in all of our departments. From Betty Murphy in Costs Analysis to Mike Burroughs in Media Relations, Joseph has earned our admiration for his commitment to quality work for our clients. Who else could have persuaded us to redo the entire Simpson account in less than two months? Who else could have enticed us with pizzas to get us to stay late and finish? Joe is committed to our clients and to our colleagues. The focal point of his work has been to help us all better understand the needs of the members of the various departments who populate our company. Joseph has helped us come together to look at

specific ways we could meet the needs of diverse departments, and he has provided us with opportunities to give expression to our common frustrations and concerns that revolve around quality products for our clients.

Presenting an Award

The following approach can serve as a framework for creating interesting, enthusiastic award presentations:

"Success isn't measured by where you are, but by how far you've come from where you started." These words exemplify the spirit of the Most Improved Player award *[States the name and nature of the award]*. Each year, players have the privilege and difficult task of voting for the player whom they believe is the most improved. The winner of this award must have demonstrated to their teammates spirit and commitment and must have shown improvement and refinement in skills *[States the criteria for selection]*. This is not an easy task. Always spurring others on and never giving up even when we were down 14–7 against the Bulldogs, this year's winner went from being unable to stop a goal to stopping six goals in our last championship game *[Builds suspense by withholding honoree's name; Provides specific examples of how the recipient meets the criteria]*. So, Mary Lee, it is with gratitude and delight that I present to you from your teammates the Most Improved Player award *[Names award winner and makes them the center of attention]*.

Accepting an Award

The following remarks, given by the head of a volunteer committee that had a profitable fundraiser, illustrate how an award acceptance presentation can be sincere, easy, and effective:

You have really surprised me today. When I said I'd help plan the auction, the last thing on my mind was an award. Raising scholarship money was our goal, and breaking last year's fund-raising record was the only reward I'd hoped for. Getting this special thank you is more than I had ever expected, and I am deeply honored *[Expresses sincere gratitude]*.

I'm also a little embarrassed to be singled out like this. We couldn't have broken that record without a tremendous amount of hard work by everybody. Chris and her committee rounded up an incredible bunch of auction items. Ben and his gang provided food and entertainment that we'll be talking about for years. Darnelle's publicity team brought in the donors. And Leo's talents as an auctioneer squeezed every last dollar out of those items. With wonderful people like this, how could we have gone wrong? *[Acknowledges contributors]*

I'm going to put this plaque in my office, right above my desk. Whenever I'm feeling tired and discouraged about human nature, it will remind me how generous and hard-working people can be for a good cause. It will also remind me how lucky I am to know you all and to have worked with you *[Describes how the award will make a difference]*.

So thanks again for this wonderful award. You're a great bunch of people, and I can hardly wait until we do it all again next year! *[Offers one last word of thanks]*.

appendix V
Crisis Communication

At some point in your career, you may find yourself in the midst of a **crisis**. On a regular basis, companies must recall products, prepare and respond to natural disasters, and address upset customers and community members. Entrepreneurs, self-employed professionals, and public figures also experience crises, as their personal and professional actions may be called into question by others.

A crisis has several defining characteristics:

- *It is unexpected.* An organization's leadership may anticipate the possibility of a crisis, but they can never identify the exact moment that a crisis will occur, nor can they predict the nuanced details of the situation.

- *It creates uncertainty.* Both the organization and the public will know little information about a crisis when it first emerges. The organizational leadership may be concerned about potential threats to its core values, operations, reputation, and financial standing. Depending on the type of crisis, the public may also be concerned about the health, safety, privacy, or financial stability of themselves and their loved ones.

- *It is a turning point.* As we discussed in Chapter 5, conflict presents both danger and opportunity. As a result of effective crisis communication, an organization may emerge even stronger than it was before the crisis occurred.

Understanding and mastering the steps involved in each of the stages of crisis communication are crucial for business professionals. Even the most successful companies with the most humanitarian values are susceptible to crisis. The impact of a crisis is exacerbated by social media—one simple tweet can go viral around the world and become a news story within minutes.[1]

Furthermore, organizations can be held liable for failing to have a crisis plan. In February 2021, the Michigan Occupational Safety and Health Administration (MIOSHA) cited 16 workplaces for failure to have a crisis preparedness and response plan for COVID-19. Related violations included a lack of employee training on infection-control practices, use of personal protection equipment (PPE), and steps they must take if they experience symptoms or receive a positive diagnosis. The companies were issued fines of up to $7,000 for these violations.[2]

Another example is the April 17, 2013 explosion at the West Fertilizer Company in West, Texas, that killed 15 people. As a result of this crisis, the company faced federal fines totaling $118,300 for two dozen serious safety violations, including its lack of a crisis plan.[3]

There are three stages of crisis communication: prevention, response, and evaluation. The tips presented in this appendix will help you successfully navigate each stage of a crisis situation in your workplace.

Prevention

Although we cannot anticipate every potential crisis we will face, it is important that we do our research in an attempt to prevent as many crises as possible. Crisis prevention consists of the following steps[4]:

- Anticipate crises that may occur based on the industry, location, size, operations, and personnel of your organization. Consider crises that may occur at nearby facilities and how those incidents might affect your organization. Also, consider how a crisis at a similar or competitor company might put your organization in the spotlight.

- Monitor the current social and political landscape. Consider whether certain issues that are gaining traction could pose threats to the company.

- Monitor the organization's reputation. Are there patterns of complaints that have gone unaddressed? Would the public perceive the organization to be part of the fabric of the community? Are the promises made in your mission statement and company materials (e.g., a commitment to diversity and inclusion) being upheld? When it comes to the public's willingness to trust your organization's response to a crisis, having a neutral reputation may be just as bad as having a poor reputation.

- Talk to your stakeholders and determine their expectations for your organization. What do your employees, employees' family members, board of directors, unions, investors, customers, suppliers, community leaders, regulators, legislators, and media expect? Most crises begin as a simple violation of stakeholders' expectations.

- Research crises that have occurred at your organization and at organizations that are similar to yours in terms of industry, size, and operations. A crisis that has occurred in the past or has affected a similar organization is likely to be repeated.

- Assemble a crisis team that includes members representing each of the departments within your organization. This crisis team should meet often and be tasked with developing and regularly updating a written crisis plan, anticipating issues, monitoring social media and public commentary, attempting to resolve issues before they become crises, and training employees on what to do during a crisis.

- Train at least two spokespersons on how to engage with the media and the public. The tips presented in Chapter 9 will be useful in this training.

Response

Each crisis situation calls for a unique response based on the organization's reputation, crisis history, perceived responsibility, legality, and other factors. Nevertheless, all crisis response statements should meet the following standards[5]:

- *Be timely.* The public will expect a response almost immediately. A good rule of thumb is to issue an initial statement, letting the public know that the organization is aware of the crisis and is gathering details, within one hour after identification of the crisis. In this initial statement, a specific date and time for release of a follow-up statement (typically within 24 hours) should be provided. It is important to know media deadlines, as journalists will often want a comment for their stories within a certain time frame. If your organization does not comment within this time frame, it leaves the door open for speculation and rumors. The longer it takes an organization to respond, the guiltier the public will likely perceive it to be.

- *Be honest.* Your statement should consist of facts. You should not speculate about the cause of the crisis or attempt to make excuses for the organization. If you do not have enough information, be honest about that fact, and let the public know that you will update them as soon as you do have information.

- *Be empathetic.* Demonstrate sincere concern for your public, even if you do not agree with their perspectives. Use nonverbal expressions that communicate empathy, and use supportive verbal communication that demonstrates regret. While it may be acceptable to apologize for a rogue tweet sent out by an employee, you must be careful with what you say during serious crisis situations that may become legal matters. Although you may want to apologize to demonstrate empathy, such a statement could be perceived as an acceptance of responsibility or an admission of guilt by an organization. Consulting with a legal team will help you make judgments about how you can express regrets.

- *Be interactive*. Encourage two-way communication, or dialogue, with your stakeholders. Listen to and address their concerns. Solicit their feedback. Communicate with them using the channel(s) they trust. Make them feel like insiders who matter.

Research has shown that an effective crisis response statement will also explain confirmed crisis facts (what, when, where, why, and how) and tell stakeholders what they need to do to physically protect themselves during the crisis.[6] It is also important to tell the public what the organization is doing to correct the wrongdoing and prevent future occurrences.

Consider the following statement issued by former Blue Bell Creameries CEO and president Paul Kruse during a *Listeria* outbreak traced to the company's ice cream[7]:

[Explains what the company is doing to correct the wrongdoing]

We're committed to doing the 100% right thing, and the best way to do that is to take all of our products off the market until we are confident that they are all safe. At every step, we have made decisions in the best interest of our customers based on the evidence we had available at the time. We have brought in one of the world's most respected food safety microbiologists to inspect our plants and systems to help us get to the bottom of this issue.

[Provides confirmed facts; demonstrates honesty]

Through further internal testing, we learned today that *Listeria monocytogenes* was found in an additional half gallon of ice cream in our Brenham facility. While we initially believed this situation was isolated to one machine in one room, we now know that was wrong. We need to know more to be completely confident that our products are safe for our customers.

[Explains what is being done to prevent future occurrences]

As Blue Bell moves forward, we are implementing a procedure called "test and hold" for all products made at all of our manufacturing facilities. This means that all products released will be tested first and held for release to the market only after the tests show they are safe.

In addition to the "test and hold" system, Blue Bell is implementing additional safety procedures and testing including:

- Expanding our already robust system of daily cleaning and sanitizing of equipment
- Expanding our system of swabbing and testing our plant environment by 800% to include more surfaces
- Sending samples daily to a leading microbiology laboratory for testing
- Providing additional employee training

At this point, we cannot say with certainty how *Listeria* was introduced to our facilities. We continue to work with our team of experts to eliminate this problem.

[Provides customers with information about how to protect themselves; corrects the situation by offering a refund; opens the door for interaction]

We urge customers who have purchased Blue Bell products to return them to the place of purchase for a full refund. Consumers with any concerns or questions should call 979-836-7977 Monday–Friday 8 a.m.–5 p.m. CST or go to www.bluebell.com for the most up-to-date information.

[Expresses empathy]

We are heartbroken about this situation and apologize to all of our loyal Blue Bell fans and customers. Our entire history has been about making the very best and highest-quality ice cream, and we intend to fix this problem. We want enjoying our ice cream to be a source of joy and pleasure, never a cause for concern, so we are committed to getting this right.

We cannot overemphasize the importance of being honest when responding to a crisis. Even the most well-articulated statements will fall apart once dishonesty is detected. As a result of the *Listeria* crisis, Blue Bell agreed to pay over $19 million in fines for shipping contaminated ice cream, and Kruse was charged with conspiracy in a scheme to cover up the incident.[8]

Evaluation

The final step in the crisis communication process occurs after an organization has suffered a crisis. It is important for the crisis team to convene and evaluate the strengths and weaknesses of the crisis prevention and response. Damages to life, property, financial standing, reputation, and business continuity should be discussed. The goal should be to retain what worked and identify an action plan for resolving the issues that did not work. It is also important to make sure that the organization's stakeholders are satisfied with the crisis response. If any issues are left unresolved, the crisis could be reignited.

references

1. Leopold, T. (2012, March 6). In today's warp-speed world, online missteps spread faster than ever. *CNN*. Retrieved from http://www.cnn.com/2012/03/06/tech/social-media /misinformation-social-media/
2. State of Michigan (2021, February 19). 16 employers cited for COVID-19 workplace safety violations [Press release]. *Michigan.gov*. Retrieved from https://www.michigan.gov/coronavirus /0,9753,7-406–552492–rss,00.html#:˜:text=of%20Algonac%2C%20MI%20was%20fined, maintain%20six%20feet%20of%20social
3. Covert, B. (2013, October 11). Fertilizer plant that exploded in West, Texas faces $118,300 in fines. *ThinkProgress*. Retrieved from https://thinkprogress.org/fertilizer-plant-that-exploded -in-west-texas-faces-118-300-in-fines-f12d9d0d5230/
4. Maresh-Fuehrer, M. M. (2013). *Creating organizational crisis plans*. Dubuque, IA: Kendall Hunt.
5. Maresh-Fuehrer, M. M. (2013). *Creating organizational crisis plans*. Dubuque, IA: Kendall Hunt.
6. Coombs, W. T. (2012). *Ongoing crisis communication* (3rd ed.). Thousand Oaks, CA: Sage.
7. Blue Bell. (2015, April 20). Statement from Blue Bell CEO and president Paul Kruse. Retrieved from http://cdn.bluebell.com/ceo-video-message
8. The United States Department of Justice (2020, May 1). Blue Bell Creameries agrees to plead guilty and pay $19.35 million for ice cream Listeria contamination—former company president charged [Press release]. *Justice.gov*. Retrieved from https://www.justice.gov/opa/pr /blue-bell-creameries-agrees-plead-guilty-and-pay-1935-million-ice-cream-listeria

glossary

A

active listening Nonverbal and verbal attentiveness to a speaker. (3)

agenda A list of topics to be covered in a meeting. Agendas also usually note the meeting's time, length, location, and the members who will attend. Complete agendas provide background information and outcome goals. (8)

analytical listening A listening style that focuses on scrutinizing messages from a variety of perspectives. (3)

anchor A listener's preexisting position on an issue being advocated. (11)

asynchronous communication Communication that occurs with a delay between sending and receiving of a message; for example, text messaging or e-mail. (1)

audience feedback Non-verbal, verbal, spoken, or written information from the audience that helps a speaker improve their presentation skills. (12)

audition interview A type of interview in which a prospective employer asks the candidate to demonstrate (rather than describe) his or her ability to perform a job-related task. (6)

authoritarian leadership style A leadership style in which the designated leader uses legitimate, coercive, and reward power to control members. (7)

award presentation A type of presentation in which the speaker describes an award and explains the reasons the recipient is receiving it. (9)

B

Baby Boomers The generation born between 1946 and 1964 who shaped the 1960s social reforms and who value achievement, accuracy, and performance. (2)

bar chart A visual exhibit consisting of horizontal or vertical bars that depict the values of several items in comparative terms. (11)

behavioral interview An employment interview in which the candidate is asked to give concrete examples of past behaviors that show how he or she behaved in certain situations. (6)

biased language A statement that seems objective but actually conceals the speaker's attitude. (4)

bona fide occupational qualification (BFOQ) A job requirement deemed reasonably necessary for the performance of a particular job. In employment interviewing, only questions exploring BFOQs are lawful. (6)

boundary turbulence When rules for the sharing of private information are not mutually understood by co-owners. (5)

brainstorming A decision-making approach that encourages free thinking and minimizes conformity. (8)

briefing An informative presentation that succinctly informs listeners about a specific task at hand. (9)

C

career research interview An informational interview to help a candidate define and achieve career goals. (6)

cause-effect pattern An organizational arrangement that shows that events happened or will happen as a result of certain circumstances. (10)

cautious shift A type of conformity in which group members take positions that are more conservative than their individual positions. (7)

channel The method or medium used to deliver a message (e.g., face-to-face communication, blog, text message). (1)

chronological pattern An organizational arrangement that presents points according to their sequence in time. (10)

claim A statement asserting a fact or belief. (10)

closed question Question that restricts the interviewee's responses, usually to yes or no, a number, an item from preselected items, or an either-or response. (6)

co-culture A group that has a clear identity within the encompassing culture. (2)

coercive power The ability to influence others that arises because one can impose punishment or unpleasant consequences. (7)

cohesiveness The degree to which group members feel part of and want to remain with the group. (7)

collectivist culture A culture with a strong social framework in which members of a group are socialized to care for one another and for the group as a whole. (2)

column chart A visual exhibit consisting of vertical columns that depict the quantity of one or more items at different times. (11)

communication apprehension Anxiety about communicating before and/or during a presentation that may result in feelings of nervousness, sweating, a shaky voice, skin flushing, or other symptoms. (10)

communication networks Regular patterns or paths along which information flows in an organization. *See also* formal communication networks, informal communication networks. (1)

comparative advantages pattern An organizational strategy that puts several alternatives side by side and shows why one is the best. (10)

comparison A type of support in which the speaker shows how one idea is similar to another; may be figurative or literal. (11)

compromise An orientation toward negotiation that assumes each side needs to lose at least some of what it was seeking. (5)

conflict phase The second of four group problem-solving phases; characterized by members taking strong stands that result in conflict within the group. *See also* storming. (A3)

connection power The ability to influence that arises because of one's connections and associations inside and outside the organization. (7)

consensus A collective group decision that every member is willing to support. (8)

contingency approaches to leadership Leadership theories that assert the most effective leadership style is flexible, changing as needed with the context. (7)

counterfeit question A statement that appears to ask for information but actually offers advice or criticism. (3)

credibility The persuasive force that comes from the audience's belief in and respect for the speaker. (11)

crisis An unexpected event that creates uncertainty for an organization and its stakeholders and serves as a turning point in the organization's future. (A5)

criteria satisfaction pattern An organizational strategy that sets up standards (criteria) the audience accepts and then shows how the speaker's idea or product meets the criteria. (10)

critical incident question Interview question that asks the interviewee about a specific situation rather than a hypothetical one. (6)

critical listening A listening style of evaluating messages for accuracy and consistency, with the purpose of accepting or rejecting them. (3)

cultural intelligence The ability to adapt to and work effectively in new cultural settings; also referred to as *cultural quotient* or *CQ*. (2)

culture The set of values, beliefs, norms, customs, rules, and codes that leads people to define themselves as a distinct group, giving them a sense of commonality. (2)

cyber incivility Rude/discourteous behaviors occurring through communication technologies such as e-mail, text messages, and social media. (5)

cybervetting The use of internet information and social networks to screen prospective job or internship applicants. (6)

D

decision-making meetings Meetings held with the purpose of deciding to take some action or make changes to existing policies or procedures. (8)

decoding The process of attaching meaning to words, symbols, or behaviors. (1)

definition A form of support that explains the meaning of a term that is unfamiliar to an audience or is used in a specialized or uncommon way. (11)

democratic leadership style A leadership style in which the designated leader encourages members to share decision making. (7)

descriptive statement Statement that describes the speaker's perspective instead of evaluating the sender's behavior or motives. *See also* "I" language, "you" language. (5)

designated leader A leader whose title indicates a leadership role, either by appointment or by group selection. (7)

direct question (in a meeting) A question that is aimed at a particular individual, who is addressed by name. (8)

direct question (in an interview) Straightforward question that asks exactly what the interviewer wants to know. (6)

disfluencies Vocal disruptions such as stammers (uh, um) or filler words (ya know, like, OK) that distract audiences and interfere with understanding. (4)

downward communication Communication that flows from leaders or managers to lower-level employees. (1)

E

emergence phase The third of four group problem-solving phases; characterized by an end to conflict and emergence of harmony within the group. *See also* norming. (A3)

emergent leaders Rather than being appointed or elected to the leadership role, the leader emerges over time as a result of the group's interaction. (7)

emotional intelligence (EQ) Aptitude and skills needed for interacting well with others. Refers to interpersonal communication skills rather than cognitive or intellectual abilities. (5)

employment interview An interview designed to judge the candidate's qualifications and desirability for a job. (6)

encoding The intentional process of creating a message. (1)

equivocal terms Words with more than one generally accepted meaning. (4)

ethics Standards of behavior expected by audiences and professional colleagues. (11)

ethnocentrism The tendency to view life from the perspective of one's own culture and to judge one's own culture as superior to other cultures. (2)

example Brief illustration that backs up or explains a claim. (11)

expert opinion A decision-making method in which a single person perceived as an expert makes a decision for the group. (8)

expert power A decision-making method in which a single person perceived as an expert makes a decision for the group. (7)

extemporaneous presentation A type of delivery in which the major ideas are planned and rehearsed but the speech is given spontaneously from notes. (12)

external audience Individuals or groups outside of and not closely related to the organization that may affect or be affected by the organization. (9)

F

factual question Question that asks for verifiable, factual information rather than opinion. (6)

fallacy An error in the logic of an argument. (11)

feasibility report A type of presentation that evaluates potential action steps and makes recommendations about how to proceed. (9)

feedback The recognizable response to a message. (1)

feminine culture A culture in which gender roles are not highly differentiated and members value feelings, cooperation, and harmonic relationships. (2)

final report Report delivered upon completion of an undertaking. (9)

flip chart A large pad of paper, attached to an easel, that is used to create and/or display visuals. (11)

formal communication networks Officially designated paths of communication designed by management to indicate who should communicate with whom. (1)

forming A phase in problem-solving groups characterized by tentative statements and getting-acquainted types of communication. *See also* orientation phase. (A3)

functional roles Types of behavior that are necessary if a group is to do its job effectively. *See also* relational roles, task roles. (7)

G

gatekeeper A person, such as a personal assistant or a receptionist, who manages access to another person. (1)

genderlects Distinct and different styles of speaking that characterize masculine and feminine speech. (4)

general goal A broad indication of the purpose of a speech, generally to inform, instruct, persuade, or entertain. (9)

Generation X The generation born between 1965 and 1980, whose members are comfortable with technology, and who value work–life balance and creativity. (2)

Generation Z The generation born 1997–present, which is independent, entrepreneurial, and comfortable with technology and social media. (2)

goodwill speech A speech with the primary aim of creating a favorable image of the speaker's cause in the minds of the audience. (9)

graph A visual exhibit that shows the correlation between two quantities. (11)

groupthink A condition in which group members are unwilling to critically examine ideas because of their desire to maintain harmony. (7)

H

handout Document(s) distributed during or after a presentation. (11)

hidden agenda A group member's personal goal that is not made public. (7)

high-context culture A culture that relies heavily on the social and physical context and nonverbal cues to convey meaning and maintain social harmony. (2)

high-level abstractions Terms that cover a broad range of possible objects or events without much detail. (4)

horizontal (lateral) communication Communication in which messages flow between members of an organization who have equal power or responsibility. (1)

hostile work environment A form of sexual harassment where verbal or nonverbal behavior interferes with someone's work or creates an intimidating, offensive, or hostile environment. (5)

hypothetical question Question that asks an interviewee how he or she might respond under certain circumstances. (6)

I

"I" language Language in which the communicator describes his or her feelings, needs, and behaviors without accusing others. (5)

identity management The practice of presenting yourself in ways that produce a preferred image and distinctive sense of self. (1)

immediacy Verbal and nonverbal behaviors that indicate closeness and liking. (4)

impromptu presentation A type of delivery in which the speaker has little or no preparation time before presenting their remarks. (12)

incivility The exchange of seemingly inconsequential, inconsiderate words and deeds that violate the conventional standards of workplace conduct. (5)

indirect question Question that gets at information the interviewer wants to know without asking for it directly. (6)

individualistic culture A culture whose members tend to put their own interests and personal choices ahead of social or group concerns. (2)

informal communication networks Patterns of interaction that are based on proximity, friendships, and shared interests. (1)

information power The ability to influence that arises because of one's access to otherwise obscure information. (7)

information-sharing meetings Meetings held with the purpose of exchanging information, such as brainstorming, sharing updates, and gaining additional knowledge or training. (8)

instrumental communication Messages designed to accomplish a task. (1)

internal audience Individuals or groups that are members of or are closely associated with an organization. (9)

interpersonal communication An exchange of verbal and nonverbal messages between two people. (5)

interview A two-party interaction in which at least one party has a specific, serious purpose and that usually involves the asking and answering of questions. (6)

J

jargon Specialized terminology used by members of a particular group. (4)

job burnout A syndrome of physical, emotional, or mental exhaustion that is often caused by prolonged exposure to stressful situations. (5)

L

laissez-faire leadership style A leadership style in which the leader gives up power and transforms a group into a leaderless collection of equals. (7)

latitude of acceptance The range of positions or arguments a person would accept with little or no persuasion. (11)

latitude of noncommitment The range of positions or arguments a person neither accepts nor rejects. (11)

latitude of rejection The range of positions or arguments a person opposes. (11)

leader–member exchange (LMX) A theory that views leadership as a collection of multiple relationships with members, each one unique. (7)

leading question Question that directs the interviewee to answer in a certain way, often by indicating the answer the interviewer wants to hear. (6)

long-term orientation A cultural orientation that emphasizes long-lasting goals rather than short-term gratification. *See also* short-term orientation. (2)

lose–lose approach An approach to negotiation in which one party's perceived loss leads to an outcome with negative consequences for the other parties. (5)

low-context culture A culture that employs language to express ideas and directions clearly and logically; members pay less attention to contextual clues for meaning. (2)

low-level abstractions Concrete statements that provide specific details or descriptions. (4)

M

majority vote A vote that achieves the support of most of the members. (8)

manuscript presentation A type of delivery in which the speaker reads word for word from prepared remarks. (12)

masculine culture A culture with highly differentiated gender roles in which members value performance, individual success, and advancement. (2)

meeting minutes A written record of a meeting. (8)

memorized presentation A type of delivery in which the speech is memorized and recited word for word from memory. (12)

message Any symbol or behavior from which others create meaning or that triggers a response. (1)

microaggression Subtle and commonplace verbal or behavioral actions that communicate negative or stereotypical attitudes toward culturally marginalized groups, whether intentional or not. (2)

Millennials The generation born between 1980 and 2000 who are technologically skilled, ethnically diverse, ambitious, and globally focused in their worldview. (2)

mindful listening A style of listening in which one is fully present, focused, and attentive. (3)

mindless listening A manner of listening habitually or mechanically and without thoughtfulness. (3)

minority decision A few members make a decision affecting the entire group. (8)

moderately structured interview A flexible interview in which major topics, their order, questions, and probes are planned but not rigidly adhered to. (6)

monochronic time orientation A cultural orientation that values time, efficiency, promptness, and chronological order over personal relationships. *See also* polychronic time orientation. (2)

motion A specific proposal for action. (8)

motivated sequence pattern An organizational strategy that presents a topic in terms of five sequential concepts: attention, need, satisfaction, visualization, and action. (10)

motivational speech A speech aimed primarily at generating enthusiasm for the topic being presented. (9)

multicommunicating Managing multiple conversations at the same time. (5)

N

negotiation Discussion of specific proposals for the purpose of finding a mutually acceptable agreement or settlement. (5)

networking The process of meeting people and maintaining contacts to give and receive information, advice, and job leads. (1)

news conference A meeting organized with the purpose of sharing important information about an organization with the media and giving journalists an opportunity to ask questions. (9)

news release A form of written communication released to the media with the purpose of turning an announcement into a news story. (A2)

noise Any factor that interferes with a message (also called *barriers* or *interference*). (1)

nonverbal communication Communication by nonlinguistic means, whether visually, physically, or vocally. (4)

norming A phase in problem-solving groups characterized by an end to conflict and emergence of harmony within the group. *See also* emergence phase. (A3)

norms Informal rules about what behavior is appropriate in a group. Explicit norms are made clear by speaking about them or writing them out. Implicit norms are not openly discussed but are known and understood by group members. (7)

O

open question Question that invites a broad, detailed response. *See also* closed question. (6)

opinion question Question that seeks the respondent's judgment about a topic. (6)

organizational chart A figure that displays hierarchical reporting relationships in an organization. (1)

organizational climate A relatively stable picture of an organization that is shared by its members. (5)

organizational culture A relatively constant and collective system of behaviors and values within an organization. (2)

orientation phase The first of four problem-solving phases of groups; characterized by tentative statements and getting-acquainted types of communication. *See also* forming. (A3)

overhead questions A question directed at all members of a group, inviting a response from any member. (8)

P

panel interview An interview conducted by a group of questioners with whom the candidate will work, who are commonly from different levels within an organization. (6)

paralanguage Nonlinguistic vocal qualities such as rate, pitch, volume, and pauses. (4)

paraphrasing A response style in which the receiver restates the sender's content in his or her own words. (3)

parliamentary procedure A set of rules that govern the way groups conduct business and make decisions in meetings. (8)

peer-influence exit tactics Messages and behaviors that employees intentionally communicate for the purpose of influencing their peer coworkers to leave the organization. (5)

performing A phase in problem-solving groups characterized by members' active endorsement of group decisions. *See also* reinforcement phase. (A3)

persuasion The act of motivating an audience, through communication, to voluntarily change a particular belief, attitude, or behavior. (9)

pictogram A visual exhibit that consists of an artistic or pictorial variation of a bar, column, or pie chart. (11)

pie chart A round visual exhibit divided into segments to illustrate percentages of a whole. (11)

podcast A downloadable/streaming audio presentation designed to share information and connect with new and existing audiences. (9)

polychronic time orientation A cultural orientation in which people and personal relationships are more important than appointments and efficiency of time. *See also* monochronic time orientation. (2)

position power The ability to influence that comes from the position one holds. (7)

power distance A measure (high or low) of how comfortable a culture is with differences in distribution of authority. (2)

presentation software/apps Computer software programs (e.g., PowerPoint, Keynote) and apps (e.g., Canva) that create displays used in presentations. Such programs typically include capabilities for creating special audio, visual, and transition effects; speaker notes; and handouts. (11)

press conference A meeting organized with the purpose of sharing important information about an organization with the media and giving journalists an opportunity to ask questions. (9)

press release A form of written communication released to the media with the purpose of turning an announcement into a news story. (A2)

primary question Interview question that introduces a new topic or a new area within a topic. *See also* secondary question. (6)

problem-oriented message Message that aims to meet the needs of both the sender and the other party. (5)

problem–solution pattern An organizational arrangement in which the speaker first convinces the audience that a problem exists and then presents a plan to solve it. (10)

problem-solving meetings Meetings held with the purpose of analyzing a situation or issue and identifying potential solutions. (8)

proposal A type of presentation that advocates for a particular position or action. (9)

Q

quid pro quo sexual harassment A form of sexual harassment that implies a job benefit or penalty is tied to an employee submitting to unwelcome sexual advances. (5)

quotation A form of support that uses the words of others who are authoritative or articulate to make a point more effectively than the speaker could on his or her own. (11)

R

rapport talk Language that creates connections, establishes goodwill, and builds community; more typically associated with a feminine language style. (4)

receiver Any person who perceives a message and attaches meaning to it, whether or not the message was intended for that person. (1)

referent power The ability to influence because one is respected or liked by the group. (7)

reflective-thinking sequence A seven-step problem-solving approach developed by John Dewey. (A3)

reinforcement phase The fourth of four group problem-solving phases; characterized by members' active endorsement of group decisions. *See also* performing. (A3)

relational communication Messages that create and reflect the attitudes people have toward one another. (1)

relational listening An empathic listening style, primarily concerned with feelings. (3)

relational roles Functional roles that help facilitate smooth interaction among members. (7)

relative words Terms that have meaning only in relationship to other (unspecified) terms. (4)

relay question In groups, a question asked by one member that the leader then addresses to the entire group. (8)

relevancy challenges Tactfully asking a group member to explain how an apparently off-track idea relates to the discussion. (8)

report An informative presentation that describes the state of an operation. (9)

report talk Language that conveys information, facts, knowledge, and competence; more typically associated with a masculine language style. (4)

reverse question In groups, a question asked of the leader that the leader refers back to the person who asked it. (8)

reward power The ability to influence that arises because one can induce desirable consequences or rewards. (7)

rhetorical question A question that requires listeners to think, but does not call for an overt response. (10)

risky shift A type of harmful conformity in which groups take positions that are more extreme (on the side of either caution or risk) than the positions of individual members. (7)

ritual activities Meetings or other activities focused on allowing organizational members to socialize, celebrate, and collaborate with one another. (8)

S

sales presentation A type of presentation aimed at persuading others to purchase a product or service. (9)

scannable résumé A résumé prepared in plain text format with clear keywords and phrases to be "read" and evaluated by software to screen potential job candidates. (6)

secondary question Interview question that seeks additional information about a topic under discussion. *See also* primary question. (6)

self-directed work teams Groups that manage their own behavior to accomplish a task. (7)

self-monitoring Paying close attention to one's own behavior and using these observations to shape the way one behaves. (4)

sender Someone who transmits a message, either intentionally or unintentionally. (1)

servant leadership Serving subordinates by emphasizing their needs. (7)

short-term orientation A cultural orientation that values quick payoffs over long-range goals. (2)

sincere question A genuine request for information, aimed at helping the receiver understand the sender's message. (3)

situational leadership model An approach to understanding leadership that suggests that a leader's style should be adapted to the ability of the individual or group the leader is attempting to lead. (7)

social intelligence The ability and skills of interacting well with other persons. *See also* emotional intelligence. (5)

social loafing The tendency of individual group members to put forth less effort when they are part of a group than when working alone. (10)

spatial pattern An organizational arrangement that presents material according to its physical location. (10)

specific goal A concrete statement of what response a speaker is seeking as the result of their remarks. (10)

speech of introduction A type of presentation that prepares the audience to listen to another speaker by emphasizing the upcoming speaker's qualifications or importance of the topic. (9)

speech of tribute A type of special-occasion presentation that honors a person's or group's achievements or characteristics. (9)

statistics Numbers used to represent an idea. (11)

status report The most common type of informative presentation; sometimes called a progress report. (9)

stories Detailed descriptions of incidents that illustrate a point; may be factual or hypothetical. (11)

storming A phase in problem-solving groups characterized by members taking strong stands that result in conflict within the group. *See also* conflict phase. (A3)

stress interview An employment interview in which the candidate is subjected to the pressures typically encountered on the job. (6)

structured interview An interview that consists of a standardized list of questions that allow only a limited range of answers with no follow-up. (6)

style approach to leadership An approach to studying leadership based on the assumption the designated leader's style of communication affects the group's effectiveness. (7)

supporting material Material that backs up the claims made in a presentation. (11)

synchronous communication Communication that occurs without a time lag between sending and receiving a message; for example, face-to-face communication. (1)

T

task roles Functional roles needed to accomplish a group's mission. (7)

task-oriented listening A listening style concerned with understanding information that will facilitate accomplishing the task at hand. (3)

team A group that is especially cohesive and effective because of clear and inspiring goals, a results-driven structure, competent members, unified commitment, a collaborative climate, standards of excellence, external support and recognition, and principled leadership. (7)

thesis statement A single sentence that summarizes the central idea of a presentation. (10)

toast A type of tribute that expresses appreciation and/or honors the accomplishments of an individual or a group. (9)

topical pattern An organizational arrangement in which ideas are grouped around logical themes or divisions of the subject. (10)

training presentation An informative presentation that teaches listeners how to perform a task. (9)

trait approach to leadership An outdated leadership theory based on the belief that all leaders possess common traits that make them effective. (7)

transformational leadership A type of leadership in which leaders' vision and personality traits enable them to inspire subordinates to work toward common goals and empower subordinates to exceed their normal levels of performance. (7)

transition A statement used between parts of a presentation to help listeners understand the relationship of the parts to one another and to the thesis. (10)

trigger words Terms that have strong emotional associations that set off intense emotional reactions in certain listeners. (4)

U

uncertainty avoidance A measure of a culture's tolerance for ambiguity, lack of structure, and novelty. (2)

unstructured interview A flexible interview with a goal, and perhaps a few topical areas in mind, but no list of questions or follow-ups. (6)

upward communication Communication that flows from the lower levels of hierarchy to upper levels. (1)

V

virtual meeting fatigue Feelings of tiredness, fatigue, and burnout associated with overuse of virtual platforms of communication. (8)

virtual team A team that conducts most or all of its work via electronic channels. (7)

Voice of Employee (VoE) The expression of ideas, grievances, and suggestions to upper-level management by employees. (1)

W

webinar A presentation, lecture, workshop, or seminar that is transmitted over the web with limited audience interaction. (8)

welcoming remarks A type of special-occasion presentation in which the speaker welcomes an individual or group, indicating the significance of the visit and setting the tone for the occasion. (9)

win-lose approach An approach to negotiation that assumes any gain by one party is possible only at the expense of the other party. (5)

win–win approach A collaborative approach to negotiation that assumes solutions can be reached that meet the needs of all parties. (5)

wireframe A layout of the background image of an infographic, used to plan its structure and content. (11)

workgroup A small, interdependent collection of people with a common identity who interact with one another, usually face-to-face over time, to reach a goal. (7)

work-life balance The extent that an organization supports the harmony between its employees, work and personal lives. (5)

workplace bullying Intense, malicious, ongoing, and damaging words or deeds that violate the conventional standards of workplace conduct. (5)

workplace dignity People's ability to gain a sense of self-respect and self-esteem from their jobs and to be treated respectfully by others. (5)

Y

"you" language Language that often begins with the word *you* and accuses or evaluates the other person. (5)

index